THE
AMBIGUOUS IROQUOIS
EMPIRE

By Francis Jennings

The Covenant Chain

The Invasion of America: Indians, Colonialism, and the Cant of Conquest

The Ambiguous Iroquois Empire: The Covenant Chain Confederation of Indian Tribes with English Colonies from Its Beginnings to the Lancaster Treaty of 1744

Empire of Fortune: Crowns, Colonies, and Tribes in the Seven Years War in America

The Founders of America

Edited
　With William R. Swagerty:
　　The Newberry Library Center for the History of the American Indian
　　Bibliographical Series

　With William N. Fenton and Mary A. Druke:
　　The History and Culture of Iroquois Diplomacy: An Interdisciplinary Guide to the Treaties of the Six Nations and Their League

　　Iroquois Indians: A Documentary History (microfilm)

THE
AMBIGUOUS IROQUOIS
EMPIRE

The Covenant Chain Confederation of Indian Tribes with English Colonies

from its beginnings to the Lancaster Treaty of 1744

by FRANCIS JENNINGS

W · W · NORTON & COMPANY · New York · London

I am grateful to the Public Record Office of Great Britain for permission to use crown copyright materials; and to the following institutions that have granted permission to reproduce and provided photographs of materials in their possession or under their copyright: The Franklin D. Roosevelt Library; the *Handbook of North American Indians* of the Smithsonian Institution; the Historical Society of Pennsylvania; the New York State Museum; the Pennsylvania Academy of the Fine Arts; the Pennsylvania Historical and Museum Commission; the University of Pennsylvania Press.

The text of this book is composed in Janson, with display type set in Janson.
Composition by The Maple-Vail Book Manufacturing Group.

Library of Congress Cataloging in Publication Data

Jennings, Francis, 1918–
    The ambiguous Iroquois empire.

    Continues: The invasion of America. 1976, C1975.
    Bibliography: p.
    Includes index.
    1. Indians of North America—Government relations—
To 1789.   2. Iroquois Indians—Government relations.
3. United States—History—Colonial period, ca. 1600
–1775.   I. Title.
E93.J44   1983   974'.02   82-22452

ISBN 0-393-30302-0 PBK.

W. W. Norton & Company, Inc., 500 Fifth Avenue, New York, NY 10110
W. W. Norton & Company Ltd, 10 Coptic Street, London WC1A 1PU

567890

For Della Bierman Jennings
First Teacher

CONTENTS 🦢

ILLUSTRATIONS ❧

The popular impression that disproof represents a negative side of science arises from a common, but erroneous, view of history. The idea of unilinear progress not only lies behind the racial rankings that I have criticized as social prejudice . . . ; it also suggests a false concept of how science develops. In this view, any science begins in the nothingness of ignorance and moves toward truth by gathering more and more information, constructing theories as facts accumulate. In such a world, debunking would be primarily negative, for it would only shuck some rotten apples from the barrel of accumulating knowledge. But the barrel of theory is always full; science works with elaborated contexts for explaining facts from the very outset. Creationist biology was dead wrong about the origin of species, but Cuvier's brand of creationism was not an emptier or less-developed world view than Darwin's. Science advances primarily by replacement, not by addition. If the barrel is always full, then the rotten apples must be discarded before better ones can be added.

Scientists do not debunk only to cleanse and purge. They refute older ideas *in the light of* a different view about the nature of things.

Stephen Jay Gould, *The Mismeasure of Man*

It moves nevertheless.

Galileo Galilei

PREFACE &

Some years ago I climbed the steep flights of stairs to the fourth floor of Lehigh University's Linderman Library in order to pay homage in person to that venerable historian of the eighteenth-century British Empire, the late Lawrence Henry Gipson. He sat in his eyrie, nestled among books and piles of papers more like an ancient little owl than an eagle, and he whispered the wisdom of nearly ninety years of living. "You know, Mr. Jennings," the soft voice confided, "when I started to write my history of the Revolution, I decided it would need a chapter of introduction." He paused to savor the coming joke. "Well that chapter became nine big volumes"—a vague wave of the ancient hand toward *The British Empire Before the American Revolution*, the anticipated classic, and a dry chuckle.

I felt a premonitory chill. I, too, intended a chapter of introduction to my subject. It does not seem likely that I have shouldered so great a burden as Gipson's, but neither have I ever felt hugely confident of lasting till ninety. *My* chapter of introduction grew into a full book and about a quarter of this one, just to get the poor thing born. Tristram Shandy managed better.

This book, like its predecessor *The Invasion of America*, is part of a history of how Euramericans and Amerindians shared in the creation of the society that became the United States of America. In that long process, different strategies were adopted by varied Indian tribes and European colonies in order to cope with the presence of all the others. The strategy of Puritan New England was armed conquest. I described it in *Invasion* with the intention of also writing a description of the strategy of accommodation used in the "middle colonies" of New Netherland and its English successors: New York, Pennsylvania, New Jersey, and Delaware. The material outgrew the book, so *Invasion* was confined to a general introduction and a narrative of New England. Here now is a balancing supplement. Complete in itself, it is also a continuation of the history of the peoples who formed a Covenant Chain of formal cooperation between Indian tribes and British colonies. This is a history impossible to conceive under the assumptions traditionally held by American historians until only a few years ago. The Covenant Chain has played no role in "frontier" histories devoted to demonstrating implacable hostility between "savage" Indians and "civilized" Europeans.

The fallacy of thinking that enmity was inevitable between the two groups is demonstrated by comments such as Robert Livingston's letter of May 13, 1701: "of the Five [Iroquois] Nations, I need not enumerate the advantages arising from their firmness to this Government [of New York], they having fought our battles for us and been a constant barrier of defence between Virginia and Maryland and the French, and by their constant vigilance have prevented the French from making any descent that way."[1] The British crown's Lords of Trade and Plantations presented a similar view to Secretary Stanhope in 1715: "We desire you will please to represent to His Majesty that New York being in the center of His Majesty's other Provinces on the Continent of America, and extending in breadth to the Lakes, and St. Lawrence, or Canada, River, has been always reputed as a Frontier to the British Empire there. That the Five Nations of Indians lying on the back of New York, between the French of Canada and our settlements, are the only barrier between the said French and their Indians, and His Majesty's Plantations as far as Virginia and Maryland."[2] References to the Covenant Chain abound in both colonial and imperial sources, but frontier historians have not seen their importance.

The Chain seems to have been equally beyond the ken of anthropologists: the Smithsonian Institution's authoritative *Handbook of North American Indians* makes no mention of the Chain except in passing in a brief article by myself on another subject. Anthropologists have been filiopietistically uncritical of the first American student of the Iroquois tribes, Lewis Henry Morgan. His work has dominated the field since he published *League of the Ho-dé-no-sau-nee, Iroquois*, in 1851, but one has to understand it not only as the work of a sensitive and sympathetic mind, but also as the product of an era. As friend and champion of the Iroquois, Morgan gained intimate personal knowledge of the tribes' internal structures and customs; but as a formally educated lawyer hankering for a world view, Morgan blindly perpetuated some lethal myths of his time and culture. For example, he was obsessed with the false notion that the Iroquois and their "surrounding nations" had lived "a hunter life," and that this was "the true reason why the red race has never risen, or can rise above its present level."[3] Apart from the moral drawn by Morgan, his facts were

1. Livingston to Council of Trade and Plantations, May 13, 1701, *Calendar of State Papers, Colonial Series, America and West Indies, Preserved in the Public Record Office*, ed. W. Noel Sainsbury et al. (London: Her Majesty's Stationery Office, 1896–), vol. 1701, p. 234. Series hereafter cited as *CSPA&WI*.

2. Whitehall, November 18, 1715, *CSPA&WI*, vol. 1714–15, p. 345.

3. Lewis H. Morgan, *League of the Ho-dé-no-sau-nee, Iroquois* (Rochester: Sage and Brother, Publishers, 1851). I have worked with the facsimile reprint with introduction by William N. Fenton (New York: Corinth Books, 1962). Quotes on pp. 58, 57. Similar remarks at pp. 137, 139, 346.

wrong in this respect, and this is the more puzzling because he frequently cited Cadwallader Colden's eighteenth-century book that remarks on its first page, "The Adirondacks [Algonquins] . . . imploy'd themselves wholly in Hunting, and the Five Nations made Planting of Corn their whole business, by which means they became useful to one another."[4] More to the present point, Morgan reported as historical fact a considerable amount of nonsense that became embalmed in history after being embroidered and passed on by Francis Parkman. Morgan created an empire for the Iroquois that never existed.

The so-called Iroquois empire was the Covenant Chain. The Chain was a confederation between English colonies and Indian tribes. It came into existence in 1677 through two treaties negotiated at Albany, New York. The first treaty, between the Iroquois Five Nations and the colonies of Connecticut and Massachusetts Bay, terminated New England's Second Puritan Conquest, commonly called King Philip's War. I have described it in this book's predecessor volume.[5]

The second treaty originating the Covenant Chain was negotiated between the Iroquois and Delawares, on the one hand, and an envoy representing Maryland and Virginia, on the other hand, to make peace between those colonies and the Susquehannocks and Iroquois. It is described herein. In both instances the Iroquois acted as spokesmen for other tribes; New York's governor supervised the proceedings and enforced the rules of negotiation.

Out of these treaties emerged a confederation whose membership and power changed with much volatility until 1784 when, after the American Revolution, the Treaty of Fort Stanwix effectually ended all possibility of the Chain's continuation. During that time the member parties pursued their own interests but generally had the most lasting success when they worked in concert. The Chain is the reason there was peace between colonies and tribes in the "middle colonial" region during the long period from 1677 to 1755. The Chain organized trade between Indians and colonials over a vast region, sometimes openly, sometimes clandestinely. It recruited warriors in joint struggles of Indians and English colonials to conquer New France. It organized systematic retreats of Indians from defeats in New England and the southern colonies into sanctuaries in New York, Pennsylvania, and Iroquoia. Chain negotiations covered the peaceful retreat of Indians from eastern Pennsylvania to the Ohio region beyond the Appalachians. And Chain arrangements opened the west to English settlement. The Chain's arrangements, rather than incessant ferocious war,

4. Cadwallader Colden, *The History of the Five Indian Nations Depending on the Province of New-York in America* (1727–1747), reprint ed. (Ithaca, N.Y.: Great Seal Books, 1958), p. 3.

5. Francis Jennings, *The Invasion of America: Indians, Colonialism, and the Cant of Conquest*, published for the Institute of Early American History and Culture (North Carolina, 1975; rpt., New York: W. W. Norton, 1976), pp. 324–26.

explain how the Iroquois achieved leadership and occasionally the power of command over other tribes. Contrary to legend, the Iroquois were frequently defeated in battle, by other tribes as well as by French troops, but their exceptional ability in treaty negotiations recouped their lost power.

Contemporary European statesmen and their colonial deputies recognized the Covenant Chain as a political, military, and economic power capable of tipping the scales of dominance in North America, and they entered into formal treaties with the Chain's tribes in the form of contracts between peers. This book rests heavily upon the evidence of those treaties—evidence too often ignored. The Chain was conceived and gradually tacked together through a painful learning process, with an amoebalike change of shape during its century of existence. Though its parties confederated as formal peers, their actual relationships became those of colonial patrons and tribal clients. Much ambiguity marks their relationships. As Sir William Johnson once remarked, the British crown claimed dominion over tribes, which it could not enforce "with 10,000 of the best troops in Europe."[6] The tribes, on the other hand, often flaunted independence from colonies whose trade they needed for survival. As with other diplomatic relationships, the language of Chain treaties requires careful examination of the realities behind the language.

Fuller analysis of the Covenant Chain's structure and functions is given where appropriate in the text. Here, however, may be noted the reason for calling this bicultural confederation the *Iroquois* Covenant Chain. It is not to be confused with the League of the Five Nations or Houdénosaunee, nor yet with the League's extended tributary system. From its beginnings, the Chain's membership simultaneously included governments in both tribal and state forms. But the Iroquois immediately recognized the Chain as a means of enhancing their own status and power, and they maintained proprietary management of it throughout its wobbly life. To tell the history of the Chain, therefore, is to tell the external political history of the Iroquois Five Nations and much of the history of New France and the English colonies. Let me just add that this was not merely a history of "Indian-White relations." It was equally a history of the Iroquois vis-à-vis other tribes. To portray the Chain in terms of race would be to reduce it to falsifying caricature. Because of the mass of available material, the book follows the Chain's history only to the Treaty of Lancaster, Pennsylvania, in 1744. Another book will be required for the tumultuous events from the Seven Years War through the American Revolution.

Lewis Henry Morgan's Iroquois informants remembered the term *cov-*

6. Johnson to John Tabor Kempe, Sept. 7, 1765, in *The Papers of Sir William Johnson*, ed. James Sullivan et al., 14 vols. (Albany: University of the State of New York, 1921–1965), 11:925.

enant chain but had evidently forgotten its full significance. Perhaps Morgan failed to grasp it. His work includes no recitation of a history such as was frequently narrated by Iroquois orators at treaty conferences, and his account of relationships between the Five Nations and their Delaware tributaries merely demonstrates that the keepers of Iroquois traditions tidied up their ancestors' behavior as busily as the most dutiful Euramerican historian. What emerges, therefore, from Morgan's *League* is a highly romanticized "golden age" of super-Iroquois.[7]

This, too, needs correction. The Iroquois of the seventeenth and eighteenth centuries, like the European invaders of America, were human in the usual simple and complex ways. Allowing for cultural pressures, one finds heroes, villains, fools, and quite ordinary persons among their people in a recognizably human distribution. The reader of this book will encounter no fabulous "hantayoyos."

Anthropology and history have come a long way since the days of Morgan and Parkman. The controlling conception of race that then defined roles and dominated social thinking has been rejected, to be replaced by the conception of culture. The Covenant Chain can be seen today because new light has been generated by the patient work of a great many scholars in many disciplines, based on the unsung but indispensable collection and organization of source documents. As presented, my subject is new in itself, but in what follows I make no pretense to extraordinary powers of discovery; my findings go simply another step beyond the many solid studies on which I have relied. I hope that step is in a forward direction.

The book is not presented as a definitive work. On the contrary, I regard it as exploratory and experimental. Because it attempts to outline a subject new to formal history, it omits much of the matter long regarded as essential to other treatments of colonies and tribes in the "colonial era." The selection and organization of the data will be unfamiliar to most readers. Though I have tried to keep the Five Nations and their Indian allies in focus, the nature of the subject requires discussion also of developments within the colonies. It is a history neither of the tribes nor of the colonies, but rather of the Covenant Chain that bound them together. Just as the Chain underwent great changes in structure and function over the years, so the book may appear to be an essay on evanescence, but it was an evanescence with the power of a hurricane (which is also a relatively fleeting phenomenon).

I have been rather startled by how many of the book's findings are at odds with those of renowned and eminent scholars. Some of those scholars have been men of ill will whose malicious falsities have been exposed with satisfaction. But I take no pleasure in revising those many others who

7. Morgan, *League*, pp. 336, 338 et passim.

have acquired their fame justifiably through long and patient years of self-less labor, and whose regrettable errors I attribute to preconceptions more cultural than personal. I hope that these distinctions will be clear.

I do not doubt that my own turn to be corrected will come, both in fact and in interpretations. This book states its positions positively in the hope of stimulating alternative views and reasoned disagreement; that is the only good road to knowledge. Because the book sprawls over much space and time, and many kinds of documentation, I cannot dare to hope that it is entirely free from factual error. *C'est la vie.* I have checked and double-checked, and pestered friends to read the manuscript. To James Axtell, William N. Fenton, and Dorothy V. Jones, who read the first draft all through, I owe much gratitude. Grudgingly, but inescapably, I must accept responsibility for the errors that remain, sometimes despite their kind advice.

I have been working in and around the subject for more than twenty years, during which time I have written a dissertation and a number of articles more or less directly on point, besides the book that I was dissuaded (thank goodness) from naming Prolegomena to the History of the Covenant Chain. Though I have not hesitated to crib from the dissertation and the articles, because each had been researched to clear up certain issues relevant to the book as well, this book is not an anthology of previous essays. Its theme and structure are new, so new in fact that it has required numerous redraftings to bring order out of the confusion and to achieve as much unity as the subject will allow.

My debts are many. Most are acknowledged specifically in the notes. Here I must thank the American Philosophical Society for two research grants; the Rockefeller Foundation for a month of free writing time and magnificent hospitality at its Villa Serbelloni in Bellagio, Italy; the National Endowment for the Humanities for its support of the Newberry Library Center for the History of the American Indian and my project on Iroquois historical documentation; and the Newberry Library itself for generous allowances of free time for research and writing. The Philadelphia Center for Early American Studies granted a month of fellowship for research in this book and the one next to come; and I owe gratitude to the Henry E. Huntington Library for six months of fellowship for the same purpose.

In the Iroquois documentary history project I have had the privilege of association with my office colleague Mary A. Druke and with joint editor William N. Fenton, the revered dean of Iroquois scholars. Another colleague, William R. Swagerty, has expertly assumed many administrative and editorial duties to allow me to give more attention to the study.

It would be ungrateful to fail to acknowledge the indispensable help given by successive members of the staff of the manuscript department of the Historical Society of Pennsylvania. Twenty-odd years ago, these were

Catherine Miller and Harry Givens. More recently Linda Stanley and especially Peter Parker have guided me to long-buried treasure. Other professional debts are so numerous that they have been acknowledged at appropriate places in the notes.

I have been blessed with the best of friends and associates. I must mention especially two who helped much in early stages of the work: those doughty Free Writers of Quakertown, Alexander Crosby (now, sadly, deceased) and Nancy Larrick Crosby, provided an ideal residence and neighborhood for eight years. From beginning to end, Joan W. Jennings has been editor of first instance as well as constant companion and steadfast partner.

The heavy array of institutional support has amused one of my colleagues who charges that I have "joined the Establishment." This is a little disconcerting to a one-time radical who prefers to think that a part of the Establishment has joined him. However, there are still plenty of critics, which is as it should be.

September 1982   The Newberry Library and
                                        Chilmark, Massachusetts

TECHNICAL NOTE ❧

This book spans the period when various nations changed their dating system from the Old Style, Julian, calendar to the present New Style, Gregorian, calendar. With one class of exceptions, no effort is made herein to adjust citations to show the effect of these changes. Documents are cited as of the dates shown on them. The exceptions are dates in January, February, and early March falling at the end of the year in the Old Style calendar. These have been cited at the beginning of the following year in conformity with present practice. Thus March 10, 1674, Old Style, becomes March 10, 1675 (often given elsewhere as March 10, 1674 / 1675).

Quotations generally follow the original in spelling, capitalization, and interior punctuation, but spelling and punctuation have been sparingly modernized in some instances to clarify sense. Abbreviations have been spelled out; the ampersand (&) has been expanded to *and;* and *ye* and *yt* have been given in full as *the* and *that* as intended. Typography conforms to modern usage. No words are omitted except where indicated by three dots, and none are added except in square brackets. With these modifications, quotations are as they appear in the cited sources.

ABBREVIATIONS ❧

Most abbreviations and short titles are given so as to be easily recognizable. A few exceptions are listed below for quick reference. All works are cited in full in the Bibliography.

CSPA&WI: Calendar of State Papers, Colonial Series, America and West Indies. Volumes bear inclusive dates rather than numbers.

Doc.Hist.N.Y.: The Documentary History of the State of New-York.

HSP: Historical Society of Pennsylvania.

Johnson Papers: The Papers of Sir William Johnson.

Md. Arch.: Archives of Maryland.

Northeast: Volume 15 of *Handbook of North American Indians.*

N.Y.Col.Docs.: Documents Relative to the Colonial History of the State of New York.

Pa. Arch.: Pennsylvania Archives.

Pa. Assembly Minutes: Votes and Proceedings of the House of Representatives of the Province of Pennsylvania, Pennsylvania Archives, 8th Ser.

Pa. Council Minutes: Minutes of the Provincial Council of Pennsylvania.

Pa. Property Minutes: Minutes of the Commissioners of Property in *Pennsylvania Archives,* 2d. ser., vol. 19, and 3d ser., vol. 1.

Part One ❧ TRANSITORY CONDOMINIUM

Chapter 1 ❧ DISTINCTIONS in DEED and THOUGHT

"With ink, anyone can write anything."

Eleventh-century squire quoted in
Marc Bloch, *The Historian's Craft*

      The first massive fact about the European invasion of America is that physical contact between the societies of the two continents took place almost wholly on American soil. Only a handful of visitors traveled from the Americas to Europe, and most of those went involuntarily. Europe had the initiative, and Europeans never had to worry about retaliatory invasion from America.

The North and South American frontiers differed significantly therefore from the engagement of peoples in the Old World, where Christian Europeans faced Muslim Asiatics and Africans who could and did send massive invasions into Europe. The Spaniards who sailed with Columbus had inherited the seven hundred-year tradition of the Reconquest of Spain from the Moors. The implications of the difference between Old World frontiers and those of the New World have never been systematically explored. Certainly they must have included a respect by Europeans for Muslim power and culture that was withheld from the cultures of the natives of America. St. Thomas Aquinas tried to assimilate into his theology all that seemed valuable in Muslim science. Bartolomé de Las Casas confined himself to demanding Christian justice for people who, though barbarous, were teachable.[1]

The crusaders who fought so long to create Spain might hate Moors but were not apt to underestimate them.[2] These crusaders appreciated much of Moorish culture, as the survival of the Alhambra beautifully evidences.

---

1. "Aquinas, Thomas," in *Encyclopaedia Britannica*, 11th ed.; Bartolomé de Las Casas, *In Defense of the Indians*, trans. and ed. Stafford Poole (DeKalb: Northern Illinois University Press, 1974), ch. 4. Another unexplored issue: Why did Islam not develop the racial doctrines and distinctions that became so prominent in Christendom?
2. Derek W. Lomax, *The Reconquest of Spain* (London: Longman, 1978).

Their descendant conquistadores, however, vaunted a crucial military advantage, marched where they pleased, took what they wanted, and destroyed Tenochtitlan utterly, a city greater than any in Spain. The evidence of the Moors in Spain is in Spain. The evidence of the Aztecs before Spanish rule is largely under ground. Such differences inspired among Europeans generally a sense of absolute superiority over native Americans that expressed itself more usually as contempt than outright hatred. Its effect was as morally and intellectually corrupting on Europeans as it was destructive physically to native Americans.

In the Americas, Europeans had the initiative in conceptualizing and explicating the processes of invasion, and they used the advantage to create rationalizations favorable to themselves.[3] The terminology so developed took its place in the arsenal of conquest. *Sovereignty*, for example, which had been invented to justify kings' conquests of their own peoples, lent itself readily to export.[4] The legal implications of the one-way traffic to America did not escape Francisco de Vitoria, who once remarked that an Indian "discovery" of Spain would not have justified Indian sovereignty over Spain. But he lost the argument.[5]

Europeans could choose where they would land to colonize the world that was so new to them. Indians could choose only to try to expel the newcomers or to accept them. Experiment disposed quickly of the first option; a reasonably well-organized beachhead colony of Europeans could be maintained indefinitely against resentful natives. Having learned this much, Indians moved to the question of terms upon which European neighborhood could be accepted. In this respect also, power gave initiative to the Europeans, and they flaunted their power tyrannically until they discovered need for Indian help in coping with the natural environment of this new, strange land. Just as urgently, the Europeans needed help

---

3. A large literature expresses diverse interests and interpretations. A sampling: Lewis Hanke, *All Mankind Is One: A Study of the Disputation Between Bartolomé de Las Casas and Juan Ginés de Sepúlveda in 1550 on the Intellectual and Religious Capacity of the American Indians* (DeKalb: Northern Illinois University Press, 1974); Hugh Honour, *The New Golden Land: European Images of America from the Discoveries to the Present Time* (New York: Pantheon Books, 1975); Cornelius J. Jaenen, *Friend and Foe: Aspects of French-Amerindian Cultural Contact in the Sixteenth and Seventeenth Centuries* (New York: Columbia University Press, 1976); H. C. Porter, *The Inconstant Savage: England and the North American Indian, 1500–1660* (London: Duckworth, 1979); Karen Ordahl Kupperman, *Settling with the Indians: The Meeting of English and Indian Cultures in America, 1580–1640* (Totowa, N.J.: Rowman and Littlefield, 1980); Robert F. Berkhofer, Jr., *The White Man's Indian: Images of the American Indian from Columbus to the Present* (New York: Alfred A. Knopf, 1978); Bernard W. Sheehan, *Savagism and Civility: Indians and Englishmen in Colonial Virginia* (Cambridge University Press, 1980).

4. Frederick Pollock, *An Introduction to the History of the Science of Politics* (1890), rev. ed. reprinted (Boston, Mass.: Beacon Press, 1960), pp. 43–68; Wilcomb E. Washburn, *Red Man's Land / White Man's Law: A Study of the Past and Present Status of the American Indian* (New York: Charles Scribner's Sons, 1971), Part I.

5. Ibid., pp. 9–13. Lewis Hanke, "Indians and Spaniards in the New World: A Personal View," in *Attitudes of Colonial Powers Toward the American Indian*, eds. Howard Peckham and Charles Gibson (Salt Lake City: University of Utah Press, 1969), p. 5.

against each other, for they were only "European" as members of an abstract category. In social relationships and their own consciousnesses, they were Spaniards, Frenchmen, Dutchmen, Englishmen, and Swedes, and they were every bit as determined to conquer each other as to acquire dominance over the native peoples of America.[6]

It seems necessary to draw attention to these national differences because of the distortions created by the racial category of "White" and the study called "Indian-White relations." Race may be studied legitimately as part of the history of ideas, but only as such. As a category referring to real people it is genetically invalid and historically misleading.

Indian also is a category that can mislead. As opposed to "White," *Indian* is a racial term. The real persons who were natives of this continent knew themselves by tribal names that usually translate to "the people" or "the people of such and such a place." The very word *Indian* is a European classification, and evidence of a serious geographical mistake, at that. It may be used with caution for convenience, in default of a better, as long as it is understood to be the counterpart of *European* rather than of *White*.

The difference is more than a quibble. We know Europeans to be a conglomeration of peoples, but Whites are presumed to be homogeneous. Racially categorized Indians are homogeneous and mythical; there never were such people. However, Indians considered as a mixture of peoples and cultures can be considered historically because that is what all the evidence shows them to have been.[7]

These differentiated Indians, like Europeans, competed against each other. There was no such thing as racial solidarity in the early seventeenth century; even the conception did not exist.[8] Anthropologist George W. Stocking, Jr., and historian Reginald Horsman agree that the category of

6. David B. Quinn, *North America from Earliest Discovery to First Settlements: The Norse Voyages to 1612* (New York: Harper and Row, 1977), ch. 10; ———, "James I and the Beginnings of Empire in America," *Journal of Imperial and Commonwealth History* 2:2 (Jan. 1974), pp. 135–52; Samuel Hazard, *Annals of Pennsylvania from the Discovery of the Delaware* (Philadelphia: Hazard and Mitchell, 1850), pp. 148–51, 183–97, 356–65; 405–7; 410–13.

7. In a sympathetic, thoroughly researched study, Robert F. Berkhofer, Jr., has assailed the uniformity erroneously attributed to Indians but seems, inconsistently, to accept the homogeneity of Whites. E.g., "To what extent do these old [homogenizing] approaches to the *Indian* still constitute the chief White views of Native Americans even today?" Berkhofer, *White Man's Indian*, pp. 3–25, quotation on p. 25. But the "White" language does not appear in Ray Allen Billington, *Land of Savagery, Land of Promise: The European Image of the American Frontier in the Nineteenth Century* (New York: W. W. Norton and Co., 1981).

8. Professor Kupperman argues that "English colonists assumed that Indians were racially similar to themselves and that savagery was a temporary condition which the Indians would quickly lose. The really important category was status." *Settling with the Indians*, p. 2. For strong contrast see Winthrop D. Jordan, *White Over Black: American Attitudes Toward the Negro, 1550–1812*, published for the Institute of Early American History and Culture (Chapel Hill: University of North Carolina Press, 1968), ch. 6. My own view is that colonial Englishmen used the language of savagery to mean different things at different times, as their descendants still do, but always with a clear implication of inferiority. Jennings, *Invasion of America*, ch. 5.

race did not become important in the history of ideas until the nineteenth century. Horsman attributed the lag to Christian doctrine: "Those who thought in terms of inherent racial inferiority had to cope with the orthodox Christian view of the unity of man—of one human race descended in less than six thousand years from Adam and Eve—and with the eighteenth-century natural philosophers who saw mankind as capable of indefinite improvement. Until the 1830s, whatever the views of the frontiersmen, most American intellectuals regarded the Indians as having the ultimate potential of equality with the whites." But all that changed radically so that by the later nineteenth century (in Stocking's words), "race and culture were linked in a single evolutionary hierarchy extending from the dark-skinned savage to the civilized white man."[9]

The histories resting on such conceptions are as fallacious as the conceptions. In the seventeenth-century colonizing era, religious and local interests held rank in men's minds far above consciousness of race or even of nationality. The distinctions *within* each continental society made possible cooperation *between* particular tribes and particular colonies.[10] Tribe and colony negotiated accommodation, each for its own purposes.

Because of such arrangements at this specific place and at that specific time, it is almost idiotic to talk of European conquest of all the Indians, let alone conquest of the wilderness. From earliest days the peoples collaborated. Europeans generally assumed leadership and gave direction to intersocietal partnerships, but not always, and leadership must not be conceived simplistically as military conquest. In one aspect, the entire history of the Iroquois league and its Covenant Chain shows Indian initiatives being pushed to the limits of feasibility and sometimes beyond. But the Indians could never overlook the technological superiority of European weaponry nor the rapid growth of colonial populations.

Indians were as rational as Europeans. Such praise is not lavish, considering the crazes, obsessions, superstitions, and fantasies prevalent in Europe. Faced with European power, Indians understood that they could maintain a degree of freedom only by maneuver. Early on, they discovered that competition between Europeans was opportunity for Indians, just as Europeans lived by the maxim, "divide and conquer." In hindsight one may see that the major strategic problem for Indian leaders therefore became that of uniting their own tribal peoples to deal with the constantly

9. Reginald Horsman, "Scientific Racism and the American Indian in the Mid-Nineteenth Century," *American Quarterly* 27:2 (May 1975), pp. 125–68, quotation on p. 154; George W. Stocking, Jr., *Race, Culture, and Evolution: Essays in the History of Anthropology* (New York: Free Press, 1968), p. vii. See also William Stanton, *The Leopard's Spots: Scientific Attitudes Toward Race in America, 1815–1859* (Chicago: University of Chicago Press, 1960).

10. See *The History and Culture of Iroquois Diplomacy: An Interdisciplinary Guide to the Treaties of the Six Nations and Their League*, eds. Francis Jennings, William N. Fenton, and Mary A. Druke, published for the Newberry Library Center for the History of the American Indian (Syracuse, N.Y.: Syracuse University Press, forthcoming).

increasing strength of the colonies. This was a difficult task for tribal peoples whose political organizations were founded on kinship and locality and who had no sense of racial solidarity.[11] They often chose instead to ally with a European colony against tribal enemies.

Disparity in power between tribe and colony was more than a matter of differential technological development. The political aspect of the invasion of America was a series of encounters between governments in the state form and governments in the tribal form. Regardless of its many virtues, the kin-structured tribe is incapable of concentrating human power as well as the coercive, hierarchically structured, bureaucratic state. Iroquois leaders could devise a league of friendship and mutual assistance, but it was a league of consultation and contract rather than a government capable of legislative command. The individual Iroquois tribes never gave up their power of individual decision. Often they struggled for dominance within the league, and sometimes (though rarely) they came to blows with each other.[12] These phenomena were also to be observed among colonial towns and villages, but whereas the Iroquois tribes maintained local independence throughout their existence, the colonies gradually came under more and more effective central controls.

In the long run, government in the state form proved capable of subduing and sometimes shattering government in the tribal form. The impersonal institutions of the bureaucratic state, aided to be sure by a tide of immigration from Europe, could mobilize greater strength, extend themselves over greater territory, and maintain themselves intact after internalizing more conflicts than kin-based tribal government could manage. This is an issue quite apart from the quality of life enjoyed by persons living under those powers.

Many tribes tried to solve the problem of disparate power by soliciting the friendship and protection of nearby colonies in return for services rendered.[13] No matter how amicable, such a relationship becomes by its nature a partnership of patron and client. The stronger partner dominates, and the client tribe using a colony for protection finds itself being used in turn in a variety of ways, the net effect of which is to increase the patron's strength still more while further weakening the client.

The Iroquois learned how to stave off this process of perpetual deteri-

11. See William N. Fenton, "Locality as a Basic Factor in the Development of Iroquois Social Structure," in *Symposium on Local Diversity in Iroquois Culture*, ed. W. N. Fenton, Bureau of American Ethnology Bulletin 149 (Washington, D.C.: Smithsonian Institution, 1951), pp. 35–54.

12. Elisabeth Tooker, "The League of the Iroquois: Its History, Politics, and Ritual." In *Handbook of North American Indians*, gen. ed. William C. Sturtevant, 20 vols. planned (Washington, D.C.: Smithsonian Institution, 1978–), vol. 15; *Northeast*, ed. Bruce G. Trigger (1978), pp. 430–37. Cited hereafter as *Northeast*.

13. For example: the Chickahominies with Jamestown; the Wampanoags with New Plymouth; the Narragansetts with Massachusetts Bay; the Susquehannocks with New Sweden; the Algonquins and Hurons with New France.

oration, though they paid a high price for the lesson. At some undetermined time, but apparently between 1400 and 1600 A.D., they formed their League of the Houdénosaunee, or Five Nations.[14] In historic times this League moved rapidly through a series of political developments. Its first phase was a brash effort by Mohawks and Senecas to expand their individual tribal memberships and territories through simple predatory conquest of tribes outside the League. What happened then is conventionally called the Beaver Wars, and it has often been described in bombastic rhetoric about vast savage empires. In point of fact, however, great strains developed within the League during the Beaver Wars, and the wars' ultimate outcome was something less than imperial triumph.[15]

The League was only the beginning of Iroquois experimentation in expanding tribal government beyond the merely local "kinship state."[16] A number of generations—no one knows certainly how many—went by before the Five Nations solved most of the problems of keeping their League united. By the time of English conquest of New Netherland in 1664, the Five Nations had ceased to fight against each other, and they acted as a unit for defense though internal strains continued throughout the League's existence. When the English came, the Iroquois allied to them in the multiparty confederation of the Covenant Chain. By affiliating other tribes directly to their League, and thus indirectly to the Chain, the Iroquois increased their own importance. The word *tributary*, usually used to identify these allied tribes, is convenient in default of a better, but it must not be understood in the European legal sense. These tribal tributaries varied from time to time and among themselves in degree of subordination to the Five Nations. No general rule can be applied, but duality or reciprocity was the principle operating throughout Iroquois political structures; what Europeans called tributaries were known by the Iroquois as *brethren*, *cousins*, or *nephews*—statuses that involved Iroquois responsibilities as well as privileges. The full implications of political distinctions involved in these kinship terms are not yet understood by students of the Iroquois.[17] Each tributary's condition must be studied throughout the changes in its history, and change sometimes occurred very rapidly.

However, one rule may be laid down confidently with respect to the Chain as a whole. Despite heroic efforts by the Iroquois to acquire tributaries from New France's protectorate, they never succeeded for very long. The French always moved quickly and decisively to disrupt alliances of their client tribes with the Five Nations. Though the Iroquois themselves,

14. Tooker, "League of the Iroquois," p. 420.
15. See ch. 5 below.
16. "The Iroquois remain the classic example of a kinship state." William N. Fenton, "Locality as a Basic Factor," p. 39.
17. William N. Fenton, "Northern Iroquoian Culture Patterns," in *Northeast*, p. 314.

as individual tribes and as a league, negotiated treaties repeatedly with New France, the Covenant Chain remained throughout its life a system limited by the effective jurisdictions of colonies of Great Britain.

The Covenant Chain was the product of a specific region. It would have been—was, in fact—impossible of invention in New France, New England, or Virginia. Though Europeans of the Atlantic coast "middle colonies" were no less determined than the others to establish dominance over the natives, their accommodation strategy generally avoided use of naked force. The New Netherland Dutch tried conquest on the pattern of New England and botched it.[18] In the sequel, they and their English successors of New York postponed subjection of their neighboring Indians and were content with exploitation. In their vicinity, Indian chiefs and councils continued through the seventeenth century and most of the eighteenth to function and be chosen in the ways hallowed by custom. Cooperation between Euramerican and Amerindian was effected through military alliance, intersocietal trade, formal treaty negotiations, late-coming missions, and the judicious outlay of presents and bribes. As James H. Merrell observes in a recent essay, "Between the two extremes of violent repudiation of European cultures by powerful tribes or meek acceptance of it by shattered ones lay a broad area in which accommodation was possible for many who were neither powerful nor shattered."[19]

But power helped. If accommodation was to be kept from degenerating into subjection and assimilation, an Indian tribe needed to preserve a land base—a territory, no matter how small—in which the tribe could live in some degree of autonomy and thus maintain its sense of identity.[20] The Iroquois were fortunate in this respect. They lived in a region where colonial population, and therefore colonial land craving, grew slowly. Dutchmen and Swedes never poured into their "middle" colonies in numbers comparable to those of the English of Virginia and New England; and even the English who arrived later showed little desire, at least for a while, to fill up New York after they had conquered New Netherland. Englishmen began to colonize massively in this region only after the founding of Pennsylvania in 1681. There was no significant crowding of the Iroquois homeland until the 1720s. That the Iroquois were able, for another half century, to cope with the inexorable pressures of speculators, homesteaders, and squatters is testimony to their remarkable political and diplomatic skills.

18. Allen W. Trelease, *Indian Affairs in Colonial New York: The Seventeenth Century* (Ithaca, N.Y.: Cornell University Press, 1960), ch. 3.

19. James H. Merrell, "Cultural Continuity among the Piscataway Indians of Colonial Maryland," *William and Mary Quarterly*, 3d ser., 36 (Oct. 1979), p. 570.

20. Imre Sutton, *Indian Land Tenure: Bibliographical Essays and a Guide to the Literature* (New York: Clearwater Publishing Co., 1975), pp. 1–4.

Chapter 2 ❧ AN EMPIRE of CONVENIENCE

The version of American history that is essentially New England local history writ large is, in the final analysis, a version of a genteel Anglo-Saxon racism. . . .
In effect, the exaggerated emphasis on New England gives us to ourselves as a single people. The insistence on the primacy of the middle-colonial pattern [by contrast] calls us to a reconfiguration of ourselves as a plural people, and calls us as well to the intricate untangling and ultimate acceptance of those multiplicities.

Michael Zuckerman, *Friends and Neighbors: Group Life in America's First Plural Society*

It does seem that New England occupies a distortingly central position in American historiography. . . . Whatever the reasons are, the fact remains that the strength of the New England myth has increased, is increasing, and ought to be diminished.

Hugh Kearney, in *The Westward Enterprise*

Conquest by decree

If the Covenant Chain was the reality, how did the idea of an Iroquois empire become so firmly fixed in the histories? The first response to that question is to be found in the title of Cadwallader Colden's *The History of the Five Indian Nations Depending on the Province of New-York in America*.[1] It suggests the major premise of a syllogism: the Iroquois "depended" on New York, which was in turn a dependency of the British crown. Therefore, if the Iroquois had an empire, it belonged to Britain.

The syllogism was preserved through the long life of Robert Livingston, New York's first secretary of Indian Affairs, who functioned, informally or officially, from 1675 until he wangled the post for his son Philip in 1721.[2] His convenient logic was quickly adopted by crown officials locked in struggle with France for sovereignty over the Great Lakes–Mis-

1. Part I was published in 1727; Part II, in 1747. Each was written as justification for English policy during a time of aggressive expansion. I have used the Great Seal Books edition that includes both parts (Ithaca, N.Y.: Cornell University Press, 1958).

2. *The Livingston Indian Records, 1666–1723*, ed. Lawrence H. Leder (Gettysburg, Pa.: Pennsylvania Historical Association, 1956), pp. 6, 8; Lawrence H. Leder, *Robert Livingston, 1654–1728, and the Politics of Colonial New York*, published for the Institute of Early American History and Culture (Chapel Hill: University of North Carolina Press, 1961), p. 258.

sissippi Valley region. As will be shown, the Iroquois did penetrate that region but were unable to maintain a presence there, much less achieve a domination that could be interpreted as an empire. But an Iroquois empire was the British syllogism's essential minor premise. Everyone knew that the French had been first of Europeans in the trans-Appalachian regions (always excepting DeSoto), so Britain could not claim by "right of discovery." Equally obvious was the maintenance of a French presence there in the seventeenth century to the practical exclusion of English traders, let alone settlers; so Britain could not claim a "right of possession." What was left available in the diplomatic arsenal of the day was "right of conquest," and the British clearly could not claim conquest of territory they had not even seen. But if the Iroquois had conquered the western tribes who held indigenous "natural right," and had thus set up a "savage empire," Britain would have the Iroquois rights of conquest because Iroquois dependency meant that what belonged to the Iroquois belonged to Britain. Lacking a reasonable alternative until the French could be forced off the continent, the British donated an empire to the Iroquois in order to claim it for themselves.[3] It was not the first, nor the last, example of creative history by diplomats, and it was swallowed whole by generations of partisan historians.

Joseph Henry Smith has remarked that no legal precedent existed for defining English jurisdiction over Indian tribes, which was "accordingly left to the fumbling of administrative officials." He continues, "This meant, of course, that no clear-cut solution was ever reached, if, indeed, in those quarters it was thought necessary or desirable. The prerogative of the crown over its overseas dominions was sufficiently large and unrestrained for long-continued evasion of definition to be feasible."[4] One reason for leaving the issue fuzzy was the desire to make the most of territorial claims based on rights attributed to Indians affiliated to Britain in ways that could be construed as subjection. As early as 1688, after a truce between Britain and France, the British crown sent instructions to governors of its colonies, including New York and New England, requiring, for the information of its commissioners to settle boundaries with the French, "an exact account and full information of the boundaries and limits thereof, *and of the Indians and territories depending thereon,* which you are to do with all

---

3. Cf. George E. Ellis's typically cynical remark: "In all the negotiations between the Indians and Europeans, including those of our own government, the only landed right recognized as belonging to the savages was that of giving up territory." Ellis, "The Red Indian of North America in Contact with the French and English," in *Narrative and Critical History of America,* ed. Justin Winsor, 8 vols. (Boston: Houghton Mifflin and Co., 1889), 1:300. In reality the situation was more complex than that. See Sutton, *Indian Land Tenure,* and Francis Jennings, "Virgin Land and Savage People," *American Quarterly* 23:4 (1971), pp. 519–41.

4. Joseph Henry Smith, *Appeals to the Privy Council from the American Plantations* (1950), reprinted (New York: Octagon Books, 1965), pp. 417–18.

convenient speed." This instruction should be read with the knowledge that "upon mature consideration we have thought fit to own the Five Nations or Cantons of the Indians, viz: the Maquaes, Sinecas, Cayougues, Oneydes, and Onondagues, as our subjects, and resolve to protect them as such."[5]

Having established the syllogism, the crown's officials clung to it with the same tenacity that the kings of England claimed still to be kings also of France, and in 1697 a flowering of the imagination bloomed among those officials. The Lords of Trade and Plantations prepared a memorial "relating to the Right of the Crown of Great Britain, to the Sovereignty over the five Nations of Indians bordering upon the Province of New York." Ostensibly a historical summary, it is a model of how a few thin facts can be stretched into "history" by ignoring the evidence that confutes them.

"From the first settlement of the Colony of New York (which we take to have been about the year 1610 [in 1609 Henry Hudson had looked into the countryside from the deck of his ship]) the five Nations of Indians commonly known by the names of Maquoas, Oneydes, Cayouges, Onondagues and Seneques, possessing the Lands to the Westward, and North West of that Plantation [vague enough to include Ohio and Ontario], have by many acknowledgments submissions, leagues or agreements, been united to, or depended on that Colony.

The said five Nations being the most warlike in those parts of the world, held all their neighbouring Indians in a manner of Tributary subjection, they went sometimes as far as the South Sea, the North West Passage and Florida, to war, and extended also their conquests over that part of the Country now called Canada."[6] It is not hard to see how "facts" of this sort could be used to argue British sovereignty over all of known North America.

Defeat of the Iroquois by the French and their allied Indians set the myth back for only a very short time. Though great alarm was caused in New York by the Franco-Iroquois peace treaty in 1701, the Yorkers saved their syllogism by taking a "deed" from the Iroquois for the region centering upon Detroit, which, though reduced from the vast territories endowed earlier upon the Iroquois by the Lords of Trade, was still respectable in scope, including arguably all of what is now Ontario and the Midwest

5. *Royal Instructions to British Colonial Governors, 1670–1776*, ed. Leonard Woods Labaree, 2 vols. (1935) reprinted (New York: Octagon Books, 1967), 2:715, 463.

6. *Documents Relative to the Colonial History of the State of New York*, eds. Edmund B. O'Callaghan and Berthold Fernow, 15 vols. (Albany: Weed, Parsons and Co., 1856–1887), 5:75. The French had refuted this argument ten years earlier. Ibid. 3:507–8. Cited hereafter as *N.Y.Col.Docs.*

states of the United States.[7] The "right" asserted in this so-called deed was the right of conquest, which failed to impress the French, whose allies had chased the Iroquois out of the territories in question.

Not bothered in the slightest by mere facts, Colden revived the empire-of-conquest myth in 1727 with Part I of his book, thus contributing his bit to a revived Board of Trade policy of aggressive expansion, and when hostilities broke out between Britain and France in King George's War (1743–1748), Colden went back to his files to produce Part II with a significantly altered title: *The History of the Five Indian Nations of Canada, Which Are Dependent on the Province of New-York in America.*[8] His propaganda was highly successful in attaining popular currency if we may judge by John Bartram's retelling of the conquest myth in 1751.

"The honour of first discovering these extensive fresh water seas [the Great Lakes] is certainly due to the French, who are at this time in possession of settlements at Fort Ponchartrian, on the strait between Lake Erie and the Lake Huron and at Misilimahinac between the latter and the upper lake, but as these can give them no title against the original inhabitants or the five nations, Conquerors of all the adjacent nations, so it is difficult to conceive by what arguments these small posts, inhabited by no subjects of France but soldiers, can be extended to mark any possession beyond the reach of their gun's, or land actually cultivated, except by such as must intitle the crown of Great Britain to all North America, both as prior discoverers and prior planters, without a subsequent desertion."[9] Bartram had the whole syllogism down pat and he was a private gentle-

7. Deed, July 19, 1701, *N.Y.Col.Docs.* 4:908–11. A curiosity in this document is the purported Iroquois claim that "our predecessors did four score years agoe totally conquer and subdue [seven nations of Indians called Aragaritkas] and drove them out of that country." Aragaritkas were Hurons. (*Northeast*, p. 405.) This date was clearly imaginary. It would have put the Iroquois conquests of western Iroquoian nations, including the Hurons, Neutrals, Eries, and Petuns, at about 1621. Those indisputable victories did not take place until the middle of the century. (Ch. 6, below.) An English motive is apparent for setting the date so far back.

8. My emphasis. See Preface to Part II, p. 77, of Great Seal ed. The reprints are with revised title: *The History of the Five Indian Nations of Canada, Which Are Dependent on the Province of New-York in America, and Are the Barrier Between the English and French in That Part of the World* (London: T. Osborne, 1747); same title, 2 vols. (London: L. Davis, 1755). Colden's interest in expansion was not lessened by his speculations in land. See Wilbur R. Jacobs, "Cadwallader Colden's Noble Iroquois Savages," in *The Colonial Legacy*, ed. Lawrence H. Leder, 4 vols. (New York: Harper and Row, 1971–1973), 3:34–58.

9. John Bartram, *Observations on the Inhabitants, Climate, Soil, Rivers, Productions, Animals, and other matters worthy of Notice, Made by Mr. John Bartram, In his Travels from Pensilvania to Onondago, Oswego and the Lake Ontario, In Canada* (1751), reprinted facsimile as *Travels in Pensilvania and Canada* (Readex, 1966), pp. 51–52. The connection between Colden and Bartram was direct and personal. See Collinson to Colden, March 5, 1741, and Colden to Collinson, March 13, 1742, in *The Letters and Papers of Cadwallader Colden*, 9 vols. (1918–1937), reprinted (New York: AMS Press, 1937), 2:208, 280.

man, without government office, whose consuming interest was botany.

Despite the many occasions when the Iroquois had begged for succor from both British and French governments to prevent their "destruction" by enemy tribes, they were neither immune to Colden's portrayal nor averse to his imperial endowment. Their self-conception could reach such heights as Mohawk Chief Hendrick's boast in 1755, "We are the six confederate Indian nations, the Heads and Superiors of all Indian nations of the Continent of America."[10] Unfortunately some rude dissidents killed him within hours of his utterance.[11]

Regardless of how little impressed the Indians were by the claim of Iroquois supremacy, English propaganda kept it alive. In 1755 cartographer Lewis Evans published his General Map of the Middle British Colonies in America with an *Analysis* giving much attention to the boundaries of the Six Nations "Confederates," which he generously extended to the Mississippi River.[12] A map appeared in London at about the same time, marking Britain's boundaries in America even more generously than had Evans and relying as he did on claims to the territories of "Subjects, or Allies."[13]

In negotiations with a French ambassador in 1755, the British negotiator insisted, "What the court of Great Britain affirms and insists on is that the Iroquois Five Nations, recognized by France as subjects of Great Britain, are by origin or by right of conquest legitimate proprietors of the Ohio River and its territory in question"; and in 1759 the British Lords of trade and Plantations exulted officially over the *recovery* "to the Dominions of the Crown" of "a great and valuable part of the Country, included in the [Iroquois] Deeds of 1701 and 1726."[14]

Myths assume lives of their own, so it is possible that by 1759 the statesmen of Britain had come to believe in this one, forgetting the circum-

10. Milton W. Hamilton, *Sir William Johnson: Colonial American, 1715–1763.* (Port Washington, N.Y.: Kennikat Press, 1976), p. 160.

11. T. Pownall to Lords of Trade, Sept. 20, 1755, *N.Y.Col.Docs.* 6:1008.

12. Evans's *Analysis* and map are reprinted facsimile in Lawrence Henry Gipson, *Lewis Evans* (Philadelphia: Historical Society of Pennsylvania, 1939). For Iroquois comment, see the remarks on the face of the map and in the text, pp. 155–57, 208.

13. The British and French Dominions in North America, ca. 1755, in mss. dept., HSP, call no. Of 301. It appears to be based on John Mitchell's famous map. Under the pseudonym of "An Impartial Hand," cartographer Mitchell published a claim to British sovereignty based largely on the assertion that a vast territory was "the property of the Five Nations of Indians . . . which they have made over to the crown of Great Britain . . ." [John Mitchell], *The Contest in America between Great Britain and France* (London: A. Millar, 1757), p. 174.

14. English Answer of June 7, 1755, in *Anglo-French Boundary Disputes in the West, 1749–1763*, French Series, vol. 2, *Collections of the Illinois State Historical Library* 27:242; Board of Trade to the Privy Council Committee, June 1, 1759, in *The Papers of Benjamin Franklin*, eds. Leonard W. Labaree, et al. (New Haven: Yale University Press, 1959–), 8:388.

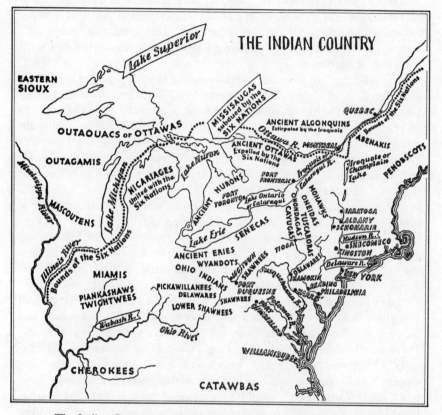

MAP 1. The Indian Country, based on a map of the British and French settlements of North America (London, 1755), showing the "Bounds of the Six Nations." REPRODUCED FROM P.A.W. WALLACE, *Conrad Weiser*, BY PERMISSION OF THE UNIVERSITY OF PENNSYLVANIA PRESS.

stances of its origin. The possibility, however, is none too likely. In 1760 the man who styled himself Lord Stirling discussed the practice of the Crown's giving by charter "what it was not itself possessed of." Though his remarks were made in another connection, their relevance to our immediate interest is apparent: "the policy of the English Court, fond of extending their Territories in America, induced them to leave the [sea to sea] Boundaries of the Colony of Connecticut as open as possible, in order to justify these people to possess themselves of their Encroachments . . . westwards."[15] In an age of aggressive territorial expansion, the end justified many devious means.

When the myth of Iroquois conquest ceased to have practical use, it was abandoned by the very well-connected and informed British colonial administrator Thomas Pownall. In 1776 he reprinted Lewis Evans's map of 1755 with its observation that the Iroquois had surrendered to Britain their hunting territory by their deeds of 1701 and 1726; but Pownall's accompanying text, though it quoted liberally from Evans's *Analysis*, omitted all mention of Iroquois conquests and boundaries.[16] For Britain the myth had become an irrelevance.

In America also, the myth died temporarily when the American Revolution brought about a review and reevaluation of tribal alliances. At Fort Stanwix in 1784, hard-nosed commissioners from the United States Congress would hear no talk of claims based on Iroquois conquest. For them the only conquest that mattered was the one made by the United States. Among the Iroquois themselves, some disillusion had set in about their League's claim to empire. At Fort Stanwix, Mohawk Captain Aaron Hill was given short shrift when he tried to set himself up as spokesman, not only for the Six Nations, but also for "the Ottawa, Chippewa, Hurons, Potawatamas, Messasaugas, Delawares, Cherokees, Shawanese, Chickasaws, Choctaws, and Creeks," who would have comprised a tidy little empire if Hill's pretensions had had any factual basis. Even Seneca Captain O'Bail (Cornplanter) would have none of such nonsense. He separated himself from Hill's position with the pointed remark that "as to the territory westward, you must talk respecting it with the Western Nations towards the setting of the Sun—*They* must consult of what part *they* must cede to the United States."[17]

15. Lord Stirling's letter, Dec. 18, 1760, mss., Penn Mss., Off. Corr. 9:154, HSP. These encroachments were on New Netherland.

16. Thomas Pownall, *A Topographical Description of Such Parts of North America as are Contained in the (Annexed) Map of the Middle British Colonies, &c.*, *in North America* (1776), reprinted with some patriotic fervor as *A Topographical Description of the Dominions of the United States of America*, ed. Lois Mulkearn (Pittsburgh: University of Pittsburgh Press, 1949). I have paged through Pownall to review his quotations from Evans. Neither the selected quotations nor Pownall's own text refers to Iroquois conquests or boundaries.

17. Journal of the Commissioners, mss., Wayne Mss., Indian Treaties, 1778–1795, B. Hist. Soc. of Pa. My emphasis.

Cornplanter's realism was confirmed by the western nations' refusal to accept orders from anybody. They remained at war with the United States for another decade, defeating two American expeditionary forces, until General Anthony Wayne forced them to sue for peace by his victory at Fallen Timbers. In the treaty that followed, at Greenville in 1795, not a single Iroquois was present as the westerners ceded some territories and received Wayne's confirmation of their just right to others. *All* the territories thus assigned had been part of the imaginary Iroquois empire,[18] but the Iroquois reaction to the news of its disposition was limited to a statement that their feelings were hurt![19]

The myth's revival

Nevertheless the myth did not die. Having diverged in two directions during the eighteenth century—through Anglo-American historiography and Iroquois tradition—it converged again in the 1850s. The double movement from a single source is hidden behind the reemergence of the Iroquois tradition as a "fact" determined by the fledgling science of anthropology. Lewis Henry Morgan, the man who is often called the founder of American anthropology, cited both a Seneca informant and Cadwallader Colden's history to support his finding of an Iroquois "empire which they reared over Indian nations."[20] It must be noticed that the Seneca informant was Ely S. Parker, a man so well educated that he became a brigadier-general under Ulysses S. Grant and was appointed later by Grant to the post of United States Commissioner of Indian Affairs. Far from being an illiterate "blanket Indian," he was as capable of reading Colden's history as Morgan himself, and I think he had. As we have been

18. See Pickering to Wayne, April 8, 1795, in *Anthony Wayne, A Name in Arms: Soldier, Diplomat, Defender of Expansion Westward of a Nation; The Wayne-Knox-Pickering-McHenry Correspondence,* transcribed and edited by Richard C. Knopf (1960), reprint ed. (Westport, Conn.: Greenwood Press, 1975), pp. 393–403. Treaty terms in *The New American State Papers: Indian Affairs,* ed. Thomas C. Cochran (Wilmington, Del.: Scholarly Resources, 1972), 4:150–52.

19. *The Correspondence of Lieut. Governor John Graves Simcoe, with Allied Documents Relating to His Administration of the Government of Upper Canada,* comp. and ed. E. A. Cruikshank, 5 vols. (Toronto: Ontario Historical Society, 1923–1931), 1:218–29;4:88.

20. Lewis Henry Morgan, *League of the Iroquois,* with introduction by William N. Fenton (New York: Corinth Books, 1962), p. 8. Except for the introduction this is a facsimile reprint of Morgan, *League of the Ho-Dé-No-Sau-Nee, Iroquois* (Rochester: Sage and Brother, 1981). Throughout this book, Morgan referred repeatedly, if somewhat inconsistently, to Iroquois empire. On p. 14, it is a condition of "nominal subjection" for the conquered, but the Iroquois "exercised a constant supervision" over them. This as of 1700 A.D. when the Iroquois were at their lowest ebb. On p. 144, Morgan has them "rapidly building up an empire, which threatened the absorption or extermination of the whole Indian family east of the Mississippi," and this "at the epoch of Saxon occupation," whenever that may have been. Whatever his virtues as an ethnologist, Morgan was one of the world's worst historians.

told by his grandnephew, Parker imbibed Colden's theses indirectly from Samuel G. Drake, who passed them on without question. These Colden-derived "traditions" were sharply at variance with more authentically tribal traditions to be mentioned further on. They call to mind the experience of a colleague who asked an Iroquois lady informant where she had gotten her account of a tradition. "Right here," said the lady, taking a book from its shelf.[21]

At almost exactly the same time that Morgan published, historian Francis Parkman delivered a gothically lurid tale of Iroquois ferocity and terrorism that cannot be fully appreciated without direct quotation. His Iroquois "extended their conquests and their depredations from Quebec to the Carolinas, and from the western prairies to the forests of Maine. On the south, they forced tribute from the subjugated Delawares, and pierced the mountain fastnesses of the Cherokees with incessant forays. On the north, they uprooted the ancient settlements of the Wyandots; on the west they exterminated the Eries and the Andastes, and spread havoc and dismay among the tribes of the Illinois; and on the east, the Indians of New England fled at the first peal of the Mohawk war-cry."[22] It is almost undiluted Colden and there is hardly a word of verifiable truth in the whole frenzied outcry.

Morgan and Parkman should not be confused with each other although they both accepted White supremacy as natural and inherent in the varied endowments of what they took to be races. It must be stressed that both thought in terms of racial categories. (Anthropologists do not like being reminded of Morgan's adherence to race doctrines, but the idea of culture had not yet been developed as the refutation of those evils.)[23] But Morgan

21. Another case of "tradition" coming from a book is reported in Robert E. Bieder, "Anthropology and History of the American Indian," *American Quarterly* 33:3 (1981), p. 309. Parker's career: "Parker, Eli Samuel," in *Handbook of American Indians North of Mexico*, ed. Frederick Webb Hodge, 2 vols. (Washington, D.C.: Government Printing Office, 1907), 2:203–4. His reading of Drake: Arthur C. Parker, *The Life of General Ely S. Parker, Last Grand Sachem of the Iroquois and General Grant's Military Secretary*, Buffalo Historical Society Publications 23 (Buffalo, N.Y., 1919). Drake on Iroquois empire and Delaware "women": Samuel G. Drake, *Biography and History of the Indians of North America, from Its First Discovery*, 11th ed. (same as first of 1841, stated preface, p. 3), (Boston: Benjamin B. Mussey and Co., 1851), pp. 500, 514–15. Curiously, Arthur C. Parker himself avoided statement of Iroquois conquests, except for the well-documented reality of the 1650s, and said nothing about the Delawares being women. See his *An Analytical History of the Seneca Indians, Researches and Transactions of the New York State Archeological Association* 6:nos. 1–5 (Rochester, N.Y.: Lewis H. Morgan Chapter, 1926).

22. Francis Parkman, *The Conspiracy of Pontiac and the Indian War after the Conquest of Canada* (1851), reprinted in New Library Edition, 2 vols. (Boston: Little Brown, and Co., 1909), 1:9–10.

23. For Morgan on race see *League*, pp. 3, 8, 10, 13, et passim, esp. p. 145. At one point Morgan contradicted his usually optimistic outlook by giving "the true reason, why the red race has never risen, or can rise above its present level," p. 57. In his later book he concluded

was a humanitarian concerned to better the lot of the Iroquois, whom he knew personally, although, like many an anthropologist since, he tended to take the side of "his" Indians against others; his scorn for the Delawares and their traditions was not restrained by any concern for objective inquiry. In sharp contrast, Parkman was a racist of the venomous type who did not hesitate to falsify his source materials to make them support his Social Darwinian preconceptions.[24] Parkman wished to show that the Iroquois were the "highest type" of Indians only in order to condemn that height for being so irredeemably low. Ironically Morgan, who was as free-enterprise capitalistic as they come, was picked up by Friedrich Engels and thus established as the founding father of international Marxist ethnology as well as the profession of anthropology in the United States.[25] The combination of Morgan and Marxism with Parkman and Social Darwinism was irresistible; it swept all criticism and dissidence aside.[26] Without need for a pedestal of evidence—in outright defiance of the evidence—the idea of Iroquois empire was enthroned.

J. N. B. Hewitt, a Tuscarora, remarked in the Bureau of American Ethnology's authoritative *Handbook of American Indians North of Mexico* (1907) that the Iroquois "were able to extend their conquests over all the neighboring tribes from Ottawa River to the Tennessee, and from the Kennebec to Illinois River and Lake Michigan."[27] Thus everywhere that an Iroquois raiding party hit and fled became a conquest even if the retreat followed after a bloody defeat. Writers in the Smithsonian Institution's revised and enlarged *Handbook of North American Indians* (1978) have quietly dropped such talk, but without commenting on its falsity and without mentioning the Covenant Chain by which the Iroquois genuinely achieved

that "The Aryan family represents the central stream of human progress, because it produced the highest type of mankind, and because it has proved its intrinsic superiority by gradually assuming the control of the earth." It is a sentence that could have been written by Joseph Goebbels. *Ancient Society, or Researches in the Lines of Human Progress from Savagery through Barbarism to Civilization* (1877), reprint ed. Eleanor Burke Leacock (Cleveland: World Publishing Co., 1963), pp. 562–3.

24. For evidence of Parkman's professional misconduct see Francis Jennings, "A Vanishing Indian: Francis Parkman Versus His Sources," *Pennsylvania Magazine of History and Biography* 87:3 (July, 1963), pp. 306–23; and Howard H. Peckham, "The Sources and Revisions of Parkman's *Pontiac*," *Papers of the Bibliographical Society of America* 37 (1943), pp. 293–307.

25. Friedrich Engels, *The Origin of the Family, Private Property and the State* (1884), trans. Ernst Untermann (Chicago: Charles H. Kerr and Co., 1902), pp. 9–11; Eleanor Burke Leacock, introduction to Part I of Morgan, *Ancient Society*, pp. I.vi–I.vii, I.xv.

26. Strangely, there is no mention of Parkman in Richard Hofstadter, *Social Darwinism in American Thought* (rev. ed. Boston: Beacon Press, 1955), although the book focuses strongly on Parkman's disciple John Fiske. The disciple was not so reticent. See John Fiske, "Francis Parkman," *The Atlantic Monthly* 73 (1894), pp. 664–74, which was reprinted almost verbatim as the "Introductory Essay to *The Works of Francis Parkman*, Champlain edition, 20 vols. (Boston: Little, Brown and Co., 1897), 1:xi–xli.

27. "Iroquois," in *Handbook*, ed. Hodge, 1:618. For Hewitt see *Northeast*, pp. 8, 9.

a degree of influence over other tribes through diplomacy rather than conquest. The popular *American Heritage Book of Indians* (1961) succumbed abjectly to Parkman's lush rhetoric and added some of its own. Writer William Brandon enthroned the Iroquois as "king of the hill. . . . In the paramount area of conflict between rival European invaders, the Great [Iroquois] League now stood alone, the ruling power, holding the key to the entire interior of the continent." Iroquois depredations rolled on, "toppling ancient societies, uprooting peoples, tumbling together fugitives and invaders. . . . The land was filled with Ishmaels."[28]

Contradictory traditions

The myth did not go unchallenged. French statesmen refuted it. Canadian authors have generally ignored it.[29] The *Jesuit Relations*, year by year, chronicled Iroquois defeats as well as triumphs. A direct refutation was issued in 1872 by an amateur historian of Newburgh, New York, who found that "there is scarce a recorded conquest by them [the Iroquois] that is not tinged by the unmistakeable fact that the subjugated tribe was contending against civilized as well as savage foes."[30] Interestingly, this writer, E. M. Ruttenber, did not use the language of race and did support his findings with documented research. But he was a mere printer by trade,[31] and the professionals ignored him.

Though Morgan laid much stress on "Indian tradition" as his source for

28. *The American Heritage Book of Indians*, ed. Alvin M. Josephy, Jr., Introduction by former President John F. Kennedy, narrative by William Brandon (New York: American Heritage Publishing Co., 1961), pp. 191–95.

29. Canadian William J. Eccles remarks in a letter to me dated Nov. 3, 1981, that "nailing the proverbial jelly to the wall is easy compared to defining their [French] policy" in regard to Indian nations. . . . I would say that the French, in fact, recognized the Five Nations as independent and sovereign, not subject to anyone, but rejected their claims to lands beyond those they had occupied when the French moved into the St Lawrence valley. . . ." For that rejection, and evidence that the French understood English policy perfectly, see Denonville to Seignelay, June 12, 1686, *N.Y.Col.Docs.*9:295; Galissonière to Clinton, Aug. 25, 1748, ibid., 6:489; treaty minutes, Quebc, Nov. 2, 1748, ibid., 10:186–88; Rouillé to Mirepoix, Feb. 3, 1755, in *Anglo-French Boundary Disputes in the West*, p. 107; Feb. 19, 1755, ibid., p. 123.

30. E. M. Ruttenber, *History of the Indian Tribes of Hudson's River; Their Origin, Manners and Customs; Tribal and Sub-Tribal Organizations; Wars, Treaties, etc., etc.* (Albany: J. Munsell, 1872), facsimile reprint (Port Washington, N.Y.: Kennikat Press, 1971), pp. 52–53.

31. A good friend of mine has tried to excuse Morgan's racism because "everyone was racist in those days." With unfeigned respect to my friend, that sounds to me like the argument used by children to do something forbidden: "All the other kids are allowed to do it." Besides which, Ruttenber's example proves that not everyone was racist. Other examples might be cited among the abolitionists of the mid-century, many of them were against race distinctions as well as slavery. Wendell Phillips and Thaddeus Stevens come to mind. But it is undoubtedly true that life scientists and social scientists were under the spell of the race

the conquest myth, various traditions disregard or contradict it. Strictly speaking, all traditions categorized as "Indian" are firstly tribal, and tribes other than Iroquois preserved different accounts of Iroquois status and the means used to achieve it. Mahican and Delaware traditions, as recorded by Moravian missionaries David Zeisberger and John Heckewelder, firmly rejected every suggestion of Iroquois conquest and supremacy.[32] They have been ridiculed out of court, but when the basis for ridicule is examined closely it turns out to be only a speech made at Easton in 1742 by Onondaga chief Canasatego and some tampering with documents performed by the Pennsylvania allies whose bidding he was carrying out.[33]

Ojibwa tradition, as told by the Christian convert George Copway (whose Indian name was Kah-ge-ga-gah-bowh), went far beyond Delaware assertions to claim defeat and rout of the Iroquois from Ontario by an alliance of western tribes in which the Ojibwa Mississaugas were prominent.[34] Morgan, Parkman, and Copway published almost simultaneously. In later years Parkman referred approvingly to Morgan but never mentioned Copway.[35] Morgan later referred to Parkman's "brilliant" histories; he, too, remained silent about Copway.[36]

Parkman had met Copway personally, and knew of the latter's preparations for publishing his Ojibwa history and legends, but Parkman dismissed them contemptuously before reading them. "Between you and me I shall have no great faith in them," he wrote to his friend E. G. Squier.

concept. See William Stanton, *The Leopard's Spots: Scientific Attitudes Toward Race in America, 1815–59* (Chicago: University of Chicago Press, 1960); Stephen Jay Gould, *The Mismeasure of Man* (New York: W. W. Norton and Co., 1981). This issue is inexcusably skirted by Curtis M. Hinsley, Jr., in his *Savages and Scientists: The Smithsonian Institution and the Development of American Anthropology, 1846–1910* (Washington, D.C.: Smithsonian Institution Press, 1981). For more enlightenment see George W. Stocking, Jr., *Race, Culture, and Evolution: Essays in the History of Anthropology* (New York: Free Press, 1968); Reginald Horsman, *Race and Manifest Destiny: The Origins of American Anglo-Saxonism* (Cambridge, Mass.: Harvard University Press, 1981).

Ruttenber's identification as a printer is in the entry for his *History of the County of Orange* (Newburgh, N.Y.: E. M. Ruttenber and Son, Printers, 1875).

32. John Heckewelder, *An Account of the History, Manners, and Customs of the Indian Nations Who Once Inhabited Pennsylvania and the Neighbouring States* (1819), rev. ed., Memoirs of the Historical Society of Pennsylvania 12, ed. Wm. C. Reichel (Philadelphia: HSP, 1876), pp. 56–67. The Delaware tradition was recited by Chief Tatamy to Conrad Weiser in 1856. See *Pa. Council Minutes*, March 5, 1757, 7:431.

33. For instance, in Horatio Hale, *The Iroquois Book of Rites* (1883), reprinted with introduction by William N. Fenton (Toronto: University of Toronto Press, 1963), pp. 92–94. For an example of tampering, see Francis Jennings, "The Constitutional Evolution of the Covenant Chain," *Proceedings of the American Philosophical Society* 115:2 (April, 1971), pp. 93–94. And see Appendix B, below.

34. George Copway, *The Traditional History and Characteristic Sketches of the Ojibway Nation* (London: C. Gilpin, 1850), ch. 6–8. Reprinted (Boston: B. F. Mussey and Co., 1851).

35. Francis Parkman, *The Jesuits in North America in the Seventeenth Century* (1857), New Library ed. (Boston: Little Brown, and Co., 1909), n. 2, pp. 44–45.

36. Morgan, *Ancient Society*, p. 157n.

"Copway is endowed with a discursive imagination and facts grow under his hands into a preposterous shape and dimensions."[37] It was relatively easy to brush aside the Ojibwa traditions, despite their being republished in Boston in 1851, because they were supported only by the credit of an individual, and an Indian at that. But the Delaware and Mahican traditions had been reported by John Heckewelder in 1819 at the request of the prestigious American Philosophical Society. Not being able to ignore them, Parkman resorted to denunciation. He attacked Heckewelder as "simple minded" and eliminated the Delaware tradition passed on by Heckewelder as "utterly unworthy of credit."[38] Yet he did not criticize the Parker version of Seneca tradition when it was passed on by Morgan.[39] It seems that, by passing through Morgan, the Parker account had been "laundered" free of its Indian taint. Like divinity, science can sometimes perform miracles that surpass comprehension.

Subtly involved were the pretensions of Boston's brahmins to omniscience in history. Bostoner Parkman was trumpeted by his associates as America's greatest historian—and this nonsense is still maintained by persons who do not compare his writings with their sources. Albany's Joel Munsell published E. M. Ruttenber's contradiction of Parkman, and the Historical Society of Pennsylvania reprinted missionary Heckewelder's book after Parkman's denunciations.[40] But Boston, Social Darwinism, Marxism, and Iroquois bragging carried the day.

Yet discordance and discrepancy existed, not only in the traditions of Indians other than Iroquois, but even in the Iroquois traditions actually recited by the chiefs in source documents. These were sometimes concocted to meet the policy objectives of the moment, especially when uttered by such an orator as Canasatego. In 1742 he thundered against the Delawares, who had been troubling his friends of Pennsylvania with demands for compensation for their lands. Previous to that time, the Iroquois had called the Delawares *women*, but had never claimed a conquest. Canasa-

37. Parkman to Squier, Boston, Nov. 18, 1849, in *Letters of Francis Parkman*, ed. Wilbur Jacobs, 2 vols. (Norman: University of Oklahoma Press, 1960), 1:65–66. Parkman's condescension showed itself in an insult to Copway that guaranteed the Indian's withdrawal of further communication: in a letter of introduction Parkman "accompanied it with a hint that he was not to trouble you with any application, direct or indirect, for pecuniary aid." It appears that the letter of introduction was never used by Copway. Parkman to Charles Eliot Norton, Nov. 10, 1850, ibid., 1:78.

38. The request by APS is noted in Heckewelder's dedication to Caspar Wistar, president of the society. For Parkman's attacks, see his *Jesuits*, n. 75–76 and *Conspiracy of Pontiac* 1:34n.

39. "Indian traditions are very rarely of any value as historical evidence." *Jesuits*, p. 545n. But Parkman repeated the conquest theme in *Count Frontenac and New France under Louis XIV* (1877), New Library ed. (Boston: Little, Brown, and Co., 1909), pp. 78–79. In the same book he repeated, "Indian traditions of historical events are usually almost worthless," p. 164.

40. Revised by William C. Reichel. Hist. Soc. of Pa. Memoirs 12, 1876.

tego concocted one on the spot.[41] In 1744, at the treaty of Lancaster, Canasatego made a convoluted claim of conquest over the Susquehannocks. Knowing that the Marylanders present were well aware that they themselves had driven the Susquehannocks out of their lands in 1675, Canasatego claimed that his people had "conquered" them afterward. He neglected to mention that the Susquehannocks had negotiated with his people for refuge in Iroquoia after their defeat by troops of Maryland and Virginia. When "tradition" becomes this creative, it must be treated exactly the same way that a careful historian approaches the works of predecessors whom he knows to have been special pleaders.[42]

The "Great Binding Law" of the Iroquois, which was a *re*constitution of Iroquois traditions as remembered in the nineteenth century (and remembered in several versions), makes no mention of an empire or even of tributaries; it provides only for war against other Indian nations until they accept the Iroquois Great Peace, after which they may be adopted into the Iroquois League. Even the Covenant Chain has vanished from this tradition despite its tremendous importance to the Iroquois of the colonial era.[43]

The Cayugas of Grand River Reserve, in Canada, have preserved an oral tradition to the present day that directly contradicts the Colden-Parker-Morgan-Parkman thesis of Iroquois conquest of the Delawares. On May 22, 1980, at the Newberry Library, Cayuga traditionalist Chief Jacob E. Thomas recounted that the Delaware nation had been adopted by the League as peacemakers to cement alliance between Iroquois and Algonquian nations. He noted that the Mohawks had raised some objection because the Delawares went "over the wall" to the Cayugas instead of "through the eastern door" kept by the Mohawks. One could wish for specific dates, but the process described has nothing to do with conquest

41. Treaty minutes, July 12, 1742, *Minutes of the Provincial Council of Pennsylvania* (often cited as *Colonial Records* because of title on spine, but herein cited as *Pennsylvania Council Minutes*), ed. Samuel Hazard, 16 vols. (Harrisburg and Philadelphia, 1838–1853), 4:579–80. Cf. Francis Jennings, "The Delaware Interregnum," *Pennsylvania Magazine of History and Biography* 89:2 (April, 1965), pp. 174–98; and "Constitutional Evolution," cited n. 33, above.

42. Treaty minutes, June 26, 1744, *Pennsylvania Council Minutes* 4:706–8. Cf. Francis Jennings, "Glory, Death, and Transfiguration: The Susquehannock Indians in the Seventeenth Century," *Proceedings of the American Philosophical Society* 112:1 (Jan., 1968), pp. 33–45. For comment on tradition, see George S. Snyderman, "An Ethnological Discussion of Allegany Seneca Wampum Folklore." *Proceedings of the American Philosophical Society* 126:4 (1982), pp. 316–26. "In reality, the tales were a teaching device used to strengthen the acceptance of Seneca lifeways. . . . No one seemed alarmed with changes if the Indian content remained intact." Pp. 318–19. "Indian" should be read as "tribal."

43. See Arthur C. Parker, *The Constitution of the Five Nations or The Iroquois Book of the Great Law* (1916), reprinted in facsimile (separately paged) in *Parker on the Iroquois*, ed. William N. Fenton (Syracuse, N.Y.: Syracuse University Press, 1968). See Fenton's comments, pp. 43–47.

or subjection; and interestingly, it conforms in essentials to the Delaware tradition reported by missionary Heckewelder and Delaware Chief Tatamy.

Perhaps myths should be separated into various kinds. Lately the general category seems to have found favor among some historians. William H. McNeill is distressed because "our historians have dodged their myth-making responsibilities."[44] Richard Drinnon deplores "a narrow rationalist definition" that focuses on proving parts of myths true or false and falls short of understanding their function as metaphorical wholes within cultures."[45] It does not seem credible that such remarks are meant to advocate outright lying, so perhaps they refer to a kind of myth that does not flout available evidence. My strictures are directed against the kind that does *and* against the "metaphorical whole" of inherent inequality that justifies automatic privilege for some human groups based on their exploitation of others. What follows herein is not merely an attempt to expose the rottenness of a false and hurtful myth. It substitutes a new synthesis, supported by documentary evidence. This sort of rationalism seems preferable to concocting still another myth.

44. William H. McNeill, "Make Mine Myth," *New York Times*, Dec. 28, 1981, Op-Ed p. A19.
45. Richard Drinnon, "Ravished Land," *The Indian Historian*, fall, 1976, p. 25.

Chapter 3 ❧ A MIXING of PEOPLES

Before we present you the matters of fact, it is fit to offer to your view the Stage whereon they were acted: for as Geography without History seemeth a carkasse without motion; so History without Geography, wandreth as a Vagrant without a certaine habitation.

Captain John Smith, *Travels and Works.*

Habitations and highways

Many Indian peoples, some of them known today only by rumor or artifact, lived along the river and bay valleys of northeastern North America. The rivers offered easy transportation and subsistence. The alluvial soils of their flood plains were rich and loose, game flourished near the stream, and fish were plentiful. Jean Gottman has observed that still today, after forests have been cut, game hunted nearly to extinction, and fish poisoned by pollution, abundant water remains the great natural resource of eastern North America.[1] In the seventeenth century its value was multiplied by the teeming life it was then permitted to maintain. In the midst of such plenty, human lives multiplied also, but the bulk of Indian population was nearly always a bit beyond the ken of the scribes of Europe. Even the names of the upstream tribes that came to be conventional in European discourse were usually not the tribes' own names for themselves; the European would accept names given by Indians near to him for those farther away. No one is quite sure, for example, where the name "Iroquois" came from, but it certainly was not from any of the Indians who were called by it.[2] Clarity is not helped by the ethnocentricity of the tribes. They did not hesitate to refer to their hostile neighbors with pejoratives equivalent to "stinkers" or "cannibals." Much confusion has resulted regarding the identities and relationships of the interior tribes, and where the pen has proved inadequate the historian can only hope for enlightenment from the archaeologist's spade.

1. Jean Gottman, *Megalopolis: The Urbanized Northeastern Seaboard of the United States* (New York: Twentieth Century Fund, 1961), pp. 8, 43, 81–85, 94.
2. Gordon Day, "Iroquois: An Etymology," *Ethnohistory* 15:4 (fall, 1968), pp. 389–402.

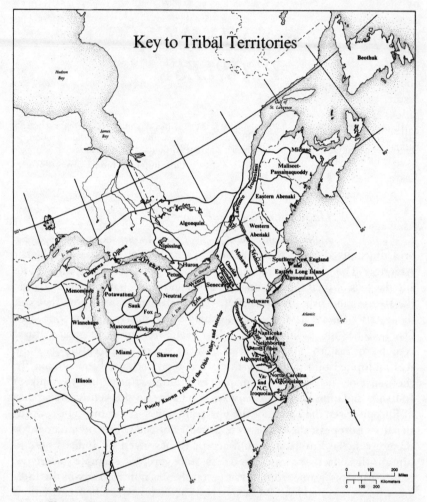

MAP 2. Key to Tribal Territories. REPRODUCED FROM *Northeast*, VOLUME 15 OF *Handbook of North American Indians*, BY PERMISSION OF GENERAL EDITOR WILLIAM C. STURTE-VANT.

Sometimes, however, the archaeologist is more hindrance than help. It was not bad enough that Indians of the Susquehanna Valley were called Susquehannocks by the English, Andastes by the French, and Minquas by the Dutch and Swedes.[3] Now the archaeologist notices from the evidence of a dig that they had culturally distinct neighbors, identified by the dig's site as "the Shenk's Ferry people." The Europeans apparently had no knowledge of the existence of these Indians.[4] Indeed the whole region of the upper Susquehanna is murky with hints and conjectures about the peoples who lived out yonder: Champlain's Carantouanais, the Jesuits' Atrakwaeronnon, the Swedes' Black Minquas, Tehaque, Skonedidehaga, and Serosquacke, which may or may not have been the tribes called by Maryland Englishmen the Ohongeoguena, Unquehiett, Kaiquariegahaga, Usququhaga, and Sconondihago. The last name may even have been an Iroquoian identification of the Nanticokes of Maryland's Eastern Shore.[5]

The Susquehanna remained for long the most mysterious river, but it was not unique. As far as the fall line, Europeans used rivers as their gateways to the interior; beyond the falls, all was murky. Even the well-traveled valley of the Hudson became hazy beyond the head of navigation at present-day Troy, New York. Somewhere up there were "Northern" Indians, so vaguely named at least until 1676. Vagueness also characterized the European consciousness of the mountainous territory surrounding the modern town of Port Jervis, where New York, New Jersey, and Pennsylvania meet. Like the territory, the people who lived in its center were called Minisinks (sometimes Minsi, later Muncy or Munsee). They confederated loosely, from time to time, with Algonquian neighbors in the lower Hudson and Delaware valleys and along the smaller streams of northern New Jersey. They learned early the dangers of European neighborhood and successfully barred colonials from entering their territory until nearly 1730. Because they protected themselves so well, they appear

3. Francis Jennings, "Susquehannock," in *Northeast*, p. 367. A bibliographic note: *Northeast* is essentially an anthology of articles by independent authors fitted into a general plan but not unified in outlook. Speaking generally, it represents the state of the art of ethnology when the several articles were completed rather than when the volume was published. It is indispensable for a student but must be used with care. As with other compendia of plural scholarship, its contributors have diverse purposes and interpretations.

4. Henry W. Heisey and J. Paul Witmer, "The Shenk's Ferry People," in *Foundations of Pennsylvania Prehistory*, eds. Barry C. Kent et al., Anthropological Series 1 (Harrisburg: Pennsylvania Historical and Museum Commission, 1971), pp. 477–79.

5. Jennings, "Susquehannock," pp. 362–63; Heckewelder, *History*, p. 92. Heckewelder says that the Iroquois called the Nanticokes *Sganiateratieh-rohne*, meaning tide-water people, or sea-shore settlers. A lot of guesswork enters into these identifications from written sources because reporters of different nationalities heard with differently attuned ears, and orthography was anything but dependable.

seldom in written sources.[6] These Minisinks have been regarded conventionally as the "Wolf" division of the Delaware tribe, with which they sometimes acted in concert in the eighteenth century. But most evidence shows them making their own decisions and going their own way.[7]

With such difficulties of perspective, it is prudent to name and locate the aboriginal populations of the river valleys with diffidence. There had apparently been considerable movement of communities before European contact. The Europeans observed more such movement after their arrival, and there is much reason to infer massive shifts of population beyond their observation, both in quantities and locations.

In a most general way the Indians of this large region are classed nowadays in two great linguistic stocks: Algonquian and Iroquoian. The spelling of both names must be watched closely to avoid confusion with particular ethnic groups called Algonquin and Iroquois—a confusion often repeated in the older literature before the modern convention became standard. Knowing as little as we do about the aboriginal relationships between tribes, scholars have been forced to group them according to their linguistic affinities. To call a gathering of tribesmen "Algonquians" is simply to say that they belong to tribes speaking related languages. They may or may not have been affiliated politically. The same rule applies to Iroquoians.[8] When Cartier visited the St. Lawrence in the early sixteenth century, he found Iroquoians at the sites of Quebec and Montreal, but they had withdrawn by the time Champlain arrived in the seventeenth century. Traditions reported by Jesuit missionaries speak of Huron attacks driving away the Iroquoians, who had lived where Montreal was later built.[9] When the Dutch arrived on the Hudson, the valley was occupied

6. The most thorough study of the Minisinks is Robert Steven Grumet, " 'We Are Not So Great Fools,' Changes in Upper Delawaran Socio-Political Life, 1630–1758," Ph.D. diss., Rutgers, The State University of New Jersey, 1979.

7. The Minisinks are noted frequently as coming to New York City instead of Albany to treat with the English. In 1681 a Minisink speaker stated this explicitly and added that his people always negotiated in the presence of the sachem of Tappan, an Algonquian. Minisink and Tappan negotiators appeared again in 1686. New York land records show purchases of Minisink lands being made without intervention by Iroquois. *N.Y.Col.Docs.* 13:550; New York Council Minutes, Aug. 7, 1686, mss. 5:163; *Calendar of New York Colonial Manuscripts Indorsed Land Papers in the Office of the Secretary of State of New York: 1643–1803* (Albany: Weed, Parsons and Co., 1864), 2:224, 238; 3:83, 84, 107, 136, 159, 167, 179; 4:8, 177; 5:40; 7:68. These are *Calendar* citations for convenience. I have inspected most of the references in the original mss.

8. Political organization of the Delawares and Minisinks has posed a particularly difficult problem, not yet solved, although Grumet's model of local groups allying in "maximal organization" for dealing with maximal issues is promising. See Grumet, "We Are Not So Great Fools," ch. 3. Iroquoian communities were highly mixed ethnically because of adopting captives and sometimes whole villages of defeated enemies.

9. The withdrawal of the Laurentian Iroquoians cannot be attributed to any one factor, but several possibilities have been identified. Epidemic disease was certainly one element. It had to be something other than scurvy because the Indians taught Cartier how to cure that—

by communities affiliated linguistically as Algonquians. So also in the Delaware Valley and Chesapeake Bay area. Iroquoians lived farther inland and upstream. The Iroquoian Susquehannocks lived north of the Chesapeake Bay on the Susquehanna River, which pours into it. The Iroquois Five Nations lived west of the Hudson River, their Mohawk component occupying the Mohawk Valley, which joins the Hudson from the west. Lying along a westward-extending line were the other four of the Five Nations—the Oneidas, Onondagas, Cayugas, and Senecas—living in the Finger Lakes region as far west as the Genesee River. Clustered at the western end of Lake Ontario and the eastern end of Lake Erie were the Wenroronons, Eries, and Neutrals, and at the eastern end of the Georgian Bay of Lake Huron were the Tionnontates (or Petuns) and the Huron confederation.[10]

Early in the seventeenth century, Europeans sailed up the St. Lawrence, Hudson, Delaware, and Chesapeake-Susquehanna to the heads of

so some Laurentian Iroquoians "withdrew" by dying, probably of European-introduced diseases. Another factor influencing withdrawal may have been the hostility of surrounding Algonquian tribes. Cadwallader Colden reported a tradition that this caused "the Five Nations" to retire "to the Southward of Cadarackui Lake [Lake Ontario], where they now live." Bruce G. Trigger thinks this "impossible," reviews the literature on the issue, and suggests that some Laurentians may have found refuge among the Hurons.

The Jesuit Relations of 1642 note that an aged Indian told a missionary that his grandfather had "tilled the soil on the spot [Montreal]." Two companions who "belonged to the nation of those who had formerly dwelt on this Island" remarked that "The Hurons, who then were our enemies, drove our Forefathers from this country. Some went towards the country of the Abnaquiois, others toward the country of the Hiroquois, some to the Hurons themselves, and joined them."

In 1646 Father Jerome Lalemant was told by an aged Indian that Montreal "is my country. My mother told me that while we were young, the Hurons making war on us, drove us from this Island; as for me, I wish to be buried in it, near my ancestors." These Indian testimonies sound convincing.

According to contemporary historian Marc Lescarbot, the Iroquoians of Hochelaga [Montreal] were driven away by attacks of the Iroquois proper at about 1600. These attacks could be consistent with Huron raids as well.

Carl Ortwin Sauer, Sixteenth Century North America: The Land and the People as Seen by the Europeans (Berkeley: University of California Press, 1971), pp. 90–91; The Voyages of Jacques Cartier, trans. and ed. H. P. Biggar, Publications of the Public Archives of Canada 11 (Ottawa, 1924), pp. 204–5, 207, 212, 214–15; Colden, History, pp. 5–6; Bruce G. Trigger, The Children of Aataentsic: A History of the Huron People to 1660, 2 vols. (Montreal: McGill-Queen's University Press, 1976), 1:180, 214–28; Trigger, "Hochelaga: History and Ethnohistory," in Cartier's Hochelaga and the Dawson Site, eds. James F. Pendergast and Bruce G. Trigger (Montreal: McGill-Queen's University Press, 1972), pp. 1–93; Barthelemy Vimont and Jerome Lalemant, Relations of 1642 and 1646, The Jesuit Relations and Allied Documents: Travels and Explorations of the Jesuit Missionaries in New France, 1610–1791, ed. Reuben Gold Thwaites, 73 vols. (1896–1901), reprinted facsimile in 36 vols. (New York: Pageant Book Co., 1959), 22:215; 29:173; Marc Lescarbot, The History of New France (1609), trans. W. L. Grant, 3 vols., Publications of the Champlain Society 1, 7, 11 (Toronto, 1907–1914), 3:267–68.

Further comment has been made in Francis Jennings, "On Doing Interdisciplinary Work," a paper presented at Cherry Hill Forum (Albany), Sept. 24, 1982. To be published in the forum proceedings.

10. See the maps in Northeast, pp. 345, 419.

navigation, where they soon planted their most advanced trading posts; but for the most part they refrained from voyaging by canoe into the rivers' upper reaches. The headwaters beyond falls and rapids were the "back country." Colonization also moved upstream. Although Europe's expansion has been characterized justly as seaborne and coastbound, river coasts were part of it. Usually the compass direction was north or west, but tributary streams could carry settlers east or south as well. In southern New Jersey, Europeans settled from the Delaware River eastward. The Dutch settled northward along the Hudson, as did Marylanders along Chesapeake Bay. In the eighteenth century, the Shenandoah Valley was colonized by a stream of settlers moving south from Pennsylvania.

For the most part, riverine Indians of these regions pulled their communities back upstream (or were pushed) as European populations became denser and more aggressive. East of the Appalachians the retreat of the Indians was to and beyond the watersheds, or "divides," between river systems. Over the grand vista of the centuries one may see a westward march of Anglo-American political institutions (which are not to be equated with "civilization"). In the seventeenth century, however, Europeans of varied nationalities moved in varied directions, and it is well worth remembering that Frenchmen were in the Mississippi Valley and on the Gulf of Mexico long before Englishmen—not to speak of the even earlier marches of Spaniards inland from Florida and Mexico.[11] In the eyes of particular men who lived at particular times and places, river valleys were more important indicators of direction than compass points.

Division by watersheds

A number of watersheds in New York and Pennsylvania gave direction and structure to demographic movements and politico-economic developments in the early seventeenth century. Of those in New York, three require particular notice. The first lies transversely between the southern end of Lake George and the Hudson River at Glens Falls. From here, at a distance of less than ten miles apart, two great streams flow in opposite directions in a trough between extensive ranges of mountains. Lake George pours its waters northward into Lake Champlain, which empties into the Richelieu River, which joins the St. Lawrence, which flows to the Atlan-

11. The best review of these early "discoveries" is David B. Quinn, *North America from Earliest Discovery to First Settlements: The Norse Voyages to 1612*, New American Nation Series (New York: Harper and Row, 1977). For more elaborate discussion of maps and movements, Justin Winsor's notes and "critical essays" are still useful—much more so than the narrative authors' ethnocentric contributions in *Narrative and Critical History of America*, ed. Justin Winsor, 8 vols. (Boston: Houghton, Mifflin and Co., 1889).

tic Ocean at Newfoundland. From Glens Falls southward, the Hudson
carries its mighty stream to the Atlantic at Manhattan, and the Hudson
was navigable to seventeenth-century ocean vessels as far upstream as what
is now called Troy, just above Albany. There is no single name for the
channel whose waters flow both north and south, but its significance as a
total entity leads me to propose that it be called by the name of its most
prominent tribal inhabitants of the era of first European contact. These
were the Mahicans, who lived in the vicinity of the modern city of Albany
and traveled extensively up and down their channel on all its waterways.
As European colonists increased in numbers—French in the St. Lawrence
Valley and Dutch and English in the Hudson-Valley segment of the Mahican Channel—the northern segment became a much-traveled route in times
of both peace and war. It has been called the warpath of nations; it was
also a commercial artery. Large cargoes of furs were carried south from
Canada to be exchanged for Dutch and English dry goods, hardware, and
arms; at other times the arms were carried in either direction by marching
men intending to kill and conquer. The Mahican Channel is unique in
North America. No other fissure cuts so directly through a broad mass of
mountains to send water from its highlands to ocean bays distant from
each other by more than a thousand crowflight miles.[12]

A second watershed, near Rome, New York, divides the eastward-flow-
ing Mohawk River from creeks flowing into Oneida Lake and thence to
Lake Ontario. The "water level route" through the Mohawk Valley to the
west has been improved by the Erie Canal, the New York Central Rail-
road, and the New York State Thruway, immense engineering works that
follow routes first traversed by canoe and moccasin. The historical importance of this gateway to the continental interior is attested by the amount
of construction that has since been laid along it, but it remained shrouded
in mystery to Europeans until toward the end of the seventeenth century.
On merely physical considerations, it should have been the direct road to
the west for English colonization, but the power of the Iroquois Five
Nations kept it closed to Euramerican colonization until the American
Revolution blasted it open.

A third watershed extends in an arc across lower middle New York,
from headwaters of the Delaware River, near Ellenville and Prattsville,
across to the Finger Lakes and headwaters of the Genesee River. Reaching
between these two extremes are branches of the vast "treetop" of the Susquehanna River, which also extends branches in western Pennsylvania
almost to the headwaters of the Allegheny River. North of this third
watershed, the streams and lakes flow a short distance northward to empty

12. "New York is pre-eminently a divide region." Ralph Stockman Tarr, "New York;
Drainage," *Encyclopædia Britannica*, 11th ed. 19:595–96. The state's great valleys were gouged
out by glacial action.

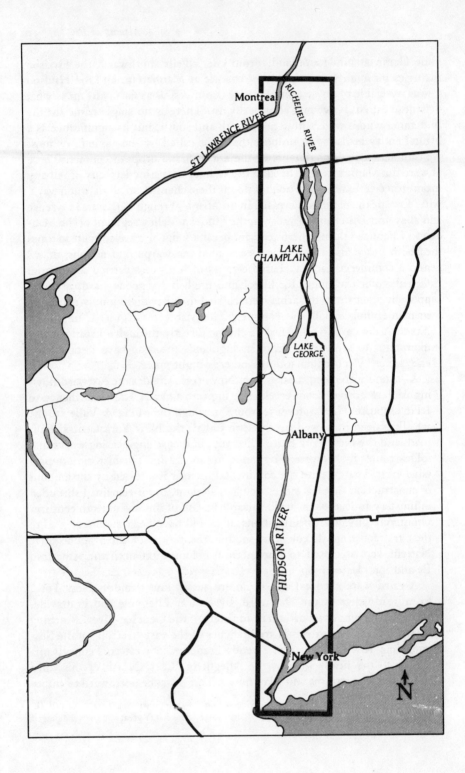

into Lake Ontario. The generally southerly flow of the Susquehanna from the watershed does not stand out so visibly on the map as does the Mahican Channel because the mountains of the region are piled up in a disorderly jumble of peaks and plateaus. Their valleys go every which way, but water from the peaks makes great rivers, which were just as navigable by Indian canoes as were the Hudson River or Lake Champlain. On its western side the Susquehanna's tributary "treetop" intertwines with that of the Allegheny River, which joins the Monongahela at Pittsburgh to make the Ohio. On its eastern side the Susquehanna's treetop interlaces with the Delaware's. There is no single straight valley to catch the eye, and the crosswise tilt of the Appalachian Mountains confuses appearances: one tends to assume that mountain ridges are themselves watersheds. But the Susquehanna and Delaware headwaters wend ultimately southward, bent this way and that by the mountain walls but always getting through. In a manner of speaking, Pennsylvania and New Jersey are simply the supporting structures of giant pipelines funneling New York's water (and their own) to the sea.

Trade moved on those waters. European ships traveled up the trunk streams. Indian light-draft canoes traversed the tributary streams as well as the main trunks, and canoes could be picked up and carried short distances—portaged—from one river system to another. For such travel, the Iroquois Five Nations had an advantageous position. Their homeland in the Finger Lakes region spread over two watersheds and lay close to a third. They could journey by canoe, if they wished, directly to the Great Lakes and from there to the St. Lawrence. Or they could paddle down the Delaware or Susquehanna rivers to their bays—or down the Allegheny, Ohio, and Mississippi to the Gulf of Mexico. No record tells of their making the longest of these voyages—there was, after all, the task of paddling or trudging back—but they were constantly busy within a radius of about 500 miles from Iroquoia.[13]

Foot traffic also moved between tribal communities, sometimes along hilltop ridges as well as valley floors. Paul A. W. Wallace has mapped 131 trails and systems of trails in Pennsylvania alone, and Morgan has traced a number of Iroquois trails, one of which he calls "one of the great natural highways of the continent."[14]

Some Iroquoians lived on the St. Lawrence when Jacques Cartier win-

13. See Cadwallader Colden, "Answers to Queries of the Lords of Trade," Feb. 14, 1738, in *N.Y.Col.Docs.* 6:122.

14. Paul A. W. Wallace, *Indian Paths of Pennsylvania* (Harrisburg: Pennsylvania Historical and Museum Commission, 1965). Morgan, *League*, pp. 47–48, 414–42, and appendix map.

MAP 3. (facing page) The "Mahican Channel."

tered in their village of Stadacona (Quebec) in 1534–1535. We know only that they spoke a language of the Iroquoian stock, to be distinguished from the Algonquian family of languages spoken by surrounding tribes. Between Cartier's time and the arrival of Samuel de Champlain in 1603, the Stadaconans had abandoned their village for an unknown destination. Some probably joined their brother Iroquoians, the Hurons, near the present site of Toronto. Many were certainly wiped out in an epidemic, as were the Indians whom the Pilgrims replaced at New Plymouth. Others of the surviving Stadaconans probably traveled south to join another set of linguistically affiliated tribesmen, the Iroquois proper. Although Stadaconans (Quebec) and Hochelagans (Montreal) are usually lumped together as Laurentian Iroquois, there is no reason to deny the possibility that they might have gone in different directions.[15]

The Iroquois Five Nations

When the curtain rises on the recorded history of the Five Nations, we find them living in stockaded villages, sometimes called "cantons," often inflated to "castles" by the English. Nearest to Albany were the Mohawks—*Kaniengehaga* in their own language—who held the status in the confederacy of the "Keepers of the Eastern Door." As such, they especially had responsibility for relations with both the coastal Algonquian tribes and the eastern European colonies. New Netherland's regime looked upon the Mohawks with ambivalence, but the English conquest of New Netherland would result in a highly favored Mohawk status as the most faithful allies of New York.

15. See no. 9 above. At the 1981 meeting of the Conference on Iroquois Research, archaeologists James Pendergast and William Ritchie contended warmly over the issue, resting their arguments on the evidence of materials found in digs. It seems that pots went north of Lake Ontario, but pipes went south. Pendergast appealed to sexual division of labor. Contending that pots were made by women, and pipes by men, he noted that digs at St. Lawrence Iroquoian sites had turned up Huron pots and pipes, and concluded that Huron captives on the St. Lawrence had been of both sexes. But digs at Huron sites exposed no St. Lawrence Iroquoian pipes though pots from that region were found. Therefore, Pendergast argued, the Hurons took only women captives from the St. Lawrence and massacred the men, thus explaining the observed depopulation of that region. Ritchie denied the assumption that labor was divided so rigidly and thus reopened the whole question. It seems to this writer that other explanations might also account for the absence of men among Huron captives, if indeed there were none. For instance, they might have been away hunting when their women were seized. Certainly some survived to take up residence elsewhere, or their descendants would not have existed to talk to Jesuit missionaries. Probably the wrangle will go on. It is so satisfactorily inconclusive that its participants are unlikely ever to agree to give it up. An amused observer of a similar argument on another occasion expressed a caution *sotto voice* against relying for a conclusion on "a few cracked pots." Appellants to archaeology for conclusive evidence need to remember that consensus in that profession is a sometime thing.

Westward were the Oneidas, "younger brothers" of the Mohawks and possibly originating as a split-off. Possessed of full membership in the Five Nations league, the Oneidas were still rather junior in comparison with the Mohawks and lacked an imposing title. Nevertheless, they seem to have assumed (along with the Cayugas) a special interest or responsibility toward the regions south of the Five Nations homeland.

In the middle were the Onondagas, whose central position geographically was also the central political capital of the League. At Onondaga burned the sacred metaphorical "fire" of the Iroquois League, and an actual fire was kindled periodically for the solemn convening of the League's grand councils. The Onondagas, whose inclinations toward alliance wavered between England and France, are often reputed to have been the League's wisest leaders, but the Mohawks also aspired to that honor.

West of the Onondagas were the Cayugas, "younger brothers" of the westernmost Senecas. Like the Oneidas, the Cayugas held no special title or responsibility, and they attempted to make up for the formal deficiency by busying themselves intensively to the southward.

West of them, the Senecas were the Keepers of the Western Door, especially responsible for relations with the "far Indians," and their remote position long saved them from the full debilitating effects of having European neighbors. While war and disease reduced the populations of the eastern tribes drastically in spite of compensatory adoptions of prisoners of war, the Senecas' share of the total Iroquois population increased proportionately; in the historical records, the Senecas outnumber all the other Iroquois combined and Seneca influence grew among the tribes in the eighteenth century as a counterweight to the previously dominant Mohawks and Onondagas. Some of the difficulties of research are shown by the Seneca name, which, according to J. N. B. Hewitt, was "the Anglicized form of the Dutch enunciation of the Mohegan rendering of the Iroquoian ethnic appellative *Oneida*, or, strictly, *Oneniuteaka*, and with a different ethnic suffix, *Oneniuteronnon*, meaning 'people of the standing or projecting rock or stone.' "[16]

It is more difficult to establish population figures than names. Gunther H. Michelson has compiled tables in which 1660 A.D. is the first date with estimates for all five nations. Expressed in numbers of warriors, the Mohawks had 500, the Oneidas about 100, the Onondagas 300, the Cayugas 300, and the Senecas 1,000. To get a reasonable approximation of total populations, each of these figures should be multiplied by a factor for the warriors' families. Again, we are not sure how large those families were. Some scholars will multiply warriors by three, some by five, in order to get figures for total populations. At maximum, the total *Iroquois* popula-

16. J. N. B. Hewitt, "Seneca," in *Handbook*, ed. Hodge, 2:502.

tion in 1660, according to Michelson's estimates, would be 10,000. But William A. Starna has gone behind Michelson's compilation chronologically for the Mohawks and has found that "the traditional and often repeated population estimates for the aboriginal and early historic period are too conservative." Using a combination of historical, ethnographic, and archaeological evidence too complex to recite here, Starna calculates the pre-epidemic population of the Mohawk tribe alone within a range of 8,258 to 17,116. The wide range takes into consideration our ignorance of the *rate* of death caused by epidemics and the *ratio* of persons per warrior in those early warrior counts. But the minimum figure of Starna's estimate is more than three times the minimum to be derived from Michelson's figures, and the maximum is about seven times as great. Certainly the issue has not yet been settled, though the tendency in recent demographic research is toward higher numbers than heretofore. Another certainty is that the total Iroquois population declined drastically from aboriginal times as the consequence of epidemics and wars.[17] (In relatively recent times, however, the population has grown once more, and there now seem to be more living Iroquois than ever previously known.)[18]

Nation and tribe

The name of the Five Nations requires explanation. *Nation* is generally reserved for a country with a state form of government, but terminology was less fixed in the seventeenth century. As *nation* was used then, it often referred to a polity of sufficient integrity and importance, regardless of internal political structure, to warrant diplomatic recognition and negotiation.[19] Thus the term at that time could be applied to kin-structured communities as well as to the impersonal bureaucratized structures of nation-states; indeed, kinship was still very important in the feudal state gradually being transformed into the nation-state. Englishmen distin-

17. The most convenient compilation of Iroquois population estimates as given in historical sources is Gunther Michelson, "Iroquois Population Statistics," *Man in the Northeast* 14 (fall, 1977), table 1, p. 4. Cf. William A. Starna, "Mohawk Iroquois Populations: A Revision," *Ethnohistory* 27:4 (fall, 1980), pp. 371–82. The estimates under different tribal headings in *Northeast* are the judgments of the authors, who take into account other factors besides historical sources.

18. The most reliable current figures have been compiled by Mary A. Druke in a special study that included questionnaires to Iroquois community governments. It is available from The Newberry Library Center for the History of the American Indian, 60 W. Walton St., Chicago, Illinois 60610.

19. E.g., in John Smith's *Map of Virginia* (1612), the "Massawomekes" are "a great nation," and the Chickahominies are "that dogged nation," *The Jamestown Voyages under the First Charter, 1606–1609*, ed. Philip L. Barbour, 2 vols., Works issued by the Hakluyt Society, 2d ser., 136–37 (Cambridge: Cambridge University Press, 1969), 2:401, 416.

guished the government of their own emerging nation-state from the governments of Indian nations by calling their own a *civil* government. Indians were not acknowledged to have civil governments and could not become "civilized" until they lived under one and obeyed all its regulations. The issue for them was not so much structure as sovereignty.

The term *tribe* was then often used to refer to kin groups that today we would call clans. There has been much contention among anthropologists recently over proper usage of *tribe*. Some seem inclined to define and refine the term out of meaningful existence.[20] In this book it denotes a community having all the exterior characteristics of a state—possession of territory, diplomacy, powers to wage war and make peace—but structured internally on kin relationships instead of impersonally defined bureaucratic functions. It is what William N. Fenton paradoxically called a kinship state. Some tribes were fragmented into bands; some were composed of persons of varied ethnic stocks—as, for instance, the Iroquois tribes when they held masses of not-yet-assimilated adoptees. Most members of a tribe usually spoke the same language or dialects thereof. Most tribes maintained territorial boundaries. All recognized themselves as a distinct community cemented by genetic and/or fictive kinship and ritual and distinguished themselves from outsiders.

This concept is cultural rather than racial. It differs sharply from the legal definitions in force in United States courts today, which define tribal membership (and therefore the aggregate tribe) as persons of one-half, one-quarter, one-eighth, etc., "blood." Under this legal definition, tribes such as the Iroquois, which depended heavily on adoption / naturalization to replace casualties, might have vanished entirely long ago. No one has the faintest idea of what proportion of the Iroquois gene pool today goes back to aboriginal Iroquois ancestors. The record is clear that it contains contributions from many other Indian and European sources. The obvious reason persons of such varied degrees of synethnicity can constitute a tribe is that they did and do.

Tribal polities based on relationships of genetic or fictive kin range widely in form and activity. Such diversity need not bother historians any more than we are upset by other phenomena of nationhood and nationality that include nations disappearing and reemerging, such as Ireland, Poland, and Israel. One can pettifog about such matters to his heart's content, but Ireland and Poland are very much with us, though most Irishmen speak English and there is considerable dispute at the moment about where their nation's proper boundaries lie; certainly Israel is functioning regardless of the millennia-long hiatus of the Diaspora. Poland's historic boundaries

20. See *Essays on the Problem of Tribe: Proceedings of the 1967 Annual Meeting of the American Ethnological Society*, ed. June Helm (Seattle: University of Washington Press, 1968). My thanks to Mary A. Druke for calling this to my attention.

look like the antics of an amoeba in heat. What, indeed, shall we properly call the variform and culturally complex historical entity known as the United States of America?

Two specialists writing for the *International Encyclopedia of the Social Sciences* hint at what is needed. One of them sees "little profit in drawing a rigid line across the continuous spectrum and insisting that all peoples above that line are nations and those below are not." The other looks from a different direction to get much the same vision: "The concept 'tribal society' . . . although having general utility as an idealized type of society, is in no sense an absolute category. Some societies are merely more or less tribal than others."[21] At such an impasse, one sends for Humpty Dumpty. The terms used in this book mean what I say they mean—in this book. Political phenomena are too multifarious and fluctuating to encourage a hope that any scheme of nomenclature will achieve universal validity. One can only state circumstances and purpose, and use terms operationally as working tools. The essential requisite is that the terms validly distinguish and identify the sets of data to which they are applied, regardless of whether they conform to any preconceived scheme.

Only by strict (even dogmatic) adherence to this rule can the Covenant Chain be conceded to have existed at all, for there is no existing theory or ideology that has room for it. Probably that is the reason it has not yet been recognized for itself in spite of its massive documentation. The Chain is impossible in the legal theory of sovereignty that dominates so much historical thought, because the Chain flouts the basic legal principle that there can be no *imperium in imperio.*[22] Principle or no principle, the kings of England who claimed sovereignty over the Iroquois League also recognized the League as an independent entity (as they previously had recognized various Irish kings who were nominally vassals to the English Lord of Ireland). In the legally absurd words of the royal commission issued to Sir William Johnson in 1756, the Iroquois were the English crown's "subjects *and* allies."[23] The absurdity, however, was only a contradiction in

---

21. Dankwart A. Rustow, "Nation," in *International Encyclopedia of the Social Sciences*, ed. David L. Sills, 17 vols. (New York: Macmillan Co. and Free Press, 1968), 11:7–14; I. M. Lewis, "Tribal Society," ibid., 16:148. See also Morton H. Fried and Frederick M. Watkins, "State," ibid., 15:143–57.

22. See the sensible discussion in Sir John Macdonell, "Sovereignty," *Encyclopaedia Britannica*, 11th ed., 25:519–23, esp. 521. See also Francis Jennings, "Sovereignty in Anglo-American History," in *Indian Sovereignty: Proceedings of the Second Annual Conference on Problems and Issues Concerning American Indians Today*, ed. William R. Swagerty, Newberry Library Center for the History of the American Indian Occasional Papers (Chicago: The Newberry Library, 1979).

23. *The Papers of Sir William Johnson*, eds. James Sullivan et al., 14 vols. (Albany: University of the State of New York, 1921–1965), 2:434–35. The phrasing is more notable because it does not appear in Johnson's earlier commission, issued by General Edward Braddock, which evades the issue by authorizing Johnson "to have the sole Management and direction of the Affairs of the Six Nations of Indians and their Allies." Commission, April 15, 1755, *Johnson Papers* 1:465–66.

theory. The crown's statesmen knew what they were doing, and so did Johnson, who busied himself with persuading those supposed subjects to act as genuine allies.

Long before Johnson became active, the assembly of South Carolina dissected the issue, saying that "His Majesty, by commanding a Treaty and League to be made with the Indians, esteemed them the friends and allies of his people in America, and not as subjects to the Crown of Great Britain."[24]

Perhaps anthropologists have been reluctant to recognize the Covenant Chain because it violates *their* theories as well as legal dicta. It does not fit an evolutionary scheme of any kind because it was unique. It does not fit well in the functional analysis of given cultures because it was bi-societal and bi-cultural. Some anthropologists are so addicted to synchronic studies (i.e., snapshots of a culture) that they have simply defined historical complexities out of bounds. There are always exceptions: one perplexed linguist has remarked, "We need to build a theory of language that starts from what we can see to be actually the case in the world." What else, I wonder, is new?[25]

Following that good advice in building a theory about the Covenant Chain, we may observe that it existed historically with a precise beginning, a complex development, and a *de facto*, if rather frazzled, end.

The Iroquois League

It is necessary to trace the antecedents of the Chain's beginning. Prominent among them is the formation of the Iroquois League of Five Nations. No written documents record it. According to Iroquois tradition, the League had been founded by the legendary culture hero Hiawatha. Unfortunately, Indian traditions, though they deserve respectful consideration of the substantive information cloaked in metaphor and myth, are not strong on chronology. We do not know precisely when the League started; but most suggested dates fall between 1400 and 1600 A.D.[26] Recent thinking by some scholars places its origins in the sixteenth century: i.e., within the period of early general contact between Europe and America, and perhaps in response to the conditions generated by that contact.[27]

Their League protected each of the Five Nations from attack by the

24. Lt. Gov. Broughton to Council of Trade and Plantations, Aug. 6, 1736, *CSPA&WI*, 1735–36, no. 376, p. 264.

25. Dell Hymes, "Linguistic Problems in Defining the Concept of 'Tribe,' " in *Essays on the Problem of Tribe*, ed. Helm, p. 42.

26. Elisabeth Tooker, "The League of the Iroquois: Its History, Politics, and Ritual," in *Northeast*, pp. 418–22.

27. Bruce G. Trigger, "Early Iroquoian Contacts with Europeans," in *Northeast*, p. 344; Anthony F. C. Wallace, "Origins of the Longhouse Religion," in *Northeast*, pp. 447–48.

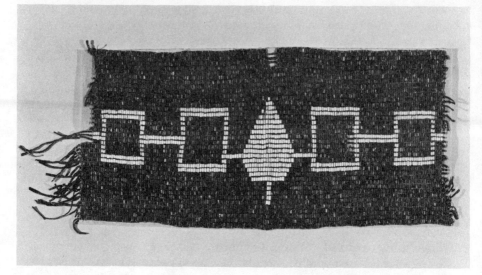

FIGURE 1. The Hiawatha Wampum Belt. Symbolizing the founding of the Iroquois League, this belt represents the Five Nations with the Tree of Peace at Onondaga in the center. COURTESY OF THE NEW YORK STATE MUSEUM.

others; though it did little more than that in its early years, it acquired stronger functions later.

Their backs protected, the Iroquois tribes were hostile to all others. It is notorious that Champlain found many tribes of Canadian Indians at war with them in 1603.[28] Delaware tribal tradition insisted that all the Algonquian-speaking peoples of the east were allied against the Iroquois. It is also apparent that the Iroquois were not perceptibly gaining ground in intertribal warfare, but it would seem that their enemies had not been able to invade their mountain fastnesses successfully.[29]

28. *Of Savages* (1603), in vol. 1, *The Works of Samuel de Champlain*, gen. ed. H. P. Biggar, Publications of the Champlain Society, 6 vols. (1922–1936), reprinted facsimile (Toronto: University of Toronto Press, 1971), pp. 100–103.

29. Bruce G. Trigger, "Champlain Judged by His Indian Policy: A Different View of Early Canadian History," *Anthropologica*, n.s., 13:1 (1971), p. 105; Colden *History*, pp. 5–6; Heckewelder, *History*, p. 60 et passim.

Nearly two centuries before Heckewelder wrote, Jesuit Jerome Lalemant recited the same tradition: "they have no Libraries other than the memory of their old men; . . . What we learn from these living books is that, toward the end of the last [sixteenth] century, the Agnieronnons [Mohawks] were reduced so low by the Algonkins that there seemed to be scarcely any more of them left on the earth. Nevertheless, this scanty remnant, like a noble germ, so increased in a few years as to reduce the Algonquins in turn to the same condition as its own. But this condition did not last long; for the Andastogehronnons [Susquehannocks] waged such energetic warfare against them during ten years that they were overthrown for the second time and their nation rendered almost extinct, or at least so humiliated that the mere name Algonkin made them tremble, and his shadow seemed to pursue them to their very firesides.

The arrival of Europeans changed all the rules of Indian warfare, but the time and place of first contact between the Iroquois and Europeans is difficult to pin down. David Quinn has found hints that ships from Bristol, England, may have voyaged to America even before Columbus.[30] As early as 1535, Jacques Cartier led a party of Frenchmen to the village of Hochelaga, inhabited by Iroquoian speakers, where the city of Montreal now stands, and Cartier found natives who were already well acquainted with European trade.[31] French traders plied the St. Lawrence throughout the rest of the sixteenth century.[32] French trade goods circulated widely among many tribes; as far south as Chesapeake Bay, in 1608, Captain John Smith found French goods in the possession of the Iroquoian Susquehannock Indians.[33]

Champlain's attacks

It seems probable, therefore, that the Five Nations had gained indirect knowledge of Europeans in the sixteenth century, but we do not know of specific direct contact until Samuel de Champlain joined their Algonquin and Huron enemies to defeat them in battle in 1609. We do know that the battle was fought on Champlain's initiative. "I had come with no other intention than to make war," he wrote, "for we had with us only arms and not merchandise for barter, as [the Indians] had been led to understand."[34] Champlain was carrying out a policy formed before 1603, when the French contracted an offensive alliance against the Iroquois.[35] Its rationale was coldly commercial. The Canadian Indians were New France's

"That was at the time when the Dutch took possession of these regions and conceived a fondness for the beavers of the natives, some thirty years ago." Relation of 1659–1660, *Jesuit Relations* 45:205.

30. Quinn, *North America from Earliest Discovery*, pp. 60–64. But cf. the discouraging survey of evidence in Patrick McGrath, "Bristol and America, 1480–1631," in *The Westward Enterprise: English Activities in Ireland, the Atlantic, and America, 1480–1650*, eds. K. R. Andrews, N. P. Canny, and P. E.H. Hair (Detroit: Wayne State University Press, 1979), pp. 81–102.

31. *Voyages of Jacques Cartier*, ed. H. P. Biggar, Publications of the Public Archives of Canada II (Ottawa: F. A. Acland, 1924), pp. 148–72.

32. H. P. Biggar, *The Early Trading Companies of New France: A contribution to the History of Commerce and Discovery in North America*, University of Toronto Studies in History (Toronto: University of Toronto Library, 1901), pp. 104–6.

33. John Smith, *A Map of Virginia* (1612), in *The Jamestown Voyages under the First Charter, 1606–1609*, ed. Philip L. Barbour, 2 vols., works issued by the Hakluyt Society, 2d ser., nos. 136–37 (Cambridge: Cambridge University Press, 1969), 2:407–8.

34. Champlain, *Voyages* (1613), in *Works* 2:71; Trigger, "Champlain Judged by His Indian Policy," p. 87. Samuel Eliot Morison bent the sources a bit to stress that Champlain was only "helping" the Algonquin and Huron Indians, but he conceded that the French might then "depend on them for trade." *Samuel de Champlain: Father of New France* (Boston: Little, Brown and Co., 1972), pp. 107–8.

35. Marcel Trudel, "Champlain, Samuel de," in *Dictionary of Canadian Biography*, eds. George W. Brown et al. (Toronto: University of Toronto Press, 1966–), 1:190.

source of peltry, and Iroquois warfare interfered with trade. The same hard logic prevailed during New France's entire existence. Champlain attacked the Iroquois once more in 1610, and again in 1615, and it is not strange that thereafter the Iroquois became hostile to the French. But one must not attribute all subsequent foreign policy of the Iroquois to these incidents. Even if the excuse be accepted that Champlain was nobly rushing to protect the presumably more virtuous northern Indians from the onslaughts of ferocious Iroquois, the simple fact evident to the Iroquois was that the French had struck them thrice, and that fact rankled—but not enough to make them lose their senses. When circumstance and interest later dictated accommodation with the French, the Iroquois went more than half way to arrange it.

The French knew what they were doing. The Iroquois could not fulfill the role desired by the French—that of primary collector of furs for French merchants. This role was preempted by confederated Huron tribes of what was then the far west. Huron territory lay between Lake Simcoe and the eastern tip of Lake Huron's vast Georgian Bay. The Hurons had concentrated a relatively large aboriginal population in a place strategic for intertribal trade.[36] Their territory lay at the northern edge of the Ontario plains, with easy access by canoe into the mountainous Canadian Shield. Almost too far north for practicable horticulture, they were still within a region where large crops could be produced to trade with the hunting Algonquians of Lake Nipissing for meat, skins, and dried fish; and the Hurons maintained the friendship essential to trade by sheltering the hunters during the bitterest winter months.[37]

When French traders appeared on their distant horizon, the Hurons developed existing commercial and diplomatic skills and expanded their trading circuit. Journeying among other Iroquoian tribes they acquired cargoes of maize and tobacco to supplement their own production. After meeting with these suppliers they headed north through a network of lakes and streams to exchange the horticultural products for great quantities of skins to be carried to the French, from whom trade goods were brought back to begin the circuit all over again.[38]

36. For discussion of Huron population, and references to varied views see above, ch. 6, n. 9, and Francis Jennings, *Invasion*, p. 25, n. 27.

37. Trigger, *Children of Aataentsic*, 1:62–63.

A bibliographic note: Trigger's scholarship in this book and numerous articles is exemplary, and I have relied much upon it as my notes will show. The notes also detail some differences of interpretation in relatively minor matters.

38. The Huron trading circuit was graphically revealed in George T. Hunt, *The Wars of the Iroquois: A Study in Intertribal Trade Relations* (Madison: University of Wisconsin Press, 1940), ch. 5, and map between pp. 7 and 8.

A bibliographic note: This study was Hunt's doctoral dissertation; he died young and wrote nothing else. It is a remarkable book for its challenge to assumptions of primitive savagery, and it forced rethinking about Indian economics, but it leans too heavily toward

According to Colden, the horticultural Five Nations, like the Hurons, had traded in aboriginal times with the hunting Algonquins, maize for meat, but this trade had stopped when the two peoples began to war against each other. Then, says Colden, the Five Nations retreated from the St. Lawrence valley to their historic locations south of Lake Ontario where they were found by Europeans to be frequently at war with the tribes on all sides. But archaeologists now say that some Iroquois had lived in that Finger Lakes region from much earlier times.[39]

Iroquois strategy

The Iroquois fought without allies. It is clear, however, that after they were beaten by French-aided enemies, they digested the lessons of Champlain's firearms and their own defeat. When the Dutch arrived on the Hudson, the Iroquois Mohawks swallowed injury and insult to remain on trading terms with the Dutch. When the English conquered the Dutch in 1664, the Mohawks hurried to ally with New York, and in 1677 all of the Five Nations joined in making the Covenant Chain with New York, Massachusetts Bay, Connecticut, Maryland, and Virginia. In short, the Iroquois League joined strategic politics and trade to militarily strategic location. Thus strengthened, the Five Nations launched an intermittently successful career of conquest and tribal hegemony marked by violently alternating triumphs and defeats. Sometimes only one of the tribes would pursue its own interests. Sometimes several would join in a campaign. Sometimes the whole League combined for a common goal. The League was not monolithic. It must be stressed, however, that although the Iroquois pursued objectives of their own, they achieved durable success only when backed up by European allies, who had goals of different sorts.[40]

When the Iroquois forgot the requirement for European patronage and assistance, they took terrible beatings from other Indians as well as hostile Europeans. There is little substance in the old myth, so sedulously cultivated by Colden and Morgan, that the name of Mohawk was so dreaded that other tribes would flee upon a mere rumor of Iroquois approach.[41]

economic determinism and is often erroneous in detail. It is wide of the mark in its chapters on the Susquehannocks and the Illinois, and its pro-Dutch bias makes other serious errors. Recognizing its important contributions as of its day, one must caution against relying upon it without verification from other sources.

39. James A. Tuck traces Iroquois culture complexes back to approximately 1000 A.D. "Northern Iroquois Prehistory," in *Northeast*, pp. 322–33.

40. "The trade and aid from Albany therefore were indispensable components of Iroquois greatness," in Allen W. Trelease, *Indian Affairs in Colonial New York: The Seventeenth Century* (Ithaca, N.Y.: Cornell University Press, 1960), p. 24.

41. Morgan, *League*, pp. 12–13.

As will be shown, many tribes fought back—for example, Mahicans, Sokokis, Susquehannocks, Missisaugas, Potawatomis, Ottawas—often quite successfully. It was sagacity rather than ferocity that elevated the Iroquois to leadership among the tribes allied to Great Britain. Other tribesmen were their peers in courage and fierceness. When the Iroquois made errors in judgment, they paid dearly, regardless of reputation.

They achieved their greatest successes by a judicious combination of war and negotiation. Fundamental to their system of dealing with other tribes were the relationships established between the Iroquois League and the colonial powers of New Netherland, later New York, and New France. The Iroquois made themselves into intermediaries between other Indian tribes and the Dutch and English colonies. They often tried to create the same function for themselves with the French, but the French would have none of that.

The instrument of negotiation was the treaty council and the agreement arrived at during the council (both called *treaties*). Much of what transpired at these councils has been misinterpreted because of Indian figures of speech being read too literally. The language seems childishly picturesque and has been too easily passed over as something appropriate to people in "the childhood of society." But Iroquois leaders were not children and not childish. They were (and are) mature adults who bargained hard in matters about which they were well informed, and their metaphors were no more childish than the legal fictions abounding in the opinions of the Supreme Court of the United States (whose constantly quarreling members, by the way, address each other as *brethren*). The metaphors of Indian treaties tell us what the Indian parties understood the treaties to mean.[42]

Metaphorical terms of address were used by Indians to distinguish relationships of parity or subordination. *Grandfather* expressed ceremonial deference but no obligation to obey; it was used by Algonquians and Iroquoians alike in referring to the Delawares and appears in some records as addressed by mixed tribesmen to the Hurons, but no one called the masterful Iroquois grandfathers. *Father* is a more difficult word. Among the Iroquois, fathers had no power to command children, but among Europeans they did. The Iroquois quickly came to understand this difference. Colden tells of an incident when a suspicious governor of New York reproached the Iroquois with their formal behavior when treating with New France's governor. "How came you to call him Father? For no other Reason, they replied, but because he calls us Children. These Names

<hr />

42. A brief description of the treaty process is in Jennings, *Invasion*, pp. 118–24. Comprehensive descriptions are in *The History and Culture of Iroquois Diplomacy*, eds. Jennings, Fenton, and Druke.

signify nothing."[43] In fact, however, the names signified much. The real reason behind the *father* image in New France was that French governors would not treat at all without it. The Iroquois refused the same term of address to English governors. They understood the statuses implied to Europeans in father-children terminology, and they knew that the English needed their alliance too badly to force the issue. (Ignorance of this simple political metaphor has led one writer into a morass of Freudian-Jungian exploration of Indian psyches.)[44]

The ordinary tributary relationship, involving an obligation to protect, on the one side, and a reciprocal obligation to heed counsel on the other, was expressed in terms of *uncles* and *nephews*. Special attention must be given to the reciprocity of this relationship; nephews were not subjects comparable to those of a nation-state, and uncles were not privileged to dispose of tributaries as they pleased.[45] Each had something to offer to the other, and their relationships were kept within the bounds of the Indian toleration of secession and tribal inability to prevent it. William N. Fenton has remarked about Iroquois political structure that "duality or reciprocity is the principle that operates throughout."[46]

Brothers were equals, although distinctions occurred between *older brothers* and *younger brothers* as, for instance, between the older brother Mohawks, Onondagas, and Senecas, and the younger brother Oneidas and Cayugas. Because of this significance, the Iroquois almost invariably insisted that English governors address them as brothers. I have found only one exception, and it caused a great row.[47]

Indian metaphor is irrelevant to European logic. The Iroquois sometimes addressed the Delawares in the same meeting as grandfathers and nephews. They had not gone idiotic; they were simply referring to different sorts of relationship, ceremonial and political.

There was also a special term *women*, which has caused much controversy. It seems to have meant originally a nation that was assigned a political role of neutrality so as to be able to assume the peacemaker's role when warring tribes wanted to end their strife without losing face.[48] Although

43. Colden, *History*, p. 159.
44. Michael Paul Rogin, *Fathers and Children: Andrew Jackson and the Subjugation of the American Indian* (New York: Alfred A. Knopf, 1975). Aside from the psycho-dogmas, the book offers some valuable research.
45. Morgan did not understand treaty relationships at all. He writes of them as "absolute supremacy of the Iroquois over other Indian nations," *League*, p. 12.
46. Fenton, "Northern Iroquoian Culture Patterns," p. 314.
47. See ch. 10, below.
48. Morgan made much of the women status to imply a condition of subjugation, but he is contradicted not only by Delaware tradition reported in Heckewelder, but also by a Cayuga oral tradition recited by Chief Jacob E. Thomas in seminar at the Newberry Library, May 22, 1980, which agrees in substance with the Delaware tradition. Morgan, *League*, p. 15.

this nation-tribe was a woman, its individual members were as much warriors as the Iroquois themselves, as is demonstrated by the trouble the
Iroquois took to recruit them for campaigns. In the mid-eighteenth century the woman metaphor became corrupted by European notions of female
subordination, which were wholly at odds with such Iroquois customs as
the power of clan matrons to make and unmake chiefs.[49]

The study of these metaphors is in its infancy, and controversy continues. I have written positively in order to force the issue.

49. This issue will be dealt with at length in following chapters. See the remarks in Anthony
F. C. Wallace, *King of the Delawares: Teedyuscung, 1700–1763* (Philadelphia: University of
Pennsylvania Press, 1949), pp. 195–96, and "Woman, Land, and Society: Three Aspects of
Aboriginal Delaware Life," *Pennsylvania Archaeologist* 17:1–4 (1947), entire issue. Among
modern historians, C. A. Weslager has argued the theory that the Delawares were reduced
to "woman" status as the reult of conquest by the Iroquois, or alternatively because of conquest by the Susquehannocks, who were in turn taken under Iroquois authority. He and I
have had many friendly wrangles. Though we still do not see eye to eye, we are not really
eyeball to eyeball either. Weslager has considerably modified earlier views in his *The Delaware Indians: A History* (New Brunswick, N.J.: Rutgers University Press, 1972), ch. 9; some
of my own earlier views have also changed a bit. See chs. 17 and 18, below.

Chapter 4 🐦 AN IRON DUTCH CHAIN

The country is well calculated and possesses the necessaries for a profitable trade. First, it is a fine fruitful country. Secondly, it has fine navigable rivers extending far inland, by which the productions of the country can be brought to places of traffic. The Indians, without our labour or trouble, bring to us their fur trade, worth tons of gold, which may be increased, and is like goods found.

> Adriaen Van der Donck (1655)

They say, we have been here before and made an alliance. The Dutch, indeed, say we are brothers and are joined together with chains, but that lasts only as long as we have beavers. After that we are no longer thought of, but much will depend upon it when we shall need each other. They thereupon give two beavers.

They say, the alliance which was made in this country, who can break it? Let us always maintain this alliance which was once made. Give thereupon two beavers.

> Mohawk treaty propositions, 6 September 1659

Dutch trade

After Henry Hudson's voyage of discovery for the Dutch East India Company in 1609, independent Dutch merchants began to trade on the Hudson River and along the Atlantic coast, and a Dutch trading company built Fort Nassau, ca. 1614, on Castle Island (near Albany) as a year-round trading post. Thus, five or six years before the founding of New Plymouth, Dutchmen had taken advantage of the Hudson's deep stream to build a habitation over 160 crowflight miles west of Plymouth Bay.[1]

---

1. Simon Hart, *The Prehistory of the New Netherland Company: Amsterdam Notarial Records of the First Dutch Voyages to the Hudson* (Amsterdam: City of Amsterdam Press, 1959), p. 27. Hart says, "there is good reason to believe that this fort was erected by the crew of the Van Tweenhuysen Company." Trelease attributes it to the New Netherland Company. *Indian Affairs*, p. 32. Van Cleaf Bachman also attributes it to the New Netherland Company but dates it at 1615. *Peltries or Plantations: The Economic Policies of the Dutch West India Company in New Netherland, 1623–1639*, Johns Hopkins University Studies in Historical and Political Science, 87th ser. (Baltimore: Johns Hopkins Press, 1969), p. 11 and n. 31. The New Netherland Company was chartered to begin operations on 1 Jan 1615. Bachman, p. 10. I am indebted to the late Philip L. Barbour for his gift of Hart's rare book.

Thomas J. Condon relies on Hart's *Prehistory* to build Fort Nassau in 1614, which seems

At Fort Nassau, the Dutch were surrounded by some 1,600 warriors and families of the Mahican tribe (Algonquian), whose friendship with other Algonquian tribes along the Mahican Channel gave them control over access to the fur trading that had already become institutionalized in the St. Lawrence Valley.[2] The Dutch immediately resolved to make the northern passage into a conduit for delivery of peltry to themselves. Since the Mahicans controlled the way, the Dutch naturally turned to them for cooperation. The Mahicans refused at first to sell land to the Dutch, but they permitted the traders to live among themselves as valued guests, and, about 1618, they entered into an agreement with whatever traders were then on the scene. The Indians regarded it as a treaty of friendship, or nonaggression. In their metaphor, they tied the Dutch ships to their shores "with a rope."[3]

In this early era, the great potential had not yet been discovered of the east-west passage through the Mohawk Valley to the Great Lakes, and the Mohawk Indians west of Fort Nassau seemed less important than the Mahicans to the traders. Some trade was apparently carried on with the Mohawks, implying the existence of an agreement. Whether either that possible agreement or the documented negotiation of the Mahicans should be regarded as a treaty between the tribes and "the Dutch" depends on how one looks at the situation. The Dutch traders of that early era represented nobody but themselves, and they were a semi-piratical lot of rough and tough individuals who certainly did not regard themselves as bound by their competitors' agreements—or, as often as not, by their own. The documented 1618 agreement would probably have been negotiated by a representative of the Van Tweenhuysen Company, which quickly passed out of existence. Until the formation of the Dutch West India Company in 1621, no Dutch business organization was capable of maintaining continuity of policy.

In 1617 Fort Nassau was abandoned because it flooded when the river rose.[4] In 1621 new energy, resources, and purpose were assured for the whole Hudson Valley by the organization of the Dutch West India Company, and in 1624 the company built Fort Orange at the site of Albany,

to be the proper date. *New York Beginnings: The Commercial Origins of New Netherland* (New York: New York University Press, 1968), p. 28 and n. 82.

2. Account of Rensselaerswyck, 20 July 1634, in *Van Rensselaer Bowier Manuscripts*, trans. and ed. A. J. F. van Laer, New York State Library 90th Annual Report, vol. 2, supplement 7 (Albany: University of the State of New York, 1908), p. 307. Reckoning of the total population of the Mahicans at this early period depends on the average number of persons in each warrior's family. At a minimum average of 3, the total becomes 4,800. If the average was 5, the total becomes 8,000.

3. "Propositions made by the Schaahkooks Indians," in *The Livingston Indian Records, 1666–1723*, ed. Lawrence H. Leder (Gettysburg: Pennsylvania Historical Association, 1956), p. 191. Also available as *Pennsylvania History* 23:1 (Jan., 1956), identical paging.

4. Trelease, *Indian Affairs*, p. 34.

thus beginning the longest lasting "frontier town" in eastern America. The company's agents at Fort Orange apparently renewed efforts to exploit traffic along the Mahican Channel, and the Mohawks promptly launched war against the Mahicans in order to acquire a role in the north-south trade.[5]

In 1626 the Dutch helped the Mahicans with men and arms, only to be humiliatingly ambushed by Mohawks armed with bows and arrows. The deaths in battle of commander Daniel van Krieckebeeck and three of his men taught discretion to the Fort Orange Dutch. Withdrawing from the Indians' quarrel, they patched up a truce with the Mohawks and waited for the winner to emerge. The Mohawks were only too willing to avoid further conflict with Fort Orange. They wanted to prosper from it rather than destroy it. By 1628 the Mohawks triumphed decisively; the Mahicans fled temporarily to the Connecticut Valley; and the Dutch had acquired a problem.

The Mohawks did not intend their defeat of the Mahicans to be simply a means of opening free trade. They destroyed Mahican controls in order to substitute their own—much to the detriment of Dutch trade. Kiliaen van Rensselaer, the irascible patroon of the giant Rensselaerswyck estate, adjacent to Fort Orange, drew the conclusion that more Dutch manpower was needed on the scene. He argued with the directors of the Dutch West India Company: "the savages, who are now stronger than ourselves, will not allow others who are hostile and live farther away and have many furs to pass through their territory, and . . . this would be quite different if we had stronger colonies . . . the Maquaas [Mohawks], who will not allow the French savages who now trade on the river of Canada and who live nearer to us than them [the French] to pass through to come to us, might through persuasion or fear sooner be moved to do so and . . . from these savages more furs could be obtained than are bartered now in all New Netherland. This is only one of many things, but should be well considered as it can be accomplished in no other way than by establishing colonies."[6]

---

5. Bruce G. Trigger, "The Mohawk-Mahican War (1624–28): The Establishment of a Pattern," *Canadian Historical Review* 52 (Sep., 1971), 276–79. See also Isaack de Rasière to the Amsterdam Chamber, Sept. 23, 1626, in *Documents Relating to New Netherland, 1624–1626, in the Henry E. Huntington Library*, trans. and ed. A. J. F. van Laer (San Marino, California: The Huntington Library, 1924), 212–15.

6. Memorial of Kiliaen van Rensselaer, Nov. 25, 1633, in *Van Rensselaer Bowier Manuscripts*, p. 258. For elaboration of the Company's difficulties and policies, see Bachman, *Peltries or Plantations*, pp. 131–32; and Trigger, "Mohawk-Mahican War" pp. 283–86. Note: Van Rensselaer's translator used the English word *savage* to convey the Dutch *wilden*. The words are not really identical in meaning. Adriaen Van der Donck explained *wilden* thus: "The original natives of the country (for now there are native-born Christians also), although they are composed of different tribes, and speak different tongues, all pass by the appellation of (*Wilden*) wild men; and this name was given them as far as we can learn, at the first discovery

Some of the defeated Mahicans later returned to the Hudson Valley—
or perhaps some had never left. At any rate, a new set of statuses was
established. In return for peace, the Mahicans agreed to pay wampum
tribute to the Mohawks. This was a minor consideration in comparison to
freedom of access to Fort Orange's trade. After two years of tribute payment, the Mahicans "got drunk and lost the pouch," but the Mohawks did
not "take it hard."[7] Land tenure was not involved at all. Though the Mahicans moved off a wary distance, they sold territory to the Dutch without
Mohawk interference.

In the sequel, both the Mohawks and the Dutch showed astonishing
willingness to forget the incident. Having satisfied their honor and gained
their point, the Mohawks came back to Fort Orange to trade. Dutchman
Peter Barentsen heard their justification—and traded.[8] What is most
unusual about it is not the Indians' forbearance but the Dutchmen's. Indians everywhere frequently swallowed abuse and violence to keep the
advantage of trade relationships, but Europeans of varied nationalities
usually made it a point of pride to take revenge for every affront, no matter the provocation given. The whole Van Krieckebeeck affair typified the
future existence of the settlement founded before Boston and destined to
become the capital of the state of New York. An uneasy co-existence of
Europeans and Indians centered upon Fort Orange and its successor,
Albany, marred frequently by quarrels, punctured occasionally by individual acts of violence, but always renewed through trade. Albany
remained immune from Indian attacks while New England's frontier towns,
fifty miles away in the Connecticut Valley, were burning. Dutch Fort
Orange remained at peace while Dutch Fort Amsterdam was fiercely
embattled with eleven tribes.

New Netherland was distinctive in many respects. Though the Dutch
came late upon the North American scene, they came prepared. The

of the country, which for various reasons seems very appropriate. First, on account of their
religion, of which they have very little, and that is very strange; and secondly on account of
their marriages, wherein they differ from civilized societies; thirdly, on account of their laws,
which are so singular as to deserve the name of wild regulations. And the Christians hold
different names necessary to distinguish different nations, such as Turks, Mamelukes, and
Barbarians; and as the name of Heathen is very little used in foreign lands, therefore they
would not distinguish the native Americans by either of these names; and as they trade in
foreign countries with dark and fair coloured people, and with those who resemble ourselves,
in distinction from negroes, and as the American tribes are bordering on an olive colour, the
name of *wild men* suits them best." Ignoring this explanation, the translators of Dutch documents including Van der Donck's have consistently substituted *savages* for *wild men*. Adriaen
Van der Donck, *A Description of the New Netherlands* (1653), trans. Jeremiah Johnson, ed.
Thomas F. O'Donnell reprint ed. (Syracuse, N.Y.: Syracuse University Press, 1968), 73.
   7. "A Glimpse of Iroquois Culture History through the Eyes of Joseph Brant and John
Norton," ed. Douglas W. Boyce, *Proceedings of the American Philosophical Society* 117 (1973),
290.
   8. Trelease, *Indian Affairs*, p. 47.

directors of the Dutch West India Company chose their location carefully. After consulting the reports of coastal traders, they equipped their colonists with all necessities, they approached the natives diplomatically, and they financed the project amply. Their intention was to create a base for profitable trade on a large scale, for which they had resources and organization superior to those of any other European country. Dutch bottoms carried three-quarters of Europe's trade within Europe. Dutch and Flemish industries produced the sort of goods that Indians most desired. ("Duffels" cloth, for instance, was made in Antwerp's suburb of that name.) Dutch merchants were rich and venturesome, and the Dutch navy guaranteed protection. In 1624 the Dutch West India Company established its colony of New Amsterdam without suffering a "starving time" or an Indian war.[9]

This was the most propitious of beginnings. From New Amsterdam, Dutch shippers added to their fur trade a carrying trade between the other colonies modeled after the carrying trade in Europe. The primary trade with Indians yielded lucrative returns—"worth tons of gold," exclaimed Adriaen Van der Donck—[10] and the Indians themselves were accommodating. Besides their furs, provided at absurdly low prices, they sold land and worked as farm laborers, also cheaply. The Montauk natives of Long Island made wampum, which those who lived in the interior accepted for peltry and food products. The Dutch had placed themselves unerringly in a spot where a large and varied working population was immediately available for the controls of commerce. Had they all observed the restraints preached to them by their Company directors in Europe, the rest of New Netherland might, like Fort Orange, have escaped the wounds of war; but greed and arrogance are international, and there were Dutchmen with their full share. How revealing it is to hear some of them complaining that their governors had abused them past tolerance: "the Christians are treated *almost like Indians* in the purchase of necessaries which they cannot do without; this causes great complaint, distress and poverty."[11]

Even in the exposed situation of Fort Orange there were occasional early adventurers, such as Jacob Eelkens and Hans Jorisz Hunthum (or Hontom), who kidnapped Indian chiefs for ransom. The Mohawks threatened both with death. After Hunthum was appointed commissary of Fort Orange in 1633, they burned one of the West Indian Company's yachts and managed thereby to get some attention. An official investigator asked

9. Bachman, *Peltries or Plantations*, pp. 81–86; C. A. Weslager, in collaboration with A. R. Dunlap, *Dutch Explorers, Traders and Settlers in the Delaware Valley, 1609–1664* (Philadelphia: University of Pennsylvania Press, 1961), 48–57.

10. Van der Donck, *Description*, p. 131.

11. "Remonstrance of New Netherland," July 28, 1649, in *N.Y.Col.Docs.* 1:297. Emphasis added.

the following question of Hunthum's successor in the post and got the reply shown below:

" 'Whether, although the ransom was paid by the chief's subjects, Hunthum, in spite of his promise, did not emasculate the chief, hang the severed member on the stay and so killed the Sackima.'

'Yes.' "[12]

Brutality seems to have been fairly common. As late as 1660, Mohawk chiefs asked the magistrates at Fort Orange "to forbid the Dutch to molest the Indians as heretofore by kicking, beating, and assaulting them, in order that we may not break the old friendship which we have enjoyed for more than thirty years." The magistrates were obliged to proclaim a ban on "the ill behavior toward them [the Mohawks] on the part of the Dutch who on horseback go up and down in the woods and not only take away their beavers by force and carry them, leaving the Indians to run after them, but also knock and throw them around, as is shown more fully in the complaint of the said Maquas made to the court." Several observations may be made about this incident. The first is that the Indians concerned were Mohawks—supposedly the most ferocious savages on the continent—and the ultimatum that they presented to the magistrates was that they would "go away and not be seen" any more by the Dutch if the violence against them were not stopped. It is also notable that the Fort Orange court accepted for the record the Mohawks' account of assaults and thefts, but brought no Dutchman to trial for any one of them. The utmost reach of its justice took it only to a ban on future misconduct. In such an atmosphere it is not strange to hear Mohawk sarcasm: "The Dutch . . . say we are brothers and are joined together with chains, but that lasts only as long as we have beavers."[13]

Dutch war

As a general rule, however, the authorities at Fort Orange made efforts to respond to Indian complaints. In this respect they differed from Willem Kieft, their governor-general at Fort Amsterdam. Kieft had looked toward New England and marked the Puritan colonies' easy conquest of the Pequot Indians from 1636 to 1638. After that conquest the Puritans received massive quantities of wampum in tribute.[14] Kieft wanted similar income, and

12. Examination of Bastiaen Jansz Krol, June 30, 1634, in *Van Rensselaer Bowier Manuscripts*, pp. 302–4.

13. *Minutes of the Court of Fort Orange and Beverwyck (1652–1660)*, trans. and ed. A. J. F. van Laer, 2 vols. (Albany: University of the State of New York, 1922–23), Sept. 6, 1659, 2:211–12; Oct. 19, 1659, 2: 222; June 26, 1660, 2:269–70. The western Iroquois made similar complaints: treaty minutes, July 25, 1660, ibid., p. 285.

14. *Acts of the Commissioners of the United Colonies of New England*, ed. David Pulsifer, vols. 9 and 10 of *Records of the Colony of New Plymouth in New England*, eds. Nathaniel B. Shurtleff

he began in 1639 to make demands on the Algonquian tribes surrounding Manhattan and on Long Island.[15] In 1643 he launched a terrorist campaign against Weckquaesgeeks and Tappans camped among the Hackensacks at Pavonia (Jersey City, New Jersey). Kieft's official example was quickly followed by colonists on Long Island who plundered corn from the Marechkawieck Indians who had previously been friendly but now rose up in arms. Suddenly, New Amsterdam and its outlying communities were at bloody war with eleven Indian tribes.[16]

But not so with Fort Orange or its nearby village of Rensselaerswyck. In 1642 Fort Orange had sent a delegation into the Mohawk country to ransom a captive Jesuit missionary.[17] The Indians refused to give him up, but negotiations continued. A Dutch delegation later dated "the first treaty of friendship and brotherhood" between the Mohawks and "all the Dutch" at 1643.[18]

Dutch-Mohawk alliance

The text of this treaty of 1643 has not come to light, but the language in which it was later mentioned must be heeded carefully. It was the first Mohawk treaty with *all* the Dutch. Thus there may have been, and probably were, previous arrangements made by the Fort Orange Dutch to facilitate trade. Some such agreement would have been necessary after the Mohawks drove away the Mahicans (whom the Dutch had helped) in 1628. Mohawk chiefs spoke in 1660 of "the old friendship which we have enjoyed for more than thirty years." This statement may be reconciled with a first treaty with all the Dutch in 1643 if the earlier date is seen as a treaty with only the Fort Orange Dutch about 1628–1630.[19]

Perhaps there were even earlier negotiations, but that is doubtful. It is unlikely that van Krieckebeeck would have been helping Mahicans in 1628 to war against the Mohawks if the Dutch at that time had been on trading terms with those Mohawks. One must be exceedingly careful about

and David Pulsifer (Boston, 1859), 2:141; *The Winthrop Papers*, ed. Allyn B. Forbes, 5 vols. (Boston: Massachusetts Historical Society, 1929–47), 3:500; William B. Weeden, *Indian Money as a Factor in New England Civilization*, Johns Hopkins University Studies in Historical and Political Science, 2d ser., 9–10 (Baltimore, 1884), p. 407.

15. New Netherland Council Minutes, Sept. 15, 1639, mss., New York State Archives, Albany. A. J. F. van Laer's typescript translation from the Dutch, p. 60; minutes, Aug. 9, 1640, typescript p. 89.

16. New Netherland Council Minutes, mss., Feb. 25, March 4, Sept. 15, Oct. 17, all 1643. Typescript pp. 185–89, 203, 207. Report of the Board of Accounts, Dec. 15, 1644, *N.Y.Col.Docs.* 1:150–51; Trelease, *Indian Affairs*, pp. 66–82.

17. Extract of a letter of Arent van Corlaer, June 16, 1643, *N.Y.Col.Docs.* 13:15; Father Isaac Jogues to the Jesuit Provincial, Aug. 5, 1643, in *Jesuit Relations* 39:223.

18. Dutch reply to Mohawks, Sept. 24, 1659, *N.Y.Col.Docs.* 13:112.

19. Mohawk speech, June 26, 1660, *Court Minutes of Fort Orange* 2:269.

accepting alleged treaties supposed to have been made as early as 1618. A "deed" signed by sachems of the Five Nations in 1701 contradicts the earlier Mohawk speech by stating that "wee have lived peaceably and quietly with the people of Albany our fellow subjects above eighty years when wee first made a firm league and covenant chain with these Christians that first came to settle Albany on this river."[20] Internal evidence as well as external circumstance demonstrates this deed to be worthless in substance. In dealings with the Dutch, neither the Indians nor the Dutch had ever used the term covenant chain, and the phrase "our fellow subjects" gives the game away. This "deed" was concocted by Robert Livingston as part of his strategy of claiming the west country for England by virtue of the Five Nations' purported conquests there. The situation is described in chapters 2 and 10 herein.

A "treaty" purportedly made in 1613 has recently made a small stir. It has been published,[21] but this so-called treaty could not possibly have obligated any Dutchmen except those of a trading ship, and we have seen what they were like. A notebook containing minutes of ancient negotiations with the Iroquois seems to add substance to the "treaty" document, and Daniel K. Richter, who recently found the notebook, suggests that Jacob Eelckens, the elusive "Jacques" of Iroquois tradition, could have been the negotiator.[22]

More substantial evidence exists of a treaty in 1618. The so-called River Indians of the upper Hudson projected the Covenant Chain back to that date in their traditional histories: in 1703 the Schaghticokes stated that their contact with "the first Christian" had occurred eighty-five years earlier. "Then we tied them with a Roap," said the Schaghticokes, "but now they are fastned with an Iron Chain to the tree of welfair so that wee hitherto have stood firm to the Covenant Chain with our father."[23]

The "River Indian" Schaghticokes were neither Mohawk nor Iroquoian, and I have shown how they came into the Chain in 1677 as a mixture of refugee Indians, some of whom were Mahicans, others being fragments of tribes broken by the Second Puritan Conquest.[24] Their 1618 tradition of a real event evidently originated with the Mahicans and became linguistically confused when Covenant Chain language was picked up from the Mohawks or New Yorkers. Historians formerly succumbed to the

20. July 19, 1701, *N.Y.Col.Docs.* 4:909. The text of the full document should be read, pp. 908–10.

21. L. G. Van Loon, "Tawagonshi, Beginning of the Treaty Era," *Indian Historian* 1:3 (1968), pp. 23–26.

22. Daniel K. Richter, "Rediscovered Links in the Covenant Chain: Previously Unpublished Transcripts of New York Indian Treaty Minutes, 1677–1691," *Proceedings of the American Antiquarian Society* 92.pt. 1(1982), pp. 45–85, esp. 49–54.

23. Treaty Minutes, Sept. 24, 1703, *Livingston Indian Records*, p. 191.

24. Jennings, *Invasion*, pp. 318, 321–23.

confusion and identified the 1618 treaty as a Mohawk-Dutch affair, but the Dutch set 1643 as the date of their first alliance with the Mohawks.[25] The historians' error was understandable in the circumstances, occurring as it did during the prolonged disappearance of the *Livingston Indian Records*, in which the 1618 date was identified with the River Indians rather than the Mohawks.

Apart from clearing up the identity of the participants, the Schaghticokes' language, when scrutinized closely, clarifies the 1618 treaty as an affair preceding formation of the Chain. Our clue is the metaphor of the rope. It is one of a series of metaphors expressed at various times by both Iroquois and Algonquian speakers. The series indicates varying degrees of relations starting with a rope, being strengthened by a chain of iron, made suddenly splendid as a chain of silver, and even occasionally transformed to a chain of gold. The figures of speech are not always identical in different recitations, but the patterns are similar enough so that inferences can be drawn confidently.

Iroquois traditions, repeatedly recited and recorded in the seventeenth and eighteenth centuries, affirm a progression of alliance with the Dutch from rope to iron chain.[26] Certainly the Indians distinguished between the significance of the two kinds of bond. As we shall see, their traditions distinguish also between a chain made of iron and a chain made of silver. Leaving the silver chain for later attention, I offer this interpretation of the rope as what would nowadays be called a nonaggression pact, sufficient to permit trading relationships, the chain escalating it to a mutual assistance pact. The iron chain of 1643, as subsequent events demonstrated, locked Dutchmen and Mohawks in each others' embrace, despite mutual dislike, because they needed each other.

For the Dutch, internal strife was decisive. Although the precise terms of the 1643 treaty remain enigmatic, the Mohawks suddenly gained a great quantity of arms in trade that were denied to other tribes.[27] A more informative affair followed in 1645. Indeed, there were two treaties in 1645. The first was made at Fort Orange in July when Governor Kieft secured the friendship of Mahicans as well as Mohawks. The second treaty,

25. Propositions, Sept. 24, 1659, *Minutes of the Court of Fort Orange and Beverwyck, 1652–1660*, trans. and ed. A. J. F. van Laer, 2 vols. (Albany: University of the State of New York, 1920–23), 2:215.

26. For example: "In the days of old when the Christians came first into this river we made a covenant with them first with the bark of a tree, afterwards it was renewed with a twisted withe, but in processe of time, least that should decay and rott the Covenant was fastened with a chain of iron which ever since has been called the Covenant Chain and the end of it was made fast at Onnondage which is the Center of the five Nations." Onondaga speaker, treaty minutes, Aug. 15, 1694, Penn Papers, Indian Affairs, mss., 1:14. Hist. Soc. of Pa., Philadelphia.

27. Report, Dec. 15, 1644, *N.Y.Col.Docs.* 1:150.

negotiated at Fort Amsterdam, in Manhattan, discloses why Kieft needed them. It proclaimed a general peace with all of New Netherland's Indians, with particular relevance to the rebellious Esopus tribe, "in the presence of the Maquas [Mohawk] ambassadors, *who were solicited to assist in this negotiation, as arbitrators.*"[28]

It seems clear that this train of diplomacy had been set in motion by Arent van Corlaer's 1642 journey from Fort Orange to the Mohawk village of Caughnawaga and the lost treaty that followed in 1643. It is certain that Corlaer acquired the Mohawks' admiration, which they reverently preserved in tradition as though he had been one of their own great chiefs: they made the name Corlaer into a title by which they later addressed respected governors of the English colony of New York.

It remains to be seen why the Mohawks, who were fully involved in on-off hostilities with New France, should have bothered to do favors for the Dutch. In 1642 the French began construction of Fort Richelieu, near the northern end of the Mahican Channel, to prevent the Mohawks from hijacking the cargoes of New France's Indian allies voyaging along the St. Lawrence River. Simultaneously the French founded the settlement of Ville Marie, on Montreal Island, to serve as a sanctuary and mission for the Canadian Indians—and thus to protect their trade. The Mohawks instantly recognized these threats to their mode of subsistence that rested substantially on plundering Canadian trade, and they reacted violently.[29] It would be very strange if the Dutch had not also recognized that the new French strategy threatened to reduce drastically the quantity of furs that Mohawks could bring to Fort Orange.

No love was lost between Calvinist Dutchman and Catholic Frenchman in those days of religious fanaticism. Some of the Jesuits of Canada, who dominated New France's Indian policies in the early 1640s, had urged the French government to conquer New Netherland and thus deprive the Iroquois of their primary source of arms. Paris was sympathetic to the proposal but overcommitted already to the Thirty Years War in Europe.[30] The Dutch could hardly have been unaware of French antagonism, and they did provide a market for Iroquois piracy on French commerce. Dutch and Mohawk interests coincided very closely. In the making of their alliance, what is still unknown concerns the identity of the initiators and the precise provisions that the Dutch preferred not to commit to paper. The general tendency of the alliance is clear.

28. Van der Donck, *Description of New Netherlands*, p. 35; *N.Y.Col.Docs.*, Aug. 30, 1645, 13:18; John Romeyn Brodhead, *History of the State of New York*, 2 vols. (New York: Harper and Brothers, 1853–1871) 1:408–9.

29. Percy J. Robinson, Introduction to François de Creux, *The History of Canada or New France*, Publications of the Champlain Society 30 31 (Toronto, 1951) 1.xviii xix, Trigger, *Children of Aataentsic* 2:639–40.

30. Lalemant to Charlet, Feb. 28, 1642, *Jesuit Relations* 21:269–73.

As then made, the alliance was strictly a two-party affair. Its functions appear to have been to provide arms for the Mohawks, to repress the rebellious tribes of New Netherland, to damage New France, and to insure delivery of furs to Fort Orange. A by-product that worried Dutch Governor Peter Stuyvesant after he took office in 1647 was the elevation of the Mohawks to a position of superiority over the other Indians of New Netherland.[31] Though Indian custom sanctioned the intervention of third parties to mediate peace between warring tribes, the Mohawks' intervention between the Dutch and the hostile Esopus tribe in 1645 edged a bit beyond the traditional pattern, for the Mohawks came in not as neutrals but as Dutch allies doing Dutch business. Mohawk "mediation" was Mohawk arm-twisting, and the resultant agreement was more in the nature of a Dutch victory than a fully voluntary peace settlement.[32]

It was not the Dutch intention to make the Mohawks a favored instrument of policy in Indian affairs. Like the French, the Dutch treated with each tribe separately and permitted none to become spokesman for others. But Dutch dependence on the Mohawks grew in much the same measure as Mohawk dependence on the Dutch. No Algonquian-speaking tribe apparently could or would deliver the quantities of good furs that Mohawks acquired by their hunting and pillaging and through their close ties with the more western Iroquois tribes. Through the dim murk of self-serving Dutch-written sources, it also seems that the lower Hudson River Algonquians were kept in sullen subservience by the alliance. From time to time the Esopus tribe broke out in open war again, and always the Mohawks made themselves useful for their suppression.

In the period immediately following the treaty of 1645, however, the Dutch were comparatively free of internal Indian troubles, and they turned their attention to profit and the chief obstacle thereto: their competitors in New France.

31. Van Corlaer's letter, June 16, 1643, *N.Y.Col.Docs.* 13–15; treaty minutes, Sept. 24, 1659, *Minutes of Fort Orange and Beverwyck* 2:215; Stuyvesant to the directors, June 25, 1660, *N.Y.Col.Docs.* 13:176.

32. Treaty minutes, Aug. 30, 1645, *N.Y.Col.Docs.* 13:18. The Esopus Indians complained in 1661 that the Mohawks "were the cause, why they had lost so many men in the war against the Dutch." Treaty minutes, Jan. 22, 1661, *N.Y.Col.Docs.* 13:191.

Chapter 5 ֍ LOGISTICS of INTERSOCIETAL COMMERCE

The history of the fur trade is the history of contact between two civilizations, the European and the North American, with especial reference to the northern portion of the continent. The limited cultural background of the North American hunting peoples provided an insatiable demand for the products of the more elaborate cultural development of Europeans. The supply of European goods, the product of a more advanced and specialized technology, enabled the Indians to gain a livelihood more easily—to obtain their supply of food, as in the case of moose, more quickly, and to hunt the beaver more effectively. Unfortunately the rapid destruction of the food supply and the revolution in the methods of living accompanied by the increasing attention to the fur trade by which these products were secured, disturbed the balance which had grown up previous to the coming of the European. The new technology with its radical innovations brought about such a rapid shift in the prevailing Indian culture as to lead to wholesale destruction of the peoples concerned by warfare and disease.

Harold A. Innis, *The Fur Trade in Canada*

As the French writers make very explicit, the necessity of holding onto allies made the continuation of Indian rivalries not only desirable, but essential. If the hostile Iroquois had not existed, the French would have had to invent them.

Bruce G. Trigger, "The Mohawk-Mahican War"

The inclusive frontier

The frontier was a society in transition, but so are all societies. The point is that the frontier was indeed a distinct society with a distinct culture. Perhaps it would be more correct to say that there were several distinct frontiers—that of the Great Lakes region was not quite the same as that which prevailed east of the Appalachians—but they all shared several traits. They were places where peoples of different continental origins did business with each other. This much has sunk into historical consciousness under the misleading name of the fur trade, but a comprehensive history of intersocietal commerce has yet to be written. What is only now emerging is the revelation that those peoples mingled, married, and begot joint offspring who blended their varied cultural heritages in distinctive regional patterns. By racist definitions the new generations and their ways were merely degenerates: impure, spoiled specimens of their parent stocks—"half breeds," "mulattoes," and a multitude of pejorative epithets.

One of those terms has been turned around by the people upon whom it was fastened, and inquirers into their history are now exploring its implications. The métis of New France and Louisiana—born of French and Amerindian and sometimes African ethnic stocks—have stubbornly preserved an identity, not as imperfect reproductions of what they are not, but as what they are. These are the true descendants of the frontier. The frontier, rather than a European or Amerindian society exclusively, molded them. The commerce between the societies here, as everywhere in the world, became necessarily an association of persons, and nature took its course. Persons as well as culture became synethnic.[1]

A number of scholars, veteran and fledgling, have quite suddenly begun to reveal the outlines of this different frontier. J. Leitch Wright, Jr., has capped a career with *The Only Land They Knew: The Tragic Story of the Indians in the Old South*. The title is unfortunate, for his massive researches disclose more than tragedy, much though there was of that. Wright shows how even the English of the race-proud southern colonies mingled with Indians and Africans to create a new people for whom their vocabulary had no word except insults.[2]

It is clear now that Frederick Jackson Turner's Line Between Civilization and Savagery, though its intellectual ancestry was ancient, never existed, except where legal sanctions and political institutions enforced segregation. Even in such places, for example, as early Virginia and Puritan New England, clandestine coupling was more frequent than has ever been acknowledged by the literary guardians of racial purity. The invention of that ideological line, with its dazzling flattery of self-conscious Whites, has blinded historians to the facts of frontier life. Our proper task is not to glorify ideology, but to investigate actuality. There was indeed in America a social frontier, a special place. It was not a place of confrontation of imagined ideal attributes. The force that created it was the common urge of persons from both societies to exchange goods, genes, and ideas.

Aboriginal Amerindian tribal society no longer exists as it was then.

1. Scorners and condemners aside, the pioneer study of North American synethnics is Marcel Giraud, *Le Métis Canadien: Son Role dans L'Histoire des Provinces de L'Ouest* (Paris: Institute d'Ethnologie, 1945). The first interdisciplinary conference on the métis was held at the Newberry Library Center for the History of the American Indian, Sept. 3–5, 1981.

2. J. Leitch Wright, Jr., *The Only Land They Knew: The Tragic Story of the American Indians in the Old South* (New York: The Free Press, 1981). The descendants of these mixed people have been traced in *Southeastern Indians Since the Removal Era*, ed. Walter L. Williams (Athens: University of Georgia Press, 1979). For aboriginal society in the region see Charles Hudson, *The Southeastern Indians* (Knoxville: University of Tennessee Press, 1976).

Neither does European colonial society. Their frontier no longer exists. But the frontier's synethnic descendants still do exist. For generations they were condemned by racist institutions to live on the other side of the imagined line that nineteenth-century ideologists had determined to enforce—in reservations, barrios, ghettoes, and books. In history they became nonpersons. But they have a history, an exceedingly interesting and important one which is as integral to American history as the sermons of all the Puritan dogmatists and has had far more effect on the shaping of the American empire.[3]

The multitude of questions raised by synethnicity per se cannot be considered within the scope of this study, which must be confined to the processes of accommodation that produced it. Commerce began it. As Frederick Jackson Turner remarked before his vision was blurred by a rhetorical line, "The history of commerce is the history of the intercommunication of peoples."[4] As in all commerce, traditions and motives other than economic entered into the processes of American frontiers, but the outline of their interplay is the pattern of commercial intercourse and its attendant politics, whether conducted for purposes of profit, prestige, power, or simply subsistence. The relationships of commerce created a distinct frontier culture in the vast regions where Europeans met and mixed with Indians. It was a culture neither "White" nor "Red," neither "Civil" nor Tribal, but rather a blend. More precisely, one should speak in the plural of frontiers and frontier cultures, for the blending varied in different regions according to the particular peoples contributing to it. But it was always distinctively itself.

Commodity exchange between societies

The intricate machinery of commodity exchange, so basic to frontier cultures, requires attention to the roles of its varied participants and the

3. Recent studies include Jennifer S. H. Brown, *Strangers in Blood: Fur Trade Families in Indian Country* (Vancouver: University of British Columbia Press, 1980); Jacqueline Louise Peterson, "The People in Between: Indian-White Marriage and the Genesis of a Métis Society and Culture in the Great Lakes Region, 1680–1830," Ph.D. diss., University of Illinois at Chicago Circle, 1981. ———, " 'Wild' Chicago: The Formation and Destruction of a Multiracial Community on the Midwestern Frontier, 1816–1837," in *The Ethnic Frontier: Essays in the History of Group Survival in Chicago and the Midwest*, eds. Melvin G. Holli and Peter d'A. Jones (Grand Rapids, Mich.: William B. Eerdmans Publishing Co., 1977), pp. 25–71; William R. Swagerty, "Marriage and Settlement Patterns of Rocky Mountain Trappers and Traders," *Western Historical Quarterly* 11:2 (April, 1980), pp. 159–80. See also papers in *Old Trails and New Directions: Papers of the Third North American Fur Trade Conference*, eds. Carol M. Judd and Arthur J. Ray (Toronto: University of Toronto Press, 1980).

4. Frederick Jackson Turner, *The Character and Influence of the Indian Trade in Wisconsin: A Study of the Trading Post as an Institution* (1891), reprint eds. David Harry Miller and William W. Savage, Jr. (Norman: University of Oklahoma Press, 1977), p. 85.

vast spaces over which the commodities moved. Management of the personnel and control over this movement preoccupied the attention and required the cooperation of teams of politicians and businessmen on both sides: Indian and European. Within each team the partners acted in distinct ways, guided by their different cultures.[5]

So much has been written about "the fur trade" that it is necessary to say it is a misnomer. What is usually meant by the phrase is exchange between Indians and Europeans, Euramericans, or Euro-Canadians. There were many kinds of such exchange, involving many different commodities, transacted in different ways at different times and places, and by persons of variously mixed ancestry. One may class them all abstractly as the institution of intersocietal exchange, but abstract categories confuse by subsuming diverse phenomena under one rubric. The multiple processes of this institution in North America share certain characteristics with colonial economics elsewhere. Natives worked at extractive industries to produce goods to exchange for the products of European processing industries. Though ambipendent (i.e., interdependent in some degree, but capable of surviving separately), colonists and natives differed in the degree of their dependence on each other. Natives could free themselves of dependence on trade only by reverting to precolonial subsistence methods, and many natives had lost knowledge of the skills and techniques of those methods. Europeans, however, had alternatives in other markets.

The goods exchanged and the conditions of commerce varied greatly. European traders were often provisioned by Indians with maize, meat, fish, fowl; but there were times when Indians had to purchase provisions from the trading post.[6] Indians sometimes labored in mines,[7] and often as

5. The interrelations between commerce and politics stand out vividly in the following: W. J. Eccles, *Frontenac the Courtier Governor* (Toronto: McClelland and Stewart, 1959); Yves F. Zoltvany, *Philippe de Rigaud de Vaudreuil, Governor of New France, 1703–1725*, Carleton Library 80 (Toronto: McClelland and Stewart, 1974); Thomas Elliott Norton, *The Fur Trade in Colonial New York, 1686–1776* (Madison: University of Wisconsin Press, 1974); Bernard Bailyn, *The New England Merchants in the Seventeenth Century* (Cambridge, Mass.: Harvard University Press, 1955); Verner W. Crane, *The Southern Frontier, 1670–1732* (Ann Arbor: University of Michigan Press, 1929). For analysis of the trade as intersocietal see Francis Jennings, *The Invasion of America: Indians, Colonialism, and the Cant of Conquest*, published for the Institute of Early American History and Culture (1975; New York: W. W. Norton and Co. 1976), ch. 6.

6. Samuel de Champlain, *Works*, ed. H. P. Biggar (Toronto: The Champlain Society, 1936), 6:41–44; Edmund S. Morgan, *American Slavery, American Freedom: The Ordeal of Colonial Virginia* (New York: W. W. Norton and Co., 1975), pp. 73–74; William Bradford, *Of Plymouth Plantation*, ed. Samuel Eliot Morison (New York: Alfred A. Knopf, 1966), pp. 114–15; *The Instruction for Johan Printz, Governor of New Sweden*, trans. Amandus Johnson (Philadelphia: The Swedish Colonial Society, 1930), pp. 111, 117; D. W. Moodie, "Agriculture and the Fur Trade," in *Old Trails and New Directions*, pp. 272–90.

7. Velma Garcia-Mason, "Acoma Pueblo" in *Handbook of North American Indians* 9:456; Edward H. Spicer, *Cycles of Conquest* (Tucson: University of Arizona Press, 1962), pp. 120, 305.

transporters of cargo. Some Indians raided others to take prisoners for sale as slaves.[8] In the American Southwest, turquoise was an important commodity.[9] Indians sometimes labored as slaves, sometimes as hired hands, sometimes as indentured servants, sometimes as free men trading independently for themselves.

The staple of exchange north of Mexico, most of the time and in most places, was animal hides, with or without fur. What follows in this chapter applies to intersocietal exchange in the North American northeastern region in the seventeenth and eighteenth centuries. Different descriptions would be required for other regions in the same era, not to speak of later times.[10]

Indians usually combined multiple roles in one person. As the trade developed, some Indians became hired hands to carry goods in the employ of colonial traders or merchants;[11] but allowing for these and such outstanding independent traders as the Hurons, the Indians who hunted were as likely as not to be also the Indians who traded. They transported and guarded the goods themselves; they negotiated rights of way and peaceful accommodation; and, when all else failed, the same Indians fought the wars generated by commercial competition.

European roles displayed the principle of division of labor. At the point of exchange stood the trader. He was usually a sturdy, adventuresome fellow with little or no capital and less scruple, often operating on credit advanced by an urban merchant who was also not overwhelmingly scrupulous. The trader might be ethnically wholly European; but often, especially in New France, he was a métis offspring of mixed marriage.[12] In either case he was compelled by his role to learn tribal languages and thus become an important mediator between the societies. Typically without

8. Crane, *Southern Frontier*, ch. 2; Wright, *Only Land*, ch. 5, 6.

9. Charles H. Lange, "Relations of the Southwest with the Plains and Great Basin," in *Handbook of North American Indians* 9:202.

10. Much of what follows is adapted from part of Francis Jennings, "The Indian Trade of the Susquehanna Valley," *Proceedings of the American Philosophical Society* 110:6 (Dec., 1966), pp. 406–24.

11. Caughnawagas ("French Mohawks") were employed in the trade between Montreal and Albany: Norton, *Fur Trade in New York*, p. 126; Carolinians hired Indian burdeners "to carry peltry as much as 200 or even 500 miles," Wright, *Only Land*, p. 161.

12. For discussion of the social issues raised by the traders' mixed ethnicity see Cornelius J. Jaenen, *Friend and Foe: Aspects of French-Amerindian Cultural Contact in the Sixteenth and Seventeenth Centuries* (New York: Columbia University Press, 1976), esp. 108–15. Jennifer S. H. Brown, in *Strangers in Blood*, has explored in great detail the effects of mixed union on the children and social structure in nineteenth-century Canadian trading regions. The two books are fascinatingly contrapuntal. For still other aspects see Daniel Usner, Jr., "Frontier Exchange in the Lower Mississippi Valley: Race Relations and Economic Life in Colonial Louisiana, 1699–1783," Ph.D. diss., Duke University, 1981; and Marcel Giraud, *A History of French Louisiana*, vol. 1, *The Reign of Louis XIV, 1698–1715* (1953), trans. Joseph C. Lambert (Baton Rouge: Louisiana University Press, 1974).

much formal education, and frequently barely literate, this trader became indispensable in negotiations between tribe and colony because the classically educated men of higher status disdained the "savage" languages without written literatures.[13] Every English colony acquired a corps of trader/interpreters whose prominent services enhanced their prestige among the Indians with whom they did business.[14] Every governor had to depend on their good will and good faith, which were sometimes highly suspect. As no one was capable of checking up on the interpreter, he could slant speeches in ways advantageous to himself and his merchant partner/protector. The documents written by this interpreter, or transcribed from his utterances, present problems of analysis and verification; and generally historians have no means at all of knowing what he spoke to the Indians in their own tongues.

Traders sometimes participated in wars, but they did not as a rule mass together and go off on raiding parties as did the Indians.[15] Among colonials, wars were fought either by militias—sometimes volunteer, sometimes impressed—or by professional soldiers who could also be divided into different types: the small-scale mercenaries of New Netherland as distinguished from the standing regiments sent by Louis XIV to New France.

A particular class of traders became so independent and so influential among the Indians as to constitute a significant power in intercolonial and intertribal affairs. These were the coureurs de bois of New France. Rebels against monopoly, whether chartered or conspiratorial, they left the shoestring settlements along the St. Lawrence to penetrate deep into the interior of the continent, sometimes wandering from tribe to tribe, sometimes settling with one Indian community and becoming part of it.[16] Their hallmark was individualism. French officials tried to suppress them from

13. E.g., New York's Robert Livingston and Pennsylvania's James Logan always used interpreters in dealing with Indians. Livingston often had to retranslate the interpreter's Dutch into English. Logan annotated his books in Latin, Greek, Hebrew, and Arabic but never bothered to learn the language of the people by whom his city was surrounded. Logan's books may be seen in the Library Company of Philadelphia. See Edwin Wolf, II *The Library of James Logan of Philadelphia, 1674–1751* (Phila.: Library Co. of Philadelphia, 1974), pp. xi–xii, xxix–xxx.

14. Examples: Connecticut's Thomas Stanton, New York's Arnout Viele, Pennsylvania's Conrad Weiser.

15. In 1704 James Moore and fifty "Goose Creek men" of South Carolina led one thousand warriors in a slave raid against the Indians of Apalachee. Wright, *Only Land*, pp. 1113–14. In 1715 Canada's Michel Bisaillon led hundreds of Illinois warriors against the Foxes. Vaudreuil to Council of Marine, Oct. 14, 1716, in *Collections of the State Historical Society of Wisconsin*, ed. Reuben Gold Thwaites, 16 (Madison, 1902), pp. 341–42.

16. W. J. Eccles, *Canada under Louis XIV, 1663–1701*, Canadian Centenary Series (Toronto: McClelland and Stewart, 1964), pp. 93–94, 109–10, 244–48; Allen W. Trelease, *Indian Affairs in Colonial New York: The Seventeenth Century* (Ithaca, N.Y.: Cornell University Press, 1960), pp. 246–47.

time to time, only to see them change coats and trade with the English.

Médard Chouart Des Groseilliers and Pierre-Esprit Radisson opened up the Hudson Bay area to French trade; when mistreated by politically powerful competitors, they joined the newly formed English Hudson's Bay Company and taught it how to work.[17] New York's Governor Edmund Andros was embarrassed by refugee traders from Montreal whom he did not trust, but his successor, Thomas Dongan, recruited them for commercial expansion to French Michilimackinac.[18] Refugee coureurs de bois Martin Chartier and Pierre Bisaillon established a foundation for the expansion of Pennsylvania's trade over the Appalachian Mountains.[19] Coureurs de bois who migrated from Canada to set up new bases in Louisiana spread French influence and commerce up the Mississippi Valley, but in their own independent fashion; some made deals with English traders from Charleston when the price was right.[20] For most Indians of the Mississippi Valley and Great Lakes regions, these rough adventurers were the true vanguard of "civilization," scattering themselves farther and wider than even the most dedicated missionaries.

They have been accused by Francis Parkman and his like of reverting to savagery.[21] Translated, this phrase means that they lacked feelings of race hatred that were deemed proper to civilized men by writers of Social Darwinist persuasion.[22] That very lack enabled them to mix freely and securely among warlike peoples hundreds of miles distant from other Europeans. Open minded as they were, they could understand and adapt to strange cultures and intermarry freely with the peoples among whom they traded. Their willingness to accept Indian humanity resulted in com-

---

17. Grace Lee Nute, "Chouart Des Groseillers, Médard," in *Dict. Can. Biog.* 1:223–28; ———, "Radisson, Pierre-Esprit," ibid., 2:535–40.

18. Trelease, *Indian Affairs*, pp. 250–51, 269; Denonville's reports, *N.Y.Col.Docs.* 9:275, 287, 290–91.

19. Francis Jennings, "Bisaillon, Peter," in *Dict. Can. Biog.* 3:65–66.

20. Ramezay to the Minister, Sept. 18, 1714, in *Wisconsin Historical Collections* 16:303; Verner W. Crane, *The Southern Frontier, 1670–1732* (1929), reprinted (Ann Arbor: University of Michigan Press, 1956), p. 66; Charles Edwards O'Neill, *Church and State in French Colonial Louisiana: Policy and Politics to 1732* (New Haven: Yale University Press, 1966), p. 42; Giraud, *A History of French Louisiana* 1:80–84, 221, 361–64.

21. Samples of Parkman: Many of the coureurs de bois, "shaking loose every tie of blood and kindred, identified themselves with the Indians, and sank into utter barbarism." A "mongrel race of bush-rangers." "Many a lawless half-breed, the mongrel offspring of the colonists of Detroit and the Indian squaws." But the English traders supposedly were superior to such degeneration: "Though they became barbarians, they did not become Indians; and scorn on the one side and hatred on the other still marked the intercourse of the hostile races." Francis Parkman, *The Conspiracy of Pontiac and the Indian War after the Conquest of Canada* (1851), rev. New Library ed. 2 vols. (Boston: Little, Brown, and Co., 1909), 1:82–83, 68, 223, 84.

22. Parkman held consistently to Social Darwinian attitudes and sometimes used the terminology explicitly. E.g., "survival of the fittest," Francis Parkman, *Montcalm and Wolfe*, 2 vols. (1884), New Library ed. (Boston: Little, Brown, and Co., 1909), 1:217.

mercial profit and political power as the Indians reciprocated by accepting them.

The roles of merchants

The role of wholesaler was performed by the well-capitalized urban export-import merchant whose credit stood well abroad and whose scale of operations enabled him to withstand competitors and calamities at home. His way of working knew very few distinctions between business and politics. Ever the advocate of freedom in the abstract, he constantly strove to monopolize the trade for himself, and he was likely to use every available device to that end, legal or not. When his friends controlled government, he advocated licensing of traders—his own traders—with fines and imprisonment for unlicensed competitors. When the merchant's friends were out of office, he bribed the placemen and flouted the laws. He kept in touch with courtiers and imperial influence wielders to secure decrees from the crown advantaging his own province and trade to the detriment of others. All in all, the custom of the time was to combine law and larceny in what we today would call a protection racket. Strange things happened to traders without the proper merchant protector. They might find themselves jailed on suspicion of treason—who could say certainly that they were not conspiring with enemy agents deep in the woods?[23] Or perhaps some happy Indians would find themselves authorized to plunder unlicensed—i.e., nonsyndicate—traders.[24] The great merchant monopolist and his silent partner in the governor's office sometimes knew how to discipline their competitors though the law was never strong enough to reach their own men.

Second only to the need for political power was that for a successful merchant to maintain constantly a large stock of the right kind of trade goods.[25] When traders and Indians appeared unannounced in town, the merchant had to be ready to supply them before competitors could get to them. Obviously he had to be able to pump large funds into his warehouse inventory. A further strain on his finances was the practice, which had become common by the eighteenth century, of extending goods on credit.[26]

---

23. Petition, mss., endorsed Jan. 6, 1693/4, Penn Letters and Ancient Documents 3:9, Amer. Phil. Soc.; *Pa. Council Minutes*, Feb. 24, 25, 1707, 2:403–5; Aug. 22, 1711, 2:539.

24. French memoir, 1686, *N.Y.Col.Docs.* 9:803. Dongan denied that this order to pillage traders was intended against the French. Dongan to Denonville, Dec. 1, 1686, *N.Y.Col.Docs.* 3:463. But his order to seize English traders from colonies south of New York is on record. *Livingston Indian Records*, 107.

25. Albright G. Zimmerman, "The Indian Trade of Colonial Pennsylvania," Ph.D. diss., University of Delaware, 1966, pp. 115–25. This is the most highly detailed exploration of its subject.

26. See James Logan's Account Book, 1712–1719, and James Logan's Ledger, 1720–1727, mss, Hist. Soc. of Pa.

It efficiently guaranteed that the harvest of a trader's season would come to the lending merchant, and in that respect it practically converted the trader to the status of an employee. But the test of credit is repayment. Traders borrowed stock to carry to their remote posts, where they passed the loan along to equip Indian customers (workmen) for the hunt. If all went well, the merchant reaped two gratifying profits on the same overall transaction: he gained once on the price he charged for the goods he had sent out, and he gained again on the price at which he accepted the furs taken in payment. Things did not always work out so well. Indians, like other people, died at unanticipated times without estate; occasionally they decamped or defaulted. Traders might be given credit by a cynical businessman, but they deserved trust only from fools. Wars and plundering added to the hazards of accident and human frailty. The merchant who watched his capital being packed off into the woods each fall slept lightly and nervously until his peltry appeared in the spring. Great merchants could minimize the effect of loss through the insurance principle of distribution of risk. Obviously these were the same men who also could wield the necessary political power to protect their organizations.

Despite his power, however, the merchant's organization had its taproots out in Indian country, and he could not succeed without expert trading personnel.[27] Not every Tom, Dick, or Harry knew how to get along in the villages, where personal relationships were prerequisite to trading relationships. Good traders knew at least one Indian language, better traders had the hang of the dialects, and some of the veterans were multilingual.

A "good" trader could cheat Indians without getting caught at it, and the trouble with that sort of fellow was that he would cheat the merchant, too, if he could. Rum bulked large in the goods of men who drank copiously along with their customers, with no appreciable gain to either physique or efficiency. In New France, the trade in brandy was a perpetually sore issue.[28] Journeys were often long and hazardous. Attitudes of financial responsibility appeared intermittently if at all. Debts piled up. Trader mortality was high, and trader business mortality even higher. No mer-

27. Norton, *Fur Trade*, ch. 6; Zimmerman, "Indian Trade," ch. 6. For detailed lists see Charles A. Hanna, *The Wilderness Trail, or The Ventures and Adventures of the Pennsylvania Traders on the Allegheny Path*, 2 vols. (New York: G. P. Putnam's Sons, 1911), 1:chs. 5, 7, 11; 2:326–43.

28. W. J. Eccles believes that many Iroquois defected to Canada in "the desire to avoid the Albany rum traders." He may be right—certainly Jesuit missionaries and the clergy generally waged a valiant battle against intoxicants—but Eccles has also reported how French brandy flowed into the Indian villages not controlled by the missionaries. W. J. Eccles, *The Canadian Frontier, 1534–1760* (New York: Holt, Rinehart and Winston, 1969), p. 88; idem., *Canada under Louis XIV, 1663–1701*, Canadian Centenary Series (Toronto: McClelland and Steward Ltd., 1964), pp. 14–15, 72, 87–89.

chant could recruit a staff of traders with assurance that that part of his work had been done. Perpetually, means had to be found to recoup loss caused by death or bankruptcy of indebted traders and to enlist competent new men.[29]

Certain personal qualities were as necessary to the merchant as others were to the trader. No merchant could establish the routines of his business and then delegate responsibility while he turned attention elsewhere. His business changed every year. On the one hand, his supplies from Europe were subject to interruption by reason of war, piracy, navigation hazards, and the competence and honesty of supplying exporters. On the other hand, the merchant's source of peltry might be cut off for much the same sort of reasons. Just to conduct day-to-day business, the merchant had to keep himself ceaselessly and accurately informed about a thousand details in the world at large as well as in his personal affairs.

Among other matters, the merchant had to steep himself in Indian politics and diplomacy. It is trite to say that until nearly the nineteenth century the North American fur trade was always a trade with Indians, but it reminds us that the basic strategy of all European traders and merchants was not to get at the animals, but rather to get at the Indians. Two methods were possible: to go to the Indians or to attract the Indians to journey themselves to centers of trade. Both methods were used.

Traders' travels

To see this is to see through the foolish and tedious myth that the Indians' reliance on hunting forced their retirement before the "advance of civilization." On the contrary, Indians who hunted for commerce were drawn by their own inclinations, as well as the settled policy of colonial merchants and statesmen, into the vicinity of posts or markets maintained by the colonies.[30] The rule was simple: the more Indians under a colony's influence or control, the more trade the colony could expect to have. Far from wanting to drive Indians away, trading colonies offered hospitality and enticements.[31] When those Indians later "retired," the pressures forc-

29. Pennsylvania's James Logan was especially fertile in expedients. See Jennings, "Indian Trade," pp. 418–24.

30. The process is vividly described in Paul A. W. Wallace, *Indians in Pennsylvania* (Harrisburg: Pennsylvania Historical and Museum Commission, 1961). But distinctions must be made. Wallace's Indians were fragments of broken tribes. Sedentary Indians who maintained tribal integrity clung to their own territories.

31. The Shawnees were especially in demand. For many details about them, rather chaotically presented, see Charles A. Hanna, *The Wilderness Trail; or The Ventures and Adventures of the Pennsylvania Traders on the Allegheny Path*, 2 vols. (New York: G. P. Putnam's Sons, (1911), 1:ch. 4; and see ch. 10, herein. No comprehensive history of the wandering Shawnees

ing them back were more substantial than the moral force of European culture or irreconcilable differences of technology. They retreated because their lands were seized from them by purchase, voluntary or coerced—or by force, fraud, or uncontrolled encroachment.

Very much like Europeans of all nationalities, some Indians used an intermediate position in trade to turn a profit and control the flow of goods.[32] Neither the European merchant nor the interior tribesman hunter was content with this situation, and each sought direct contact with the other. Europeans developed a strategy of traders' leapfrog. They bypassed tribes on the ocean coast by sailing far inland to the heads of navigation of great rivers: French voyages up the St. Lawrence were emulated early in the seventeenth century by Dutch traders on the Hudson, Connecticut, and Delaware rivers, and Englishmen on Chesapeake Bay. (One must not forget that the Chesapeake, quite apart from its tributary streams, is navigable for as great a distance as the Hudson River.) Having learned to leapfrog over tribes, Europeans practiced the art on each other. On the Delaware River especially, Swedes, Dutch, and English traders pushed beyond each other to intercept the trading tribes before competitors could get to them. Dutch and English colonists played the same game on the Connecticut River. In both places the playing became rough, and the stronger competitors got rid of the others by armed force.[33] For many decades, however, few Europeans would venture far from waters navigable by the ocean-going ships that carried their lifeline to Europe, and no matter how deeply they penetrated upstream the neighboring tribes immediately closed around them to control access.

has yet been published. The sketch "Shawnee" by Charles Callender in *Northeast* (pp. 622–35) is disappointingly ahistorical for the most part and frequently erroneous when it attempts superficial history, but its map (p. 623) reveals the migrations that have daunted historians.

32. Harold A. Innis seems to have been first to recognize the importance of the phenomenon of tribal interposition. There has been some argument as to which tribes acted as "brokers" of peltry purchased from other tribes, but the effort by tribes close to European trading posts to control access to the posts is now generally accepted. Harold A. Innis, *The Fur Trade in Canada: An Introduction to Canadian Economic History* (1930) rev. ed. (Toronto: University of Toronto Press, 1956). Charles Howard McIlwain, "Introduction," in Peter Wraxall, *An Abridgment of the Indian Affairs Contained in Four Folio Volumes, Transacted in the Colony of New York, from the Year 1678 to the Year 1751*, ed. C. H. McIlwain (1915), reprint (New York: Benjamin Blom, 1968), p. xliv; Allen W. Trelease, "The Iroquois and the Western Fur Trade; A Problem in Interpretation," *Mississippi Valley Historical Review* 49 (1962), pp. 32–51; Bruce G. Trigger, *The Children of Aataentsic: A History of the Huron People to 1660*, 2 vols. (Montreal: McGill-Queen's University Press, 1976), 2:617–23.

33. C. A. Weslager and A. R. Dunlap, *Dutch Explorers, Traders and Settlers in the Delaware Valley, 1609–1664* (Philadelphia: University of Pennsylvania Press, 1961), ch. 6–10; C. A. Weslager, *The English on the Delaware: 1610–1682* (New Brunswick, N. J.: Rutgers University Press, 1967); Francis Jennings, "Indians and Frontiers in Seventeenth Century Maryland," in *Early Maryland and the World Beyond*, ed. David B. Quinn (Detroit: Wayne State University Press, 1982), pp. 216–41. Francis Jennings, "Virgin Land and Savage People," *American Quarterly* 23 (1971), pp. 519–41.

Interior Indians therefore had no choice but to accept the intermediate tribes' terms or fight through. Some negotiated, some fought. Pertinent to present concerns, the Hurons fought their way into the St. Lawrence valley from their homeland between Lake Huron and Lake Simcoe, and the Susquehannocks overpowered the Delawares to gain access to the traders of Delaware Valley. We have already seen (in chapter 3) how the Mohawks drove through Mahican interference on the upper Hudson.

Having gained their own access, these strong interior tribes in turn assumed the role of privileged middlemen. This role could be played in various ways. The Hurons and Susquehannocks made themselves into brokers. Little is known about the Susquehannocks except that they traveled great distances to acquire furs to bring back to the Swedish and Dutch traders on the Delaware River. Huron practices are better documented. From their homeland, lying between Lake Huron's Georgian Bay and Lake Simcoe, they made a great circuit of the Iroquoian Neutral, Erie, and Tionontate (Petun) tribes on the shores of lakes Ontario and Erie, and thence up to the Algonquian hunters at Lake Nipissing, whence they might get to Quebec either by journeying overland to the Saguenay River and down it to the St. Lawrence or by the more direct route of the Ottawa River to the St. Lawrence. Vast distances were traversed, and great quantities of fur eventually delivered to Quebec.[34] If Huron culture had permitted capital accumulation, some of these Indians would naturally have become merchants and possibly might have followed that process through the logical development of a state form of government. But their culture stressed sharing instead of investment, and they remained individual tribal traders instead of acquiring employees and hoarding wealth.

Huron traders dealt with French merchants. After their long circuit the Hurons brought an annual accumulation of furs to the French market at Quebec and (after 1642) Montreal. Perhaps these markets ought rather to be called fairs. They burst into frenzied activity briefly in the spring when a great fleet of Huron or Ottawa canoes brought in the winter's peltry collection, and subsided back into normal routines during the rest of the year.[35]

After Champlain established direct alliance with the important Canadian tribes, the French were not troubled by local tribes attempting to monopolize trade at the markets. They had plenty of trouble, however, with Iroquois depredations.

34. See George T. Hunt, *The Wars of the Iroquois: A Study in Intertribal Trade Relations* (Madison: University of Wisconsin Press, 1940), ch. 5 and map between pp. 7 and 8; Trigger, *Children of Aataentsic* 1:335–44; Conrad Heidenreich, *Huronia: A History and Geography of the Huron Indians, 1600–1650* (Toronto: McClelland and Stewart, 1971), ch. 7.
35. [Louis-Armand de Lom d'Arce] Baron de Lahontan, *New Voyages to North-America* (1703), ed. Reuben Gold Thwaites, 2 vols. (Chicago: A. C. McClurg and Co., 1905), pp. 92–95.

In the latter seventeenth century many individual French Canadians ventured out into Indian territory to become traders themselves. Official trading posts were also established by government policy at important crossroads, the most distant of which was Michilimackinac at the junction of lakes Superior, Michigan, and Huron.[36] The primary collectors in the backwoods, whether individual French coureurs de bois, Indian traders, or employees of great merchants, gathered cargoes that sometimes weighed tons and required transportation in canoes that seem huge by comparison with the modern sport canoe. (Some of the working boats would take crews of fourteen men.)[37] Quebec and Montreal continued through the eighteenth century to serve as the markets where these cargoes were bought by great export-import merchants for trans-shipment to Europe.

At these base towns, political authorities regulated the trade, ostensibly to prevent abuses and maintain Indian good will. In actuality the controls were often imposed to create effective monopolies in which the regulating authorities participated surreptitiously.[38] But every regulation could be evaded out in the bushes. Freelance traders simply ranged into the interior and gained concessions from competing merchants. The wilderness entrepreneurs, called coureurs de bois, submitted to no binding discipline. Threatened with punishment for their illegal activities, some of them turned their coats and took up business in Albany and at trading centers in Pennsylvania on the Schuylkill and Susquehanna rivers.[39]

36. The point of upper Michigan's peninsula juts out as a natural center of communication for the western Great Lakes region. It was originally the site of habitation by various Indian tribes. Father Jacques Marquette founded the mission of Saulte Ste. Mare in 1668 on the strait through which Lake Superior empties into Lake Huron. When his charges fled from Indian enemies, he followed them to found the mission of St. Ignace on the strait through which Lake Michigan empties into Lake Huron. Fur traders were attracted to the vicinity, and, about 1683, Daniel Greysolon Dulhut built Fort Michilimackinac on the strait. Location is in *A Historical Atlas of Canada*, ed. D. G. G. Kerr, 2d ed. (Don Mills, Ont.: Thomas Nelson and Sons Ltd., 1966), p. 20. Site chart in Lahontan, *New Voyages* 1:36/37.

See Raphael N. Hamilton, S. J., *Marquette's Explorations: The Narratives Reexamined* (Madison: University of Wisconsin Press, 1970), pp. 16–17, 164; Yves F. Zoltvany, "Greysolon Dulhut, . . . Daniel," in *Dict. Can. Biog.* 2:263; W. J. Eccles, *Canada under Louis XIV*, pp. 104, 108–9.

37. George Irving Quimby, *Indian Culture and European Trade Goods* (Madison: University of Wisconsin Press, 1966), p. 164.

38. W. J. Eccles, *Frontenac: The Courtier Governor* (Toronto: McClellan and Stewart Ltd., 1959), ch. 5; Yves F. Zoltvany, *Philippe de Rigaud de Vaudreuil: Governor of New France, 1703–1725*, The Carleton Library 80 (Toronto: McClelland and Stewart Ltd., 1974), ch. 11; Jennings, "Indian Trade."

39. Denonville's letters, 1687, *N.Y.Col.Docs.* 3:471, 9:326; Evelyn A. Benson, "The Huguenot LeTorts: First Christian Family on the Conestoga," *Journal of the Lancaster County Historical Society* 65:2 (Spring, 1961), p. 99. I owe thanks to Mrs. Benson for guidance in this matter and on James Logan's Indian trade.

Intersocietal partnerships

French and Dutch markets functioned in ways varying according to national and tribal policies. Perhaps the national policies derived from the opposite fates of Champlain and Van Krieckebeeck. Champlain won against the Mohawks and could carry out a policy of direct leadership of all the Canadian tribes. Van Krieckebeeck lost against the Mohawks, whereupon the Fort Orange Dutch withdrew from efforts at grand policy and confined themselves to dealings with particular tribes for particular purposes. After Governor Willem Kieft's disastrous adventurings at Manhattan, the Dutch became more and more dependent upon the Mohawks in ways that New France never experienced with any particular tribe.

After Louis XIV took personal charge of the French government in 1661, New France was regarded in Paris as a potential empire worth the expenditure of large sums to develop. In Amsterdam, however, the Dutch West India Company looked upon its New Netherland colony as worthless if it could not produce an immediate profit. The different attitudes extended into the colonies with significant consequences. Some Dutch colonials dreamed of becoming great lords, but few held dreams of imperial glory. Dutchmen were businessmen. As such, when fighting was to be done they hired mercenary soldiers, including English colonials and Indians of all tribes, and they coped with situations as each arose. For French policymakers trade was a means to the end of empire as well as an end in itself. Aspiring to achieve political control over the peoples of the New World, instead of just doing business with them, the French had a clear understanding that military force would be required to attain their goals. Under direction from Paris, New France formed tough militias and braced them with sporadic reinforcements of professionals from the royal armies.[40]

On the tribal side, the Mohawks also had a dream of empire, of a sort, that contrasted with the predominately commercial outlook of the Hurons. The Mohawks challenged French dominance while the Hurons adapted to it. The Mohawks could get along with the Dutch, on the other hand, because the Dutch left them alone except for business transactions. And the Dutch were very useful to them. Increasing Dutch dependency on Mohawk military strength led to an increase of help by the Dutch to build that strength. If the Dutch lacked the desire to extend domination over distant tribes, the Mohawks more than made up for the lack.

Though occasionally acting as brokers (apparently as hired hands for

40. Marcel Trudel, *The Beginnings of New France, 1524–1663*, Canadian Centenary Series (Toronto: McClelland and Stewart, 1973), p. 140; W. J. Eccles, *France in America*, New American Nation Series (New York: Harper and Row, 1972), ch. 3.

Dutch merchants) Mohawk men seem to have alternated most of their activity between hunting and plundering, and they jealously controlled traffic by other tribes—even their Iroquois brethren—to the Dutch merchants. They were middlemen in a different sense from that of the brokerage of the Hurons. A middle position in the trade could be exploited in various ways: one example is that of the Kichesipirinis, who occupied Allumette Island in the Ottawa River and charged tolls on traffic passing by.[41] Mohawk intentions went far beyond making a profit.

Huron traders were especially vulnerable to Mohawk brigandage. Their long journeys took them through unprotected wilderness trails and along many narrow waterways where ambush was easy. Nor were the Hurons wholly secure in their home villages, for the Iroquois Senecas—the westernmost tribe of the Five Nations—picked up the habit of raiding at even that distance.[42]

These tribal policies and actions lead to a number of conclusions. First, the arrival of European traders stimulated intertribal competition and warfare between systems of trade at the same time that it promoted cooperation within each system. Though sources of initiative varied, conflict occurred not merely between tribes or between colonies; it manifested itself as a partnership of tribe and colony versus another partnership of tribe and colony.

Second, European merchants and their governors retained final control over the trade through their control of the manufactured goods which were its reason for being, and their ability to withhold such goods from enemies. But their control existed only in the abstract aggregate. Indians could also withhold from enemies the furs desired by the Europeans, and so long as Frenchman competed against Dutchman, Swede, and Englishman, Indians willing to travel could influence prices and the flow of exchange—always with the understanding that extensive travel involved extensive diplomacy.

Third, geography and the logistics of transport were essential to the shape of the trade's growth and development. We have noticed the importance of controls over Indian access to European trading posts. This was matched by the importance of traders' access to hunting Indians, especially those of the Great Lakes, Hudson's Bay, and Mississippi Valley regions—and by the necessity for security of traffic between the sources of furs and the sources of trade goods. Strategic interposition meant much in every phase of the trade.

We may glance briefly at Hudson Bay before consigning it to the

41. Trudel, *Beginnings of New France*, p. 144; Hunt, *Wars of the Iroquois*, p. 44; Elisabeth Tooker, "The League of the Iroquois: Its History, Politics, and Ritual," in *Northeast*, pp. 430–32. For the Kichesipirinis see Trigger, *Children of Aataentsic*, 1:341–42.
42. Trigger, *Children of Aataentsic* 2:658–60.

oblivion of regions beyond further consideration. After the founding in 1670 of the English Hudson's Bay Company, the French organized a competitive Compagnie de la Baie du Nord. English presence became a constant magnet attracting Indians from a vast surrounding region and compelling New France to incessant diplomatic and military measures.[43] These proved fruitless, and the Hudson's Bay Company is still with us as a going concern. But the conditions of trade at Hudson Bay were very different from those in the regions of our interest, and very remote.[44] We may pass them by without damage to our central concerns.

The southern frontier

The earliest frontier was that at the opposite extreme from Hudson Bay. In its initial phase, the *entrada* of De Soto, the Southern frontier was one of military confrontation. The Spanish occupation forces in due course set up the Franciscan mission systems of the South Atlantic coast and interior Apalachee. English traders destroyed the missions, after the founding of Carolina in 1670, by inciting independent tribes to raid the mission for slaves. Although deer skins bulked large in the *fur* trade of South Carolina, J. Leitch Wright remarks that "it is impossible to comprehend the remarkable expansion of the Indian trade without taking slavery into account." In the early years of South Carolina, "Indian slavery became a mainstay of the colony's economy."[45]

After the founding of Louisiana at the turn of the century, French traders competed with the Carolinians as the latter tried to force their way into the Mississippi. Valley. All the European colonials set up extensive systems of alliance with the tribes living between them, and the tribal territories became arenas of intercolonial competition and conflict. But it is well to notice also that distinctive regional patterns of accommodation and synethnicity developed within each alliance system. In South Carolina, plantations and plantation slavery came to dominate the economy, but Professor Daniel Usner has documented a new conception of the effects of trade in the lower Mississippi Valley: "Plantation agriculture and Indian trade in this region and perhaps in other colonial regions did not belong to two separate economies. Instead, they evolved as interconnected parts

---

43. Eccles, *France in America*, pp. 93–94.

44. The standard history is E. E. Rich, *The History of the Hudson's Bay Company, 1670–1870*, 2 vols., Hudson's Bay Record Society Publications 21, 22 (London, 1958–1959). New issues and problems now claim researchers' attention, as evidenced in Arthur J. Ray, *Indians in the Fur Trade: their role as trappers, hunters, and middlemen in the lands southwest of Hudson Bay, 1660–1870* (Toronto: University of Toronto Press, 1974) and *Old Trails and New Directions*, eds. Judd and Ray.

45. Wright, *Only Land*, pp. 46–47, 138–45. Quotation at p. 138.

of a single regional economy, providing inhabitants with varied economic alternatives and producing a variable set of export commodities."[46]

It is tempting to speculate that the southern frontier may have been partially responsible for the historical development of the regional self-consciousness of the American South. Carolinians' attention was drawn southwestward from the time of the colony's founding, whereas the Northern colonies had Canada to contend with and were required therefore to face northward and northwesterly. From the beginning, the Southern and Northern English colonies were obliged by French competition to face outward to their frontiers in such wise that they were almost back to back.

Northern trading systems

Our main business in this study is with the northern frontier region. Its complex trading systems between the Great Lakes and the Atlantic were interlinked by the exigencies of topography. Frenchmen had a direct route to the interior via the St. Lawrence and Ottawa rivers as well as the lakes, but the Dutch and English colonies faced the great physical obstacle of the Appalachian mountain wall. There were trails through the mountains, but waterways delineated the main channels of communication, whether by canoe or on the well-worn paths that followed alongside the streams. These waterway systems converged to "trunk lines" through the hills. Thus, physical conditions limited sharply the number of commercially worthwhile long-haul routes.

For convenience of description, let us start inland. There were three great systems for coming from the far interior to the northeastern trading settlements. Over the French system, trading Indians coming from Huronia used as their main route Georgian Bay, French River, Lake Nipissing, and the Ottawa River to the St. Lawrence, down which they traveled northeasterly to Quebec. After the dispersion of the Hurons, the Ottawa Indians used the same route as far as Montreal until the establishment of western trading posts made the journey unnecessary.[47]

A second system moved goods along a more southerly route. In this system, which may be called the Susquehanna for short, a canoeist could paddle from the Mississippi up the Ohio to the Allegheny River. At several points en route, he might be joined by travelers from Lake Erie: for instance, voyagers who had left the lake at the site of modern Cleveland

46. Daniel Usner, Jr., "Frontier Exchange in the Lower Mississippi Valley: Race Relations and Economic Life in Colonial Louisiana, 1699–1783," Ph.D. diss., Duke University, 1981, p. 152.

47. Heidenreich, *Huronia*, p. 245; Trigger, *Children of Aataentsic* 2:821.

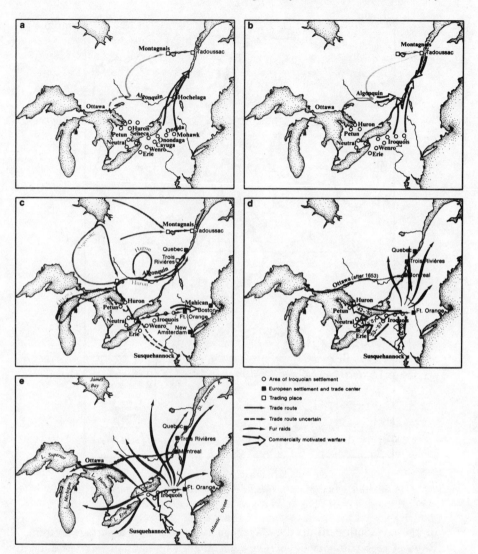

MAP 4. Tribal Trade and Warfare, Prior to English Conquest of New Netherland. Area of settlement, warfare, and trade: a. late 16th century; b. by 1603; c. 1615–1640; d. 1642–1657; e. 1659–1663. REPRODUCED FROM *Northeast*, VOLUME 15 OF *Handbook of North American Indians*, BY COURTESY OF GENERAL EDITOR WILLIAM C. STURTEVANT.

MAP 5. Susquehannock Major Canoe Routes. REPRODUCED FROM
Northeast, VOLUME 15 OF *Handbook of North American Indians*, BY
PERMISSION OF GENERAL EDITOR WILLIAM C. STURTEVANT.

to journey southward up the Cuyahoga River and over a portage to the
Beaver Creek tributary of the Ohio, or others who had left Lake Erie in
the vicinity of the modern city of Erie to get onto the French Creek branch
of the Allegheny. From several headwaters of the Allegheny, short portages could be made to the Juniata River or West Branch tributaries of the
Susquehanna Bay or paddle northward over the Susquehanna's North
Branch to its source, whence a portage of 14 miles took the voyager to the
Mohawk River and on to Albany. This Susquehanna system linked into
Delaware River waterways over three short portages (and longer ones were
also possible): among the intertwining headwaters of the Delaware and
the Susquehanna's North Branch; more significantly for western travel-

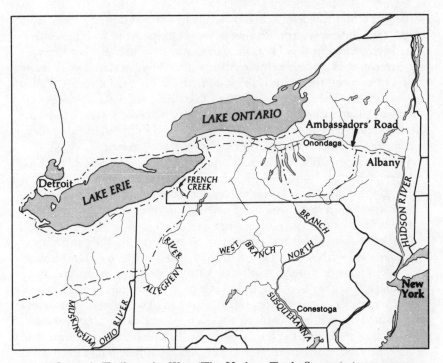

MAP 6. Iroquois Trails to the West (The Hudson Trade System). (ADAPTED FROM P.A.W. WALLACE, *Indians in Pennsylvania*, P. 42, BY COURTESY OF THE PENNSYLVANIA HISTORICAL AND MUSEUM COMMISSION.) The dashed lines mark footpaths traveled by Iroquois warriors, traders, and diplomats.

ers, lower down via creeks to the Schuylkill River branch of the Delaware; and still further downstream, across the narrow peninsula between Chesapeake and Delaware bays.[48] These terminal bays witnessed intense international and intertribal competition, and their methods of trade were conditioned by their circumstances. In the early seventeenth century, trading posts were built along them by Dutchmen, Swedes, and Englishmen of various provinces. Competition prevailed at the bays even after English jurisdiction became established over the whole region, but relatively orderly operation of the trade there was maintained after 1677 by the Iroquois Covenant Chain.

48. Cadwallader Colden, "Observations on the Situation, Soil, Climate, Water Communications, Boundaries &c. of the Province of New York," Feb. 14, 1738, in *Documentary History of the State of New-York*, ed. E. B. O'Callaghan, 4 vols. (Albany: Weed, Parsons and Co., 1849–1851) 4:173–74. I have supplemented Colden's description from other sources to produce the map in *Northeast*, p. 362. Reproduced herein.

Between the St. Lawrence and Susquehanna transport systems lay a third, the Hudson system, distinct in itself but linked to both the others. The key location in this Hudson system was its center at Fort Orange–Rensselaerswyck, which became Albany after English conquest. Albany was a hub. From the north it drew traffic from the St. Lawrence Valley by way of the Richelieu River, Lake Champlain, and Lake George. Fort Orange–Albany was thus in a position to receive trade diverted from the St. Lawrence trading system either by way of the Richelieu River–Lake Champlain route or by way of the Mohawk Valley route.[49]

It was also accessible from the Susquehanna system by way of the Susquehanna River's North Branch, and from New England via footpaths through the mountains. Access to New England meant access to the Connecticut Valley, a lesser avenue of north-south trade parallel to the Hudson that functioned in its own distinct fashion.

The advantage of Albany's position was enhanced by the proximity of the Iroquois Five Nations allied to the merchants of Albany. The "castles" of the Iroquois (i.e., their stockaded villages) stretched westward along the Mohawk Valley and Finger Lakes region. From this center the Iroquois were able to travel with relative ease and swiftness in almost any direction. Like medieval banditti on heights overlooking caravan routes, the Iroquois could raid the traffic on the St. Lawrence, Susquehanna, and Connecticut systems, diverting peltry to Albany, although that town stood apart from the other main systems. The Iroquois were not only able to raid Indians traveling to other markets, but they could also intercept the "far Indians" coming from the west to trade at Albany. For several decades in the seventeenth century, the Iroquois Mohawks, who were closest to Albany, exploited their location even at the expense of other Iroquois nations.[50]

During the early years of Dutch occupation, the Hudson system's benefits upriver were matched by a great asset downstream. Until the mid-1630s the Dutch had a virtual monopoly on the wampum produced by the Montauk Indians of Long Island.[51] Although other coastal Indians of lower New England also made wampum, the great quantity and superior quality of the Montauks' product established the Long Islanders in the forefront of wampum mintmasters. Inland Indians lacked the raw materials to make their own wampum—the periwinkle shellfish—so were obliged to obtain their supplies by trade and plunder.[52]

49. Cadwallader Colden, "Memoir on the Fur Trade," Nov. 10, 1724, N.Y.Col.Docs. 5:729–30.

50. Tooker, "League of the Iroquois," Northeast, 430–32.

51. Isaack de Rasières to Samuel Blommaert (ca. 1627), New-York Historical Society Collections, 2d ser., 2 (1849), p. 350; Benjamin F. Thompson, The History of Long Island, 2d ed., 2 vols. (New York, 1843), pp. 85–89; Bradford, Of Plymouth Plantation, p. 155.

52. Bradford, loc. cit.; Heidenreich, Huronia, p. 228; T. J. Brasser, "Mahican," in Northeast, p. 203.

The French lacked access to wampum producers, but they had their own powerful advantage of position. Having started their colonizing along the St. Lawrence River, the French had moved into the spout of the funnel that drained the whole Great Lakes Basin. It did not take them long to discover the wealth that poured through that funnel, and when they pursued it to its sources they found ways also into the Mississippi basin. With a very small resource of ethnically French population, the French colonies amplified their manpower by tolerating and assimilating the children of intersocietal liaisons.[53] These offspring of mixed unions became especially valuable in the basic French strategy of controlling large native populations by planting a network of forts and trading posts among them. By the end of the seventeenth century the French had created and mastered a politico-economic empire extending over the vast regions of the Mississippi Valley and the Great Lakes environs, precisely the territories where the bulk of commercial peltry originated.[54]

"Mastered," however, is too strong a word. The French did manage, most of the time, to dominate, but they could not often dictate to their tribal allies. Violent rebellions broke out, notably among the Fox bands, and the Iroquois made a bloody farce out of French claims to formal sovereignty over them. Nevertheless, the French learned how to cope with Indian warfare and forced even the Iroquois to their knees by 1700. A different kind of insubordination proved more threatening to French control in the long run. This was the unsuppressible desire of all Indians to get the best bargains possible in their trading. The stark reality was that the French could not compete successfully in price with the Dutch and English. In the equation of European goods with furs, trade goods were usually dearer, and furs cheaper, at Montreal and Quebec than at Albany and on the Chesapeake and Delaware bays.[55] Tribes within the French political system were attracted to the English economic system, and tensions were thus created that produced perpetual diplomatic negotiation, violence, and smuggling.

The Iroquois tribes exploited these tensions. They alternated their incessant struggles with New France between armed conflict and efforts to seduce French tribal allies. The Indians of the two networks had deal-

53. Jaenen, *Friend and Foe*, ch. 5. But toleration of synethnics did not become acceptance on terms of equality except in Indian territory.

54. *A Historical Atlas of Canada*, ed. D. G. G. Kerr, p. 22.

55. W. J. Eccles disputes this finding in "A Belated Review of Harold Adams Innis, *The Fur Trade in Canada*," *Canadian Historical Review*, 60:4 (1979), pp. 425–30. With due respect to a master historian, I have encountered in the sources the statement about English prices being lower so often as to regard the fact as commonplace, though there were exceptions. Western tribes repeatedly defied their alliance with Canada in efforts to trade with Albany because better bargains awaited them there. Why else would they want to? See Cadwallader Colden, "Memorial concerning the Fur Trade," *N.Y.Col.Docs.* 5:730; Callière's price list, 1689, ibid., 9:408–9; Louis XIV to Denonville and Champigny, March 30, 1687, ibid., 9:323.

ings with each other that both French and Dutch authorities were powerless to prevent. Fort Orange merchants were ambivalent about the Iroquois aggressiveness. They approved of Iroquois efforts to bring "French" Indians into their own trading orbit, and of Iroquois raids on cargoes traveling along the St. Lawrence and Susquehanna routes, but Dutchmen disliked Iroquois interposition against "far Indians" coming from the west to trade. Fort Orange's dilemma was the Iroquois' advantage. To reap the benefits of plundering expeditions, the merchants had to arm their fractious allies, and there was no way of preventing the same arms from being used also to demand tolls from customers.[56]

The importance of firearms

Why did the trade begin? We have noticed the familiar motive among Europeans of profit as a means to accumulate wealth. In European cultures, wealth could be transformed into capital and so breed more wealth. But Indian cultures resisted formation of capital because of their strong sharing ethic. Among Indians, wealth was accumulated only briefly by individuals, and quickly passed on. Indians of the early trading era did not become rich.[57]

The primary reason for Indians engaging in exchange with Europeans was the technological superiority of European implements. A steel hatchet did not shatter as stone often did; a copper kettle could be transported easily so that it need not be remade at each new campsite; woven cloth was superior to animal skins as garments worn next to the skin; and, of course, firearms were crucial.

Some students have argued that the gun was not intrinsically superior to the bow—was indeed inferior functionally to the poor guns of the early seventeenth century. According to this line of argument, an arquebus or musket aimed badly and took a long time to reload; its only possible advantage therefore had to be the psychological effect on Indians of its noise and smoke.[58]

This argument, if it was known to the Indians, failed to convince them. However much the noise and smoke might scare enemy Indians into running away, it had precisely the same effect on game when that effect was the opposite of desirable. But Indians took guns to the hunt instead of bows and arrows. There had to be a reason. The records clearly show Indians everywhere demanding guns in trade, not only for war but for the

56. Details in ch. 6, below.
57. See Jennings, *Invasion*, ch. 6.
58. The argument was advanced by Dr. Karl Schlesier in a paper delivered at the 1976 meeting of the American Society for Ethnohistory in Albuquerque, New Mexico.

hunt as well. It is not necessary to rely on argument. They were vocal and explicit about this demand.

A Dutch board reported in 1644 that "not only the Colonists, but also the free traders proceeding from this country [Holland], sold for furs in consequence of the great profit, fire-arms to the Mohawks for full 400 men, with powder and lead; which, *being refused to the other tribes when demanded, increased the hatred and enmity of the latter.*"[59] In 1711 Five Nations chiefs were recorded as saying, "If Powder and Lead keeps so dear with you how shall we defend ourselves if attacked? With Bows and Arrows we cannot. Let us not want Powder and Lead."[60]

In intertribal strife, Indians wanted guns at first in order to achieve superiority over their enemies. The latter then had to acquire them for defense. Iroquois triumphs in the mid-seventeenth century were all marked by the use of firearms against enemies lacking them. When both sides acquired parity in arms, victory seesawed back and forth.[61]

The net effect of Indian appetites for European implements, weapons, cloth, and that luxury firewater was to make Indians dependent on trade and therefore on European trading partners. Of late there have been efforts to psychoanalyze those Indians to discover some sort of weird kink in Indian mentality that I can only interpret as a revival of savagery mythology;[62] but Indian dependency was the outcome of rational decisions by rational persons caught up in an objective situation that limited choice. The Indians simply could not foresee the implications of their initiative for the trade in guns. By the time its effects in dependency became clear, the Indians had lost their power of choice.

Accommodation with violence

Position gave the Iroquois the opportunity to demand alliance and guns, which they used to great advantage against tribes without firearms. Indeed their dramatic victories during the brief decade or so of this advantage have served as the substantial foundation for their rhetorical empire. However there was something more. When other tribes acquired equivalent armament, they trounced the Iroquois as often as not. If arms had been the only factor in Iroquois ascension, they would soon have declined

59. *N.Y.Col.Docs* Dec. 15, 1644, 1:150.
60. Wraxall, *Abridgment*, p. 86.
61. Cf. ch. 6 and 9, below.
62. Cf. the labored construction of an Indian "war against the game" with its refutation by a symposium of anthropologists. Calvin Martin, *Keepers of the Game: Indian-Animal Relationships and the Fur Trade* (Berkeley: University of California Press, 1978); *Indians, Animals and the Fur Trade: A Critique of Keepers of the Game*, ed. Shepard Krech III (Athens: University of Georgia Press, 1981).

into insignificance. But they possessed uncommon political talent as well. Alternately resorting to war, alliance, and neutrality amidst the Europeans, and constantly maintaining all possible pressure on unaffiliated Indians, the Iroquois extended their Covenant Chain confederacy in every direction after its organization in 1677 and maintained their own status between Canada and New York with as much political independence as was inherently possible considering their state of technological and economic dependence.

Wars and hijacking gave momentary advantage to merchants of one side or the other, but businessmen prefer orderly, dependable operations. As early as the 1680s, English and French colonials began to trade clandestinely with each other in defiance of imperial policies and conflicts. Montreal's merchants swapped to Albany's the furs that came cheaply to Montreal for the trade goods that came cheaply to Albany, and Indian porters carried the cargoes both ways. After the peace of 1701, this trade grew to large proportions.[63]

Besides the well documented north-south traffic between Montreal and Albany, there are strong indications of a similar clandestine trade in the latter seventeenth and early eighteenth centuries between Frenchmen in the west and Albany and Philadelphia in the east.[64] Renegade French coureurs de bois established bases among the English from which they continued to do business as before with their kinsmen and partners in the backwoods.

A student must constantly remember the distinction between commercial expansion and political imperialism. Even today, they originate in different sectors of the polity, and their objectives are not identical. This is to be seen readily enough when the imperialist proposes to tax the merchant's profits. Although trade marches with the flag for part of the journey, the merchant's interest diverges from the politician's when either assumes to dictate the other's policies. The merchant demands and will pay for protection, but he resists subjection, and the measure of his resistance is the history of smuggling. In the seventeenth century the mystique of national loyalty was much less strong than it is today, and certainly weaker than the lure of personal interest; and governments had no means in the backwoods to control the officers and agents who were supposed to be implementing the governments' policies. Who could take care of the caretakers?

Considering all the tensions and conflicts, it might seem almost outrageous to call their aggregate the process of accommodation between soci-

63. Norton, *Fur Trade*, ch. 8.
64. Yves Zoltvany, "New France and the West, 1701–1713," *Canadian Historical Review* 46:4 (Dec., 1965), pp. 301–22; Jennings, "Bisaillon, Peter," *Dict. Can. Biog.* 3:65–66.

eties. Certainly the process was rough and painful. Nevertheless, it was different in substance from the ways that Cortés and De Soto hacked their progress through Indian nations; the Indians who were sought in trade retained personal and tribal freedom, however much it cost. The vast web of intersocietal exchange persists in some regions even to the present day. During its entire life it has functioned wherever European and Indian met to draw them together in some sort of collaboration. It is the everlasting refutation of the myth that "savagery" and "civilization" could not be reconciled.

Chapter 6 ❧ THE IROQUOIAN "BEAVER WARS"

I have not given up the hope, if the Lord will grant me a few years more, of diverting to the colony a large part of the furs of the savages who now trade with the French in Canada, and nothing grieves me more than that we now dispute with one another about formalities and do not even touch what is to yield profits.

Kiliaen van Rensselaer, June 6, 1641

[Father Le Jeune] has obtained ten thousand écus, with which to send men over there to fortify against the Iroquois, and prevent their incursions. Indeed, he would also have desired more effectual assistance, in order to drive away those who are sustaining the said iroquois in this war, and furnishing them with firearms. But this enterprise has been deemed very hazardous. . . .

Father Charles Lalemant, February 28, 1642

It is especially said of the native inhabitants of these territories that they must be governed with kindness, and the former wars [with the Dutch] incline us to believe it; we would have preferred to avoid these wars, for we notice that the savages have thereby come to a knowledge of their strength and they are consequently very anxious to provide themselves with guns, powder and lead; they ask for them to be used for hunting purposes, but we presume that is only a pretext. We remark, however, that they are so bent upon it that we must apprehend, they would rather begin a new war against us than to be entirely deprived of it, and considering that under our present circumstances a war would be utterly unadvisable, we would think it best to provide these people, but sparingly, we mean by the Company's officers, without giving such a permission to any private parties.

Directors of the Dutch West India Company, April 7, 1648

The intersocietal trade was a web of relationships, within tribes and colonies as well as between them. No more than what we call capitalism or socialism can it be reduced to simplistic economic explanation. This trade between Indians and colonials was the means for one tribe to gain power over another, and this motive far outweighed a hope of gaining wealth. Through the trade one colony could acquire many Indian clients and thus also gain power, not only as against other tribes but more desirably as against other colonies. For some colonials, of course, wealth was a primary lure, and there were times when purely mercenary colonials clashed with imperialist officials.

To get power, men use not only the seduction of riches and the menace of force, but also the mesmerism of religion. This, too, became a powerful force among the Five Nations as well as among the Hurons. Thus, to speak of the trade is to speak of the whole public existence of the trading tribes and some of the most dominant concerns of the trading colonies.

Control of the trade implied control of the peoples. Ultimate control remained always with the Europeans who supplied the goods and weapons demanded by Indians, but subsidiary controls over access to the Europeans and their goods became the central issue of a mélange of conflicts in the mid-seventeenth century. As wars over trade were frequent and widespread, this particular set should properly be distinguished as the *Iroquoian* Beaver Wars because of the prominence of Iroquoian speakers among its participants.

Tribal competition

As the trade bound tribe and colony together, it divided tribe from tribe and colony from colony. In that fact lies a tragedy of epic proportions. In their competition to gain advantage in the trade, tribes rejected the impulse to unite against invading colonials, and their strivings were incited further by competing colonials. No feasible way existed in the conditions of that era to prevent the competition from heightening to bloodshed. Even in Europe the larger scale nation-states solved their problems by repeated wars, as they do today.

In the early seventeenth century, while the colonies were still tiny outposts of empire scrabbling precariously for existence in an alien world, wars over the intersocietal trade were fought by decision of the tribes whose members overwhelmingly outnumbered the wholly surrounded Europeans. The population of New France grew so slowly that as late as 1650 it totaled only some 2,000 persons in scattered tiny villages and isolated habitations along the thousand-mile length of the St. Lawrence River.[1] They existed and grew, despite heavy casualties, because of the sufferance of nearby Indians who desired their trade.

More distant Indians also desired that trade. French officials preferred to have all the tribes competing for it, but the tribes individually tried to exert controls, each for its own advantage. As early as 1535, Jacques Cartier's hosts at Stadacona [Quebec] tried to prevent his traveling on to Hochelaga [Montreal], and the St. Lawrence tribes tried to dissuade Champlain from venturing onward to Huronia. They had good reason. When Hurons and Frenchmen discovered each other, a special relationship came into existence, based on the size, power, and trading proclivities

1. Eccles, *France in America*, p. 51.

of the Huron Confederation. We begin to learn about them from Samuel de Champlain, who spent the winter of 1615–1616 among them and estimated their population at about 32,000, a number later confirmed by the Recollect missionary Gabriel Sagard.[2]

As we have seen, the Hurons were traders in aboriginal times, and they quickly adapted their great trading circuit to the intersocietal trade. Despite opposition by intervening tribes, the Hurons allied to Quebec and annually brought there a great fleet of heavily laden canoes. They aimed to control and monopolize the trade among the western tribes, reserving the role of intersocietal broker to themselves.

Perhaps they might have succeeded if nature had been kinder. They cultivated political friendships in their trading circuit in order to facilitate the trade, and they maintained final control only over the last leg of their roundabout journey to Quebec. Such a web of political and economic relationships might have developed naturally into a tribal empire of truly imperial proportions. As Marcel Trudel remarks, "In the interior of the continent, the Hurons played the role that the little city of Venice played in the Mediterranean, or the Dutch in international commerce.[3]

French policies

Though the French rejoiced over Huron efficiency in delivering furs, they chafed at their dependency. "It was political control that they would have to aim for," Trudel has written, "and because of the nature of the Indian trade network, control not only of one nation but of a whole complex of nations. This, far more than colonization or evangelization, appears to have been the overriding immediate goal of the French in the period 1604–1627."[4]

But colonization and evangelization were the means to that end, and control of the western tribes had to begin with control of the Hurons. Contact began simply in 1609 and 1610, after which the French took care to maintain agents regularly in Huronia.[5] Despite mutual advantage in

2. *Works of Samuel de Champlain* 3:122; Gabriel Sagard, *The Long Journey into the Country of the Hurons* (1632), ed. George M. Wrong, trans. H. H. Langton, Publications of the Champlain Society 25 (Toronto, 1939), pp. 91–92; Jerome Lalemant to Richelieu, March 28, 1649, in *Jesuit Relations* 17:223.

A bibliographic note: Editor of *Jesuit Relations* Thwaites cautions in prefaces that his voluminous compilation is a *selection* of the Jesuits' writings (1:viii–ix), and that "the several reports which together form the *Relation* each year were first edited by the superior at Quebec, before transmission to France; and, before publication, were again freely edited by the provincial in Paris" (21:10). The purposes of such repeated editing require no comment.

3. Marcel Trudel, *The Beginnings of New France, 1524–1663*, Canadian Century Series (Toronto: McClelland and Stewart, 1973), p. 144.

4. Ibid., p. 140; Champlain, *Works* 5 (1632):61–65, 69f., 81f.

5. Trudel, *Beginnings of New France*, ch. 11; Champlain, *Works* 2 (1613):138–42.

the Huron–New France liaison, tension strained it as each party tried to dominate the other. The possibility that either might abandon the other to trade instead with the Five Nations kept suspicion alive. At first it was French suspicion of Huron intentions. While Mahicans still controlled the Mahican Channel there was little contact between the Five Nations and the French, but the possibility was credible that the Iroquois might be drawn into the Huron trading circuit. This would have been fatal to Quebec's business, for in that case the trade of Huronia could have flowed naturally through Iroquoia to the higher prices and better goods of the Dutch at Fort Orange. To block such rapprochement the French dispatched in 1623 a special mission of eleven laymen and three Recollect priests. Thus began the Catholic missions in Huronia.[6]

This action was in full accord with long-term French policy, adhered to closely from Champlain's first encounter with the Iroquois until the political extinguishment of New France. The iron rule was that the Iroquois must be kept from close association with the Indians of Canada, for, if such friendship should ever develop, the Iroquois would drain away the peltry and tribal alliances that kept New France alive. The long antagonism between the French and the Five Nations was created by the French, not by the Iroquois, as a deliberate implementation of divide-and-conquer strategy. Every effort by the Iroquois at reconciliation was rebuffed or evaded until finally they exploded. From another point of view, one might say that on the whole, and with certain unsavory exceptions of realpolitik, the French faithfully supported their Indian allies against the Iroquois— after the Iroquoian Beaver Wars taught French colonials how closely their own fate was bound up with that of their allied Indians'.

On the other hand, in 1626, the French attempted to evade Huron controls in order to develop a direct trade with the Neutral tribe already being served as part of the Huron circuit. To check this gambit the Hurons exploited the religious status and garb of the French emissary, Father La Roche Daillon. By spreading a rumor that he was an evil sorcerer, they so incensed the Neutrals that he was forced to leave hurriedly to avoid assassination.[7]

Disastrous effects of French missions

Daillon had coincidentally opened a new era by escorting two Jesuits to Huronia.[8] With the growth of the Jesuit mission, the formerly prosperous

---

6. Trudel, *Beginnings of New France*, p. 145; Trigger, *Children of Aataentsic* 1:401; Frederic Gingras, "La Roche Daillon, Joseph de," in *Dict.Can.Biog.* 1:420–21.
7. Trudel, *Beginnings of New France*, p. 146.
8. René Latourelle, "Brebeuf, Jean de," and J. Monet, "Noue, Anne de," in *Dict.Can.Biog.* 1:121–22, 521; Charles to Jerome Lalemant, Aug. 1, 1626, *Jesuit Relations* 4:221–23.

Huron Confederation was wracked by intensified factionalism. The missionaries sowed discord by demanding that their converts reject and denounce the traditional religious rituals binding the people in unity. As the French presence grew in Huronia—traders, missionaries, and the laymen servicing the missions—the newcomers unwittingly sowed epidemic diseases that reduced the population traumatically to about 10,000 persons in the period 1630–1640, and this calamity was blamed by traditionalist Hurons on the missionaries and the mission religion. As Father Paul Le Jeune explained to his superiors, the missionaries had much trouble "to disabuse the people of the rumors spread by some Huron Apostates, who attribute to the Faith all the wars, diseases, and calamities of the country. They allege their own experience in the confirmation of their imposture; they assert that their change of Religion has caused their change of fortune; and that their Baptism was at once followed by every possible misfortune. The Dutch, they say, have preserved the Iroquois by allowing them to live in their own fashion, just as the black Gowns have ruined the Hurons by preaching the faith to them."⁹ At least one Jesuit inclined also to this view, interpreting it with a theological twist: "With the Faith, the

9. *Jesuit Relations*, 1656–57, 43:291. The total loss of Huron population depends upon which estimate one uses as the pre-contact base. If the Champlain-Sagard figures are adopted, the Hurons lost about 20,000 people in a decade, not to speak of what they incurred after the Iroquois destroyed their homeland. In his earlier writings, Bruce G. Trigger used the Champlain figure but has since scaled downward to approximately 18,000 pre-contact Hurons, largely because of findings by geographer Conrad Heidenreich and from archaeological digs. It seems to me that archaeology can only establish minimums; after another dig, the minimum goes up. I think also that both Trigger and Heidenreich have too readily attributed missionary Sagard's confirmation of Champlain to mere copying of Champlain. Heidenreich acknowledges that only "much of what Sagard wrote" was copied and notices that Sagard had differentiated the component regions of Huronia as Champlain had not, which definitely means, I think, that Sagard was not merely copying Champlain. Heidenreich carefully itemized the discrepancies between Sagard and Champlain in "Huron," in *Northeast*, p. 370. I think also that there is some inconsistency in Trigger's reasoning and calculations.

Supposing, however, that the low figure is correct, the Hurons lost approximately half their population, or 9,000–10,000 people, in ten years, rather than the two-thirds indicated by Father Lalemant. The difference is a matter of degree; the substance of catastrophe is clear either way. Bruce Graham Trigger (high estimate): "The Destruction of Huronia: A Study in Economic and Cultural Change, 1609–1650," *Transactions of the Royal Canadian Institute* 33 (1960), pp. 16, 29; (low estimate): *The Huron: Farmers of the North* (New York: Holt, Rinehart and Winston, 1969), pp. 11–13; *Children of Aataentsic*, pp. 31–32, 578, 589; Conrad Heidenreich, *Huronia: A History and Geography of the Huron Indians, 1600–1650* (Toronto: McClelland and Stewart, 1971), ch. 4.

The issue of the relative values of different sorts of evidence remains substantial and is directly traceable, I think, to the assumptions laid down in different disciplines of scholarship. Trigger is an anthropologist; Heidenreich, a geographer. Both are historically aware, but neither seems to accept wholeheartedly the historian's axiom that the observations of historical phenomena made by contemporary observers must normally be given greater weight than those of persons more distant in time unless substantial contrary evidence can be shown. It seems apparent to me that the consistently reported figure of 30,000 pre-epidemic Hurons is drawn from repeated interrogation of the Hurons themselves—not from mere copying of Champlain. I credit them with the ability to count their own people.

scourge of God came into the country; and, in proportion as the one increased, the other smote them more severely."[10]

The decade of the 1630s witnessed a fearful scourge of epidemic desease among all the Iroquoian tribes that spread from the Hurons through the Five Nations to the Susquehannocks and reduced their populations catastrophically by half or more. As a by-product of this horror, the tribes became increasingly dependent on trade goods from Europe, and the corollary of this dependence was heightened competition in trade.

Iroquois initiatives and French repulses

For the Five Nations, who had access to Dutch merchants at Fort Orange and Rensselaerswyck, increased competition meant greater efforts to get furs. Three methods were possible: expansion of trade with other tribes, expansion of hunting territories, or plunder. In 1638 an Iroquoian tribe called the Wenroronons began to abandon its territory west of the Senecas under pressure from other tribes—just which ones is not clear. Their movement signaled the outbreak of the Iroquoian Beaver Wars. The Wenroronons sought refuge among the Neutrals and Hurons, undergoing great hardships in forced migrations, and were assimilated into the host tribes who were also Iroquoian speakers.[11]

At the opposite, eastern end of the Iroquois League, the Mohawks struggled for viable relationships with trading Europeans. Although they had access to Dutch markets, they did not yet have a treaty of alliance with the Dutch who at the time considered them obstructions to trade with more distant Indians. Kiliaen van Rensselaer, the great patroon of Rensselaerswyck, wanted to get around the Mohawks to make direct contact with the "far Indians.[12] The Mohawks, for their part, had no great love for people who treated them as roughly as did the Dutch: "Those people are cruel," they complained to a captive Frenchman.[13] This from the tribe reputed to be the bogey men of all the eastern Indians.

In 1741 the Mohawks journeyed to Trois Rivières in New France to propose peace with the French and all their allied tribes and to request that the French set up a trading post in Iroquoia. They addressed the French as "uncles," a term of deference, and offered to "give a kick to the Dutch, with whom they no longer wished to have any intercourse." The French and their Indian allies suspected treachery. An Algonquin chief

10. Francesco Gioseppe Bressani, *Jesuit Relations* (1653) 39:141.
11. Trigger, *Children of Aataentsic* 2:562–63, 623–24.
12. Kiliaen van Rensselaer's memorial, Nov. 25, 1633, in *Van Rensselaer Bowier Manuscripts*, p. 248.
13. Paul Le Jeune, Relation of 1640–41, *Jesuit Relations* 21:33.

denounced the Iroquois as liars. The Jesuit reporter gave thanks to God instead of the Iroquois for their sparing the lives of two French captives.[14] Governor General Montmagny considered his options and found an Iroquois peace less desirable than an Iroquois war. Peace seemed to imply abandonment of his Huron and Algonquian allies, and that could mean "a more dangerous war than that which we wished to avoid; for if these [allied] peoples, with whom we live day by day, and who surround us on all sides, attacked us, as they might do should we abandon them, they would give us much more trouble than the Hiroquois." Montmagny also considered the trade: "if the Hiroquois had free access to our ports, the trade of the Hurons, of the Algonquins, and of the other tribes who come to the warehouses of the Gentlemen of New France would be entirely stopped." Montmagny's reasoning was reported by Jesuit Father Paul le Jeune, who added a thought that seems to have been his own: "After all, neither Monsieur our Governor, nor any of the Frenchmen could decide on throwing into the jaws of the enemy the new Christians who publicly profess themselves Frenchmen"—and were recognized by the King of France as his subjects. Whatever reason loomed largest to Montmagny, his approach to negotiation was challenging rather than conciliatory. He refused to present the Mohawks with requested firearms (arquebuses), demanded the surrender of an Algonquin prisoner, and resolved "to put them completely in the wrong before coming to hostilities."[15] The result, naturally, was the anticipated hostilities.

Perhaps Montmagny was right. Certainly he has been praised enough in the histories, and the Mohawks were as capable as the French of tricky diplomacy. But when the internal history of New Netherland is taken into account, with its clearly documented episodes of cruelty and brutality toward Indians of all tribes, the possibility that the Mohawks were genuinely reaching for an accommodation with New France seems at least credible. Our only report of their approach to Montmagny is the plainly slanted account by Le Jeune. One yearns for a Mohawk report for balance. What the Mohawks intended toward the Canadian tribes is problematical and probably would have been tough. What they intended toward the French seems to have been genuinely to get a French trading partner as an alternative to the Dutch. Any such hope was blasted by Montmagny's response, and the skirmishing that it triggered "marked the beginning of the first open warfare of the Iroquois against the French."[16] It was to continue vigorously, with truce pauses, for sixty years, and to fester as a rankling grudge for sixty more.

14. *Jesuit Relations* 21:29–55.
15. Ibid., pp. 55–59.
16. Gustave Lanctot, *A History of Canada*, trans. Josephine Hambleton and Margaret M. Cameron, 3 vols. (Cambridge, Mass.: Harvard University Press, 1963–1965), 1:172.

The founding of Montreal

New France's Jesuit missionaries perceived the Iroquois at this time as an extreme threat. Paul le Jeune, who observed and reported the Mohawks' dealings with Montmagny, set off for Paris to get help. His aim was twofold: "to send men over there to fortify against the Iroquois and prevent their incursions" and "to drive away those [Dutch colonials] who are sustaining the said iroquois in this war and furnishing them with firearms." To fight the Iroquois he got 10,000 ecus, but to fight the Dutch he got only vague words of encouragement nullified by specific cautions for prudence.[17] The French would think twice before engaging openly against the naval power of the Dutch West India Company, especially while they were deeply embroiled in the Thirty Years' War.

Instead, therefore, of chastening the Iroquois by conquering New Netherland, New France was committed to backwoods Indian war of a kind not yet well understood by colonials, and the outcome was not always certain. By 1642 the whole of New France included only 300 persons of ethnically French stock, women and children included, who straggled along the St. Lawrence in four tiny settlements.[18] These would have been but a mouthful for the Iroquois if not for fortifications and Indian allies. Assistance for the French came also in the form of new settlers sent by a religious society in France to found the community of Ville Marie on Montreal Island. Religious in motivation, Ville Marie coincided with, and became a part of, further developments in trade and the Iroquois war. Its religious leader, Jesuit Father Charles Lalemant, worked simultaneously to establish the mission and to build new fortifications.[19]

As an outpost about 150 miles upriver from Quebec, the new settlement at Montreal represented more than just a sanctuary for Indians trying to escape Iroquois raids, and more than pious concern for their souls. They were trading Indians, and Montreal could be as good a place to trade as Quebec, and so it became. This potential had been perceived in Quebec, where strenuous efforts were made to dissuade the new settlers from going on to Montreal.[20] One must wonder whether Quebec Frenchmen were less concerned than Montreal Frenchmen about savage salvation.

Despite such obstructions the new colony was founded in 1642, and its strategic position instantly became a powerful factor in intercolonial and intertribal affairs. Montreal Island sits at the junction of the Ottawa and St. Lawrence rivers, and an armed force located there could do much to

17. *Jesuit Relations* 21:269–71.
18. Lanctot, *History of Canada* 1:172; Eccles *Canadian Frontier*, p. 2; Richard Colebrook Harris, *The Seigneurian System in Early Canada: A Geographical Study* (Madison: University of Wisconsin Press, 1968), ch. 2.
19. Eccles, *Canadian Frontier*, pp. 39–40; Trigger, *Children of Aataentsic* 2:629.
20. Lanctot, *History of Canada*, 1:176.

hinder the Iroquois from raiding up the Ottawa. Not far downstream from Montreal is the junction of the Richelieu River with the St. Lawrence—where the Mahican Channel connects to the mainline of French trade. The French thoughtfully accompanied Montreal's founding with the erection of a new fort—Fort Richelieu—near the junction. The Mohawks understood strategy, too, and they attacked the fort immediately while it was still under construction.[21]

But the fort was built, and Montreal grew. While the Mohawks found ways to circumvent these strong points, raiding Canada successfully and often, they continued to take initiatives for accommodation. The French, on the other hand, could not long remain cooped up in their forts without succumbing to economic suffocation. The warring parties came to terms in 1645 in a great treaty conference at Trois Rivières.[22]

Mohawk aims

That conference's agreements bound only the Mohawks and the French. A peace was concluded, but it did not extend to the other tribes of the Iroquois Five Nations, nor did it include non-Christian Indians allied to the French. Governor Montmagny continued to feel the force of obligation to protect Catholic Indian subjects, but he changed his mind about abandoning Indian allies who clung to their traditional faiths. He distinguished: "Without the former [converted Indians], it is certain, we do not make a peace; as for the latter [unconverted], they themselves are the masters of their own actions, nor are they united with us like the others." Montmagny's remark was spoken in secret conference with Mohawk chief Le Crochet in response to the latter's demand for the French to "abandon the Algonquins without shelter." To someone unaware of this circumstance, the casuistry could be persuasive, for the converts were recognized as French subjects and gave obedience to their priests, while the traditionalists managed their own affairs in total independence. Yet when this has been said, there is still the awkward matter of the alliances in which French protection had been pledged, and the failure of the French to inform the abandoned tribes that protection had been withdrawn. Montmagny's private deal with the Mohawks cannot really be made to smell sweet by any sort of rationalization, and it is not improved by the recorded casuistry of Jesuit missionaries Vimont and Le Jeune. It would seem that the demands of honor gave way to those of faith and expedience.[23]

21. *Jesuit Relations* (1642) 22:275–79.
22. Trigger, *Children of Aataentsic* 2:647–49.
23. *Jesuit Relations* 27:1–31 6:51 28:149 31, 133, 313. It is difficult to argue with a masterpiece, but my interpretation differs from Trigger's in *Children of Aataentsic* 2:647–49. Trigger

The Mohawks, however, made separate treaties with Canada's allied tribes, the purport of which one can only try to guess. George T. Hunt thought they were centered on trade relations. Bruce G. Trigger rejects this interpretation to explain them as arrangements for an intertribal truce during which prisoners could be exchanged. It seems to me that the tribes might have had both objectives in mind; they are far from being irreconcilable. Whatever the true intention, the peace or truce between the Mohawks and Canada's allied tribes lasted only a couple of years—long enough to free the prisoners and long enough for the Mohawks to discover that peaceful hunting was not as lucrative as looting and plundering.[24]

A third Mohawk purpose is hinted by a letter of Isaac Jogues, the Jesuit who fearlessly ventured into Iroquois villages remote from help and soon found martyrdom in one of them. "The design of the Iroquois," he wrote in 1643, "as far as I can see, is to take, if they can, all the Hurons; and, having put to death the most considerable ones and a good part of the others, to make them both but one people and only one land."[25]

One people in one land is a constant theme in Mohawk history. Tradition ascribes to a Mohawk the initiative for creating the League of the Five Nations, and the Great Law of that League still today asserts the principle that alien peoples must bow to Iroquois terms. "When the council of the League has for its object the establishment of the Great Peace among the people of an outside nation and that nation refuses to accept the Great Peace, then by such refusal they bring a declaration of war upon themselves from the Five Nations. Then shall the Five Nations seek to establish

says that Jerome Lalemant "later recorded in his journal that the story of this secret agreement as rumoured by the Mohawk, was false, 'at least for the most part.' " But that seems to me like a red herring drawn across the trail. Lalemant did not deny the statements made by Governor Montmagny in secret to the Mohawk chief. Montmagny himself reported them to Lalemant, who recorded them in Latin instead of the customary French, in order the better to keep the secret. What Lalemant wrote about falsity is as follows: "On the 23rd [of February 1646], Pierre Boucher arrived and Toupin his brother-in-law,—also an Annieronon [Mohawk] from 3 rivers, who came to see his companion and take him away. They brought letters and Confirmed the idea that *everything which the Huron Tandihetsi had said was false*,—at least, in the main." Montmagny himself is the authority for Montmagny's desertion of the Algonquins, and Lalemant did not accuse him of falsity.

A bibliographic note. Lanctot omits all reference to the secret episode, writing only that Montmagny "formally concluded peace with the Mohawks in the name of all Frenchmen, Hurons, and Algonquins." This is fairly typical of Lanctot's way of sweeping French scandals under the rug. His bias against "savages" is strong and undisguised. *History of Canada* 1:187.

24. Cf. Trigger, *Children of Aataentsic* 2:650–52, and Hunt, *Wars of the Iroquois*, pp. 78, 81–82. Hunt is often wrong, but Trigger seems to have been a little unfair to him here. I do not read Hunt as suggesting "that any interpretation but his own is meaningless," although many scholars might find it hard to refute such a charge; and I do not follow Trigger's interpretation of Iroquois intentions on p. 651, sentence beginning sixth line from bottom of page.

25. June 30, 1643, *Jesuit Relations* 24:297.

the Great Peace by a conquest of the rebellious nation."[26] This is the doctrine of a Chosen People.

Forms and methods changed, but the grand dream dominated Mohawk and Iroquois political thought through phases of voluntary association, military conquest, and combinations of the two in confederation with tributary allies. Even after total military defeat, the Iroquois Grand Council still meets—the oldest governmental institution still maintaining its original form in eastern North America—and it still keeps the dream although most Iroquois now prefer other governments. I think it likely that the Mohawks in 1645 were motivated by more than material interests. Theirs was a dream of empire.[27]

But! Not empire as conceived by Europeans. The Iroquois thought themselves the wisest of Indians, pointing to their League as evidence, and thus rationalized their role of hegemony over other tribes. It was for the latters' own good—not an unfamiliar argument among imperialists. But the Iroquois also generally took seriously their role as protectors of tributaries and only rarely debased their power to exploit the weaker tribes. No multitudes groaned under the hobnailed moccasin. The cultural trait, widespread in North American Indian cultures, that forbade capital accumulation and demanded of leaders that they impoverish themselves for the benefit of their people was integral to Iroquois society; and it made impossible an empire of wealth and exploitation, quite apart from the handicap of inadequate technology.[28] Whoever heard of emperors in rags? Mohawk chieftains were seen so, even at the height of their tribe's ascen-

26. *The Great Law of Peace of the Longhouse People* (Mohawk Nation at Akwesasne: White Roots of Peace, 1971), article 80. The identical article is to be found in Arthur C. Parker, "The Constitution of the Five Nations, or The Iroquois Book of the Great Law" (1916) in *Parker on the Iroquois*, ed. William N. Fenton (Syracuse, N.Y.: Syracuse University Press, 1968), p. 52 (paged separately from other contents of the volume).

A bibliographic note. Several versions of the Iroquois traditional Great Law were recorded in the 19th and 20th centuries; none exists in writing from an earlier time. The White Roots of Peace reprint of Arthur C. Parker's rendition of Seth Newhouse's version seems to me to put upon it a sufficient imprimatur by modern traditionalists to warrant citation for some purposes. Other versions support it substantially in the matters of concern in this study. Note that it is a *re*constitution, and that it is not accepted by all traditionalists. It bears signs of European influence, and it must not be taken as authentic for aboriginal society. Fenton discusses the sources of the variant texts of the Great Law in his introduction to *Parker on the Iroquois*, pp. 38–46, and in "The Lore of the Longhouse; Myth, Ritual and Red Power," *Anthropological Quarterly* 48:3 (July, 1975), pp. 131–47. See also the Hiawatha myth in *The Iroquois Book of Rites*, ed. Horatio Hale (1883), facsimile reprint (Toronto: University of Toronto Press, 1963), p. 22. Hereinafter a citation to *Great Law* is by articles rather than pages and can be found either in *Parker on the Iroquois* or in the White Roots of Peace pamphlet.

27. *Great Law*, articles 76–77. These articles make amply clear, and the historical record confirms, that the Five Nations were to be the only voting members determining the policies of the Great Peace. Even the Tuscaroras, who became the adopted Sixth Nation of the League, have never been permitted to vote.

28. See Governor Hunter's ethnocentric letter of March 14, 1713, *CSPA&WI, 1712–14*, p. 158.

dancy. Morgan deplored the Iroquois lack of "the desire to gain," which had "never roused the Indian mind." Without it, he thought, Indians could never achieve the civilization of "our race."[29]

The Iroquois "melting pot"

The original conception of the Mohawks was the melting pot—that favorite image of superpatriots everywhere. They would not *create* an empire but rather *become* one by incorporating conquered peoples in themselves and literally remolding them into Mohawks through adoption into families and thus "naturalizing" them as full "citizens" of the tribe. This practice never ceased. Cadwallader Colden described it thus: "It has been a constant Maxim with the Five Nations, to save the Children and Young Men of the People they Conquer, to adopt them into their own Nation, and to educate them as their own Children, without Distinction; These young People soon forget their own Country and Nation; and by this Policy the Five Nations make up the Losses which their Nation suffers by the People they loose in War."[30] By 1668 two-thirds of the Oneida village were assimilated Algonquins and Hurons "who have become Iroquois in temper and Inclination."[31] Bruce G. Trigger estimates that "500 to 1,000 Tahontaenrat [Hurons] joined the Seneca in 1651, and about 400 Huron later left Quebec to join the Mohawk and Onondaga. While no figures are available concerning the number of Huron who joined the Iroquois between 1648 and 1650, several thousand must eventually have been incorporated into Iroquois society in addition to the many hundreds who had been taken prisoner previously."[32] In 1657 Jesuit Father Paul LeJeune reported that "At Onondaga there are Indians of seven different nations permanently established; and, among the Senecas, of no less than eleven."[33]

With time, another idea was joined to the melting pot; that is, the concept of a chain of nations linked together by agreement or covenant. But this is running ahead of events, and we must return now to 1645.

It was not a time for simple solutions to simple problems. While the Mohawks made peace, the other Iroquois tribes continued to wage war. The Senecas especially continued to batter at Huron villages even after acquiring the territory of the Wenrononons, and after only two years of peace with New France the Mohawks again went on the warpath. There

29. Morgan, *League of the Iroquois*, p. 139.
30. Colden, *History*, p. 8; Morgan, *League of the Iroquois*, pp. 341–42. Cf. Le Jeune, Relation of 1656–57, *Jesuit Relations* 43:187.
31. Ltr. from Jacques Bruyas, Jan. 21, 1668, in *Jesuit Relations* 51:123.
32. Trigger, *Children of Aataentsic* 2:826.
33. *Jesuit Relations* 43:265.

are no documents explaining this, unless one accepts French denunciations of perfidy, savagery, bloodlust, and so on, all of which would be equally applicable to seventeenth-century Europeans. Hunt speculates that changing conditions of the trade motivated the Mohawks to renew war.[34] Trigger interprets the renewal as merely the end of a truce that the Mohawks had regarded from the beginning as a temporary device.[35] My thought is that the Mohawks discovered they could not achieve ascendancy over New France's Indian allies so long as New France insisted on direct management of the client tribes. Unlike the Dutch, the French would not tolerate intermediaries. Nor were the client tribes willing to accept Mohawk superiority. In 1645 the Mohawks played different roles at Fort Orange and Trois Rivières. For the Dutch they became pacifiers and policemen of rebellious tribes. With the French, however, the utmost of their achievement reached only to permission to make peace individually with Canada's allies. This, I think, was not enough to satisfy Mohawk aspirations.

Jogues's mission and assassination

Clearly they did not persuade the Algonquins to knuckle under, and they were much disturbed by the actions of Father Isaac Jogues when he came to them in June 1646 to confirm the peace and begin a mission. Jogues was no stranger to the Mohawks: he had earlier been captured and tortured by them, and had only been released by Dutch ransom in 1643. Forgetful, it seems, of Mohawk pride, Jogues now assumed attitudes approaching those of a viceregent. He approached some visiting Onondagans to prepare the way formally for a French embassy directly to their tribe and suggested alternative routes besides the road through Mohawk territory. This did not sit well with Jogues's Mohawk hosts. "It is necessary," they said, "to take the road which Onontio has opened"—the road through Mohawk territory, which would keep the proceedings under Mohawk control. (Onontio meant "Great Mountain," which meant Governor Montmagny.) Not content with his indiscretion with the Onondagans, Jogues lectured the Mohawks, "very pertinently" according to his Jesuit reporter, but very impertinently according to Mohawk etiquette, on their error in permitting other Iroquois tribes to march to war through their territory.[36] They passed it by with vague promises to do better, intending plainly to do nothing.

Jogues might have survived even these gaffes, but his religious zeal

34. Hunt, *Wars of the Iroquois*, p. 91.
35. Trigger, *Children of Aataentsic* 2:652.
36. J. Lalemant, Relation of 1645-46, *Jesuit Relations* 29:57-59.

intensified the factional spirit between the pro- and anti-French clans in the Mohawk villages, and he frightened the hostiles into thinking that he was working spells of witchcraft upon them. When he returned to Trois Rivières after a stay of eleven days among the Mohawks, he left a small chest of clothes behind in the Indian village, and the Bear clan concluded that it held the Devil "who had caused their Indian corn to be devoured." When Jogues came back to the Mohawks, they slew him and his attendant, and that was the end of peace with New France. The former pattern of raids and plunder resumed.[37]

Superstition seems to have played at least as great a part as policy and interest in Jogues's martyrdom, but it was not wholly irrational superstition and it was not monopolized by the Indians. Jesuit Jerome Lalemant summarized one major issue concisely: "The Algonquins and Hurons, and next the Hiroquois, at the solicitation of their captives have had, and some have still, a hatred and an extreme horror of our doctrine. They say that it causes them to die, and that it contains spells and charms which effect the destruction of their corn, and engender the contagions and general diseases wherewith the Hiroquois now begin to be afflicted. . . . Moreover, it is true that, speaking humanly, these Barbarians have apparent reasons for thus reproaching us, inasmuch as the scourges which humble the proud precede us or accompany us wherever we go."[38]

News of Jogues's death did not reach Quebec until June 5, 1647, and was delayed longer in arriving at Huronia.[39] Meanwhile the Hurons worked diplomatically to exploit the dissension that had manifested itself among the Iroquois tribes. The four other Iroquois tribes had received the Mohawk peace with New France with mixed emotions. In Onondaga especially, a fear prevailed that the Mohawks "who become insolent in their victories, and who make themselves unbearable even to their allies, may become too much so and, in time, may tyrannize over them if the Hurons, relieved from a portion of their wars, do not unite all their forces against them."[40] Hurons and Onondagans exchanged embassies amicably. Father Paul Ragueneau at mission Sainte Marie in Huronia dared to hope that the middle three Iroquois tribes—the Cayugas, Onondagas, and Oneidas—might come to peace with his Huron charges, leaving only the Senecas at war with them. From the south another important trading tribe, the Susquehannocks, promoted the peace cause actively.[41]

37. J. Lalemant, Relation of 1647, *Jesuit Relations* 31:115–19; Trigger, *Children of Aataentsic* 2:654–56.

38. *Jesuit Relations* 31:121–23.

39. *Jesuit Relations* 30:175.

40. Paul Ragueneau, Huron relation, 1647–48, *Jesuit Relations* 30:175.

41. Ibid., pp. 123–25, 133.

Susquehannock intervention

The maneuver had some prospect of success. At this point in history, the Iroquois tribes were far from united in their policies and interests. The central tribes fiercely resented Mohawk controls over their access to Fort Orange. Appealing to this mood the Susquehannocks aimed at setting up a sort of grand Indian cartel in the trade, whose participants would serve an ultimatum on the Mohawks: join or fight. Propositions made by the Susquehannocks for a peace that "would not hinder the trade of all those countries with one another" seem fair to a modern mind, but the effects of such a peace would have been to rob the Mohawks of their hard-won special advantage and to reduce them to parity with the other participants. Indeed, freedom of trade would convert the advantage of their location into a disadvantage. Their market at Fort Orange was more distant from the best hunting country, and more difficult to reach with heavy cargoes, than either the Hurons' market at Montreal or the Susquehannocks' market then on Delaware Bay. The flow of rivers dictated that the bulk of trade of the four "upper" Iroquois tribes would have been drawn from Dutch Fort Orange to either French Montreal or Swedish Fort Cristina on Delaware Bay.[42] Under such circumstances the Mohawks might have been able, if willing, to make a viable, though humiliating, adjustment to parity—though most likely it would have degenerated into subordination to the Hurons—but the Dutch merchants at Fort Orange would have been ruined.

Assault on Huronia

Up to this point the Dutch do not seem to have interfered by design in the politics of the trading Indians (except for their aborted pro-Mahican intervention in 1628). Their formal responses to Mohawk demands for guns were equally responses to internal conditions of New Netherland, and informal sales by individual traders were simply a matter of taking profit where it could be maximized. But a change in Dutch policy now became apparent. Although Governor Peter Stuyvesant distrusted the growing power of the Mohawks, he queried his Company directors in

---

42. The four western nations lived on or near streams that fed into Lake Ontario, by means of which canoe traffic could move easily to the St. Lawrence and down the river to Montreal. Living near the headwaters of the Susquehanna River they could travel by canoes to the Chesapeake and Delaware bays more rapidly than they could get to Albany. "Draught of the Susquehannes River and how soon the Indians westward can come there," Sept. 7, 1683, in *Livingston Indian Records*, pp. 69–70, and facsimile map following p. 70. See also the minutes of the Albany Commissaries, Sept. 7, 1683, and Commissaries to Dongan, Sept. 8, 1683, in *Doc. Hist.N.Y.* 1:393–95.

cryptic terms and received authorization directly from Holland to reverse the rules about trading guns to Indians. As of April 7, 1648, the directors told him to sell guns to the Mohawks officially rather than by authorization to individual traders, and with the suggestively phrased private understanding that the Indians' desire for the guns "for hunting purposes" was "only a pretext." With his eyes wide open to the real purposes for the guns, Stuyvesant promptly sold the Mohawks 400 of them.[43]

They did not disappoint him. Joined by Senecas to a total of about 1,000 warriors, they marched to Huronia and descended upon its outermost villages in March 1649. What happened thereafter destroyed the Hurons for an era as a viable political entity and ruined their trading circuit.[44]

The Huron confederation broke up. Villages and individual families went off in different directions: some to flee as far as possible, some to seek a defensible island position nearby, some to seek refuge among allied Neutral and Tionnontate nations, some to surrender voluntarily to the Iroquois in order to join captive kinsmen, and some to accompany their missionaries eventually to the protection of far off Quebec. The great Huron trading system was smashed. The Hurons themselves were scattered in many directions, and tragically many died.

The motive for Mohawks attacking Huronia could not have been acquisition of territory. Because of location, Huron lands would have to come

---

43. *N.Y.Col.Docs.* 13:23–24.
A bibliographic note. Hunt decried the "Jesuitical and Parkmanesque interpretation" that "cast the Iroquois and the Dutch together as complementary parts of a military machine that ruined New France," and he credited New Netherland with a "truly moderate and always humane attitude toward its French competitors." *Wars of the Iroquois*, pp. 165–66. Hunt's argument, beginning on these pages, about "The Dutch Trade in Firearms with the Iroquois" is seriously in error. He describes the official gun trade of the Dutch as beginning in 1649, after the ruin of the Hurons, but he skipped over the directors' letter of April 7, 1648, just cited, which definitely establishes official authority for the gun trade well before the Iroquois climactic raid on Huronia. Other Dutch documents show that four hundred guns were officially traded through governor Stuyvesant himself, at what private merchants regarded as outrageously low prices. Hunt knew of these transactions but apparently thought they happened after a *second* authorization to trade, which bore a 1649 date. He was encouraged in error by a lie of the directors in Holland, who when reproached by a dissident group of colonists for having ordered the sale of firearms, flatly denied having done so. The date on the dissidents' "Remonstrance" establishes that the guns had been sold in 1648, and the Remonstrance notes that "the Director [Stuyvesant] . . . exhibits the Company's order" to sell guns. Stuyvesant and the Iroquois were wary and distrustful of each other, but, speaking objectively, they were indeed complementary parts of a military machine in the same manner as New France and its Indian allies. The Iroquois fought with weapons and ammunition supplied by the Dutch. "Remonstrance of New Netherland," July 28, 1649, *N.Y.Col.Docs.* 1:311–12; "Short Digest," ibid., p. 337; "Answer of the West India Company," ibid., p. 337; "Observations," ibid., pp. 373–74; Stuyvesant to the directors, June 25, 1660, ibid., 13:176.
44. My description and interpretation of the Huron breakup are based on Trigger, *Children of Aataentsic*, ch. 11.

under Seneca domination, and Mohawk hunting there would be conditioned by Seneca controls as Seneca access to Fort Orange was controlled by the Mohawks. It seems to me that the Mohawk motive in this attack was primarily to destroy the Hurons' special partnership with New France and thus to make possible a Mohawk assumption of that relationship. Other motives, such as plunder and acquisition of prisoner-adoptees, seem secondary. In material terms the Senecas got the lion's share, although the Mohawks had acquired the guns that assured success. The myth is that ever after Champlain's joining with Mohawk enemies all the Iroquois preserved a permanent savage grudge against the French, and that this led them to attack New France's allies. More probably the Mohawks attacked French allies in order to try to make a place for themselves as the most privileged French ally. They were doing the same thing in New Netherland.

The great raid of 1649 was not militarily decisive in itself because Huron reistance compelled the attackers to retreat without achieving any overwhelming victory in battle. Moreover, it was by no means the first time that Iroquois raiders had struck in Huronia: the *Jesuit Relations* report previous Seneca raids that had become so numerous that Huron outpost villages had been abandoned in alarm and their residents resettled among the safer towns. But the 1649 raid was critical for its revelation to the Hurons that their territory had become indefensible. Their food reserves had dwindled because of drought, and the prospect of repeated Iroquois attacks meant that future cultivation would be risky at best and probably unproductive. Huron society had been deeply riven by a Jesuit mission so that leaders could no longer command a united following even for defense, and morale was almost nonexistent. The Jesuits, obsessed by their doctrines, rejoiced in misfortunes that drove the desperate Hurons to clutch at the reed of Christian salvation. And overshadowing all was the sure knowledge that the Iroquois would return.

Nineteenth-century historians followed the lead of Francis Parkman in conceiving this disintegration as extermination, attributing it all to the savage ferocity of the Iroquois stimulating an equally savage, irrational panic by the Hurons. Neither kind of emotion is apparent in the events, though cruelty and atrocity were rife. The Iroquois had a carefully planned strategy that exploited Huron weaknesses. The Hurons acted as logically in the end as anyone could be expected to do in their circumstances. In reality they had lost before the Iroquois began to attack. What defeated them was the very strategy of alliance with New France by means of which they aimed to grow strong, for it brought within their homeland the disintegrative force of the Jesuit mission. With the missionaries came disease, faction, and demoralization. In the end, many traditionalist Hurons blamed the Black Robes more than the Iroquois for their troubles, and some went so far as to join the Iroquois in order to take revenge upon all Frenchmen.

This is not to disparage the courage or dedication of the missionaries. One must carefully distinguish these admirable virtues from certain other missionary traits. Humility, for instance, was highly directional. No persons on earth were more humble toward their god and their church than these Jesuits, but such humility did not infuse their attitudes toward Indians.[45] There is a hint here, in another form, of the zealotry of the Inquisition in which the salvation of souls justified means leading to the destruction of bodies. The greatest service possible to the Indians, in missionary understanding, was to convert them at any cost, including that of death. In justice, it must be noticed that the missionaries were willing to sacrifice their own lives as well as those of the Indians. Their assumptions led to actions designed deliberately to weaken traditionalist government and leaders: they withheld firearms from traditionalists while arming Christian converts; they withdrew converts from participation in the rituals by which the tribe confirmed its unity; they instigated converts to attack the institutions and leaders of traditional society. It appears also that as the Jesuits acquired a following they assumed privilege, taking up residence in separate compounds with better defenses than were built for the Huron villagers and reserving special supplies of food for themselves while Hurons were in literal fact starving to death. Even the strong discipline of the Jesuit order could not wholly stamp out differences in its members' personalities. Some missionaries were heroic in their faith, some less so. All were undeniably dedicated, and the irony is that their dedication wrought devastation in ways unintended and unforeseen.

Downfall of Huron allies

The fall of the Hurons exposed their Indian partners and allies in the trading system they had so elaborately conducted. These had not been disrupted to the same degree by missionary activity, but they had no firearms. In December of the same year, 1649, Mohawks and Senecas struck again, this time at the Huron ally called the Petun nation (also called "Tobacco Nation" or Tionantati). The raiders destroyed an almost undefended Petun village in the absence of its warriors. Demoralized, but not panic-stricken, the Petuns emigrated westward in fairly orderly fashion, maintaining their tribal identity intact. After half a century of wandering, they settled along the Detroit River in 1701, where they mingled with

45. See Cornelius J. Jaenen, *Friend and Foe* ch. 2; J. H. Kennedy, *Jesuit and Savage in New France* (New Haven: Yale University Press, 1950), ch. 4.

Hurons to become known under the name of Wyandots.[46]

Five Nations warriors followed up these victories with a two-pronged offensive against more former allies of the Hurons. The Senecas attacked and dispersed the tribe of Neutrals, adopting large numbers (or perhaps the whole tribe) as members of the Seneca tribe. The Mohawks turned southward to the remaining major opponent, the Susquehannocks. The whole region around the shores of Lake Erie was emptied of human habitation by death, flight, and capture. As before, the Iroquois lost heavily in these constant wars but rebuilt their own numbers by adopting and assimilating persons from the defeated tribes.

Resistance of eastern tribes

The Five Nations' overwhelming western success in the Beaver Wars—which they could not repeat ever again—seems due to ample supplies of firearms that their western enemies lacked. This is the more notable because of their outstanding failures to conquer and scatter certain eastern tribes: the Mahicans who were the Mohawks' nearest neighbors, the Sokokis of the upper Connecticut Valley, and the Susquehannocks. These were all tribes that possessed guns and lacked missionaries. Mahicans and Sokokis had access to English trade at the Pynchon trading post at Springfield, Massachusetts, and Susquehannocks were bountifully supplied with guns and expertise by the Swedes on Delaware Bay. All three of these tribes maintained their independence and territory against Iroquois onslaughts until attacked by English colonials and Indian allies in 1675–1677, and all three inflicted severe defeats on the Iroquois at various times. Mahicans and Susquehannocks separately invaded Iroquois territories. Sokokis nearly wiped out a large Mohawk raiding party. On at least one occasion the Mohawks pleaded with the Dutch to compel their eastern enemies to make peace.[47]

The extra factor in the Iroquois western successes—the only one that can be isolated as unique in both west and east—was the special alliance between the Dutch and the Mohawks, and the supplementary Dutch treaties with the other Iroquois tribes. In the east, Dutch help to the Mohawks was offset by English and Swedish help to their enemies; in the west, French aid to the Hurons was as much liability as asset, and it did not extend to the other western tribes. The indispensable help of the Dutch was the more remarkable because the Dutch were anything but enthusiastic about it. Governor Stuyvesant's ambivalence was more than matched

46. Charles Garrad and Conrad E. Heidenreich, "Khionontateronon (Petun)"; Elisabeth Tooker, "Wyandot," in Northeast, pp. 394–406.
47. Mohawk proposals, July 23, 1672, in Livingston Indian Records, pp. 35–36.

by that of the inhabitants of Rensselaerswyck, the settlement neighboring Fort Orange. Rumors reached them in September 1650 that the Mohawks, inflated with their recent triumph over the Hurons, were organizing a conspiracy to "kill" the Dutch "when the ice was on the water." Rensselaerswyck borrowed cannon from the fort and voted political measures. The language of its court minutes is instructive.

"The insecurity of our lives and property oppresses us continually, living as we do under the unrestrained domination of inhuman people and cruel heathen. And while, indeed, we had some intimation of this last year, it shows itself particularly at present through evident indications and plausible predictions and earnest warnings which are communicated to us, not by the aforesaid parties, but by far distant Indians. Which being the case, although some think it advisable to have recourse to arms and resistance, and to exchange our weak position for that of their superior strength, their honors, the directors, commissioners and councilors, realizing the need, have resolved and determined, for the welfare of the colony of our lord patroon, the preservation of the commonwealth and the protection of our wives and children to commission and empower . . . a present to the Maquas [Mohawk] country, to renew the former alliance and bond of friendship."[48]

Without further evidence, the distant Indians' statements about Mohawk conspiracies against the Dutch must lie open to question. Starting such rumors was a much-used Indian device to sow discord and stimulate attacks upon their enemies. (Compare the example of Uncas, the Mohegan who triggered the First Puritan Conquest with tales about his enemies the Pequots.)[49] In the present instance, the "far distant Indians" included a Tappan, a member of one of the Hudson Valley tribes policed by the Mohawks for the Dutch. His tale is suspect, but not wholly incredible. Dutch response in this instance was the very opposite of the Puritan colonies' war against the Pequots, perhaps because of the tiny population of the Dutch settlements. The Puritans, in their thousands, could afford valor. The Dutch, in their hundreds, chose discretion. Probably similar discretion, under similar conditions, had been partially responsible for their earlier provision of arms for the Mohawks.

With their new presents, the Iroquois launched a two-pronged offensive against the former allies of the Hurons. As we have seen, the Senecas attacked and dispersed the tribe of Neutrals, incorporating large numbers among themselves, including many Hurons who had fled to the Neutrals

48. *Minutes of the Court of Rensselaerswyck, 1648–1652*, trans. and ed. A. J. F. van Laer (Albany: University of the State of New York, 1922), Sept. 21–23, 1650, pp. 127–29. Cf. Stuyvesant to the Directors, June 25, 1660, *N.Y.Col.Docs.* 13:176.
49. Jennings, *Invasion*, pp. 202–3.

for refuge.[50] The Mohawks meanwhile turned south to attack the Susquehannocks.

Unfortunately we have no source of information within the Susquehannock towns comparable to the Jesuits among the Hurons, but from what those distant Jesuits picked up we learn that the Mohawks tried in the winter of 1651–1652 to make a lightning conquest of the Susquehannocks. Here, however, they found their match. Though the Susquehannocks seem to have taken very heavy losses at first, they neither panicked nor surrendered. In the wake of their first defeat, they reorganized their diplomatic front to concentrate future energies against the Five Nations, and they fought on.[51]

Mohawk mixed fortunes were overshadowed by the great triumphs of the western Iroquois who seized the moment to reorganize their own diplomatic front. Faced with the still formidable Erie tribe and desiring to circumvent Mohawk control over access to Dutch trade goods, the Senecas, Cayugas, Onondagas, and Oneidas in 1653 initiated peace negotiations with Quebec via Montreal. Whereupon the Mohawks, encircled by active enemies, asked for peace also—but via Trois Rivières, separately from the other Iroquois.[52] In an unsubtle maneuver the Mohawks tried to have Trois Rivières designated as the future location of all Iroquois-French negotiations. This trading village lay midway between Montreal and Quebec at the junction of the St. Maurice River with the St. Lawrence. It was much closer to Mohawk territory than to Onondaga, and in time of war the western Iroquois might have been cut off from access except through Mohawk lands. The Mohawks evidently aimed at the same control over access to French treaty-making that they held already over access to Fort Orange. Their effort failed, but it did not contribute to harmony and sweet reason within the League.

The French were overjoyed by the peace initiatives. Iroquois attacks had destroyed their commerce and many of their habitations, and had killed ethnic Frenchmen as well as Indian allies and subjects. In no position to dictate terms, the French could only temporize as both Onondagans and Mohawks separately demanded delivery to themselves of Huron refugees under French protection. Meanwhile the Iroquois factions strengthened themselves, each in its own way.

In December 1653, a month after their peace treaty at Trois Rivières, a Mohawk delegation came to Fort Orange to request that the Dutch communicate certain important information to the Governor of Canada; namely, that the Dutch were "well pleased" with the French peace, fur-

---

50. Ragueneau relation of 1650–51, *Jesuit Relations* 36:177–79.
51. See ch. 7, below.
52. Trelease, *Indian Affairs*, p. 121; François Le Mercier, relation of 1652–53, *Jesuit Relations* 40:161–69, 183–91.

ther, according to the minutes, that if the Mohawks "again got involved in war with the French savages, that the French should keep out of it." A letter of greatest urbanity was dispatched, making no explicit threats but conveying by juxtaposition and indirection the idea that the Dutch thought it best for the Mohawks to be humored. The magistrates wrote to Canada's Governor Jean de Lauson, rejoicing at the peace. "This nation of the Maquas [Mohawks] has even this day promised us that as far as it is in their power they will observe and carry out the [terms of] peace . . . and they have requested us to ask your honor that the same might be done on side. Furthermore, if they, the Maquas, should become involved in any war or trouble with your honor's savages, they request that your honor and your honor's nation would not interfere. . . . On our part we shall not fail to make every effort in our power to keep the Maquas disposed to continue the recently concluded peace. . . ." The magistrates did not need to add that the Mohawks' disposition would depend on the French government's behavior.[53] In the following summer the Fort Orange Dutch made an extraordinary collection of funds from their "most favorably disposed" citizens in order to send a large present to the Mohawks. It included gunpowder.[54]

Mohawk-Onondaga friction

The western Iroquois invited the French to establish a trading and missionary settlement at Onondaga. To this the French gave glad assent, and on August 10, 1654, Father Simon Le Moyne gave to each of these four tribes a metaphorical hatchet " to be used in the new war in which they were engaged with the Cat Nation [the Eries]."[55] If standard practice was followed, the metaphorical weapon was accompanied by a present of real weapons. The ensuing campaign began the destruction of the Eries as an identifiable tribe and gained great numbers of captives.

But the Mohawks enjoyed no such triumph and were deeply angered by rising Onondaga power. Although Iroquois tradition stimulated Onondaga as the place of the central council fire where all joint decisions of the League must be made, it also stipulated that the Mohawks were "the head

53. *Court Minutes of Fort Orange*, Dec. 25, 1653, 1:90–92. In the perpetual game of diplomatic musical chairs, France and the Netherlands were momentarily at peace with each other while England was at war with the Dutch. French Canadians had information that the Mohawks were leaguing offensively and defensively with the Dutch against the English, "who have declared war on them." *Jesuit Relations* 38:191. The cited document shows, however, that the Iroquois were intent on their own objectives.

54. Twenty-five pounds of powder were presented to the Iroquois on August 11. *Court Minutes of Fort Orange*, July 15 and August 11, 1654, 1:170–71, 175.

55. Le Moyne's journal, *Jesuit Relations* 41:111.

and the Leaders" of the League.[56] An obvious compromise, the arrangement reduced formal competition only to stimulate informal struggle. Each
of the Five Nations was free to make war and peace separately, and the
Mohawks had exploited their position near Fort Orange to exert considerable de facto control over the other Iroquois regardless of formal rules.
Now the Onondagas's new friendship with the French threatened to erase
all the Mohawks's hard-won gains. Not only did the Onondagas arrange
for trade to bypass Mohawk territory, but they stipulated that their own
town of Onondaga "would be thenceforth the scene of the assemblies and
parleys relating to the peace" with New France.[57] With this neat twist
they destroyed opportunities for the Mohawks to deal separately with New
France. In short, they undermined the Mohawks politically as well as
commercially.

The Mohawks had apparently foreseen this development and had tried
beforehand to divert Father Le Moyne from his embassy to Onondaga. A
Mohawk chief in Quebec asked rhetorically, "Ought not one to enter a
house by the door, and not by the chimney or roof of the cabin, unless he
be a thief, and wish to take the inmates by surprise? . . . Well, then, will
you not enter the cabin by the door, which is at the ground floor of the
house?" His point was that the Mohawks were the closest geographically
to the French of the Iroquois tribes and held the title of Keepers of the
Eastern Door of the metaphorical Iroquois Long House. A hint of menace
crept into his speech as he continued. "It is with us Anniehronnons
[Mohawks] that you should begin; whereas you, by beginning with the
Onnontaehronnons [Onondagas] try to enter by the roof and through the
chimney. Have you no fear that the smoke may blind you, *our fire not
being extinguished*, and that you may fall from the top to the bottom, having
nothing solid on which to plant your feet?"[58]

The Jesuits debated anxiously for more than a year the advisability of
setting up a formal mission at Onondaga. Huron converts advised earnestly that the missionaries would be going to their death. The situation
was so hazardous because the Mohawks "manifested a jealousy almost
verging on fury, because we wished to dwell with those people [at Onon-
daga]; for it was greatly to the benefit of their trade, that the Onondagans
should always be compelled to pass through their country." On the other
hand, if the French rebuffed "those [Onondaga] Barbarians, by refusing
what they so urgently demanded, they intended to unite at once with the
Mohawks, to fall upon the French, to wage endless war against them, and,
if possible, to exterminate them entirely." The "authority and the opinion
of Monsieur our Governor" won the debate. He "saw very well that it was

56. Iroquois League *Great Law*, article 6.
57. Le Moyne's journal, August 10, 1654, *Jesuit Relations* 41:117.
58. Le Mercier, relation of 1654–56, *Jesuit Relations* 41:85–89.

necessary to perish in order not to perish; and to expose oneself to dangers of all kinds, in order to avoid all dangers." Notably, however, this Governor Lauzon did not volunteer to expose his own self. He soon took ship for France, preferring to expose himself to a sea voyage's danger in order to avoid others. As Lanctot dryly observes in another connection, Lauzon was "more prudent than energetic by nature."[59]

The French refused to change their course. On July 11, 1656, about fifty lay Frenchmen, accompanied by four Jesuits, arrived at Lake Onondaga, where they established their mission settlement at a prudent distance of "five short leagues" from the village of Onondaga.[60] They did not stay long.

Events in New France and New Netherland, in different ways, strengthened the Mohawks' inclinations to take the offensive once more. In New France a fierce internal dispute between religious orders, and the assumption of office by a new governor, resulted in temporary loss by the experienced Jesuits of management of the colony's Indian policies.[61] The aggressive new governor, d'Ailleboust, initiated new belligerence. He was outraged by the frontier incidents that marred the Iroquois peace—occcasional killings and thefts without apparent plan but clearly bespeaking Iroquois contempt. On October 21, 1657, d'Ailleboust called an assembly of the inhabitants at Quebec "at which it was Resolved, by common consent of all the habitants and of the Sieur Governor, that the French should defend themselves against the Indians of both the upper and lower Iroquois; And that no one should be allowed to commit a Theft or robbery or any other act of hostility, under pretext of peace."[62] Three days later he renewed protection for the nearby Hurons and Algonquins and freed them "to defend themselves or to attack first."[63] Early in November he received eleven Mohawks who had been seized "by subtlety" at Trois Rivières because of the murder of three Frenchmen there. Holding nine as hostages, he sent two back to their own country "to warn their people of their detention and of the cause of it.[64] (According to another source, some of these hostages were Onondagas.)[65]

The French sources naturally give a rather one-sided picture of the events. Relying wholly upon them, one would conclude perforce that the traps and ambushes of Mohawk "savagery" were qualitatively different from the traps and ambushes of French "subtlety." A different story

59. Jean de Quen, relation of 1656–57, *Jesuit Relations* 43:127–33; Lanctot, *History* 1:215–16.

60. Relation of 1656–57, *Jesuit Relations* 43:157–61.

61. Lanctot, *History* 1:226–29.

62. Journal, *Jesuit Relations* 43:61.

63. Ibid., p. 65.

64. Ibid., p. 69.

65. Relation of 1657–58, *Jesuit Relations* 44:155–57.

appears in Dutch sources. The Dutch heard Mohawks "complain bitterly about the French, because the French do not keep the peace with them, for whenever they are out hunting, they are attacked by the French savages, among whom are always concealed parties of Frenchmen, who meanwhile beat them."[66] It seems possible that blame for peace breaking ought to be shared by both sides.

While Canada thus became tougher with the Mohawks, New Netherland warmed up to them. Discord between Mohawks and other Iroquois had already become so great by June of 1657 that on the sixteenth the Mohawk sachems came to Fort Orange to request "as old friends" that the Dutch should help to repair their stockades and should give refuge to their wives and children "in case they should be involved in war with the Sinnekes"—that is, other Iroquois whom the Dutch did not yet distinguish by particular tribal names. The Dutch assented, with the "hope that it will not be necessary."[67] Nevertheless, as the Jesuits heard, "the two sides fought with each other until the ground was stained with blood and murder."[68]

Mohawks and Dutchmen became ever more useful to each other. In 1655 the Dutch conquered New Sweden on the Delaware and thus robbed the Mohawks' Susquehannock enemies of their chief means of military support. Later, the Susquehannocks confessed that they were forced "to submit to the Dutch or hide."[69] But while Governor Stuyvesant was conquering on the Delaware, the Algonquian tribes near his own headquarters at New Amsterdam rose in the revolt called the "Peach War," whereupon the Dutch upriver at Fort Orange "prudently renewed the ancient alliance between the Dutch and the Mohawks."[70]

Their rear secure, the Mohawks reopened their front against the French. Curiously they began by marching against Onondaga. In February 1658 they moved to destroy the new mission at Onondaga, and apparently the mission had so divided the Onondagans that some were ready to join the attack. Forewarned, the French decamped.[71]

This odd episode raises puzzling questions about motives all too frequently answered by gratuitous allegations of savage mentality. It is too easy to slur the Iroquois as does Lanctot, who thinks that "They had won the war against the Neutrals and the Cat people [Eries] and no longer needed the French habitation at Gannentaha as a refuge in the event of

---

66. *Court Minutes of Fort Orange*, Sept. 24, 1659, 2:218.
67. Ibid., June 16 and 21, 1657, 2:45, 47.
68. *Jesuit Relations* 44:149.
69. Treaty minutes, Oct. 15, 1658, *N.Y.Col.Docs.* 13:95.
70. John Romeyn Brodhead, *History of the State of New York*, 2 vols. (New York. Harper and Brothers, 1853–1871), 1:606–11.
71. *Jesuit Relations* 44:155–61.

defeat."[72] This is sheer nonsense; no shadow of a hint exists that Onondaga feared an onslaught from the Neutrals or Cats or that either of those nations contemplated one. They would have had to fight through the territories of Senecas and Cayugas to get at Onondaga, and they had no guns. The "enemies" against whose attack the Onondagas wanted a French refuge were the Mohawks, who simultaneously entreated the Dutch to provide refuge from Onondaga attack.

An anonymous Jesuit expressed honest bewilderment and incredulity about "the subterfuges and intrigues imputed to" the Onondagas. He believed that they had been sincere in their urgent requests for a mission and speculated that "they desired some of the French for the sake of obtaining firearms from them, and having them mend such as should be broken. Furthermore, as the Mohawks sometimes treated them rather roughly when they passed through their Village to go and trade with the Dutch, they wished to free themselves from this dependence by opening commerce with the French. And that is not all. As they were constantly at war, they asked our Frenchmen to build a large Fort in their country, to serve as a retreat for themselves, or at least for their wives and children, in case their enemies should press them too hard."[73]

There seems to have been cause for other motives to expel the French after sincerely inviting their presence. Father Ragueneau, who had been one of the Onondaga missionaries, rejoiced that even though forced to flee, "We bear in our hands more than five hundred children, and many adults." He meant their souls, for he added, "most of whom died after Baptism."[74] What this signifies is that epidemic came to Onondaga with the Black Robes as it had formerly accompanied them to Huronia. The sudden deaths of nearly 500 persons could not have endeared them to the community, regardless of politics. How many civilized communities would not have wanted to get rid of such deadly visitors?

Renewed war in New Netherland

In May of the same year, 1658, the Esopus Algonquians, whose territory lay midway along the Hudson between New Amsterdam and Fort Orange, became restless as Dutchmen intruded upon their lands. Incidents in that vicinity seem to have heightened the sensitivities of the Fort Orange people, farther upriver, on which the Mohawks played shrewdly. A delegation came to the fort in August to request help. They wanted an

72. Lanctot, *History* 1:229.
73. Relation of 1657–58, *Jesuit Relations* 44:149–51.
74. Ragueneau to Renault, Aug. 21, 1658, *Jesuit Relations* 44:155.

interpreter to accompany them to Canada to negotiate the freedom of the hostage held at Quebec. Significantly, the Mohawks were avoiding negotiation with the French at Onondaga, thus violating the Onondaga-French accord of 1653, which the Mohawks simply refused to recognize.

The Fort Orange court demurred. It was a long journey. "They did not know whether any one could be found among them who would be willing to undertake such a journey. Whereupon," the minutes continue, "the said Maquas explained that at the time of the war with the Indians [on the Hudson River] they had gone down to the Manhatans and done their best to bring about peace and that it was our duty to do the same in such circumstances for them, *promising in the future to do their best between us and other Indians.*" With a quick look over their shoulders toward Esopus, the court members dug up a hundred guilders and provided the requested interpreter.[75]

Faced with the likelihood of renewed Indian wars of their own, the Dutch reached out for all the help they could get. In October they summoned the Susquehannocks to counsel peace to the refractory Esopus tribe. In September 1659 they sent a mission to the Mohawk village of Caughnawaga, and a month later Fort Orange received a Mohawk delegation that spoke bluntly. "You say you have no war and that you do not wish to go to war against any savages." The speaker grew angry. "You and the Manhatans are one. Suppose the Esopus savages came now or in the spring to kill the country people, what would you do then? You have no sense." He sent a messenger from the Mohawks to the hostile Esopus "in order that the Esopus savages should do no harm to the Dutch here and at Katskil and release the Christian prisoners, or else to proclaim war against them."[76] What he meant by this ambiguously reported speech was that the Esopus must make peace with the Dutch or have war with the Mohawks.[77]

But the Esopus war continued, and a new conference was held on July 15, 1660. This time both the Susquehannocks and the Mohawks joined in reproving the Esopus.[78] That doughty and desperate tribe stayed on the warpath nevertheless, having found support among the Minisink Indians, whose adjacent territory offered ample hiding places. The Susquehannocks seem only to have offered advice to the Esopus. The Mohawks, however, took the field against them, if rather halfheartedly. The Mohawks' main attention was reserved for New France. In the end, which

75. Brodhead, *History of New York* 1:650; *Court Minutes of Fort Orange*, Aug. 13, 1658, 2:149–50. Brodhead omits the Mohawks' promise about the future.

76. *Court Minutes of Fort Orange*, Sept. 24, and Oct. 19, 1659, 2:215–18, 222–23.

77. Stuyvesant to van Rensselaer, Nov. 5, 1659, *Correspondence of Jeremias van Rensselaer, 1651–1674*, trans. and ed. A. J. F. Van Laer (Albany: University of the State of New York, 1932), p. 186.

78. Brodhead, *History* 1:678–79.

did not come till 1664, it was the Dutch themselves who conquered the Esopus with the proven colonial strategy of devastation of their country.[79]

A turning point

The Mohawks had both won and lost. They won the special relationship with the Dutch that enabled them thereafter to control at will the traffic of western Indians to Fort Orange. They lost what may have been the greater goal, the same sort of special relationship with the French to control traffic to Montreal. While, together with the Senecas, the Mohawks succeeded in destroying the Hurons' special relationship along with the Hurons' trading system, the French did not bend with the storm as the Dutch had done. They had plenty of other Indian allies who were eager to trade. From the west the great Ojibwa family of Algonquian nations— the most populous in North America—took up the challenge. These Ojibwas, Chippewas, Missisaugas, Ottawas, and Potawatomis, with French support, were more than a match for the Iroquois and their colonial supporters. In the course of time they would drive the Five Nations out of all the territories north of Lake Erie and west of present-day Cleveland, that had been conquered during the Iroquoian Beaver Wars.[80]

In all this weary welter of attack and maneuver and shifting alliances, a historical turning point had been reached. Though the Iroquoian Beaver Wars began and long continued for reasons of the Indians' own, Europe's colonies gained strength and people while the Indians suffered severely damaging casualties that were only temporarily ameliorated by the captives adopted by the victorious tribes. The power of decision was passing from Indians to colonists.

It did not happen overnight. The Iroquois remained a force to be reckoned with in intertribal and intercolonial affairs, and they never lost the formal power to run their own affairs for their own purposes. But the growth of colonial populations implied a proportionate growth of colonials' power. The limits and numbers of Iroquois political choices constantly declined until and beyond Governor Thomas Dongan's taunt in 1687: "you know that we can live without you, but you cannot live without us." It was not full dependence. Dongan might have said more accurately that the Iroquois could not live *as they wanted to* without his help. Nevertheless his comment contrasts sharply to a sturdy young Powhatan's

79. Trelease, *Indian Affairs*, pp. 164–68.
80. Robert E. Ritzenthaler, "Southwestern Chippewa," and E. S. Rogers, "Southeastern Ojibwa," in *Northeast*, pp. 743, 760–62; Donald B. Smith, "Who Are the Mississauga?" *Ontario History* 17:4 (Dec., 1975), p. 217; Leroy V. Eid, "The Ojibwa-Iroquois War: The War the Five Nations Did Not Win," *Ethnohistory* 26:4 (fall, 1979), pp. 297–324.

defiance of Captain John Smith about three-quarters of a century earlier: "we can plant any where, though with more labour, and we know you cannot live if you want our harvest, and that reliefe wee bring you."[81]

The great victories of the Iroquois took place only in the west, against opponents lacking effective European support, and were confined to the brief span of 1649 to 1655. After that the Iroquois had nothing but exhausting, debilitating, inconclusive conflict.

Yet it was not wholly profitless. They had learned that not all Indians could be absorbed and assimilated, but that many would accept strong leadership if allowed a measure of autonomy. The entire Tahontaenrat band of Hurons was accepted among the Senecas in the separate village of Gandougarae, where they were permitted to take in other refugees and maintain their own customs in amity.[82] Captives of all tribes intermarried and gradually became Iroquois in culture as well as name. Bruce G. Trigger's thoughtful comment is worth quotation. "As a result of the conflicts engendered by the fur trade, the Iroquois must have killed, either directly or indirectly, several thousand Huron, although not nearly so many as died of European diseases. Ironically, however, they also provided homes and an acceptable life for more Huron than were to survive anywhere else. Having been pitted against one another in the earliest phases of European activity in eastern North America, the aboriginal Iroquois and these assimilated Huron were henceforth to confront as one people the growing power of Europeans to direct their lives. Conquerors and conquered were to share a single destiny."[83]

81. Treaty minutes, Aug. 5, 1687, *N.Y.Col.Docs.* 3:439; John Smith, *A Map of Virginia* in *The Jamestown Voyages under the First Charter, 1606–1609,* Hakluyt Society Publications, 2d ser., 136–37, 2 vols. (Cambridge: Cambridge University Press, 1969), 2:443–44.
82. Trigger, *Children of Aataentsic* 2:828.
83. Ibid., 2:840.

Chapter 7 ❧ ODD MAN OUT

If we attempt to define at any period during the seventeenth and eighteenth centuries the conflicts between the savages and Europeans on this continent, we have to look for the explanation of any special change in the relations of the Indian tribes to the varying interests and collisions of the different foreign nationalities in rivalry here.

> George E. Ellis, D.D., LL.D. (Pres., Mass. Hist. Soc.)
> "The Red Indian of North America in Contact with the French and English,"
> in *Narrative and Critical History of America*.

The power of the Iroquois cannot be understood without an attempt to see the League from the Iroquois point of view. Other Indian confederacies had risen and taken in nations by conquest. The Iroquois had more in mind than that. They believed themselves destined to conquer because they had a mission to take in all nations. In their own eyes they were not simply part of a powerful political confederacy. They were nothing less than agents of universal peace.

> Dorothy V. Jones, *License for Empire*

Iroquois interests and strategies extended in all directions from the Five Nations homeland. When the Hurons and other western tribes had been dispersed, the Iroquois turned their attention to the Susquehannocks, the surviving Iroquoian tribe of the Hurons' former trading system. It is impossible, however, to narrate the conflict as a purely intertribal affair. Many European parties and issues became involved in it—so many that the Franco-Dutch competition in the north seems comparatively simple and straightforward. It is necessary to backtrack and introduce the participants in turn and to repeat some occurrences already discussed, but to do so from different viewpoints.

Southward from Iroquoia

As the drainage basin of the Great Lakes and the St. Lawrence River was previously the theater of action, so three eastern rivers now come into focus: the Hudson, the Delaware, and the Susquehanna. All descend in roughly parallel courses, north to south, from the mountain wall that separates coastal lowlands from the great basin of the Mississippi; and all empty their waters into the Atlantic Ocean. The interlacing tributary streams of the Hudson, Delaware, and Susquehanna formed one large transportation system for canoeists, and (with their bays) each river's mainstream was navigable by ocean-going ships for hundreds of miles. The opportunities thus offered for penetration of the land and contact with trading Indians attracted early colonization by three European nations in the seventeenth century, in addition to the aborted sixteenth-century effort by Spain.[1] These colonies were no less aggressively competitive than the Indians involved in the beaver wars, and each colony allied itself to the tribes that seemed to promise the most advantage. All of them became mixed up together in a confusion of conflicts and negotiations. The peoples living amidst that network of waters could not avoid each other. When European colonies appeared on the bays and at the heads of navigation, the whole system instantly became a commercial hinterland of their settlements. But economics and nature were at odds. Although the system was a natural unit, its human inhabitants were not. They struggled for preeminence and control, and gradually they sorted themselves out (as the peoples farther north were also doing) into effective partnerships of colony and tribe, each of which competed strenuously against other combinations of the same sort.

One underlying pattern may be discerned: each of these rivers' headwaters originated in or near Iroquoia. The parties involved were thus geographically related to each other along a gradient from the colonial villages on the broad waters, through an intermediate succession of Algonquians and Iroquoian Susquehannocks, upstream to the vicinity of the Five Nations. In varied ways and on different timetables the Europeans came into direct political contact with the interior Five Nations. Through these processes the Covenant Chain took shape. There was no set rule of procedure. Each link was added in circumstances peculiar to its own moment and place. Each individual history must be noted, however briefly. One factor, however, was common to them all: Five Nations strategies influenced the events and at critical moments often became decisive.

In this region the Five Nations acquired their most durable and reliable tributaries—tribes so important in the total structure of the Covenant Chain that the Iroquois called them their "props." (One must not try to apply formal European principles of rhetoric to Indian figures of speech; it bothered no one to hear the clashing of metaphors in a chain having some of its links as props.) The tributaries represented an important change in Iroquois policy. The Five Nations' objectives in their western beaver wars had been to capture some members of enemy tribes for adoption and assimilation and to drive the rest away. In the southern region adoption continued to be an Iroquois objective, but there the Iroquois developed a

---

1. For the Spanish debacle see Quinn, *North America from Earliest Discovery*, pp. 281–83.

new method of enhancing their power; they began to strive for a system of alliances in which they would hold general leadership and more or less of control. They thus multiplied their available military manpower and gradually became a formidable force capable of tipping the balance in struggles between European empires.

Not all at once. The process was gradual and drawn out over a long period of time as the Five Nations digested the lessons of each new effort. It is easy to see growth of sophistication, decade by decade. Iroquois attacks upon the Susquehannocks were set in the pattern of the Iroquoian beaver wars, but the Mohawks dropped out of that contest, as we shall see. Although the central fire of the League burned at Onondaga, the competition continued between Onondagas and Mohawks for precedence in the League's councils. This was not the only tension within the League, but it is the one most evident in the source documents.

Recorded history for our purposes begins on Chesapeake Bay with the founding of Jamestown. Captain John Smith has told how he journeyed in 1608 to the head of the bay, nearly 200 miles inland from its mouth and a little less than 100 miles west from the nearest Atlantic shore. Smith was astonished to find Susquehannocks there brokering French goods to the Tocwoghs of the bay.[2] The location remained a busy trading center for 70 more years.

Smith estimated the Susquehannocks at 600 able men, implying a total population of 2,400 to 3,000, but his figure seems much too low.[3] Three decades and at least one epidemic later, a Canadian Jesuit put 1,300 warriors in "a single village" of the Susquehannocks, implying a population of 5,200 to 6,500.[4] As early as 1615 they had been numerous enough to spare 500 warriors to aid Samuel de Champlain in an attack on the Five Nations.[5]

Virginian William Claiborne began to trade with these Susquehannocks at Kent Island (opposite today's Annapolis) in 1630–31 and extended his operations seven years later to Palmer's Island at the head of the bay. Claiborne put up buildings at each location and staffed them with traders. Obviously such arrangements were made with Susquehannock cooperation. But just as Claiborne was getting settled, the king of England chartered the new colony of Maryland with boundaries embracing Claiborne's establishments. Claiborne refused to surrender them to Maryland, claim-

2. John Smith, *A Map of Virginia* (1612), in *The Jamestown Voyages under the First Charter, 1606–1609*, ed. Philip L. Barbour, 2 vols., Works issued by the Hakluyt Society, 2d ser., nos. 136–37 (Cambridge: Cambridge University Press, 1969), 2:407–8.
3. Ibid., p. 343.
4. Paul Ragueneau, "des Hurons," April 16, 1648, *Jesuit Relations* 33:129.
5. Samuel de Champlain, *Voyages and Discoveries* (1619), in *Works*, ed. Biggar, 3:53–54.

ing that his priority of settlement gave him priority of possession. Virginia backed his claims, which became part of territorial boundary disputes between Virginia and Maryland, but the crown overruled him. While the issue was being argued at court, it was fought out in the bay. Cecilius Calvert, second Lord Baltimore, sent his brother Leonard to seize Claiborne's posts by force, whereupon—according to Maryland sources—Claiborne instigated the Susquehannocks to hostility. Supposedly, as Leonard Calvert asserted, the Susquehannocks had been part of Claiborne's "conspiracy" against Maryland and had continued after his overthrow to harass Maryland's allied Indians.[6]

Susquehannocks and Delawares

Information is scanty, but there is no doubt that the Susquehannocks were at war with many tribes of the region. They later claimed to have conquered the indigenous tribes of large territories on both shores of Chesapeake Bay. As early as 1626 they were struggling to get past the interference of the Algonquian tribes of the Delaware Valley in order to trade with the Dutch at Manhattan,[7] and their dispute was a full-scale war in 1634 when the Englishman Thomas Yong sailed up the Delaware. He reported that the Susquehannocks had chased the Delaware Indians across the river, making them abandon their villages on the west bank.[8] Yong's understanding of the situation was imperfect, as is evidenced by the gullibility of his men and the ease with which they were tricked by Dutch traders.

Yong had been seeking a Northwest passage to the orient. Encounters with Delaware refugees and Susquehannock pursuers made him and his crew apprehensive about their own safety. When Dutch traders arrived and expostulated over Yong's presence in their company's claimed jurisdiction, he displayed a royal charter with a massive seal and claimed the Delaware River for England. The wary Dutch retreated to New Amster-

6. *Archives of Maryland*, eds. Wm. Hand Browne et al. (Baltimore, 1883–), 3:64–73. I am obliged to Garry Wheeler Stone for copies of the following additional documents: Gov. Leonard Calvert to Lord Baltimore, April 25, 1638, in *Calvert Papers, Number One*, Fund Publication no. 28 (Baltimore: Maryland Historical Society, 1889), pp. 182–88; "A relation of a voyage made by Mr. Cyprian throwgood to the head of the baye," Young Collection, document 7, mss., Maryland Dept., Enoch Pratt Free Library, Baltimore, Md.

7. Isaack de Rasière to the Amsterdam Chamber, Sept. 23, 1626, in *Documents Relating to New Netherland, 1624–1626, in the Henry E. Huntington Library*, trans. and ed. A. J. F. Van Laer (San Marino, Calif.: The Huntington Library, 1924), pp. 192, 211.

8. "Relation of Captain Thomas Yong, 1634," in *Narratives of Early Pennsylvania, West New Jersey, and Delaware, 1630–1710*," ed. Albert Cook Myers (New York: Charles Scribner's Sons, 1912), pp. 39–44.

dam for instruction. In their absence, Yong seized their empty Fort Nassau, garrisoned it with a handful of men, and returned to his own base in England. The Dutch traders returned to play upon the isolated greenhorns' nerves. As told by one of the Englishmen: "the English inquiring of the Dutch what was the great concourse or meeting of the Indians, it was replied by the Dutch that it was undoubtedly to cut them off (meaning the English that were then seated). Then the English, for fear of the Indians, procured the Dutch to carry them away and the next year the Dutch, having that opportunity by the English being forced to forsake the place, came themselves and seated it."[9] Like the merchants of New Plymouth, the Dutch knew how to create an Indian Menace to serve their purpose.

They could not work the same trick when the colonists of New Sweden appeared in 1638 because the governor of New Sweden was as experienced as they. Peter Minuit had been the second director-general of New Netherland, serving from 1626 to 1632, and he knew the Indians' ways. He knew Dutchmen's ways, too. He understood perfectly well that the Dutch West India Company's charter did not include a grant of territory, and that the company had attempted to legitimize its territorial pretensions by purchases of land cessions from Indians. If the Dutch could purchase territory, so could the Swedes. Minuit promptly met with Delaware sachems and bought a tract of land. The deed is not available today. Four crewmen of the Swedish ship deposed that it transferred "all the land, as many days' journeys on all places and parts of the river as they [the Swedes] requested; upwards and on both sides."[10] This was clearly false. Delaware sachem Mattahorn, who had been one of the participants in the transaction, gave a more plausible report to the Dutch in 1648 and 1651. He stated that Governor Minuit had bought only a small piece of land—as much as was contained within "six trees"—"to plant some tobacco on it." The rest of the lands occupied by the Swedes had been "stolen."[11]

Several Susquehannock sachems had been present when Minuit made his purchase, and their presence, together with their apparent victory over the Delawares in 1634, has convinced some scholars that the Delawares had become tributary to the Susquehannocks. Whether there was some sort of subordinate relationship, I cannot say, but there is plenty of evidence to show that whatever it may have been did not involve Susquehannock claims to Delaware territory. The Delawares were the landlords of

9. James Waye's Deposition, April 18, 1684, in Weslager, *Dutch Explorers*, pp. 300–302.
10. Affidavit of four men from the *Key of Calmar* (1638), in *Narratives of Early Pa.*, ed. Myers, pp. 86–89.
11. Report of Andries Hudde, Nov. 7, 1648, in *The Instruction for Johan Printz, Governor of New Sweden*, trans. and ed. Amandus Johnson (Philadelphia: Swedish Colonial Society, 1930), p. 274; *N.Y.Col.Docs.* 1:598.

the Delaware Valley and were recognized as such by Swedes, Dutchmen, Englishmen, and the Susquehannocks themselves.[12]

It is not possible to say how many Delawares there were at that time. In 1641 an English observer counted 800 warriors in the towns along the lower part of their river, implying a total population there of 3,200 to 4,000 persons, but there were many more uncounted communities upstream and along tributary creeks.[13]

It seems likely that the issue involved in the Susquehannock-Delaware fighting had been freedom of transit for Susquehannock traders over Delaware territory. The sources clearly indicate that the Susquehannocks were the major fur-trading tribe of the region, and Minuit placed his Swedish colony strategically at the mouth of Christina Creek in order to intercept Susquehannocks before they could get to Dutch traders on the Delaware.[14] What the Swedes called Christina Creek was known by the Dutch as the Minquas Kill (meaning the Susquehannocks' Creek) because the Susquehannocks were accustomed to canoe from Chesapeake Bay up to

12. Charles A. Hanna, *The Wilderness Trail*, 2 vols. (New York: G. P. Putnam's Sons, 1911), 1:106–7; C. A. Weslager, *The Delaware Indians: A History* (New Brunswick, N.J.: Rutgers University Press, 1972), p. 99. For discussion of the sources and their significance see Francis Jennings, "Glory, Death, and Transfiguration: The Susquehannock Indians in the Seventeenth Century," *Proceedings of the American Philosophical Society* 112:1 (Jan., 1968), pp. 19, 50–53.

A bibliographic note: Hanna was an amateur who pursued every scrap of printed paper available in his time that dealt with relations between colonial governments, Indian peoples, and traders in the region between the Chesapeake and Delaware bays and the Ohio River. His volumes are alike indispensable and exasperating: indispensable because they quote from so many sources that one cannot be certain of having seen all the evidence until Hanna has been checked; exasperating because the material is a hodgepodge so badly organized that checking thoroughly almost requires memorizing the whole book—though there is a usable index. Hanna's attitudes were narrowly ethnocentric—not only characterized by notions of White supremacism but displaying the peculiarly ugly bigotry of the narrow Calvinist toward all other faiths. He slurs with little restraint, and his quotations should be checked in context of the originals because of frequent distortion by truncation.

13. Robert Evelin's letter (1641) in Beauchamp Plantagenet [Edmund Plowden], *A Description of the Province of New Albion* (1648), reprinted in *Tracts and Other Papers*, comp. Peter Force, 4 vols. (1836), vol. 2. *Description* is separately paged, p. 22. (I have used the more recent facsimile reprint by Peter Smith: Gloucester, Mass., 1963.) The inadequacy of Evelin's population figures is shown in a variety of ways. His overall estimate of 800 warriors is exceeded by the sum of his own individual village estimates, which comes to 890 (p. 22). A much greater number of villages is shown on the map in Weslager, *The Delaware Indians*, p. 38. On this subject of population: James Mooney's oft-cited estimates of Indian populations are not worth a damn and should be sent to limbo instead of being constantly resurrected as in the *Encyclopaedia Britannica*. Mooney, "The Aboriginal Population of America North of Mexico," in *Smithsonian Miscellaneous Collections* 80 (Washington, D.C., 1928), p. 7; Douglas H. Ubelaker, "The Sources and Methodology for Mooney's Estimates of North American Populations," in *The Native Population of the Americas in 1492*, ed. William M. Denevan (Madison: University of Wisconsin Press, 1976), pp. 243–92, discussion of Delawares on p. 256; F. Jennings, *Invasion of America*, ch. 2. It is disheartening to see Mooney's attitude still visible in Ives Goddard, "Delaware," in *Northeast*, p. 214, but Goddard's article was completed in 1973, before Ubelaker published.

14. Weslager, *Dutch Explorers*, 117–18, and ch. 6.

Elk River via a short portage to Christina, or Minquas Creek, and down it to the Delaware. Minuit was lucky enough to start business at just the moment when Maryland was seizing the trading posts of William Claiborne on the Chesapeake. It appears that the Susquehannocks immediately diverted their trade to New Sweden.[15]

This did not please the Dutch, who would have been the recipients of that trade if the Swedes had not suddenly appeared.[16] They protested vigorously as Minuit had anticipated, but he knew that relations between Sweden and the Netherlands in Europe were such that the Dutch West India Company would be obliged to refrain from using its overwhelming power against him. Had he not been protected by the current diplomatic balance, he could not have held out with his tiny force against a single Dutch ship.

By 1640 on the Delaware, then, there were Dutch and Swedish presences and the promise of an English return.[17] Tensions existed between Susquehannocks and Delawares, but since Susquehannock sachems had quietly witnessed the Delaware cession of the land for Fort Christina, some sort of accommodation had been reached.[18] Through bluff and luck, as well as Minuit's experienced skill, tiny New Sweden, whose total population never reached as many as 400 persons, had captured the lion's share of the Delaware Bay trade in competition with New Netherland and Maryland. Neither the Dutch nor the English would long accept that state of affairs.

Maryland's defeat by Susquehannocks and New Sweden

In 1642 the Maryland English declared war on the Susquehannocks.[19] An early historian of Maryland attributes the war to Maryland's desire to stop Susquehannock incursions against the colony's clients, the Piscataway and Patuxent tribes "and probably the Yoamacoes, with whom, it would seem, the Susquehannocks had never ceased to wage uninterrupted

15. *Virginia and Maryland* (1655), in *Tracts and Other Papers*, ed. Peter Force, vol. 2, separately paged, p. 5. For what follows, see also Francis Jennings, "Indians and Frontiers in Seventeenth-Century Maryland," in *Early Maryland in a Wider World*, ed. David B. Quinn (Detroit: Wayne State University Press, 1982), pp. 216–41.

16. Samuel Hazard, *Annals of Pennsylvania from the Discovery of the Delaware, 1609–1682* (Philadelphia: Hazard and Mitchell, 1850), pp. 47–50.

17. See C. A. Weslager, *The English on the Delaware, 1610–1682* (New Brunswick, N.J.: Rutgers University Press, 1967), ch. 7–10. I have omitted the story of the New Haven English on the Delaware in order to simplify an already overcomplicated narrative; it led to nothing. Weslager's is the fullest account.

18. Deed, July 19, 1655, in *N.Y.Col.Docs.* 1:599–600.

19. Council minutes, Sept. 13, 1642, *Md.Arch.* 3:116–17.

hostilities ever since the first settlement of the Maryland colony at St. Mary's."[20]

Whatever the reason, Maryland's troops marched sometime between July 1643 and June 1644. Two campaigns were undertaken, in the first of which the Susquehannocks fled from the militia's gunfire.[21] But the Swedes rallied to the Indians' aid, and the Susquehannocks won the second round, routing Maryland's troops and capturing fifteen prisoners, whom they killed with horrifying brutality. The governments of both Maryland and New Sweden were reticent about the affair. Maryland's records specify the colony's campaigns, become silent about their outcome, then suddenly give instructions to a negotiating officer "for restoring as much as you can gett of the armes and other goods lost or left in our last march upon [the Susquehannocks], at least the two feild pieces." These two cannon, so casually "lost or left" appear again in Swedish sources as having been abandoned in the Marylanders' flight.[22] But the Swedes had their own reasons for taciturnity. Aid by Europeans to Indians for hostilities against other Europeans was always clandestine and always denied. "Covert operations" did not wait till the twentieth century to be invented, and neither did lying about them. The Swedes did not want the odium of helping Indians against Christians, and the Marylanders did not want the disgrace of a defeat that might provoke intervention by the crown (as had happened in Virginia after the Indian uprising of 1622). We learn about the actual battle from an obscure pamphlet written by the unofficial English visitor.

The Swedes certainly gained by Maryland's defeat. Thereafter the Susquehannocks were committed to market their large stocks of furs exclusively at New Sweden. The tribe remained in an inactive state of war with Maryland until 1652, which precluded trade in that direction; it was also at odds with the Dutch because of friendship with a Hudson River tribe warring against the Dutch. But the Swedes did not always have enough goods to exchange for all Susquehannock furs. Banished from trade on the Chesapeake and at New Amsterdam, the Susquehannocks smug-

20. John Leeds Bozman, *The History of Maryland, from Its First Settlement, in 1633, to the Restoration in 1660*, 2 vols. (Baltimore, Md.: James Lucas and E. K. Deaver, 1837), 2:161–62.

21. Plantagenet, *Description*, p. 24; Matthew Page Andrews, *Tercentenary History of Maryland*, 4 vols. (Chicago: S. J. Clarke Publishing Co., 1925), 1:167.

22. Report of Governor Johan Printz (1644), in *Narratives of Early Pa.*, ed. Myers, p. 102; council minutes, June 18, 1644 and June 28, 1652, *Md.Arch.*, 3:149–50, 276, 277; Peter Lindestrom, *Geographia Americae with an Account of the Delaware Indians, Based on Surveys and Notes Made in 1654–1656*, trans. and ed. Amandus Johnson (Philadelphia: Swedish Colonial Society, 1925), pp. 241–44. Lindestrom calls it a battle with "the English of Virginia," but Virginia was the name he used for all Englishmen on the Chesapeake, which he called the Bay of Virginia. His mention of the field artillery corresponds with that detail in *Md.Arch.*, Council minutes, June 18, 1644, 3:149. Report of Gov. John Rising (1655), in *Narratives of Early Pennsylvania*, ed. Myers, pp. 157, 159.

gled some of their peltry to the Dutch through the Delawares, who made a good thing out of the situation. The Delawares got trade goods from the Swedes, either on credit or in exchange for maize, traded the goods for surplus Susquehannock furs, took the furs to New Amsterdam for the high Dutch prices, and had a neat profit from the cycle. The Swedes had not relied on circumstance to monopolize Susquehannock trade. In 1645, according to Minuit's successor, Governor Johan Printz, the Swedes "bought" the whole of the Susquehannocks' country—"only for the sake of trade." This equivocal comment asserts confidently an agreement for exclusive trading relationships while insinuating through its curious choice of language a claim on territory.[23]

Mohawk war and Maryland peace

The inherently unstable situation was soon disturbed. The Mohawks, flushed with triumphs from the Beaver Wars in the west, turned southward in the winter of 1651–1652 to overwhelm a people known only as the Atrakwaeronons. Whether the name was some intervening tribe's term for the Susquehannocks or whether it identified a separate tribe of allies is not clear, but the results of the Mohawk raid are plain. On the one hand, the Mohawks marched victoriously home with a great haul of captives said to number 500 to 600.[24] On the other hand, the Susquehannocks prepared quickly for a war against some or all of the Five Nations; it dragged on for twenty-five years.[25]

To protect their rear, the Susquehannocks initiated diplomacy with Maryland. In 1652 they negotiated a treaty of peace subscribed by sachems Sawahegeh, Aurotaurogh, Scarhuhadih, Ruthcuhogah, and Wathetdianeh (who appears in later records as Wastahandow). In return for arms and the safety of their southern flank, they ceded to Maryland large territories on both shores of Chesapeake Bay.[26] Supposedly these lands were occupied by tribes who had been conquered by the Susquehannocks, but this statement in the treaty seems a little inflated since Mary-

23. Report of Gov. Johan Rising, 1655, in *Narratives of Early Pa.*, pp. 157, 159; Printz to Oxenstierna, Aug. 1, 1651, in *Instruction for Johan Printz*, pp. 181–82.

24. Journal of the Jesuit Fathers, March 10, 1652, June 5, 1652, July 1652, *Jesuit Relations* 37:97, 105, 111.

25. An ambiguous entry in the Journal of the Jesuit Fathers for August 21, 1653, states that the Susquehannocks were "engaging in war between" the Mohawks and Senecas. *Between* is a translation from *entre*, which might also be rendered *among*. *Jesuit Relations* 38:189–91.

26. Treaty text: *Md.Arch* July 5, 1652, 3:277–78. There may be some significance in the fact that the man who made this treaty on Maryland's behalf was a commissioner from the Parliamentary Council of State in England who had previously reduced Maryland to obedience on March 27, 1652. Bennett Bernard Browne, "Historical and Genealogical Notes, *William and Mary Quarterly*, 1st ser., 3:3 (Jan., 1895), pp. 206–7.

land had been acting as those tribes' protector. What seems more likely is that the Susquehannocks offered to quit claim to rights of any sort, and the Marylanders made the quitclaim into a transfer of "rights of conquest," thereby acquiring the appearance of legal possession without having to pay off the resident tribes. In that era, rights of conquest were featured prominently in the body of diplomatic arguing points comprising the so-called law of nations, and much effort was put into devices for acquiring such "rights." If they could be obtained without the risk and expense of actual combat, so much the better. They will appear frequently in the course of this narrative.

Dutch conquest of New Sweden

The 1650s were an exceedingly turbulent time. While the Susquehannocks were making peace with Maryland in 1652, England went to war with the Netherlands, and the Delaware River Swedes seized the opportunity to "conquer" the few Dutch traders on the river.[27] This was foolish audacity. England and the Netherlands made peace in 1654, whereupon the Dutch of New Netherland, who were no longer distracted, sent a fleet to terminate New Sweden's legal existence in 1655. The Swedish fort capitulated to the Dutch fleet, and the Swedish settlers came under Dutch government.[28]

Though the removal of New Sweden's government eliminated one active agent in the universal violence, plenty of others were left. The French of Canada menaced New Netherland from the north. From the east, New England's Puritan governments coveted and encroached upon Dutch Long Island and the upper Hudson Valley. Anglican Virginia and Roman Catholic Maryland strove with each other over conflicting claims around the Chesapeake Bay, and Protestants in Maryland challenged the Catholic governing class—some getting hanged for subversion. The Catholic lords of Maryland also laid claim to all of Calvinist Dutch Delaware Bay. In Old England, Cavaliers and Roundheads continued to harass each other until the Stuart Restoration, and Englishmen fought Irishmen and Scots. Puritans and Royalists agreed upon hostility to Dutch commercial supremacy and fought a series of wars with the Dutch, beginning in 1652.

Amid all these struggles the Indian tribes pursued their own interests

27. Hazard, *Annals of Pa.* 146–51. A version is given by Amandus Johnson that sounds almost like an effusion from a Swedish ministry of propaganda. *The Swedish Settlements on the Delaware: Their History and Relation to the Indians, Dutch and English, 1638–1664*, 2 vol. (Philadelphia: University of Pennsylvania Press, 1911), 2:581–87.

28. Hazard, *Annals of Pa.* 178–203. Hazard quotes both Dutch and Swedish sources reporting the fact of Dutch conquest.

as well as they were able. We have already noticed the bloodshed and destruction of the Iroquoian beaver wars and the involvement in those wars of trade rivalry between New France and New Netherland. The Susquehannocks in turn became involved in intercolonial rivalries, forcing upon them a dilemma that only catastrophe could resolve.

Dutch policies and practices

What happened among Indians after the suppression of New Sweden depended largely on what happened in New Netherland. For a period, Dutch centers at Fort Orange and Manhattan, on the North River (Hudson), and New Amstel, on the South River (Delaware), controlled the great bulk of the intersocietal trade south of New France. With control over markets they gained powerful influence over tribal policies and activities throughout a vast area. But the Dutch were not quite sure what to do with their influence according to any general plan. They dealt with each tribe separately, and each situation pragmatically, as it arose. The metaphorical chain binding New Netherland to the Iroquois was never more than "iron."[29]

Nevertheless, the mere existence of Dutch control over the major markets for peltry forced the tribes into accommodation. The Susquehannocks could no longer sustain themselves independently of Dutch friendship. They showed their capitulation in 1658 when they, like the Mohawks earlier, exerted their influence to end the renewed wars of the Esopus Indians of Hudson River against the Dutch. Reasoning with tribes whom they called tributaries, the Susquehannocks confessed that they had been forced "to submit to the Dutch or hide."[30] Thus it came about that the Mohawks and Susquehannocks were fiercely at war in the winter of 1651–1652, pursued parallel policies in 1658, and later joined together in the same conference in 1660 to pressure the still-refractory Esopus Indians into submission.[31] The turnabout of Mohawk-Susquehannock relations, so mysterious out of context, appears supremely simple against its background. The Mohawks had not won Susquehannock surrender, but the Dutch had.

From 1658 to 1662 was the period of maximum friendship between the Susquehannocks and Mohawks, and it was a time when the Susquehan-

29. Neither iron nor chains were known to Indians aboriginally, so words had to be invented as equivalents. According to Cayuga Chief Jacob E. Thomas, the word translated as *chain* means literally "arms linked together." The distinction between a chain of iron and a chain of silver is discussed at various places herein. See the index.
30. Treaty minutes, Oct. 15–18, 1658, *N.Y.Col.Docs.* 13:95.
31. Treaty minutes and supporting documents, July 1660, *N.Y.Col.Docs.* 13:179–84.

nocks remained locked in bloody conflict with the other four of the Five Nations. Mohawks and Susquehannocks conceived their diplomatic roles in explicitly similar terms. In 1658 the Mohawks reminded the Dutch at Fort Orange "that at the time of the war against the 'savages' they had gone down to the Manhattans and had done their best to preserve peace; therefore we too [the Dutch] were in duty bound to do the same for them while they promise to exert themselves in future as mediators between us and other 'savages.' " [*Savages* is the English translator's word for the Dutch *wilden*.] The Mohawks then demanded help against other Iroquois nations who were trying to break through the Mohawk cordon around the Dutch market at Fort Orange.[32]

In 1662 the Susquehannocks asserted to the Dutch at Delaware Bay that they had "at all times let themselves be employed to mediate in differences between the Christians and the other savages, to which they still consider themselves obliged." They, too, wanted help (in the form of supplies on credit) with which to fight their non-Mohawk enemies among the Iroquois.[33] It appears that the Susquehannocks attempted to control access to the Delaware market as the Mohawks restricted access to the Fort Orange market, and both had to fight the more distant Iroquois nations that tried to break through.

Had New Netherland been organized along the lines of New France, such powerful Indian allies might have been turned against English colonies on the pattern of the Seven Years War of the eighteenth century, but the ruling Dutch West India Company was much more interested in piracy and plantation in the West Indies and Brazil than in its less lucrative colony of New Netherland. It had no plans for mainland territorial empire in North America in spite of its desire to acquire commercial supremacy, and it was constantly on the defensive against imperialist aggression from England and the English colonies, not to speak of the French in Canada.[34]

Such considerations have led some writers to absolve the New Netherland Dutch of aggressive intentions. Hunt remarked that "True expansion at Albany did not begin under the Dutch at all, but under the energetic Dongan, in 1684."[35] Trelease stated that the Dutch "had no ambition to dominate North America" and therefore refrained from wasting resources "in an international contest for continental supremacy."[36] These statements leave an unfortunate impression of a sort of peaceful store-minding not possible with the conditions of commercial competition as they were

32. Fort Orange Council minutes, Aug. 13, 1658, *N.Y.Col.Docs.* 13:88–89.
33. Wm. Beeckman to Stuyvesant, Dec. 23, 1662, *N.Y.Col.Docs.* 12:419.
34. Bachman, *Peltries or Plantations*, ch. 3, 8. Thomas J. Condon, *New York Beginnings: The Commercial Origins of New Netherland* (New York: New York University Press, 1968), pp. 144–47.
35. Hunt, *Wars of the Iroquois*, p. 172.
36. Trelease, *Indian Affairs*, p. 137.

at that time. The Dutch did have ambitions to dominate the trade of North America, and they did not hesitate to use all practicable force toward that end.

English harassment of New Netherland

New Netherland was full of contradictions. The colony's business was trading with Indians, but the Indians were mistreated and embittered. The nature of the business called for aggressive penetration of the continent, but the Dutch sat still in their villages; there were no Dutch Champlains, Perrots, Marquettes, or La Salles, and only an occasional *bushloper* (equivalent to the French coureurs de bois) appears in the sources. New Netherland's location was a geographical center of gravity for European trade and colonization, but New Netherland's Dutch population remained so small as to create almost a vacuum at the center.[37] The consequence of these contradictions of circumstance was contradiction in policy. Dutch governors vacillated between bold aggression and defensive discretion bordering on the pusillanimous. They armed the Mohawks to attack Canadian Indians, but they never dared to use the Mohawks openly against New England. They made big talk about their rights in the Connecticut Valley and permitted themselves to be pushed out without a fight. They watched New Englanders push into their close vicinity and could only think of asking the Puritan intruders to please accept Dutch jurisdiction. They conquered the Swedes on the Delaware and groveled before the English from the Chesapeake. New Netherland was really a golden goose with clipped wings, and the wonder is that it was not plucked sooner.

Its neighbors were deterred by two fears—of the Mohawks and the Dutch navy—so they encroached gradually, bit by bit, never creating an

37. Thomas J. Condon estimated the total population of New Netherland in 1664 at 10,000 "at most," including ethnically English colonists on Long Island and in Westchester County, together with other nationalities (not taking Indians into account, apparently), "which may have constituted 20 to 40 percent of the total population." Stella H. Sutherland reduced this estimate by half, allowing 5,500 White and Negro persons to "New York" and "Delaware" in 1660; leaving blanks for "Pennsylvania" and "New Jersey" she gave approximately 63,000 White and Negro persons to the surrounding colonies of Massachusetts, Connecticut, Maryland, and Virginia. Condon, *New York Beginnings*, p. 177; *Historical Statistics of the United States: Colonial Times to 1970*, ed. William Lerner, 2 vols. (Washington, D.C.: Bureau of the Census, 1975), Table Z 1–23, comp. Stella H. Sutherland, p. 1168. Apart from Sutherland's personal research, the most recent study cited by her is dated 1935 (p. 1152).

The Iroquois population by itself, may have been greater than the total of all European people in New Netherland in 1660. The Jesuits estimated a total of Iroquois on the order of 2,200 warriors, implying 6,600 to 11,000 persons altogether, depending on the size of families. When the Algonquians and Susquehannocks are added, the total of Indian peoples in the region certainly outnumbered the Europeans. Gunther Michelson, "Iroquois Population Statistics," *Man in the Northeast*, no. 14 (fall, 1977), Table I, p. 4.

occasion for the resistance born of desperation. Connecticut forced final abandonment of the Dutch House of Hope after 1641. New Haveners crept toward New Amsterdam and took over the eastern half of Long Island.[38] In 1659 a Massachusetts party proposed to settle on a northern tributary of the Hudson River and demanded right of passage up the river to facilitate their plan. Exactly how the Dutch responded to this last proposed violation of their inner sanctum is not quite clear, but they did draw the line. The directors in Holland ordered resistance by any means, and Governor Stuyvesant assured them in cryptic language that he would comply.[39] The settlement was not made. The English, meanwhile, incited New England's Indians against the Mohawks and tried to organize a general rising of New Netherlands' Indians to coincide with their own projected invasion by land.[40]

In the south, New England contingents had early attempted to bluff their way into the Delaware but were ousted by clandestine cooperation between the Swedes and Dutch.[41] That happened, of course, before the Swedes and Dutch came to blows with each other. In 1659 Cecilius Calvert, second Lord Baltimore, sent a delegation to New Amstel on Delaware Bay to demand formal surrender, giving as his reason the terms of Maryland's charter. Conceding nothing, the Dutch reacted cautiously. At New Amstel they affirmed their own right to the Delaware territory on the basis of Indian purchases and long-term possession and habitation; and Governor Stuyvesant reinforced these arguments with a stronger garrison. After further discussions in 1660, Maryland's claims were forwarded to Amsterdam for adjudication. In this case, official firmness was undermined by popular panic. Maryland's pressure caused "much uncertainty and trouble among the people," reported the colony's vice-director, who added, "everyone is trying to remove and escape."[42]

38. Deduction Respecting the Differences About Boundaries, &c., in New Netherland, Nov. 5, 1660, *N.Y.Col.Docs.* 2:134–37, 141–44.

39. *Court Minutes of Fort Orange*, Aug. 4, 1659, 2:208; Stuyvesant to directors in Holland, Sept. 4, 1659, *N.Y.Col.Docs.* 13:107; same to same, n.d., ibid., p. 126; dirs. to Stuyvesant, Dec. 22, 1659, ibid., pp. 129–30; same to same, March 9, 1660, ibid., p. 150; Stuyvesant to dirs., April 21, 1660, ibid., p. 162.

40. Dirs. in Holland to Stuyvesant, March 26, 1663, *N.Y.Col.Docs.* 13:240; proceedings at Fort Orange, Sept. 26, 1663, ibid., pp. 297–98; memo, Dec. 29, 1663, ibid., p. 322; Couwenhoven's report, March 15, 1664, ibid., pp. 363–64; proceedings at Fort Orange, July 12, 1664, ibid., p. 389; Van Rensselaer to Van Cortlandt, July 17, 1664, *Correspondence of Jeremias Van Rensselaer*, p. 356.

41. Weslager, *English on the Delaware*, ch. 7–9.

42. *Md.Archives*, 3:365–78, 426–31; *N.Y.Col.Docs.* 12:215–16,248 ff., esp. p. 255; Alrichs to De Graaff, ibid., 2:70.

Susquehannock alliance with Maryland

Because the local Indians soon became involved, one particular escapee from the Delaware colony requires our attention. He was a trader named Jacob Claeson, who, like salesmen everywhere, had nicknamed himself "Jacob, My Friend." He departed mysteriously from New Amstel "with quite a large sum of money, given to him by divers parties to trade with," and unusual efforts were made by the Dutch to get him back. The money was not their primary concern. What especially concerned them was that Jacob could speak the Susquehannock language—a rare, perhaps unique, accomplishment for a European—and he had considerable personal influence over those Indians. As the Dutch feared, he soon made himself useful to Maryland.[43]

His value was enhanced because the Susquehannocks suddenly were thrust into the center of Maryland's foreign policy. The implications of Maryland's 1652 treaty with the Susquehannocks probably had not been fully understood by the provincial negotiators. By 1660 they began to understand, at least dimly. In that year the Oneida tribe of the Five Nations killed five of the Piscatawa Indians of Maryland "for being friends" to Maryland and the Susquehannocks.[44] As it appeared to the Marylanders, their protected Indians had been attacked by "Cynegoes" [Senecas]—their vague term for any of the Five Nations (whom they could not differentiate by individual tribes). Maryland declared war on the "Cynegoes"—all the Five Nations—not being aware that the Mohawk nation had by this time ceased hostilities with the Susquehannocks and had not participated in the raids on Maryland's Indians. In 1660, therefore, the Marylanders conceived themselves to be at war with the Indian allies of the Dutch of Fort Orange while also engaged in a politer but no less determined struggle with the Dutch of Fort Amstel. One can sense the suspicions nagging the Marylanders: had the Dutch instigated the Cynegoes' raids on Maryland's Indians?[45]

Prudence dictated prompt countermeasures. The Maryland assembly decided in April 1661 that "the Sasquehannoughs are a Bullwarke and Security of the Northern parts of this Province," and within a month their existing treaty of peace was expanded into a full alliance. Jacob, My Friend, was licensed to trade with the Susquehannocks and employed as an official

43. Beekman to Stuyvesant, April 28, 1660, in Hazard, *Annals of Pennsylvania*, pp. 309–10; Stuyvesant to dirs. in Holland, June 25, 1660, *N.Y.Col.Docs.* 12:317; council minutes, April 17, July 30, Oct. 12, 1661, *Md.Arch.* 3:443, 430–31, 434–35, 453, 462. I have pieced together a brief biography of this interesting but almost invisible man in "Jacob Young: Indian Trader and Interpreter," in *Struggle and Survival in Colonial America*, eds. David G. Sweet and Gary B. Nash (Berkeley: University of California Press, 1981), pp. 347–61.
44. Memo, Dec. 20, 1660, *Md.Arch.* 3:403.
45. Act of War, April 17, 1661, *Md.Arch.* 1:406–7.

intermediary for the province, and the Indians were supplied with substantial help. Besides goods and arms, they were allotted a troop of fifty
Englishmen to help garrison their fort.[46]

The allies had different motives for their pact. The Susquehannocks
obviously wanted help for their war with the western tribes of the Five
Nations. Maryland wanted to use the Susquehannocks, not only defensively on the exposed Susquehanna River approach to the province, but
also offensively in the Delaware Valley.

To the northward, Maryland's commissioner was instructed "to informe
yourself of the processe of the Warre" between the Susquehannocks and
the Five Nations tribes "and if you finde them slack in itt, to press them
discreetly to a vigourous prosecution of it."[47] To the eastward, a Delaware
murder of four Marylanders served as a provocation; Maryland demanded
Susquehannock assistance to obtain "satisfaction" from the Delawares. The
point of this action was instantly understood at New Amstel. Dutch secretary Beeckman fretted about rights of conquest: "if the English go to
war with these savages, . . . all of the territory whence they drive out the
same will be seized as being taken from their enemies by the sword. The
English will most likely come into our jurisdiction to pursue their enemies
without having given previous notice; in case of refusal they would suspect us and treat us in the same manner."

Beeckman had good reason for anxiety. Shortly after he wrote, the
Maryland council sat down to consider a letter from Proprietor Lord Bal-
timore by which they were instructed to direct hostilities against "certaine
Ennemies, Pyratts, and Robbers," meaning the Dutch.[48]

Iroquois defeats

The general regional tension came to a climax in 1663 when 800 Senecas, Cayugas, and Onondagas besieged the home fort of the Susquehannocks. Apparently they had signaled their intentions because almost all
the Susquehannocks' fighting men were at home awaiting the attack.
Numbers were about even. A hundred Delawares had joined the 700 Susquehannock warriors to repel the attackers. According to the myths about
the overpowering ferocity and even invincibility of the Iroquois, the Susquehannocks should have shared the fate of Hurons, Tionnontates, Neutrals, and Eries. They did not. After a few sallies from the fort had
convinced the besiegers of probable failure, they lifted the siege. In less

46. Loc. cit.; council minutes, May 18, 1661, Md.Arch. 2:420–21; May, 1622, ibid., p.
453.

47. Instructions of governor and council, May 16, 1661, ibid., 3:418.

48. Treaty minutes, May 16, 1661, Md.Arch. 3:421; Beeckman to Stuyvesant, May 27,
1661, N.Y.Col.Docs. 12:343–44; council minutes, July 30, 1661, Md.Arch. 3:427–29.

than a week, the Iroquois headed home with excuses.[49]

Some implications of the battle should be noted. One is that the Iroquois had certainly not conquered the Delawares, as they were later to claim, up to this date. More important for the participants, the Susquehannocks retained gratitude for Delaware help, a gratitude that frustrated Maryland's plans for vicarious conquest of Delaware Bay.

The year 1663 was very bad for the Five Nations. Although the Mohawks repulsed an attack by "praying Indians" of Massachusetts Bay (who had been supplied with arms by Puritan mission supervisors), they met serious defeat in their own offensives.[50] In the fall a combined expedition of Mohawks, Onondagas, and Oneidas attacked the Sokoki tribe on the upper Connecticut River. After an initial repulse the Mohawks wanted to call it quits, but the others overruled them; the party returned to be calamitously beaten.[51] Adding to war's troubles, smallpox struck again. In August, Jesuit Father Jerome Lalemant reported "sad havoc" by the disease in deserted villages with only half-tilled fields. The Dutch heard of a thousand victims of the epidemic among the Five Nations. Far from being the savage rulers of a wilderness empire, the Iroquois now came "within two finger-breadths of total destruction" from the accumulated effects of famine, disease, and war.[52]

Yet the fighting continued, seemingly of its own momentum. The Indians of New England continued hostile, the Mahicans warred intermittently, and both were supplied with arms by the New England Puritans who had plans for eventual conquest of the Hudson Valley. The Mahicans were later to express public gratitude to Major John Pynchon, of Springfield, Massachusetts, because he "did as it were take us in his armes and protected us."[53] The implacable Canadian Algonquins, with French

49. This is an example of clashing traditions from different tribes. Two distinct and different versions of this battle exist in the sources. The Iroquois version, as told to Jesuit missionaries, blames defeat on the European-type fortification of the Susquehannocks and the failure of a stratagem to lure them out of their walls. The Susquehannock version (less frequently used in the histories) matches approximately equal forces of Iroquois and Susquehannock warriors, and it has the Iroquois abandon their enterprise after a few sallies from the fort had convinced them of probable failure. Jerome Lalemant, Quebec, Sept. 4, 1663, *Jesuit Relations* 48:77–79; Andries Hudde to Stuyvesant, Altena, May 29, 1663, *N.Y.Col.Docs.* 12:430; Beeckman to Stuyvesant, Altena, June 6, 1663, ibid., p. 431; Susquehannock chief Wastahandow, Sept. 27, 1663, *Md.Arch.* 1:471–72.

50. Jennings, *Invasion*, pp. 286–87; New Netherland council minutes, March 23, 1664, *N.Y.Col.Docs.* 13:363–64; court minutes of Fort Orange, July 12, 1664, ibid., p. 389; Stuyvesant to Holland directors, Aug. 4, 1644, ibid., p. 390; Van Rensselaer to Van Cortlandt, July 17, 1664, *Correspondence of Jeremias Van Rensselaer*, p. 356.

51. Trelease, Indian Affairs, pp. 129–30; Gordon Day, "The Identity of the Sokokis," *Ethnohistory* 12:3 (summer, 1965), p. 243.

52. Jerome Lalemant, Aug. 30, 1664, *Jesuit Relations* 49:147–49; John Romeyn Brodhead, *History of the State of New York*, 2 vols. (New York: Harper and Brothers, 1853–1871), 1:710.

53. *The Livingston Indian Records, 1666–1723*, ed. Lawrence H. Leder, entire issue of *Pennsylvania History* 23:1 (Jan., 1956), also published separately as a book (Gettysburg, Pa.: Pennsylvania Historical Association, 1956), pp. 39–40. (Paging identical in both forms.)

support, continued to fight, and the Susquehannocks were egged on anew by the Maryland English.

In 1664 an Oneida party struck at allies of the Susquehannocks living on Chesapeake Bay. The always-choleric aristocrats of Maryland were outraged, but the Susquehannocks were battle weary. A trader who had their confidence informed the colony's government that the Susquehannocks "would willingly Imbrace a peace if Obteyned, but are unwilling (through height of Spirit) to sue for itt." He besought Governor Charles Calvert to authorize the negotiation of a general peace, "which by every one, wee thinke, is much required and most earnestly desired." Calvert's answer was a redundant declaration of war, specifically against the Oneidas, who, as members of the Five Nations, were already among Maryland's formally declared, if not very well understood, enemies.[54]

Duke of York's conquest of New Netherland

While tribes and colonies fought and intrigued, commercial and dynastic struggles took a new turn in Europe. Charles II was restored to the English throne in 1660, and Louis XIV assumed personal government of France in 1661. Repercussions from these events transformed the world of the tribes.

In 1664 Charles II "granted" all of New Netherland to his brother James, duke of York. James commissioned a small fleet of three vessels, which cowed New Amsterdam into capitulation on August 27, 1664, by a simple show of force, and won Fort Orange the same way in September. On the first of October, Dutch Fort Amstel on Delaware Bay surrendered.[55] Just as the demise of New Sweden had transformed backwoods diplomacy, so the conquest of New Netherland now restricted even more sharply the number of genuine choices possible for the Indians. Reduced by disease, beaten in battle, and now deprived of the fundamental prop for their whole system of external politics, the Mohawks immediately sued the English conquerors for peace. So far were they from presiding over multitudes of fear-ridden subjects that when Englishmen took command at Fort Orange, newly renamed Albany, the Mohawks earnestly desired the newcomers to mediate peace with their near neighbors, "the Nations down the [Hudson] River," whom they had been attempting to bully into submission at least since 1645.[56]

54. Mathews to Calvert, June 9, 1664, Md.Arch. 3:501; Stockett, Gouldsmith, and Wright to Calvert, June 7, 1664, Md.Arch. 3:498–99; council minutes, June 27, 1664, Md.Arch. 3:502.
55. Hazard, Annals. of Pa., pp. 356–68; Brodhead, History 1:743–44.
56. Anonymous letter, Quebec, Sept. 22, 1664, Jesuit Relations 49:149–53; Indian conference, Albany, Sept. 25, 1664, N.Y.Col.Docs. 3:67–68; Nicolls to Boston General Court, July 30, 1669, ibid., p. 172.

French destruction of Mohawk towns

1664 was also the year when Louis XIV decided on a final solution to Canada's Iroquois problem. He sent the famous Carignan regiment of troops under the capable command of the veteran Marquis de Tracy with instructions "to carry war even to their firesides in order totally to exterminate them."[57] Such orders were more easily given than executed. When he arrived on the scene, de Tracy determined that his mission would be sufficiently fulfilled by an object lesson. The news of the arrival of his troops was enough in itself to motivate the four western nations of the Iroquois to send embassies to Quebec where they fearfully signed a treaty, December 13, 1665, requesting two Jesuit missionaries to be sent among them, supplicating peace and protection, offering to accept French families amongst themselves, and agreeing to send "two of the principal Iroquois families" from each of the four western nations to live among the French of Montreal, Quebec, and Three Rivers.[58]

The Mohawks held off, and the French found their nonparticipation "inexcusable," but the Mohawks were no less worried than the other nations about DeTracy's troops. They did offer an excuse of sorts for procrastinating by resorting to a fine point of protocol. Knowing very well that the French had arrived, and therefore would not accept their relayed plea of ignorance, their point was that they had not been notified *officially* by a French messenger. The Mohawks were sticklers for ritual and equally demanding that formal respect be paid to their dignity. In this instance, at least, the four western nations were ready enough to abandon them to French wrath. Their treaty stipulated that the Mohawks were to be excluded from its coverage.[59]

The treaty signed, de Tracy sent a party of troops on snowshoes to campaign against the Mohawks. Suffering greatly from the rigors of a harsh winter and a Mohawk ambush, the exhausted French gave up after arriving only twenty leagues from the Mohawk villages. They excused their return on the grounds that they had sufficiently terrorized the Mohawks by coming so close.[60] It would seem that this invasion was regarded by the Mohawks as official enough notice of the French presence. In May they sent a delegation to include their nation under the provisions of the treaty formerly made by the other four nations.[61] The

57. Instructions to M. Talon, March 27, 1665, *N.Y.Col.Docs.* 9:25.
58. Treaty minutes, Dec. 13, 1665, *N.Y.Col.Docs.* 3:121–25.
59. Ibid., p. 124.
60. French relation for the years 1655, 1666, in *Doc.Hist.N.Y.* 1:65–67; English relation, ibid., 1:71–74. The French relation discreetly omits mention of the Mohawk ambush.
61. Treaty text, July 12, 1666, in *N.Y.Col.Docs.* 3:126–27. This text takes pains to include mention of the preceding French campaign against the Mohawks, blaming its lack of success

French accepted their subscription, but de Tracy was not satisfied. He found evidence of "treachery," and resolved to lead a punishing expedition himself. I wonder. The available records have more rhetoric than evidence about that treachery. It seems credible that de Tracy simply decided that he had not done enough to satisfy Louis XIV by merely making treaties; his orders were to exterminate the Iroquois, and the record ought to show that he had at least done something toward that end.[62] Whatever his motive, he marched.

In October 1666, the aged marquis led his troops into the Mohawk country, which they found prudently vacated of occupants. The French burned and destroyed villages and crops and marched home again.[63] It was indeed an object lesson to all the Iroquois, though they may not have drawn the desired conclusion from it. The Mohawks had thought they were protected by a treaty with the French. Whatever the French may have thought about Mohawk treachery, de Tracy's disregard for that treaty made the Mohawks quite certain that they could not trust French commitments. Other parties were upset also by de Tracy's campaign: newly arrived Englishmen, who had their own treaty with the Mohawks and claimed the Mohawks as "dependents," were not happy to hear that de Tracy had erected crosses in the Mohawk villages as a sign that they and all the Mohawk territory had been "conquered from the Iroquois in the name of the King."[64]

New York inherits New Netherland's roles

It was a turbulent and violent era, and England's conquest of New Netherland did little to pacify the region. It would seem to have been a time for great rejoicing in England's older colonies—Maryland, Connecticut, and Massachusetts Bay—that had been harassed by the Five Nations; now, surely, they would be able to expand under the crown's protection to acquire the extra territories for which they had schemed and struggled

on "the mistake of their [Indian] guides." Was this just an alibi, or did those Indians mistake on purpose?

62. A summary by Intendant Talon of reasons for warring on the Mohawks was made just before Tracy marched. It is a hardnosed evaluation of the advantages to be gained by war and climaxes with the following: "the success of the expedition against the Mohawks opens the door for the seizure of Orange [i.e., Albany]." Propositions, Sept. 1, 1666, in *N.Y.Col.Docs.* 9:52–54, quote at p. 53.

63. *Doc.Hist.N.Y.* 1:68–71.

64. Act of Possession, Oct. 17, 1666, *Doc.Hist.N.Y.* 1:77–78. Col. Nicolls to Capt. John Baker, Jan. 11, 1667, in *N.Y.Col.Docs.* 3:148. The Mohawks would have every right to suspect French intentions. On Oct. 27, 1667, Intendant Talon coolly consulted Minister Colbert as to whether "a second invasion be made on those of the Lower Nation [the Mohawks], notwithstanding the treaty concluded with them." *N.Y.Col.Docs.* 9:60.

so long in former New Netherland. To make such assumptions, however, would be to misunderstand relationships between the crown and its colonies. Neither king Charles nor duke James undertook the reduction of New Netherland just to strew benevolence over the provinces. Royal commissioners sailed with York's fleet, and they had bad news for the schemers in the colonies. They had been instructed that "the reduction of the place being at his Majesties expense, you have commands to keep possession thereof for his Majesties own behoofe and right."[65] It is hardly surprising, under the circumstances, that Puritans and Marylanders greeted New Netherland's conquest with less than joy. The conquest had not eliminated their powerful competitor so much as it had substituted a still greater power in the same role. Sovereignty changed, but the functions and roles of New Netherland continued to be performed by New York, albeit rather awkwardly at first. New York also inherited the plots by the older colonies against its territorial integrity.

Naturally such schemes had to be covert, and in the circumstances of the time the agencies for their fulfilment had to be Indian. Intertribal hostilities were prerequisite, for peaceful tribes implied stable boundaries. Therefore, when New York's first governor, Richard Nicolls, tried to get peace for the Mohawks with Maryland, Governor Calvert ignored him.[66] When Nicolls's successor tried to enlist the support of Connecticut's Governor John Winthrop, Jr., for pacification of the Indian territory straddling their claimed boundaries, Winthrop politely led him down a trail of paper leading nowhere.[67] Both Calvert and Winthrop planned to expand at New York's expense through conquests and the rights of conquests of Indian surrogates.

Iroquois on the defensive

It seems that Nicolls never learned to recognize the signs of clandestine manipulation of the tribes. In his innocence he was unable to prevent instigation of Indian disruption even within his own province. The Hudson Valley Mahicans got support from New England to renew their long hostilities with the Mohawks,[68] and Maryland continued to support the Susquehannocks against the other Iroquois. Nicolls could not be blamed for all the tumults. He surely could not help it that England renewed war

65. Instructions to Sir Robert Carr, Sept. 3, 1664, *N.Y.Col.Docs.* 12:457–58.
66. Nicolls to Gen. Court at Boston, July 30, 1668, *N.Y.Col.Docs.* 3:172.
67. Lovelace's letters, July 25, 1669, Jan. 24, 1670, *Minutes of the Executive Council of the Province of New York*, ed. Victor Hugo Paltsits, 2 vols. (Albany: State of New York, 1910), 1:377–83.
68. Treaty minutes, April 24, 1677, *Livingston Indian Records*, pp. 39–40.

against the Netherlands or that France joined the Dutch in 1666 or that French enmity to England exacerbated Canadian enmity to the Five Nations. But New York's "protection" became hard to find in Iroquoia when de Tracy burned the Mohawk villages and food supply, and when the Susquehannocks, armed and urged by Maryland, destroyed an Onondaga army. Meanwhile the Mahicans "infested the roads" of the Five Nations so successfully that an Onondaga sachem pleaded with the French to call them off.[69] A Jesuit father reported that the Oneidas were continually alarmed in their villages by both Mahicans and Susquehannocks, and "a panic of terror" swept over one Cayuga village on the mere false rumor that a Susquehannock army was approaching.[70]

Violence begot more violence. The badly beaten Onondagas made revenge an obsession so intense that when a Susquehannock sachem brought proposals of peace to the Cayugas in 1670 the Onondagas instigated his murder.[71] It seemed to be a time exemplifying Thomas Hobbes's "war of all against all," but it was no Hobbesian "state of nature." In the last analysis the Indians remained dependent on European trade goods, and whenever the Europeans were able to submerge strife amongst themselves, they had it within their power to stop Indian warfare. The conflicts were no longer like the Iroquoian beaver wars of the mid-century. In those the Europeans had been backers of Indians fighting Indian wars for Indian goals. But lack of alternatives to retaliatory wars for enforcing intertribal order had subsequently made the tribes vulnerable to outside manipulation, and European firearms had changed from an offensive advantage to a defensive necessity. In 1670 a Susquehannock chief dinned this into the heads of some stubborn Delawares "and showed them, here live Christians and there live Christians; declaring to them that as they were surrounded by Christians, if they went to war, where would they get powder and ball?"[72]

There came at last a brief moment on the continent of North America when the occupying great powers could come to an understanding because France had switched sides in Europe. In 1670 Louis XIV and Charles II made a secret personal treaty of alliance, and in 1672 France and England joined in open war against the Netherlands. In the same year Canada and New York suppressed the feud between the Mohawks and the Mahicans. When the Mahicans proposed an expedition against the Mohawks, the French rejected it. The Mohawks heard of the proposal and ran to Albany.

69. Francois Le Mercier, Quebec, Aug. 20, 1668, *Jesuit Relations* 51:243; ltr., July 26, 1664, *Correspondence of Jeremias Van Rensselaer*, p. 358. "Nearly all" the Onondaga braves "perished in the war." Fremin to le Mercier, Aug. 20, 1669, *Jesuit Relations* 54:111.

70. Relation of 1668–69, *Jesuit Relations* 52:147, 175–77.

71. Ltr. of de Carrheil, June 1670, *Jesuit Relations* 54:75.

72. Examination of Indians about a murder, Oct. 6, 1670, in *Minutes of the Executive Council of N.Y.*, ed. Paltsits, 2:502.

"We have accepted the peace which has been made by you people," they said. "Speak with the Mahikanders so that they come and do as we do." Albany's magistrates promised to "take care that the peace will remain steadfast" and to "force the Mahikanders to come here," continuing with the promise of explicit sanctions: "if they come to slay one of you, then they will see that they will have to deal with us, and we will revenge it." Peace ensued. It was so reliable a peace that Mohawks could afford to get roaring drunk in Albany and stagger back home along paths formerly overrun by Mahican bushwhackers. On the French side, missionary Father Lamberville thought it was a "baleful peace" that created such opportunities for continued drunkenness, but Governor Frontenac enforced it. So it came about that when France and England leagued together, their dependent Indian allies were pacified immediately.[73]

The alliance between Stuart and Bourbon was not matched by amity between Stuart and Calvert. Intermittent and desultory war continued between the Duke of York's Five Nations and Lord Baltimore's Susquehannocks, to the apparent disadvantage of the Iroquois. In 1672 a war party of Senecas and Cayugas was routed by equal numbers of Susquehannock adolescents. In 1673 the Iroquois appealed for help from their new friends in Canada; they "earnestly exhorted" governor Frontenac to assist them against the Susquehannocks because "it would be a shame for him to allow his children to be crushed, as they saw themselves about to be . . . they not having the means of going to attack [the Susquehannocks] in their fort, which was very strong, nor even of defending themselves if the others came to attack them in their villages." (It looks as though Maryland was continuing to supply munitions to the Susquehannocks while New York was denying arms to the Five Nations.) Frontenac made no commitment to gratify his "children," and the odds are long that he did not arm them covertly: first, because it was not a time for the French to be meddling with Indian conflicts deep within English territory; second, because Frontenac's government was suffering from an acute shortage of munitions for its own defense, as he reported to France in November 1674.[74]

This is a significant date. According to old histories, the Susquehannocks were supposed to have been badly beaten by the Iroquois sometime between 1672 and 1675 although no one has ever been able to identify the presumed battle. It may be said quite confidently that the reason the battle cannot be located is that it did not take place.[75] We have seen what shape

73. Treaty minutes, July 23, 1672, *Livingston Indian Records*, pp. 35–37; Jean de Lamberville, Relation of 1672–73, *Jesuit Relations* 57:81.
74. Pierre Raffeix, June 1672, *Jesuit Relations* 56:55–57; Frontenac's journal, July 17–18, 1673, *N.Y.Col.Docs.* 9:108, 110–11; Frontenac to Colbert, Nov. 14, 1674, ibid., pp. 116–17.
75. Hunt should be credited with having understood this. *Wars of the Iroquois*, p. 143.

the Iroquois were in until 1672. The French records make it clear that the Five Nations could not possibly have launched a successful attack before July 1673 when they met with Frontenac; and they could not have obtained any considerable supply of arms from the French thereafter through November 1674. Even if we suspect Frontenac of wanting to arm the Iroquois secretly—a most unlikely supposition—he could not have done so through the winter of 1674–1675 because of the winter freeze on the St. Lawrence. It was impossible for Frontenac's appeal for an arms shipment from France to be answered before the spring thaw. As for other sources of supply, New Englanders would sooner have armed the Mahicans to reopen attacks on the Iroquois than to have supplied the Iroquois, and if New York had been willing to open its armory the Iroquois would not have had to appeal to Frontenac. There was no great defeat of the Susquehannocks because, as the Iroquois said themselves, they had not the means to fight. It may also be considered how silent they were at the time about any such occurrence. Certainly, had it taken place, they would have bragged about it from Maryland to Maine. In fact, however, they did not think to claim a victory until many years later when circumstances suggested its utility in certain negotiations.

Maryland's assaults on Delaware

The Susquehannocks did abandon their stockaded village to retire into Maryland, but this was by Maryland's desire rather than because of a Five Nations victory. To see how that came about, we must turn once more to Maryland's policies. Although that colony's expansion had been frustrated for a while after York's conquest of New Netherland, postponement did not signify abandonment. In 1672 Lord Baltimore concluded that the time was ripe to begin anew. He decreed the creation of "Worcester County, Maryland," and proclaimed boundaries for it including a settlement called the Whorekills on the west shore of Delaware Bay near its mouth—an area previously taken into the jurisdiction of New York. Having thus laid his legal claim, Baltimore commissioned one Thomas Jones as captain and commander in chief of the newly proclaimed county, with instructions to suppress all "mutinies, Insurrections, and Rebellions whatsoever," which meant the officers and supporters of New York. Jones promptly took a troop of thirty horsemen to raid the Whorekills, picking up some plunder for himself and settling some personal scores.[76] New York's bumbling

76. Whorekills inhabitants' affidavits, May 16, 1683, *Pa. Mag. of Hist. and Biog.* 74 (1950), p. 477; Elizabeth Merritt, Introduction, *Md. Arch.* 45:xxiv–xxviii; session of provincial court, Dec. 11, 1672, ibid., pp. 50–55; council minutes, April 20, 1672, *Md. Arch.* 5:106–7; proclamation of Worcester Co., June 19, 1672, ibid., pp. 108–9; commissions, June 20, 1672, ibid., pp. 109–11.

Governor Francis Lovelace was incredulous and then apoplectic at the news, but Baltimore had timed the raid with luck because England and the Netherlands were at war again.[77] While Lovelace fumed, a Dutch fleet descended upon him and reconquered all of former New Netherland, including Delaware Bay. Stripped of power, Lovelace could not punish Baltimore.

However, Baltimore wanted the Whorekills for himself, not for the Dutch, and he struck again in December 1673. He sent forty troopers this time—a large force for that time and place. Under the command of Captain Thomas Howell they took the place by a simple show of force. Howell entertained himself by torturing a merchant into confessing the location of his peltry hoard and by committing sundry other "barbarous cruelties." On Christmas Eve he summoned all the Whorekills inhabitants together, took their arms from them, and informed them of his instructions from Baltimore to destroy everything on fifteen minutes' notice—"that he must not Leave one stick standing." His men set fire to the place, standing guard to prevent anyone from rescuing even a single possession. The bewildered people—their boats and horses taken away as well as their arms and food, and with some of their women pregnant—stood aghast. Survivors recalled that "the Indians that Lived here about wept when they saw the spoil that the Inhabitants had suffered by their owne native country men," and it appears that those supposedly menacing Indians kept the victims alive till help could be summoned from Manhattan.[78] When news of the attack finally reached Governor General Colve, the new chief of the revived New Netherland, he ordered immediate "means of support" to be given to the victims, English as well as Dutch. In his indignation he ordered further "proper arrangements" to prevent "such cruel tyranny" thereafter, and he put the inhabitants of Delaware Bay into a state of military emergency.[79]

Now it was the turn of the Lord Baltimore's people to feel fear. The Dutch of Manhattan were far away, and the Dutch of Delaware Bay were weak; but, given some prodding and arms, the Indian allies of the Dutch might become terrible indeed, and the Indians were in a highly volatile state. Continual seizure by Virginians and Marylanders of Indian lands had led some of the Delaware sachems to contemplate preventive war to hold their own at Delaware Bay. A couple of Englishmen had been killed by the Indians. Before the Dutch reconquest, the English had decided to wage a conquest of the Delawares in the spring of 1673, and they had been making plans for it when the Dutch overthrew their government.

77. See the docs. in *Minutes of Exec. Council of N.Y.*, ed. Paltsits, 2:669–83, esp. Lovelace to Philip Calvert, Aug. 12, 1672, and Lovelace to Carr, Oct. 7, 1672, pp. 678–79, 680–82.
78. Leon de Valinger, Jr., "The Burning of the Whorekill, 1673," *Pa. Mag. of Hist. and Biog.* 74 (1950), pp. 473–87; Howell's commission, Oct. 1, 1673, *Md.Arch.* 15:27–29.
79. Proclamation, Jan. 14, 1674, *N.Y.Col.Docs.* 12:511.

One suggestion that had been made by the Bay Englishmen to their distant governor in New York is worth noting. If possible, they had asked, fifty or sixty "North Indyans"—that is, Iroquois—should be hired, "who will doe more than 200 men in such a warr." Such notions could not well have escaped the attention of the Marylanders, who had many informants at Delaware Bay; and certainly, if the English at the Delaware might have contemplated bringing in Iroquois to attack other Indians, there could be small reason to doubt the possibility that the new Dutch government might bring them in to attack the Maryland English with whom both the Iroquois and the Dutch were formally at war.[80]

We have to distinguish between the facts of record and the facts as they appeared to the people of that time. No record that I have seen shows, and no recorded event suggests, that the Dutch did actually arm and instigate the Five Nations in this situation. But let us see how it looked to contemporaries. In 1673 there was an Indian population around the bays that had become embittered against the English. There was Dutch Governor Colve at Manhattan, under strong provocation, proclaiming defensive measures at Delaware Bay. Governor Colve was allied by treaty to the Five Nations Indians and presumably could supply them with weapons. The use of Indians for covert warfare had long been accepted as one of the facts of colonial life, and Maryland had rejected former overtures by the Iroquois for peace. It seems reasonable to suppose that Lord Baltimore's people began to be nervous about the Iroquois. A pair of dates are on the record: in January 1674 Governor Colve proclaimed his state of emergency, and on the first day of June 1674 the Maryland Assembly voted unanimously that it was "necessarie that a Peace be Concluded" with the Iroquois.[81]

Having made that decision, the Assembly had to face up to its implications. Rather, the Lower House of the Assembly had to be manipulated by the Upper House to accept the implications—more particularly, the financial implications. Maryland's executive branch of government consisted of a governor and council. In the legislative process the executive council's members sat as an upper house to dominate the elective lower house. As council, the upper house was always privy to executive plans and decisions that were disclosed to the lower house at discretion and with less than total candor. Thus after the lower house had safely voted to seek peace with the Iroquois, the upper house released some previously undisclosed information. Its process of disclosure was to initiate sequel legislation to empower the governor and council to make and finance war even outside the provincial boundaries "forasmuch as that Peace [with the Iroquois] may bring a Warre with the Sasquehannoughs."[82]

80. Various documents, *Minutes of Exec. Council of N.Y.* 2:501, 508, 594, 602–3.
81. Proclamation, *N.Y.Col.Docs.* 12:511; resolution, *Md.Arch.* 2:377.
82. Minutes, June 1, 1674, *Md.Arch.* 2:378.

This was a jolt. Two weeks dragged on while the lower house withheld its response. Final agreement, when it came, included reference to "credible Informations of the many murthers and Outrages committed upon the persons and Estates of divers of the good People of this Province in Baltemore County by the Susquehanna Indians *and other their Confederate Indians by them countenanced and protected contrary to the Articles of Peace.*" No bill of particulars accompanied the accusation. Curiously the charge was advanced not so much to justify punishing the Susquehannocks as to justify making peace with the Iroquois. It was worded neatly for Baltimore's maximum flexibility in defense or offense, for its mention of the Susquehannocks' "Confederate Indians" meant the Delawares, and an expedition against the Delawares would be a march on Delaware Bay with the prospect of rights of conquest claims on the entire bay region. Such a march would indeed have brought on the possibility of war with the Delawares' Susquehannock allies. Having made its findings so conveniently, the assembly voted a supply for the expenses of either peace or war.[83]

Maryland "invites" the Susquehannocks to the Potomac

A hiatus ensues in the records that must be filled by inference from subsequent events. Maryland's Governor Calvert held a conference with the Indians "at Mattapanie"; no further information about it is given. Afterward, in February 1675 the Susquehannocks—all of them—showed up at St. Mary's in Maryland, "and being asked their Business they desired to know what part of the Province Should be allotted for them to live upon." The language of the record is startlingly abrupt. Indians were normally more roundabout and deferential in negotiations, especially when asking for favors. And these were the Susquehannocks, who supposedly had been committing murders and outrages against Maryland's people. Even more strangely, the upper house formally asked the lower house's opinion about what to do with the Indians, and the lower house raised no hint of seizing and punishing these presumed murderers who had placed themselves so artlessly in the hands of the government. Rather confusedly the lower house suggested sending the Indians to "a Place above the falls of Potomack. There being time enough . . . to clear Ground enough to Plant Corn this year which is the only thing they Seem to desire to live among the Neighbour Indians for." The Susquehannocks, "after Some tedious Debate," agreed to go to the junction of a creek with the Potomac just south of present-day Washington, D.C., where they took up residence in an abandoned Piscatawa stockaded village.[84]

83. Act, June 16, 1674, *Md.Arch.* 2:462–63. Italics added.
84. Minutes, Feb. 19, 1675, *Md.Arch.* 2:428–30. No date is given for the Mattapanie conference. I have been unable to find other references to it.

This is the retirement of the Susquehannocks that has been variously explained as the consequence of defeat or pressure by the Iroquois. Such explanations rest solely on extrapolation and imagination; there is not a scintilla of evidence in any contemporary document of a major battle with the Iroquois at this time, nor is there any contemporary signal of increased Iroquois strength from the miserable state the Five Nations had confessed to Frontenac in 1673. Instead of noting a rise in hostilities between the Iroquois and the Susquehannocks, Maryland's lower house expressed suspicions of the two peoples having "private Correspondence together." The enigma is solved for us by a remark of William Penn in a retrospective debate in 1684 with Lord Baltimore's nephew and acting governor, George Talbot. Penn charged that the Susquehannocks had been "betrayed out of their Lives by Inviteing them downe among the English," and Talbot, who recorded the dialogue, put the remark down without challenge.[85] This seems to be the explanation for the mysterious meeting of Charles Calvert with the Susquehannocks "at Mattapanie" before the Indians came into Maryland. It appears that Calvert gave the Susquehannocks an ultimatum to withdraw from their home fort and retire into Maryland. Failure to comply would be interpreted as grounds for war. By thus forcing the Susquehannocks to retire into Maryland, Calvert could clear the way to make peace with the Iroquois. With the Iroquois nullified and the Susquehannocks under control, he would be able to renew his effort to conquer Delaware Bay.[86]

But—what embarrassment!—in November 1674 an English fleet once again took over New Netherland in consequence of a new peace settled between the Dutch and the English in Europe, and once again both the Iroquois Indians and the Delaware Bay came into the government of the Duke of York. By the time the Susquehannocks had responded in February 1675 to their "invitation" to reside in Maryland, the reason for moving them there had ceased to exist.[87] Now there was nothing for Maryland to

85. George Talbot, "Report of a conference between Coll. Talbot and William Penn," 1684, *Maryland Historical Magazine* 3 (1908), p. 25. Penn's remark is confirmed by a paper of Charles Calvert, May 15, 1682. Calvert, then third Lord Baltimore, warned two treaty negotiators not to "abandon our ffriend Indians" for fear of causing them to "break the peace in reveinge of our breach of Articles and Deserting them, as wee see the small remnant of the Susquehannohs have done." Instructions to Henry Coursey and Philemon Lloyd, May 15, 1682, *Md.Arch.* 17:98.

86. The confused and distorted rumors of Baltimore's Protestant opposition were sent to England as a "Complaint from Heaven with a Hue and crye," 1676. *Md.Arch.* 5:134. The document has drawn some historical attention, but its only value is as evidence of popular misinformation.

87. The relevant events on record are as follows: Jan. 14, 1674, Proclamation by Dutch governor Colve of military preparation in Delaware Bay; June 1, 1674, Maryland Assembly resolves on necessity of peace with the Iroquois. June 16, 1674, Maryland Assembly enacts support for expenses of peace or war. Date unknown, Baltimore, at Mattapanie, invites Susquehannocks into Maryland. Nov. 3, 1674, Governor Andros writes to Governor of

do except go through the comedy of assigning a place in the province for the Susquehannocks to live, and so it came about that the lower house found itself so abruptly and confusingly consulted.

An illusion of peace

Peace was in the air. The agitating presence of the Swedes and Dutch was gone. The Duke of York's energetic new governor, Edmund Andros, was determined to stabilize a turbulent situation. In the north he pacified the Mohawks and Mahicans with renewed English protection for them both.[88] He interceded for the Mohawks with the French "not to molest them without Cause and forthwith to release any Hostages," and he affirmed that he would never permit "the Prosecution of any Indyans under the Proteccon of this Government."[89] On Delaware Bay he won the friendship of the Delaware sachems so that they afterward became his agents of mediation with other Indians—a status implying no subordination of the Delawares to other tribes.[90]

The Susquehannocks were not immune to the mood of the moment, and their susceptibility to peace overtures apparently was made known to the Iroquois. In April 1675, Governor Andros in New York received word that the Mohawks were "ready to deliver" seventeen Susquehannock prisoners, and in June he received and aided a neutral sachem traveling as mediator from the Mohawks to the Susquehannocks.[91] Andros noted that the Iroquois nations were divided: the farther Iroquois were "wholly adverse" to a peace, but the Mohawks hoped that the Susquehannocks might even be won to peaceful amalgamation with them.[92]

Once more, chance intervened. Circumstances utterly beyond the control of New York or New York's allies caused nearly simultaneous eruptions in New England on the one side and Virginia and Maryland on the other. This book's predecessor volume has shown how Andros intervened in New England and forged the Covenant Chain in the crucible of King

Maryland about the English resumption of administration of New York "and dependencies." Andros mentions it is his first opportunity to write. *N.Y.Col.Docs.* 12:513–14.

88. Andros's "Short account," ca. 1678, *N.Y.Col.Docs.* 3:254; *Livingston Indian Records*, Feb. 14, 1675, pp. 37–38.

89. Council minutes, April 16, 1675, *N.Y.Col.Docs.* 13:483.

90. Treaty minutes, May 13, 1675, *N.Y.Col.Docs.* 12:523–24; Andros to Cantwell, Dec. 10, 1675, ibid., p. 542; Logan Papers, Records of the Court at Upland, mss., March 13, 1677, p. 16, Hist. Soc. of Pa.

91. Interview minutes, April 20, 1675, New York Colonial Mss., vol. 24, in *Third Annual Report of the State Historian of the State of New York, 1897*, ed. Hugh Hastings (New York: Wynkoop Hallenbeck Crawford Co., 1898), p. 302; Indian visit, June 28, 1675, ibid., pp. 345–46.

92. Andros to gov. of Md., Oct. 1, 1675, *N.Y.Col.Docs.* 13:491.

Philip's rising, thereby guaranteeing the integrity of New York's eastern boundary.[93] With exquisitely attuned strategy, he intervened in the southern conflicts also, picking out of them more links for his Covenant Chain and outmaneuvering Maryland's efforts to seize the Delaware Bay.

A new era was about to begin. Under Andros's protection and supervision, the Iroquois would renew their strength and develop more sophisticated political techniques. But the day had passed when they could dream of independent empire with any real hope of achieving it. The dream died hard, and it had yet to be put to the test of a showdown with New France, but the Iroquois were never again to launch a successful war on their own initiative. They did not stop fighting, but, despite all the fantasies about stupendous feats of war, they did not win. Their victories, when those transpired, were accomplished by diplomacy and maneuver, which meant that in order to gain their own goals they had to make themselves useful to greater powers.

93. Jennings, *Invasion*, ch. 17, 18.

Part Two ❧ *WARRIORS*

Chapter 8 ✑ A SILVER ENGLISH CHAIN

Brethren: You are come here to this Prefixed Place [Albany] which is by the Christians appointed to be the house of Treatty for all Publique Bussinesse with us the Five Nations, and doe Return you many thanks for your Renovacon of the Covenant chain which is not of Yron now as it was formerly, but of Pure Silver, in which chain are Included all there Majesties Subjects from the Sinnekes Countrey quite to the Eastward as farr as any Christian Subjects of our great king lives and from thence Southward all along New England quite to Virginia.

> Mohawk Chief Sachem Tahaiadoris, September 23, 1689

Brethren of the five Nations, I will begin upon a thing of a long standing, our first Brothership. . . . I found out some of the old Writings of our Forefathers which was thought to have been lost, and in this old valuable Record I find, that our first Friendship Commenced at the Arrival of the first great Canoe or Vessel at Albany, at which you were much surprized but finding what it contained pleased you so much, being Things for your Purpose . . . you all Resolved to take the greatest care of that Vessel that nothing should hurt her Whereupon it was agreed to tye her fast with a great Rope to one of the largest Nut Trees on the Bank of the River. But on further Consideration in a fuller meeting it was thought safest, Fearing the Wind should blow down that Tree, to make a long Rope and tye her fast at Onondaga which was accordingly done and the Rope put under your feet That if anything hurt or touched said Vessel by the shaking of the Rope you might know it, and then agreed to rise all as one and see what the Matter was and whoever hurt the Vessel was to suffer. After this was agreed on and done you made an offer to the Governour to enter into a Band of Friendship with him and his People which he was so pleased at that he told you he would find a strong Silver Chain which would never break, slip, or Rust to bind you and him forever in Brothership together, and that your Warriours and ours should be as one Heart, One Head, one Blood &ca.

> Sir William Johnson to the Six Nations
> Onondaga, April 25, 1748

Virginia and Maryland attack the Susquehannocks

In the same month of July 1675 that the Second Puritan Conquest began, similarly violent events were in the making in Virginia. A wealthy planter got into a dispute with some Doeg Indians over money matters. The argument turned violent, some of the Indians were killed, and their tribesmen retaliated by killing an English herdsman employed by the planter. The local militia mobilized and pursued the Doegs. As usual in

such situations, the militia paid little attention to tribal affiliations or juris-
dictional lines. Crossing into Maryland, they killed not only Doegs but
Susquehannocks as well. Instead of overawing the Indians, this indiscrim-
inate vengeance stirred up the hitherto friendly Susquehannocks, and soon
there were Indian raids on outlying settlements of both Virginia and
Maryland.

Virginia mobilized once again, this time with a "request" for assistance
from Maryland. Such a request mandated its answer because conquest of
Indians on Maryland's territory might possibly be converted into a rights-
of-conquest claim on that territory, and the two colonies' history of
boundary disputes was far from moot. Maryland responded with 250
troops, and the combined militias went in pursuit of the Susquehannocks.[1]

The thousand militiamen found a hundred warriors and their families
at the junction of Piscataway Creek and the Potomac River in the stockaded village that Maryland's assembly had appointed as their home. Even
at ten-to-one odds, the Susquehannocks' reputation inspired a certain discretion in the English, who decided to lay siege instead of storming. The
Indian chiefs were twice called out to parley. On their second appearance,
five were seized in violation of their safe conduct and put to death on the
orders of Maryland's Captain Truman, urged or abetted by Virginia's
Colonel John Washington. The atrocity has not been condoned in either
Virginia or Maryland, but considerable energy has been expended in each
place to prove that primary responsibility lay in the other. It is only fair
to add that Maryland's assembly tried and convicted Captain Truman for
his part in the affair, although he seems never to have suffered any actual
penalty except a security bond. Washington was not inconvenienced in
any such way.[2]

The besieged Susquehannocks, despite the overwhelming odds against
them and the loss of their chiefs, held out for six more weeks. Then, one
dark night, they all walked silently through the English camp, taking toll
of ten sleepers on the way, after which they launched a fury of revenge
on the isolated cabins of the backwoods. In the wake of these events,

1. Except where otherwise noted, the Virginia-Susquehannock episodes rely on Wilcomb
E. Washburn, *The Governor and the Rebel: A History of Bacon's Rebellion in Virginia* (Chapel Hill:
University of North Carolina Press, 1960), through which I was guided to the primary
sources. This reference is to pp. 20–22. As Washburn has aroused some hostile critics, it
may be well to mention that I spent a day at Longleat House spot checking his Coventry
Papers manuscript sources and found no fault.

2. Ibid., pp. 22–23. Minutes and depositions in Truman's case, *Md.Arch.* 2;481–83, 485-
86, 494, 500–501, 504, 511–13. Baltimore lifted Trueman's bond later, saying, "I have no
desire that the said Trueman should imagine I have the least malice or prejudice to his person
. . . what I formerly did order was only occasioned by the great exigency of affaires att that
tyme." Baltimore to Notley, Aug. 10, 1678, *Md.Arch.* 15:182–83.

Virginia's governor Berkeley was overthrown by a demagogue named Nathaniel Bacon. After the fashion of demagogues, Bacon promised to do the impossible with the intention of doing the unmentionable. He took a troop of volunteers on a campaign ostensibly to exterminate the Susquehannocks. On finding the Susquehannocks, they avoided the risk of fighting those fierce warriors; instead they massacred friendly Occaneechees, who were unfortunate enough to be possessed of a quantity of valuable peltry.[3]

Bacon solved the awkward legal problems raised by his insurrection by dying of natural causes in 1676. The historical problems had just begun. On the one side, the sordid story of avarice, treachery, and slaughter was converted through the mystiques of the frontier and racism into a heroic saga of primitive democracy aborning. Bacon—a criminal aristocrat living in enforced exile—was apotheosized into a sort of Siegfried of the settlers. On the other side, the responsibility for attacking and dispersing the Susquehannocks was displaced from the English colonials to the Iroquois, and it became yet another instructive example of the ferocity of savages in general and the Iroquois in particular.

How that myth was created can best be explained by telling what happened to the Susquehannocks after they broke out of their besieged stockade in Maryland. The narrative depends on English documents, and it must therefore begin, as they did, by losing the Susquehannocks in the backwoods whence they emerged only to take sudden vengeance and vanish again.

Thus, by January 1676, the Wampanoags and Narragansetts in New England and the Susquehannocks in the Chesapeake region had both been forced into enmity by colonial attacks upon them; both had retaliated. For the representatives of royal authority, the coincidence raised a frightful danger.[4] Virginia's Governor Berkeley and New York's Governor Andros, with a breadth of vision denied to bellicose colonial contemporaries, looked beyond their immediate jurisdictions to the horrible prospect of a universal rising of the tribes against all Englishmen.[5] Berkeley's efforts to prevent so great a disaster were negated by Bacon's rebellion. Andros, however, preserved his freedom of action.

3. "A Discription of the Fight between the English and the Indians in Virginia in May 1676," mss. P.R.O., C.O.1/36, 5184, ff. 211–12; Va. gentlemen to Board of Trade, May 31, 1676, mss., Coventry Papers 67:95, Longleat House; Washburn, *Governor and Rebel*, pp. 40–46.
4. See the report of the royal commission of inquiry, "Narrative of Bacon's Rebellion," *Virginia Magazine of History and Biography* 4 (1896), 117–54; Washburn, *Governor and Rebel*, pp. 37–38, 42–46.
5. Ibid., pp. 25–26; Andros, "A Short Account of the General Concerns of New-York," 1678, in *N.Y.Col.Docs.* 3:254–55.

Andros's first Covenant Chain treaty
for New England

A full account of how Andros intervened in New England's wars has been given in *The Invasion of America*.[6] Here it is enough to say that he instigated and armed the Mohawks to strike a decisive blow against King Philip and his allies. Many old adversaries of the Mohawks were among them, including the Mahicans, and the Mohawks performed their task with such brutal efficiency as to reduce the Mahicans to a shadow of their former strength. But Andros did not purpose the destruction of the tribes; in his own words, that would be a "loss" to the English colonies. He wanted only their defeat, and he offered refuge to former enemies who would come into his territory and submit to his jurisdiction.[7] Thus the Mahicans in defeat became his "children" and he their "father," and he set aside a sanctuary for them at Schaghticoke, about ten miles north of present-day Troy, New York. When Connecticut and Massachusetts demanded the blood of the refugees, Andros permitted the New Englanders only to make peace without vengeance.[8]

In one respect, however, he gave way to them, and his concession was pregnant with the future. The New England delegates refused to let Andros simply order the Indians to be at peace "as being under or part of" his government. They insisted that a treaty conference should be held in April 1677, at which the Puritan colonies would deal with the tribes themselves, face to face (under Andros's chaperonage), and in which each of the parties would be responsible for its own obligations. Such proceedings fitted well into Puritan notions of convenanting. They also implied recognition of the tribes as free agents, *not* under New York's government, and thus open to the possibility of one day coming under the government of Massachusetts or Connecticut. For the sake of getting a peace, Andros permitted proceedings he much disliked, and he came to regret the sequel. He had never before made treaties with "his" Indians but had simply assumed authority and issued commands. Following the New Englanders' treaty-making, he complained that his neighboring Indians had become "insolent," and "now all my hope is Regulations and Orders from the King, as the only means to keep us well in peace and preserve or defend us if wars."[9]

Andros was no man to whine and wait. If his only hope was in the king, he nevertheless got on with his business, and if he could no longer simply

6. Ch. 17, 18.
7. Instructions to Capt. Delavall, May 30, 1676, N.Y.Col.Mss. 25:121. New York State Archives, Albany.
8. Jennings, *Invasion*, p. 323.
9. Andros to Blathwait, Oct. 12, 1678, mss., P.R.O., C.O.5 / 1111, 43–44 (fol.24).

issue orders to Indians, he adjusted to the treaty-making process. Thus the Covenant Chain was forged as a multiple alliance binding tribes and colonies in a "silver" chain of friendship.[10] Except for one fragment and some references, the records of the event have vanished. Fortunately it was followed within months by a better-documented treaty that sheds much more light on what was involved.

Andros's approaches to the Susquehannocks

At the first opportunity, Andros moved to repair the damage done by Virginia and Maryland. In February 1676 he received a report from his officer on Delaware Bay of the presence of a Susquehannock in that vicinity. Andros immediately scolded the officer, one Captain Cantwell, for failing to make immediate contact with the Indian.[11] Cantwell thereupon exerted himself and produced two Susquehannock sachems in New York on June 2, 1676. Andros came directly to the point with them. If the Susquehannocks would return to live "anywhere" within his government, he said, "they shall be welcome and protected from their Enemys."[12]

This astonishingly bold offer can be appreciated fully only by reference to surrounding circumstances. The enemies in question were English. Andros had already promised refuge, only three days previously, to all the "North Indians" embattled with Connecticut and Massachusetts. Now he was offering at the same time to protect the Susquehannocks against Virginia and Maryland! His resources for the assumption of all this protection were scant. New York's European manpower useful for military purposes was almost nonexistent. Andros's tangible assets were the Indians themselves and the arms of Albany's merchants. His intangibles included the disunity among his quarreling colonial opponents, the indirect power of second-hand royal authority derived from the king's brother rather than the crown itself, and his own superlative sense of strategy. What he did with these resources was to convert the possibility of intercolonial disaster into the actuality of economic, military, and political windfalls for New York.

Admirable though the strategy was, its execution was difficult. Winning the Susquehannocks taxed even Andros's powers of maneuver. He promised to make peace for them not only with Virginia and Maryland

10. Mohawk sachems' speech, June 6, 1683, *Minutes of the Court of Albany, Rensselaerswyck and Schenectady 1668–1673*, trans. and ed. A. J. F. van Laer, 3 vols. (Albany: University of the State of New York, 1926–1932) 3:363; Mohawk speech, Sept. 23, 1689, *Livingston Indian Records*, p. 154.
11. Andros to Cantwell, Feb. 22, 1676, mss., Dreer Collection, Governors of Colonies 1:2. Hist. Soc. of Pa.
12. Minutes of interviews, June 2–3, 1676, N.Y.Col.Mss. 25:124.

but also with their Iroquois enemies within his government. He passed on a Mohawk invitation for the Susquehannocks to move in as guests. All was to be entirely as the Susquehannocks themselves desired: "They should say whether they will come into the Government or no. If they will not, it is well; if they will, he will make provision for them." The Susquehannocks departed "well satisfyed"—small wonder—but they had not been empowered to conclude a treaty. They returned for consultation with their "folks," who were living in sanctuary provided by the Delaware Bay Indians.[13] These Delaware hosts, we may remind ourselves, were themselves inhabitants and allies of Andros's government at that time, and their sachem Renowickam was recognized by Andros as an especially close friend among the Indians.[14] He was to play an important role in the events to follow. For the moment it is enough to say that his Susquehannock guests spread word of Andros's proffered protection; and their scattered people began to drift in, some to their homeland on the Susquehanna River, others to join the nucleus on the Delaware. Still others emerged from Virginia's backwoods, raided Maryland settlers, and fled to the Iroquois for shelter.[15]

Maryland's threat to Delaware Bay

As Andros's designs became known, opposition formed. In spite of the late hostilities, the Marylanders still wanted "their" Indians within their own jurisdiction. Lord Baltimore had not relinquished his claims to the Delaware Bay territory governed from afar by Andros,[16] and the Susquehannocks under Andros's orders could have exactly the same frustrating effect on Baltimore's expansionism that the Iroquois had had in New Netherland's time: in the absence of an effective Indian force of his own, Baltimore would not dare to seize the Delaware Bay while Andros had veteran warriors at command. Besides the politico-military considerations of Maryland's government, there were economic issues posed by the proposed disposition of the Susquehannocks. These were trading Indians, it

13. Loc. cit.
14. Conference minutes, Newcastle, May 13, 1675, in *N.Y.Col.Docs.* 12:523–24. The Delaware Sachem Renowickam was a man whose considerable importance has escaped notice, partly because of variant spellings of his name in the sources. He was regarded by contemporaries as "emperor" of the Delawares and had been one of the landowners who sold Wicaco (a site in present-day South Philadelphia, in the fork of the Schuylkill and Delaware rivers) to the Dutch in 1646. Deed, Sept. 25, 1646, in Weslager, *Dutch Explorers*, p. 307; Andros to Cantwell, Dec. 10, 1675, *N.Y.Col.Docs.* 12:542–43.
15. Coursey to Notley, May 22, 1677, *Md.Arch.* 5:247–48.
16. In veiled and polite terms, Andros warned Baltimore to refrain from further molesting the inhabitants of the Whorekills. Ltr., May 15, 1675, N.Y.Col.Mss. vol. 24, in *Third Annual Report of the State Historian of N.Y.*, p. 314.

will be remembered, whose peacetime annual commerce in furs had been large.

At Andros's meeting with the Susquehannock chiefs in June, his offer of protection had been gratefully received, but no binding treaty had been agreed upon. Peace with Maryland had yet to be arranged. On August 4, 1676, the Susquehannocks came with Maryland's interpreter, Jacob Young (who had been New Netherland's soldier-trader "Jacob, My Friend"), to the head of the Chesapeake (probably at Young's trading post) to send a message to the Maryland council. They were accompanied also by Andros's local commander, Captain Cantwell. The Indians asked for "peace and trade as formerly with the [Maryland] English." The council observed that Andros had already made peace between the Susquehannocks and their Indian enemies, the Iroquois, "so that now they are at Ease and out of our reach." "This notwithstanding," the Susquehannocks seemed to desire "to treate of a peace with the English in Generall." It was a "blessing from God unhoped for," according to the council. "Wee thought it not to be Slighted." A safe conduct was dispatched at once.[17]

Apparently a truce was negotiated to give the Maryland council time to consult the province's allies, whereupon new complications arose. When the council informed its allied Indians of the Susquehannock peace overture, the allied Piscatawa and Mattawoman tribes objected strenuously. They had joined the Maryland militia in pursuit of fleeing Susquehannock bands, and they feared retaliation. They wanted the war continued until the Susquehannocks could not possibly survive as a serious threat. Faced with this opposition, the Maryland council sensed opportunity and asked whether the allies would march under Maryland's officers against the Susquehannocks in "the new fort they have built, or otherwise to pursue the Susquehannoughs." The allies agreed.[18] The special significance of this arrangement lies in its geographical implications. The Susquehannocks had retired into Andros's jurisdiction and had been guaranteed his protection. The agreement's "or otherwise" clause obliged Maryland's allied Indians to go wherever the colony's officers directed, including the long-coveted Delaware Bay. "Hot pursuit" of the Susquehannocks would justify invasion there, and Maryland's grasp on the Delaware territory would not easily be pried loose after it had been fastened. In sum, Maryland's negotiations for peace with the Susquehannocks turned into negotiations for revitalized war against them.

17. Minutes, Aug. 6, 1676, *Md.Arch.* 15:120–24.
18. Minutes, Aug. 17, 1676, *Md.Arch.* 15:125–26.

Andros's response

Someone informed Andros what was afoot. With his usual decisiveness, he immediately reorganized his administration at Delaware Bay; he commissioned Captain John Collier as replacement commander on the Delaware; and he brought different sorts of pressure to bear in different directions. He ordered Collier to deliver a polite but unmistakable ultimatum to Maryland. Either the Susquehannocks were to be actually received within Maryland or some acceptable reason for keeping them dangling in an unconfirmed truce would have to be given to Andros. (But Andros planned to dispel his fears of invasion in either case.) Failing Maryland's compliance with his terms, Andros would take the Susquehannocks permanently into his own jurisdiction "rather than hazard their being obliged to refuge with a grudge and rancour in their hearts, further off, if not wholly out of our reach." However, if he were to assume formal jurisdiction over the Susquehannocks, Andros intended not to leave them within reach of a strike from Maryland. The ultimatum to Maryland was matched by another to the Susquehannocks. Captain Collier was ordered to persuade as many of those Indians as possible to remove immediately northward out of Delaware Bay and into New York proper. The rest were warned that "though they shall receive no harme from the Government" Andros would not "now undertake to Secure them from others where they are." [19]

Andros also wrote a suitably diplomatic letter to Deputy Governor Notley, of Maryland, couched in language more equivocal and less abrupt than that of the ultimatum prepared for oral delivery. In the letter he added pressure of a kind calculated to stir genuine concern in the Marylanders. The Susquehannocks, he wrote, "if some course bee not speedily taken . . . must all necessarily Submitt" to the Mohawks and other Iroquois "which passionately desire it, but might prove of a bad consequence." The Maryland gentry could hardly fail to agree that a uniting of the Susquehannocks and the Iroquois would be worrisome. Maryland was still formally in a state of war with all the Iroquois. Until the colony had joined Virginia to attack the Susquehannocks, those Indians had been Maryland's first line of defense against possible Iroquois attack. Were the Susquehannocks now to join the Iroquois, Maryland's frontiers would be open to devastating raids. The situation was critical, suggested Andros, but it might yet be saved. All that the Maryland government need do was to tell him its desires and let him manage matters. "I have some interest with the Maques and Siniques," he noted, "which can best deale with

19. Commission and instructions, Sept. 23, 1676, in *N.Y.Col.Docs.* 12:556–57.

them, and they apprehend, and I shall be ready to use all fitting means for the best."[20]

Andros's blandly realistic offer was ignored. Bacon's rebellion in Virginia stirred up sympathetic turmoils in Maryland, but the uprising there was quickly suppressed and the hanging of two ringleaders left the council free once more to turn its attention to Indian affairs. Taking precedence even over the hangings, "the most considerable affair" that Deputy Governor Notley could report to proprietor Lord Baltimore was "a small encounter at Jacob Young's house" between the Iroquois and the Susquehannocks. Notley's cryptic comment was intended to convey a message to his master without revealing it to prying eyes in case the letter miscarried. That the "encounter" was not a matter of hostilities between the Indians is practically certain; Notley would have rejoiced at conflict between the colony's proclaimed enemies, and he surely would have commented on a rupture of the Iroquois-Susquehannock peace previously established by Andros. That the "encounter" took place at Jacob Young's house is suggestive, for Jacob was then very much engaged in Maryland's interest and had long been a friend to the Susquehannocks. It would appear to have been a kind of negotiation. Notley concluded from his private intelligence of what had occurred that "if wee be not timely in adjusting all matters with them, we shall be surprised by them, and your Lordshipp's Province will receive much damage . . . therefore I shall take all imaginable care to be at peace both with the Sennico and Susquahannock."[21]

Maryland's "peace" strategy

This decision, reported to Baltimore in January, 1677, did not signify that Notley had decided to accept Andros's offer of mediation made the preceding September. Rather, Notely still hoped to invade Andros's subprovince at Delaware Bay. Soon even the "common people" of Maryland were gossiping about their government's intention to lay hands on the lower Delaware, as an inhabitant of that region reported to Andros.[22]

The details of Notley's plan can only be conjectured, but the management of Indians was surely a factor in it. It would be especially necessary, Notley told Baltimore, to win the friendship of the Iroquois because "they being the greatest and most considerable nation . . . our league with them will occasion our security from the Delaware or Masquas Indians *especially if those two Nations should warre upon each other.*"[23]

20. Andros to deputy gov. of Md., Sept. 25, 1676, in *N.Y.Col.Docs.* 12:558.
21. Notley to Baltimore, Jan. 22, 1677, *Md.Arch.* 5:152–53.
22. Wiltbank to Andros, Feb. 26, 1677, in *N.Y.Col.Docs.* 12:571.
23. See. n. 21. Observe the name *Masquas* for the Delawares. It becomes critical to the interpretation of an important document. Cf. pp. 159–62, below.

This is a most remarkable notion. That Notley was serious about it is underscored by his omission of the Delawares when he named the tribes with which he would seek peace. What would lead him to believe that the Iroquois and the Delawares—currently on peaceful terms and both within the jurisdiction and under the protection of New York—might turn to war? It would appear that Notley had learned of conflicts developing over the disposition of the fragmented and now faction-plagued Susquehannocks.

Disposition of the Susquehannocks

Andros had told the truth when he said that the Iroquois wanted the Susquehannocks to "submit" to them. It must not be assumed, however, that submission meant a state of servile subjection. In the Susquehannocks' dispersed and disorganized state, they were incapable of maintaining a stable, independent tribal identity, which was the reason so many had sought shelter among their old allies, the Delawares. The Iroquois wanted to "adopt" the fragments of the former Susquehannock tribe, as they had earlier adopted Hurons and other western tribesmen, to strengthen and enlarge the Iroquois confederation. As a rueful Maryland emissary was to see by hindsight, the Iroquois had no desire to hurt the Susquehannocks, "for every one of the [Iroquois] fforts strive what they can to get them to themselves, and Governor Andros to get them to the Mohawks, for it was told me . . . that if they had them they would make warr immediately with the ffrench."[24] One of the obstacles to this endeavor was Delaware opposition, and perhaps some Iroquois hints of the Delaware resistance were what had encouraged Notley to think that war might break out between Iroquois and Delawares. The Delawares wanted to keep the Susuqehannocks who had settled among them, for precisely the same reason that the Iroquois wanted to woo them away. Acquisition of the Susquehannocks would mean an increase in manpower and therefore in tribal importance. No conquest was implied in these processes; they were a competition for allegiance rather than a process of repression.

The relative statuses of the client Indian nations of New York were still in a state of flux. The Mohawks were governor Edmund Andros's favored instrumentality for intervention in New England's Second Puritan Conquest, but Andros had depended on the Delawares for intermediation with the Indians in the southern region of his jurisdiction. At this stage, Iro-

24. See n. 15 in this ch.

quois and Delawares were rivals for Andros's favor and the advantages to be had from it.

To settle the Susquehannock issue, a great intertribal treaty conference met at the Delaware village of Shackamaxon, where Philadelphia now stands. It began without publicity, and it has passed unnoticed in the histories. In early February 1677, the Susquehannocks passed by New Castle, on the Delaware, on their way "up the River." (New Castle was the third name of the settlement that had been called New Netherland's Fort Casimir and then New Amstel.) In mid-March, some Iroquois Indians came to Shackamaxon "to fetch" the Susquehannocks. The Delawares contested this move, and the Susquehannocks themselves split into factions. Two of them had previously fled to the Iroquois for sanctuary as others had come to the Delawares, and these two accompanied the Iroquois to Shackamaxon, seemingly to plead the Iroquois cause. The Delawares appealed to Andros's magistrates at Upland (Chester, Pennsylvania) to intervene. Delaware "Emperor" Renowickam, who had previously treated with Andros on other matters, suggested to Captain Collier and the magistrates that they join the Shackamaxon conference with a proposal to have Andros arbitrate the issue. The magistrates agreed. Collier and an undisclosed number of the magistrates joined the conference from March 14 to March 18, but no indication exists that Renowickam's suggestion of a delegation to Andros was adopted. Perhaps the Iroquois could say that they already knew Andros's mind.[25] Collier surely knew that Andros wanted the Susquehannocks out of the Delaware Bay region because of the threat of renewed attacks from Maryland. Indeed, Andros sent orders three weeks after the treaty's end that the Susquehannocks still remaining at the Delaware should locate themselves anywhere they pleased within his government *except* among the Delawares, "it being dangerous to both."[26] The danger apprehended by Andros was not from the Iroquois with whom he was on such excellent terms; rather, he was responding to fear of Maryland's intentions. His fears were soon confirmed by intelligence that the government of Maryland had just sent surveyors to lay out thousands of acres within Andros's jurisdiction.[27]

It is clear that the Iroquois had not come to Shackamaxon with warlike intentions toward anybody, and they certainly were not ready to jeopardize their friendship with Andros by any rash gestures of defiance. They

25. New Castle Justices to Andros, Feb. 8, 1676/77, Records of the Court at New Castle, 1676–1681, Liber A, p. 71, mss. photostats, Hist. Soc. Pa.; minutes, March 13, 1676/77, and June 14, 1677, mss., Records of the Court at Upland, mss., Logan Papers, pp. 12, 20, HSP; Coursey to Notley, May 22, 1677, *Md.Arch.* 5:246–48. Note: Hazard misinterpreted the date of this occurrence as 1676 because of the difference between Old Style and New Style calendars and thereby confused a sequence of events. *Annals of Pa.*, pp. 423–24.
26. Order of council, April 6, 1677, *N.Y.Col.Docs.* 12:572.
27. Wiltbank to Andros, June 11, 1677, *N.Y.Col.Docs.* 12:576–77.

did propose to make peace with Maryland, probably at the urging of Jacob Young, but their method of approach to this delicate subject could give small comfort to Andros's enemies, for the Iroquois offered to make peace through the agency of Andros's deputy, Captain Collier. The proposal died at birth. Collier shrugged them off with the story of what had happened when he had earlier taken Andros's mediation offer to Maryland. The response he had received was that "Maryland would make warr or peace att their own pleasure." Andros had been "incensed" at the rejection, and Collier would wait for Andros's orders.[28]

The main issue at Shackamaxon was the disposition of the Susquehannocks, and despite the myth of Iroquois conquest and tyranny it is clear that the Susqehannocks themselves made the decisions. Some of them agreed to go off with the Iroquois, but twenty-six families insisted on remaining with the Delawares.[29] Neither group lived as captives or prisoners, but both were submerged politically in the tribal organizations of their hosts. Although Susquehannock tribal polity had been "exterminated" by the attacks of Maryland and Virginia (as the Huron polity had previously been destroyed by the Five Nations), individual members of the broken tribe remained very much alive among the Iroquois and Delawares. This was a diaspora. It is not possible to say certainly whether the Delawares obeyed Andros's post-Shackamaxon order to evict their Susquehannock guests. However, the order was dated April 6, 1677, and as of May 22 some Susquehannocks were still on the Delaware, with no evident intent to depart. The likelihood is that the general peace settlement beginning at that time permitted them to remain in their adopted home.

The details of the Shackamaxon treaty were carefully shielded from Maryland. Notley must have learned enough, however, to convince him, as the leaders of Connecticut and Massachusetts had previously been persuaded, that the agency of Edmund Andros was indispensable to an Iroquois treaty. On April 30, 1677, Notley's council resolved to send an ambassador to Andros and "by his meanes to come to a treaty with the Cinnigo Indians at ffort Albany or elsewhere as opportunity shall offer."[30] On this difficult mission, Major Henry Coursey set off in mid-May for New York by way of New Castle. It was the beginning of a long and expensive journey that produced a treaty, an illusion, a triumph, and an organization. The expense and the illusion came to Maryland. The triumph and the organization were shared by Andros and the Indians. The treaty was the means of all.

There was no welcome mat for Coursey at New Castle. Alarmed by

28. Coursey to Notley, May 22, 1677, Md.Arch. 5:247–48.
29. Loc. cit.
30. Minutes, April 30, 1566, Md.Arch. 15:149.

reports of his large escort of mounted gentlemen, and "not knoweing Certainly uppon what accompt" he came, Captain Collier mustered the militia to man the fort, "there to bee uppon their Garde and Receive such further order as shall be found necessary."[31] On arriving, Coursey got little information and less help. Captain Collier, he found, had been an "evill Instrument" to Maryland, and Collier showed no signs of change. After several frustrating days, Jacob Young arrived, through whom Coursey was able to talk to some of the Indians of the vicinity. Delaware "emperor" Renowickam introduced four Susquehannocks who declared their desire for peace with Maryland and promised to "endeavour to speak" with any Iroquois party that might come to the region, thus "to prevent any mischeife that may be done" either by the Iroquois or by any Susquehannocks accompanying them. Both the Susquehannocks and the Delaware sachem were pleased with Coursey's mission; they promised to send representatives of their own to New York to join the grand treaty in the making there. This fell short of what Coursey had aimed for. He had hoped to persuade all the Delaware Bay Susquehannocks, rather than just representatives, to *accompany* him, but the cautious Indians agreed only to send two of their chief men to *follow* him "with all haste."[32] They were not ready to risk the sort of pressures he could apply on such a journey.

Andros disciplines Maryland's envoy

Arrived in New York, Coursey was hazed by Andros as the New England commissioners had been disciplined a few months earlier. Much of June was spent in haggling over the terms Coursey would be permitted to present to the Indians.[33] Something of the sort had been anticipated by Maryland's council, so Coursey's formal instructions had been prepared in reproachless form. Coursey was to be sure to include Virginia and all the allied Indians in a "universal" peace. He was to make indemnity to the Iroquois for "injuries done by our [Indian] Neighbours to them unknowne to us." He was to explain to the Iroquois that Maryland's hostilities had all been provoked by deceptions practiced by the wicked Susquehannocks: "we afterwards found out that those very murders which the Susquehannocks fathered upon the Cinnigos were committed by the Susquehannocks themselves, and that was the real cause of the war."

31. Minutes, May 15, 1677, mss. Records of the Court of New Castle, 1676–1681, Liber A, p. 87. Hist. Soc. Pa.
32. See n. 28 of this ch.
33. Council minutes, June 6, 1677, in *N.Y.Col.Docs.* 13:507–8; Baltimore to Blathwait, March 11, 1682, *Md.Arch.* 5:349. Note that the New York council still referred to the "Maques and Sinnekes Indyans," lumping the four non-Mohawk Iroquois nations under the "Seneca" label although the existence of "five Respective Castles" was known.

Coursey was also to demonstrate Maryland's purity of heart: all this effort was being made "for to settle our owne peace, nothing [being] more to the decreasing of his Majesty's Customs than such distractions as take the people from Planting." As a final sign of Lord Baltimore's good will, Coursey was "to make a present of One hundred pounds Sterling to the Governor of New York as a token of his Lordshipps thankfulness for his care and kindness shewn to this Province."[34]

The last sentiment could not have failed to stir Andros's sense of humor, for he had received a report, while in the process of negotiations, that Maryland's surveyors were at work in the Delaware Bay. The same Maryland Council that was so thankful for Andros's care had decided to "grant" 8,000 acres of land within "this Province [of Maryland] on the Seaboard side" in order to combat settlers who "doe pretend to be under the Government of New York." Discreetly the council decided to postpone "a right understanding" with New York about the disputed territory until after Henry Coursey should return with his treaty safely signed.[35] The record does not show whether Andros accepted Maryland's proffered bribe, but he surely did not give money's worth in return.

The damage that Maryland proposed to inflict upon the Duke of York's interests was hidden no better by Coursey than by the trespassing surveyors. Coursey proposed to make a speech to the Indians in which he would assume a haughty, browbeating tone contrasting strongly with the placating phrases of his formal Instructions. In the intended speech, Coursey would have boasted that Maryland had "fallen upon" the Susquehannocks "and have now so near destroyed them that they are forced to seek shelter under you [the Iroquois] who were before their Enemies." As the price of peace, Coursey wanted to demand that the Iroquois police the Susquehannock refugees in their villages. Any Susquehannock suspected by the Maryland government of criminal activity would have to be delivered up by the Iroquois for adjudication and punishment within Maryland and under Maryland law.[36] The effect of such terms would be to make the Iroquois formally responsible to Maryland instead of New York. Three months earlier, New England's commissioners had aimed at the same sort of goal with demands for surrender of the refugees from the Second Puritan Conquest.

Coursey got as much satisfaction as they. What Andros finally approved for actual delivery to the Indians was a homily that kept well within the

34. Commission and instruction, April 30, 1677, Md.Arch. 5:243-46.
35. Wiltbank to Andros, June 11, 1677, in N.Y.Col.Docs. 12:576-77; minutes, June 24, 1677, Md.Arch. 15:153-54.
36. Proposal to the Indians, n.d., indorsed "Copy of the Govr. and councill in order to Coll. Henry Courcy to be made use of at the Congress the July 15, 1677," Md.Arch. 5:251-52.

peace and good will formula of Coursey's instructions. Not only was the brag about destroying the Susquehannocks deleted; all reference whatever to those Indians was suppressed. (This circumstance undoubtedly contributed to the later myth about Iroquois conquest of the Susquehannocks.) The treaty became in form a negotiation between Maryland on the one side, and the Iroquois and Delawares on the other side. The sanctions that Coursey had wanted to impose turned into a mild request for good faith: "Wee are willing that all what is Past, be buryed and forgott, you takeing care (as we shall on our Parts) that your Indians, nor none liveing among you or comeing through your Countrey, doe for the future Injure any of our Persons (Piscataway or other our Indians liveing with us) or goods, and if any ill Person should doe any harm, that there be Present full Satisfaction given, for all Injuries or dammages."[37]

Coursey tried to recover lost ground by getting to the Iroquois directly. He arranged through Jacob Young—thus circumventing Albany's official interpreters and censors—to hold a private meeting in his own room. There he proposed to the sachems that a new conference be held the following year at Onondaga, away from New York's supervision. The western Iroquois agreed; but, for some unknown reason, Maryland does not seem to have fulfilled the arrangement with an actual embassy.[38] Perhaps it was because the Mohawks insisted, as they had previously when the French set up Onondaga as a treaty site, that negotiators from the colonies must come through the Mohawk "door." The record shows Mohawks demanding of Coursey that "if the Senekes now or any time hereafter, should appoynt any other place for to Speake with you In ther own Cuntry or else wher Wee desyre that it may not be accepted off bot that this [Albany] be and remane the only appoynted and preffixed place."[39]

Role of the Delawares

Anticipating issues to be discussed later, we should note that the Delawares participated in this treaty as an independent tribe, unlike the Susquehannocks who had been reduced to anonymity among their Iroquois and Delaware hosts. So far as the records show, the Iroquois did all the speaking at the treaty, but Maryland's proclamation of the treaty text names the Delawares as responsible participants and subscribers. Although Gov-

37. Propositions of Henry Coursey, *Md. Arch.* 5, 254. Cf. text in *Livingston Indian Records*, June 30, 1677, p. 42. Apparently the *Livingston Indian Records* text, which is even milder than the speech finally delivered by Coursey, was Andros's original bargaining stance. The *Maryland Archives* text seems to be the outcome of all the haggling and to have been actually delivered on July 20, at Albany.
38. Minutes, Oct. 6, 1679, *Livingston Indian Records*, p. 51.
39. Treaty minutes, Aug. 6, 1677, ibid., p. 46.

ernor Notley did not mention the Susquehannocks, he included among the "Severall Nations" of the treaty: "The Sinnondowannes, Cajouges, Onondages, Onneydes, Maques, and Mattawass or Delaware Indians."[40]

Apart from the negotiations between Indians and colonials, this treaty conference seems also to have been the occasion for some unrecorded tribal arrangements. As I read the scattered evidence, Iroquois and Delawares agreed on a division of responsibilities and prerogatives. The Iroquois, as adopters of the bulk of the Susquehannocks, acquired a recognized right to most of the Susquehanna Valley, which they soon afterward placed under the protection of New York. But they never claimed below the falls on the Susquehanna River although that more southerly region had been as indisputably a Susquehannock territory as were the lands upriver.[41] A Delaware sold land below the falls to William Penn in 1683, without Indian protest.[42] I conclude that the Delaware right below the falls derived from their adoption of a minority of the Susqehannocks.

Besides this territorial division, there seems to have been an assignment of political responsibilities. Probably reluctantly and under pressure from Andros, the Delawares accepted the Five Nations (particularly the Mohawks) as spokesmen between themselves and the colonial governments. In doing so, they became "tributaries" in the language of European politics and law, but there are implications in that term that must be rejected. As even Pennsylvania's conspiring Indian interpreter Conrad Weiser conceded, the Delawares were tributary to the Iroquois only "in an Indian sense."[43] The problem for a student is to identify the specific obligations involved in that Indian sense.

There are no records thereafter of the Delawares dealing directly, through their own chiefs, with the government of New York; and an Iroquois chief came to live, briefly, among the Delawares. The Iroquois, from time to time, addressed the Delawares as "nephews" and were addressed in reply as "uncles." Taken together, such phenomena imply a relationship in which the Iroquois were superior in certain political respects, specifically acting as spokesmen and intermediaries between the Delawares and the government of New York. They did not, as we shall see, lay any claim to Delaware territory, and when Pennsylvania came into existence four years after the Albany treaty, the Delawares treated quite independently for themselves with William Penn and his agents. Not only was there no hint of Iroquois intervention, but for many years the Five Nations were treated by Pennsylvanians as probable antagonists. The

40. Md.Arch. 5:269.
41. Onondaga and Cayuga proposition, Aug. 2, 1684, in Doc.Hist.N.Y. 1:402.
42. Pa. Council Minutes, Jan. 3, 1783, 13:464; Md.Arch. 3:402.
43. Conrad Weiser, "An Account of . . . the Six Nations," The American Magazine (Boston: Dec., 1744), p. 666.

Delawares, on the other hand, were "our" Indians. It is clear that, however subordinate the Delawares might have been to the Iroquois in the eyes and records of New Yorkers, they were not tributary in the sense of subjection. More about that later.

Perhaps one word may be allowed regarding the confusion between the Delawares as "nephews" and as "cousins" of the Iroquois. Both terms appear in the sources. Moravian missionary David Zeisberger pointed out that the term "cousin" referred to sister's children. (See the quotation below.) It would naturally have been translated into English as nephews. The confusion appears to have arisen among the interpreters rather than among the Indians.

The Delawares were also "grandfathers" to the Iroquois, which probably means that the Five Nations paid this compliment in imitation of the Algonquian speaking tribes who all regarded the Delawares as the oldest among them. In the bewildering nomenclature of fictive kinship and personal relations, the Delawares also assumed the role of "women." This was not a term of contempt as it has so often been interpreted. Women were honored in Iroquois society. Indeed the Iroquois Great Law prescribed that clan matrons held the power to make and unmake chiefs.[44] This power did not devolve upon the Delawares, but there was another important function allotted to women—the initiative for peacemaking. We have seen already that Algonquian tribes related to the Delawares had carried peace messages between the warring Iroquois and Susquehannocks. At Albany, in 1677, this function seems to have been systematized. A Cayuga tradition, kept alive to the present day, holds that the Delaware role in the Covenant Chain was to act as mediator between the Five Nations and the Algonquian speaking Indians.[45] It dovetails neatly into the usage of "grandfather" as well as "women."

The Delaware tradition has been preserved for us by the David Zeisberger who wrote in 1779–1780 about their concept of a mediator nation. "Soon after Pennsylvania had been settled by the whites, the Six Nations sent an embassy to the Delawares, opened negotiations and said: It is not profitable that all the nations should be at war with each other, for this would at length ruin the whole Indian race. They had, therefore, contrived a remedy by which this evil might be prevented while there was yet opportunity to do so. One nation should be the woman. She should

44. Articles 17, 18, 19. But one must not carry the idea too far. Men made the decisions. See Elisabeth Tooker, "Women in Iroquois Society," in *Extending the Rafters: Interdisciplinary Approaches to Iroquoian Studies*, eds. Jack Campisi, Michael K. Foster, and Marianne Mithun, forthcoming, State University of New York Press.

45. Interview, May 23, 1980, with Cayuga Chief Jacob E. Thomas. The Cayugas no longer have an organized nation in the United States. Chief Thomas, whose people live in Canada, sometimes meets with the traditionalist Grand Council of the Houdénosaunee at Onondaga.

be placed in the midst, while the other nations, who make war, should be the man and live around the woman. No one should touch or hurt the woman, and if any one did so, they would immediately say to him, 'Why do you beat the woman?' Then all the men should fall upon him who has beaten her. The woman should not go to war but endeavor to keep the peace with all. . . . Ever since then the Six Nations have called the Delawares their cousins, i.e., sister's children."[46]

This rings true to Iroquois political ideas and imagination. It goes counter to the Colden-inspired Seneca tradition reported by Lewis Henry Morgan that the Iroquois conquered the Delawares and so many other tribes as to create a vast woodland empire. The Morgan account is the one that Francis Parkman and his followers elected to believe. The evidence of the falsity of that understanding is displayed throughout this book.

The intertribal arrangements negotiated at Albany in 1677 became part of what I call the "constitution" of the Covenant Chain, but that was a flexible and changing affair, and it was disrupted seriously by the founding of Pennsylvania, as will be noticed in a following chapter. Nevertheless, the Iroquois kept the idea in mind, and relationships with their "props," the Delawares, became a continuing political preoccupation.

Iroquois legalism

In spite of all restrictions and frustrations, Maryland's Henry Coursey left Albany with an illusion of ultimate triumph. He had finally made contact with the elusive Iroquois and had provided (as he thought) for meeting some of them again on better terms. He had gotten what he thought was a full and final peace embracing Virginia and his Indian allies as well as Maryland. In both conclusions, however, he erred grievously, for there were flaws in both the structure and the stipulations of his treaty. One defect lay in Coursey's assumption of the role of spokesman for Maryland's Indian allies. In that role he persuaded the Iroquois to bury "all which is past . . . in oblivion," as the Onondagas put it. They added that when differences arose in the future, the parties should "give one another Satisfaction and not Immediatly fall in warre."[47] The word "immediately" had not been part of Coursey's proposals, but apparently he underestimated Iroquois capacities for sharp legalism and was ignorant of that part of the Iroquois Great Law respecting the admission of outside nations to the Great Peace: "When the council of the League has for its

46. David Zeisberger, *History of the Northern American Indians*, trans. Nathaniel Schwarze, ed. Archer Butler Hulbert, *Ohio Archaeological and Historical Quarterly* 19: 1 & 2 (Jan. and April, 1910), pp. 34-35.

47. Treaty minutes, July 21, 1677, *Livingston Indian Records*, pp. 43-44.

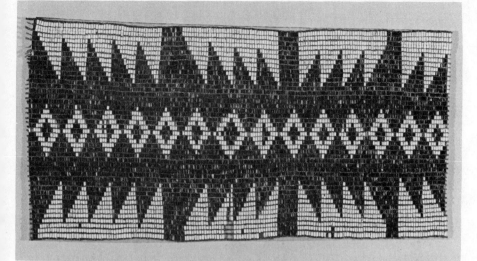

FIGURE 2. The Thadodáho, or Chain Wampum Belt. Tradition associates this belt with the founding of the Iroquois League, but there are reasons for placing it otherwise. Technically the beads have been worked in ways impossible for aboriginal tools. William N. Fenton has suggested that the design may be as old as the League. However, it could not have been associated with a chain before European contact, and the alliance system apparently represented by the belt's figures did not exist before 1677. It seems appropriate symbolism for the Covenant Chain. COURTESY OF THE NEW YORK STATE MUSEUM.

object the establishment of the Great Peace among the people of an outside nation and that nation refuses to accept the Great Peace, then by such refusal they bring a declaration of war upon themselves from the Five Nations. Then shall the Five Nations seek to establish the Great Peace by a conquest of the rebellious nation."[48] There is no allowance in that rule for third parties to arrange peace in behalf of the "rebellious" nation; it must speak for itself. Henry Coursey failed to anticipate that the Iroquois would seek future "satisfaction" directly from Maryland's allied Indians rather than indirectly through the colonial government. Soon the Five Nations were to present a demand to the Maryland tribes that the latter join the Great Peace, signifying acceptance of the peace by ceremonial presentation of presents to the Iroquois. Refusal would create a "future" difference that the Maryland tribes would fail to "satisfy," and the legalistic Iroquois might then resort to their accustomed forceful methods of persuasion. Something of the same sort also happened in Connecticut and

48. Article 80.

Massachusetts as the Iroquois demanded tributary adherence by the Indians there.

Disappearance of the Susquehannocks

The second defect in Coursey's treaty aggravated the troubles created by the first. It lay in the "extermination" of the Susquehannocks. What this amounted to was the nonrecognition for diplomatic purposes of a Susquehannock "nation." Thus, only the separately named Iroquois nations, plus the Delaware, were proclaimed as Indian parties to the finished treaty.[49] Coursey hoped to make the Iroquois and Delawares assume responsibility for their immigrant Susquehannocks by itemizing in his propositions "that no harm should be done by "your Indians, nor none liveing among you, or comeing through your Countrey," but the Onondagas had responded only that "wee" would not injure Virginians or Marylanders.[50] It may not be thought that these were casual or routine phrases. The Onondagas were committing only themselves. By their formula, the Susquehannocks were free to strike out at will while living under Iroquois protection.

Jacob Young was outraged at what seemed to be the permanent loss to New York of his best business partners. He lamented to Coursey that he would rather have lost 20,000 pounds of tobacco than have seen the Susquehannocks excluded from the peace negotiations.[51] Despite Young's opposition, the powers had their way. The Susuqehannocks themselves, though reduced in dignity and status, had certain compensations. When Iroquois demands on Maryland's Indians created new opportunities, Susquehannock warriors happily joined the southward bound raiding parties. As an Indian informant told Lord Baltimore in 1679, "the Susquehannocks laugh and jeare at the English [of Maryland] saying they cann doe what mischief they please for that the English cannot see them."[52] In this respect, at least, Coursey's treaty had provided more of privileged sanctuary than of suppression.

Baltimore's use of the treaty

The treaty did have one advantage for Lord Baltimore in that it helped him to preserve his government at a critical moment. For simplicity of

49. Proclamation of treaty terms, Oct. 5, 1677, *Md.Arch.* 15:157.
50. Treaty minutes, June 30 and 31, 1677, *Livingston Indian Records*, pp. 42–43.
51. Trial findings, Oct. 19, 1683, *Md.Arch.* 7:475.
52. Conference minutes, March 19, 1679, *Md.Arch.* 15:239.

narration, only one motive has been presented here for Baltimore's seeking of the treaty: the attraction of an Iroquois alliance as an aid to seizing Delaware. However, there had been a push as well as a pull. Lord Baltimore had been in London answering official questions ever since the outbreak of all the violence in 1675. The simultaneous Indian tumults in New England and the southern colonies had caused great concern among the statesmen of the Crown. Baltimore was in trouble anyway because of complaints about his bias against Protestants; to this perpetual vexation was now added his evident inability to protect his back settlers from Indians. To stall hostile action, Baltimore lied boldly to the Privy Council's Committee of Trade and Plantations. He told them in 1677 that the "Peace with the Northern Indians bordering upon his Province has held for twenty years and is yearly confirmed by the Indians." To his embarrassment, he was asked for evidence. Coursey's treaty at Albany gave Baltimore something in writing to offer the Lords of Trade. The treaty did not confirm his words, but it did at least seem to show signs of effort and accomplishment in stabilizing relations with the Indians.[53] The treaty was a costly humiliation—Baltimore got exactly nothing from the Indians except promises of future good behavior—but his government was protected by it against the sort of opponents that Baltimore could not brush aside.

Resurgence of the Mohawks

Though not formally a party to the treaty, Andros gained more by it than did Baltimore. As he had acquired some of New England's Indians with a "tree of peace" on the upper Hudson, now he gained important military and commercial assets in the persons of the Susquehannocks. As he had fended off the New Englanders from intruding their independent influence over Indians within New York, so now he foiled Maryland's intrigues. And as he had secured New York's boundaries against encroachment from New England, he now secured his Maryland line: so long as Delaware remained under Andros's government, Lord Baltimore confined himself to legal means of pressing his claims. Indeed, Andros's strategy had been so brilliantly successful that it laid the basis for New York to turn to aggressive expansion on its own account.

The key to all was the network of relationships established between New York and the Indians and intertribally among the Indians themselves. The 1677 treaties at Albany established what may properly be called a constitutional basis (in the English sense) for the Indians under

53. Minutes of Committee for Trade and Plantations, April 10, 1676, Dec. 18, 1677, March 26, 1678, April 15, 1678, *Md.Arch.* 5:125–30, 263, 264, 269.

New York's protection. The Mohawks grasped its significance at once. "We are glad," they told Henry Coursey, "that the Governor General hath been pleased to destinate and appoint *this place* to speake with *all* Nations in peace . . . especially that his Honor hath been pleased to grant you the *privilege* for to speake with us here . . . for the Covenant that is betwixt the Governor Generall and us is Inviolable; yea, so strong that if the very thunder shoulde breake upon the Covenant Chain, it would not breake it asunder."[54]

There was good reason for the Mohawks to rejoice. Only four years earlier, they had been a beaten, harried, almost defenseless people. Andros's aid had enabled them to turn the tables on their Mahican enemies whom they defeated so decisively as never to have to worry again about another challenge from that tribe. Now Andros's friendship restored their ascendancy within the Five Nations. Onondaga remained the site for all intra-League councils, but Onondaga had lost its bid to become the site of the League's treaties with New France.[55] Those treaties henceforth were to be negotiated in Montreal or Quebec where Onondagas and Mohawks were on an equal footing. But the all-important negotiations with the English colonies were set after 1677 to take place at Albany, the nearest Iroquois neighbors of which were the Mohawks. In such an arrangement the Mohawks would become the eyes and ears of the whole Five Nations to observe and report upon the English; they would also become the first upon the scene to speak to the English for the Five Nations. Within the Covenant Chain the Mohawks and New York became a special sort of steering committee, often resented by other colonies and tribes alike but enduring for more than half a century.

Neither Mohawk sachems nor New York's governors were shy about their roles. Only rarely were other English colonies permitted to treat with the Five Nations apart from New York's direct supervision. As for the Mohawks, sachem Hendrick flaunted their attitude without subtlety or ambiguity at Albany in 1754. "There are some of our People who have large open Ears and talk a little broken English and Dutch, so that they sometimes hear what is said by the Christian settlers near them, and by this means We came to understand that We are looked upon to be a proud Nation . . . 'Tis true and known We are so, and that We the Mohocks are the Head of all the other Nations. Here they are and they must own it."[56]

54. Mohawk speech, Aug. 6, 1677, *Md.Arch.* 5:256–58. Emphasis added. Cf. *Livingston Indian Records*, pp. 45–47. Minor variations of tendency appear, but substance of texts is identical.

55. *Jesuit Relations* 41:117. See ch. 6 herein.

56. Treaty minutes, Albany, June 28, 1754, in *Pa. Council Minutes* 6:77. The Iroquois League Great Law states, Article 6: "I, Tekanawita, appoint the Mohawk statesmen the head and the Leaders of the Five Nations League." A curiosity about Chief Hendrick's boast is that he was an adopted Mahican.

"Corlaer's" silver chain

They were grateful as well as proud. They gave a special symbolic name to Andros as a mark of high esteem. They called him *Corlaer* in memory of the Dutchman who had negotiated their first treaty of full alliance with New Netherland. The name became a title to be used when addressing subsequent governors of New York, as *Onontio* was used for reference to Canada's governors after Montmagny, but whereas Onontio was only a translation of the French name, Corlaer was a tribute, a per-petual reminder of a man whom the Mohawks "esteemed deare."[57]

Either at this treaty with the emissary of Maryland and Virginia, or more probably at the earlier 1677 treaty of the Iroquois with Massachu-setts and Connecticut, the chain of friendship between the Iroquois and the English became "silver" as it received its new name of Covenant Chain. The transformation from iron to silver is quite definite. Although most of the traditional histories recited by Iroquois chiefs at treaty councils thereafter refer to the silverness of the Chain, one identifies it specifically as English, and all contexts suggest that the Englishman who originated it was Edmund Andros. At Lancaster in 1744, Onondaga Chief Canasatego specified that "about two years after the arrival of the English," a governor came to Albany to renew the league that formerly existed between the Iroquois and the Dutch. He told the Iroquois "he would give us a Silver Chain, which would be much stronger and would last for ever."[58] The time fits the *second* arrival of the English, late in 1674, after the second brief existence of New Netherland. From fall of 1674 to spring of 1677 is little more than two years. The negative evidence is that nothing of any great consequence developed between the Iroquois and Andros's prede-cessors during New York's first incarnation.

The Covenant Chain remained silver from Andros's time onward, and from then on it remained also a multi-party confederation. But the Cove-nant Chain agreements did not mean that thereafter all would be sweet-ness and light between the Iroquois and the English colonies. All the parties to those treaties were looking after their own interests and pursuing their own objectives. These were so far from identical that the Iroquois had had good private reasons for the careful legalism of the terms on which they subscribed to the Chain treaty.

57. Trelease, *Indian Affairs*, pp. 116, 249; Mohawk orator, Sept. 20, 1688, *N.Y.Col.Docs.* 3:559.
58. Treaty minutes, *Pa. Council Minutes*, June 26, 1744, 4:707.

Susquehannock revenge

They had in mind the anonymous Susquehannocks refuging among them. Safely out of reach in Iroquois sanctuary, the Susquehannocks instigated vengeance, with Iroquois help, against the tribal auxiliaries of Maryland who had attacked them in the 1675–1677 war. Iroquois leaders looked on the Susquehannock pursuit of revenge as a means of extending Iroquois hegemony over southern tribes. Already by June 1678, rumors reached Maryland that the "Senecas" intended to war upon Maryland's Piscatawa allies and "scoure the heads" of Virginia's river valleys "by Instigation of the Remaineing part of the Susquesahannoghs now amongst them."[59]

The raids began. In March 1679, a Piscatawa Indian who had been captured by the Iroquois appeared before Lord Baltimore with a message from the Senecas. They declared themselves blameless and instructed their messenger to tell Baltimore "who it was had Done the English all the mischiefe, and that those two nations with whom the Susquehannohs lived would certainly yett doe more mischiefe." The Susquehannocks had full freedom to travel about in Iroquoia "as ffriends and netopps [tribal members] and were "of such a turbulent bloody mind that they will never cease Doeing mischiefe both to the English and Pascattoway Indians soe long as a man of them is left alive." Baltimore asked whether the Iroquois hosts of the Susquehannocks were "of the same bloody mind." The messenger replied that "at ffirst they were not but by the insinuation and instigation of the Susquehannocks he does believe that they are now become all One." The Piscatawas present requested badly needed arms and ammunition because they were expecting attack daily.[60]

Maryland's frustrations

Only one document even hints that Maryland tried to treat independently with the Iroquois through interpreter Jacob Young. But New York's vigilant Governor Andros issued a summons to Young, and the effort at negotiation failed.[61]

The raids continued, expanding to include the Mattawoman tribe as

59. *Md.Council minutes*, June 13, 1678, *Md.Arch.* 15:175–76. Note that in January 1678 a party of Senecas and Oneidas had attacked the Susquehannocks still remaining in Virginia's back country. The attackers later excused themselves on grounds that they had not learned of the Covenant Chain treaty. The incident probably explains why the Susquehannocks later preferred friendship with the Cayugas and Onondagas. Sec. Nicolls to Albany magistrates, January 15, 1678, *N.Y.Col.Docs.* 13:516.
60. Conference at Manahowickes Neck, March 19, 1679, *Md.Arch.* 15:238–42.
61. Andros to Captain Cantwell, June 12, 1680, *Pa.Arch.*, 2d. ser., 5:719–20.

well as the Piscatawa/Conoys.[62] The bewildered Indians were caught between two powers. They wanted to negotiate a peace. The Piscatawas informed Lord Baltimore that they intended to ask the Delawares [Mattwas] to mediate for them.[63] But Baltimore would not tolerate the reduction of his own authority implied by direct negotiations between "his" Indians and the Iroquois, more especially because the mediating Delawares had been violently resisting encroachments by Marylanders on their lands. Baltimore insisted that his government must negotiate for his Indian allies.[64] But he temporized and dallied, and the ravages grew worse. By 1682 he could stall no longer. Once more Henry Coursey journeyed to Albany, accompanied this time by Philemon Lloyd; they entered into a prolonged wrangle with the Albanians. Coursey and Lloyd proposed that New York should threaten to cut off trade with the Iroquois and even make war upon them if they would not keep the peace. Albany refused point blank: "it is not in our Power to Perform, in such manner and methods as you prescribe in your Proposalls."[65]

The resulting treaty was highly unsatisfactory to the Marylanders, so much so that Coursey tried to get the Iroquois to come to Maryland, where New York's chaperonage could be evaded. Fourteen Mohawks actually followed up the invitation and treated with Baltimore at Coursey's house, after which they visited the Maryland Indians. But this

62. *Md.Arch.* 15:280–300.

63. Md. Council minutes, March 31–April 1, 1680, *Md.Arch.* 15:277–80. The series of texts in *Md.Arch.* 15 deserves more detailed attention than can be given here. Two of them confirm the Delaware and Cayuga traditions of the Delawares ("Mattwas") as go-betweens to make peace with the Iroquois. In this instance the Delawares promised the Piscatawas to make peace with the Oneidas "or hazard their owne Lives for them." It does not sound as though they had been reduced to helpless femininity, and this occurred while the Delawares and Iroquois were simultaneously under the protectorate of New York.

Other documents show that Maryland wanted the Mattawomans to remove to the Eastern Shore of the Chesapeake for safety, but this solution was refused by the Indians, partly because "by their goeing thither they should be dispossessed of their Lands, and that the English woulde seat the same." The stubborn and too sadly wise Mattowomans insisted that they had incurred the enmity of the Susquehannocks and "all other Indians through our [Maryland's] means and for that reason will not leave us." After defending themselves as long as possible, "when they can hold out no longer, they will thrust themselves among the English" (pp. 299–300).

64. *Md.Arch.* 15:287–88; 329, 353–54, 375–76, 407–9. Baltimore's officials were well informed compared to the confusion of the common colonials. Cf. the deposition of June 15, 1681: "Mr. Nicholas Bodkin . . . saith that he was present when the said Mordecai said that he heard that the boy reported that the Indian said that the English called Romans and the Sinniquos were to joine and kill the Protestants." *Md.Arch.* 15:420. It seems that the distrust of the Protestant settlers for the Catholic gentry was still another element in the muddle.

65. Gov. and Council of Md. to Capt. Anthony Brockholes, March 4, 1682, *CSPA&WI, 1681–1685*, no. 437.i, p. 207; Instructions of Lord Baltimore to Coursey and Lloyd, May 15, 1682, *Md.Arch.* 17:96–102; Resolutions of Henry Coursey and Philip [i.e., Philemon] Lloyd, June 13, 1682, mss., Gratz Collection, Case 4, Box 6, folder Coursey, Henry, HSP; *Minutes of the Court of Albany, Rensselaerswyck and Schenectady,* July 1682, 3:266, 272.

embassy did not help matters much, for "On the return voyage 9 of the 14 suddenly died, from which it is presumed that they were poisoned by the Maryland Indians, about which they are much discontented."[66]

The major issue in all this seeming chaos lay in conflicting assertions of authority. Yorkers were not going to let Maryland get a handle on *their* Iroquois. The Iroquois were not going to let Maryland take over *their* Susquehannocks. Maryland was not going to let the Iroquois acquire *its* Piscatawas and Mattawomans. As we have seen, Lord Baltimore assumed a right to speak in behalf of his Indian allies, but the Iroquois conceived that he had only the right to speak in behalf of his own people, the English colonists of Maryland. In Iroquois theory, the Piscatawas and Mattawomans were free Indians who would be required to commit themselves by their own act to Covenant Chain membership by way of the Chain's substructure, the Iroquois tributary system. Regardless of Baltimore's pretensions, his deliverable power was inadequate for his purposes, and the Iroquois had their way. Peace came at last for the Piscatawa/Conoys in 1685 when they sent three chiefs to Albany "to Stay here in Corlaers house till the Indians as far as onnondage come here to Speak with us about the Covenant."[67]

In discussing Maryland's troubles with the Iroquois, I have omitted mention of Virginia's similar difficulties in order to keep the narrative uncluttered.[68] In both cases, the troubles were caused by the colonies' war of 1675–1677 against the Susquehannocks, and by the participation of the colonies' Indian allies. In both cases, the Iroquois used vengeful Susquehannocks as willing instruments to force southern tribes into the Iroquois "Great Peace." Throughout the subsequent treaty negotiations, and for many decades thereafter, the Iroquois insisted that tribes must speak for themselves through their own chiefs, no matter what sort of sovereignty or overlordship might be claimed by English or French officials.

Thus, in Iroquois theory, the Indian tribes of the Covenant Chain composed a confederation with the Five Nations at its head. This theory did not preclude the tributaries from treating separately with their respective colonial governments or with other tribes until later years when some

66. Ibid., Dec. 19, 1682, 3:307; Treaty minutes, Aug. 3–4, 1682, *N.Y.Col.Docs.* 3:321–28.
67. Propositions of Md.Indians, Aug. 7, 1685, *Livingston Indian Records*, p. 83.
68. See letters from Col. Ludwell to the Privy Council, July 22, 1681, and to Lord Culpeper, July 26, 1681, *CSPA&WI, 1681–1685*, no. 184 and 185, pp. 92–94; New York colonial manuscripts, July 1679, 28:120, 121, 125a, New York State Archives, Albany; treaty records, Sep.–Nov. 1781, *Livingston Indian Records*, pp. 49–61. It is amusing and instructive to see how much of the material in the Livingston records was omitted from Colden, *History* (pp. 28–32). Colden slanted his account and justified his tilt with a barefaced lie: to wit, that "None of their [the Iroquois] Answers appear upon the Registers, except the Mohawks, which we have given" (p. 31). The Livingston records, which were Colden's source, give extensive, but embarrassing, responses in the treaty from Oneidas and Onondagas.

English colonies, for purposes of their own, thrust upon the Iroquois the role and responsibility of spokesmen for other tribes. These developments are discussed further on, in chapters 15–17. Much was to transpire before they occurred.

Chapter 9 ☙ EXPANSION and REACTION

To preserve the Beaver and Peltry Trade for this and Albany and to bee an encouragement to Our Beever Hunters I desire I may have order to erect a Campagne Fort . . . *upon the Susquehanna where his Majesty shall think fit Mr Pens bounds shall terminate.* And another at Oneigra near the Great Lake in the way where our people goe a Beaver hunting or trading or any where else where I shall think convenient it being very necessary for the support of Trade, maintaining a correspondence with the further Indians, and in securing our right in the country the French making a pretence as far as the Bay of Mexico, for which they have no other argument than that they have had possession this twenty years by their [missionary] fathers living so long among the Indians. They have fathers still among the five Nations aforementioned . . . and have converted many of them to the Christian Faith and doe their utmost to draw them to Canada, to which place there are already 6[oo] or 700 retired and more like to doe, to the Great prejudice of this Government if not prevented. (Italics added.)

Governor Thomas Dongan, March 1687
(Emphasis added.)

In its early years, the Covenant Chain's role and functions were not very clear. For governor Edmund Andros the Chain was an expedient to pacify the backwoods of New England and the Chesapeake Bay colonies. For the Mohawks, it was the means of enhancing their status in the Iroquois League by confirming their control over access to Albany and Albany's goods. For the western Iroquois, it confirmed their acquisition of the refugee Susquehannocks and opened an unobstructed path to the south. As far as the French were concerned, the Chain was a nullity; they saw only an alliance between the Iroquois and New York.

Soon, however, the Chain acquired definition as a factor in the policies of expansionist statesmen. Bolstered by New York's support, the Iroquois aimed at repeating their great conquests of the Beaver Wars; they colonized the north shore of Lake Ontario and sent raiding parties westward all the way to the Illinois country. But their activity coincided with French exploration of the vast Mississippi Valley, which the French designed to

---

᛫ Thanks are due to Lawrence H. Leder for listening patiently to a crude early draft of this chapter. He may not recognize it now, partly because his expert criticism mandated revisions.

rule over themselves. French explorers were also French traders, and they were soon followed by French forts and garrisons, and claims of French protection over the resident tribes.

Neither New York nor the Iroquois looked kindly on such activity by the French. The Iroquois alternately negotiated and fought for their own domination over the western tribes, and the Yorkers construed Iroquois raids into conquests warranting a British claim to sovereignty. Besides the political possibilities of Iroquois alliance, its commercial implications were very well understood: Iroquois peltry, whether acquired by trade or raid, would be brought to Albany.

One can oversimplify; the full reality in both New France and New York included internal opposition to expansion; and in Iroquoia there were divisions between tribes as well as within them. Among colonials and Iroquois alike, internal divisions formed over the basic issue of geographical direction. Should trade be developed along the north-south route of the Mahican Channel, or should it be concentrated east and west? Advocates of business-as-usual in Montreal and Albany preferred the north-south route, and many Mohawks agreed. Advocates of imperial expansion strove westward, with support for expansionist Yorkers coming especially from the Senecas.

Because English claims to western sovereignty depended so heavily on Iroquois accomplishments, real or fancied, it was necessary for the Yorkers to establish Iroquois status as that of subjects to the English crown. As will be shown, the Iroquois reacted ambivalently. They were willing to claim English protection but firmly resisted every attempt at English rule, regardless of the Yorkers' explanations that protection could not be separated from rule. In consequence, the Covenant Chain confederation wore a double aspect during its early years, with the Yorkers seeing it rather differently than the Iroquois; strains developed as the allies pulled in different directions.

Frontenac and La Salle

It will be remembered that the long war with the Susquehannocks had drained the strength of the western Iroquois tribes, and that the latter had pleaded with the governor general of New France for aid in 1673. He gave them no military assistance, but he opened a trade with them that had ramifications for the future. He was noble, this governor general. His full name was Louis de Buade de Frontenac et de Palluau, Comte de Frontenac; he was godson to Louis XIV; and he had pretensions and tastes expensive enough to uphold the honor of the name. His reason for being thousands of miles away from the Sun King's court was an aristocratic lack of concern about paying his bills. Had his name and connections been less long, he would have stayed in France in debtors' prison instead of being exiled in pretentious poverty to lord it over the peasants and wild men of France's distant outpost.[1]

There was a direct connection between Count Frontenac's impecuniosity and a lull in tensions between New France and the Iroquois, for the Count had decided that trade with Indians was the remedy for his poverty. In 1673 he built a so-called fort, in reality a trading post, where the Cataracoui River empties into Lake Ontario (modern Kingston, Ontario), and put it in charge of an iron-willed henchman whose nobility and name were not quite as impressive. René Robert Cavelier Sieur de La Salle renamed the post Fort Frontenac and intercepted the western Indians as they headed toward the market at Montreal.[2] The merchants of Montreal promptly went into opposition to the Frontenac–La Salle regime.[3]

Fort Frontenac, or as the Indians called it, Cadaraqui, seemed at first to be a boon to the western Iroquois. Standing where Lake Ontario finds its outlet into the St. Lawrence River, it provided an alternative market to Albany without blocking traffic between the Iroquois and the western tribes along the lake's south shore. But, just at the moment when the Covenant Chain was renewing Iroquois strength, La Salle threatened to deprive the Five Nations of their new opportunities by a new maneuver in the old game of trader's leapfrog. Late in 1678 he began to build a large sailing vessel to cruise and trade in the Great Lakes, and early in 1679 he began construction of a fort on the Niagara River between lakes Erie and Ontario.[4] He launched his vessel, *Griffon*, in August 1679, cruised extensively around the lakes to collect a cargo of furs, and left the ship with orders to return to Fort Niagara while he explored the interior. The ship disappeared. There is a tradition that it was surprised and destroyed by the Iroquois. A modern scholar who retraced its voyage in a small boat believes that it was lost in a storm on the always treacherous waters of these lakes.[5] La Salle did not immediately learn of his loss. Elated with his seeming mastery of transportation on the lakes, he journeyed inland to stake out claims to the empire he envisioned, ranging from Green Bay (Wisconsin) on upper Lake Michigan southward through the country of the Illinois Indians.

1. The standard (and very good) biography is W. J. Eccles, Frontenac, *The Courtier Governor* (Toronto: McClelland and Stewart, 1959). Eccles has also written the concise life in *Dict.Can.Biog.* 1:133–42.

2. Eccles, *Frontenac*, pp. 38, 78–81.

3. Yves F. Zoltvany, "Aubert de La Chesnaye, Charles," in *Dict.Can.Biog.* 2:29.

4. Celine Dupré, "Cavelier de La Salle, René-Robert," in *Dict.Can.Biog.* 1:176–77.

5. George Quimby, *Indian Culture and European Trade Goods: The Archaeology of the Historic Period in the Western Great Lakes Region* (Madison: University of Wisconsin Press, 1966), ch. 4, "The First European Trade Ship on the Western Great Lakes." This essay is a model of combination of historical records with nondocumentary kinds of evidence.

Heroic as all this appears in the histories of Europeans, it appeared to the Iroquois as a menace to their power and even their livelihood. They had recognized the *Griffon*'s threat immediately. Regardless of how that ill-fated craft actually perished, the Iroquois were determined to do it in somehow; its builders had had to maintain twenty-four-hour guard to keep it from being burnt on the stocks.[6] The Iroquois also quickly recognized La Salle's Fort Niagara as a barrier between themselves and the western tribes of upper Canada. They were slower, but not less angered, to learn of La Salle's journey to the Illinois country; when they discovered that he had extended New France's nominal protection over tribes that had long been Iroquois enemies, the challenge became unmistakable.[7]

Senecas frustrated in the Illinois country

South of the Great Lakes, the Five Nations' strategy was directed first against the distant Illinois bands in the Mississippi Valley. In 1680 the Iroquois launched full-scale war against them. Strictly speaking, this was something more complex than the earlier Iroquois wars. The beaver wars had been fought for hunting territories and controls over trade. War with the Illinois involved European territorial jurisdiction as well as trade, although the Iroquois were somewhat astonished to find that out. It came home to them on their first campaign when they attacked an Illinois village and discovered they had wounded and captured Henri de Tonty, lieutenant to La Salle. Hostilities with New France were more than the Iroquois had intended or desired at that time, so they let Tonty go. The Illinois were not to be let off so lightly. In spite of Tonty's declarations of New France's alliance and protection for them, war continued against the Illinois.[8]

Count Frontenac hesitated also to precipitate Franco-Iroquois war. Quickly sensing his reluctance, the emboldened Iroquois launched raid after raid into the Mississippi Valley. But here, as with the Susquehannocks, the beaver war pattern of conquest could not be achieved. After initial reverses, the Illinois acquired arms and allies, and they remained doughtily in the field in spite of severe decline in population. The legend that they succumbed to the Iroquois is not true. When they finally went down to defeat, their conquerors were the Potawatomis, a third component of the numerous and widespread Ottawa-Ojibwa-Potawatomi "Three Fires."[9] (To call them a confederation is stretching language a bit, but

6. Ibid., pp. 46–47.
7. Hunt, *Wars of the Iroquois*, pp. 149–50; Duchesneau's memoir, Nov. 13, 1681, *N.Y.Col.Docs.* 9:163.
8. Loc. cit.
9. R. David Edmunds, *The Potawatomis: Keepers of the Fire* (Norman: University of Oklahoma Press, 1978), pp. 48–49.

they recognized kinship with each other, and their bands frequently allied for particular objectives.)[10]

Mohawks divided by mission

While the western Iroquois were troubled by the imperialist ventures of Frontenac and La Salle, the Mohawks in the east suffered from a different instrument of French policy. The Mohawks had carefully avoided overt hostilities with New France since de Tracy's campaign in 1666 had captured and burned all the Mohawk villages and their winter food supply. One of the conditions of the peace then imposed upon the Mohawks was acceptance of Jesuit missionaries in their villages. These made remarkably quick progress in conversion, in part because of the favor shown to converts by the French, and they seriously weakened the Mohawk tribal structure. As in the Huron villages earlier, the missionaries required converts to reject participation in the unifying traditional rituals of the tribe, and even to heap scorn on the tribal members who remained faithful to tradition. The ensuing controversies did not always satisfy missionary desires as converts sometimes capitulated to the intense pressures exerted by their traditionalist kin. To prevent such recidivism, the missionaries changed strategy. Instead of inciting converts to proselytize within the tribe, the Jesuits withdrew the converts entirely from the tribal villages and took them to two mission reservations near Montreal, beginning in 1669. The drain took serious toll of Mohawk strength. By 1680, there were at least 400 Indians in residence at the mission villages, most of whom were Iroquois; of these, most were Mohawks. They came to be called the Caughnawaga Mohawks, French Mohawks, or simply Caughnawagas, and they acted as staunch allies of New France.[11] Their presence at the head of the Mahican Channel created a very special situation on that vital artery of transportation. Conscious of kinship, Mohawk and Caughnawaga rarely and reluctantly fought each other even when their patrons warred most bitterly. Unlike the turbulent situation in the west, trade could be carried securely along the Montreal-Albany axis because of the understandings between the dominant Indians at its ends. But, much as that gain benefited certain Albany merchants, it did little to reconcile the embittered

---

10. See James A. Clifton, "Potawatomi," in *Northeast*, pp. 725–42, esp. pp. 730–32.

11. Trelease, *Indian Affairs*, pp. 251–53, 261; Dongan's report to Lords of Trade, Feb. 22, 1687, *N.Y.Col.Docs.* 3:394; Sadeganaktie's speech, July 21, 1701, *N.Y.Col.Docs.* 4:907.

Gunther Michelson's population review suggests that there was a very substantial drain of Mohawks to Canada on the order of 20–30 percent. He lists 300 total Mohawk population at Canada's Caughnawaga in 1676, and 300 Mohawk *warriors* in Iroquoia, implying a total population there of 900 to 1500. "Iroquois Population Statistics," Table II, p. 5.

chiefs of the Mohawk nation as they watched their followers walk away to join the French.

To sum up, relations between the Iroquois and New France became more discordant with each passing year. Quite apart from English influence or instigation, the interests and policies of tribes at both ends of Iroquoia conflicted directly with French interests and policies. It was easy, therefore, for English colonial imperialists to find Iroquois leaders willing to help challenge French power. No mysterious powers of persuasion were needed; interests coincided, and the allies' most serious problem was to work out the means of implementing their joint policies.

In New York the expansionist impulse required time to develop. Albany's Dutch merchants felt no urge to venture into the wilderness as long as the Indians would come to them. When Edmund Andros became governor in 1674, the personal alliance between the royal families of Stuart and Bourbon guaranteed peace between England and France, and the peace held as long as a Stuart wore the crown. Andros's task, therefore, was to guard English interests defensively. In his conception, the Covenant Chain was a nonaggression pact rather than an alliance for aggression. He made no attempt to penetrate the French protectorate, but he was annoyed by what he perceived as French efforts to seduce the Five Nations from England. In 1678 he urged the Iroquois to evict all Frenchmen from their territories, especially the vexatious Jesuits, and he laid the foundation for the English crown's subsequent claim to the Iroquois as "subjects."[12]

Livingston and Dongan

Andros's chief assistant in Indian affairs was Robert Livingston, a man destined to become the leader of New York's aggressive expansionists. Born and reared in Scotland, Livingston had learned the Dutch language and the merchant's trade as a youth in Amsterdam. Of Presbyterian clerical stock, he took seriously the notion that the earth was intended for the elect, and he came to Albany at the age of twenty with the intention of getting his share. He started in the Indian trade, connected himself to the Van Rensselaer family and fortune by a judicious marriage, and acquired the reputation of being "the most selfish man alive."[13] His fluency in Dutch

12. Frontenac to the king, Nov. 6, 1679, *N.Y.Col.Docs.* 9:129; Andros to Blathwayt, March 25, 1679, *N.Y.Col.Docs.* 3:278; treaty minutes, July 21, 1679, *Wraxall's Abridgment*, p. 9; Mohawk sachem Sindachsegie, Aug. 6, 1687, *N.Y.Col.Docs.* 3:442.

13. For Livingston's biography see Lawrence H. Leder, *Robert Livingston, 1654–1728, and the Politics of Colonial New York,* published for the Institute of Early American History and Culture (Chapel Hill: University of North Carolina Press, 1961). The quotation is at p. 222. For the origins of Livingston Manor, on which the family based its wealth and power, see George Dangerfield, *Chancellor Robert R. Livingston of New York, 1746–1813* (New York: Har-

made him useful to Andros, who appointed him secretary of Indian Affairs in 1675, in which post Livingston observed and influenced the Iroquois until he managed to have his son Philip succeed him in 1722.[14] It was Livingston who called Andros's attention in 1678 to the dangerous French activities among the Iroquois and suggested the necessity of prompt counter measures.

Throughout Livingston's life—a long one for the times—he urged the policy of westward expansion. It fitted the western strategy of the Iroquois although Albany's Dutch merchant *handlaers* disliked its costs and risks and were supported by business partners among the export merchants in the city of New York. In 1683 Thomas Dongan arrived to succeed Edmund Andros as governor. Dongan and Livingston were kindred souls, and they immediately became political allies. In a new generation of energetic statesmen, Dongan and Livingston and their Iroquois allies challenged New France to the utmost degree permitted by English royal policy and New York's colonial resources.

La Barre

They were confronted by an equally aggressive new governor general of New France. Frontenac's successor, Joseph-Antoine Le Febvre de La Barre had arrived in New France in 1682. He was immediately advised by older residents that the Iroquois must be suppressed if France was not to lose the west. The advice implied support for the trading structures built earlier by La Salle, but it did not extend to maintaining La Salle in charge. La Barre joined the faction led by the merchant Aubert La Chesnaye, which had opposed Frontenac and La Salle all along. La Barre, as his biographer remarks, "wanted above all to get rid of La Salle, and he devoted all his efforts to making the latter's position untenable and driving him out of all the posts he had founded."[15]

With regard to the Iroquois, La Barre had two objectives. He aimed to eliminate by force the Seneca threat to French control of the west, but in the meantime he saw opportunities for quick enrichment by trading with Albany through territory controlled by the Mohawks. Close to Montreal, at the northern end of the Mahican Channel, was the seigneury of Cham-

court, Brace and Co., 1960), pp. 12–16. For the Albany Dutch see Alice P. Kenney, *The Gansevoorts of Albany: Dutch Patricians in the Upper Hudson Valley* (Syracuse, N.Y.: Syracuse University Press, 1969); and idem, *Stubborn for Liberty: The Dutch in New York* (Syracuse: Syracuse University Press, 1975).

14. Leder, *Robert Livingston*, pp. 15–16, 235–55; Council of trade and plantations to governor Burnet, June 6, 1722, in *CSPA&WI, 1722–1723*, no. 171, p. 83.

15. R. La Roque de Roquebrune, "Joseph-Antoine Le Febvre de La Barre," *Dict.Can.Biog.* 2:444.

bly, the master of which allied himself in trade with La Salle's enemy and La Barre's friend, La Chesnaye. In the authentic manner of the seventeenth century, La Barre consulted his own interest. While Franco-Seneca relations deteriorated in the west, Franco-Mohawk relations continued pacific and businesslike in the east.[16] In La Barre's mind this situation was strictly temporary; he had every intention of a series of conquests as soon as he could muster resources. "If I defeat these [Iroquois] people," he wrote in 1682, "I shall not be able to resist attacking the people at Albany, who give them arms and protection."[17]

However, while preparing for conquest, La Barre made certain lucrative arrangements: he sent official communications to Thomas Dongan that said all the diplomatically correct things about how horridly the Iroquois were behaving; however, according to La Barre's enemies, his messenger carried furs as well as letters to Albany, and Dongan's return emissaries were described as openly engaged in trade in Quebec. It is beyond doubt that a certain Sieur de Salvaye, well known as a coureur de bois, performed highly confidential services for La Barre as go-between with Dongan.[18]

Dongan, it may be seen, was also far from averse to making a little profit on the sly. He cooperated up to the point where La Barre's interests conflicted with his own. He dealt amiably with La Barre's man Salvaye, but Dongan had no intention of turning the Senecas over to the French. They were performing a valuable service to New York by disrupting Canada's hold on the western tribes; to abandon them would be to abandon English hopes for western empire. Therefore, while Dongan abetted the trade between Albany and Montreal, he also affirmed English protection for the Senecas. It was largely a rhetorical kind of protection since Dongan's military resources hardly extended beyond the Indians themselves. He had no militia of the sort that made New England's colonies formidable. The Dutch inhabitants of New York had always relied on mercenary soldiers even during New Netherland's rule. Dongan was to boast in 1687 that he

16. Leopold Lamontagne, "Jacques Duchesneau de La Doussiniére et d'Ambault," *Dict.Can.Biog.* 1:289; Jean-Guy Pelletier, "Saurel, Pierre de," ibid., p. 602; Denonville to Seignelay, May 8, 1686, *N.Y.Col.Docs.* 9:290; Lahontan, *New Voyages to North-America* 1:91; La Barre to Dongan, June 15, 1684, *N.Y.Col.Docs.* 3:447–48.

17. La Barre to ?, Nov. 11, 1682, *CSPA&WI, 1685–1688*, no. 2072, p. 641.

18. Remonstrance of Sieur de la Salle, 1684, *N.Y.Col.Docs.* 9:215. The names of two particular coureurs de bois recur several times in connection with the events discussed here, though neither is mentioned in *Dict.Can.Biog.* One hopes that they will find biographers. Gideon Petit and a man identified only as Sieur de Salvaye were deeply engaged in trade with the English. After their protector, La Barre, left office, they fled to Albany. Later they became partners briefly with Peter Bisaillon, a sometime associate of Tonty, who also took refuge among the English, but in Pennsylvania, where he became prominent. Bisaillon is in *Dict.Can.Biog.* 3:65–66. The scanty references for Petit and Salvaye are as follows: *N.Y.Col.Docs.* 9:212, 215, 326; 3:450–51, 471; *Doc.Hist.N.Y.* 1:102–5; *Livingston Indian Records*, p. 127; *Md. Arch* 20:470–71.

had 300 to 400 available soldiers "which makes as much noise as if we had six times as many."[19]. Against New France, something more than noise would be needed.

Lord Howard's treaty

In 1684 the contentions came to a climax. Iroquois raids in the west and the south roused anger simultaneously in Virginia and Canada. The Virginia raids were intended to force the Indians under that colony's protection to come into the Covenant Chain as direct tributaries of the Five Nations rather than through the intermediation of Virginia. This distinction, if it was understood by Virginia's ruling gentry, failed to impress them. The colony's governor, the improbably named Lord Howard of Effingham, journeyed personally to New York to do something effective about the Iroquois intrusions.

But Lord Howard's belligerence softened considerably when news arrived from Canada. Simultaneous to the raids in Virginia, the Senecas and Cayugas had invaded the Illinois country once more. Going beyond their standard raids on other tribes, these Iroquois had become so bold as to attack La Salle's Fort St. Louis on the Illinois River (unsuccessfully) and had pillaged a canoe manned by fourteen Frenchmen.[20] La Barre announced to Dongan his intention of waging war against the western Iroquois, while leaving the unoffending Mohawks and Oneidas at peace, and demanded that Dongan refrain from selling arms to the Indians so that they should "see the Christians united on this subject."[21] Neither Dongan nor Lord Howard shared this desire for Christian unity. Both knew that if La Barre succeeded in conquering the Senecas, there would be no more hope for English advance westward. Their instant reaction was to reassert England's claim to sovereignty over the Five Nations.

Dongan claimed that an attack on the Senecas would be an invasion of English territory.[22] Lord Howard discovered a need for reconciliation with the tribes he had intended to browbeat. At a treaty with the Iroquois, he complained indignantly about outrages and violations of the Covenant Chain compacts. He made strong verbal demands for reform of Iroquois behavior. But he exacted no reparations, offered no threats, and specified

19. Dongan to Earl of Sunderland, Oct. 31, 1687, in *CSPA&WI, 1658-1688*, no. 1494, p. 461.
20. Howard's instructions for Arnout the interpreter, ca. July 1684, in *Livingston Indian Records*, 70 71; La Barre to Dongan, June 15, 1684, in *Doc.Hist.N.Y.* 1:99-100.
21. Loc. cit.
22. Dongan to La Barre, June 24, 1684, and July 1684, in *Doc.Hist.N.Y.* 1:100-102.

no sanctions. This is the more remarkable in light of Iroquois admissions about their misbehavior in Virginia.[23]

"We will conceal nothing of the Evil," said the Mohawk speaker Odianne as he turned to excoriate the silent Oneidas, Onondagas, and Cayugas. "You are Stupid, Brutish, and have no Understanding, thus to break your Covenant. . . . we are ready to cry, for shame of you."

It is difficult to conceive the proud Iroquois relishing such a tongue lashing, regardless of its coming from one of their own people. Odianne spoke as one giving orders rather than advice.

You Oneydoes, I speak to you as Children. Be no longer void of Understanding.

You Onnondagas, our Bretheren, you are like Deaf People, that cannot hear, your Senses are cover'd with Dirt and Filth.

You Cayugas, Do not return into your former ways. There are three things we must all observe.

First, The Covenant with Corlaer [New York]. *Secondly*, The Covenant with Virginia and Maryland. *Thirdly*, The Covenant with Boston. We must Stamp Understanding into you, that you may be obedient. And Take this Belt for a Remembrancer.

The division between the Mohawks and the other tribes was never clearer. Odianne's speech was the message that the English colonials wanted conveyed. The response from the other tribes was not so satisfactory. Speaking for the others, an Onondaga sachem uttered mollifying phrases without committing them to a thing. "We Thank the great Sachem of Virginia, that he has so readily forgiven and forgot the Evil that has been done; and We, on our parts, gladly catch at, and lay hold of the Chain." Instead of retracting the policies that involved raids on Virginia, the Onondagas seized the opportunity to press for further implementation of them. "We desire that the Path may be open for the Indians under your Lordships Protection to come safely and freely to this place, in order to confirm this Peace." To force Virginia's allied tribes into the Iroquois tributary system had been precisely the point of all the fighting. No wonder, then, that "the Oneydoes, Onnondagas and Cayugas, joyntly, . . . Thank'd the Governor of New-York for his effectual Mediation with the Governor of Virginia, in their favour."[24]

The Senecas arrived several days after the treaty began. Like the Mohawks, they disavowed complicity in the raids on Virginia, and they

23. Propositions, July 30, 1684, *Livingston Indian Records*, pp. 71–73. Howard's speech is also in Colden, *History*, pp. 32–35. Curiously, it is lacking in the Virginia mss. The versions vary slightly; Colden's looks cleaned up. The full mss. minutes of this treaty are in Virginia State Library, Richmond: Colonial Papers, Folder 4, Item 2a. I have used the photocopy at the Newberry Library.

24. Colden, *History*, pp. 35–39.

agreed readily to Lord Howard's demand that "we must not come near the Heads of your Rivers, nor near your Plantations, but keep at the foot of the Mountains."[25] Agreement or not, the issue continued to rankle for more than thirty years afterward. But the Senecas had other matters on their minds. Their orientation was chiefly westward, and they were the primary target of La Barre's threats. When Dongan acquainted them with La Barre's demand for reparations for the canoe they had plundered, they became bitter.

"When the Governor of Canada speaks to us of the Chain, he calls us Children, and saith, *I am your Father, you must hold fast the Chain, and I will do the same. I will Protect you as a Father doth his Children.* Is this Protection, to speak thus with his Lips, and at the same time to knock us on the head, by assisting our Enemies with Ammunition? . . . he often forbids us to make War on any of the Nations with whom he Trades, and at the same time furnishes them with all sorts of Ammunition, to enable them to destroy us. . . . Corlaer said to us, that Satisfaction must be made to the French for the Mischief we have done them. This he said before he heard our Answer. Now let him that hath Inspection over all our Countries, on whom our Eyes are fix'd, let him, ev'n Corlaer judge and determine. If you say it must be paid, we shall pay it, but we cannot live without free Bever-hunting. . . . Have we wander'd out of the way, as the Governor of Canada says. We do not threaten him with War, as he threatens us. What shall we do? Shall we run away, or shall we sit still in our Houses? What shall we do?"[26]

Colden, who transcribed the speech from New York's Indian records, does not give Dongan's response, but Canada got no reparations.

The Senecas' speech was more challenging than humble. When their speaker turned to Lord Howard, he gave no hint whatever of humility. In return for the pledge to stay beyond Virginia's settlements, he demanded that the Virginians send one of their allied tribes to become an Iroquois tributary. "You tell us, that the Cahnawaas [Conoys] will come hither to strengthen the Chain. Let them not make any Excuse."[27]

Dongan and Lord Howard were able to extract one statement from the Iroquois—more precisely, the Onondagas and Cayugas—that they badly needed to make their case for English sovereignty, but they did not get it

25. Ibid. Colden's phrasing differs substantively from that of the Virginia mss. (n. 23, above). Colden, p. 43, has the Senecas saying that in future they will "wholly stay away *from Virginia.*" The mss., p. 12, says, "We shall not come near *your Plantations.*" As Virginia claimed territory far beyond its settled plantations—indeed, to the Pacific coast—what the Senecas promised was not what Colden said they had promised. My emphasis.

26. Colden, *History*, pp. 48–49; Va. mss., pp. 21–22 (see n. 23, above). Colden has the Senecas saying, "We speak to him that Governs and Commands us." No such unlikely phrase appears in the mss.

27. Colden, *History*, p. 43.

in quite the form they wanted. The Onondaga speaker declared, "We have put our Lands and our Selves under the Protection of the great Duke of York. . . . We have put our Selves under the great Sachem Charles, that lives on the other side of the great Lake [the Atlantic Ocean]. . . . We will not therefore joyn our selves or our Lands to any other Government but this." But then he added, "Let your Friend, the great Sachem that lives on the other side the great Lake know this," and we can imagine him staring directly into Dongan's eyes. "We being a Free People, tho' united to the English, may give our Lands, and be joyn'd to the Sachem we like best. We give this Bever to Remember what we say."[28]

To the amusement of the French, Dongan presented the Iroquois sachems with plaques bearing the duke of York's arms to be posted in the Indian villages for protection.[29] "We may suppose," remarks Colden with rare sarcasm, "they were told [these plaques] would save them from the French." The Indians went along with this comedy but knew better than to depend upon it. Apart from that gesture, Dongan assisted with information about French intentions as he obtained it from La Barre, and we may be certain that Albany continued to supply arms.

Onondaga independence

Rumors reached Dongan that the Iroquois wanted to negotiate with La Barre. He immediately forbade them to do so. Probably for different reasons, the Senecas and Mohawks obeyed his ban; but the middle tribes rejected it, and their reasons explain the basis of English policy. An Onondaga sachem was blunt: *"You say we are Subjects to the King of England and Duke of York, but we say, we are Brethren. We must take care of our selves. Those Arms fixed upon the Post without the Gate, cannot defend us against the Arms of La Barre."* It would appear from his speech that the Onondagas saw opportunity in the situation to regain a position of ascendancy in the Iroquois League. "Brother Corlaer, We tell you, That we shall bind a Covenant Chain to our Arm, and to his, as thick as that Post (Pointing to a Post of the House). Be not dissatisf'd; should we not imbrace this Happiness offer'd to us, viz. Peace, in the place of War yea, we shall take the Evil doers, the Sennekas by the hand, and La Barre likewise, and their ax and his Sword shall be thrown into a deep Water. We wish our Brother Corlaer were present, but it seems the time will not permit of it."[30]

In the circumstances, it was not exactly brotherly of the Onondaga to

28. Colden, *History*, p. 42. This agrees substantially with the mss.
29. La Barre's memoir, Oct. 1, 1684, *N.Y.Col.Docs.* 9:242:
30. Colden, *History*, p. 51.

denounce the Senecas as evil doers, but the available documents for this occasion and the treaty with La Barre that followed suggest strongly that the Onondagas were not thinking altruistically. Rather, they saw opportunity to strengthen themselves in relation to the other Iroquois nations by using alliance with Montreal as the Mohawks used their ties with Albany. Through chance, the Onondagas seemed at first to succeed. When they met with La Barre, he had blundered into their power.

La Barre's humiliation

La Barre had hoped to awe the Iroquois by a show of great force. He assembled an army at Fort Frontenac/Cadaraqui of overwhelming size: 600 soldiers and 300 allied tribesmen, to be joined by another 600 Frenchmen and Indians from the west. For once, however, an epidemic served the Indians instead of Europeans. La Barre's troops were disabled by Spanish influenza, and when he finally met the Onondagas with such troops as could still travel, the Iroquois knew that they had the upper hand.[31] La Barre heard his intended menace turned back on him by Onondaga speaker Garangula.

"Hear Yonnondio, I do not Sleep, I have my eyes Open, and the Sun which enlightens me discovers to me a great Captain at the head of a Company of Soldiers, who speaks as if he were Dreaming. He says that he only came to the Lake to smoke on the great Calumet [pipe of peace] with the Onnondagas. But Garangula says, that he sees the Contrary, that it was to knock them on the head, if Sickness had not weakened the Arms of the French.

I see Yonnondio Raving in a Camp of sick men, who's Lives the great Spirit has saved, by inflicting this Sickness on them. Hear Yonnondio, Our Women had taken their Clubs, our Children and Old Men had carried their Bows and Arrows into the heart of your Camp, if our Warriors had not disarmed them, and retained them when your Messenger, Ohquesse appeared in our Castle."[32]

Cadwallader Colden dismissed the affair contemptuously as an expensive expedition intended to terrorize the Five Nations that ended "by a Dispute between the French General and an Old Indian," but there was rather more to it than that.[33] Issues of territoriality and sovereignty came

31. Eccles, *France in America*, p. 92. Figures on the size of La Barre's army vary. I have used those in De Meulles to the minister, Oct. 10, 1684, *Doc.Hist.N.Y.* 1:120. See also Colden, *History*, p. 53; Lahontan, *New Voyages* 1:79–81; Thomas Grassman, "Otreouti," *Dict.Can.Biog.* 1:525–26.

32. Colden, History, pp. 54–55.

33. Ibid., p. 57.

A bibliographic note: The speeches in Colden and the Va. mss. that relate to Iroquois

into focus, and a new Indian conception of the Convenant Chain wholly contradictory to European conceptions of law.

La Barre accused: "The Warriors of the Five Nations have conducted the English into the Lakes which belong to the King, my Master, and brought the English among the Nations that are his Children." Garangula retorted, "We carried the English into *our* Lakes, to traffick there with the Utawawas and Quatoghies, as the Adirondacks brought the French to our Castles, to carry on a Trade which the English say is theirs. *We are born free.* We neither depend upon Yonnondio nor Corlaer. We may go where we please, and carry with us whom we please, and buy and sell what we please. If your Allies be your Slaves, use *them* as such, Command *them* to receive no other but your People. *This Belt Preserves my Words.*"[34]

The sovereignty issue is plain. For the conception of the Chain, we must hark back to the Onondagas' statement of intention as they were preparing for the treaty. They aimed at binding a Covenant Chain between themselves and Canada. They gave no sign of wanting to renounce the Chain already binding them to New York. When they succeeded in dictating terms to La Barre (including the abandonment of his Illinois allies) they transformed *the* Covenant Chain from a confederation with New York and the Mohawks at its center to a confederation with the Onondagas linking Canada and New York. For a fleeting historical moment the Onondagas thought they were at the head of an organization that included France and Britain—a strange and scandalous empire indeed.

This was an ultimate heresy in European conceptions of statecraft and law. The same organization could not include two European powers, both claiming sovereignty in theory over other members of the organization and each frustrating the other's realization of sovereignty in fact—not to speak of the link binding them together being an Indian tribe without a "civil" government. Had the Onondagas' plan worked, the Covenant Chain would necessarily have ceased to be in English theory an English property and would have become an unambiguously international as well as intercultural league. Even by rather different Indian conceptions, the Onondagas had stretched their Chain so far that it would have to snap.

putting their lands under the protection of the duke of York and the king of England are subject to a specific interpretation as well as the more general one given here, and there is some question as to how the colonial scribes may have twisted language to get the desired meaning of the Iroquois putting *all* their lands under English protection. The particular lands that the Onondagas and Cayugas referred to included most of the Susquehanna Valley involved in a contest between New York and Pennsylvania for jurisdiction. That contest has been excluded from this chapter for the sake of simplicity and comprehensibility. See chapter 12, below.

34. Ibid., pp. 52–55. My italics except for the last sentence. There is hilarious contrast between Colden's report and the one sent back to France by La Barre, printed in *Doc.Hist.N.Y.* 1:117–20. In the furtive manner usual to officialdom when embarrassed, La Barre's shame was endorsed by the minister, "These letters must be kept secret."

Chapter 10 ❧ "THEY FLOURISH and WE DECREASE."

Since the time that the Governours have been here from the Great King of England we have made a Generall and more firme covenant which has grown stronger and stronger from time to time, and our neighbours seeing the advantage thereof came and put in their hands into the same chain, particularly they of New England, Connecticutt, New Jersey, Pensilvania, Maryland, and Virginia. But since that time that all Our neighbours have put in their hands into the covenant chain We have had great struggling and trouble from the Common enemy, the ffrench. Our Brother Cayenquiragoes wrist and Ours are tyred and stiff with holding fast the chain alone while the rest of Our neighbours sit still and smoake it. The Grease is melted from our flesh and drops upon our neighbours who are grown fatt and live at ease while we become lean. They flourish and we decrease.

Onondaga chief Sadekanarktie, August 15, 1694

The Onondagas' bloodless triumph of 1684 may justly be called the zenith of Iroquois glory. Diplomacy, no matter how brilliant, is the prisoner of statistics and technology, and European mass was too much for Iroquois energy. If Governor La Barre was incompetent to generate and control the power potentially at his service, there were other Frenchmen with greater ability. Across the Atlantic the word of La Barre's disgraceful peace and "abandonment of the Illinois" stirred royal wrath. Louis XIV promptly appointed a new governor general to replace La Barre and commanded new policies.

Denonville

For the new governor, the Marquis de Denonville, the "principal object," according to the king's instructions, would be "to secure the quiet of Canada by a firm and solid peace; but in order that such a peace be permanent, the pride of the Iroquois must be humbled, the Illinois and other allies who have been abandoned by Sieur de la Barre must be sustained, and the Iroquois must from the outset be given, by a firm and vigorous policy, to understand that they will have everything to dread if they do not submit to the conditions it will be his pleasure to impose on them." Further,

Denonville "must be aware that the Governor of New-York has undertaken to assist the Iroquois, and to extend British dominion up to the banks of the River St. Lawrence, and over the entire territory inhabited by these Indians." These English activities required a carefully balanced policy. "Everything must be done to maintain good understanding between the French and English. But if the latter, contrary to all appearances, excite and aid the Indians, they must be treated as enemies when found on Indian territory, without, at the same time, attempting anything on territory under the obedience of the King of England."[1]

Apart from a certain fuzziness about the meaning of the "Indian territory" at the heart of the contentions, these instructions gave clear guidance; and Denonville, with all his faults, was an energetic man. The pattern of 1664 was about to be repeated: as the Mohawks had then been beaten, so now the Senecas would be. Both tribes escaped outright conquest, but neither ever wholly recovered its former strength.

Dongan's expansionism

Dongan, of course, could not foresee the future. Made confident by La Barre's weakness, Dongan launched a campaign to detach New France's Indian allies and bring them into his own Covenant Chain. It was essential for him to convince the Iroquois that the French themselves could not be members of the Chain. He engaged all the Chain's affiliates in the task, as well as renegade Canadian coureurs de bois and Albany's own bushlopers. Fundamental to his strategy was the assertion of the Indians' "submission" to New York. Thus the Indians who allied themselves to the Iroquois became the "dependents" of the Iroquois, who were, in Dongan's argument, the "subjects" of New York.

As this device became central to British policy and traditional American historiography, Dongan's words and their purpose must be noted well. He wrote to the President of the Privy Council: "In the last Treaty the ffrench copy has it exprest, That the savages are not to be assisted, which word being generall they lay hold of, but the English copy sayes Wilde Indians, as I conceive to make a distinction between those who submitt to [civil] government and those who doe not, which reaches not our Indians who have from time to time submitted themselfs under his Majesty's Souveraignity."[2]

Dongan continued Andros's policy of treating directly with the Algonquian Indians on the Hudson River, and he made his first gains through

1. Instructions to M. de Denonville, March 10, 1685, in *N.Y.Col.Docs.* IX, 271–72.
2. Dongan to the Lord President, Feb. 19, 1688, *N.Y.Col.Docs.* 3:511.

their means. A delegation of Mahicans living in Canada—probably refugees from Mohawk attacks in the Second Puritan Conquest—conferred with Dongan in 1684. At his solicitation they returned in July 1685 in strength (fifty-six men and one hundred women and children) to take up residence at Schaghticoke. Albany's magistrates made them welcome and asked for more: "acquaint the Rest of your nation that are Still at Conida of the good Entertainment you have here and send them this Belt of wampum as a letter from the governor who Promises them all favor and Protection and you are to use all means to Perswade them to live at Skachkook for there is land Eneugh and it shall be for you and them and Posterity after you and you need not to doubt but a firm and Strong Covenant chain Shall be kept unviolable on our Parts between us and all other of your nation that shall come and live under this government."[3]

The campaign continued. The "River Indians" visited their brethren among the Pennakooks in New England, and the Mohawks urged their Catholic brethren at Canada's Caughnawaga mission to return; to the latter, Dongan promised land at Saratoga and a resident priest.[4] Among the western tribes, Iroquois proposals for trade and alliance, alternating with Iroquois raids against holdouts, were so effective that Governor Denonville was almost in despair. "The principal affair at present," he wrote in November 1686, "is the security of this Colony which is in evident danger of perishing if the Iroquois be let alone."[5]

Perhaps Dongan could have been bought off. He requested Denonville's intervention to get him 25,000 livres supposedly owing from Dongan's prior service in France's armies. He had, in fact, performed such service, but Denonville interpreted his request as compensation for services yet to be performed. Denonville passed the request along to Versailles with a contemptuous hint that a bribe would be wasted. Dongan was "a very selfish man and, should you consider it proper, would assuredly govern himself accordingly. But the secret is, he is not master of those merchants from whom he draws money." "Those merchants," of course, were the Albanians with whom Dongan was working in close accord not only to expand future horizons of trade and territory, but more urgently to seize the Great Lakes trade at once. In 1685 ten canoes from Albany were guided to Michilimackinac by French deserters. Michilimackinac was the very hub of the French trade in the far west. Located on an island at

3. Propositions of "North Indians," July 1, 1685, and Albanians' reply, July 2, 1685; Propositions of the Senecas, Aug. 3, 1685; *Livingston Indian Records*, pp. 77–81.

4. Propositions of River Indians, Aug. 4, 1685, *Livingston Indian Records*, p. 82; Report by Onnachragewaes, Aug. 5, 1686, *ibid.*, p. 104.

5. Dongan's service: Stephen Saunders Webb, *The Governors-General: The English Army and the Definition of the Empire, 1569–1681*, published for the Institute of Early American History and Culture (Chapel Hill: University of North Carolina Press, 1979), p. 498. Denonville's remark: *N.Y.Col.Docs.* 9:298.

the conjunction of Lakes Superior, Michigan, and Huron, the post there drew Indian hunters and controlled waterborne traffic in a vast region with a radius of hundreds of miles. There was no question in anyone's mind that Englishmen at Michilimackinac would destroy French trade with the inland Indians, and with it the French empire in the west.[6]

Those who made the trip in 1685 caught the French by surprise. They made a great impression on the Huron and Ottawa tribes with their cheap goods and were escorted home by Senecas whose hope was to increase east-west traffic through their territory. In August and September of 1686, Dongan licensed a much larger expedition into the lakes country, and in December he authorized another for the following spring.[7] By this time, however, the French were ready. They captured both of Dongan's expeditions and took the traders off to Quebec for several weeks of jail before shipping them back to Albany. The Canadian turncoats who had guided them were put to death.[8]

Also in 1686, Dongan asserted a right to control the trade of all colonials: addressing the Five Nations chiefs in May, he said, "I hear there are a great many English, dutch, and french goes a hunting and Tradeing with the farr nations of Indians, without a Seale from me, I would not graunt itt," adding, "You are not to Suffer any to Trade or hunt, butt Such as have 3 little Red Seals to show, a Pattern whereof you Shall Take along with you." This was too extreme for the Iroquois. Declining to interfere with the trade of Englishmen, the Onondagas remarked, "We are affraid the seals given us put us in a new trouble." Their old trouble with the French continued to fill Denonville's dispatches.[9] Denonville missed little of Dongan's activities among the Indians, and everything that came in from his widespread intelligence network increased his apprehensions.

Denonville's attack

Denonville was no La Barre. A competent soldier, he had come to Canada with instructions to make the colony secure, whether by war or diplomacy being at his discretion. From the beginning he judged that the Iroquois would have to be beaten in war to fulfill his mandate, but two factors made him hesitate; the condition of New France was such that the

6. Denonville to Seignelay, May 8, 1686, *N.Y.Col.Docs.* 9:287–88. Trelease, *Indian Affairs*, pp. 269–70.

7. *Livingston Indian Records*, pp. 106–8; Trelease, *Indian Affairs*, pp. 269–70.

8. Eccles, *Canadian Frontier*, p. 119.

9. Treaty minutes, Aug. 30–Sept. 1, 1681, mss., reconstituted from fragments in *Doc.Hist.N.Y.* 1:403–5, and N.Y.Council Minutes, mss., 5:163, 169. Copies on file in N.Y. State Archives and the Newberry Library.

odds seemed to lie in favor of the Iroquois, and the Jesuit missionaries in Iroquois villages—particularly Father Lamberville among the Ononda-gas—seemed to have influence enough to keep the Iroquois nations divided and amenable to diplomatic maneuver. Denonville temporized, appealed for troops from France, tried to get some system into Canada's chaotic administration, and argued at length with Dongan by letter. As he reported to Minister Seignelay, "M. Dongan has written me, and I have answered him as a man may do who wishes to dissimulate, and does not yet feel himself in a condition to get angry, much less to overcome his enemy." Behind Denonville's mild manner lay the conviction, reported in the same letter, that "the Iroquois have no other design than to destroy all our allies, one after the other, in order finally to annihilate us, and in that consists the entire policy of M. Dongan and his merchants."[10]

How much longer Denonville might have stalled is an unanswerable question. Dongan forced his hand by organizing the expeditions to Mich-ilimackinac. Denonville was desperately aware that the continued success of these expeditions would cause the Indians of the west to change sides, and without their Indian allies the French would be lost. In Paris, Minis-ter Seignelay and Louis XIV agreed with him. While Denonville dis-patched a force to waylay the traders, the king commanded an army to be sent from France. Since hesitation no longer served any useful purpose, the Iroquois were to feel his Majesty's might.

Unfortunately for Denonville, the mood of the mighty was thrifty. The king sent only half the troops requested and dispatched them too late. In lieu of the remainder he sent flattery: Denonville would certainly triumph, "having to contend only with Indians who have no experience in regular war, whilst on the contrary, those whom he will be able to marshal will prove most efficient being led by a man of his ability and experi-ence."[11] Denonville's outlook was considerably more realistic. Without delusions of decisive victory, he launched his available forces against the Senecas in the minimum hope of forestalling otherwise inevitable disaster. They marched in June, 1687. Their worst enemy was distance and the hardships of movement through rough country while they preserved con-stant guard. The Senecas ambushed them once, near their objective, but Denonville's precautions rendered the attack ineffectual, and the Senecas withdrew. Denonville then systematically destroyed their villages, burn-ing, among the rest, 350,000 bushels of standing corn and 50,000 bushels of dried corn. On a post in the midst of the ruins stood the arms of England donated by Dongan for the Senecas' "protection." Denonville acted out

10. Memoir, Nov. 8, 1686, N.Y.Col.Docs. 9:297-98.
11. N.Y.Col.Docs. 9:313, 321, 323, 340-41.

the solemn farce of claiming the land for France by prior right of exploration and conquest.[12]

As Denonville had foreseen, the worst part of his war came after the campaign. Political differences among the Iroquois were set aside as the tribes harassed New France from one end to the other. In New York, Dongan fed and armed them and rallied other Covenant Chain tribes to their aid. He also harangued them on political matters. The French attack had stripped the Iroquois for the time being, of all capacity to maneuver between the empires. In full fact as well as rhetoric, they had become dependents of New York, and Dongan seized his opportunity.

Dongan and Iroquois "subjects"

He advised them on measures to win their war, which were practical enough and just happened to be dear to the hearts of the Albanians for other reasons. The Iroquois were to bury the hatchets and make a Covenant Chain with the Ottawas and Miamis (Twightwees) and other western Indians, and "open a path for them this way, they being the King of England's subjects likewise." (They lived deep in the interior of territory claimed by the French.) Dongan would permit the Iroquois to levy a toll when the distant Indians came to trade ("they paying you an acknowledgement yearly for the Path"), and they should all "joyne together against the French." The Iroquois should also forget all their former differences with Indians who had once lived with or near them. The Christian Iroquois should be persuaded to return from Caughnawaga, and the old grudge against the Mahicans and North Indians should be buried—"all means must bee used to bring them home, and use them kindly, as they passe throw your Country." Dongan would help by building "a Fort upon the Lake" for "the Brethren's security and assistance." His unspoken implication being that the times were such that the Brethren must surely welcome what they had formerly forbidden.

He lectured them also on the general principles of constitutional law and what such principles entailed. "You having two or three years agoe made a Covenant chaine with the French contrarie to my commands (which I knew, could not hold long) it being void in ittselfe amongst the Christians, forasmuch as subjects (as you are) ought not to treat with any forraigne Nation, it not lying in your power, have your selfs brought this trouble upon you." Practically speaking, these principles required the Iro-

12. Lanctot, *History of Canada* 2:104–6; W. J. Eccles, *Canada under Louis XIV, 1663–1701*, Canadian Centenary Series (Toronto: McClelland and Stewart, 1964), pp. 149–54.

quois to take Dongan's orders and stop molesting Indians in the colony of Virginia, "for all the King of England's subjects are bound to joyne with one another against any Enemy that will fall upon them." If the Iroquois failed to give satisfaction to the governor of Virginia, Dongan himself would "joyne with him and warr upon you, and then you will be totally ruined."[13]

The Iroquois ignored Dongan's rodomontade and pretensions. They conceded fault and error in particulars and accepted Dongan's strategy for dealing with other Indians. They agreed specifically not to make a peace with the French "without your Excellency's commands." But they retained for themselves the power to make treaties generally, tacitly rejecting Dongan's definition of their subject status. Politely, but firmly, they reminded him of their importance to English interest, "for the French would faine kill us all and when that is done, they would carry all the Bever trade to Canida, and the great King of England would loose the land likewise."[14]

As subjects, the Iroquois were far from abject; though they used the term often, they defined it their own way. Invariably they reserved the right to accept "orders" by voluntary decision regardless of the phrasing of their decisions. Such a reserved right is, of course, the very negation of the European conception of subjection.

Dongan understood the distinctions and adapted his style of discourse to them. He needed the Iroquois in the role of subjects in order to perform two quite separate functions. Obviously if the Indians would genuinely knuckle under there would be significant increase in Dongan's power and authority. For his second purpose, however, the substance of subjection made little difference so long as the appearance was given. This purpose was the achievement of sovereignty—as against France rather than against the Iroquois—over Indian tribes and territories. For this purpose Dongan needed only the Iroquois acceptance of proper terminology, which state lawyers would know how to employ. As long as the Iroquois would say, "We are English subjects," Dongan was satisfied. When he pressed them and they resisted, he lifted the pressure. The clue to the relationship lies in the formal terms of address used by Dongan and the Iroquois for each other. Though he told them they were the "children" of the great King of England, he addressed them as "brethren" and described himself and the other English governors as equally "subjects" of the King.

13. Dongan's speech, Aug. 5, 1687, N.Y.Col.Docs. 3:438–41.
14. Mohawk chief Sindachsegie's speech, Aug. 6, 1687, N.Y.Col.Docs. 3:441–44.

Brethren or children?

The importance of such terms is demonstrated by what happened when Sir Edmund Andros resumed the government of New York for a brief period after it became part of the Dominion of New England. Andros met with the Five Nations at Albany in 1688, and they expressed their great joy at the return of their "Brother Corlaer." Andros cut them short. It seems that he had determined to bring them under discipline. He replied in curt, even abrupt, language, addressing them as "Children." The Mohawks immediately sensed the change and made an issue of it. When they replied, they called Andros merely "Corlaer," omitting the former "Brother," and they handed him a belt of wampum "eight deep" to emphasize their comment that "The Mohawk Sachems who spoke formerly with you are dead, and wee have not soe much knowledge as they had. Nevertheless though they are buried, yett lett the old Covenant that was made with our ancestors be kept firme. Then wee were called Brethren, and that was also well kept; therefore lett that of Brethren continue without any alteration."

The other Iroquois were less bold or more ready to equivocate, but they also showed recognition of the issue. Speaking for them a Cayuga sachem said, "Father Corlaer, Wee Fower Nations, the Senekes, Cayouges, Onondages and Oneydas, accept the name of Children; but. . . ." and then rejected one of Andros's demands.

Andros overbore them all. He faced the issues squarely: "You take notice of the word Brethren and Children, but leave it to mee: they are both words of relation and friendship, but Children the nearer. What I sayd yesterday remaines upon record in this place." The contrast with Dongan could hardly have been greater.[15]

Had Andros remained in office longer, the Iroquois might have been reduced to genuine subjection, for they held him in great awe and their condition was low. But his administration was brief, and his successors discovered that they needed the Iroquois more than the Iroquois needed them. Discreetly the magistrates of Albany resumed friendship with their "Brethren," and the term remained in use thereafter, its significance underscored by the test it had survived.[16]

By 1690, therefore, two fundamental issues of Covenant Chain relationships had been decided. After their dallying with La Barre, the Iroquois had become convinced that *the* Chain had to exclude the French from membership although it solicited Indians allied to the French. And, after

15. Treaty minutes, Sept. 21, 1688, *N.Y.Col.Docs.* 3:557–61.
16. Magistrates' speeches, Aug. 28, 1689, Feb. 26, 1690, *Doc.Hist.N.Y.*, ed. E. B. O'Callaghan, 2:86, 167.

Andros's aborted effort, the English had become convinced that the Iroquois, while subjects of a sort, could be governed only by negotiation and contract. Properly speaking, they were nearer vassals than subjects, closely resembling medieval communities of freemen whose acknowledged lord perforce respected their chartered liberties. In the Indians' case, however, the liberties derived from aboriginal sovereignty.

What the Iroquois meant by acknowledging themselves subject to the English crown was plainly stated to Dongan's face by Seneca chiefs in 1687, "we being the King of Englands Subjects though ourselves no ways obliged to harken to him."[17] Dongan used weasel language to imply the tribes' subjection while acknowledging indirectly their capacity to make their own decisions; he stated to the Lords of Trade in 1687 that "the Indians annexed those lands to this Government forty years ago."[18] His antagonist Denonville argued that "the English are the principal fomenters of the insolence and arrogance of the Iroquois, adroitly using them to extend their sovereignty; uniting with them as one nation, in such wise that the English pretend to own nothing less than Lake Ontario, Lake Erie, and the entire Saguinan country, that of the Hurons if these become their allies, and the whole territory towards the Micissippy."[19] Because of the pivotal position of the Iroquois, the French took pains to assert prior claim to sovereignty over the League.

Effects of the Glorious Revolution

All colonial political processes were interrupted by the overthrow of James II in England in 1688. Dubbed by Whig historians The Glorious Revolution, it might better be called the Protestant Gentry's Seizure of Power. A king was deposed and replaced by a queen and king sharing the throne. In domestic affairs the effect of the change was to prevent change. James's efforts to bring Catholicism into the open and to enlarge the royal prerogative were aborted. Regardless of William and Mary's new pomp, ultimate governmental power remained firmly lodged in Parliament; the revolutionary event merely confirmed the conservative fact. In colonial affairs, however, the crown had long held powers unchecked by Parliament, and the change of monarchs entailed drastic alterations of colonial administrative structures and officials.

Uprisings occurred in Massachusetts, New York, and Maryland. Sir Edmund Andros was arrested and sent as a prisoner from Massachusetts to England, but he convinced the new king of his loyalty and was sent

17. Speech, Aug. 2, 1687, mss., Penn Mss., Indian Affairs 1:5, HSP.
18. *CSPA&WI, 1685–1688*, March 1687, no. 1160, p. 327.
19. Denonville to Seignelay, June 12, 1686, *N.Y.Col.Docs.* 9:297.

back to America as governor of Virginia. The Dominion of New England broke up into its component colonies. The rebels in Massachusetts gained Plymouth and Maine but lost their bid for restoration of their former chartered autonomy. New York was thrown into the confusion and factionalism of Leisler's Rebellion. Proprietaries Lord Baltimore and Mr. Penn were temporarily deprived of the governments of their colonies.

Colonial order was further disturbed after May 1689, when William III brought England into the War of the League of Augsburg. (Called King William's War by the colonials.) William's act decided Louis XIV to conquer New York as his Canadian officers were urging. Louis sent Count Frontenac for a second term as governor of Canada, with instructions to effect the conquest.

Iroquois-French War

News of England's war also influenced Iroquois policy. Until then the Five Nations had temporized, alternating small-scale brawls with halfhearted negotiations, but not hazarding all-out war. Now it seemed that the Great Sachem Across the Water would have to commit warriors of his own people at last. With a commitment of aid from New York, the Iroquois went on the offensive. Taking advantage of New France's poor communications overseas, they surprised the village of La Chine before the Canadians had learned of England's newly proclaimed enmity. At dawn on August 5, 1689, 1,500 warriors raided the village about ten miles upstream from Montreal, creating horror and panic on all sides. Yet when wild rumor finally gave way to confirmable statistics, the Iroquois raid accomplished little. Twenty-four French habitants were killed on the scene, as well as about 40 soldiers and Indian allies. An estimated 42 habitants were taken off captive—to either death or adoption in Iroquois villages. Perhaps as many as 50 more were captured but survived to return. Thus immediate losses of all descriptions numbered fewer than 200 persons, and final casualties—actual deaths—no more than 106 at most. These figures have been rhetorically inflated by the same historians who make light of the deaths of similar numbers of Indians attacked by the colonials. The Iroquois withdrew, and the French reoccupied La Chine.[20]

So it was everywhere. Iroquois harassment caused great suffering in Canada, but it fell far short of decisive triumph. The French suffered

20. Eccles, *Canada under Louis XIV*, pp. 164–66; Lanctot, *History of Canada* 2:110. Cf. Parkman's blood and thunder over Lachine: "the most frightful massacre in Canadian history." Even Trelease has multiplied the casualties. Francis Parkman, *Count Frontenac and New France under Louis XIV* (1897), reprinted (Boston: Little, Brown, and Co., 1909), pp. 185–89; Trelease, *Indian Affairs*, pp. 297–98,.

many times more deaths from epidemics than from Indian raids.[21] Only the large-scale organization of Europeans could give victory to the Iroquois, as they themselves understood. They urged their English allies constantly to take the field.

Count Frontenac hoped to forestall combined operations by spoiling attacks of his own during the winter of 1689–1690. One of these struck Schenectady, near Albany, in March 1690, killing sixty inhabitants and creating the same sort of panic in New York that the La Chine massacre had touched off in Canada. A Mohawk condolence delegation found it needful to spirit up Albanian morale. "Brethren," they said, "Doe not be discouraged. This is butt a beginning of the warr."[22] In the circumstances, it was not the cheeriest of messages.

The Indians discovered that even under conditions of open war the military enterprise of English colonials was handicapped by conflicting interests, division of counsel and authority, profiteering, lack of support and supply, and a certain amount of bullheaded stupidity. The details of great expectations and dashed hopes need not be repeated here. It is enough to say that the war dragged on in guerilla fashion, neither side being capable of occupying the other's territory. Both the English and the French attempted invasions; both bungled. Frontenac invaded Onondaga, where he destroyed houses and crops, as had become his pattern; he also mobilized the western tribes for continued harassment of Iroquois detached parties. In proportion to their population, Iroquois casualties were disastrously high.[23]

Shawnees come east

In all the dreary, bloody months of war, Iroquois prospects grew steadily more bleak. One event partially redeemed the time, a bit ambiguously, when a band of Shawnees trekked east from the Illinois country to join the Covenant Chain and were followed by others over a period of years. Their appearance was a surprise. Until then these Shawnees had been allied to Illinois enemies of the Iroquois. To understand why they came east and what sort of role they played in the Chain, we must look back a few years.

It may be recalled that the 1687 attack by Canada's governor Denonville upon the Senecas had led to close counseling between the Iroquois and

---

21. Eccles, *Canadian Frontier*, p. 119. Measles and smallpox killed over 1000 persons in a population of 11,000.
22. Treaty minutes, Feb. 25, 1690, *Doc.Hist.N.Y.* 2:165. Colden subtly altered this remark to, "This is a beginning of your War." *History*, p. 105.
23. See Eccles, *Canada under Louis XIV*, chs. 11, 12.

New York's Governor Dongan. As part of his advice, Dongan told the Iroquois to bury the hatchet with the "far Indians" allied to the French and to "open a path for them this way." Mohawk sachem Sindachsegie accepted this strategy for his own people and added, "The Mahikanders and other River Indians living here are likewise subjects of the Great King of England, whom his Excellency will be pleased to make use off and send to the Farr Nations of Indians to help to effect the Peace."[24]

The remark is informative in two ways. It shows, firstly, that the Mohawks were not issuing commands themselves to those river Indians. In addition, anticipating issues to be discussed further along, we may note that Sindachsegie's proposal accorded with the Indian custom of using nonbelligerents as intermediaries to initiate peace negotiations. This was a feminine role in Indian eyes, because warriors must not confess such humiliation, so the intermediaries were considered in diplomatic metaphor as "women." Traditions of both Iroquois and Mahicans accord the women status to the Mahicans as of the period in question, and events demonstrate that Dongan complied with Sindachsegie's request.[25]

The French soon were disturbed by "Loups" carrying English presents among the western Indians. It is not possible from the French word to identify their tribes exactly because the French applied *Loup* (or *Wolf*) indiscriminately to the related Algonquian-speaking Mahicans, Minisinks, and Delawares.[26] A French officer reported that the Miamis (or Twightwees) of the Saint Joseph River "no longer thought of anything except of opening the way to the Loups, who had opened a commerce with the English." In 1689 Nicholas Perrot resumed command of the strategic post at present-day Green Bay, Wisconsin, and found eight Loups there.[27]

At about the same time a party of five Mahicans and Minisinks journeyed to La Salle's Fort St. Louis on the Illinois River to solicit Indian friendship and trade under the noses of the alarmed French. Here they encountered a community of dispossessed and wandering Shawnees, whom they persuaded to return east and join the Covenant Chain. Commandant Henri Tonty blustered unavailingly. Minisink sachem Matasit reported the interview.[28]

" 'Then,' said Monsieur Tonty, 'you have certainly some new design;

24. Treaty minutes, Aug. 5–6, 1687, *N.Y.Col.Docs.* 3:439–44.

25. The traditions are discussed in ch. 2, above.

26. Gordon M. Day, *The Mots Loups of Father Mathevet,* Publications in Ethnology 8 (Ottawa: National Museum of Man, 1975), pp. 35–44.

27. *The Indian Tribes of the Upper Mississippi Valley and Region of the Great Lakes, as described by Nicholas Perrot, French commandant in the Northwest; Bacqueville de la Potherie, French royal commissioner to Canada; Morrel Marston, American army officer; and Thomas Forsyth, United States agent at Fort Armstrong,* ed. Emma Helen Blair, 2 vols. (Cleveland: Arthur H. Clark Co., 1911–1912), 2:81, 85.

28. Hanna, *Wilderness Trail* 1:138, quoting New York Colonial Mss. 38:165.

but all the Indians that you take along to the Ssouwenas [Shawnees] will be killed, and yourself also.'

"Then I answered: 'Come, tomorrow I will depart for New York. If you can, kill me. I fear you not.'

"Then said the sachem of Ssouwena: 'If you go, I'll go along; and I shall stop Monsieur Tonty's ears'; and told me further, 'Now I'll go with you.'

"Then I answered: 'That is good; my land shall be your land.'

"Then the sachem of Ssouwena said: 'I am afraid for the Mohawks.'

"I answered him, 'Why are you afraid; the Dutch are my friends, and Corlaer is my Father?'

"Then the said Ssouwenee said: 'We have been everywhere, and could find no good land. Where is your land?'

"I answered, 'Menissinck is my land; there shall we live.'

"The Sachem of the Ssouwena: 'Where live ye brethren?'

I answered, 'They live at New York.'

"The sachem of the Ssouwena asked: 'Your brethren, the Dutch, are they good?'·

"I answered, 'For certain they are good. When you come there you shall see that they are good.'

"Then the sachem of the Ssouwenas said: 'If they are good, we will certainly all go thither.' "

Among the Shawnees at Fort St. Louis was Martin Chartier, a coureur de bois who had been jailed by Governor La Barre, had escaped, and had remained prudently distant from Canada thereafter. Chartier adopted the Shawnees as his own people, married a Shawnee woman, and accompanied his band eastward. After a protracted and circuitous journey, swinging far southward to avoid hostile Miamis, they arrived at the head of Chesapeake Bay in August 1692. Maryland's authorities, consternated in time of war by this "Frenchman lately come in with a Parcell of strange Indians," promptly clapped Chartier in jail and sent a warning to New York to beware of the "strange Indians."[29]

Investigation calmed the Marylanders' ruffled nerves. Trader Jacob Young and Colonel Casparus Herman came from the head of the bay to report that there had been two parties of the strange Indians. (The scribe's bad ear and crabbed handwriting make their name come out in the printed transcript as *Stabbernowles*.) One party had gone north, ostensibly to join the Iroquois in their war with Canada. Chartier's party preferred to settle down and be at peace. They found unanticipated sponsors in a band of Susquehannocks who had abandoned the Iroquois wars and territory after being "reduced to a small number" and had become "as it were, newly

29. Interrogation of Chartier, Aug. 16, 1692, *Md. Archives* 8:345–47; *CSPA&WI, 1689–1692*, p. 695.

grown up." That is, the Susquehannocks had reestablished the separate tribal identity they relinquished in 1677. They now wished to "settle upon their own Land at the Susquehannah Fort and to be taken and treated as [Maryland's] Friends." They were glad to welcome the Shawnee band as neighbors.[30]

The absence of two parties from the proceedings probably contributed greatly to the sensible outcome. Lord Baltimore was in England, and the revolutionary government that had driven him out was not interested in fighting his boundary battle with William Penn, so Jacob Young could tell the Susquehannocks that "their Fort as they call it" fell within Pennsylvania's limits and was no concern of Maryland. Like Baltimore, the Iroquois were also elsewhere and so were unable to dictate terms about the Shawnees. The Indians who simply wanted to settle down in peace did so—the Susquehannocks at Conestoga, and the Shawnees a short distance farther downstream at Pequea, where Martin Chartier and his son Peter became prominent. For the time being, they were let alone.[31] They had settled within the protectorate of peaceful Quaker Pennsylvania, which, since its creation, had subscribed to its own chain of friendship but not to the Covenant Chain dominated by New York and the Iroquois.[32]

Shawnees and Iroquois

The other Shawnees, who had decided to live with the Minisinks, found it more difficult than anticipated. They proceeded to Philadelphia—startlingly without mention in Pennsylvania's records—where they were met by Arent Schuyler, the brother of Albany's mayor. He escorted them to New York City, where the colonial council treated with them.[33] This was too much for the Iroquois. As Mayor Peter Schuyler wrote from Albany,

30. Council minutes, April 11, 1693, *Md.Archives* 8:517–19.

31. Loc. cit.

32. In 1699, Robert Livingston wrote to the New York council to say that "the Indians had been at Pennsylvania to trade *in breach of the Covenant Chain.*" (My italics.) New York council minutes, Aug. 30, 1699, mss., 8:131. In 1689 the Mohawks renewed the Chain "between us and you, that is to say New England, Vergenia, Mereland, and all these parts of America." New York's part in the Chain was taken for granted because the treaty was held in Albany, but Pennsylvania's omission from the named colonies is significant. Treaty minutes, May 24, 1689, in *The Public Records of the Colony of Connecticut*, ed. J. Hammond Trumbull, 15 vols. (Hartford, 1850–1890) 3:462.

33. See the series of entries in N.Y. council minutes, mss., between Aug. 12 and Oct. 10, 1692, 6:113, 115, 116, 117, 126, 130–31. Because of mutilation of the mss. by fire, supplement these with a calendar compiled before the fire: *Calendar of Council Minutes, 1668–1783*, New York State Library Bulletin 58 [History 6], (Albany: University of the State of New York, 1902), pp. 75–76; N.Y.Colonial Mss., mss., 38:165; *Livingston Indian Records*, p. 168. Hanna's account plods through the sources and quotes extensively, *Wilderness Trail* 1:137–43.

"These Schowaenos are Indians in a public war with our [Iroquois] Indians who show great displeasure because the government makes peace with those Indians." The Iroquois were willing enough to negotiate; indeed, their disturbance arose from their involuntary nonparticipation in the negotiations. Peace with any of the common enemies of New York and the Five Nations, they recalled, could only be made legitimately by common consent. And besides, they had heard that the Shawnees had intended to negotiate with them before being intercepted at New York. How could the Christians be "so drunk in their minds as to negotiate a separate peace now without their knowledge"?[34]

Iroquois chiefs had good reason for their concern. They were far from overjoyed by Minisink and Susquehannock acquisitions of Shawnee supporters independently of their supervision. As Peter Schuyler reported, "They do not mind that those Indians come over here, but for that they first want to get the whole house together." The Shawnees were a worrisome lot.[35]

Minisink independence

Behind Iroquois concern lay anxiety about power within the Covenant Chain. The Chain had been strained badly by the French war and the Pennsylvania reorganization. Tributaries ignored Iroquois demands; the Iroquois themselves were too involved in Canada to attempt enforcement; and New York now seemed to be ignoring its most solemn obligations. Suppose the Shawnees were accepted in the Chain and they came to live with the Minisinks as invited, what then? There was an ancient tradition of war between Shawnees and Iroquois; it recounted that the Five Nations had dispersed the Shawnees and driven them out of their homeland in the Ohio Valley. The Shawnees' many scattered bands made up a numerous people, warlike by tradition and all the more effective in hunting and trading because of the wide distribution of their kinsmen. Shawnees on Minisink territory might simply strengthen the Minisinks against the Iroquois within the Chain instead of strengthening the Iroquois against the Chain's external enemies. Minisink independence is a recorded fact: when New Netherland warred against the Esopus Indians on the mid-Hudson, and all other tribes had abandoned or turned against the Esopus, the Minisinks had given them refuge and support. One of the Iroquois complaints

34. Peter Schuyler to N.Y. council, Sept. 6, 1692, in *Livingston Indian Records*, p. 168.
35. Loc. cit.

to Schuyler in 1692 was that the Minisinks "did not go to war even though they had asked them to do so."[36]

Shawnee arrival had occurred while New York was between governors. Happily for internal harmony, a new one arrived in time to make decisions. Conceding the Iroquois main point, governor Benjamin Fletcher sent those Shawnees on to Albany to "endeavour a peace" with the Iroquois Brethren before promising his own protection.[37] The gesture mollified the Iroquois who converted it into an arrangement more substantial than a gesture, but it did not resolve all the issues. While this Shawnee band submitted themselves in due form and apparently provided some warriors for the Canadian front, they continued in their determination to live with the Minisinks in the upper Delaware Valley. Thus, both the Shawnee community among the Susquehannock-Conestogas and the community among the Minisinks, while acknowledging Iroquois supervision in principle, protected themselves in practice by special ties with stronger neighbors of independent inclinations.

From governor Fletcher's point of view, the difference between Shawnees in the Mohawk Valley and Shawnees in the Delaware or Susquehannock Valley mattered little. They were all going to come under his management anyway. Mr. Penn had been in deep political trouble back in England as Fletcher departed for New York, and Penn's government was soon turned over to Fletcher to administer simultaneously with New York. In fact, Fletcher's Pennsylvania commission was sealed in England within two months after his debarkation in New York.[38] In theory, Fletcher could coordinate the two provinces for a more efficient war effort. However, as he soon found out, riding two horses works only if the horses are going in the same direction. By the necessities of war, Fletcher had to keep on good terms with his most reliable and active troops—the Iroquois—but provincial politics included Pennsylvania's interests, which pulled him away from what the Iroquois wanted.[39] Though Fletcher briefly drew Pennsylvania into the Covenant Chain, the fact created as many problems in Indian relations as it solved. The maneuvers about Shawnee affiliation highlighted them all.

Albany's merchants instantly recognized the Shawnee potential in trade. When preliminary talks had finished, and some of the Shawnee chiefs

36. Hanna, *Wilderness Trail* 1:121; *Jesuit Relations*, 1659–1660, 45:207; *Livingston Indian Records*, p. 168. The Minisink determination to have the Shawnees "settle among us . . . as our friends and Relacons" is in N.Y.council minutes, Sept. 17, 1692, mss., 6:130.

37. Fletcher's speech, N.Y. council minutes, mss., Sept. 17, 1692, 6:130–31.

38. Joseph E. Illick, *William Penn the Politician: His Relations with the English Government* (Ithaca, N.Y.: Cornell University Press, 1965), pp. 115–18.

39. Ibid., p. 119. Charles M. Andrews, *The Colonial Period of American History*, 4 vols. (1934–1938), reprinted (New Haven: Yale University Press, 1964). 3:312–15.

were ready to carry the glad news back to the west, a veteran Albanian interpreter and trader, long associated with the expansionist strategy of Dongan and Livingston, accompanied them: Arnout Viele. His assignment obviously was to see that the expected bonanza of furs carried by the large body of newcomers should not be diverted from the Albany market.

The war was going badly for the Iroquois. In January 1693, a French expedition destroyed all the Mohawk villages and captured three hundred of their people, mostly noncombatants.[40] New discipline and watchfulness in Canada reduced the effect of Iroquois raids there, and the French were even able to convoy a great fleet of canoes, loaded with a million pounds of fur, from the Great Lakes to Montreal. Realistically the Iroquois began to consider ending a war they could no longer win.[41]

While Fletcher hesitated, the Minisink tribe tested his intentions. Like the upper Hudson tribes, the Minisinks had been accustomed to treat with New York's government independently of Iroquois participation. Their treaty fire burned at the city of New York rather than at Albany, and (at least until 1681) the sachem of the Hudson River Tappan Indians, rather than those of any of the Five Nations, accompanied them when they came to "make their Covenant and speake of greate things." They quite insisted upon this arrangement; during Andros's regime they would "not runn about to other places but alwayes Come here [in New York city]. During the regime of Dongan, he ordered them to help the Iroquois with reinforcements, but the Minisinks dragged their feet. In 1693 they presented themselves to Governor Fletcher *in Philadelphia*. We must assume that they had decided to "run about," after all, for what seem to be the following reasons: to treat with Fletcher in New York was to deal with him in his capacity as governor of that colony, and it entailed dealing with the New York council also; to treat with him in Philadelphia, however, meant treating with this man of many offices in his capacity as governor of Pennsylvania, and the council of Pennsylvania was a very different lot of people from the council in New York. What the Minisinks did by going to Philadelphia was to secede from New York's protectorate in order to join Pennsylvania's, and the treaty data show that the Minisinks intended their act also as a means of preserving independence from the Iroquois. They were withholding their tribute from the Iroquois. Further, they set themselves up as spokesmen for Indians of Virginia and Maryland, in whose behalf as well as their own they asked Fletcher "to persuade the Senecas from doing them any harme in their hunting (as was done to some of them last Summer) that they may hunt in safety." Fletcher straddled; he promised to "Enjoine the Senecas and all the other Indians to peace and friend-

40. Lanctot, *History of Canada* 2:127; Eccles, *Canada under Louis XIV*, p. 192.
41. Lanctot, *History of Canada* 2:128.

ship with them," but he also expressed the hope that they would send "some of their best men up to Albany, to assist our people against the enemy"; and he quietly shanghaied them back into New York for future meetings.[42]

Fletcher's friction with the Iroquois

Up to that point, Fletcher was on good terms with the Iroquois and was trying to accommodate them, but he soon made a sharp turn in policy. If New York's council had been "drunk in their minds" to omit the Iroquois while treating with the Shawnees, they were not so befuddled as to overlook Iroquois efforts to treat with the French. Or, more strictly speaking, French efforts to treat with the Five Nations. News came in July 1693 that the Jesuit missionary among the Oneidas, Father Pierre Milet, was engaged in "Evil Practices" with the Iroquois. These consisted in advancing a proposal by Count Frontenac of "the notion of a Peace," which "hath great Influence upon them who are wearied with this long warr, and if not Prudently Prevented will lull them a Sleep."[43] Fletcher reported tersely to the crown, "I have endeavoured to my Power to hinder" it, and he admonished the Iroquois chiefs to "remove that Ill person" Milet.[44]

Despite his intense pressure, they did not;[45] and despite their assurances of absolute commitment to the war, the Oneidas sent Chief Tarriha to Frontenac with a proposal that peace negotiations should include New York as well as the Five Nations; but neither Frontenac nor Fletcher was ready to let the Indians direct foreign policy for him. Frontenac taunted them: "he had nothing to do with the Governor of New-York, he would treat only with the Five Nations; the Peace between the Christians must be made on the other Side of the great Lake [in Europe]. He added, he was sorry to see the Five Nations so far degenerated, as to take a sixth Nation into their Chain to rule over them. . . . You have done very ill, to suffer the People of New-York to govern you so far that you dare do

42. Arent Schuyler's journal, Feb. 10, 1694, *N.Y.Col.Docs.* 4:99; *Pa. Council Minutes*, May 10, 1693, 1:372–73.

43. "Remarks," ca. June or July 1693, *Livingston Indian Records*, pp. 170–71. From the French sources, Lanctot and Eccles attribute the peace feelers to an Iroquois initiative, but the English source explicitly states that Frontenac's proposal initially "amazed" and "confused" the Iroquois, and the Oneida chief who visited Frontenac returned with Frontenac's "second" peace belt. It would seem that Frontenac's dignity required some adjustment of his reports to convert the Iroquois into supplicants. Lanctot, *History of Canada* 2:128; Eccles, *Canada under Louis XIV*, p. 193; treaty minutes, Feb. 3, 1694, *N.Y.Col.Docs.* 4:88.

44. Fletcher to Blathwayt, Aug. 15, 1693, *N.Y.Col.Docs.* 4:37; treaty minutes, July 3, 1693, ibid., 4:41.

45. Fletcher to sachems of Five Nations, July 31, 1693, *N.Y.Col.Docs.* 4:51; Major Dirck Wessel's journal, ibid. 4:59–63.

nothing without their Consent." The reporter was Onondaga sachem Decanisora, who was to become one of the truly great statesmen of the Iroquois league.[46]

Fletcher was as determined as Frontenac to reduce the Iroquois to his own terms. He took certain drastic steps about which the source documents are fuzzy. A Connecticut gentleman picked up a rumor that Fletcher intended to make war himself upon the Iroquois unless they would meet with him "in 100 days." This was indignantly branded by the Connecticut council as a "false report," but Fletcher did in fact issue an ultimatum, and it did specify 100 days. Exactly what it said cannot be certainly ascertained because the speech in which he presented it was "wanting" from the records even in the eighteenth century "tho' a Blank Leaf is left for it." Whatever the details, Fletcher and the Iroquois were not working in double harness.[47] But, again, a distinction must be made between the Mohawks and the other Iroquois. The Iroquois delegation to Frontenac had been sent after a meeting of the grand council of the League, which was boycotted by the Mohawks, and in 1694 the chiefs accused Fletcher of having caused the Mohawk abstention.[48]

There was much tension at the 1694 treaty. The Iroquois were determined to preserve the right to negotiate where and when they pleased, and Fletcher was equally determined to compel them to obey his orders. Until they would knuckle under, he went about stripping them of authority over their tributaries. Although the ever-diplomatic Decanisora tried to mollify Fletcher by acknowledging him "to be the head of the covenant chain," Fletcher did not return the compliment by recognizing the Iroquois as sole spokesmen for Chain Indians; he met separately with the Mahicans at another time and place.[49]

Delaware independence

Fletcher had previously recruited the Minisinks to aid the Iroquois, but he now stepped between the Five Nations and the Delawares. It was a direct confrontation. In July, the Onondagas and Senecas had demanded

46. Colden, *History*, p. 141; confirmed by Onondagas' message, Nov. 22, 1693, *N.Y.Col.Docs.* 4:76; and treaty minutes, Feb. 2, 1694, *N.Y.Col.Docs.* 4:85.

47. N.Y. Council Minutes, July 2, 1694, mss., 7:70; July 15, 1694, 7:76; *Wraxall's Abridgment*, pp. 22–24.

48. Colden, *History*, p. 140; Trelease, *Indian Affairs*, p. 316.

49. Treaty Minutes, Albany, Aug. 16, 1694, mss., Penn Mss., Indian Affairs 1:16; treaty minutes, Kingston, Aug. 28, 1694, ibid., 1:32 The big treaty of Aug. 15–16, 1694 exists in several mss. copies. Besides the Penn Mss. copy, there is one in N.Y. Council Minutes 39:184–85, and another in N.Y.Col. Mss. 39:184. I have not compared texts. These minutes contain a recitation by Sadekanarktie of the traditional history of the Covenant Chain.

Delaware help in the war against the French. The Delawares appealed to Pennsylvania's council for protection; their appeal was relayed to Fletcher in New York, and he faced down the Iroquois with it in August. "The Sennekes of Late have sent a belt of wampum to the Indians of Delaware river requiring them to take up the hatchett of warr and fight along with them which frighted those peaceable Indians that live among a peaceable people who are no warriours and since they are in my Government of Pennsylvania I charge the Senekes not to frighten them but to lett them alone." Onondaga Chief Sadekanarktie replied evasively.[50] It is certain that Fletcher's sudden concern for the "peaceable people" of Pennsylvania was not what motivated him. His detestation of Quaker pacifists was expressed in many reports to the crown.

From the Iroquois point of view, colonial failure to provide either English troops or tributary Indian warriors to fight the French was base betrayal. Even the Mohawks, always tightest in partnership with Albany, had been angered in 1691, when New York's then-governor Sloughter exhorted them, "You must keep the Enemy in perpetual alarm." The Mohawks "took Notice of his saying '*You* must keep the Enemy in perpetual Alarm.' 'Why don't you say,' they replied, '*We* will keep the Enemy in perpetual Alarm.'"[51] In 1692 Oneida Chief Cheda took up the refrain. "Brother Corlaer, you desire us to keep the Enemy in perpetual Alarm, that they may have no Rest, till they are in their Graves; Is it not to secure your own Frontiers? Why then not one Word of your People that are to join us? . . . How comes it that none of our Brethren, fastened in the same Chain with us, offer their helping Hand in this general War, in which our great King is engaged against the French? Pray Corlaer, how come Maryland, Delaware River, and New-England to be disengaged from this War? . . . How can they and we be Subjects of the same great King, and not be engaged in the same War?"[52] It was an uncomfortably logical question, often to be plaintively echoed in the correspondence of New York's governors with the crown.

Iroquois losses

The Iroquois were desperate men, reeling in pain and shock from French blows and outraged by unfulfilled promises of campaigning by the English. Iroquois strength suffered dramatically from casualties and abandonment. Mohawk losses in 1693 had made that tribe cease to function effectively

---

50. *Pa. Council Minutes*, July 6, 1694, 1:447; private conference, Albany, Aug. 20, 1694, mss., Penn Mss., Indian Affairs 1:27, HSP.
51. Colden, *History*, p. 112.
52. Ibid., pp. 125–26.

as a fighting force, and many Mohawks went off to Caughnawaga Mission in Canada. According to Sadekanarktie, the Susquehannocks at Conestoga had "fledd" from Iroquoia, and another Indian told interested Philadelphians how a contingent of Conoys had also abandoned the Iroquois for Conestoga. Angrily, Sadekanarktie lamented that "Our neighbours sit still and smoake . . . the Grease is melted from our flesh and drops upon our neighbours who are grown fatt and live at ease while we become lean. They flourish and we decrease."[53]

News came that Arnout Viele was returning to Albany from the west with an estimated seven hundred Shawnees. Albany's young men scrambled hungrily out on the trail for first contact with all that potential profit, but the Iroquois had less reason to rejoice.[54] Eight days after his argument with Sadekanarktie, Fletcher met those Shawnees at Kingston rather than Albany, and he received them into his protection under Mahican rather than Iroquois sponsorship.[55] They constituted a relatively tremendous increase in the strength of Indians in the Covenant Chain, but whether any went off to Iroquoia is highly doubtful.

More decrease was in store for the Iroquois. Fletcher's measures with the Five Nations succeeded to the extent of preventing ratification of their proposed pact with Frontenac, and in 1696 Frontenac punished the Onondagas and Oneidas by destroying their villages as he had already assaulted the Mohawks.[56]

The stark effects of French punishment show in the available estimates of Iroquois population. By 1689 it had risen to the height of 2,570 warriors (implying 7,710–12,750 persons), apparently as the result of adoption of captives. Eleven years later, however, the number of warriors declined traumatically, to 1,230 (implying only 3,690–6,150 persons). An absolute reduction of more than 50 percent was shared by all the constituent nations though the Mohawks and Oneidas suffered most. Gunther Michelson's compilation itemizes as follows: Mohawks, a drop from 270 warriors to 110; Oneidas, down from 180 to 70; Onondagas, 500 to 250; Cayugas, 320 to 200; Senecas, 1,300 to 600.[57]

It is impossible to determine how much of the decline should be pro

53. Penn Mss., Indian Affairs, mss., 1:14; *Pa. Council Minutes*, July 6, 1694, 1:449. Sadekanarktie's bitter comment must be read with an eye to distinctions. If the English colonies generally were flourishing during the French wars, Albany was not. Between 1689 and 1698, its population dropped precipitately from 2016 to 1449. Memo, April 19, 1698, *N.Y.Col.Docs.* 4:337–38. It should also be noted that New York's governors got little response to their continual appeals for help from other colonies and the crown.

54. Peter Schuyler's speech, Feb. 6, 1694, *N.Y.Col.Docs.* 4:90; Trelease, *Indian Affairs*, p. 325.

55. Treaty minutes, Aug. 28, 1694, mss., Penn Mss., Indian Affairs 1:32, Hist. Soc. of Pa.

56. Eccles, *Canada under Louis XIV*, pp. 200–201; Lanctot, *History of Canada* 2:130–31.

57. Gunther Michelson, "Iroquois Population Statistics," Table 1, p. 4.

rated to battle casualties, disease, religious conversion, captives, refugees, or simple turncoats. Traditions of the Ojibwa Indians and their Ottawa, Huron, and Potawatomi allies tell of epic battles and great slaughter that forced the Iroquois out of Ontario. Iroquois tradition is silent on this point, but the Iroquois did retire from Ontario, leaving it in the possession of the Ojibwas. A modern historian, Leroy V. Eid, has tracked down confirming documents for the traditions of Iroquois defeats; he remarks that the French trader-statesman Nicolas Perrot "gave credence to what the old men of the Ottawas told him concerning a great defeat of the Iroquois, and there's no reason for any historian to do otherwise." His evidence is persuasive.[58]

The French exploited intertribal hostilities in several ways. We have a record of Cadillac de la Motte instigating attacks against the Senecas in the spring of 1697.[59] After England and France ended their own war by the Treaty of Ryswick in September of the same year, the French offered sanctuary to individual Iroquois who would leave their tribes for the mission villages on the St. Lawrence. In 1700 Robert Livingston mourned the effectiveness of this strategy in a report to New York's Governor Bellomont: "the Maqua's nation are grown weak and much lessened by the late war, but more since the peace [between England and France] by the French daily drawing them from us to Canada so that near two thirds of said nation are now actually at Canada with their familyes, who are kindly received, being cloathed from head to foot, are secured in a Fort guarded

58. I am deeply obliged to Helen Hornbeck Tanner for guiding me to the following sources, which have greatly altered many of my previously held views. Leroy V. Eid, "The Ojibwa-Iroquois War: The War the Five Nations Did Not Win," *Ethnohistory* 26:4 (fall, 1979), pp. 297–324; Donald B. Smith, "Who Are the Mississauga?" *Ontario History* 17:4 (Dec., 1975), pp. 211–22; Copway, *Traditional History . . . of the Ojibwa Nation*, ch. 6–8. A geographer has confirmed the Iroquois withdrawal, but he ascribes it to French pressure rather than tribal attacks. Victor Konrad, "An Iroquois frontier: the north shore of Lake Ontario during the late seventeenth century," *Journal of Historical Geography* 7:2 (1981), pp. 129–44. Professors Eid, Smith, and Konrad have kindly provided offprints of their very interesting studies.

The climactic battle of the western tribes against the Iroquois, in which "a vast number" of Iroquois were killed and "only one taken Prisoner" has been recited from Iroquois tradition by John Norton, of mixed Cherokee and Scottish descent, who became an adopted Iroquois chief and led the Grand River Iroquois in the War of 1812. [John Norton], *The Journal of Major John Norton, 1816*, eds. Carl F. Klinck and James J. Talman, Publications of the Champlain Society 46 (Toronto, 1970), pp. xxiv, lxxvi, xcix, 249.

Mississauga acquisition of tenure rights in Ontario by conquest of the Five Nations was so well recognized that when the British wished to provide refuge in Canada for the Iroquois, they were obliged first to purchase the land from the Mississaugas. Treaties, Dec. 7, 1792 and April 1, 1793, in *Canada: Indian Treaties and Surrenders from 1680 to 1890*, 2 vols. (Ottawa: Queen's Printer, 1891), 1:5–8. The present-day Grand River Reserve is a shrunken remnant of that tract.

59. Narrative of the Most Remarkable Occurrences in Canada, Oct. 18, 1697, *N.Y.Col.Docs.* 9:672. Thanks to Professor Richard Haan for calling my attention to this and for many other favors.

with souldiers and have Priests to instruct them."[60]

Tension often existed between French officials and French missionaries, but the effectiveness of the missions as instruments of state policy cannot be doubted. In 1700 New York's Commissioners of Indian Affairs solicited allied Iroquois to obtain the return of their brethren in Canada. Spokesman Sagronwadie replied, "We are now come to trade, and not to speak of religion . . . I wish it had been begun sooner that you had had ministers to instruct your Indians in the Christian faith, I doubt whether any of us ever had deserted our native country, but I must say I am solely beholden to the French of Canada for the light I have received . . . and we can be instructed at Canada, Dowaganhae [Ottawa country] or the uttermost parts of the earth, as well as here."[61] Robert Livingston wondered, "It's strange to think what authority these priests have over their Indian proselites; they carry a chain in their pocket and correct the Indians [by whipping them with the chain] upon the commission of any fault, which they bear very patiently."[62]

There can be no reasonable doubt that the Five Nations Iroquois had been beaten by the French and their Indian allies, and badly beaten. The Susquehannocks who had refuged in Iroquoia since 1677 had already taken refuge again, this time by fleeing back to their homeland at Canestoga, on the lower Susquehanna River, and it appears that they were joined by an unknown number of Senecas. According to figures available to the Lords of Trade in London, the combined effects of war and conversion reduced the population of Iroquoia from 3,500 at the beginning of the "late war" to 1,100 by 1700.[63] (These figures seem to refer to warriors rather than total population.) For the power and status of the Five Nations chiefs, the losses were genuine and catastrophic regardless of their causes. It is possible that by 1700 there were more Iroquois, under other names, in Canada than in Iroquoia. According to Robert Livingston, this had become true for the Mohawks.

Peace for the English, war for the Iroquois

The continuing weakening of the Five Nations explains the diplomatic jockeying between New York and New France after the Anglo-French peace treaty of Ryswick in 1697. New York sent a mission to Quebec to make peace for the Indians. Frontenac, knowing that his side gained

60. Livingston to Bellomont, April 1700, N.Y.Col.Docs. 4:648.
61. Treaty minutes, June 28, 1700, CSPA&WI, 1700, p. 437.
62. N.Y. Col. Docs. 4:649.
63. Bd. of Trade to Sec. Vernon, Oct. 4, 1700, CSPA&WI, 1700, p. 543. The full report shows that the Board understood the situation.

strength every day, was in no hurry. He insisted that the Iroquois were not English subjects and would therefore have to treat for themselves. Ironically he thus subscribed to a basic principle of Iroquois policy that required the parties to a treaty to meet face to face. But New York's government feared that in any such treaty Frontenac would create a basis for claiming the Iroquois as French subjects by conquest. The French refused to treat with New York for the Iroquois, and New York refused to permit the Indians to make peace for themselves. No wonder harried individuals fled to the security of the missions. Onondaga chief Decanisora thought "it was hard there should be a peace and they have no profite of it"— surely a poignant understatement.[64]

Western Indian allies of the French were hounding them relentlessly, in spite of a truce with the French government, and the Five Nations could respond only with desperate and disregarded appeals for protection.[65] About 1698 or 1699, a climactic battle took place on Lake Erie during which "a vast number" of Iroquois were killed and "only one taken Prisoner" by the western nations. The battle was reported from both Ojibwa and Iroquois traditions of the early nineteenth century but deleted from the later Iroquois tradition. By September 1699, the western Algonquians had advanced into Iroquoia and killed five Senecas "near their Castle."[66] The western Algonquian Mississaugas occupied the site in Ontario of the former Iroquois village of Kanatiochtiage, then sent an embassy to Onondaga to propose peace and an open path to Albany's trade. The Iroquois were only too happy to accede, with the fervent hope that the two peoples might "grow old and grey headed together; else the warr will devour us both." But at the meeting with New York's commissioners in 1700, the Five Nations sachems were obliged to report that "the Dowaganhaes [Ottawas] or far Nations have now again kill'd many of our people att their hunting; all which is done by the instigation of the French as the said far Indians themselves confess." The Iroquois were in an impossible situation. "The French themselves declare they will not take the hatchet out of the Dowaganhaes hands till we come and submitt to the Governour of Canada and make peace with him; which our great Brother Corlaer forbids us to do."[67]

Yorkers were panic stricken at the prospect of losing their first line of defense. After Fletcher's recall, his successor, the Earl of Bellomont, tried

64. N.Y. Council minutes, Aug. 17, 1698, *CSPA&WI, 1697–1698*, no. 749; N.Y. Council Minutes, Aug. 17, 1698, mss., 8:61. The mss. source has been partly burnt.

65. *Propositions made by the Five Nations of Indians . . . to . . . Richard Earl of Bellomont . . . in Albany, July . . . 1698* (New York, 1698), p. 4. I have used the photographic copy in HSP of a printed book in the New-York Historical Society. For some of the independent actions of the western Indians see William N. Fenton, "Kondiaronk," in *Dict. Can. Biog.* 2:320–23.

66. *N.Y.Col.Docs.* 4:597.

67. *N.Y.Col.Docs.* 4:693–95.

frantically to forestall such a loss. Yorkers knew that the peace between England and France was a mere truce, and that a new outbreak of imperial war might find them utterly exposed if French-allied Indians should be able to pass safely through Iroquoia to attack New York's settlements. Despite the Yorkers' pressures, the Iroquois at last found continuing war too high a price to pay for Albany's goods and friendship. Defying the governor's explicit ban, and circumventing the colony's many intrigues, they trudged to Montreal to capitulate in a series of negotiations in 1700 and 1701.[68]

Effectively abandoned by the English, and incapable of defending themselves against the western tribes, the Iroquois sued for peace because they had no alternative but complete collapse and disintegration. They put up a show of bravado (as always), but the treaty that ensued was dictated by the French.

The Iroquois become a barrier

Although French arms had triumphed decisively, the real victory was won by paradox. Certain unanticipated results of the war caused French treaty terms to be surprisingly lenient. French victory had been too complete. When the Iroquois were forced onto the defensive in the 1690s, French trade with the western tribes increased quickly to three times the annual volume it had had before 1675—so much, indeed, that it greatly exceeded the capacity of French commerce and industry to handle.[69] French officialdom ordered measures to reduce the influx of furs, but Canadian officialdom knew that the enforcement of such measures would bring political disaster; for, if French traders refused to accept the furs brought to their posts by western tribes, or closed down the posts as once ordered by Versailles, the western tribes would take their goods elsewhere, and their loyalties along with them. It was necessary to preserve a barrier between the western tribes and the English. Curiously, the Iroquois, who had been trying for decades to make themselves a link between the western tribes and the English, were now forced by the French into the role of barrier.

It has often been noticed that New France wanted the Iroquois as a buffer between Canada and the much more populous English colonies, but that interpretation must be modified to take into account the French desire to use the Five Nations as a means of channeling trade to Canada. The apostate Baron Lahontan expressed the situation concisely: "Those who alledge that the destruction of the Iroquois would promote the inter-

68. Trelease, *Indian Affairs*, ch. 12.
69. Eccles, *France in America*, pp. 97–98.

est of the Colonies of New-France are strangers to the true interest of that Country; for if that were once accomplish'd, the Savages who are now the French Allies would turn their greatest Enemies, as being then rid of their other fears. They would not fail to call in the English, by reason that their Commodities are at once cheaper and more esteem'd than ours; and by that means the whole Commerce of that wide Country would be wrested out of our hands." To be sure, the Iroquois struggled as before to dominate the western tribes, but they came to rely much more on diplomacy because their military power was reduced so drastically. The French were as alert to this diplomatic approach as to former displays of naked force; they carefully attended to keeping old intertribal animosities alive. As Lahontan remarked, " 'tis the interest of the French to weaken the Iroquese, but not to see 'em intirely defeated."[70]

With such intentions, the French refrained from demanding Iroquois subjection in the great treaty settlement at the beginning of the new century. They were content to require that the Five Nations formally declare peace with all their protected Indians, and that the Iroquois accept neutral independence between the colonies of France and Britain. The Iroquois were happy enough to escape, by a peace, the punishment still being inflicted upon them by the western tribes. They accepted neutrality and ratified the pact in 1701.[71] Only New York was a loser by the treaty.

Even New York, however, gained something by the treaty, for the neutrality imposed upon the Five Nations implied that French troops must not march through their territory, and Iroquoia lay between New France and New York. As a consequence, Yorkers escaped the horrors of guerrilla war in the soon renewed imperial conflicts of France and Britain, while New Englanders, who lacked the Iroquois buffer, suffered severely.

But the treaty doomed New York's grand plan of expanding westward through Iroquois instrumentality into the Great Lakes region. Robert Livingston recognized the danger and took alarm. If New York were to salvage its hopes, he thought, it would be absolutely necessary to seize the straits of Detroit where a fort could control traffic between lakes Huron and Erie besides dominating a wide hunting territory.[72] The French thought so, too, and they built first. New York's lieutenant governor Nanfan tried to strain the new Franco-Iroquois pact by urging the Indi-

70. Louis-Armand de Lom D'Arce de Lahontan, *New Voyages to North-America* (1703), ed. Reuben Gold Thwaites, 2 vols. (Chicago: A.C. McClurg and Co., 1905), 1:394, 395.
71. Eccles, *France in America*, pp. 100–101;———, *Frontenac*, ch. 19; Yves Zoltvany, "Calliere, Louis-Hector de," *Dict. Can. Biog.* 2:114. The views of these Canadian historians are signficantly different from those expressed in Anthony F. C. Wallace, "Origins of Iroquois Neutrality: The Grand Settlement of 1701," *Pennsylvania History* 24 (1957), pp. 223–35. See also the revisionist viewpoint in Richard L. Haan, "The Problem of Iroquois Neutrality: Suggestions for Revision," *Ethnohistory* 27:4 (fall, 1980), pp. 317–30.
72. Livingston to Bellomont, April 1700, *N.Y.Col.Docs.* 4:650–51.

ans to prevent completion of Fort Detroit, and the Iroquois response showed how firmly they had committed themselves to neutrality. They told the English to attack the fort themselves.

Livingston's "deed"

Because of the frequent misinterpretation given to an incident of this affair, it must be dwelt upon for a moment. The Iroquois gave a "deed" to the King of England, absurd on its face but taken seriously because it was later to be advanced in diplomacy to justify England's claims against France. This "deed" was a worthless piece of paper.[73] It purported to set forth the rights of the Iroquois to vast hunting territories in the west by rights of conquest over the Hurons and other Indians during the beaver wars, and it conveyed those asserted rights to the English Crown. But the conveyance was made precisely because the Iroquois had been driven out of those supposedly conquered lands, which the Indians wanted the King to reconquer so as to provide "free hunting" for them "for ever." Who lives by conquest, dies by it also; nothing is more common in history than the cancellation of one conquest by another.[74]

The true meaning of the Iroquois "deed" was exactly the opposite of a conveyance of property or territory. It was a challenge for the English to fight in behalf of the Iroquois for a change, instead of the Iroquois fighting for the English. The Indians were most explicit. "Wee have not power to resist such a Christian enemy" as the French, they protested; "therefore wee must depend upon you Brother Corlaer to take this case in hand."[75] Brother Corlaer failed them. In 1702 they told a new governor that the French had built a fort at Detroit with "high Pallisadoes" and "a garrison of a hundred brisk men." So far as the Iroquois were concerned, they would "leave it wholly to your Lordship to doe therein as you shall think fitt."[76] They had had enough of being catspaws.

73. Deed, July 19, 1701, *N.Y.Col.Docs.* 4:908–11. For its uses by the English, see ch. 2.

74. The language of the treaty minutes and deed refers to the lands formerly conquered by the Iroquois as those "of the Hurons" and "Tuchsagrondie." Huron territory was north of Lake Ontario, and the Iroquois were chased out of that whole territory during their wars with the French. Tuchsagrondie was an Iroquois version of the Huron Tiosahrondion, which originally referred vaguely to the whole region on both sides of the Straits of Detroit, though it was sometimes used to refer to Detroit proper. E. S. Rogers, "Southeastern Ojibwa," in *Northeast,* p. 761; James Mooney, "Tiosahrondion," in *Handbook of American Indians North of Mexico* 2:757–58.

75. Cf. Donald H. Kent, "Historical Report on the Niagara River and the Niagara River Strip to 1759," in *American Indian Ethnohistory. North Central and Northeastern Indians,* ed. David Agee Horr, *Iroquois Indians II* (New York: Garland Publishing, 1974), pp. 42 43; treaty minutes, July 19, 1701, *N.Y.Col.Docs.* 4:906.

76. Mohawk chief Onuchenanorum, July 18, 1702, *N.Y.Col.Docs.* 4:987.

By 1701 the Covenant Chain had become an empty form and the Iroquois stood almost alone. Although they had maintained their independence and had gained new flexibility for maneuver between the colonies, they had correspondingly lost the special favor of New York. Their Indian allies hardly bothered to go through the motions of formal fidelity. Pennsylvania's sanctuary protected Susquehannocks, Delawares, and Shawnees against Iroquois domination, and New York dealt separately with Minisinks, Mahicans, Schaghticokes, and other Hudson River Indians. It would seem inevitable in such ruinous circumstances that the Five Nations should have fallen to the low estate of just another set of smallish Indian villages. That they rose instead to become once more an important force among the American powers betokens keen intelligence and a rarely indomitable spirit, but these qualities might have been inadequate without the additional capacity to organize. The instrument chosen by the Iroquois for rebuilding their shattered fortunes was the Covenant Chain. They restored the gaping and scattered links of the Chain, linking themselves into it in a very special position.

Chapter 11 ❧ PERMUTATIONS

Having established strong and vigorous colonies in the trying years of the seventeenth century, the English extended their power over the Indians as occasion warranted and as the weakness of the Indians permitted. Smaller, dependent tribes were gradually amalgamated or destroyed by the eroding effects of white contact. Disease—of which the frequent small-pox epidemics were the most costly—swept away many of the smaller tribes and decimated many of the larger nations. Yet throughout the eighteenth century and into the period of the American Revolution the Indians in several areas, most notably the Six Nations in the present area of New York State, and the Cherokee, Creek, and Choctaw of the southern interior, maintained a power and an independence which kept the colonies adjacent to them watchful and respectful of their needs and rights.

Wilcomb E. Washburn, Red Man's Land / White Man's Law

In many cases, rival segments within both the indigenous society and the intrusive one compete with each other in a frontier zone. Indeed, in every contact situation, even where relationships are predominantely violent, crosscutting ties quickly develop across the major cleavage. Thus intruders acquire allies among indigenous peoples.

The Frontier in History: North America and Southern Africa Compared
eds. Howard Lamar and Leonard Thompson

Connessoa, King of the Onondagoes . . . desryed . . . That, Hospitality be shown to all strangers, and suffer them to pass, for without the assistance of the 5 Nations neither Christian nor Indian could live here for the ffrench.

Chief Decanisora in treaty, July 31, 1710

*For the Indians the Covenant Chain provided a degree of imme-*diate security from English attack and an opportunity to postpone ultimate confrontation. After 1677, when Edmund Andros offered refuge to the Indians fleeing New England's Second Puritan Conquest, the Hudson, Delaware, and Susquehanna valleys became sanctuaries for colonization by the harried and persecuted Indians of North America's east coast. Wampanoags, Narragansetts, Sokokis, and Nipmucks took shelter under the Tree of Peace planted by Andros at Schaghticoke on the upper Hudson, losing their former identities to become "River Indians" along with the Mahicans.[1] Their linkage with the Covenant Chain was directly to New York with whose governors they treated personally and directly.[2]

1. Jennings, *Invasion,* ch. 18.
2. E.g., treaties at Albany and Kingston, Aug., 1694, Penn Mss., Indian Affairs, mss., I:14–32; treaties, Aug.–Sept., 1722, at Albany, *N.Y.Col.Docs.* 5:657–81.

Schaghticoke was located in Mahican territory; consequently the Iroquois could not claim to act as spokesmen for the Indians there on the grounds of being their hosts.

After Pennsylvania was carved out of New York in 1681, the Susquehanna Valley became a major center of refuge for tribes fleeing from violence in the south. To Pennsylvania came not only refugees from New England, but also the Piscataway-Conoys from Maryland and Virginia, the Nanticokes from Delaware and Maryland, the Shawnees from widely dispersed regions of the south and west, the Tutelos from Virginia, and the Tuscaroras from North Carolina.[3] In the words of Delaware tradition, Pennsylvania became for many Indians "a last, delightful asylum."[4] The Iroquois were intensely interested in these Indians whom they regarded as guests in the valley they claimed to have conquered from the Susquehannocks. Some of the refugees on the Susquehanna were later persuaded to continue migrating north into Iroquoia. In a manner rare in history, they were all given hospitable welcome, permitted to maintain their own institutions of government, and provided with arable land for their livelihood by agreement between the pacifist Quakers and the ever-warring Iroquois!

The Iroquois learned patience in Pennsylvania because they had to. They did not dare to domineer over the strong Delaware tribe in alliance with that colony, a tribe that paid little attention to Iroquois pretensions of superiority. Despite the nonsense so often written about the Delawares as weakling "women," they constituted one of the most powerful eastern tribes in the early eighteenth century; and, as we shall see, they sometimes vied with the Iroquois for leadership. Indeed, a running contest between Delawares and Iroquois can be traced to and past the American Revolution.

Two factors brought about Iroquois triumph *in the east*. Probably the more important was the westward migration of most Delawares to the Ohio country as a consequence of colonial encroachment on their eastern lands. The Iroquois had nothing to do with this. The remnant bands remaining in the Delaware and Susquehanna valleys were adeptly outmaneuvered by Iroquois intrigues with Pennsylvanians who wanted all the rest of the Delaware lands. It was a rankly malodorous business for which colonials and Iroquois must share the blame even though their motives were different.

Precisely because of the nastiness of these transactions, they have been whitewashed and perfumed by filiopietists; in a manner altogether too common, the Delawares and their colonial friends have been turned into

3. Paul A. W. Wallace, *Indians in Pennsylvania* (Harrisburg: Pennsylvania Historical and Museum Commission, 1961), ch. 14, 15.
4. Heckewelder, *History*, p. 78.

the villains of the drama. We shall see why this was done and how completely it inverts the facts.

It may be noticed also that the Delawares were not the only tribe to escape Iroquois hegemony. Never, after the Five Nations victories in the mid-sixteenth century, did they beat down an unbroken tribe; they picked up bands and fragments of tribes that had disintegrated from wars or colonial encroachment, and as E. M. Ruttenber sensed, they always did so with direct or indirect help from a colonial ally.

Distinctions must be made between New York's protection and Pennsylvania's. Yorkers regarded themselves as a "frontier" colony—not against Indians as such, but against the French and allied Indians of Canada. For Yorkers, a chief function of the Iroquois and their allies was military, and we have seen in earlier chapters how expansionist clashing between New York and New France harmed the Iroquois and their fighting allies. In contrast, the Quakers, who founded Pennsylvania, avoided war and made no demands upon their client Indians to go to war. Indeed, they protected the clients from demands made by New York and the Iroquois. The latter were able to recruit volunteers as they marched down the Susquehanna Valley Warriors' Path to raid southern tribes, but they could not compel provision of organized war parties from the communities in the valley. In this respect the two hosts of the Susquehanna groups were at odds with each other, and the Iroquois had to bide their time.

They wanted closer association with Pennsylvania, but that desire put them at odds with New York. We shall see that Thomas Dongan frustrated William Penn from treating with the Iroquois for cession of the Susquehanna Valley.[5] A similar issue arose in 1699 when a Seneca delegation met with Penn's lieutenant governor Markham to request "a free Trade and Amity with that Government." Markham accepted and gave them two letters, which they showed to New York's commissioners of Indian affairs. In great alarm the commissioners sent the letters to governor Bellomont, denouncing this "Treaty and Negotiation . . . without the least notice given or leave obtained from the Governor of New York, who will undoubtedly take it very ill"; and secretary Livingston called it a "breach of the Covenant Chain," ordering the attorney general to "draw up a Rebuke to the said Indians for the same."[6]

Both Penn's people and the Iroquois were losers by New York's exclusivity. Pennsylvanians were blocked from some sources of fur for their

5. Ch. 12.
6. New York commissioners' minutes, Aug. 23, 1699, in Peter Wraxall, *An Abridgment of the Indian Affairs . . . from the Year 1678 to the Year 1751*, ed. Charles Howard McIlwain, Harvard Historical Studies 21 (Cambridge, Mass.: Harvard University Press, 1915), p. 33; New York Council Minutes, Aug. 30, 1699, mss., 8:131, New York State Archives, Albany. The offending negotiations have not been preserved in Pennsylvania's official records, to my knowledge.

trade. The Iroquois were blocked from negotiating an alliance that might be used to support their claims to hegemony over the Susquehanna Indians. Although ceremonial links seem to have been maintained, supervisory controls were generally shattered.

So much attention has been given to Pennsylvania as a sanctuary of religious toleration (which it was) that stress must be laid upon its functioning as a new entry in colonial competition for the potential wealth of America. Founder William Penn was a profoundly religious man, but he was also a great lord very much aware of his position and powers and determined to take his place as the full equal, at least, of every other colonial lord. Penn's lack of a noble title on the peerage establishment of England, Ireland, or Scotland left him unconcerned; he scorned "vain and empty" titles. However, his title as True and Absolute Proprietary of the Province of Pennsylvania, while it smacks somewhat of vanity, was certainly not empty. He told the Lords of Trade in 1707 that the governing power "was all the Crown gave me for making a Colony to it, having bought the Land of the Natives at dear Rates."[7] Writing to his son in 1701, he was even more explicit: "it was the Government which engaged me and those that adventured with me, for as to Land, it is the Natives', and I could have bought that of them on my own account, but that would not have engaged us to have gone above 3,000 miles off to convirt a meer Desert into an improved and faithful country."[8]

Penn wanted the powers of government in order to use them. He wanted to be a *good* lord who would radiate benevolence and win the love of his people while enjoying all the perquisites of position, but he could not accomplish this aim without contending against other powers having contrary tendencies. There were the other lordships of surrounding colonies, the libertarians of his own province striving against his paternalistic rule,and the Iroquois Indians with their incessant effort to usurp *his* powers over *his* Indians.

The Indians of Pennsylvania were in the middle of all these struggles. Their recognized native rights to land ownership became issues in the colony's boundary disputes, and these rights were also to generate inter-tribal antagonisms after William Penn's death.[9] Among the Pennsylvania provincials, traders and merchants evaded Penn's controls over commerce with the Indians and acquisition of Indian lands. Some of these struggles are considered in subsequent chapters below. More immediately pertinent here is Penn's assertion of his lordship over the client Indians of his province, which entailed rejection of the prior rights claimed by the Iroquois and their patron in New York.

7. Penn to Lords of Trade, July 2, 1707, mss., PRO, CO5 / 1764, ff. 16–17.
8. Jan. 2, 1701, *Pa. Archives*, 2d ser., 7:11.
9. Ch. 12, 14.

Though Pennsylvania and New York differed in regard to military adventuring, they were similarly motivated in regard to adventures of the commercial type. Penn and his colony quickly entered into direct competition with New York for the trade of all Indians within reach, and the colonies' competition necessarily involved the Iroquois and Iroquois pretensions to hegemony over other tribes.

The rivalry between Albany and Philadelphia, like that between Albany and Montreal, created both difficulties and opportunities for the Five Nations. Changes in status of their Delaware and Susquehannock tributaries presented problems but left room for maneuver and possible recovery of lost advantage. Pennsylvania was not such an implacable adversary to the Iroquois as was New France. On the contrary, its new and vigorous center of trade positively invited maneuver and intrigue. Alternatives to Albany meant reduction of Iroquois dependence on Albany, and the Onondagas, especially, kept looking for an alternative center of alliance and trade in order to bypass Mohawk controls over access to Albany.

Pennsylvania's alternative swiftly became real and powerful. Within four years, a great wave of immigration delivered about 8,000 immigrants to the new province. By 1685, therefore, as Gary B. Nash remarks, there had occurred "a population buildup unmatched in the annals of English colonization."[10] Pennsylvania continued to grow during the period of New York's heavy involvement in King William's War, in which Albany's numbers shrank from 2,016 in 1689 to 1,449 in 1698.[11]

The Iroquois interest in the major new power to the south was matched by the Yorkers. Iroquois friendship with Pennsylvania had to be developed with great discretion for fear of provoking Albany's wrath against the Five Nations and the crown's ire against Pennsylvania. In an open dispute between the proprietary colony and the royal one, there could be little doubt which side the crown would take. Penn was an accomplished courtier, but his ambitious thrust into the Indian trade alarmed the duke of York, who derived substantial revenue from that trade as conducted in New York.[12] The duke's disfavor grew to the point where, as James II, king of England, he initiated proceedings to deprive Penn of his much

10. Gary B. Nash, *Quakers and Politics: Pennsylvania, 1681–1726* (Princeton: Princeton University Press, 1968), p. 50.

11. Unsigned memorandum, April 19, 1698, *N.Y.Col.Docs.* 4:337–38.

12. Sir John Werden to Dongan, March 10, 1684, *N.Y.Col.Docs.* 3:341. In the second year of his reign, James II sent instructions to governor Dongan that required him, among other things, to preserve the Indian trade for New York and Albany, though "Wee are informed that some of the Colonys adjoyning to Our said Province under color of Grants from Our Self, or upon some other groundless pretenses, endeavor all they can to obstruct the Trade of New York and Albany." Clause #51, instructions, May 29, 1686, PRO, CO5 / 1111, p. 125 (f.65).

cherished government.[13] Penn managed to stall until 1692 when William III canceled his charter and put Pennsylvania under New York's Governor Fletcher. The charter and Penn's government were restored in 1694, but the sequence of events makes clear that Penn, great magnate though he was, had to deal circumspectly thereafter with New York.[14]

It is understandable, though provoking, that his province's official records are scant and spare for the early years of contact between Pennsylvania and the Iroquois. One must supplement their taciturnity with a variety of private papers and make some admittedly speculative inferences from documented situations. It is indisputable, however, that rapprochement gradually grew up, in a process that the Indians of the Delaware and Susquehanna valleys watched with notable ambivalence.

13. Minutes, May 30, 1687, *Acts of the Privy Council of England, Colonial Series, 1613–1783,* eds. W. L. Grant and James Munro, 6 vols. (London, 1908–1912), 2:92.
14. Nash, *Quakers and Politics,* pp. 182–83, 187.

Part Three ❧ DIPLOMATS

Chapter 12 🐛 A LINK LOST

· A description of Pennsylvania

This Province Pennsylvania takes its name
ffrom Wm. Penn Proprietor of ye same.
A barbarous nation first ye land did own
Who with ye English are confederate
Carefull to keep their trust inviolate.
Twixt heat & cold ye air is temperate;
Warm Southern winds ye cold does mitigate.
The Northwest wind ye rains and clouds does clear,
Bringing fair weather & a wholesom air.
　　Here we in safety live without annoy;
Each one his right securely does enjoy.
Whilst sad New England hence not very far
Have greatly suffered by their Indian war. . . .

　　　　　　　　　　　　　Thomas Makin, 1728

"O Pennsylvania! what hast thou cost me? above £30,000 more than I ever got by it, two hazardous and most fatiguing voyages, my straits and slavery here, and my child's soul almost."

　　　　　　　　　　　　　William Penn to James Logan, n.d.

Penn's plans

　　We have been following the history of the Iroquois alliance with New York, and the northern frontier between those allies and New France. Turning now to the Iroquois southern frontier, we must backtrack to the traumatic change of relations after the founding of Pennsylvania in 1681. The creation of the new province took the Delaware and Susquehanna valleys out of the jurisdiction of New York; simultaneously it took the Indian tribes of those valleys away from New York's protectorate and put them under Pennsylvania's. Such drastic changes posed new political problems for the Five Nations. An understanding with the new colony was urgently called for.

　　Its founder, William Penn, was more than willing. Before setting sail for America in 1682, Penn sent ahead a letter to "the Emperor of Canada,"

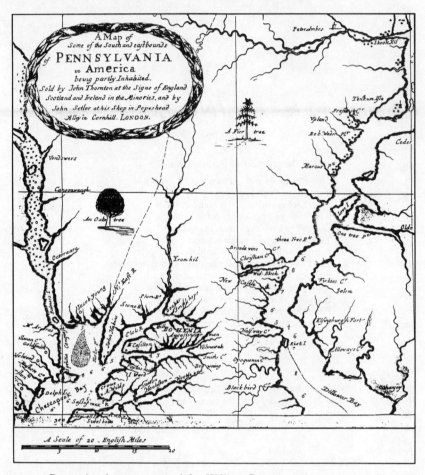

MAP 7. Promotional map engraved for William Penn in 1681. DETAIL REPRODUCED FROM A COPY REPRINTED BY THE HISTORICAL SOCIETY OF PENNSYLVANIA.

by which grandiose title he meant the leading chief at Onondaga. It was very businesslike. "I have set up a society of traders in my province to traffic with thee and thy people, for your commodities, that you may be furnished with that which is good, at reasonable rates; and that society hath ordered their president to treat with thee about a future trade."[1] Few things could have more interested the Onondagas or more alarmed the Albanians.

1. Samuel Hazard, *Annals of Pennsylvania, from the Discovery of the Delaware, 1609–1682* (Philadelphia. Hazard and Mitchell, 1850), p. 579; James Claypoole to Brother Norton Claypoole, July 14, 1682, in *James Claypoole's Letter Book: London and Philadelphia, 1681–1684*, ed. Marion Balderston (San Marino, Calif.: The Huntington Library, 1967), pp. 132–33.

Penn planned, while still in England, that the trade with Indians would play an important role in financing his colony, and he needed the revenue from it to help defray his staggering expenses.[2] But competitors were already on the scene, and Penn was to find that it was easier to get jurisdiction and commercial privileges by charter grant than to realize them in practice. His charter granted all the lands of New York west of the Delaware River between two highly disputed northern and southern lines, and he bought the Three Lower Counties of Delaware in a separate transaction. He immediately raised up frontier opponents on all sides, and all were English.[3]

Claiming jurisdiction under his charter to a long stretch of the Susquehanna River, Penn informed himself about tribal rights and moved promptly to obtain Indian quitclaims by purchase.[4] He encountered antagonism from both Maryland and New York. Penn planned to build a city on the Susquehanna, sister to Philadelphia on the Delaware, and he claimed that the head of Chesapeake Bay lay within his charter grant. Lord Baltimore objected that the prior charter of Maryland gave the head of the Chesapeake to him, besides which he claimed rights of conquest over the Susquehannocks.[5] Penn offset the latter claim by a strategic move to buy the Indian right to the place "from Maclaloha, owner of said lands" and acquired with it the undying enmity of Maryland's proprietary Calvert family.[6]

2. As early as 1686, Penn had a deficit of £5,000 in his provincial finances. Penn to James Harrison, Sept. 23, 1686, mss., Penn Mss., Letters of Wm. Penn copied by J. Francis Fisher, HSP. For his planned trade see Hazard, *Annals of Pa.*, pp. 577–80.

3. Penn's charter claims are simply described in the pamphlet, William A. Russ, Jr., *How Pennsylvania Acquired Its Present Boundaries* (University Park, Pa.: Pennsylvania Historical Association, 1966). The duke of York's deeds, Aug. 24, 1682, for the Three Lower Counties of Delaware are in Hazard, *Annals of Pa.*, pp. 588–93. See also the mss. in Cadwalader Collection, Thomas Cadwalader, folder Coates List no. 18, HSP. Penn's charter is in Hazard, *Annals*, pp. 488–99.

4. For Penn's understanding of lands open for purchase from Indians, see Instructions to Capt. Markham respecting Lord Baltimore, ca. Sept. 1683, mss., Cadwalader Collection, Thomas Cadwalader, Coates List no. 12, HSP. An extract deserves quotation: "It hath been the Practice of America, as well as the Reason of the thing itself, even among Indians and Christians, to account not taking up, marking and (in some degree) planting a reversion of Right; for the Indians do make People buy over again that land [which] the People have not seated in some years after purchase, which is the Practice also of all those [colonial] Governments towards the People inhabiting under them." The full document is conveniently accessible in *The Papers of William Penn*, eds. Richard S. Dunn, Mary Maples Dunn, et al. (Philadelphia: University of Pennsylvania Press, 1981–), 2:471–79.

5. Baltimore to Blathwait, March 11, 1682, *Md.Arch.* 5:349; Baltimore's account of a private conference with Penn, May 29, 1683, ibid., pp. 399–400.

6. *Pa. Council Minutes*, Jan. 3, 1783, 13:464; *Md.Arch.* 5:402. According to William Hunter (personal conversation, Aug., 1966), Maclaloha was a Delaware, and some controversy has existed over what right he may have had to sell the lands in question. Several issues are involved. Were the Susquehannocks conquered in a legal sense by either Maryland or the Iroquois? After their dispersal, did they retain any right in native custom to their former

The Iroquois and the Susquehanna

To northward, Penn claimed a charter boundary that would have included Iroquoia if he had ever been able to make it good. In 1683 he sent commissioners William Haig and James Graham to Albany to obtain Iroquois quitclaims to the Susquehanna Valley, and the commissioners hired Albany's veteran interpreter Arnout Viele to go to the Mohawks with an invitation to negotiate.[7]

Viele spoke with chiefs of all the Iroquois nations except the Senecas. The one point of unanimity among them was their absolute willingness to accept Penn's presents and release whatever pretensions they had. This became stunningly clear to the merchants of Albany through their independent investigation. While Viele interviewed Indians in a Mohawk village, the Albany magistrates interrogated two Cayugas and a Susquehannock in the courthouse. Suppose trading houses were set up on the Susquehanna, asked the magistrates. Would the Iroquois like that, and would they be able to travel easily to the new markets? The Indians responded enthusiastically that such trading posts would be much closer and more convenient than those at Albany. They would be delighted to see such a settlement. The magistrates panicked. Penn became to them a menace more dire than the French. They protested immediately by express

territory? Did rights go proportionately to those seeking sanctuary among the Iroquois and those who stayed with the Delawares? Further complications might arise through intermarriage with their Indian hosts, about which nothing is known. My interpretation is that Penn established the Indian right "below the falls" of the Susquehanna as separate from the rest; he offered to make separate purchases from the Delawares and the Iroquois. The Iroquois themselves claimed only southward to the falls. (See n. 12, below.) While all is muddled by the colonies' overlapping charter claims, it is pretty plain that the Indian jurisdiction and property rights of the land below the falls depends on whether one accepts Maryland's claim of conquest or the Susquehannocks' insistence that although dispersed, they never capitulated. They had earlier ceded lands to Maryland by treaty, but these lay farther south on the Chesapeake Bay; the particular territory at issue was never ceded. Under the Susquehannocks' interpretation, the Delawares would have as a good a right to dispose of the land share of "their" Susquehannocks as the Iroquois claimed later over the larger share north of the falls. Contrariwise, if Maryland's claim was valid, neither the Iroquois nor the Delawares had any rightful claim. Maryland's later silence with regard to the Iroquois claim weighs negatively against Maryland's own claim. Claims and counterclaims aside, the issues were settled in the last analysis by power and influence.

The location of "the Greatest Fall" is shown on John Thornton's "First Map of Pennsylvania Under William Penn, 1681," ed. Albert Cook Myers (Philadelphia, 1923). Thornton mistakenly placed it above the 41st degree of latitude, which should have been the 40th. The mistake was to cause Penn much grief. "The [Iroquois] Confederates never claimed but to the Conewaga Falls": Lewis Evans (1755), in Lawrence Henry Gipson, *Lewis Evans, to which is added Evans' A Brief Account of Pennsylvania* (Philadelphia: Historical Society of Pennsylvania, 1939), p. 156.

7. Gary B. Nash, "The Quest for the Susquehanna Valley: New York, Pennsylvania, and the Seventeenth-Century Fur Trade," *New York History* 48 (1967), p. 6; Wm. Penn to Capt. Brocles and Jo. West, July 3, 1683, *Pa. Arch.*, 2d ser., 7:3. See also *The Papers of William Penn* 2:466–71, 479–80, 481–82, 487–89, 492–94.

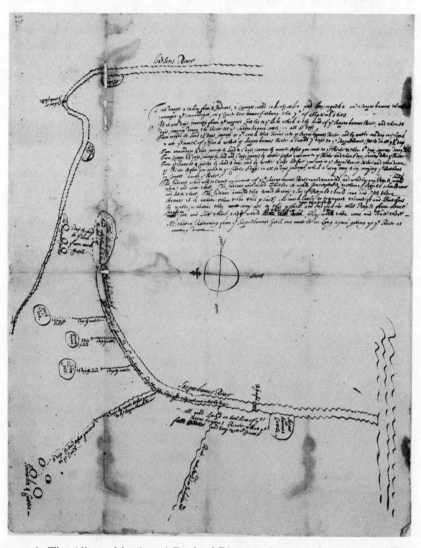

MAP 8. The Albany Merchants' Draft of Distances between Conestoga and Iroquois "Castles." REPRODUCED FROM THE LIVINGSTON MANUSCRIPTS BY COURTESY OF THE FRANKLIN D. ROOSEVELT LIBRARY, HYDE PARK, N.Y.

messenger to newly arrived Governor Dongan at the city of New York that "they that setle upon said [Susquehanna] River will be much nearer to the Indians then this Place, and consequently the Indians more Inclinable to goe there, where the accommodation of a River is to be had, then come by Land here." Deferentially the magistrates added that "the Expedient that is to be found for Preventing the Same, is Left to your honour's Consideracon.[8]

Two weeks later, no answer having been received, the magistrates wrote again, more urgently. Delegates from four of the Iroquois Five Nations would arrive in Albany on the morrow, and "Wee are credibly Inform'd of there willingnesse to dispose of the Susquehanne River. . . . if Wm. Penn buys said River, it will tend to the utter Ruine off the Bever Trade, as the Indians themselfs doe acknowledge. . . . The french its true have Endevourd to take away our trade, by Peace meals but this will cutt it all off att once. . . . [We] shall Putt a Stopp to all Proceedings, till wee have Received your honour's Commands."[9]

Dongan remaining silent, the magistrates concocted their own expedient. They reached an understanding with the Cayuga sachem Oreouache (or Ourehaouare). Suddenly Cayugas and Onondagas remembered that they had given the Susquehanna to New York's Governor Andros four years earlier "to rule over it," and three Cayuga sachems "now" gave it again "to the Governor Generall or to them that now Represent him." The magistrates "thankfully" accepted without an instant's delay, producing a few presents on the spot and promising more in the governor's name "when occasion permits." Dongan happily cooperated in this interesting procedure and "advised" William Penn to stay out of the Susquehanna Valley because "they have all of them agreed to Give Sesquehannah River to me and this Government."[10] Dongan later claimed to have granted the Indians " a large consideration."[11] For the time being, Penn was balked. Notably, he was excluded from the Covenant Chain.

The nature of the Iroquois grant should be noted carefully. It was neither a cession of territory nor a sale of real property, but rather a trust that could be taken from one governor and placed in the hands of another. Dongan, however, managed to give it a different construction. In his vir-

8. Minutes, Sept. 7, 1683, and Commissaries to Dongan, Sept. 8, 1683, *Doc.Hist.N.Y.* 1:393–94; draft and explication, *Livingston Indian Records*, pp. 69–70.

9. Magistrates to Dongan, Sept. 24, 1683, in *Doc.Hist.N.Y.* 1:395–96.

10. Propositions, Sept. 26, 1683, mss., Dreer Collection (boxes), folder Robert Livingston, HSP; various, *Doc.Hist.N.Y.* 1:396–403; Dongan to Penn, 1683, *Pa.Arch.*, 1st ser., 1:76–77. Apparently Dongan and Lord Baltimore were cooperating against Penn, which situation helps to explain the contradictions in their claims to Indian propriety. See Wm. Haig to Penn, Aug. 29, 1683 and Sept. 4, 1683, mss., Society Collection, HSP.

11. Dongan to Lords of Trade [1685], *CSPA&WI, 1685–1688,* #1160, p. 327. Because of Dongan's later claim to have been granted the Susquehanna lands personally, his language here is noteworthy: "the Indians annexed those lands to this Government forty years ago

tuous way, he later extorted from Penn a price of £100 for lands "lately Purchased or had given *him*" by the "Seinneca Susquehaneh Indians"—the impersonal government of New York had disappeared from the picture.[12] It is but fair to add that the duke of York approved of Dongan's frustrating Penn, although one may question whether York would have approved Dongan's technique for acquiring private property.[13] Dongan did not see fit to bother him with all the details.

The Iroquois had made no genuine conquest in the Susquehanna Valley, and they knew it. Only four years earlier, in 1679, the Oneidas' speaker had told an agent for Virginia that "the Susquehannes are all destroyed for which wee Return you many thanks."[14] Even earlier, the Mohawk sachem Canondondawe gave Maryland's commissioners, in August 1677, "hearty thanks for the releasing of the two Sonnes of Canondondawe, and likewise that you beheaded the sachem of the Susquehannocks named Achnaetsachawez who was the cause of their being taken prisoners."[15] As time went on, Iroquois imagination flowered in a tale of having won the Susquehanna Valley "by the sword," originating a myth that countless writers have preferred over the clear and plentiful evidence of its falsity.

The development of this "conquest" can be traced from humbler beginnings. As we have seen, before Penn's agents approached the Iroquois, the Indians thanked Maryland and Virginia for the colonists' defeat of the Susquehannocks. When Penn's men hired Albany's interpreter Arnout Viele to invite the Iroquois to Albany for purchase negotiations, the Indians claimed "that the Susquehanna River did belong to them in ancient Times, and secondly that they did Chase them away in the time of the warr."[16] "Chasing away" was one false step beyond thanking other people for a victory, but only after Albany's officials and Governor Dongan per-

[i.e., in 1645, during New Netherland's jurisdiction] and have renewed the annexations with every Governor, Dutch or English, and with myself in particular, who granted them a large consideration for them." No such "annexation" of territory appears in the sources concerning New Netherland's 1645 treaties with the Five Nations. See ch. 4, n. 28, above.

12. Dongan's deed contradicts Iroquois statements in two important particulars. (1) Though Dongan claimed personal property, the Onondagas and Cayugas stated at their treaty with Lord Howard, of Effingham, in 1684: "We have put our Lands and our Selves under the Protection of the great Duke of York, the Brother of your great Sachem. . . . [We now] put the Susquehana River above the Wasuhta [the falls] and all the rest of our Land under the great Duke of York, *and give that Land to no body else.*" Colden, *History*, p. 41. My emphasis. I have some reservations about the phrase "all the rest of our Land;" see ch. 10, n. 58. (2) Although the quoted passage from Colden shows that the Iroquois had not even claimed the Susquehanna below the falls, Dongan's deed included the entire river from headwaters to bay, thus adding to Dongan's claim about 60 miles of the lower river more than what the Iroquois claimed. Deed, Jan. 12, 1696, mss., Gratz Collection, Governors of Pennsylvania, Case 2, Box 33-a, HSP.

13. Werden to Dongan, Aug. 27, 1684, *N.Y.Col.Docs.* 3:350.

14. Treaty minutes, Oct. 31, 1679, *Livingston Indian Records*, p. 56.

15. Treaty minutes, Aug. 6, 1677, ibid., p. 47.

16. Viele's minutes, Sept. 7, 1683, transcribed by Robert Livingston, mss., Dreer Collection (boxes), folder Robert Livingston, HSP.

formed their secret rites did the Iroquois escalate to full conquest on their own.

"In the Maquase Land," on September 7, 1683, the Mohawks, Oneidas, Onondagas, and Cayugas told Viele that the Susquehannocks had been chased by 120 Mohawks "of the 3d Castle called Tionondoge, joyned with thirty onnondages," and the Cayugas "said they were also owners of old." All agreed that "the Sinnekes nation had nothing to doe with itt." But when the same four nations' delegations showed up at Albany, the Cayugas and Onondagas told the magistrates on September 26 that "The aforesaid Land belongs to us, Cayugas and Onnondagas, alone; the other three Nations, vizt. the Sinnekes, Oneydes and Maquaas have nothing to do with it."[17]

As the other nations did not protest, one must assume that some sort of intra-league accommodations probably had occurred beyond the observation of European scribes. It may have made good politics, but there are too many contradictions to make good history. The Cayugas and Onondagas repeated their exclusive claims at a treaty with Virginia's governor in 1684. It was on this occasion that the Iroquois discovered they had "won with the sword" the lands they entrusted to New York.[18] It was a good trick for warriors who fought with knives and hatchets when they were not using firearms. The phrase clearly had its origin in someone other than an Indian, but it served the purpose for which it was contrived.

Trade on the Schuylkill

Penn's trading competition included a new center of trade within his own colony. It developed on the Schuylkill River rather surprisingly amidst the Delaware Indians, who had retired upstream after ceding the lower Schuylkill for the site of Philadelphia. This new center was just as obnoxious to the Albany merchants and Thomas Dongan as if it had been Penn's personally, and they moved reflexively to suppress it. Once more, as at the Susquehanna, Dongan's chosen instrument was the Covenant Chain, but the circumstances at the Schuylkill were rather different than at the Susquehanna, and so were the results.

In terms of Penn's chartered powers, there was no difference. He claimed the Schuylkill Valley by the same document that gave him the Susquehanna. What altered the legal situation was the question of individual tribal right, and what decided the outcome was the power and favor of the Delaware Indians whose friendship Penn had won.[19]

17. Loc. cit.; extract from minutes of treaty, Sept. 26, 1683, *Doc.Hist.N.Y.* 1:396.
18. Colden, *History*, p. 41.
19. The Delawares' original name for themselves was *Lenni Lenape*, which translates to something like "the real, or common, people." Their river was the *Lenapewihittuck*. The

The Schuylkill trade was started by a partnershp of Dr. Daniel Coxe, Sir Matthias Vincent, and Major Robert Thompson. These partners and their associates obtained a grant from Penn of 30,000 acres on the Schuylkill near present-day Phoenixville in 1685. They hired a Huguenot refugee family headed by Captain Jacques Le Tort to operate their trading post, and Le Tort went to work in the most energetic and venturesome manner. About 1687 or 1688, tenants of Dr. Coxe, presumably led by Le Tort, made their way in a canoe across the Schuylkill's French Creek to the headwaters of the Susquehanna's Conestoga Creek. They then followed the Susquehanna main trunk up to and along its West Branch (or perhaps the Juniata tributary), portaged from there to a branch of the Allegheny, descended to the Ohio and the Mississippi, and paddled up that father of waters to a "great yellow river," which they ascended. We now know confidently that this 'yellow river' was the Missouri, and its ascent by Le Tort's men took them much farther west than the famous exploits of La Salle, Marquette, or Joliet.

Thus, well more than a century before the Lewis and Clark expedition, traders from the Schuylkill Valley explored the Missouri Valley. They did so without official patronage or support and without publicizing the details of their adventures. Indeed, all the circumstances of the time prevailed toward secrecy to avoid helping competitors and to keep from alarming French officialdom into measures that would prevent trade in those distant parts. Subsequent generations can only mourn the price of this secrecy, for it has cost us knowledge of the aboriginal societies along the route of that epic journey, not to speak of the epic itself.

On their return, the adventurers began a friendship with "over forty

English explorer Captain Thomas Argall named the river "Delaware," in honor of Lord de la Warr, governor of Virginia, and a reverse twist occurred. Instead of the river being named for the people, the people became named for the river. Note that the Delawares called Penn *Miquon,* meaning feather or pen. The Iroquois called him *Onas,* which meant the same thing in their language.

A bibliographic note. The senior historian of the Delawares still practicing is C. A. Weslager. See his *The Delaware Indians: A History* (New Brunswick, N.J.: Rutgers University Press, 1972); and *The Delawares: A Critical Bibliography,* published for the Newberry Library (Bloomington: Indiana University Press, 1978). For specific identifications of persons and groups see William A. Hunter, "Documented Subdivisions of the Delaware Indians," *Bulletin of the Archaeological Society of New Jersey* 20 (1978), pp. 20–40; but Hunter's interpretation of events and relationships is significantly different from the one given herein. Ives Goddard, "Delaware," in *Northeast,* pp. 213–39, is a valuable overview with a significantly different view of Delaware-Iroquois relations from that herein. An older study of merit is William W. Newcomb, Jr., *The Culture and Acculturation of the Delaware Indians,* Anthropological Paper 10 of the Museum of Anthropology (Ann Arbor: University of Michigan, 1956). A valuable collection of papers appears in *A Delaware Indian Symposium,* ed. Herbert C. Kraft, Anthropological Series 4 (Harrisburg: Pa. Hist. and Museum Commission, 1974).

Two studies by Anthony F. C. Wallace are required reading: *King of the Delawares: Teedyuscung, 1700–1763* (Philadelphia: University of Pennsylvania Press, 1949); "Woman, Land, and Society: Three Aspects of Aboriginal Delaware Life," *Pa. Archaeologist* 17 (1943), entire issue.

nations" of Indians, according to Coxe.[20] Seemingly they had also made contact with dissident Canadian coureurs de bois, whom they impressed with the opportunities for free enterprise. One of these, Peter Bisaillon, either returned with them or came to the Schuylkill soon afterward.[21] Another, Martin Chartier, came later.[22]

Governor Dongan regarded the traders from Pennsylvania in the same light as the French of Canada. Perhaps he did not know that Dr. Daniel Coxe was physician to king Charles II; more likely he did not care. In May 1686 Dongan ordered the Iroquois not to "Trade or Traffique, or Enter Into any Covenant Chain with any Christians french or English as to matters of Trade or Traffique without my Consent and approbation," and "not to Suffer any to Trade or hunt" except with Dongan's license.[23] The Iroquois considered the matter for several months and decided not to meddle with Englishmen's trade.

Because of truce between Britain and France, Dongan actually became rougher with the Pennsylvania traders than with the French. He instructed one of his great western trading expeditions "not in Any wise to meddle with or Disturb Any ffrench Indians, or Any others Whatsoever *Except* Such as be Traders from Pensilvania, East and West Jerseys, whom they Are hereby Empowred to Apprehend and bring to his Majesty's Citty of New Yorke."[24]

Dongan also suggested to the Iroquois that they should pretend to the

20. Dr. Coxe's memorial of 1719 to the Lords of Trade retrospectively claims and describes the journey. I have named the specific creeks in eastern Pennsylvania from knowledge that they were commonly traveled by Indians and traders, and known to William Penn. Curiously, this journey into the "Illinois country" was made at about the same time Dongan sent his great trading expeditions to Michilimackinac, but French officialdom seems not to have caught on to the intrusion of Coxe's men into their claimed territory. The fact suggests collusion between Coxe's men and other free enterprisers in the Mississippi Valley. HSP transcripts, Bd. of Trade Papers, Proprieties, 1697–1776, X92), Indorsed Q:186. See also Evelyn A. Benson, "The Huguenot Le Torts: First Christian Family on the Conestoga," *Journal of the Lancaster County Historical Society* 67 (1961), pp. 99–100. Identification of the "great yellow river" as the Missouri is in Donald Jackson, *Thomas Jefferson and the Stony Mountains; Exploring the West from Monticello* (Urbana: University of Illinois Press, 1981), p. 8. Could there possibly be a Le Tort journal hidden away somewhere?

A bibliographic note: Alvord and Bidgood have disparaged Coxe's claims on the assumption that he was only concocting another speculative "bubble," but his details are confirmed from other sources and his geographical data could have been acquired only from direct exploration. These authors seem to have wanted to establish primacy in English exploration beyond the Appalachians for Virginia's Governor Alexander Spotswood, who was really very late on the scene, lagging long after the Carolina traders as well as Coxe's crew. They print the Coxe memorial in a different sequence from that of the HSP transcript, but with the same material. Clarence W. Alvord and Lee Bidgood, *The First Explorations of the Trans-Allegheny Region by the Virginians, 1560–1674* (Cleveland: Arthur H. Clark Co., 1912), pp. 231–49.

21. Francis Jennings, "Bisaillon, Peter," in *Dict.Can.Biog.* 3:65.

22. See. ch. 10.

23. Treaty minutes, May 20, 1686, *Livingston Indian Records*, p. 100.

24. N.Y. council minutes, Sept. 30, 1686, ibid., p. 107.

ownership of the Schuylkill Valley as they had already claimed the Sus-quehanna: "I take it very ill that those Indians that the Bretheren has given leave to live upon the Schoolkill and the Susquehanna Should bring Bever and peltry to Philadelphia which is Contrary to the agreement Brethren has made with us. I desire of the Bretheren not to suffer any Indians to live there longer but on Condition not to trade any where but att Albany. Also that the Bretheren would take Such French and English they shall finde going up those Rivers without my Lycence or pass and bring them tyed to Albany, and there deliver them to the Magistrates—for which the Bretheren shall have all the goods they finde belonging to Such persons to themselves."[25] In short, Dongan declared clandestine war on Penn, not only in the remote back country of Penn's colony, but up to the outskirts of Philadelphia.

The Iroquois knew very well that they had not "given leave" to the Delawares to live in the latter's native country. They also knew that the Delawares had been, and might become again, their most numerous and powerful "props," and they quite obviously did not care to risk converting such important people into enemies. The Iroquois had their hands full already with the French. They were hoping for Delaware aid instead of hostilities. What they thought of Dongan's idea of diplomacy can only be conjectured. What they did was to ignore all his instructions pertaining to the Schuylkill. They very carefully confirmed obedience to his orders about the Susquehanna, and they equally carefully omitted the Schuylkill from their confirmation.

Turncoat coureurs de bois

When Dongan realized that he could not impose his will in this matter, he tried another tack. In July 1687 he licensed runaway coureurs de bois Petit and Salvaye "to goe up by the way of Susquehanna and trade amongst the Indians." How successfully this competitive venture turned out is not clear, but there is a hint in the records that the men who had fled Canada were also capable of transferring loyalties from Albany. At some time within the next few years they formed a partnership with Schuylkill-based

25. Dongan tried twice to have the Iroquois raid the Schuylkill trading center (only about 25 miles from Philadelphia). His first effort is recorded in the treaty of Aug. 30, and Sept. 1, 1686, which I have reconstituted from two incomplete texts: New York Council Minutes, mss., 5:163, 169 (mutilated by fire) and *Doc.Hist.N.Y.* 1:403–5 (extracts made before the fire). Dongan's second effort, from which my quotation is given, is recorded as of April 25, 1687, in the *Livingston Indian Records*, pp. 112–13. Copies of the reconstituted treaty are deposited in the New York State Archives and the Newberry Library Iroquois treaty archive. O'Cal-laghan's excisions from the complete mss., which he had at his disposal, are tendentious, but he did show omissions with leaders.

Peter Bisaillon, who was also a runaway from Canada.[26] This partnership miscarried, and the future careers of Petit and Salvaye are not known to this writer. Bisaillon never became Albany's man. Dongan's effort to seize the Schuylkill Valley from Penn died without a whimper, possibly without Penn's knowing that the effort had been made.

Dongan's loss was not Penn's gain. Although the Schuylkill was within Penn's jurisdiction, the traders there picked up their goods at Burlington, New Jersey, instead of Philadelphia, and transmitted their furs to Dr. Coxe, not to Mr. Penn. Coxe sold his property in 1692 with a prospectus that boasted, "I can Exclude the Inhabitants of Pensilvania from this ffurr trade,"[27] and the new owners were organized in the West Jersey Society. The actual operators of the business continued to be Frenchmen, and their presence gave the name French Creek to the stream that joined the Schuylkill at their site. Jacques Le Tort returned to England in 1696, where he made Penn's acquaintance and testified to the Lords of Trade in Penn's behalf.[28] Le Tort's wife and son, James, continued the business with the apparent assistance of Peter Bisaillon and perhaps some other coureurs de bois.

Bisaillon was undoubtedly a key figure, but much of his activity can only be surmised. Before changing sides, he had traveled down the Mississippi with Henri de Tonty in search of La Salle, and he had later become chief factor for Colonel Daniel Quary, who briefly dominated the trade at Delaware Bay and was also a bitter political opponent of Penn.[29] Bisaillon had probably met the employees of Dr. Coxe during their western voyage. Besides being widely traveled he was exceedingly well connected. His brother Michel was an important trader in the Illinois country. Brother Richard was reported active in the Carolinas. Another brother was situated at La Prairie, just outside Montreal. The brothers kept in touch with

26. Bisaillon had squatted on Schuylkill Valley land that Jacques Le Tort took over in the names of Sir Matthias Vincent and Dr. Caniel Coxe. The large tract is shown on Thomas Holme's 1687 map of Pennsylvania under the names of Vincent, Coxe, and two other proprietors. Map in Hist. Soc. of Pa. Denonville to Seignelay, June 8, 1687, *N.Y.Col.Docs.* 9:326; Denonville to Dongan, Aug. 22, 1687, ibid., 3:471; Remonstrance of La Salle, 1684, ibid., 9–215; Information of Col. Herman, May 1, 1696, *Md.Archives* 20:406; Wm. Markham to Gov. Nicholson, n.d., ibid., 20:470–71. Benson, "Huguenot Le Torts," is an excellent discussion of the French traders in Pennsylvania.

27. Markham to Nicholson, *Md.Archives* 20:470; Daniel Coxe, "Account of New Jersey," *Pa. Mag. of Hist. and Biog.* 7 (1883), p. 328. Coxe tried to be a mover and shaker on the grand scale. Besides his trading center on the Schuylkill, he set up a company in 1686 with the ambitious goal of acquiring a vast tract of land on Lake Erie. It never functioned. Albright G. Zimmerman, "Daniel Coxe and the New Mediterranean Sea Company," *Pa. Mag. of Hist. and Biog.* 76 (1952), pp. 86–96.

28. Markham to Nicholson, *Md. Archives* 20:470; Le Tort to Wm. Penn, London, May 4, 1702, HSP Bd. of Trade Papers transcripts, Proprietaries, vol. 6², 1–43.

29. Albright G. Zimmerman, "The Indian Trade of Colonial Pennsylvania," Ph.D. diss., University of Delaware, 1966. Pp. 54–58. Quary had learned the trade while formerly a resident of South Carolina. Crane, *Southern Frontier*, pp. 77, 143.

each other, and one cannot doubt that their association was commercially advantageous in ways that evaded regulations of all governments. They were concerned more with prosperity than patriotism, and their first loyalty was to each other rather than to any flag.[30] It appears that when the French market became glutted with furs, the brothers helped ease the strain by diverting furs to the English. As New France's historian Gustave Lanctot has remarked, since English prices for furs were twice as high as Canadian, "it was inevitable that large quantities of furs should find their way into the hands of the Indians to be sold in the English markets."[31] Another Canadian historian has documented a smuggling trade from French Detroit to Albany.[32] It appears that Peter Bisaillon channeled some of it to competitive English markets in Pennsylvania.[33]

Another renegade Canadian married a Shawnee woman and settled with her band on the lower Susquehanna.[34] Like Bisaillon, Marin Chartier had intimate, first-hand knowledge of the Illinois country from a sojourn there at La Salle's Fort St. Louis. These were experienced men who knew their business and had contacts with Indians and other coureurs de bois, and perhaps some smuggling contacts also with certain French officials. It would be a mistake, however, to attribute Pennsylvania's rise in the intersocietal trade entirely to the traders, important though they were. The Indians themselves were the first requirement of the trade. Thus, when the Susquehannocks fled from the slaughter of the Iroquois wars with Canada and Canada's Indian allies and resettled in their old homeland, the colony gained an economic resource of incalculable value—further enhanced by Shawnees settling with the Susquehannocks. William Penn knew the worth of these Indians and moved to reap its advantages.

A problem was to get through the barrier of the trust deeded to Dongan by the Iroquois. Dongan had converted it to a claim of personal ownershp of the whole Susquehanna Valley, and he maintained the claim after retirement from the governorship. Penn sought him out in Ireland and paid him off to eliminate the nuisance. The price paid shows that Penn did not believe in the legitimacy of Dongan's claim—only £100 for the whole valley was a small fraction of the rate Penn was paying to the Indians of the Delaware Valley for relatively small tracts of their territories.[35]

30. Jennings, "Bisaillon," pp. 65–66.

31. Lanctot, *History of Canada* 2:223.

32. Yves F. Zoltvany, "New France and the West, 1701–1713," *Canadian Historical Review* 46(1965), pp. 301–22.

33. See Francis Jennings, "The Indian Trade of the Susquehanna Valley," *Proceedings of the American Philosophical Society* 110:6 (Dec., 1966), pp. 406–24.

34. Hanna, *Wilderness Trail* 1:126–29.

35. Deed, Dongan to Penn, Jan. 12, 1696, Gratz Coll., Govs. of Pa.., mss., Case 2, Box 33–a, HSP. Though all records show the Iroquois claiming only to "the falls" of the Susquehanna River, Dongan's personal deed to Penn conveyed both sides of the river, from the "fountain or heads" to Chesapeake Bay. It thus included territories that subsequently were

Having disposed finally of Dongan, Penn came to his province a second time, arriving in December 1699, and arranged a treaty with the Susquehannocks living at Conestoga (and soon to become known as Conestogas). He had two purposes: (1) to build another city on the Susquehanna, sister to Philadelphia on the Delaware; (2) to gain for Pennsylvania exclusively the trade of the Indians on the Susquehanna. Both purposes threatened Albany. The loss of trade from the Susquehanna region might not be too serious, but the possibility of Iroquois trade being drawn to their new center was ominous. Without Iroquois commerce, Albany would become merely a sleepy country village.

Penn's treaty with the Susquehannock / Conestogas

Albany was powerless at the time. Penn's charter gave him indisputable royal right to the Susquehanna; and the Iroquois, who might otherwise have been manipulated to obstruct Penn's negotiations, were at their lowest ebb. The year was 1701, and the Iroquois were in no condition or mood to challenge anyone. Penn nailed down his right to the Susquehanna Valley by obtaining still another deed, this one from the Susquehannock-Conestogas—notably without Iroquois protest at the time—and early in the spring of 1701 the sachems of the motley bands living there came to Philadelphia to make a great treaty. Unlike his treaty with the Delawares at Shackamaxon, which exists only in tradition, the record of the Susquehanna treaty has survived in full text. Its eleven articles provided for a lasting peace, the cession of the Susquehanna Valley, and a monopoly for Pennsylvanians of the trade there.

Thus were the tables turned on Albany and New York. But the treaty was important in other respects as well. While the territory had been ceded, Article Three provided what the Indians took to be a guarantee that they might live on those lands in parity with the colonial inhabitants: the Indians were to have "the full and free privileges and Immunities of all the Said Laws [of the province] as any other Inhabitants." From later developments it appears that the Indians understood this treaty language to mean also that some lands would always be reserved for their own communities. Perhaps an explicit promise to that effect was made orally at the treaty; it would fit with Penn's practices elsewhere, and long after all par-

defined as parts of New York and Maryland. See also Dongan's reply to what was apparently a recrimination by Penn, Jan. 25, 1708, mss., Penn-Forbes Coll. 2:67, HSP. Cf. Onondaga Chief Canasatego's speech at Lancaster: *Pa. Council Minutes*, June, 26, 1744, 4:708. His remarks are quoted in ch. 18, below.

ties were dead a deed of some sort came to light that provided a tract of 500 acres for the Conestogas.[36]

Other articles in the treaty promised mutual information about activities concerning the parties, with advice and counsel; the regulation of trade and a guarantee of adequate supplies of goods for it; prevention by the Indians of settlement west of the Susquehanna by "strange Nations of Indians"; and sanctuary for the Conoys, who were having difficulties with Maryland. The treaty was subscribed by Conestogas, Shawnees, and Conoys, as well as by Ahookasoongh, the Onondaga "brother to the Emperor" of the Five Nations. Whatever the height of his status at home, this Ahookasoongh was not the great man of the occasion in Pennsylvania. He seems instead to have been an observer testifying to knowledge and approval of the treaty rather than a participant negotiating it. No similarity existed between this treaty and the 1677 treaty at Albany, where the Iroquois had so dominated the proceedings that the Susquehannocks in their midst were not even mentioned by name. It follows from all the foregoing that this 1701 treaty was not a Covenant Chain agreement. It spoke of a chain of friendship but did not use Covenant Chain terminology or refer to its tradition. The Iroquois were not mentioned except for Ahookasoongh's signature, which was placed, inconspicuously, sixth on the document, and an assertion in the text that he was acting "for and in Behalf of the Emperor." Iroquois pretensions to the Susquehanna Valley were simply ignored, and no mention is made of their being raised by Ahookasoongh. Great Penn extended his protection over the tribes on the Susquehanna, against all other peoples, not excluding the Iroquois. He had previously protected the Delawares, and the Delawares promptly stopped sending tribute to the Five Nations. Pennsylvania's protection at this stage meant peaceful disruption of a major segment of the Covenant Chain. During Benjamin Fletcher's earlier tenure as simultaneously governor of New York and Pennsylvania, Fletcher had pronounced Pennsylvania to be part of the Chain, but nothing could be clearer than William Penn's determination to break off his link.

The local tribes were pleased. In June 1701 Penn repaid the Indians' Philadelphia visit by making a courtesy call on the Susquehanna where he "pretty well traversed the wilderness." Perhaps cartography was mixed in with the courtesy. One of Penn's companions, councilor Isaac Norris,

36. Deed, Sept. 13, 1700, mss., Cadqallader Coll., Box 12, Fol. Penn Indian Deeds, HSP. Copy in Philadelphia Deed Book F–8:242, Phila. City Hall. Printed in *Pa. Archives*, 1st ser., 1:133. Treaty text, April 3, 1701, Penn Papers, Indian Affairs, mss., 1:45, HSP; printed in *Pa. Council Minutes* 2:14–18. Deed and treaty printed again in ibid., Aug. 2, 1735, 3:599–603. One may notice that the survival of the Susquehanna Treaty was as advantageous to Penn's successors as was the disappearance of the Delaware treaty. Reservation of Conestoga Manor: *Pa. Archives*, 1st ser., 9:49–50.

reported that "We lived nobly at the King's palace in Conestoga."[37] The language is unique. No other colonial record describes an Indian long-house as a palace.

In October a delegation from Conestoga came back to Philadelphia again in solemn state after the Indians had learned that Penn was "to our great Grief and the trouble of all the Indians of these parts obliged to goe back for England." (His enemies had been busy in London.) The chiefs of the Conestogas, the Shawnees, and the Conoys paid tribute to Penn, acknowledging that he had been "not only alwayes just but very kind to us . . . and careful to keep a good Correspondence with us, not suffering us to receive any Wrong from any of the People under his Government, Giving us as is well known, his Hous for our Home at all times and freely entertaining us at his own Cost and often filling us with many presents of necessary Goods." The rhetoric was obviously helped out by the English scribe. A document showing harmony in Penn's colony would be useful in his political difficulties. This particular document would lay any ghost of New York's claim to the Susquehanna. The Indians expressed hope that Penn and his children would "alwayes Govern these parts." An inter-esting reason was expressed by the Indians: if Penn governed, they would have confidence not only of good treatment but also that they would "be encouraged to live among the Christians according to the Agreement that he and We have solemnly made for us and our Posterity."[38] This is the first indication that I know of formal encouragement in an English colony for integration of the peoples. From the time of John Smith in Virginia and the Pilgrims at New Plymouth, the rule had always been the segre-gation that had become policy during the Elizabethan conquest of Ireland, and that policy was enforced by law as well as custom in the American colonies. As Edmund Plowden summarized in 1648, "fair and far off is best with Heathen Indians."[39] "Racial" segregation preceded African slav-ery in English America.

37. Isaac Norris to David Zachary, June 21, 1701, *Correspondence Between William Penn and James Logan, and Others, 1700–1750. From the Original Letters in Possession of the Logan Family.* With notes by the late Mrs. Deborah Logan. Ed. Edward Armstong, 2 vols., Memoirs of the Historical Society of Pennsylvania 9–10 (Philadelphia: J. B. Lippincott and Co., 1870–1872), 1:43. Apparently Griffith Owen and Edward Shippen were also of the party. J. Logan to W. Penn, July 9, 1702, mss., Logan Papers 1:122, HSP.

A bibliographic note: *The Penn-Logan Correspondence*, to use its short title, is a convenient compendium but must be used with some care. It is no exception to the rule that descendants compiling ancestors' papers usually tidy them up to rid the ancestors of their blemishes. As almost all of the Logan Papers are now at HSP, comparison of the printed transcripts with the manuscripts is possible. It reveals that while the printed work seems reliable enough in what it transcribes, it truncates and extracts tendentiously, often without signalling omis-sion.

38. Address of Indian Kings, ca. Oct. 7, 1701, mss., Penn-Forbes Coll., HSP.

39. Quotation: Plantagenet, *Description of New Albion*, p. 25. For the transition of policy from Ireland to Virginia, and the reasons therefore, see Nicholas Canny's very important

Tentative dealings with the Iroquois

Penn did not wish to make enemies of the Iroquois. At the 1701 treaty, Penn apparently tried to arrange a rapprochement with the Five Nations through unrecorded conversations with Ahookasoongh. The other Indians were less than zealous in encouragement. To follow up, Penn gave a wampum belt and an unrecorded message to the reluctant Delawares to carry to Onondaga for him. They delayed the journey for eleven years. They also neglected during the same period to present whatever tribute the Iroquois may have thought they owed. Nothing dreadful happened to them. If tributary status had any operational meaning at all during that period, it surely was not a condition of grinding servitude to anybody. If the Iroquois were in a position to demand tribute, they surely were the world's pokiest tax collectors.[40]

In May 1704 the Onondagas sent messengers to Philadelphia with a tentative offer to trade. This caused considerable excitement, but Peter Bisaillon sobered the council with a report that the Iroquois intended to carry off the Shawnees, "they being colonies of a nation that were there enemies." Council considered the matter "fully"—rather more fully than it cared to record—and decided to send an embassy to protect the Shawnees "as the Shawannahs are as of our selves." A coda tantalizes: "and that all the Belts of Wampum be procured and sent up that were collected among the Indians three years agoe for that purpose."[41]

What belts and what purpose? The remark seems to allude to William Penn's off-the-record conversations with Ahookasoongh at Conestoga. Whatever was going on, the Onondagas were not dictating terms. They came to Philadelphia at the end of August, and they left without the Shawnees. The official minutes of the affair are so lean as to be almost invisible. They report the arrival and then dispose of all business in a single sentence: "the Secretary, by order, made a speech to them, which being interpreted, [Onondaga chief] Kagundonoyagh answered, and Presents were made on both sides."[42]

Secretary James Logan reported privately to Penn that the Iroquois "at length arrived here very seasonably, after we were furnished with goods . . . and had a treaty with us, which we hope may prove of service." He spelled out the reason for so much official taciturnity: "it is by no means agreeable to [Governor] Lord Cornbury, who, with all the government of

essay, "The permissive frontier: The problem of social control in English settlements in Ireland and Virginia, 1550–1650," in *The Westward Enterprise: English activities in Ireland, the Atlantic, and America, 1480–1650*, eds. K. R. Andrews, N. P. Canny, and P. E. H. Hair (Detroit: Wayne State University Press, 1979), pp. 17–44.

40. *Pa. Council Minutes*, May 19, 1712, 2:548.
41. Ibid., May 9, 1704, 2:140; May 18, 1704, 2:145.
42. Ibid., Aug. 28, 1704, 2:158–59; Sept. 1, 1704, 2:159.

York, is jealous that we should have any thing to do with these people."[43] Penn was well aware of the situation. He had previously remarked to Logan that, in regard to the Five Nations, "New York . . . draws the Line of Jealousy over Us, and fear into the Bargain."[44]

Perhaps Logan's way of keeping records preserved the trade secret from Yorkers, but news got around quickly on the moccasin telegraph. Several months after the Iroquois departure, there arrived in Philadelphia two Shawnees of the upper Delaware—those who lived under the wing of the Minisinks. "Considerable numbers of that and some other adjoining Nations designed to come down hither to trade," they were reported as saying, and they asked about prices. The council responded that "at all times we Should be glad to trade with them."[45] The point is, these were Indians whose trade had formerly been monopolized by New York.

The period yields very little information about the Iroquois. Their approach to Pennsylvania speaks clearly of neglect by New York, in spite of the fact that huge quantities of furs were being smuggled from Canada (or perhaps because of that fact). The bulk of that smuggling seems to have gone by way of Montreal to Albany, and the Indians who carried it between the two towns were merely hired hands, not traders. The houses provided for Indians actually trading at Albany had deteriorated by 1705 to the point of being uninhabitable.[46]

All in all, it appears that New York lost interest because the Iroquois were bound to neutrality by their 1701 treaty with New France. So weak were they, in fact, that when a large hunting party of Senecas was ambushed by Ottawas in 1704, with a loss of thirty men, the Senecas complained to Canada's Governor Vaudreuil instead of striking back.[47]

Penn's personality and status

What happened in Pennsylvania's Indian relationships after William Penn's second and final return to England in 1699 was largely dominated by the steward he left behind to look after his interests in the colony, a young Scotch-Irish Quaker named James Logan. In spite of their common adherence to the Society of Friends, Penn and Logan were very different people. What would have happened if Penn had been permitted by circumstance to spend more time in Pennsylvania is debatable. He was a rare

43. Logan to Penn, Sept. 28, 1704, mss., Logan Letter Books 1:163, HSP.
44. Penn to Logan, Dec. 4, 1703, mss., Penn Mss., Ltrs. of the Penn Family to James Logan 1:15, HSP.
45. Pa. Council Minutes, March 6, 1705, 2:183.
46. Norton, Fur Trade, pp. 56, 67.
47. Yves F. Zoltvany, Vaudreuil, p. 53.

and special person. His Indian policies reflected the unique blend of the practical, the pious, and the decent that was Penn's mind. Recent scholarship has tended to compensate for previous hagiography by emphasizing his political side, some of which has already been shown here.[48] Nevertheless he was a devoutly believing member of the Religious Society of Friends—so renowned that there are people today who can name him as such though they would stammer before being able to name a second Quaker—and there is no understanding Penn or his colony without taking the Friendly faith into account. Penn's Quaker faith was his reason for being interested in the New World.[49] Quakers were pacifists and tolerationists. Pennsylvania became a colony without an army or militia, in which persons of all religions—even Catholics, Jews, and heathen Indians—could worship without official hindrance. The Quakers launched no military campaigns and therefore required no Indian warriors to aid in such campaigns, and they sent out no missions to persuade or persecute the tribes into religious factionalism.

Courtier, mystic, spendthrift, great magnate, intellectual, and practical man of the world, Penn was an extremely complex man, and the complexities of his character were almost matched by the variety of his functions as True and Absolute Proprietary of Pennsylvania. He had refused a title, on principle, but he was a great lord in powers. By the terms of his charter, Penn held the province as a feudal fief. He had two distinct rights: he owned all the land, subject to the performance of his feudal due to the crown (no mention of Indian right intruding in the charter), and he had full power to govern so long as his laws were consented to by the colony's freemen and were consistent with the laws of England.[50] Insofar as law could prescribe, Indian relations were absolutely under Penn's personal control. As governor he had full power to conclude treaties with the Indians on his own authority, and in secrecy if he so desired. As proprietor, he voluntarily obliged himself to extinguish all native claims to the land in order to sell his own patents of land "free from any Indian incumbrance."[51]

48. See Mary Maples Dunn, *William Penn: Politics and Conscience* (Princeton: Princeton University Press, 1967); Joseph E. Illick, *William Penn the Politician: His Relations with the English Government* (Ithaca, N.Y.: Cornell University Press, 1965).

49. Frederick B. Tolles, *Quakers and the Atlantic Culture* (New York: The Macmillan Co., 1960), p. 45; William C. Braithwaite, *The Second Period of Quakerism*, 2d ed., ed. Henry J. Cadbury (Cambridge: Cambridge University Press, 1961), pp. 55, 402–3.

50. Among other places, the charter may be found in Hazard, *Annals of Pa.*, pp. 488–99.

51. William Penn, "Some Account of the Province of Pennsilvania" (1681), in *Narratives of Early Pa.*, ed. A. C. Myers, p. 208.

Penn's policies toward Indians

Penn's interest in the Indians transcended his legal powers and responsibilities. He saw them in five distinguishable aspects: souls to be shown the Truth by example, exotic objects for study, native owners of the soil, objects of government, and trading partners. He founded no missions, believing instead in converting the Indians by a display of righteousness in practice. He followed the precepts of the founder of Quakerism by admonishing the first settlers of Pennsylvania, "Don't abuse [the Indians], but let them have Justice, and you win them," ending with the comment, "It were miserable indeed for us to fall under the just censure of the poor Indian Conscience, while we make profession of things so far transcending."[52] Such a humble equation of consciences was rarely to be found in the seventeenth or eighteenth century.

To say that Penn was interested in the Indians as objects for study is inadequate. On his first visit to his colony, he "made it my business to understand" the Delaware language, "that I might not want an Interpreter on any occasion."[53] In itself this fact distinguished Penn sharply from upperclass Englishmen in all the colonies except Rhode Island, and equally from Penn's own stewards and successors in Pennsylvania. He joined in Indian activities, gave and accepted hospitality, and studied Indian manners and customs with such admirable perception that his descriptions are respected by modern anthropologists. But these Indians studied by Penn were not merely objects to him; they were human persons. Penn defined them as human within the law of moral obligation, and he dealt with them according to his conception. In 1681, after he had received the grant of his colony, he wrote a letter for his agents to read to the Indians in anticipation of his coming. It is an earnest and moving statement, unique in the literature of Indian-European relations.[54]

My friends—there is one great God and power that hath made the world and all things therein, to whom you and I, and all people owe their being and well-being, and to whom you and I must one day give an account for all that we do in the world; this great God hath written his law in our hearts, by which we are taught and commanded to love and help, and do good to one another, and not to do harm and mischief one to another. Now this great God hath been pleased to make me concerned in your parts of the world, and the king of the country where I live hath given unto me a great province, but I desire to enjoy it with your love and consent, and that we may always live together as neighbours and friends, else what

52. "A Letter from William Penn . . . to the Committee of the Free Society of Traders" (1683), in *Narratives of Early Pa.*, ed. A. C. Myers, p. 236. Cf. the repressive missions of John Eliot in Massachusetts. Jennings, *Invasion*, ch. 14.
53. Ibid., p. 230.
54. Hazard, *Annals of Pa.*, pp. 532-33.

would the great God say to us, who hath made us not to devour and destroy one another, but live soberly and kindly together in the world? Now I would have you well observe that I am very sensible of the unkindness and injustice that hath been too much exercised towards you by the people of these parts of the world, who sought themselves, and to make great advantages by you, rather than be examples of justice and goodness unto you, which I hear hath been matter of trouble to you, and caused great grudgings and animosities, sometimes to the shedding of blood, which hath made the great God angry; but I am not such a man, as is well known in my own country; I have great love and regard towards you, and I desire to win and gain your love and friendship, by a kind, just, and peaceable life, and the people I send are of the same mind, and shall in all things behave themselves accordingly; and if in any thing any shall offend you or your people, you shall have a full and speedy satisfaction for the same, by an equal number of just men on both sides, that by no means you may have just occasion of being offended against them. I shall shortly come to you myself, at what time we may more largely and freely confer and discourse of these matters. In the mean time, I have sent my commissioners to treat with you about land, and a firm league of peace. Let me desire you to be kind to them and the people, and receive these presents and tokens which I have sent to you, as a testimony of my good will to you, and my resolution to live justly, peaceably, and friendly with you.

I am your loving friend,

William Penn.

Penn's complexity did not include hypocrisy. He meant what his letter said, and while he exerted effective control over his province, the Indians had good reason for gratitude.

In sending his commissioners to buy Indian lands, Penn accepted one variant of "Law of Nations" theory—the Dutch variant given its classic expression by Hugo Grotius. Implicitly Penn rejected the virgin land and *vacuum domicilium* propositions of Samuel Purchas and John Winthrop. The Indians, he wrote, "are as exact Preservers of Property as we are . . . and that the Indians are true Lords of the Soil, there are two Reasons; 1st because the Place was never conquer'd. 2dly That the Kings of England have alwaies comanded the English to purchase the land of the Natives . . . which it is supposed they would never have done, to the prejudice of their own Title, if the Right of the Soil had been in them, and not in the Natives."[55] (That the kings of England had not "always" so commanded has been demonstrated elsewhere,[56] but Penn apparently believed his erroneous statement and acted upon it.) Guided by his moral impulse, he showed unprecedented generosity in his payment for Indian quitclaims. By 1685 he had paid out at least £1,200 in presents and purchase money.[57]

55. Wm. Penn's Instructions to Capt. Markham respecting Lord Baltimore (ca. 1683), mss., Cadwalader Coll., Thos. Cadwalader. Coates List #12, HSP.

56. Jennings, *Invasion*, ch. 8.

57. Wm. Penn, "A Further Account of the Province of Pennsylvania" (1685), in *Narratives of Early Pa.*, ed. A. C. Myers, p. 276.

For this sum he had obtained extensive good will and lands that were much less extensive. The territory thus freed of Indian claim was sharply limited to a small corner of the grant made by King Charles. When it is considered that Penn had been granted the whole province in discharge of a royal debt of £16,000, the startling fact emerges that he paid the Indians at a higher rate than he had, in effect, paid his king. It was another of Penn's unique distinctions. Other Europeans had bought land from Indians but never at such rates.

I have said that Penn conceived the Indians, in one capacity, as objects of government, being obliged to use the word *objects* because of semantic difficulties. The Indians were not "subjects" to Penn, and they were not "aliens" living within his government. They were "natives," having their own governments, and Penn observed the operation of those governments with ungrudging respect: " 'Tis Admirable to consider, how Powerful the Kings are, and yet how they move by the Breath of their People. . . . I have never seen more natural Sagacity . . . and he will deserve the Name of Wise, that Outwits them in any Treaty about a thing they understand." Penn adopted Andros's laws, adding his own refinement that in differences between the English and the Indians, "Six of each side shall end the matter."[58] This was not a mixed jury, as is often averred, because it did not operate under English law or in English courts. There are no records of Indian jurymen in Pennsylvania. Nor was "six of each side" a sentimental invention. Rather, it shows Penn in the aspect of a legal scholar with ability to see current problems in a historical context. Early in the tenth century the march lords of England and Wales had composed their differences with arbitration by six on each side.[59] The identical numbers suggest that Penn knew the tradition and planned to adapt it for his own use; but the Indian treaty institution prevailed instead.

Recognizing Indian chiefs as "kings," Penn nevertheless followed the historical pattern of Ireland whereby clan kings had abounded but were nominally subject to the sovereign overlordship of the king of England. Like other colonials, Penn assumed that his charter from that civil sovereign gave him a subordinate overlordship above the Indian "kings." In his political treaty of 1701 he required the Indians to "behave themselves Regularly and Soberly, according to the Laws of this Government while they live Near or amongst the Christian Inhabitants thereof." He conceded to the Indians "the full and free privileges and Imunities of all the Said Laws" without making provision for them to be instructed in what the laws provided, "they Duly Owning and Acknowledging the Authority of the Crown of England and Government of this Province." The treaty did not

58 Wm. Penn, "Letter to the Society of Traders," pp. 235–36.
59. Doris Stenton, *English Justice between the Norman Conquest and the Great Charter, 1066–1215*, Jayne Lectures for 1963 (Philadelphia: American Philosophical Society, 1964), p. 7.

FIGURE 3. *Penn's Treaty with the Indians*, by Benjamin West, 1771. COURTESY OF THE
PENNSYLVANIA ACADEMY OF THE FINE ARTS.

provide for reciprocity: Pennsylvanians living amongst the Indians were
not required to observe Indian custom.[60]

The Great Treaty with the Delawares

Although the 1701 document is Penn's only political treaty to have survived, it is apparent that he had negotiated an earlier one with the Delawares having much the same terms. In 1685 he wrote that "if any of [the
Indians] break our Laws, they submit to be punisht by them: and to this
they have tyed themselves by an obligation under their hands."[61] The fact
that no political treaty has survived with a date earlier than 1701 does not
signify that none was made. Indeed there is much reason to believe the
legend of the Great Treaty of friendship made by Penn with the Dela-

60. *Pa. Council Minutes*, April 23, 1701, 2:16.
61. Wm. Penn, "A Further Account," p. 276.

FIGURE 4. The Great Treaty Wampum Belt. Pennsylvania Quaker traditions associate this belt with William Penn's Great Treaty with the Delawares, ca. 1682, under an old elm tree at Shackamaxon (Philadelphia). It was presented by descendant Granville Penn to the Historical Society of Pennsylvania, through whose courtesy it is reproduced here. The figures symbolize size and importance rather than an attempt at photographic realism. William Penn was not fat at the time of the treaty.

wares under a spreading elm at their village of Shackamaxon. The legend has been so strong that Benjamin West painted a tremendous anachronistic canvas of the imagined scene; Voltaire quipped that it was the only agreement between Europeans and Indians never sworn to and never broken; and Edward Hicks was inspired in the nineteenth century to paint the scene repeatedly in Biblical symbols of the lion and the lamb lying down together in *The Peaceable Kingdom*. School texts uniformly are illustrated with pictures of the wampum belt supposedly given by the Delawares to Penn on the occasion, and the belt itself was given by one of Penn's descendants to the Historical Society of Pennsylvania, in whose library it is now on display. That some such treaty took place is almost certain.[62] Besides Penn's remark, already quoted, about the Indians' tying themselves to an obligation to observe English law, there is his earlier report (in 1683) of "Treaties for Land, and to adjust the terms of Trade." For Indians, trade relations were concomitant with political relations, and Penn added to his remark about the treaties that "great Promises past between us of Kindness and good Neighbourhood, and that the Indians and English must live in Love, as long as the Sun gave light."[63] Nearly a

62. A well-balanced and reasonably accessible discussion of the Great Treaty tradition is in J. Thomas Scharf and Thompson Westcott, *History of Philadelphia, 1609–1884*, 3 vols. (Philadelphia: L. H. Everts and Co., 1884), 1:104–8. The tradition is discussed in detail in articles in *Memoirs of the Historical Society of Pennsylvania* 3 (Philadelphia, 1836); see especially Peter S. Du Ponceau and J. Francis Fisher, "A Memoir . . .," pp. 141–203.

63. Wm. Penn, "Letter to the Society of Traders," pp. 235–36.

century later, the Delaware old men recalled their tradition that at Miquon's "first arrival in their country, a friendship was formed between them which was to last as long as the sun should shine, and the rivers flow with water." Penn's account is confirmed by the Delaware tradition.[64]

Two other documents speak directly to the issue, and to my mind they clinch the case beyond cavil. In 1728 governor Patrick Gordon addressed chief Sassoonan and some other Delawares who had appeared "in the Name of all the Delawares, Shawanese and Mingoes [Conestogas] amongst us." Gordon, who was new in the province, undoubtedly spoke words written by James Logan, the veteran provincial secretary. He mentioned "the Links of the Chain made between William Penn and you" and recited "the nine Articles or links of the Chain, as in the Treaty held at Conestogoe." In 1731 Gordon was even more explicit. Speaking again to Sassoonan and retinue, he recited: "When William Penn first arriv'd here with his people, He immediately called together the Chiefs of the Indians, and told them he was come over to them with leave of the great King of England and had brought a great number of good people to live amongst them who should furnish them with what they wanted, that they should be his brothers and his people and the Indians should be the Same. They exceedingly rejoyced at this. They bid him and his people welcome. He made a Strong Chain of Friendship with them which has been kept bright to this day."[65]

In the language of Indian diplomacy, a Chain of Friendship was an alliance that could be made only by a formal treaty, and Gordon's reference to the likeness between this Chain and the one that he had "remembered" at Conestoga establishes their substance as similar to that of the 1701 treaty with the Susquehannocks. It also makes quite clear that the Delaware Chain of Friendship with Pennsylvania had nothing to do at that time with the Iroquois *Covenant* Chain.[66]

As will be shown, Pennsylvania's Indian policies took a sharp turn after 1732 that made written evidence of the Chain of Friendship with the Del-

64. Heckewelder, *History*, p. 66. The phrase about the sun shining, in both accounts, does not appear in the 1701 treaty with the Indians on Susquehanna. It is specific to the Delaware treaty.

65. *Pa Council Minutes*, Oct. 11, 1728, 3:336; Indian treaty held at Philadelphia, Aug. 17 and 18, 1731, in James Steel's Letter Book, mss., 2(1730–1741), p. 274, HSP. The 1731 document was not printed in Pennsylvania's provincial records although a substitute was printed in *Pa. Council Minutes* 3:404–6. A copy of Steel's mss. is in Penn Papers, Indian Affairs 1:35, HSP, with a superscription in James Logan's writing, "This is Copied from JL's rough draught uncorrected." It is apparent that what got into the official record had been "corrected." Note that there is discrepancy in dates: the Penn mss. copy and the printed version date the event at August 13 instead of Steel's August 18.

66. At Conestoga in 1728, governor Gordon "remembered" nine "Chief Heads or Strongest Links" of the Chain of Friendship made with the Susquehannock/Conestogas in 1701. Curiously, he omitted the articles or links requiring a monopoly of the trade there for Pennsylvania's traders. *Pa. Council Minutes*, May 26, 1728, 3:311–12. Cf. ibid. 2:14–18.

awares inconvenient and awkward for the province's officials. The easiest way to eliminate the awkwardness would be to eliminate the document. The tradition, however, could not be disposed of so easily.

James Logan

After Penn finally departed from his province, his powers were distributed between a deputy governor, who acted in his place as legislator and public executive, and a secretary who administered his estates and acted as watchdog secretary of the provincial council. Deputy governors came and went, but Secretary James Logan retained office for two decades, during which time he became, in one scholar's words, "a sort of permanent under-secretary for *all* affairs.[67] Among the rest, he took effective charge of relations with the Indian tribes. This was formally a function of the deputy governors, but these seldom acted without Logan's advice and rarely deviated from his suggestions.

Logan had as brilliant an intellect as Penn's. It was probably what had won him Penn's interest and confidence. Unfortunately he did not share Penn's scruples. Like Penn, he launched neither war nor mission, but short of those extremes he conducted Indian policies much like those of other colonies, and with similar long-run effects. He made exorbitant profits from trade with Indians, and he cheated them in land transactions. Logan became the architect of tacit understandings with the western Iroquois that gradually developed into a full-scale alliance in the Covenant Chain, rivaling the partnership between the Mohawks and New York. On the way to that culmination, he systematized the intersocietal trade in Pennsylvania with which he gained great leverage over the tribes and founded a fortune.

67. Joseph E. Johnson, "A Quaker Imperialist's View of the British Colonies in America: 1732," *Pa. Mag. of Hist. and Biog.* 60(1936), p. 103.

Chapter 13 &dotsdot; MENDING CHAIN

"Mr. Logan still goes on briskly, and as no man living knows better how to puzzle the state of an account, perhaps it will be no easy matter to unravel the artfull Confusion already Introduced in those affairs."

Sir William Keith, July 5, 1722

The warriors' path southward

The Iroquois were ambivalent about Pennsylvania. During their wars with New France, the Quaker colony had refused contributions of any kind and had obstructed recruitment of the Indians under its protection. On the other hand, it had resources that the Iroquois needed. The Susquehanna Valley was good hunting territory in its northern and western reaches. It was becoming populous with hunting and trading Indians near Conestoga. It was the through highway from Iroquoia to the Chesapeake Bay, the Potomac and Shenandoah valleys, and the back country of the Carolinas.[1]

Though Pennsylvania's officials refused to consider positive alliance, they were highly amenable to various sorts of tacit accommodation, and the Iroquois responded in kind. So long as the Five Nations refrained from violence within the colony, they might come and go as they pleased. This privilege was so highly valued by the Iroquois that they carefully avoided creating incidents in Pennsylvania of the sort that made them obnoxious in Maryland and Virginia.

The Susquehanna tribes were valuable both defensively and offensively. When outraged southern Catawbas tried to retaliate against Iroquois onslaughts, the Susquehanna tribes took the brunt of Catawba wrath; Iroquoia remained undisturbed. Although the Susquehanna tribes had no stomach for war against the French, their young men were willing enough, even eager, to join Iroquois parties raiding southward.[2] Pennsylvania's

1. William B. Marye, "Warriors' Paths," *Pennsylvania Archaeologist* 13:1 (1943), pp. 4–26, and 14:1 (1944), pp. 4–22; end papers map and supporting text in Paul A. W. Wallace, *Indian Paths of Pennsylvania* (Harrisburg: Pennsylvania Historical and Museum Commission, 1965); Spotswood to Keith, Jan. 25, 1720, in *Pa. Council Minutes* 3:82–89.
2. *Pa. Council Minutes* May 9, 1704, 2:138; July 12, 1720, 3:92, 95–97.

249

government admonished its client tribes but took no decisive action, and the Iroquois made the most of their opportunities.

New York's government made no serious effort to stop the Five Nations' southern raids. Governor Robert Hunter rather encouraged them. He boasted that "There are above 2,000 Indians to the southward and westward who are tributaries of the said 5 nations and under their command"—which would certainly have been news to the Iroquois.[3] They could have used those warriors in their no-win difficulties with New France's client tribes. As Hunter was well aware, his bragging did not reduce his importance in the eyes of crown officials, and Hunter's ambitions transcended his post in New York.[4] Iroquois raids forced southern governors to appeal to him as the only person able to curb the Indians, a situation that also did nothing to hurt his status. Ironically, when southern tribes rose in rebellion, the governors wanted Iroquois help, which meant to them Hunter's help. He boasted to the Lords of Trade in 1715, "I have sent messengers to our Five Nation Indians to perswade them to make warr upon those who have lately attacked Carolina, as also to the Indians on Sesquahanna to encourage them to goe on in their attempts upon 'em, these have lately brought home 30 prisoners. This I take to be the effectual way to put an end to that war."

Hunter hinted that he would be ready to assume larger responsibilities: "It is matter of wonder that hitherto noe effectual method has been thought of for uniteing the divided strength of these Provinces on the Continent for the defence of the whole."[5]

His suggestive letter reveals information highly pertinent to Pennsylvania's concerns. Hunter was sending Iroquois warriors through Pennsylvania's jurisdiction quite as though the other colony did not exist; and Hunter was pressuring the tribes on the Susquehanna to resume the subordination to Iroquois leadership that had been broken by William Penn's treaty of 1701. In that status the Susquehanna tribes would become New York's clients more effectively than Pennsylvania's. But the Iroquois, though willing enough to assert intertribal superiority, kept their own interests foremost.

3. Order from governor Hunter, May 13, 1712, *Livingston Indian Records*, pp. 220–21.
4. Stephen Saunders Webb, *The Governors-General: The English Army and the Definition of the Empire, 1569–1681*, published for the Institute of Early American History and Culture (Chapel Hill: University of North Carolina Press, 1979), pp. 483, 500–501.
5. Hunter to Council of Trade and Plantations, July 25, 1715, *CSPA&WI, 1714–15*, p. 243.

Trade and hospitality at the Susquehanna

The Susquehanna tribes were becoming a center of commerce for Pennsylvania's traders and merchants. As an alternative to Albany, this new center interested the western four Iroquois tribes. They repeatedly suggested to Pennsylvania negotiators that good prices could attract their business. The real responses to these overtures are difficult, if not impossible, to unearth from records that were always written to mislead Albany and generally succeed in bemusing a student.[6]

For half a century, the Mohawks took no interest in Pennsylvania. Albany was, and continued to be, the Mohawks' base of operations; and, insofar as they looked elsewhere for colonial connections, it was toward Boston. All the other Iroquois tribes busied themselves from time to time along the Susquehanna, but one leader stands out in the rebuilding of Iroquois strength in this location. Onondaga chief Decanisora was a brilliant and subtle diplomat whose achievements command deep respect. Had he been able to work with the resources of a European nation, he would have shaken the balance of European power. As it was, he painstakingly laid the basis for his tribesmen to weigh heavily in the colonial balance of power.[7]

In their weakened condition after the French wars, the Iroquois could no longer grow by destroying enemy tribes and absorbing their remnants. Forced to rely on diplomacy, they acquired new strength by mediating between colonies and other tribes. To follow that process in the Susquehanna Valley we must give some attention to the growth of the region's intersocietal trade.

Nowhere else it is so clear that the advance of Euramericans to the interior was a product of intersocietal cooperation. Treaty negotiations and tacit accommodation facilitated demographic change. The trade with Indians acquainted speculators both with the best routes for transportation and communication and with the most desirable sites for new communities. It is hugely ironical that this institution of trade, which served as the very foundation of intersocietal accommodation, was self-destructive in the long run. One must distinguish. It was not primarily the hunting to extinction of fur-bearing animals that wrought such ruin. Indians were willing to travel hundreds of miles to new hunting grounds if they could return to undisturbed home villages. It was the trade's very success

6. James Logan to William Penn. July 26, 1704, Sept. 28, 1704, in Logan Letter Books, mss., 1:158, 163, HSP; *Pa. Council Minutes*, Aug. 28, and Sept. 1 1704, 2:158–59.

7. W. J. Eccles's biography of Decanisora is in *Dict. Can. Biog.* 2:619–23, under the French spelling "Teganissorens." Under either spelling it is the same name and the same sound, more or less. Probably the French spelling is closer to accuracy when pronounced with the French values of the syllables. Like French, Iroquoian languages are somewhat nasal although English renditions often look guttural. Thanks to W. N. Fenton for elucidating this.

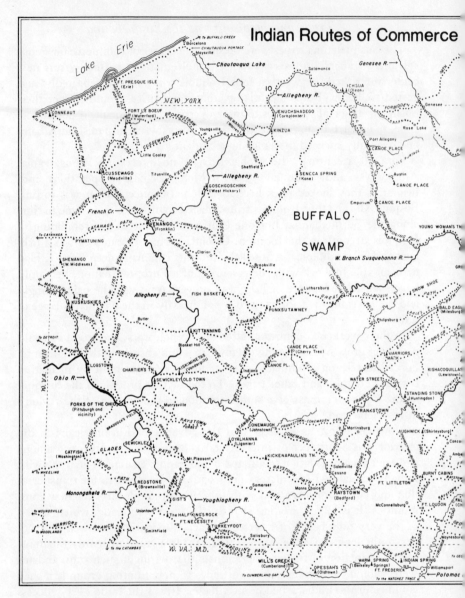

MAP 9. Indian Routes of Commerce and War in Early Pennsylvania. REPRODUCED
FROM THE END PAPERS OF PAUL WALLACE, *Indian Paths of Pennsylvania*. HARRISBURG: PENN-

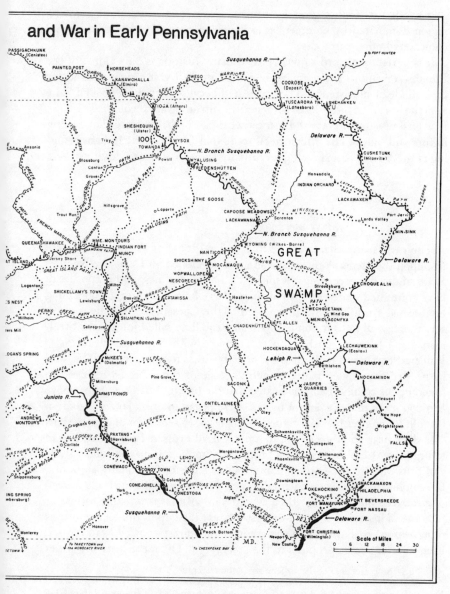

and War in Early Pennsylvania

SYLVANIA HISTORICAL AND MUSEUM COMMISSION, 1961, BY COURTESY OF THE PUBLISHER.

that spoiled it, for its growth attracted crowds of new colonials to the region dominated by commercial exchange instead of war. But the newcomers had other purposes.

It is perfectly absurd to write, as so many historians have done, of the Indians retiring to the west because they needed vast ranges of land for their mode of subsistence. They retreated because they were pushed. The appetite for ever more land belonged to intruding new colonials, whose new goal was to cultivate and market wheat and tobacco instead of dealing in furs and hides. The intersocietal trade that first brought Indians refuging *to* the Susquehanna Valley eventually created pressures to drive them *from* it.[8]

Logan as merchant

The earliest merchants in the intersocietal trade of Pennsylvania were late upon the scene. A thriving trade had developed on Delaware Bay and River under the preceding Swedish and Dutch regimes, and it appears to have continued under English auspices.[9] We have seen how Jacob Young established a trading post at the head of the Chesapeake Bay; his successors there seem to have come from Maryland: one called John Hans Steelman (or Tilghman) pushed up to compete with the Pennsylvanians.[10] William Penn hoped to develop a trading business for his own profit because he needed the money badly to defray some of the debts he incurred in founding his colony. Penn calculated that the province had cost him "above £30,000 more than I ever got by it."[11] He began to press James Logan, in his first letter after his final return to England, to send bear and buck skins "for they bear an advance."[12] In 1703 a hard-pressed Penn asked Logan to urge the assembly to grant a proprietary monopoly in the Indian trade and thus obviate the need for "any levy, excise, or tax for my account." He emphasized the request with the cry, "O that we had a fur-trade instead of a tobacco one, and that thou wouldst do all that is possible to master furs and skins for me. . . . I earnestly press thee upon this one point, as thou desirest to assist me in the readiest and surest way." Logan refused even to offer such a proposal to the assembly. "The merchants will never

8. These processes are detailed in Jennings, "Indian Trade."

9. Weslager, *Dutch Explorers*, chs. 6, 7; Johnson, *Swedish Settlements*, passim, see index; Francis Jennings, "National Policies: Sweden and Netherlands," in *History of Indian-White Relations*, ed. Wilcomb E. Washburn, vol. 4 of *Handbook of North American Indians* (forthcoming).

10. For Steelman see index in Charles A. Hanna, *The Wilderness Trail*, 2 vols. (New York: G. P. Putnam's Sons, 1911).

11. Penn to Logan, n.d., *Penn-Logan Corr.* 1:280, It should be noted, however, that Penn was extravagant in all his affairs.

12. Penn to Logan, Jan. 4, 1702, *Penn-Logan Corr.* 1:73,

bear it," he responded. "Contrivance and management may give thee a share with the rest, and more is not to be depended on."[13]

Logan was already practicing contrivance and management in the most devious way. At the time he responded to Penn so discouragingly he had already entered trade personally with a planter-trader named Edward Farmer, whose estate at Whitemarsh lay a dozen miles north of Philadelphia. Farmer, in turn, had diverted to himself at least some of the trade of the Le Tort establishment farther up the Schuylkill. James Le Tort solicited employment with Farmer in 1703, and Peter Bisaillon apparently had begun earlier to trade with him.[14] Through Farmer the Frenchmen became associated *sub rosa* with Logan.

The alliance was mutually profitable, but it required secrecy. In this time of intermittent war between England and France, all Frenchmen were suspect in Pennsylvania. In 1701 William Penn himself had denounced "two Frenchmen, Louis [Lemoisin] and P. Besalion, who have been suspected to be very dangerous persons in their Traffique with the Indians in this Troublesome conjuncture of Affairs."[15] In 1702 formal war broke out between the empires, and in 1703 "Louis" brought tales to Philadelphia that caused the council to call in Bisaillon and James Le Tort for questioning. Logan's intervention preserved them from jail even though they had to post security bonds in the relatively enormous amounts of £500 sterling each. Le Tort's bond was posted by Edward Farmer.[16]

13. Penn to Logan, Feb. 20 and 24, 1703, *Penn-Logan Corr.* 1:163–64, 170; Logan to Penn, July 9, 1703, ibid., 1:202.

Penn's difficulties with the trade were compounded by the hostility of Col. Robert Quary, an Anglican crown official who conspired constantly against Penn in both politics and business. Quary was for a while "the greatest Merchant or Factor in the Province," and he tried unsuccessfully to obtain a legal monopoly of the Indian trade in the American colonies. Zimmerman, "Indian Trade of Colonial Pa.," pp. 54–57. A series of Board of Trade papers from 1702 demonstrates Quary's harassment of Penn. HSP transcripts, Bd. of Trade Papers, Proprieties, Vol. 6², I-14, I-17, I-19, I-20, I-28, I-43, K8, K9.

14. A bibliographic note: Farmer's connection with Logan has remained unnoticed because of Logan's desire to keep his personal interest in the fur trade as secret as possible from critics in the colony, and because of subsequent bibliographic complications. Logan noted in a letter to Edward Farmer the fact of Bisaillon's involvement in their arrangements (May 20, 1703, mss., Logan Letter Books 2:25), but this letter was miscataloged under "H" because of the elaborate flourishes on the initial F. Logan was not trying to hide his trade from Penn, who constantly urged him onward in it, so Logan could acknowledge to Penn that Farmer was the man "with whom chiefly I deal." This statement was omitted from the printed copy of his letter in *Penn-Logan Corr.* 1:199—not, by any means, the only fault in that compilation. Cf. the mss. in Logan Letter Books 1:100, HSP. For Farmer's background, see Howard M. Jenkins, "The Family of William Penn," *Pa. Mag. of Hist. and Biog.* 21 (1897), pp. 335–36 and note; William J. Buck, *History of Montgomery County within the Schuylkill Valley* (Norristown, Pa., E. L. Acker, 1859), pp. 68–69, 114. Farmer's estate is shown on Thomas Holme's map of 1687.

15. *Pa. Council Minutes*, May 17, 1701, 2:18–19.

16. *Pa. Council Minutes*, Aug. 17, 1703, 2:100; Logan to Penn, Sept. 2, 1703, mss., Logan Letter Books 1:115, HSP.

In 1704 Le Tort was employed by the council to translate for the messengers from Onondaga, but the Pennsylvanians' nerves were jangled by a morale-shattering blow of French-allied Indians against Deerfield, Massachusetts, and Le Tort suddenly found himself in jail. No charge was lodged against him, but bail was set at £1000.[17]

Meanwhile Pennsylvania's trade was migrating to the Susquehanna, and Logan took some trouble to clear the river of competitors. In October 1705 he journeyed to Conestoga to allay the restlessness of the Indians who had been aroused by hostilities of Maryland and Virginia against the Conoys still resident in Maryland. Logan welcomed the refugees to Pennsylvania, exhorting them to be on their good behavior with all British subjects, and proceeded from statecraft to business. Logan had heard that Maryland's John Hans Steelman was building a trading post among the Indians, which was against Pennsylvania's regulations. The Indians should not let Christians settle among them without permission of the governor of Pennsylvania (which meant, in effect, Logan's permission). Logan's desire was heeded. Steelman was not permitted to build outside Maryland, and Logan's men became dominant thereafter in spite of their French handicap.[18]

Logan had enemies in the assembly who impeached him in 1707. Their Remonstrance accused him, among other things, of countenancing the French traders. "Two of them, viz. Nichola, and Letort" were "reckoned very dangerous Persons," in the assembly's view. "All three have been at Canada, and yet are permitted to trade with the Indians."[19] The continuance of Queen Anne's War made the change serious.

Logan rolled with the punch. On the same day that the assembly voted impeachment, Logan's political ally, Governor Evans, told the uneasy Conestoga Indians of his confidence in the traders. Evans set out for Conestoga to mend fences. At the Shawnee village of Pequehan he was entertained at the home of Logan's trader Martin Chartier. After treating with the Susquehanna tribes, Evans journeyed upstream to Paxtang, where he enlisted James Le Tort's help to seize "one Nicole [Godin], a French Trader . . . against whom great Complaints had been made to the Governor."[20] Le Tort had been named by the assembly along with Nicole;

17. *Pa. Council Minutes*, Oct.–Nov. 1704, 2:163, 170, 171–72.

18. Logan's report, *Pa. Council Minutes*, June 6, 1706, 2:244–47. In suppressing Steelman, Logan was following Penn's policy. Penn himself, in 1701, had confiscated goods belonging to Steelman and had banned him from trading in Pennsylvania. Hanna, *Wilderness Trail* 1:144.

19. Articles of Impeachment, Feb. 25, 1707, and Remonstrance, June 10, 1707, *Votes and Proceedings of the House of Representatives of the Province of Pennsylvania, 1682–1776*, 8 vols. *Pennsylvania Archives*, 8th ser. (Harrisburg, 1931–1935), 1:715–19, 770. Hereinafter *Pa. Assembly Minutes*.

20. *Pa. Council Minutes*, Feb. 24 and 25, 1707, 2:403–5.

yet here was the governor not only failing to seize Le Tort, but acting in close cooperation with him. The upshot was that the assembly got a sacrificial victim in such a way that authorities in London could be told that Pennsylvania's government was alert and responsive to backwoods threats, while the Le Tort-Bisaillon-Chartier-Logan trading association eliminated another competitor.

There is often an aesthetically satisfying quality about the economy and audacity of Logan's political maneuvers. He frequently contrived to serve two or more interests at the same time, one of which was always his own, and he had mastered the art of turning defensive operations to positive advantage.

At the height of the hue and cry against him, Logan still controlled the commissioners of property—who were solely responsible to the proprietary—as though the elected assembly did not exist. In 1708 Peter Bisaillon requested "free liberty" to build a house and plant fields "on any of the Lands above Conestoga not Possesst or made use by the Indians," and the commissioners were pleased to grant his request. Tenure was to be held at their pleasure. The rent was one deer skin yearly.[21] But Bisaillon needed protection. When Logan finally fled to England to escape arrest by the assembly, a new governor, one who was not Logan's friend, seized Bisaillon's goods. Until Logan returned, Bisaillon and Le Tort repeated the security bond and jail term routine.[22]

Logan had placed his men in the most strategic spot in the province for Indian affairs. The watchful Iroquois did not interfere, and trade flourished. During Logan's absence in England, uncontrollable distant events pressed Pennsylvanians and Iroquois into closer relations. Though the colonials still avoided open alliance, the Iroquois grasped cleverly at the opportunity to regain power.

Botched plan to invade Canada

An attempted invasion of Canada from New York, organized by a gentleman-adventurer named Samuel Vetch, provided the Iroquois with an occasion to recoup their loss. In 1709 Vetch convinced the English crown to authorize a campaign to be supported by men and money from a number of colonies and launched from Albany. New York's commissioners of Indian Affairs were instructed to mobilize the Five Nations and

21. Minutes, Oct. 11, 1708, Book G, *Minutes of the Commissioners of Property*, in *Pennsylvania Archives* 2d ser., vol. 19, and 3d ser., vol. 1. This reference is to (2)19:496. Hereinafter *Pa. Property Minutes*.
22. *Pa. Council Minutes*, March 18, 1710, May 28, 1711, Aug. 22, 1711, 2:509, 531, 539. Logan returned March 22, 1712. Logan Parchment Letter Book, 1712–1715, mss., p. 1, HSP.

their tributaries. On paper the plans looked grand. Unfortunately they assumed, erroneously, that the expected contributors would share Vetch's ardor for the campaign. New Jersey's assembly rejected all participation, while Pennsylvania's got into a wrangle with its governor and stalled.[23] The Minisink Indians refused to send warriors even after a second message went to them accompanied by the ultimate in symbols of importance—"seven hands of wampum." The Minisinks remained unmoved; they replied that they were "only Squas and no fighting men."[24] The Indians of the Susquehanna received conflicting messages from Philadelphia. Together with the Delawares they made some personal inquiry in the city and discovered the government's divided state; they promptly decided that the time had become "too late for them to proceed in their Journey Northwards, because they would not be able to return before the Cold weather sett in."[25] That was in July. In brief, Vetch's expedition failed to get started in 1709, and the disgusted Onondagas who had rallied to his colors sent deputies secretly to Canada's Governor Vaudreuil "to solicit my friendship."[26]

Tuscarora negotiations

While Vetch's men marched uphill and down in New York, there was movement of a different kind in the Carolinas. The large but divided Tuscarora tribe became fearful as English colonists seized its lands and kidnapped its people for sale into slavery in the West Indies. At the same time, Iroquois raiding parties made the woods unsafe for Tuscarora hunters. The harried Tuscaroras decided to secure at least one of their flanks by sending a delegation up to Conestoga in June 1710 "to treat with the

23. G. M. Waller, *Samuel Vetch: Colonial Enterpriser*, Published for the Institute of Early American History and Culture (Chapel Hill: University of North Carolina Press, 1960), pp. 124-25, 135-38.

24. New York Council Minutes, mss., July 19, 1709, 10:696, N.Y. State Archives. This summons, like that to the Long Island Indians, was made directly by New York's government, without Iroquois participation. See *Calendar of Council Minutes, 1668-1783*, New York State Library Bulletin 58 [History 6] (Albany: University of the State of New York, 1902), item for June 21, 1709, p. 229, and entry for same date in *Calendar of Historical Manuscripts in the Office of the Secretary of State, Albany, N.Y.*, ed. E. B. O'Callaghan, Part II: English Manuscrips (Albany: Weed, Parsons and Co., 1866), p. 365. The Iroquois were not asked to join the Canada expedition until June 29. See that date in ibid., p. 365. Waller states that "The Indians were promised rewards and threatened with being turned over 'to the resentment of the Mohawks and the rest of the Five Nations' if they did not obey," but that resentment was hard to find among the Senecas who were among the tribes failing to appear. Waller, *Samuel Vetch*, pp. 148-49.

25. *Pa. Council Minutes*, June 15, 1709, 2:467; July 25, 1709, 2:469-70; June 26, 1709, 2:470-71.

26. Vaudreuil to Pontchartrain, May 1, 1710, *N.Y.Col.Docs.* 9:842.

Christians and Indians of this Government" and to send peace proposals forward to the Five Nations. With the sponsorship of the Conestogas and Shawnees, the Tuscaroras requested permission to settle in Pennsylvania. Unhappily the colony's suspicious negotiators demanded a certificate of good behavior from North Carolina before giving the requested permission. This was like asking the Carolinians to give up their trade in slaves.[27] A few weeks later the chiefs of all five Iroquois nations arrived at Conestoga under the leadership of the renowned Onondaga chief Decanisora.

Decanisora's secret treaty

Although the Tuscaroras had already departed, Decanisora included them among his other business. The surviving manuscript record demonstrates that this was an important council. Seventy Indians were present, including the chiefs of the Conestogas, the Shawnees, the Brandywine Delawares, and the Conoys, besides Governor Charles Gookin of Pennsylvania, attended by members of his council and other gentlemen of standing. It is also evident that the Pennsylvanians were not eager to advertise their participation. The minutes of the affair were excluded from the colony's official records, and the manuscript in which they appear does not have the conventional form of a treaty contract. Instead it appears as a monologue by Decanisora addressed to all the Indians present and interrupted at several points with objections made by the colony's Colonel John French. His silence on the others implied tacit consent by the governor and council witnessing the proceedings.[28]

No explanation was offered for these curious arrangements, but Decanisora mentioned one issue that neither the Iroquois nor the colonials would want noticed in New York. He referred to Governor Gookin's "verry acceptable" proposal "that a free trade be granted so as the Buyer purchases where he best likes."[29] Considering Albany's perpetual efforts to monopolize Iroquois trade, this was not so trivial a matter, but we cannot be certain what bargaining produced the agreement.

Proposition 12 of the treaty was less innocent than its wording appeared. In a large, general way it specified that because "the land belonged to the five Nations . . . Indians might settle wherever corn could be made." More specifically it meant that the Tuscaroras could come into the Susquehanna Valley and take refuge. Naming them would have exposed Pennsylvania

27. J.N.B. Hewitt, "Tuscarora," in *Handbook of American Indians North of Mexico*, ed. F. W. Hodge, 2:843; Report of Conference dated June 8, 1710, in *Pa. Council Minutes*, June 16, 1710, 2:511–12.
28. Treaty minutes, July 31, 1710, Penn Papers, Indian Affairs, mss., 1:34, HSP.
29. Ibid., clause 23.

to recriminations from the colonies hostile to the Tuscaroras. Another good reason for Pennsylvania's suppression of the treaty text was the colony's agreement to permit the Iroquois freedom of transit along the warriors' path to the south.[30] Maryland and Virginia would not look kindly on such facilitation of Iroquois raids on their client Indians.

The treaty council seems also to have produced an agreement—tacit or at least unwritten—that Pennsylvania would recognize a qualified Iroquois right to give orders to some of the Indians within Pennsylvania's jurisdiction. If such an agreement had been made, however, it stopped short of allowing the Iroquois to impress warriors from the colony's client tribes.

Decanisora pushed his ordering device too far when he claimed the Susquehanna Valley as Iroquois territory. Here Colonel French objected and cited William Penn's purchases, but French did not object to Indians settling there. And when the chief announced grandiosely (with some justice) that the Iroquois were the only protection of both Christians and Indians against the Canadians, the embarrassed colonel sputtered that the Queen of England could look after her own subjects "wherever Settled."[31] Incidentally there is no use of "red man" or "white man" in this document, nor even of nationalist terms. The English colonials are *Christians* and the Indians just Indians.

Canadian invasion bungled again

While the Indians thus quietly enhanced their influence in Pennsylvania and opened the door to Tuscarora alliance, Samuel Vetch continued his ill-starred schemes for invading Canada. He managed once more to mount the beginnings of an offensive in 1711. Again, the Iroquois were summoned, but their independent behavior had made them untrustworthy for English purposes.[32] Or perhaps it was their inability to deliver what was wanted. Whatever the reason, recruiting of other Indians was accomplished directly by government order rather than through Iroquois agency. Once more, the Governor of New York ordered the Indians "Inhabiting in or near the Province of Pensilvania and on Susquehanna River" to join in. It was not a message calculated to rouse ardor from the government of Pennsylvania, and it is curious to see what happened to it. The Indians of the Susquehanna Valley marched bravely into *Philadelphia*, because, as they said, Colonel French had asked them to go to Delaware's *New Castle* (where they would probably have embarked for New York). They

30. Ibid., clause 18.
31. Ibid., French's response to clause 29.
32. N.Y. Council Minutes, March 29, 1711, and April 24, 1711, mss., 10:581, 590.

announced that they were responding to the order of the governor of New York, "but they expected Coll. French to go with them." Since Colonel French had decided, for unrecorded reasons, not to go, the Indians withdrew to "further Consider amongst themselves." They stayed home.[33]

It is hard to imagine what they might have done if they had gone. The many parties assembled by Samuel Vetch for his campaign were working at such cross-purposes that once again the project disintegrated before the march began. In the midst of the other crosscurrents, the Iroquois arrived in camp with 682 warriors, 26 of them Shawnees "under the Senecas"—habitat unknown.[34] Decanisora played the role of a Talleyrand. While making his brave display of support for the English invasion, he again sent a message to the governor of Canada warning of the preparations for attack.[35]

There was considerable tension between New York and the Iroquois in 1711. The Five Nations were more concerned at this time to extend themselves westward than to support English schemes against Canada. They had concluded an alliance with the Fox tribe, newly established in a village at Detroit, and they demanded ammunition from New York in March in order to war against the "Waganhaes" (probably Ottawas). Governor Hunter rejected the demand, whereupon the Onondagas received three French officers and thirty men. If they wanted by that act to get Hunter's attention, they succeeded. He hastily dispatched Peter Schuyler to forbid further communication with the French—except in his presence. The qualification, like the whole situation, shows the extent of Hunter's incapacity for issuing genuine commands.[36] Decanisora's secret message to Canada confirms the inference. He was not being simply treacherous. The Onondagas had had too much experience of fighting New York's wars. They had no wish to repeat previous situations in which they had borne the brunt of Canadian retaliation. All things considered, perhaps it was just as well for Samuel Vetch that his heterogeneous "army" failed to get out of base camp.

Although the campaign never got going, its preparations demonstrated

---

33. N.Y.Council Minutes, mss., June 27, 1711, and June 30, 1711, 10:598, 602; N.Y. Col. Mss., June 30, 1711, and July 4, 1711, 55:73, 83; *Pa. Council Minutes*, Aug. 1, 1711, 2:537.

34. Speeches of 5 Nations, Aug. 25 and 26, 1711, *N.Y.Col. Docs.* 5:270, 272. Waller has over 800 warriors arrive at Albany on Aug. 24, 1711. Waller, *Samuel Vetch*, pp. 215–16.

35. Vaudreuil to Pontchartrain, Oct. 25, 1711, *N.Y.Col.Docs.* 9:859. W. J. Eccles remarks, "Only when English interests coincided with those of the Five Nations did Teganissorens further them." "Teganissorens," *Dict. Can. Biog.* 2:622. The remark might be narrowed further. Teganissorens, or Decanisora, was an Onondaga chief, and the documents of the period show much division of policies in the Iroquois League. Onondagas, Mohawks, and Senecas negotiated independently of each other for quite different objectives.

36. *N.Y.Council Minutes*, mss., March 29, 1711, 10:581; April 24, 1711, 10:590; Lanctot, *History of Canada* 2:162.

anew how heavily the English depended upon the Iroquois for military strength. New York's orders to the tributary Indians were to join the Iroquois. Pennsylvania's recognition of Iroquois ascendancy was hedged with a final restriction, but it still contributed to the Five Nations' prestige. Vetch's grand schemes came to total failure for himself, but the Iroquois had gained something from the way he failed.

Hospitality for Tuscaroras and Mennonites

Iroquois strength was increased further by the real war that broke out in 1711 between the Carolina colonies and the Tuscaroras. In this war the colonies mobilized quickly and effectively to inflict a smashing defeat upon the tribe. Fleeing northward to Iroquois hospitality and sanctuary, bands of Tuscaroras paused in Pennsylvania, then made their way to Iroquioia to become the League's Sixth Nation. Their manpower added significantly to its military strength.[37]

James Logan returned to Pennsylvania from England in 1712 to find that the trading base he had so carefully prepared at Conestoga had been joined by the Iroquois. To his annoyance, a number of Swiss Mennonites had also moved to about five miles from the Susquehanna to settle their town of Strasburg on the river's Pequea Creek.[38] Not being one to mourn to no purpose, Logan assessed the changes and helped them along. Recognizing that the Mennonites would be followed by more settlers, he acquired rights to nearby lands in order to profit when the newcomers should arrive.[39]

Delawares and Iroquois

Recognizing that the Iroquois could perform useful functions, Logan cautiously helped their campaign to re-achieve ascendancy over Pennsyl-

37. Verner W. Crane, *The Southern Frontier, 1670–1732* (orig. pub. 1929. Ann Arbor: U. of Michigan Press, 1956), pp. 158–61; N.Y. Council Minutes, mss., various dates in 1712, 11:69, 81, 98, 100, 110, 113, 115, 117; Paul A. W. Wallace, *Indians in Pennsylvania* (Harrisburg: Pa. Historical and Museum Commission, 1964), pp. 110–12.

38. H. Frank Eshleman, A. K. Hostetter, and Charles Steigerwalt, "Report on the True Character, Time and Place of the First Regular Settlement in Lancaster County," *Publications of the Lancaster County [Pa.] Historical Society* 14 (1910), pp. 21–71.

39. Logan's dealings in this vicinity are discussed and documented in detail in Francis Paul Jennings, "Miquon's Passing: Indian-European Relations in Colonial Pennsylvania, 1674 to 1755," Ph.D. diss. (U. of Pa., 1965), pp. 154–72; ———, "The Indian Trade of the Susquehanna Valley," *Procs. of Am. Phil. Soc.* 110:6 (Dec. 1966), pp. 416–20.

vania's Indian clients. An indication of rising Iroquois prestige, and of Pennsylvania's acquiescence in it, was the Delawares' decision in May 1712 to bring their overdue wampum presents to Onondaga along with the belts entrusted to them by William Penn in 1701. The Delaware delegation stopped near Philadelphia to consult about the messages that had been "read into" the wampum. Logan interviewed them and recorded the minutes of the occasion. His editing has helped befuddle students of Delaware history and culture ever since. According to the original manuscript draft, Delaware Sachem Scollitchy told Logan that his tribesmen were "friends of the 5 Nations" bearing "presents"—which would have meant the sort of things exchanged between parties of equal status at treaty conferences. Logan later altered the language to make Scollitchy's statement appear to have been that the Delawares were "friends *and Subjects* of the 5 Nations" who were bearing "tribute." When the minutes were published the printer naturally set Logan's amended version, and it became evidence for the mythical notion that the Iroquois had made the Delawares "women" by conquest.[40]

Partly because of such tampering with the sources, the precise relationship of the Delawares to the Five Nations during the early eighteenth century is murky. On their return from Iroquoia in 1712, the Delawares reported, by a wampum belt from the Senecas, that presents sent from Pennsylvania to the Five Nations "when Captain Cock was living" had been intercepted by "those of Albany, through a suspition that a Correspondence with us would be injurious to that Trade."[41] But this does not explain why the Delawares themselves had failed to deliver until 1712 the belt entrusted to them by William Penn in 1701. This delay contrasted sharply with the behavior of the broken tribes living along the Susquehanna who sent wampum tribute to the Five Nations and received acknowledgment belts in return.[42]

It must be noted that the Delawares were not a united body. The Brandywine Delawares met separately from the Tulpehocken Delawares with Pennsylvania's government; and the Brandywines, under chief Chechochinican, contended more than twenty years without noticeable help from the Tulpehockens to get compensation for lost lands. Similarly, when the Tulpehockens, under Chief Sassoonan, negotiated about their lands, the Brandywines were nowhere to be found. Later still, the Jersey Delawares,

---

40. Cf. *Pa. Council Minutes*, May 19, 1712, 2:546, with photostat of mss. of same document in Society Collection, HSP, and with formal mss. record at Pa. Hist. and Museum Commission, Harrisburg. The mss. draft is in Logan's own handwriting.

41. *Pa. Council Minutes*, Oct. 14, 1712, 2:557–58.

42. *Pa. Council Minutes*, June 6, 1706, 2:246–47; July 22, 1707, 2:387–88; N.Y.Council Minutes, mss., April 25, 1709, 10:301; treaty minutes, July 31, 1710, mss., Penn Papers, Indian Affairs 1:34, HSP; Five Nations speeches, Aug. 26, 1711, *N.Y.Col.Docs.* 5:272.

under Chief Nutimus, dealt separately with Pennsylvania and New Jersey about yet other lands.[43]

There seems also to have been some competition between the Tulpehockens and the Five Nations for preeminence in the region of eastern Pennsylvania. When the Conoys removed from Maryland, they first announced their intention of settling among the Tulpehockens, but the Five Nations took charge and ensconced them instead near Conestoga.[44] On one occasion Delaware Chief Sassoonan represented himself as speaking "in behalf of all the Indians on this side of Sasquehanna, Excepting those of Conestogo."[45] It looks as though Sassoonan was contending to be Philadelphia's head client in somewhat similar fashion to the Mohawks' relationship to Albany.

What ultimately gave the prize to the Iroquiois was the policy of James Logan.

For personal reasons, Logan pressed constantly to repress the Delawares by any available means, and his control of the colony's records gave him opportunity to suppress the true situation. For example, when Delaware Chief Sassoonan called officially in 1718, Sassoonan remarked, "he remembers when he was but small their [Delaware] Nation was look'd on as dependant on the five Nations, but those Nations have their own Lands and Countrey and these here have theirs, and each of them are to Manage their own concerns." The remark is in Logan's private papers in his own hand, but it never got into the official records in his custody.[46] It appears to me that the period of Delaware dependence on the Five Nations when Sassoonan "was but small" would have been the period 1677–1681, between the founding of the Covenant Chain and the founding of Pennsylvania; certainly there was no Iroquois conquest of the Delawares during that period. Nor is there evidence of one during any other period until 1742.

---

43. Brandywines: *Pa. Property Minutes*, Bk.G, Sept. 23, 1707, *Pa. Archives*, 2d ser., 19:491; 1st ser., 12:281; *Pa. Council Minutes*, June 16, 1718, 3:45; Logan to James Steel, July 20, 1725, mss., Hazard Family Papers, fol. James Logan, HSP; Brandywine Indians' complaint, n.d., Logan Papers, mss., 11:13, HSP; *Pa. Council Minutes*, May 20, 1728, 3:310. Tulpehockens: Draft minutes of Indian treaty, Sept. 15, 1718, mss., Logan Papers 11:7, HSP; *Pa. Council Minutes*, June 4, 1728, 3:316; Logan to T. Penn, Aug. 16, 1733, *Pa. Archives*, ser. 2, 7:145; Logan to T. Penn, July 7, 1734, ibid., pp. 168–69. Jersey Delawares: See ch. 14, below.

I am indebted to C. A. Weslager for introduction to the Brandywines' troubles. See his *Red Men on the Brandywine* (1953), reprinted facsimile (Wilmington, Del.: Delmar News Agency, 1976).

44. *Pa. Council Minutes*, May 12, 1705, 2:191; treaty minutes, July 31, 1710, mss., Penn Papers, Indian Affairs 1:34, HSP, clause 5.

45. *Pa. Council Minutes*, June 14, 1715, 2:600; June 22, 1715, 2:603.

46. Draft minutes of Indian treaty, Sept. 15, 1718, mss., Logan Papers 11:7, HSP.

Logan's supremacy

The Pennsylvania–Five Nations rapprochement of 1710 soon took effect on the Shawnees of the Susquehanna. Their "king" Opessa abdicated and departed from them in 1711, disgusted with their ungovernability. What specific issues led to his decision are not clear, but the date suggests a possible unrecorded connection to the recruiting for Samuel Vetch. What is on record is the "new Elected King" who got the position in 1714. He was named Carondawana; he had not been "elected" by the Shawnees and was not a Shawnee himself. He had been chosen by the Conestogas at their newly created outpost of the Covenant Chain, by what process is not mentioned, and he was an Oneida of the Five Nations.[47]

That this happened with James Logan's consent cannot be doubted. Logan had skillfully seized on the opportunities presented to him by coincidence as well as by policies, making himself the preeminent authority in the Susquehanna Valley—as indeed he was in Philadelphia as well. While in England, Logan had been made the agent for the receivers who took over the estates of bankrupt William Penn—including his propriety of Pennsylvania—and in 1712 Penn suffered a series of disabling strokes.[48] In 1713 England and France made peace at the Treaty of Utrecht, thus opening trans-Appalachia to unhampered movement by the Iroquois and their Indian allies.[49] By 1714 the surplus of furs that had ruined French trade in the west had rotted in storage, and trade revived.[50]

For Logan, all this coincidence meant prosperity. With his powers as commissioner of property and agent of Penn's receivers, he involved himself heavily in Indian affairs, having as his motto the classically simple view that "All men of business think it unnatural to be doing something for nothing."[51] Dominating the Susquehanna Indians with the benevolent acquiescence of the Iroquois, Logan soon expanded his dabblings in the Indian trade to large-scale operations that outstripped all other merchants in the colony. Between 1712 and 1720 he amassed one of the larger for-

47. *Pa. Council Minutes*, Oct. 1, 1714, 2:573–74. The printer transformed Carondawana into Cakundawana, but the identification is given elsewhere in the minutes.

48. Robert Proud, *The History of Pennsylvania*, 2 vols. (1797–1798), reprinted Pennsylvania Heritage Series 2–3 (Spartanburg, S.C.: The Reprint Co., 1967), 2:58. Penn was stricken while in the midst of a letter of bitter complaint to Logan about the latter's failure to forward funds. The broken off manuscript gives startling immediacy and intimacy to the tragedy. Wm. and Hannah Penn to Logan, Oct. 4 and 13, 1712, mss., Penn Mss., Letters of the Penn Family to James Logan 1:50, HSP.

49. An extract from the treaty is in Lanctot, *History of Canada*, 3:215–17. Article 15 provides that "The subjects of France inhabiting Canada, and others, shall hereafter give no hindrance or molestation to the Five Nations or cantons of Indians, subject to the dominion of Great Britain, nor to the other natives of America, who are friends to the same."

50. Zoltvany, *Vaudreuil*, p. 144.

51. Logan to J. Penn, June 26, 1728, mss., Penn Mss., Off. Corr. 2:9, HSP.

tunes in Pennsylvania, multiplying his wealth more than five times.[52]

More important to the colony was the importance of that trade for currency exchange with England. The colony's commerce was perpetually inhibited by its unfavorable overall balance of trade with England, which resulted in a constant drainage abroad of hard coin; in consequence, export goods for which London merchants would pay in sterling were as important to the general economy as they were to their particular dealers. The products of the Indian trade held this special importance.

Stephen H. Cutcliffe has researched the Import and Export Ledgers of the British Customs Office to tabulate the value of fur and skin exports to London. His tables show that during Logan's most energetic years as a trader the exports of deerskins from Pennsylvania rose sharply in absolute value though it declined in proportion to all other exports. (This applies only to the direct trade to London.) In 1713 the skin trade was worth only £168,, but it formed 93.9 percent of Pennsylvania's shipments to London. In 1714 the percentage declined to 40.7, but value increased to £1,083, and in 1715 it increased again to £1,485. Value for 1716, a banner year, was £2,641. Though absolute value dropped in 1717 to £1,675, the skin trade's share of total direct exports increased to 71.5 percent. From that time until the beginning of the Seven Years War with France, export of furs and skins never made up less than 20 percent of Pennsylvania's direct exports to London. They rose to 82.2 percent in 1730 and generally ranged above 30 percent.[53]

It was during Logan's most active trading years that the Indian population of eastern Pennsylvania, enlarged by the conjoint hospitality of the provincial government and the Five Nations, rose to its historical maximum. But all was not wine and roses, for the population of Pennsylvania colonials increased too, faster than the Indians' and more expansively. Pennsylvania differed from other colonies by continuing William Penn's original policy of compensating Indians for the lands from which they migrated—sometimes, however, long after they had left under pressure. Penn's example of honesty and fair dealing with the Indians was *not* followed, but the Pennsylvanians held to their Quaker heritage by not launching war against their neighboring tribes—not, that is, until the Seven Years War upset their tradition.

52. Logan's accounts show his worth at £2,261 as of March 25, 1712, and at £11,889 as of March 1, 1720. Logan's Account Book, mss., pp. 1–2; James Logan's Ledger, 1720–1727, mss., p. 11, both HSP.

53. Stephen H. Cutcliffe, "Colonial Indian Policy as a Measure of Rising Imperialism: New York and Pennsylvania, 1700–1755," *Western Pennsylvania Historical Magazine* 64:3 (July 1981), Tables 1 and 2, pp. 240–44.

Logan as land speculator

Logan's touch was everywhere. Here we shall attend to only one of the effects of his trading organization: its encroachment on the communities of Indians on the Susquehanna. Logan regarded his Indian trade as a profitable business in itself and as a means to the even more profitable business of land speculation. Indeed "speculation" is a misnomer for his way of acquiring and selling lands. He always had a sure thing before he laid out any money of his own; the expense of risk was always someone else's. He saw, like everyone else, that land-hungry immigrants kept coming into Pennsylvania. Unlike most people, however, he had the power and purpose to determine where they should locate; he sent them where he had already acquired land to be resold.

The effect on the Indians of Logan's land hunger can hardly be exaggerated. The "fur trade interest" in Pennsylvania, which became preeminently James Logan, was not a social and political factor protecting Indians from the encroachments of settling farmers, as allegedly was the case in other colonies. Rather, in Pennsylvania the trade was a means of *accelerating* settlement. Logan-the-merchant put his traders as close to Indian villages as he could: his store at Conestoga, for example, was next to one Indian village and on the abandoned site of another.[54] Through the trade, Logan amassed the capital and resources to become a magnate of lands. In effect, the Indians performed pioneer labor for him, clearing wilderness sites—which he later acquired—for their villages and establishing lines of communication and transportation. But a dilemma arose. Since the real estate value of land increased in direct proportion to the number of Europeans in the vicinity, Logan's lands would become spectacularly more valuable when surrounded by masses of land-hungry people. In such circumstances continued residence by Indians would become difficult or impossible. Thus there was conflict inherent in the motivations of Logan's different functions. As merchant, he wanted to keep as many Indian customers and suppliers as possible, as long as possible; but in the long run, the interest of Logan-the-land-speculator required Logan-the-merchant to transform the character of the land. His genius is revealed in the devices he used to reconcile his varied ambitions to consistent advantage. The effect of his activities on the Indians was first to draw them to the Susquehanna region in pursuit of trade, then to push them ever farther west, destroying the sedentary agricultural functions of their economy and magnifying the importance of hunting and nomadism. Certainly, settlement by colonials would have taken place anyway—Logan cannot be held responsible for that—but the advance of settlement was profoundly influ-

54. Jennings, "Indian Trade," pp. 418–20.

enced by him. To a considerable extent, he controlled the direction of the advance; and, both as merchant and as provincial officer, he controlled the Indians.[55]

What happened in the Susquehanna Valley contradicts the thesis that frontier regions must be wild and lawless. When colonial settlers began to surge into the valley, they did not escape law or authority. They moved instead into territory where Logan's agents were omnipresent, informed, and effective. This frontier, within the limits that mattered to Logan, could be and was disciplined. His final control of controls was the hunger of the settlers for good title to their lands, a hunger that could be satisfied only by the Commissioners of Property, dominated by Logan. The land available for settlement was limited in quantity by reasons of topography, law, and diplomacy. The upper reaches of the Susquehanna River, as well as its farther side, were in Indian territory; every settler there would have over his property the encumbrance of Indian claims—and over his head, the hazard of Indian resentment. The lower reaches of the river were spoiled for stable and knowledgeable farmers by the uncertainty over land titles in a large area disputed between Pennsylvania and Maryland. Penniless immigrants went there and squatted, but those who could pay good money went where the Land Office would sell with conveyance of clear title unencumbered by Indian or other colonial claimants.

Encroachment at Conestoga

Even so clever a man as Logan could not keep the Indians contented while colonials occupied the land. A Palatinate Mennonite immigration of 1717 flowed into Conestoga Manor, and surveyor Taylor's maps show that Logan allocated lands as far as the border of the Indian village.[56] In the midst of settlement, some anonymous cynic, drunk, or prophet—an English resident near Conestoga—told the Indians that the king of Great Britain and the regent of France had agreed to "cut off" the Indians of North America to make room for surplus Europeans. The rumor flew along the river. By June, 1717, the Five Nations chiefs had heard it three times and were confronting New York's governor with it. They told him they did not really believe it, but if there should be anything to it, they would not allow themselves to be pushed over easily. They betrayed the

55. Albright G. Zimmerman disagrees sharply with my interpretation of Logan. See his "New Approaches to the Indian History of Early America," *Hayes Historical Journal* 3:3 (spring, 1981), pp. 49–61, esp. 53–55.

56. *Pa Property Minutes* April 8, 1717, *Pa. Archives*, 2d ser., 19:622–24. The survey was actually made on Oct. 11, 1717; Taylor Papers, mss., 16:3349; Penn Mss., Large Folio, mss., 32(5). But the warrant for survey was not issued until Feb. 1, 1718: Cadwallader Collection, Thomas Cadwallader, Box 6a, Misc. Land Papers, mss., HSP.

uneasiness beneath their bravado, however, by an angry insistence that they would find out who was spreading smallpox among them and seek to "disswade" that evil person "from such pernicious practices."[57]

"Invaders" from Maryland increased the tension. The Provincial Council resolved that their friends, the Indians in the Conestoga neighborhood, must have been very much disturbed by the settlers from Maryland "near the thickest of our settlements." While Logan continued to encourage settlers who bought land under Pennsylvania law, the council magniloquently commissioned Colonel John French as Ranger and Keeper of the Marches of the Province, authorizing him to apprehend the Marylanders.[58]

In January, 1718, the Commissioners of Property decided that "The late Settlements on and near Conestoga Creek hath made it necessary that the Indian ffields about the Town Should be enclosed by a good ffence to secure the Indians Corn from the Horses, Cattle and Hoggs of those new Settlers that would otherwise destroy it and thereby cause an uneasiness in those Indians."[59]

Alienation of Chartier's Shawnees

At the same meeting, the commissioners granted a warrant to Shawnee Peter Chartier to buy the three hundred acres on which his father, Martin, had located and was currently operating a trading post. It would appear that this action was also intended to placate the Indians, for Martin Chartier had lived among the Shawnees since their entry into Pennsylvania, and Peter was his son by a Shawnee wife. But Martin died in April, and, according to Logan's accounts, Chartier owed the sum of £108.19.3¾. It was not an especially large sum, compared with other traders' accounts; indeed, there were movable goods on the premises sufficient to discharge the debt more than three times over. But Logan, as "principal creditor," not only informed young Peter Chartier that the son was accountable for his father's debts, but also seized all of Martin Chartier's property, real, as well as personal. Logan extracted a deed from Peter for his recently inherited three hundred-acre tract with improvements (which appears to have been hitherto unpaid). Then Logan evicted Peter and established another trader, Stephen Atkinson, in his place. The ethics of the transaction, not to speak of its legality, would be questionable by any standards. Among other things, Logan's haste to get Chartier's debt discharged was not matched by any dispatch in paying his own; although Stephen Atkin-

57. Private conference, June 13, 1717, *N.Y.Col.Docs.* 5:486–87.
58. *Pa. Council Minutes*, Feb. 15, 1718, 3:37.
59. *Minutes of Property*, Bk. H., Jan. 2, 1718, *Pa. Archives*, 2d ser., 19:626.

son paid Logan £30 for the Chartier tract in 1720, Logan did not pass the money along to the Proprietaries until 1727.[60] We must imagine the Shawnees' reaction. How could the eviction of one of their chief men be reconciled with William Penn's solemn encouragement to live among the Christians?

Even the sharply edited official records betray the Indians' dismay. According to the treaty minutes, when the Susquehanna Indians called at Philadelphia in June of 1718, they had only sweet words of friendship and regard. But, though the editor of the minutes removed from the Indians' expressions all reference to land, he permitted Governor William Keith, on the following day and page, to answer the questions that ostensibly had never been asked. Suddenly we become aware of a dialogue that had been in progress for some time. Keith reminded the Indians "That in Referrance to the Surveys of Lands, they Cannot but be sensible of the Care that has been taken of them. *They had Expressed a willingness to Retire from Conestogoe;* Yet the Government here had perswaded them to Continue near us." Keith pointed out how the Indians' fields at Conestoga had been fenced off for them; but, instead of satisfying the Indians, this reminder merely stimulated them to ask that the Shawnee and Conoy villages should be fenced, too, "with Lines at the distance of ffour miles from the River."[61] Keith's motives and policies are detailed in chapter 14.

Logan somehow managed to temporize. Ever fertile in expedients, he permitted Peter Chartier to trade on credit from the Conestoga store. Eventually Chartier was able to establish a new trading post higher up the Susquehanna, at Paxtang. But references to Chartier in Logan's business correspondence hint at an antagonism that never really ended. Decades would pass before any serious outbreak of Shawnee violence against Pennsylvanians, but it was Peter Chartier's band that first turned hostile, in 1745—ten years before the outbreak of the Seven Years War. Logan's seizure of Chartier's homestead cannot be held the direct cause of an event so remote in time; nevertheless, in an accumulation of grievances a man would remember being deprived of what he understood to be his birthright, and Indian memories were long. The trade that had drawn to Pennsylvania the Shawnee band of Martin Chartier evolved in such a way that it helped to drive them out again with his son Peter.

60. Draft of survey, n.d., Taylor Papers, mss., 13:2731; J. Logan to I. Taylor, April 26, 1718, Taylor Papers 14:2875; instructions of Logan regarding Martin Chartier's estate, mss., Logan Papers 10:110; "Martin Chartier's Estate," mss., James Logan's Ledger, p. 35, foregoing all HSP; *Pa Property Minutes* Bk. I, April 26, 1727, *Pa. Archives,* 2d ser., 19:749; "Inventory of Martin Chartier's Estate," *Publications of the Lancaster County Historical Society* 29(1925), pp. 130–33.
61. *Pa. Council Minutes,* June 16, 1718, 3:48–49.

Logan and the Delawares

The Delawares were not so important in trade as the Conestogas and
Shawnees, but they occupied valuable lands closer to the earliest colonial
settlements. Logan understood, as did many of his contemporaries, that
the quickest way to get rich was to seize Indian lands for little or no compensation. He began to build his own wealth from Delaware Indian lands
before he entered the Indian trade, almost instantly after William Penn's
second departure from the colony in 1701. Logan was compelled both by
Penn's policies and by Quaker principles to act secretly, but Penn was far
away and easily misinformed. Other local Quakers joined Logan in compromising their principles to share in the processes of enrichment. In the
private papers of Logan and his henchmen we see a very different picture
from that he described to Penn.

Logan's first Indian victims were the Delawares, who lived on a reservation Penn had set aside for them along Brandywine Creek. In February
1702, the Commissioners of Property, dominated by Logan, issued a warrant to survey the Brandywines' land for sale to one of Logan's closest
friends. The Brandywines protested; Logan even conceded the justice of
their protest at one point, but he continued to whittle away at their reserved
lands until none were left. Most of the Brandywines thus dispossessed of
their homeland removed to the Susquehanna and Ohio regions, where
they told their story of fradulent dealings to anyone who would listen.[62]

Naturally enough, the much-encroached upon Susquehanna tribes did
listen, and they watched in alarm as Logan directed new communities of
European immigrants to settle closer and closer to the Susquehanna villages. He acted secretly and illegally, often using some of his close associates as front men to disguise how he was personally profiting.

It must be stressed that Logan fully understood the injustice and inhu-
manity of what he was doing, as well as its illegality under Pennsylvania
law; and he knew also its possible drastic consequences. He moralized
movingly when an enemy's similar encroachment maneuvers resulted in
the dispossession and emigration of another Delaware band: "These poor
People were much disturbed at this, yet finding they could no longer raise
Corn there for their Bread they quietly removed up the River Sasquehannah, though not without repining at their hard usage. Not long after, most
of their Hunters retired for the Sake of better Game to Ohio." More than

62. Checochinican to Gov. Gordon, June 24, 1729, *Pa. Arch.*, 1st ser., 1:239–40; Charles
I. Landis, "Postlethwaite's and our First Courts," *Publications of the Lancaster County* [*Pa.*]
Historical Society 19 (1915), p. 231; Christopher Gist's Second Journal, Dec. 7, 1751, in *George
Mercer Papers Relating to the Ohio Company of Virginia*, ed. and comp. Lois Mulkearn (Pittsburgh: University of Pittsburgh Press, 1954), p. 34; C. A. Weslager, *Red Men on the Brandywine* (1953), reprinted (Wilmington, Del.: Delmar News Agency, 1976), ch. 6–8, maps on
pp. xviii–xix; Jennings, "Miquon's Passing," pp. 107–14, 235–45.

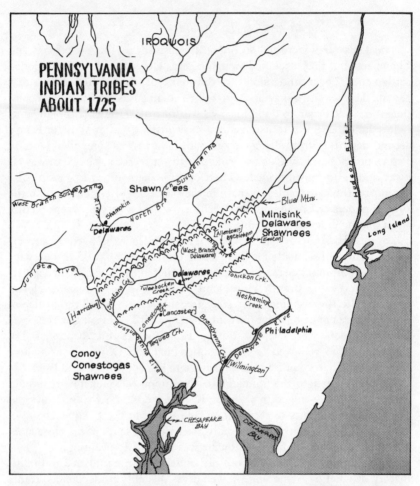

MAP 10. Pennsylvania Indian Tribes about 1725. Adapted from P.A.W. Wallace, *Indians in Pennsylvania*, p. 136. The valley between the Blue Mountains and South Mountain is part of the Great Valley of the Appalachians. In Pennsylvania, it is called Lebanon Valley east of the Schuylkill River, and Lehigh Valley along the Lehigh River. Very fertile, it was a natural place for Indians to settle when retreating from colonial expansion.

the desire for open spaces motivated the Indians' removal. Their unfenced corn had been destroyed by the cattle "of these new-comers whom they knew not." In view of Logan's whole history, it is startling to see how clearly he understood the moral issue. " 'Tis certain," he wrote, "they have the same reason to resent this as all those other Indians on this Continent have had for the foundation of their Wars that in some places they have carried on so terribly to the destruction of the European inhabitants."[63]

By the 1720s there was general discontent among the Delaware clients of Pennsylvania, including, besides the issues described above, another issue of encroachment on the lands of Delaware Indians in the Delaware Valley, north of Philadelphia. It will be discussed in the following chapters. Here we review the regions of discontent: they formed a great arc around Philadelphia, sweeping from Brandywine Creek westward to the Susquehanna, northward along that river, then eastward again to the Schuylkill's Tulpehocken Creek, and eastward again, by slightly south, to the Tohickon Creek that flows directly into the Delaware.[64] Had the Indians of these regions joined together to avenge their wrongs at that time, the consequences would have been terrible indeed. Pennsylvanians had good reason, without knowing it, to be thankful that their client Indians remembered William Penn's benevolence and could distinguish between one and another kind of colonial. Too many histories have failed to make the same distinction, with the consequence that when they get to the eventual outbreak of Delaware resentment during the Seven Years War, the occurrence comes as a great surprise, explainable only in terms of savage ingratitude and bloodlust. They are absolutely false. The Delawares had plenty of grievances. It is only remarkable that they waited so long to exact retribution.

Markets and immigrants

The process was not preordained or predetermined; it was the outcome of conscious choices made by interested persons. The lands themselves dictated only what uses could *not* be made of them, leaving open a range of possible options and combinations. The option adopted by incoming Europeans was not (as so often stated) the life of yeomen subsistence farmers. Had that been so, there would have been land enough, and to spare, for the Indians as well, and their hunting and fishing abilities could have fitted neatly into such a mode. What occurred instead can be seen abstractly as a struggle between two voracious markets: peltry and wheat. As Thomas

63. Logan to John Penn, Aug. 2, 1731, mss., Penn Mss., Off. Corr. 2:181, HSP.
64. I have made individual studies of each region. Brandywines: "Miquon's Passing," pp. 107–14, 235–45, 290–91, 422; Susquehannas: "Indian Trade of the Susquehanna Valley"; Tulpehocken or Schuylkill Delawares: "The Delaware Interregnum" and "Incident at Tulpehocken"; Nutimus's "Jersey" Delawares: "The Scandalous Indian Policy of William Penn's Sons: Deeds and Documents of the Walking Purchase." The present book culls from these studies and adds insights learned since they were published, but in the interest of readability I have not tried to reproduce everything. Readers wanting more detail are referred to the earlier studies.

C. Cochran has reminded us, the farmer in America has always been a businessman.[65] The new farmers of Pennsylvania's Lancaster County were soon shipping cargoes of first-class wheat to the West Indies and Europe besides feeding their families. *To produce that much wheat, great quantities of land were required.*

The old historiographical myth has it that Indians needed vast amounts of land for their subsistence and therefore had to retire before the advancing agriculturalists of Europe, with the implication that the colonials were more efficient in land use. Whether this may have been true in some corners of the country, I cannot say. In Pennsylvania the myth is many ways wrong. After European arrival the Indians did not hunt for subsistence; they hunted for the peltry market. They hunted mostly in the lands westward of the Susquehanna River rather than those occupied by immigrant colonials. The colonials wanted the buffer lands between Indian and colonial settlements, and when they got these they demanded Indian croplands and village sites. The colony's political authorities shared their inclinations and made all necessary arrangements for dispossessing and displacing the resident Indians, who until they were pushed, desired nothing more than to stay where they were. As Quaker and Mennonite principles precluded the crudely violent means used by Anglican Virginians and Puritan New Englanders, Pennsylvania's officials resorted to techniques made possibly by the Covenant Chain.

Immigrants continued to come. Their livestock got into the Indians' unfenced crops, and the resentful Indians were cowed by the great numbers, wealth, and power of the intruders. Even so, the Susquehanna River continued to be the limit line for all but a few colonial settlers until 1732, and Logan's organization dominated the region's affairs almost absolutely, except for a period when he and Governor William Keith were enemies. When the next great surge of immigration took settlers across the Susquehanna River, they passed over trails beaten by Logan's traders through towns built on Logan's lands (always recognizing that the trails and lands had been Indian before association with Logan). If the immigrants encountered the law, it was in courts manned by justices who had been appointed by governors but chosen by Logan. And when at last the immigrants drove their Conestoga wagons onto Logan's ferry (equipped with the Pennsylvania rifles also made by German immigrants at Conestoga), they were carried to the other side of the river, where once again they found his traders' trails, leading to a new western empire.

They also found there the Indians who had been forced out of eastern Pennsylvania and were in no mood to migrate again.

65. Thomas C. Cochran, "The History of a Business Society," *Journal of American History* 54 (1967), p. 7.

Chapter 14 ❧ A VISE MADE IN EUROPE

As we are entirely of opinion, that the Indian trade, if fairly carried on, would greatly contribute to the increase of your Majesty's power and Interest in America, we should humbly propose, that the same may be put under as good regulations, as the nature of the thing will admit, for on the successful progress of this trade the enlargement of your Majesty's dominions in those parts doth almost entirely depend, in as much as all the Settlements, that may at any time hereafter be made beyond the Mountains, or on the Lakes, must necessarily build their hopes of support much more upon the advantage to be gained by the Indian trade, than upon any profits to arise from planting at so great a distance from the sea. . . .

And that your Majesty's subjects may be the more easily induced to extend this trade as far Westward, upon the lakes and rivers behind the Mountains, as the situation and ability of the respective Colonies will permit; forts should be built, and garrisons settled in proper places to protect them.

Board of Trade Report to the King, 8 September 1721.

Keith versus Logan

Sir William Keith came of the northern Scottish family of Powburn, and his grandfather had become a baronet, without estate, of Nova Scotia. William's genteel poverty led him to Queen Anne's court, where he picked up the post of Surveyor General of the Customs for the American colonies, with an attached salary of £500 sterling. On such a sum a gentleman might live well and cultivate appetites, and in such a post he could become acquainted with all the crown's officials concerned with the New World. But when Anne died in 1714 and the Whigs took over under George I, Keith lost his post and his income. He retained the appetites and the acquaintances.[1]

In 1715 he visited Pennsylvania. He seemed to be just what the colony needed. The Quaker-dominated government had suffered from Anglican harassment ever since its beginning; it needed friends at court. The difficulty of the Quaker oligarchy had been to find such a man who would be

---

1. Joshua Francis Fisher, ed., Introduction to Andrew Hamilton, "Narrative of Sir W. Keith's coming to the Govt. of Pennsylvania," *Memoirs of the Historical Society of Pennsylvania* 2:pt.2 (Philadelphia: Lea and Carey, 1827), p. 26.

sufficiently compliant while they exercised actual rule. Keith's very poverty made him eligible; he could not afford to be independent. He eagerly solicited the Deputy Governor's post (William Penn being the absentee Governor as well as Proprietary), and he apparently gave the important Quaker gentlemen to understand that his own membership in the Church of England would not close his mind to their special problems. Penn's supporters sent recommendations, and Penn commissioned Keith as Deputy. Keith arrived in Philadelphia on May 31, 1717. It did not take him long to see that the direct source of his income was the elected House of Representatives, commonly called the Assembly, and that this Assembly was dominated by an anti-Proprietary faction of Quakers. Keith soon upset the calculations of the pro-Proprietary group who had gotten him the post.[2]

Logan tried to use the appointed Council to dominate resentful Keith, who quarreled with Logan almost at once. Logan charged that Keith was ungrateful to the persons who had secured his appointment and that the ingrate was wooing the Assembly to assure his "support"; i.e., salary.[3] Certainly Keith succeeded more than any previous governor in untying the Assembly's purse strings. By his own estimate he averaged £1,400 yearly during his nine years in office, and his opponents raised that estimate substantially.[4] It was a huge sum for the time, but Keith was an extravagant spender who always needed more.

William Penn's contested inheritance

Under earlier conditions Logan probably would have found ways to bring Keith to terms, but aged William Penn died on July 30, 1718, and his death transformed all. Even dying was for Penn a complicated affair. A long struggle ensued over the succession. Ordinarily Penn's estate would have descended to his eldest son, but the eldest son by Penn's first wife had become "debauched" and Anglican. Urged by Logan, Penn disinherited this William, Jr., by a will made in 1712, and he bequeathed the estate, including Pennsylvania, to John, Thomas, and Richard, his sons by his second wife, Quaker Hannah.[5]

William Penn, Jr., contested this will. After his father's death he

2. Hamilton, "Narrative," ibid., 36–41; James Logan to Hannah Penn, April 27, 1716, *Pa. Archives*, 2d ser., 7:49–50; Keith to Hannah Penn, Sept. 10, 1716, mss., Penn Papers, Off. Corr. 1:53, HSP; commission, Nov. 29, 1716, mss., Misc. Mss. Coll., APS.

3. *Pa. Council Minutes*, Feb. 2, 1718, 2:28–29; *A Letter from Sir Wm. Keith . . . to Mr. James Logan*, Dec. 13, 1725 (Philadelphia: Andrew Bradford, 1725), p. 14; James Logan, *Remarks on Sir William Keith's Vindication* (Philadelphia, 1726), pp. 10, 18–19.

4. William Keith, *A Just and Plain Vindication of Sir William Keith, Bart., Late Governour of Pennsilvania* (Philadelphia: Samuel Keimer, 1726); Andrew Hamilton, "Narrative," pp. 35–36.

5. Copy of the will, May 27, 1712, mss., Penn-Forbes Coll. 1:28, HSP.

attempted to seize control of Pennsylvania's government by sending a commission to Governor Keith, whose appointment to office had technically died with William Penn, Sr. If Keith had accepted William Junior's commission, his recognition might have supported the young man's battle for recognition by the courts as heir to the estate. Young William baited his proffered commission with accompanying instructions to Anglican Keith to "be careful" of the interest of the Church of England in the colony "and Employ where you can Deserving members of that Comunion, ffor I think they ought to have at Least an Equall share in the administration of Public Offices with their Neighbours of other Perswasions."[6] Considering Pennsylvania's previous history of court-connected Anglicans trying to take over, young William's ploy appears to have been a committee product rather than his own inspiration. It bore implied promise of support for Keith at court. What it implied for the Quakers need not be spelled out.

Keith informed the Assembly of young William's gambit, and his amusement at the Quakers' dismay smiles with urbane assurance through even the official records. The situation held opportunities that interested him more than did a triumph over heretics, and he never forgot where his money came from. Young William had made a strategic error in failing to mention alternative sources of income. When the Assembly requested Keith to suppress young William's commission to "Contribute to the peace of this Government," Keith held out his hand, palm side up, and cooperated.[7] He had previously hinted secretly to the crown that the time might be ripe for converting the anachronistic feudal propriety to a royal province. Now he wrote again for instructions. The Lords of Trade and Plantations were interested. They authorized him to continue in office independently, separate from any and all Penns until the lawyers should work their way through all appeals.[8] From the secure bases of crown authority and Assembly financing, Keith squared off against Logan. Keith discovered, like Logan before him, that other income could be supplemented by judicious speculation in Susquehanna lands. The two men locked in struggles that were to disturb all the Indians on the river and result in the first leap of colonial settlement over the river barrier.

6. Instructions of Wm. Penn, Jr., in *Pa. Council Minutes*, Dec. 16, 1718, 3:63–64.

7. *Pa. Council Minutes*, April 28, 1719, 3:64–67; May 11, 1719, 3:67–68. Keith's demands for "support" are scattered through *Pa. Assembly Minutes* 2. See also William R. Shepherd, *History of Proprietary Government in Pennsylvania*, Ph.D. diss., Columbia University, 1896.

8. Keith to Lords of Trade, Sept. 24, 1717, *CSPA&WI, 1717–1718*, no. 101; Keith to Sec. Craggs, May 14, 1719, *CSPA&WI, 1719–1720*, no. 285–i, ii; Lords of Trade to Lords Justices, July 21, 1719, ibid., no. 319; Mr. Delafaye to Lt. Gov. Keith, July 30, 1719, ibid., no. 344; Keith's proclamation, Nov. 9, 1719, *Pa. Archives*, 1st ser., 1:169–70.

Virginia complains about the warriors' path

Every year, Iroquois war parties descended the Susquehanna on their way to raid Cherokees and Catawbas in the south. Every year, the Iroquois recruited warriors from the Susquehanna villages. After harrying the southern Indians, the war parties would return, often pursued by vengeance-bent Catawbas. The Shawnees especially were unable or unwilling to curb their young men's compulsion to prove their manhood in combat, and the Conestogas had lost their Oneida supervisor in a raid sometime before May 1717.[9]

Shortly after Keith took office, his friend governor Alexander Spotswood of Virginia sent an emissary to Pennsylvania to make a treaty with the Indians on Susquehanna in order to halt further raids on Virginia's allied Indians. Keith responded that "he did not conceive it to be necessary or usefull that any persons whatsoever should be permitted to treat with the Indians, Except the Government of that Colony, to which the Indians Respectively Belonged," but that he would treat personally in Spotswood's behalf. The result was a series of familiar admonitions to the Indians to behave themselves.

According to Spotswood, Five Nations warriors had joined Tuscarora attacks on Virginia colonials in 1712 and 1713. He charged further (accurately) that the defeated Tuscaroras had been given asylum near the Susquehanna; that a Five Nations party had attacked an unarmed Catawba peace delegation treating with Spotswood and under his protection in 1717; that raiding parties in 1719 were so bold as to march home through the colonial settlements of Virginia, stopping at the Conoy town on the Susquehanna to display their prisoners to John Cartlidge; "and that they expected to have free recourse for their People amongst the English Plantations whilst they were making war."[10]

9. *Pa. Council Minutes*, June 16, 1718, 3:45–47; ibid., Conestoga, July 19, 1717, 3:21–25.
A bibliographic note: Curiously these Conestoga minutes close with the statement that "These leaves were out when delivered to [Secretary] Richard Peters. This is written on a fragment of one of the torn out leaves which are three in number." In another record appears "Extracts from Council Book E, 18th July, 1717. Fo. 12. Gov. Keith's Treaty with the Chiefs of the Conestogoe or Mingoe Indians, the Delawares, the Shawnois and Ganawoise, wherein are no Complaints about land," and that is all. *Pa. Archives*, 1st ser., 1:168. In the light of their history, it is just about a dead certainty that the Susquehanna Indians did complain about encroachments on their lands. Cf. *Pa. Council Minutes*, June 16, 1718, 3:48–49, and *Pa. Property Minutes* Bk. H, Jan. 2, 1718, *Pa. Archives*, 2d ser., 19:626.
10. Gov. Spotswood to Pres. Schuyler, Jan. 25, 1720, in *Pa. Council Minutes*, March 3, 1720 (1719 Old Style), 3:82–89. Spotswood was frustrated by a situation in which authority was divided and the buck was passed freely. Pennsylvania's Col. John French had met with the Indians on Susquehanna, June 28–29, 1719, to exhort them to be at peace and to refuse hospitality to Five Nations war parties; and they had formally agreed to his demands. But the Commissioners of Indian Affairs at Albany contented themselves with communicating to the Five Nations the wishes of Pennsylvania's government to stop the war parties down the Susquehanna. The Albany commissioners did not add their own authority to this. Instead,

The Iroquois had complaints of their own. The breach between the Carolinas and the Tuscaroras had come about, they said, because Indian lands had been seized without payment and because Indian children, bound out to colonials for instruction, had been transported away and sold into slavery. The Iroquois claimed that they had wanted to make peace with the Catawbas as early as 1714, but that an Iroquois peace delegation had been assassinated treacherously by the Catawbas.[11]

Perils at Conestoga

To Pennsylvanians the feuding was senseless, dangerous, and sickening. When news arrived of a raiding party's having tortured a prisoner to death in one of the Susquehanna villages, Colonel John French was sent to command the sachems of all the towns that "no person whatever offer after this time to put any man to Death by Torture here, for whoever does it must answer to the Governour and Government at their peril." French was horrified; in unmistakably sincere and eloquent words he pleaded with the Indians to remember their common humanity. Be it said to the credit of the Pennsylvanians that, until the horrors of the Seven Years War, torture was practiced surreptitiously if at all in their colony. The gory accounts so common to New England, New York, Canada, and Virginia simply do not exist in Pennsylvania's annals.[12]

James Logan went to Conestoga in 1720 to explain to the Susquehanna tribes the suicidal nature of their involvement in the north-south conflict, and to exhort them to avoid it entirely. The Five Nations, Logan pointed out, were drawing the angry southern Indians directly to the Susquehanna towns by retreating through them. Revenge parties would fall directly on the hapless bystanders while the Five Nations were secure at home.[13]

The Susquehanna Indians were in a truly impossible situation. By 1719,

they suggested to New York's governor that Pennsylvanians could themselves "prevent and hinder" the Five Nations from raiding southward, "but it seems that they are rather Inclind to trouble your Excellency and put this province to Expence with what they may Easily prevent themselves if they be at a little Expence." It should be added that a Five Nations chief said that "one of the principal men at Fort Christiana" in Virginia had given them powder and lead and incited them to attack.

Pa. Council Minutes, Nov. 9, 1719, 3:78–81; ltr. of transmittal and treaty minutes, June 19, 1719, mss., N.Y.Col. Mss. 61:147–48. See also the earlier effort by Spotswood and Keith with which New York refused to cooperate. N.Y. Council Minutes, Sept. 4–5, 1717, mss., 11:426–27.

11. Heathcote to Townsend, July 16, 1715, *N.Y.Col. Doc.s* 5:433; Five Nations speech, June 17, 1717, ibid., p. 490.

12. *Pa. Council Minutes,* Nov. 9, 1719, 3:79.

13. *Pa. Council Minutes,* July 12, 1720, 3:95–96.

as Logan remarked, they were "animated in a manner that has never been known here before."[14] Logan's chiding only made the situation worse. Not only did the powerful Iroquois demand help that drew retaliatory wrath from the south, but now the Pennsylvanians who controlled the necessities of life threatened further trouble. Conestoga Chief Civility dictated a letter of expostulation to Governor Keith. The Indians were in a fearful state, Civility said. They recognized their danger from the southern tribes, but they feared also to incur the wrath of the Senecas against both themselves and the back-country Christians. Civility was positive that the Senecas "do not bear true affection to your Government, and some of them are already very bold and impudent to the Christian inhabitants and us also." To Logan, privately, Civility was more explicit. He disclosed that some of the Five Nations Indians, especially the Cayugas, were expressing "a Dissatisfaction at the large Settlements made by the English on Sasquehannah, and that they seemed to claim a Property or Right to those lands."[15] Apparently unaware of the long shadow of Thomas Dongan thus thrown across the colony from the past, Governor Keith blamed the French when he told his Council that he had grounds to "apprehend that the ffive Nations, especially the Cayoogoes, did entertain some secret Grudges against the advancing of our Settlements upon Sasquehanna River."[16]

A frontier line proposed

All parties recognized the need for a resolution of the chronic crisis. In 1721, Keith journeyed to Virginia to confer with his friend Spotswood. The latter proposed an utterly simple solution—too simple, it was to prove—and Keith accepted it. Spotswood proposed to keep the northern and southern Indians entirely apart. If a line were drawn between them, which they would be forbidden to cross, they could no longer fight, and peace would be automatic. The line proposed by Spotswood ran from the mouth of the Potomac River to its headwaters, in the Appalachians, then followed the mountains' course to the south and west. Spotswood guaranteed to keep Virginia's client and subject Indians below the river and within the mountain fence, provided that the northern colonies would keep "their" Indians above and outside.[17]

Meanwhile the Five Nations had also been discussing the matter. Shortly

14. Logan to Gov. Hunter, June 4, 1719, mss., Logan Letter Books, 2:213, HSP.
15. *Pa. Council Minutes*, July 12, 1720, 3:97–98; July 20, 1720, 3:103.
16. *Pa. Council Minutes*, July 19, 1720, 3:98–102. Keith or Logan may have gotten word of the offer made by the Cayugas in August, 1719, to sell the Susquehanna Valley to New York, "in preference to any other Government." *Wraxall's Abridgment*, pp. 120–21.
17. *Pa. Council Minutes*, March 22, March 28, June 3, 1721, 3:113–18.

after Keith's return from his visit to Spotswood, he received word that an Iroquois delegation headed by Seneca Sachem Ghesaont had arrived at Conestoga to treat with him. He responded grandly at the head of seventy-odd well-armed horsemen, accompanied by some presumably unarmed Friends from his Council.[18]

After ceremonial greetings, Keith took charge and asserted his authority. In a bold but tactful maneuver to instruct the *Iroquois* without giving them such a direct order as they would resent, he met with the *Conestogas* to explain his agreement with Spotswood about the line of separation. The Iroquois were thus not required to respond, and they did not. When Keith turned to them, however, they raised issues of their own. Seneca speaker Ghesaont "remembered" their previous treaties with Pennsylvania, then came directly to the point: trade. Goods cost too much, and traders misbehaved. He desired Pennsylvania's help in getting higher prices for the Indians' skins and furs. Keith betrayed his lack of experience in Indian affairs by dismissing Ghesaont's complaint with an airy platitude about free trade, evading entirely the issue of prices; he then took splendid leave.[19]

Iroquois soundings about trade

Logan knew better, and Logan stayed behind. After sitting and chatting for a day longer, "with a Pipe and some small mixt Liquors," he passed on to Keith and the Council as much as he thought good for them to know. Ghesaont had trade on his mind; Logan had land on his. The Iroquois were poor, said Ghesaont; some kind of trouble at Albany was making goods there hard to get. Young Iroquois men went to war in order to plunder goods and clothing from their enemies. Having provided appropriate justification, he came to the heart of the matter: the chiefs were resolved to see if they could not trade with other English governments besides New York. No news could have interested Logan more. His formal record, however, shows no response other than a remark that the Iroquois could best be supplied by Albany. We may allow ourselves a certain skepticism.

For his own part, Logan wanted Ghesaont to know that the Five Nations had no legitimate claim to lands along the Susquehanna. These lands, said Logan, had been given up long previously. Conestoga Chief Civility was bold enough at this point to speak up for his own people. The old men, he said, remembered their joy on hearing that William Penn had "brought back" their lands, and they had confirmed all their right to Penn. Ghe-

18. *Treaty with the Five Nations at Conestoga, 5 July 1721* (Philadelphia: Andrew Bradford, 1721), p. 1.
19. *Pa. Council Minutes*, July 5–8, 1721, 3:121–30.

saont was affably noncommittal. Nothing was decided.[20]

The Iroquois chiefs had a journey yet to make. Their primary mission was to sound out the southern tribes on prospects for peace. Logan arranged safe conduct and an escort to take them to Virginia. It seemed as though the Susquehanna Valley might at last become really neutral and peaceful territory. The Iroquois were ready to treat with Virginia and trade with Pennsylvania. The outlook, however, was rosier than the reality.

Conflicts of interest

In spite of the seeming chaos of events, patterns may be discerned. One dominant pattern showed itself in the difference between what colonials wanted to do and what their imperial rulers commanded them to do. Colonials struggled to enrich themselves, and they resented imperial interference whether it took the form of taxes or of limiting controls of wealth-producing activities. Imperialists aimed for an expanding empire and demanded that individual colonials sacrifice their short-term interests to that end. The resulting struggles were governed by the greater power of the imperialists so that colonials chose evasion rather than confrontation. They argued legalistically over interpretation of the laws. Colonial officials delayed enforcement while requesting further instructions via long sea voyages; often they succeeded in getting their way in effect by the time responses were received. Traders and squatters did what they pleased out in Indian country beyond the view or reach of officialdom. And merchants smuggled, by sea and by land. The empires ground on toward their greater goals, but the long-range intentions of imperialists to make North America all French or all English were often frustrated by their insubordinate subjects. In one aspect the American Revolution was merely the culmination of a long process. Despite all the crowns' pretensions to sovereignty, colonials and Indians alike strove constantly for as much autonomy as was possible in the conditions of their lives.

However, one can overstate the degree of that autonomy. It varied with circumstance, and imperial powers frequently threw the plans of colonials and Indians into confusion. Decisions made in France and England, as well as happenstance in America, were soon to present Logan, Keith, and the Iroquois with new problems and new opportunities.

We must backtrack once more for perspective and sequence. After the long War of the Spanish Succession ended, in 1713, the Treaty of Utrecht recognized the Iroquois Five Nations as subjects of Great Britain, but the Iroquois did not. The treaty also permitted free trade by English-allied

20. *Pa. Council Minutes*, July 20, 1721, 3:130–34.

Indians anywhere in New France, but French-allied Indians, who had had no part in making the treaty, had no intention of letting the Iroquois take over the trade in their territories; beaver wars continued under other names.

Yet the imperial strategies held firm. It was not a conflict of races that dominated these years, but rather a confrontation of empires. England's Queen Anne died in 1714, and France's Louis XIV in 1715, causing momentary loss of attention to the colonies while parties in the metropoles sorted themselves out under successor monarchs; but the pause was no more than a break in the rhythm of imperial maneuver. Even during the pause, the interests of traders from South Carolina and Louisiana collided, and the resulting Yamassee War drove English traders back to the Atlantic coast. Whether French instigation or English traders' abuses actually provoked the war is not clear, but the French had no lack of intention.[21] Either way, the result was an English setback. As Yves Zoltvany remarks, "The sudden defection of the Indians put an end to the first major British attempt to wrest the Mississippi valley from France."[22]

English penetration was more subtle and more successful at Detroit because the distant English merchants operated through French and Indian go-betweens instead of sending their own nationals to preempt and engross the trade. The brokering was wholly satisfactory and lucrative to Commandant Cadillac, whose major objective was to make himself, rather than merely France, the master of the northwest.[23] Brokering suited also the merchants of Albany and Philadelphia, but it caused contention among the tribes as the Iroquois allied with the Foxes to challenge other tribes' superior positions in the trade.[24] A French inspector, sent from Paris to get reliable intelligence, reported that Detroit had become practically a satellite of New York's commercial sphere. He added "that the Iroquois have taken advantage of the period since the founding of Detroit to win over our allies."[25] Minister Pontchartrain chose a circumspect method to downgrade Detroit by transferring Cadillac to be governor of Louisiana and substituting a known incompetent at Detroit.[26] The developing Iroquois alliance system in the west blew up in an eruption of intertribal conflict known as the first Fox War.[27]

21. Crane, *Southern Frontier*, ch. 4.
22. Zoltvany, *Vaudreuil*, p. 138.
23. Zoltvany, "New France and the West," pp. 311–12; ———, *Vaudreuil*, p. 41.
24. Lanctot, *History of Canada* 2:162; Edmunds, *Potawatomis*, ch. 2.
25. Yves F. Zoltvany, "Laumet, Antoine, *dit* de Lamothe Cadillac," *Dict. Can. Biog.* 2:354–55.
26. Louise Dechêne, "Dauphin de La Forest, François," *Dict. Can. Biog.* 2:170.
27. Edmunds, *Potawatomis*, pp. 27–29.

284 THE AMBIGUOUS IROQUOIS EMPIRE: PART THREE

Trade between Montreal and Albany

There was another smuggling trade between enterprising French and English colonials, operating by way of the Mahican Channel between Albany and Montreal. This one was frowned upon by English imperialists as well as their French counterparts because it seemed to accept and adapt to French mastery of the west. Made possible by the Iroquois policy of neutrality and the peace brought by that policy to a buffer zone between the St. Lawrence and Hudson valleys, this Mahican Channel trade rested on a solid foundation of interests shared by colonials in defiance of imperial policies. Each of the merchant communities involved had a specialty: Montreal had a superior organization for bringing in peltry; Albany had a superior source of trade goods. Certain of the preferred trade goods— especially the woollens called strouds—were made only in England. English-made goods were usually cheaper than the French, and the Hudson stayed navigable through winters when ice blocked traffic on the St. Lawrence. English manufacture and the conditions of English transportation were so greatly superior to the French that English traders could sell their goods at half the French prices and still make twice the French profit. This was the basic English advantage that the French never really could overcome, no matter how brilliantly they administered their colonies and clients. On the other hand, French explorers and voyageurs had carried political alliance to trading Indians long before Englishmen penetrated the Appalachian barrier, so the French monopolized the sources of the bulk of marketable peltry. On both sides, some merchants adjusted to the situation instead of trying to change it. Montrealers bought goods wholesale from Albanians, delivering furs in exchange, and sold retail through their far-flung network of trading posts. At the posts they acquired more furs to renew the cycle. In 1720, a former governor of New York estimated their trade at ten to twelve thousand pounds worth of Indian goods annually.[28] New England might war incessantly and fiercely; New York placidly did business with the imperial enemy.

The Iroquois tolerated the Mahican Channel trade, having no alternative but to reopen hostilities with Canada's Indians, which was not a rational option at the time; but the Iroquois were unhappy about the situation. This trade brought no profit to Iroquoia. Its traffic was carried back and forth by the Catholic Mohawks of Caughnawaga village near

28. A bibliographic note: A classic exposition of this trade is Cadwallader Colden, "A Memorial concerning the Fur Trade of the Province of New York," Nov. 19, 1724. A counter view is revealed by merchants Dirck Schuyler and John Groesbeck, Feb. 15, 1725, *N.Y.Col.Docs.* 5:552, 726-33, 743-44. An overview is in Norton, *Fur Trade*, ch. 8. The decisive importance of the trade in New York's politics is discussed in Leder, *Robert Livingston*, pp. 251-91, and in Stanley Nider Katz, *Newcastle's New York: Anglo-American Politics, 1732-1753* (Cambridge, Mass.: Harvard University Press, 1968), passim.

Montreal, who received the pay for this porterage. The resentful Iroquois were convinced that if the trade stopped, the Caughnawagas would leave Canada to rejoin their Mohawk kinsmen of the Five Nations.[29] (Whether or not they were right in this belief is beside the point.) To the Iroquois it seemed that there was no future along the Mahican Channel; to renew their glory they would have to unite the tribes of the west in their Covenant Chain. The Five Nations never ceased to think of the Great Lakes region as their own territory, won "by conquest" during the Beaver Wars; it mattered not that they had been driven out of their conquest territories by other tribes allied to Canada.[30] Iroquois goals thus dovetailed with the goals of expansionist Englishmen, who were only too ready to maintain the conquest fiction against the most obdurate facts of counter-conquest. The French understood the identity of interest between expansionist Englishmen and the Five Nations but were confident of being able to keep the Indians under control. The situation was full of tension and sporadic violence that never quite erupted into full-scale war. Though peace prevailed along the Mahican Channel, intrigue and skirmishing never ceased in the Mississippi Valley and Great Lakes regions.

English imperialists' new western strategy

Into this situation the imperialist Whigs of England thrust a new initiative. Properly speaking it began after the death of Queen Anne and the succession of George I when the Whigs came to power. Its first attempt, which took place along the southern frontier between the Carolinas and Louisiana, was baffled by the destruction of the Yamassee War. The British imperialists began their second major effort to win the Mississippi Valley from a base in New York and Iroquoia.

All unknowing, James Logan, of Pennsylvania, started the process in 1718 when Peter Bisaillon brought his brother Michel from the Illinois country to Philadelphia. In response to the English Board of Trade's circular to colonial governors inquiring about French "encirclement," Logan quizzed Michel Bisaillon and prepared an elaborate set of "suggestions" for Governor Keith to transmit to the Board.[31] Immediately (as always), complexity set in.

Keith was already his own man by then—William Penn had died, and his proper heirs had not been determined—and Keith insisted on putting

29. Norton, *Fur Trade,* 126–27, 134–35.
30. E. S. Rogers, "Southeastern Ojibwa," in *Northeast,* p. 761; Edmunds, *Potawatomis,* p. 23.
31. Lords of Trade to Sec. Addison, *CSPA&WI, 1717–1718,* no. 256; Logan to Keith, Dec. 1718, mss., Soc. Misc. Coll., Indians, Box 11–c, HSP.

some proposals of his own into his report. Here we must remember Keith's friendship and constant correspondence with Governor Alexander Spotswood, of Virginia. As Keith's report finally emerged, it was a blend of Logan's detailed information with Spotswood's variant of westward impulse, and it made so mighty an impression on the Lords of Trade that they singled out Keith for special commendation in their own subsequent report to the Privy Council. It is amusing to see Logan beaten at his own game. Keith airily acknowledged that his sources of information were "Indian traders"—anonymous.[32]

What Keith recommended for English policy was essentially a mirror image of French practice. He listed five desirable policies: (1) prevention of cheating and abuses in the Indian trade; (2) extension of the trade as far west as possible, with establishment of forts and garrisons for protection; (3) creation of a broad system of Indian alliances; (4) enforcement of intertribal peace; and (5) systematic interprovincial correspondence to coordinate policies in Indian affairs. Keith specifically proposed that forts be erected at lakes Erie and Ontario "to secure all the Indians on this side Carolina to Canada, which are settled to the eastward of the Lakes, but also open a trade with the . . . great and Numerous Nations to the westward."

Up to this point, Keith and Logan saw eye to eye, but Keith recommended two more forts "because the distance between the English settlements in these Colonies and the Lakes is too great, without the refreshment as well as security of a middle stage or resting place." These middle stages were to stand "on the head or highest fountain of Potowmack River" and "towards the head of Susquehannah River." If carried out, his recommendations for the support and control of his fort design would effectually have carved off a great chunk of western Pennsylvania from the chartered limits granted to the Penns: the fort at Lake Erie was to be directed by Virginia! (Spotswood's influence?) The one at the Potomac was to be operated by Maryland. The Ontario fort was to be New York's responsibility, and Pennsylvania was to have the Susquehanna fort.[33]

Logan objected to two of these forts, as one might expect; but the two that he chose to oppose were not so easy to anticipate. Had he been serving the Penns' interests, as he always fervently proclaimed, Logan would have fought tooth and nail against extending Virginia's occupation to Lake Erie, but he made no issue there. Instead he protested the two forts at the heads of the Potomac and Susquehanna rivers. One may well wonder what these two middle stages were supposed to be in the middle of; cer-

32. Keith's report: CSPA&WI, 1719–1720, no. 61, 61.i. "Indian traders" remark at p. 32. Lords' thanks to Keith, Sept. 8, 1721, CSPA&WI, 1720–1721, p. 436.
33. CSPA&WI, 1719–1720, pp. 37–39.

tainly they would not lie between the forts on the lakes. Keith thought that Logan's "averseness" might arise from fear of engaging the colony "more in warlike affairs than is Consistent with the principles of your friends," but Logan's conduct and writings over a lifetime make it amply clear that his pacifism (if it existed at all) was easily subverted. Early on, he acknowledged himself not to be a "good professor" of the Quaker faith, though his contacts with influential Quakers were among his most impor-tant assets.[34] The two "middle" forts were obnoxious to him because they lay in territories frequented by his traders. Even the Susquehanna fort under Pennsylvania would be under governor Keith's control rather than Logan's, and Logan had begun to understand what that might imply. His concern was magnified by his financial circumstances at the time. He had "a considerable part of my fortune in the hands of those whose abilities to make me any Return for it depends on a good understanding with the Indians."[35] Translated, this meant that much credit had been extended to traders. If competition intruded, from Keith or others, Logan could face hard times.

He was reprieved by the expense involved in Keith's program. Though the Board of Trade advocated it strongly, the Privy Council refused com-mitment. However, the Board had resources of its own for activating parts of the plan. We shall ignore its maneuvers in the southern colonies.[36] What it started in New York is more pertinent to our interests.

On the Board's recommendation, the crown commissioned William Burnet as New York's lieutenant governor in April 1720. Burnet's arrival in New York coincided with Robert Livingston's elevation to the Speak-ership of the Assembly, and signalled the revival of Livingston's old scheme to aim Albany's trade due west. Burnet had been briefed in London to pursue such a policy, and Livingston, as Speaker, made the perfect part-ner for manipulating the legislature.[37] Together they pushed through an absolute ban on the sale of Indian goods to Canada, which meant the suppression of the Albany-Montreal trade being conducted by Livings-ton's merchant competitors. Proponents of this trade were dismissed from the Governor's Council and replaced by Cadwallader Colden and James Alexander, two empire builders of the Livingston stripe.[38]

This much, the Iroquois could approve, and they were soon to be grat-ified further by a grand multicolonial treaty that reconfirmed their supe-

---

34. Logan to W. Penn, Dec. 20, 1706, *Penn-Logan Correspondence* 2:190.
35. Logan to Keith, April 8, 1719, mss., Logan Papers 10:20; Keith to Logan, April 9, 1719, mss., Penn Mss., Addl. Misc. Ltrs., 1:23; Logan to Gov. Hunter, June 4, 1719, mss., Logan Ltr. Bks., 2:213–14. All HSP.
36. Crane, *Southern Frontier*, pp. 220–34.
37. Lder, *Robert Livingston*, pp. 250–53.
38. Ibid., pp. 255–56; Norton, *Fur Trade*, p. 136–38.

rior place in the British system of Indian alliances. In the background, however, lurked the Board of Trade's determination to confront the French aggressively with new forts. A purpose of one of these forts was to "secure" the Five Nations; i.e., to deprive them of freedom to maneuver between the French and the British. That goal had been made very plain by Governor Burnet at his first meeting with the Five Nations in August 1721. He was greeted then by the famous Onondaga chief Decanisora, who had long been the foremost Iroquois advocate of neutrality between the empires. But, as Cadwallader Colden remarked, Burnet refused to treat with Decanisora because of the chief's "keeping a Correspondence with the french and going somtimes to the french settelments." Decanisora was accordingly deposed by the other chiefs, and when Burnet next spoke to all the sachems, the humiliated Decanisora "stood among the young Indians who made a semicricle round the Sachems, and lookt very much dejected. Soe that the Indians had done more than what the Governour desired. His Excellency only disliked his being speaker, and they removed him entierly from their councils."[39] It may be wondered whether Decanisora lost all influence also back in Onondaga, out of Burnet's sight, but he does not appear again in the treaty records.

For a few years the Iroquois managed to stall. Then the French and British jaws of a vise of empires closed in on them. Decanisora had predicted it. As Colden reports he had told the Iroquois, "they ought not to join either with the English against the french or with the french against the English butt to keep the ballance betwixt the two for if the English should prevaile over the french the five Nations would be of means to enslave themselves for then the english would make no more account of them than they doe now of the river or Long Island Indians butt if the five Nations would now observe an exact Newtrality they would be courted and fear'd by both sides."[40]

Wise as he was, however, Decanisora made sense only as of a particular era and its circumstances. To maintain genuine neutrality against the pressures from both sides, the Iroquois needed to increase their independent strength to match the constantly growing power of the English and French. This proved too great a task for the resources of their culture, and when they later tried to revert to the policy of neutrality, their moment of opportunity had passed.

39. "Colden's account of the Conference between Gov. Burnet and the Five Nations, 1721," in *Collections of the New-York Historical Society* 50 (New York, 1918), pp. 128–30.

40. Ibid., p. 129.

Chapter 15 ❧ DESPERATION in
IROQUOIA

The third Act of a publick nature and consequence is to prohibit all trading [of New York's merchants] with the French for Indian Goods, that is goods which the French sell again to the Indians and thereby have the supplying all the Farr Indians with our Goods who would [otherwise] come to us and trade and hence our Indians justly say the French build Forts with our goods. This Trade was so much practiced by the leading men here that the Assembly could never be brought to prohibit it untill now, but finding the use that the French made of our easiness to them [the Assembly now has] made a severe law against it—by which means either the French will be totally deprived of such goods as Strouds Duffles &c., or if they get them it must be from Boston or Europe directly at a great disadvantage in the price and with the risque of going up the River of Canada, which is of most dangerous navigation, and then the trade will be at Quebec, which is above a hundred leagues further from our Indians than Monreal, and Monreal will sink to nothing which flourishes by its Trade with Albany.

Governor William Burnet to the Lords of
Trade, November 26, 1720

Iroquois status on the Susquehanna

The long, slow rebuilding program of the Five Nations made little visible progress during the first two decades of the eighteenth century, but it avoided fresh calamity and eased the Iroquois cautiously into position to tip once more the strategic balance. Never again would they be a terror in the Mississippi Valley, where domination had passed to the Potawatomis. Never again would they raid at will in the St. Lawrence Valley, where French control was now secure. But Iroquois gains in the Susquehanna Valley, made bit by bit, without ostentation, were real. Manpower had built up there as the Conestoga allies welcomed refugees from the south and some Brandywine Delawares from the east. The Shawnees had been placed under direct supervision of a resident Oneida chief. Tuscaroras waited along the Susquehanna for the signal to journey to Iroquoia to become the Sixth nation. Conoys and Nanticokes had fled into Pennsylvania from Maryland. A little congeries of broken tribes enjoyed the joint hospitality of Pennsylvania and the Iroquois in a string of villages between the juncture of the North and West branches of the Susquehanna and its outlet, at the head of Chesapeake Bay. The Susquehanna River had been held as the limit line for expansion of Pennsylvania colonials. Along the entire river, from the Chesapeake upstream to its tributary "treetop" where it interlaced with other streams of Iroquoia, Indian occupiers more or less accepted direction of their affairs by the Iroquois; all of this gain had resulted from the neutrality policy so adroitly administered by Decanisora.

But there was a substantial change from the days when the Five Nations had dared to fling themselves independently against New France despite peace between France and Britain. The Iroquois no longer could make their own decisions wholly for their own purposes. By 1720 they were obliged always to seek allies both among other tribes and among the colonies, and the interests of their allies had to be joined with their own. No matter how circuitous the description, this is a recipe for a degree of dependency. The Iroquois had become clients of a generalized English protectorate. Cadwallader Colden called them the "Five Indian Nations Depending on the Province of New-York in America." Their dependence was not formal and legal as he implied, but it was substantial nevertheless. They preserved a degree of independence by skillfully maneuvering between one English colony and another (as well as between all the English and Canada), by using their tribal alllances to enhance their importance in the eyes of colonials, and by using their colonial alliances to overawe the tribes. It was a juggling act that can only be admired for the performers' virtuosity, but it was not the same thing as independent power. In 1722 the three colonies of New York, Pennsylvania, and Virginia were to give formal recognition to the Five Nations' renewed ascendancy, but this gratifying tribute would be eroded by imperial purposes harmful to Iroquois strength.

The murder of Sawantaeny

The Great Treaty of 1722 got started in a way not planned by any of its participants. The brutal murder of a Seneca Indian by two Pennsylvania traders created an urgent necessity for the colony's government to assuage Seneca anger with what our Anglo-Saxon ancestors called *wergeld*—the payment of a large present to expiate the crime. For this purpose the colony would have to arrange a meeting with the Seneca tribal chiefs.

The murderers were not just any run-of-the-mill traders; they were Logan's key men at Conestoga, John and Edmond Cartlidge. And the facts of the murder could not be suppressed, though Logan put all his art into the effort. It had been witnessed by too many people, both Indians and colonials. John Cartlidge was "the law" at Conestoga. A provincial justice of the peace, he functioned regularly as official interpreter of treaty negotiations and daily supervised Logan's store. Indeed he was Logan's alter ego among the Indians of the Susquehanna. The prestige and reputation of the province were represented in this person. The identity of the murdered Indian, Sawantaeny, also worsened the gravity of the offense, for his Seneca tribe was the largest, strongest, and least reliable of all the Five Nations. The scattered bands at the Susquehanna might be overawed by sufficient address, but the Senecas would have to be placated.[1]

The situation became an unexpected trump card for Governor Keith in the game he was beginning to play with Logan. Although Logan rigged an inquiry that made the murder seem like an accident, Keith took depositions from the Cartlidges' indentured servants that described the affair in damning detail.[2] Logan had enemies in the Assembly who wanted to know the truth, and they were ready to force the Cartlidges to trial under Pennsylvania law, the outcome of which would surely have been hanging.[3] The Cartlidges, on their part, were unlikely to go silently to the scaffold. What they knew about Logan's dealings at Conestoga, including his embezzlement of Penn lands, could ruin him.[4] As he well knew, his whole future depended on his ability to keep them from harm. Smiling Keith held the decision. If Keith were to withhold the evidence of murder, the Assembly would vote funds for wergeld for the Senecas. If Keith passed on to the Assembly the depositions in his hands incriminating the Cartlidges, there would be a public trial.

Breach of the Susquehanna boundary

At a later date Keith might have elected to ruin Logan, but their quarrel had not yet deepened so far. Blackmail seemed to offer the greater rewards.

1. I have given a detailed account in my dissertation, "Miquon's Passing," pp. 198–206. Cf. with the typically slanted paragraph devoted to the subject in Hanna, *Wilderness Trail*, 1:173–74.

2. *Pa. Council Minutes*, March 21, 1722, Society Misc. Coll., Indians, Box 11c, fol. 2, HSP. These mss. contain the full report written by Logan and Colonel French of their trip to Conestoga to attempt a composition for Sawantaeny's murder. They also contain the sworn examinations before Keith of the Cartlidges' indentured servants Jonathan Swindel and William Wilkins. Wilkins's testimony is especially damning and confirms that of Shawnee witnesses who would not have been allowed to testify in court against colonials. Swindel's and Wilkins's depositions were subsequently eliminated from the formal record printed in *Pa. Council Minutes*, March 21 and 22, 1722, 3:147–57.

3. *Pa. Assembly Minutes*, April 26–28, 1722, 2:1416–20.

4. Logan's personal dealings in lands were usually made through "fronts," but the sheer quantity and range of his operations made secrecy impossible to maintain entirely. An embittered enemy informed the Penns of what he knew, and as soon as feasible they relieved Logan of all control over lands. Many documents have since come to light that were secret at the time. I have traced the Penns' enlightenment in "Incident at Tulpehocken," *Pennsylvania History* 35:4 (Oct. 1968), pp. 335–55. See also Jennings, "Indian Trade," pp. 416–20.

Prolonging the inquiry (and Logan's anxiety) Keith immediately had a tract of land surveyed for himself on the west bank of the Susquehanna. It was the first breach of the line between colonial and Indian jurisdictions, and normally Logan would have risen to furious attack, but now he remained strainedly silent.[5]

Opportunist that he always was, Logan reconciled himself to necessity by trying to get some trans-Susquehanna land surveyed for himself, whereupon Keith snapped his whip. He clapped the Cartlidges in jail and told the Conestogas that the traders would be "tryed and judged by our Laws in the same manner as if they kill'd an Englishman."[6] Utterly defeated, Logan subsided. Until the Cartlidges were placed beyond reach of the law administered by Keith, he was helpless.[7]

But Keith did not have it all his own way. The Indians told Keith that they had no objection to his taking the trans-Susquehanna lands—or so his report says. They also told him, more credibly, that he would have to clear the matter with the Five Nations.[8] For his own reasons, Keith now desired as much as Logan to arrange a treaty.

With all this in the background, Keith manipulated the Assembly to pay for a large present, and he arranged to meet the whole Iroquois League—not just the aggrieved Senecas—at Albany[9] His friend Spotswood came along too, and New York's Governor Burnet chaperoned them in the time-honored tradition of New York governors. Logan stayed home.[10] It seems reasonable to guess that he had had a hint from Keith that his presence was not desired.

5. Keith to Isaac Taylor, March 25, 1722, mss., Taylor Papers 14:2976, HSP; *Pa. Council Minutes*, April 16, 1722, 3:160; survey warrant, June 18, 1722, in *Pa. Council Minutes*, June 16, 1722, 3:184–86.

6. *Pa. Council Minutes*, April 16, 1722, 3:160–61; May 11, 1722, 3:169–70; *Pa. Assembly Minutes* 2:1432.

7. The Cartlidges were never brought to trial. Pennsylvania's Supreme Court deferred hearing the case until composition with the Senecas should be made, after which the issue apparently became moot. *Pa. Council Minutes*, Aug. 1, 1722, 3:191. The trial could have been held in Chester County Quarter Sessions Court, but its still-intact records mention no charge against, or trial of, both Cartlidges or either one. They were clearly highly privileged persons. Both had been summoned on other charges to appear before several sessions of the court in 1719-1720, but neither showed up and no action was taken. Quarter Sessions Docket, 1714–1723, West Chester Court House. Pages are not numbered, but are in chronological order. Cf. with what happened when Logan's enemy Ezekiel Harlan was tried for adultery. Though declared innocent by the jury, he was assessed the costs of trial and jailed until he paid them. Quarter Session Docket, 1723–1733, mss., sessions of Nov. 29, 1726, and Feb. 28, 1727, pp. 93, 101.

8. *Pa. Council Minutes*, June 16, 1722, 3:182–83.

9. A total of £280 was laid out by the assembly. £50 paid for the inquiry into Sawantaeny's murder (so that Logan managed to make some money even out of the maneuvers to save his men and himself) £130 paid the expenses of Pennsylvania's delegation to Albany. Typically this exceeded the £100 appropriated for the wergeld to the Senecas. *Pa. Assembly Minutes* 2:143, 1443; *Pa. Council Minutes*, Aug. 7, 1722, 3:190.

10. Logan's absence is the more notable because the Five Nations had invited him specifically by name. *Pa. Council Minutes*, July 30, 1722, 3:189, Aug. 3, 1722, 3:193. Burnet's chaperonage: *Pa. Council Minutes*, Oct. 3, 1722, 3:203–6.

Keith's business at Albany

For clarity of exposition, let us stay with Keith's business, which was really a sideshow of the overall treaty, before turning to other concerns. Keith waxed rapturous in Indian metaphors as he explained his great distress over the death of Sawantaeny. He did away with all "clouds and darkness . . . that the flame of Love and Affection may burn clear in our Breasts." On this bonfire of love he heaped substantial fuel including five bolts of cloth, five casks of gunpowder, and 500 pounds of lead. The flame of love burned brightly. It illuminated the desire of the Iroquois to be as discreetly urbane as Keith. They deplored the "accident" that had happened to Sawantaeny, and they were suffused with forgiveness. "We think it hard the Person who killed our friend and brother should suffer," they said and requested Keith to free the Cartlidges.[11]

Keith's public business mixed up with some of a more private nature. He later informed his Council in Philadelphia that he had obtained a "free surrender" of "all those lands about Conestogoe which the Five Nations have claimed" as well as a "desire" from the Indians "that the same may be settled with Christians." In compensation, he quoted the Iroquois as demanding, "we . . . expect, that if any of our people come to trade at Philadelphia you will order that they be received like Brethren, and have the Goods as cheap as possible." To which Keith purportedly responded that Albany was a good place to trade, and Philadelphia out of the way, but that Iroquois coming to Philadelphia would be treated like brethren.[12]

Even after allowing for suspicious New Yorkers overseeing the proceedings, Keith's description sounds fishy. It is easy enough to accept his statements concerning Iroquois interest in trade and his own response. Keith was not a merchant; it would have amused him to take a dig at Logan's interests. But that the Iroquois would give up territory critical to their strategic deployment, on no further consideration than a vague promise to be treated well when they dropped in to visit—this is not to be believed, and for the best of reasons: it was not true. Yet Keith carried the fabrication so cleverly that not even Logan guessed its falsity until a Five Nations delegation visited Philadelphia five years later. Then Logan learned that Keith had received only a grant of the right to make his own personal settlement over the Susquehanna "and that nothing further was intended by it."[13] However Keith had accomplished it, he had penetrated the Susquehanna front nevertheless, and thereafter the main issue narrowed to which colonials would gain most by following up the breakthrough.

While in Albany, Keith transacted some other private business also, which was to take traumatic effect on the Delaware Indians living in the

11. Conference minutes, Sept. 7 and 10, 1722, *N.Y.Col.Docs.* 5:677–79.
12. *Pa. Council Minutes*, Sept. 21, 1722, 3:201–2.
13. Logan to Honoured Friend, July 10, 1727, mss., Penn Mss., Off. Corr. 1:283, HSP.

valley of Tulpehocken Creek, a segment of the Great Valley of the Appalachians lying between South and Blue mountains just west of the Schuylkill River. Keith interviewed a German named Hans Lawyer, who represented the Palatines settled in New York, and gave him "encouragement" to bring his people to Pennsylvania. This group—perhaps *band* would be the right term—had been much abused in New York, but Keith's known character suggests that something more than sympathy motivated his encouragement for them to move. However the arrangement may have been consummated, sixteen Palatine families promptly moved into Pennsylvania, with more following later.[14] They deposited themselves abruptly in the midst of the Tulpehocken Valley Delawares, whose pleas to Keith were merely verbal, and the Indians soon were forced to abandon the region.[15]

All in all, the 1722 treaty was a nice piece of business for Keith and a disaster for Pennsylvania's client Indians. Not so, however, for the Iroquois. Keith won their favor with more than presents and florid rhetoric. Whether he fully understood what he was doing is debatable, but he became the first of Pennsylvania's negotiators since Fletcher to use Covenant Chain terminology in dealing with the Iroquois, and his usage had implications for the status of the Iroquois in relation to other tribes.[16] Previously, Pennsylvanians had spoken of a chain of friendship binding the colony to the tribes, but has always stopped short of saying "Covenant Chain." The distinction was clear then and should be now. Any treaty relationship could be expressed as a chain of friendship; but the Covenant Chain was a particular set of relationships with a very special place in it for the Five Nations. Keith's terminology, and his endorsement of what the Iroquois decided at Albany with his friend Spotswood, meant to the Iroquois that Pennsylvania had now joined *the* Chain—*their* Chain.

Spotswood's ambiguous frontier line

Considering Spotswood's intentions, this was an ironic outcome of the treaty. Spotswood was far from wanting to strengthen the Five Nations. He had come to Albany with firm determination to discipline them, and the united front of the three colonial governors—Spotswood, Keith, and

14. Conference minutes, June 4 and 5, 1782, mss., Penn-Physick Mss. 6:25, HSP. This mss. contains the matter of *Pa. Council Minutes* 3:316–26, with an additional deposition of Godfrey Fidler. See also J. Mitchell to Logan, May 13, 1723, *Pa. Archives*, 2d ser., 7:77–78.

15. Logan to John Penn, Aug. 2, 1731, mss., Penn Mss., Off. Corr. 2:181, HSP.

16. *Pa. Council Minutes*, Sept. 21, 1722, 3:198. The sudden use of Covenant Chain language probably came from the influence of the Livingston family at Albany, who were hosts to the governors during the treaty. Robert Livingston boasted that "All the 3 Governors . . . have consulted me concerning their proposals." Leder, *Robert Livingston*, p. 268.

Burnet—was overtly aimed at awing the Indians into acceding to Spotswood's demands. But Spotswood met more than his match in the Iroquois
diplomats. They gave him what he wanted, he thought, but it turned out
to be not quite what he had expected.

Spotswood wanted an end to Iroquois raids on Virginia's client Indians.
To achieve this, he wanted the Iroquois to agree to a barrier line they
would not cross. He evaded a sticky question of sovereignty that hovered
in the background and neither asserted the crown's claimed rights nor
conceded any Indian right. His objective was a frontier of expedience. He
stipulated, "That the great River of Potowmak and the High Ridge of
Mountains which extend all along the Frontiers of Virginia to the Westward of the present [English] Settlements of that Colony shall be for ever
the established Boundaries between the *Indians* subject to the Dominion
of Virginia and the Indians belonging to and depending on the 5
Nations."[17] To Spotswood's outrage, the Iroquois kept him waiting a week
for their answer which, when it came, showed careful legalistic analysis
of his proposition. They agreed not to cross Spotswood's line without his
permission, but they shrewdly restated his formulation. In their terms,
the line became the "Frontiers of Virginia," and they thanked Spotswood
politely for renewing peace "As well in behalf of the Christians as the
Indians of Virginia." As Spotswood had guaranteed to keep Virginia's
Indians within his line if the Iroquois would stay outside it, the Five
Nations' restatement implied plainly that Virginia's colonials also were to
stay inside the line. Spotswood understood this and rejected it. He repeated
his own position with the remark that "the Bounds between *your Indians
and ours* are firmly agreed upon." So the English records report. There are
grounds for some doubt about their faithfulness to the event. For the Indian
records, Spotswood created a quite different impression by handing the
Iroquois two belts of wampum, "one from the Christians and the other
from the Indians of Virginia," and the Iroquois reciprocated with two
belts of their own. The agreement thus presents itself ambiguously. For a
while it worked as a practical control on dangerous traffic. Its semantic
difficulties emerged later.[18]

Iroquois responsibility for the other tribes

On the surface this agreement seemed to contain nothing but restraint
upon the Iroquois. Examined more closely, however, Spotswood's phrase

17. Treaty minutes, Aug. 29, 1722, *N.Y.Col.Docs.* 5:670. My italics.
18. Treaty minutes, Sept. 6, 1722, *N.Y.Col.Docs.* 5:671; Sept. 10, 1722, 5:673. The difference between the two parties' understandings was stated explicitly at the Treaty of Lancaster, June 27–28, 1744. *Pa. Council Minutes* 4:712–13, 717–18.

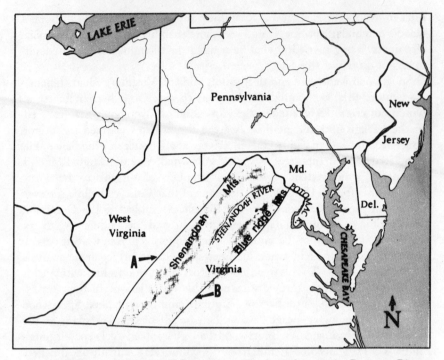

MAP 11. Spotswood's "Line" of Separation. The boundary at the Potomac River was unambiguous, but the location of the line along the mountains was disputed by Virginians and Iroquois. Negotiated in 1722 at Albany, a line was agreed upon, of which the Iroquois would stay west when traveling southward. The treaty phrases were ambiguous. Virginians understood the line to be the one marked *A*. The Iroquois understood it to be *B*.

about the Indians "depending on the Five Nations" raised interesting possibilities for future exploitation. Spotswood plainly intended it to make the Iroquois responsible for tributaries' actions, and the other governors present supported him; but responsibility implies authority, and the colonials' formal recognition of the one quality enhanced the other. The Iroquois willingly accepted both. The treaty made the colonies their partners in hegemony over a set of named tribes.

Confusion about Iroquois relationships with other tribes abounds in the sources as well as the histories. The basic dispute is over assumptions about the Iroquois' power to command obedience from their tributaries—assumptions that project upon them the powers of European imperial metropoles over colonies or conquered provinces. For example, New York's Governor Hunter had aserted in 1712 that "There are above 2,000 Indians to the Southward and westward who are Tributaries of the Said 5 Nations and under their Command."[19] Hunter was inflating his own importance as colonial official directly responsible for relations with the Iroquois. What he wrote was nonsensical bluff, as the Indians in Pennsylvania demonstrated when the Iroquois "commanded" them to send warriors to help invade Canada. The so-called command was disobeyed, and the Iroquois swallowed their pride; in 1712 their power to enforce commands was all but nonexistent.

At Albany in 1722, the Iroquois clarified the issue of their ascendancy over other tribes by listing specifically the tribal groups whom they would agree to keep away from Virginia's Indians. The listed groups—in effect, the total of tributaries under subordination—were the Tuscaroras, the Conestogas, the Shawnees, a split-off group of Iroquois with the jaw-breaking name of Octaghquanawicroones, and a group on the upper Susquehanna called the Ostanghaes.[20] Of these, the last two were negligible in importance; the Tuscaroras had come north by invitation after defeat by South Carolina and were shortly to be adopted as the Sixth Nation of the Iroquois League; the Conestogas were lineal descendants of the Susquehannocks, intermixed with some Iroquois, who had fought the Iroquois to a standstill until defeat by English colonists in 1675 forced them to seek refuge in Iroquoia; and the Shawnees had trooped from the Mississippi Valley to join the Covenant Chain but chose to reside with Minisink and Conestoga tributaries rather than in Iroquoia. Those Shawnees did not take kindly to orders from anybody. Early in 1723, Governor Keith heard that the upper Shawnees on the Susquehanna were making visits to the governor of Canada "whom they think fit to call their Father."[21] It is especially significant that the Delawares were omitted from the Iroquois list of subordinate tributaries.[22] Where were all the groaning hordes of the "savage empire"? Plainly they did not exist.

Nevertheless the precedent had now been set for intercolonial support of Iroquois pretensions to authority over other tribes, and the Five Nations chiefs would gradually exploit its potential thereafter. If the colonials were using the Iroquois for colonial ends, the Iroquois were to show considerable adroitness in using the colonials for Iroquois ends. The Treaty of 1722 must be regarded as a genuine contract by both sides—perhaps a bit slippery in some of its provisions, but what treaties are not? It was voluntarily made and faithfully, if legalistically, observed. It marks an important step in the evolution of the Covenant Chain, which is to say that

19. *Livingston Indian Records*, p. 221
20. Treaty minutes, Sept. 12, 1722, *N.Y.Col.Docs.* 5:675.
21. *Pa. Council Minutes*, May 20, 1723, 3:219.
22. In light of the myth concerning Iroquois "conquest" of the Delawares, it seems necessary to note that the myth's supporters ignore data such as this. Surely the Iroquois themselves knew their "dependent" tribes.

intertribal relations and British colonial policy were both moved by this treaty to new stages in their development.

The treaty, however, was a contract between tribes and colonies rather than between the tribes and the imperial crown that held sovereign authority over the colonies. Its varied implications must be noticed in turn. Setting others aside for a moment, let us look at events in New York. There the Board of Trade's new policy of aggressive westward expansion created special circumstances that the treaty did not take into account.

The unsuppressible Montreal-Albany trade

Up to a point, the Iroquois approved Governor Burnet's implementation of the western strategy. They were willing to see him block the smuggling trade up the Mahican Channel, believing that a revival of their own western-oriented trade would ensue.[23] To that point their interests coincided with those of the expansionists in London. Curiously the French imperialists also approved this much of the English imperialists' policy, because the French ministers believed that Montreal's commerce with Albany had retarded the growth of Canada.[24] Only the stubborn colonial participants in the smuggling trade dissented.

They were able as well as obstinate. They eluded Burnet's controls time after time. Although he obtained a law from New York's assembly in 1720 including provision for the sheriff to break into homes and search without warrant all sorts of private property, the trade continued. Burnet tried a different tactic. He built a blockhouse at the Saratoga portage on the Mahican Channel, only to discover that it became a smuggling center![25] Some traders evaded risk by taking their goods to the Mohawks in a perfectly legitimate commerce. The Mohawks carried the same goods to their Canadian Caughnawaga kinsmen, who took them on to Montreal. At every step this roundabout smuggling was completely out of reach of Burnet's enforcement officers. While the trade continued, it seems to have diminished under Burnet's assault.[26] Burnet tried to stop it at its source. He obtained stronger laws with clauses requiring merchants to swear self-incriminating oaths so rigorous that even the Privy Council found them "grievous and oppressive."[27] This went too far. The smuggling merchants—all pillars of the community—organized deputations and lobbies

23. Norton, *Fur Trade*, pp. 134, 159-60.
24. Instructions to Marquis de Beauharnois, May 7, 1726, *N.Y.Col.Docs.* 9:956-57.
25. Norton, *Fur Trade*, pp. 137-40.
26. Zoltvany, *Vaudreuil*, p. 184. Norton says that "Burnet had failed to achieve a substantial reduction in the number of beaver skins arriving from Montreal." *Fur Trade*, p. 147.
27. Burnet to Lords of Trade, June 2, 1726, *N.Y.Col. Docs.* 5:778; affidavit of John Groesbeck and Dirck Schuyler, Feb. 15, 1725, ibid., 5:743-44; *CSPA&WI, 1728-1729*, no. 1025.

to Parliament, aided by their merchant correspondents in London. Burnet lost control of his Assembly, which deposed Robert Livingston from the Speaker's post in 1725 and replaced him with an ally of the smugglers. Burnet's failures became so costly that he was replaced as governor in 1727, and all his laws aimed at blockading the Canada trade were repealed by the crown in 1729. He had been doing the crown's business, and he was rewarded with another governorship in Massachusetts Bay. But he had demonstrated only too well that even in a royal province under its direct authority the crown had to adjust imperial policies to powerful colonial interests.[28]

Competition in fort building

Iroquois disenchantment with Burnet's administration proceeded on a parallel with the resistance of the smuggling merchants, but for different reasons. Burnet tried not only to destroy the Mahican Channel trade, but to "secure" the Iroquois in alliance to New York; which, translated, meant to make them wholly dependent politically on the province. He launched a campaign to build forts in Iroquois territory. Unfortunately for him, a leisurely, careful, step-by-step procedure was inadequate against French strategic skill. By the time Burnet was installed in office and ready to act, the French were already on the scene at Niagara with a trading post and blockhouse. French control of Great Lakes traffic remained intact.[29]

Burnet still hoped to break through. Within a few months of the French occupation he met with the Iroquois to incite them to destroy the French buildings and to accept an English fort instead. The Iroquois were reluctant.[30] A French blockhouse was in their minds substantially different from an English fort. The blockhouse simply secured trade against occasional raids. A fort, however, would secure its garrison against the tribe in whose territory it stood. The distinction was very clear, though writers have often used the term *fort* indiscriminately and projected their own lack of clarity upon the Indians to enhance the irrationality of savages.

Burnet turned to a form of bribery. After a multilateral treaty at Albany in 1722, when nothing was said about forts, he organized a "Company of young men" under command of Major Abraham Schuyler "to Settle in the Sinnekes Country for a twelve month to Trade with the farr Indians

28. Norton, *Fur Trade*, p. 147. Burnet's party collapsed and an overturn in New York's politics resulted in which the traders with Canada rose to power. Leder, *Robert Livingston*, ch. 17; Katz, *Newcastle's New York*, pp. 166–68, 171–73.

29. Zoltvany, *Vaudreuil*, pp. 168–69.

30. Various docs., April–Nov. 1720, *N.Y.Col.Docs.* 5:536–37, 552, 559–61, 572–73, 576–80. Norton, *Fur Trade*, pp. 161–62.

that are come from the upper Lakes, and endeavour by all Suitable means to perswade them to come and trade at Albany or with this new Setlement." His bribe to the Senecas appears in his further instruction to Schuyler: "You are not to trade with the four hithermost [Iroquois] Nations (except for Provisions in your passage to and fro) but to carry your goods as far as the Sinnekes Country, and to trade with them or any other Indian nations that come thither."[31] The Senecas apparently were amenable to the sort of intrusion that could only enhance their own trade, but Burnet could not budge the French.

Everything Burnet attempted with the Iroquois was instantly countered by the French. His trading missions into the Seneca country provoked the French agent Louis-Thomas Chabert de Joncaire to persuade the Senecas to permit enlargement of the French defenses at Niagara. They let him build a wooden stockade sufficient for a garrison of three hundred men.[32] But then the Senecas permitted Burnet to build a fort at Oswego at the mouth of the Onondaga River on the southwest shore of Lake Ontario. The Senecas were determined that if they could not keep all colonies out, they at least would not let either one acquire a monopoly. Neutrality no longer meant only standing between the powers; it now took the form of preserving them in balance. But the Senecas were deeply disturbed because this redefinition had not come about through their own initiative. It was forced on them.[33]

Vaudreuil and Burnet agreed on Oswego's strategic value. Burnet thought that canoe-borne trade coming to Oswego could bypass French controls. Vaudreuil feared it would become a base for attacks on Niagara. Vaudreuil instantly decided to strengthen Niagara. Soon the French convinced the Senecas to allow replacement of their wooden palisade by stone. They then built a genuine fort capable of withstanding any Indian assault lacking European artillery and tactics. When the true size of this monster emerged, it alarmed the Iroquois greatly, and their reaction gives a clue to French methods of persuasion. By the time the Iroquois understood how they had been hoodwinked, the building had progressed beyond their power to stop it.[34] Never before had they felt so boxed in. Despite the political and moral authority they had so painstakingly acquired over other tribes, they had ceased to be masters in their own homeland. In revulsion they organized for their first and only attempt at interracial war.

31. Burnet to Lt. H. Vedder and Instructions for Major Schuyler, both Sept. 8, 1722, *Livingston Indian Records*, pp. 232–35.
    32. Yves F. Zoltvany, "Chabert de Joncaire, Louis-Thomas," in *Dict. Can.Biog.* 2:126.
    33. Norton, *Fur Trade*, pp. 163–64; Zoltvany, *Vaudreuil*, p. 199; Decision of the Minister, Oct. 1, 1728, *N.Y.Col.Docs.* 9:1011.
    34. De Longueuil and Begon to Ministry, Oct. 31, 1725, *N.Y.Col.Docs.* 9:952–53; private conference of Burnet with Iroquois sachems, Sept. 7, 1726, ibid., 5:786–89.

Delawares and Shawnees reject Iroquois proposals for war

In 1726 the Iroquois conferred secretly with the Indians of Pennsylvania—their allies in the Covenant Chain. As Shawnee chief Newcheconner disclosed (years later) "the five nations Came and Said, our Land is goeing to be taken from us. Come, brothers, assisstt us. Lett us fall upon and fightt with the English." (Interestingly, the Shawnees were "brothers" then, even though the Treaty of 1722 had put them under Iroquois direction.)[35]

It must not be thought that the Six Nations wished to leave the French unscathed. While the intrigue against the English was in progress, the Senecas issued an "order"—which was ignored—to all the Canadian tribes as far west as Lake Superior to attack simultaneously in all the posts against the French.[36] Had Iroquois desires been carried out, the northern tribes would have fought the French while the Shawnees, Delawares, and other Covenant Chain Indians fought the English.

The war proposal continued to circulate for several years among the Minisink Indians and the Ohio Valley tribes, but the Shawnees and Delawares rejected it. The rejection is worth careful notice. Its first significance is that Iroquois hegemony over tributary tribes was not absolute rule—not even in the case of the Shawnees. The tributaries were not so fearful of their patrons as to permit themselves to be forced into war against colonials, and the Iroquois were not so blindly ferocious as to attempt war against colonials by themselves, or to attack the tributaries.

"Women" and the west

The rejection's second significance arises out of its consequences in an alternative Iroquois policy. Newcheconner (in 1732) explained it in explicit detail. He placed the change "about a year after" the tributaries' refusal to do battle—i.e., in 1727. As he remembered, "the Five Nations told the Delawares and us [Shawnees], 'Since you have not hearkened to us nor regarded what we have said, *now* we will put petticoats on you, and look upon you as women for the future, and not as men. Therefore, you Shawnese, look back toward Ohio, the place from whence you came; and

35. Shawnee chiefs to Gov. Gordon, 1732. *Pa. Archives*, 1st ser., 1:329. This enormously important revelation is enhanced by the expertise of its witnesses. It was recorded by Edmond Cartlidge in the presence of James Le Tort and Peter Chartier.

36. Speeches at an Indian Council, 1732, in *Wilderness Chronicles of Northwestern Pennsylvania*, eds. Sylvester K. Stevens and Donald H. Kent (Harrisburg: Pa. Historical Commission, 1941), pp. 6–7.

return thitherward; for now we shall take pity on the English, and let them have all this land.'

And further said, 'Now, since you are become women, I'll take Peachohquelloman [at the Delaware Water Gap] and put it on Meheahoming [Wyoming Valley on the North branch of the Susquehanna]; and I'll take Meheahoming and put it on Ohioh [Allegheny River]; and Ohioh I'll put on Woabach [Wabash River]; and that shall be the warriors' road for the future.' "[37]

Much information is compacted in this terse statement. It reveals an Iroquois decision to divert their main thrust of military strategy from the south to the west. Their warriors' road had formerly run down the Susquehanna and over to the valleys along the Appalachian Mountains, from which valleys they could raid Cherokees, Choctaws, Creeks, Catawbas, and other southern tribes. The new locations of Shawnee villages were to provide for rest and refreshment of Iroquois parties marching westward. These valleys lay on an east-west line extending from the Susquehanna's North branch to the Wabash River; to maintain the line, the Iroquous established another village in 1728 at the forks of the North and West branches of the Susquehanna, where warriors coming down from Iroquoia by canoe would turn west. In this village of Shamokin Pennsylvania [Sunbury, Pennsylvania] they ensconced their famous deputy, the Oneida Chief Shikellamy.

Notably in all this rearranging, no orders to the Delawares appear on record. Perhaps this was because of the Delawares' strength and prestige being greater than the Shawnees'. Perhaps orders may not have been necessary. Keith and Logan, between them, had already unseated and dispersed many Delawares. Brandywines and Tulpehockens were mostly gone from their homelands by the time the Iroquois pushed the Shawnees around in 1727. Some of the Delawares seem to have moved in close to the Conestogas; others settled at Shamokin; still others, apparently most, moved west to a village called Kittanning, on the Allegheny River. Kittanning also lay along the new Warriors' Road of the Iroquois, and it probably figured in their strategic calculations. Despite all these considerations, however, there is no record or tradition of Delawares truckling to Iroquois commands at this time, although Chief Sassoonan placidly remarked in 1728 that "the five Nations have often told them that they were as Women only." On this occasion in 1728, Sassoonan quietly defied the Iroquois in public. Although the Iroquois had "desired" the Delawares "to plant Corn and mind their own private Business, for that they [the Iroquois] would take Care of what related to Peace and War,"[38] Sassoonan ignored them

37. See n. 35. I have italicized *now* to point up that the women status of Shawnees and Delawares was intermittent.

38. *Pa. Council Minutes*, Oct. 10, 1728. Sassoonan made the interesting remark, in the presence of Shikellamy, that only a few "Delaware and Brandywine Indians, and none of

and went on to treat with Pennsylvania. Indeed the Delawares themselves evicted a village of Shawnee "guests." As reported by the displaced persons, "The Delaware Indians Some time agoe bid us Departt for they was Dry and wanted to Drink the land away whereupon wee told them Since Some of you are Gone to ohioh wee will go there also. Wee hope you will nott Drink thatt away too."[39]

The new western strategy of the Iroquois implied strategic withdrawal from the lower Susquehanna. Iroquois regional headquarters were moved upstream from Conestoga to Shamokin. Newcheconner's report of the Six Nations' decision to let the English "have all this land" was confirmed by a Six Nations delegation to James Logan in the following year: 1727.

General Indian unrest

Logan had by this time got rid of troublesome Keith and was back in the saddle. One might mangle the metaphor by saying he was feeling his oats. His reception of the Iroquois offer to sell the Susquehanna was anything but receptive. He told the delegation that Pennsylvania had bought the valley previously and would not buy again. Much earlier, the Iroquois had deeded the Susquehanna to Thomas Dongan, and William Penn had bought Dongan's deed. Had not Sir William Keith confirmed the purchase at Albany in 1722?

Only then did Logan find out how Keith had fooled even him. The Iroquois sachems informed him that Keith's Albany purchase involved only five hundred acres for Keith's personal estate, and "nothing further was intended." Logan "turn'd it off and endeavoured to stagger them" by playing on the Dongan purchase, but he was stimulated to look further into the matter and soon reported to the Penns that their title was not so clear as he had thought.[40]

the Shawanese" were with him, the rest being off hunting, but that "nevertheless, he now speaks in the Name and Behalf of them all." This was very bold, considering that "Shickellamy of the five Nations" had been "appointed to reside among the Shawanese." He made no recorded protest against Sassoonan's assumption of authority, but a comment in the minutes suggests that he did some talking off the record. The minutes note that his services "had been and may yet further be of great advantage to this Government." *Pa. Council Minutes,* Oct. 11, 1728, 3:337. Cf. Gov. Gordon's statement that the Shawnees (without mention of any other tribe) were "under the Protection of the five Nations, who have sett Shakallamy over them." Gordon to H. Smith and J. Petty, Sept. 1, 1728, mss. Nead Papers, HSP.

39. *Pa. Archives,* 2st ser., 1:330.

40. *Pa. Council Minutes,* July 3–5, 1727, 3:271–76; Logan to Honoured Friend, July 10, 1727, mss., Penn Mss., Off. Corr. 1:283; Logan to J. T. and R. Penn, Nov. 16, 1729, mss. Logan Ltr. Bks. 3:312, HSP. This episode raises once again the ghost of the supposed Iroquois "conquest" of the Susquehannocks. Most of the claimant chiefs were Cayugas. As has been shown, there was no conquest, but perhaps the Cayugas claimed by virtue of having given refuge to the Susquehannocks, although Dongan had taught them the uses of conquest rhetoric.

I do not well understand how the Iroquois claimed property rights after the Susquehannocks sold to Penn in 1701 without objection. Perhaps it was a matter of distinctions between nations. Ahookasoongh, who signed the 1701 treaty, was an Onondaga. In 1727 the main Iroquois claimants were Cayugas and Oneidas.

The chiefs' visit to Logan was not harmonious in any respect. They were willing to sell off the lower Susquehanna, but their offer applied only to that area. Colonial settlements were to be forbidden above Paxtang (Harrisburg). Disputation over land rights was not the only discordant note struck by the Iroquois; they raised once more the perennial issues of the trade. The traders cheated and charted too much—they were Logan's traders—and there was too much rum being brought into the villages. The rum was expensive—a somewhat contradictory grievance—and if it continued to flow where warriors marched, there might be trouble. Logan rejected every proposal. He denied their land claims. His expensive rum continued to flow. Patrick Gordon, Pennsylvania's new governor, who was under Logan's thumb in all matters Indian, declined to limit settlements. The Iroquois departed with unimproved dispositions.

Logan's high tone at this meeting was not typical of his usual approach to the Iroquois, and he soon regretted his lapse from prudence. Mysterious troubles began to plague the backwoods. In the spring of 1728, James Le Tort, who was trading on the upper Susquehanna, picked up the news that a black war belt of wampum had circulated among the Minisinks— always reputed to be more warlike than their neighbors—and that the belt had gone the rounds of the Six Nations and the Twightwees (Miamis) of the Ohio region. The disquiet caused by this news was enhanced by Logan's awareness that Minisink Chief Manawkyhickon held a grudge against the English because New Jersey had executed a kinsman of his for murder of a colonial. Pennsylvania's Provincial Council observed uneasily that Indian affairs had been neglected lately and that the Indians "now generally thought themselves slighted." Council ordered a new round of treaties.[41]

Tension increased when some colonials wantonly murdered a family of unoffending Indians. The government took extraordinary measures to assuage the resentment caused by the killing. Governor Gordon denounced the "most barbarous Murther," and commanded Pennsylvanians to treat the Indians "with the same civil Regard" as "an *English* subject." Presents of condolence were quickly given to the victims' kin. Astonishingly, the killers were also seized and tried and (not being traders) they were hanged.[42]

41. *Pa. Council Minutes*, April 18, 1728, 3:295–98; Logan to Sassoonan, Manawkyhickon, and Mme. Montour, *Pa. Archives*, 1st ser., 1:210–11.
42. *Pa. Council Minutes*, May 6, 10, 15, 20, June 4, Aug. 6, 1728, 3:302–9, 318, 345; various docs., *Pa. Archives*, 1st ser., 1:215–21; proclamation, May 16, 1728, mss., Penn

Logan's treaties

Logan worried. More than Indian resentment was involved in the general disquiet. Although Logan was back in power in the executive branch of government, his enemies in the legislature could not be disregarded. There was a general current of restlessness among the colonial public in regard to Indian affairs. Logan's abuse of the Brandywine Delawares had been well exposed while Keith held office, and Logan himself had been loud in denouncing Keith's mismanagement of the Tulpehockens. Each had been anxious to blacken the other, and both had succeeded. Logan and his friends needed the new 1728 round of treaties to consolidate their political position as well as to manage the Indians. Logan took good care to arrange the treaties to thwart the opposition forming around the issue of Indian discontent.

The first of the new treaty conferences took place at Conestoga in May 1728. The minutes report that all was love and friendship. "Some of the Gentlemen present moved the Governor, that seeing there was now a numerous Company of our Inhabitants mett together, he would be pleased to press the Indians to declare to him if they suffered any Grievance or Hardship from this Government, because several Reports had been industriously spread abroad as if they had some just Cause of Complaint. . . . They all answered that they had no Cause of Complaint, that William Penn and his People had still treated them well, and they had no Uneasiness." Our source for this is Logan, who wrote the minutes.[43]

Less than two weeks later, Chief Sassoonan, of the Tulpehocken Delawares, came to Philadelphia for his treaty. Most of Sassoonan's people had gone off to the Ohio country. He lived at Shamokin as a guest of the Iroquois, and he was putty in Logan's hands. Before a crowd of a thousand Philadelphians—huge for that day and place—Logan and Sassoonan staged an act. Sassoonan starred, but Logan directed.

Upon urging, Sassoonan complained that the Christians "had Settled on his Lands, for which he had never received any thing." Logan radiated magnanimity. He apologized to Sassoonan for the misdeed while immediately extricating himself from responsibility. The Palatines had settled at Sassoonan's Tulpehocken without Logan's knowledge. He fiercely denounced Sir William Keith for culpability. He promised the Indians that if they would be patient and refrain from violence, he would guar-

Letters and Ancient Documents 3:23, American Philosophical Society. For tensions see also Samuel Whitaker Pennybacker, "Bebber's Township and the Dutch Patroons of Pennsylvania," *Pa. Mag. of Hist. and Biog.* 31 (1907), pp. 1–18.

43. *Pa. Council Minutes*, May 26–27, 1728, 3:309–14. The spokesman for all the tribes present—Conestogas, Brandywines, Conoys, Shawnees—was Conestoga Chief Tawenna. No Iroquois was recorded present.

antee satisfaction of their complaint. Logan was ever a virtuoso at turning attacks upon himself back upon the assailants.[44]

Shawnee flight

There were still the Shawnees to mollify. The most unreliable of the colony's clients, they seemed to need the most attention. Earlier in 1728 they had killed two Conestogas in a dispute that nearly flared into warfare. They handled a trader so roughly that he was rumored dead (falsely). And a whole village of Shawnees suddenly vanished! In September, two traders reported that the Shawnees at Pechoquealin on the upper Delaware had been collecting skins to make up a treaty present to the governor when suddenly "an Indian came from Sasquehannah with some Message, upon receiving which they with the Wives and Children, went off from Pechoquealin, leaving their Corn standing."

Pennsylvanians guessed that Pechoquealin's disappearance was connected somehow with the Iroquois delegation at Conestoga. It appeared to them as another example of the "absolute Authority" of the Iroquois, which was believed to extend to all of Pennsylvania's Indians.[45] With hindsight we know that Iroquois authority over the Shawnees was strong but not absolute. Pechoquealin's disappearance was the consequence of Shawnee refusal to war upon Pennsylvanians at Iroquois behest. It is at the same time a sign of how far Iroquois authority carried and where it stopped. (Peter Chartier's Shawnee band remained on the Susquehanna.)

Oneida Chief Shikellamy, the Six Nations deputy at Shamokin, attended Sassoonan's treaty with Logan in 1728. Shikellamy stated his function to be supervision over the Shawnees. He did not claim responsibility for the Delawares. When Sassoonan stated Delaware ownership of Tulpechocken Valley, Shikellamy remained silent; he did not present a counter claim to the valley as the Iroquois had not hesitated to do for the Susquehanna. In view of issues to be discussed further on, we must note that Shikellamy maintained hands off during the four-year period that finally produced compensation to Sassoonan for the Tulpehocken lands, and the Iroquois did not share in that compensation. Although Sassoonan was, by this time,

44. The treaty: *Pa. Council Minutes* 3:316–26; the crowd: Logan to John Page, April 17, 1731, mss., Logan Letter Books 4:245, HSP.

45. Sadowsky to Petty, Aug. 27, 1728, and Petty and Smith to Gov. Gordon, Sept. 3, 1728, *Pa. Archives*, 1st ser., 1:227, 232; *Pa. Council Minutes*, Sept. 1, 1728, 3:329–31. A number of instances scattered through the council minutes endow the Iroquois with absolute authority. I have not determined whether these were retrospective insertions by Logan to justify policies adopted in later years. Certainly the statement was untrue and sometimes downright silly. Logan once spoke in the same breath of Iroquois absolute authority over the Shawnees and Shawnee absolute defiance of it. *Pa. Council Minutes*, Aug. 4, 1731, 3:402–3.

living at Shamokin in Iroquois territory, it seems plain that his formal independence was respected. Even at the nadir of Delaware political organization, which did not come until 1742, a most knowledgeable and pro-Mohawk contemporary cautioned that the Delawares were tributary only "in an Indian sense" to the Iroquois.[46]

The Shawnees were more dependent but could be pushed only so far. As it happened, the Iroquois had blundered by sending them so brusquely westward. Distance did not make the Shawnee heart grow fonder. Squeezed between Iroquoia and Philadelphia, the bands took orders, but out in the distant west they acquired "frontier liberty." To the delight of the French, a delegation of four Shawnees arrived in Montreal in the summer of 1729 to complain of their treatment by Englishmen and Iroquois and to ask for French protection. Governor Beauharnois welcomed them and told them to negotiate with other French-allied Indians for an acceptable location "within the sound of their Father's voice." They conferred with hospitable Hurons and Ottawas. Some two hundred Shawnee families then settled on French Creek near Lake Erie, where they accepted a resident French supervisor and promised to plunder any English traders who might come after them. Some questions may be raised about the pledge because English traders do seem to have gotten to them, but of their loss to the English and the Covenant Chain there can be no doubt.[47]

Iroquois losses

One might think that such a severe blow to the strength of the Six Nations would have taught them to refrain from arbitrary and abusive policies toward their tributaries, but an illusion of power beckoned them to future repetition of the error, which, in the long run, would tear the Covenant Chain apart. In 1729, however, problems of the immediate present engaged Iroquois attention. Their far western allies, the Foxes, were attacked by large forces of Indians with French encouragement; and in a futile effort to flee to Iroquoia in 1730, the Foxes were caught and massacred.[48] Iroquois grand strategy in the west collapsed. Worse, in 1731 the French drove another salient directly toward Iroquois country by building a palisaded fort at Crown Point, on the southern narrows of Lake Champlain. In due course it would be transformed, like Niagara, into the com-

46. Conrad Weiser, "An Account of . . . the Six Nations,' *The American Magazine* (Boston: Dec., 1744), p. 666.

47. Examination of Edmond Cartlidge, Dec. 7, 1731, *Pa. Archives*, 1st Ser., 1:305; abstract of dispatches, Oct. 25, 1729, *N.Y.Col.Docs.* 9:1016; Beauharnois to Maurepas, Oct. 1, 1731, ibid., 9:1027; Louis XVI to Beauharnois and Hocquart, April 22, 1732, ibid., 9:1033; Beaharnois to Maurepas, Oct. 15, 1732, ibid., 9:1035.

48. Edmunds, *Potawatomis*, pp. 35–37.

manding stone structure of Fort St. Frederic.[49]

The English, too, were busy, though some of their proceedings were more devious. While the French built St. Frederic, the government of Albany obtained a deed from the Mohawks for a thousand acres of prime meadowland called Mohawk Flats. Supposedly the land was to be held by Albany in trust to prevent encroachment by individual colonials; but Albany reneged on its promise to provide the Mohawks with a copy of the deed and claimed to have acquired the land by an absolute quitclaim.[50] East, north, and west, the Iroquois were being battered. In their distress, many of their young men drifted off to the Ohio country, where they became known as Mingos and adopted an attitude of worrisome independence from the chiefs of the Grand Council.[51] Only toward the south, in Pennsylvania, did there seem to be any hope of maintaining a position of strength. Iroquois opportunity was created by James Logan's need for help to extricate him from his entanglements.

49. Lanctot, *History of Canda* 3:35.

50. Georgiana C. Nammack, *Fraud, Politics, and the Dispossession of the Indians: The Iroquois Land Frontier in the Colonial Period* (Norman: University of Oklahoma Press, 1969), p. 23; Gov. Wm. Cosby to Lords of Trade, Dec. 15, 1733, *N.Y.Col.Docs.* 5:960–62.

51. The name *Mingo* had been used previously for the Conestogas, apparently as a corruption of the earlier *Minquas*. In this light the question arises as to how many of the resettled "Ohio" Indians had formerly lived on the Susquehanna. Though the Conestoga tribe became extinct by a massacre in 1764, the possibility seems strong that some of its members survived in the west under the Mingo alias.

Chapter 16 ❧ A NEW FIRE

Now, since I am here with you my Self, I do assure you that the Friendship and strict Union which my Father began with all our Friends, the Indians, and his Governors after him have cultivated, I shall take Care to improve and strengthen. My Father made a Chain and Covenants for himself and his Children, and I, his Son, will to the best of my Power make that Chain yet stronger and brighter on our Parts that it may continue so to all Generations. As a Proof of this, we would now enter into a close Discourse with you on Affairs that nearly concern your own Peace and Safety; for as true Brothers that are as one Body, and have the same Interest, we lay to our harts whatever may affect and touch you.

Thomas Penn to the Iroquois, 23 August 1732

Logan's straits

In 1727 James Logan acquired a tract of land at Durham Creek, where it joins the Delaware River, and started an iron mine. What concerns us here about this transaction is only its relation to Indian affairs. The tract in question was located beyond the furthermost boundaries of Indian cessions to Pennsylvania. To say this another way, it was in Indian territory.[1] Logan had pacified the possessor, Delaware Chief Nutimus, by paying personally for the land, but such payment could not validate his ownership under Pennsylvania law because Indian purchases could be made legally only by a Penn or a duly authorized representative.[2] To be sure, Logan was authorized to make an official purchase as the Penns' agent, but the Indians in question would not deal with him in that capacity. They wanted a Penn. They remembered fondly the fairness of William Penn, and they assumed that his sons would have as much integrity as the father. They therefore insisted that they would not cede any more territory to any person, except one of William Penn's sons. Indian assumptions of virtue descending in "good" families would be sadly disproved by Penn's offspring, but this was yet to be demonstrated. Logan had to pro-

---

1. Logan to J. Penn [Jan., 1726], mss., Logan Letter Books 2:292; deed, May 15, 1727, mss., Penn Mss., Deed Box, 1702–1759, HSP; indenture describing organization of Durham company, mss., Philadelphia Deed Book G-3:240–50 (Microfilm Reel 17), Records Dept., Phila. City Hall.

2. *Statutes at Large of Pennsylvania, 1682–1809* (Harrisburg: State Printer, 1896–1915), vol. 4, ch. 312, pp. 154–56.

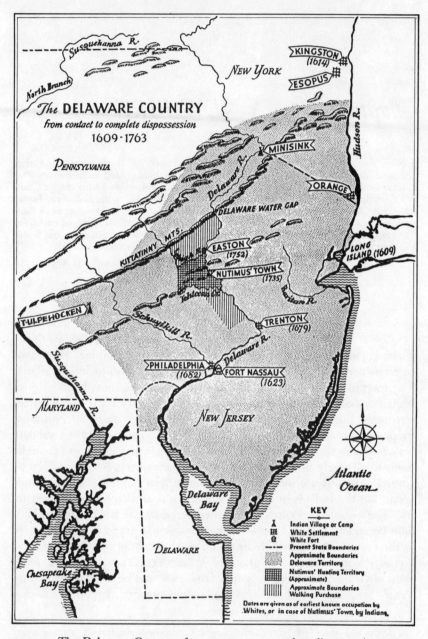

MAP 12. The Delaware Country, from contact to complete dispossession, 1609–1763. REPRODUCED FROM ANTHONY F.C. WALLACE, KING OF THE DELAWARES: TEEDYUSCUNG (1949), BY COURTESY OF THE UNIVERSITY OF PENNSYLVANIA PRESS.

duce a Penn to negotiate cession of the territory that included his iron-works·tract in order to lift the Indian "incumbency" and get clear title to his property. The land in question lay north of Tohickon Creek, and for convenience's sake I shall call the Indians involved the Tohickons, though several communities were participants in the events to be described.[3]

To the westward, Logan had attempted to overawe old Chief Sassoonan into acquiescence in the loss of Tulpehocken Valley, but the usually tract-able old man drew the line, literally, at the South Mountain on the valley's southern rim.[4] Logan tried to undercut Sassoonan politically by cultivat-ing his heir apparent, whereupon Sassoonan, "in his liquor," stabbed the young man to death.[5] According to contemporary Indian belief, drunken men were not responsible for crimes because they had been driven out of their minds by alcohol.[6] In this case, I wonder. Sassoonan seems to have known very well what he was doing. The man he killed was Logan's pro-tégé. The effect of the murder was to eliminate a threat to Sassoonan's authority.

Another effect was to elevate Pisquetomen, an "ill fellow" according to Logan, as Sassoonan's successor-to-be.[7] Pisquetomen was not someone whom Sassoonan needed to worry about. On the contrary, it is apparent that his ill character consisted of disagreement with Logan; there would be no plotting between them. In the conference at which Sassoonan intro-duced Pisquetomen to Logan, the issue of Tulpehocken lands was raised. Logan had conceded in 1728 that the Delawares had been illegally dispos-sessed so that there was no issue of legality to be debated in 1731. The only issue was the compensation to be paid the Indians by Pennsylvania. Governor Gordon, who spoke Logan's words, tried to beat down the Indi-ans' asking price by disparaging the lands' value. "Your Lands . . . were worth nothing to you before W. Penn and his People came. The English make it of Value by using it.[8] Apart from its blind ethnocentrism, this was not really the sort of comment to rouse wild admiration in a man whose native country has been seized from him. Pisquetomen interpreted for Sassoonan and seems to have added his own words of unrecorded comment. By the end of the formal proceedings, Logan knew that Pisque-tomen was his enemy. He quickly arranged for a different interpreter and

3. Logan to [J. Penn], Dec. 6, 1727, mss., Logan Papers, Corr. of James Logan 1:89; Logan to J., T., and R. Penn, July 29, 1728, mss., Logan Papers 10:45, HSP.
4. *Pa. Council Minutes*, June 5, 1728, 3:320–22.
5. Logan to J. Penn, Aug. 2, 1731, mss., Penn Mss., Off. Corr. 2:181, HSP.
6. Jacques Bruyas, April 4, 1670, *Jesuit Relations* 53:257.
7. Logan to J., T., and R. Penn, Aug. 26, 1731, mss., Penn Mss., Off. Corr. 2:191, HSP.
8. Treaty minutes, Aug. 17 and 18, 1731, mss., James Steel's Letter Book 2 (1730–1741), pp. 274–76, HSP. These minutes were discreetly omitted from the official records kept by Logan. Steel was his right-hand man in the Receiver's office. The formal draft of the earlier sessions has a superscription in Logan's writing: "This is copied from J L's rough draught uncorrected." I infer that Logan edited Steel's text. Penn Mss., Indian Affairs 1:35, HSP.

a private session with Sassoonan. As he told the Penns, "I concerted measures with Sassoonan, when return'd to my house, to have that fellow laid aside and a better Substituted in his place which, 'tis hoped, may take effect."[9] It did seem to, at the time, but Pisquetomen's submergence was more appaarent than real. More "measures" would be required throughout the rest of Logan's life.

In 1731, Pisquetomen was still a comparatively unimportant side issue. Logan was in deep hot water with the Penns, who had learned of his embezzlements of their property and had taken measures of their own to strip him of the power to continue on his course. They authorized one of his many enemies to survey and possess land in Tulpehocken that Logan had already "sold" to Palatine immigrants.[10] This arrangement, like Logan's ironworks at Durham, involved land in unceded, though occupied, Indian territory. The Iroquois claim still lay upon the Susquehanna Valley; Marylanders were settling northward up the valley in defiance of Pennsylvania's claims to jurisdiction; the Tohickon Delawares would not validate Logan's possession of his ironworks until a Penn journeyed from England to treat with them; and the Tulpehocken Delawares resisted the kind of manipulation that would enable Logan to legitimize his tangled dealings with the Palatines. Logan needed a deus ex machina to unsnarl his entanglements.

Reduction of the Tulpehockens

The gods obliged. From the heavens their car descended, and out stepped Shikellamy. He came to Philadelphia with Sassoonan and Pisquetomen for their fateful conferences with Logan in August, 1731, and Logan used the occasion to chat privately with Shikellamy about "another affair of vast importance." We have only Logan's guarded account of the meeting's outcome, which was a journey by Shikellamy to the Six Nations council at Onondaga "to invite some of their Chiefs to hasten down to treat with us." The intended subject of the treaty was "to putt them, if possible, on measures to Strengthen both themselves and us."[11] What Logan said to Shikellamy and what Shikellamy reported to Onondaga are not on record, but the Iroquois did respond with a substantial delegation in 1732. Before that, when Shikellamy reported back to Philadelphia in early December,

9. Logan to Edward Shippen, Aug. 18, 1731, mss., Logan Papers 2:8; Logan to J., T., and R. Penn, Aug. 26, 1731, mss., Penn Mss., Off. Corr. 2:191. Both HSP.
10. The situation is detailed in Jennings, "Incident at Tulpehocken."
11. Logan to J., T., and R. Penn, Aug. 26, 1731, mss., Penn Mss., Off. Corr. 2:191, HSP. This letter is revealing in several respects. Shikellamy's "absolute authority" is reduced in it to "a watch over" the tributaries, which is much closer to reality than the propaganda rhetoric. And Logan's concern with the vastly important affair is "to manage" it.

1731, he was not alone. With him came one of the Palatines settled at Tulpehocken—a man named Conrad Weiser, who had lived with the Mohawks for sixteen years and had been adopted into their tribe. Though Weiser would gradually become a henchman of Thomas Penn, Paul A. W. Wallace has observed that he entered Pennsylvania's Indian affairs in the service of the Six Nations. Logan, Shikellamy, and Weiser made themselves into a tight little steering committee for the management of Pennsylvania's relations with Indians—all Indians—and the Six Nations chiefs approved.[12]

It happened just in time to save Logan's hide. A deeply suspicious Thomas Penn arrived in Philadelphia in 1732, armed with powers to act in his brothers' behalf. After some quiet inquiry into the management of public proprietary affairs, he stripped Logan of all executive power and reorganized the provincial government with Penn's own men in key positions. There was no public quarrel or outcry; no one could afford to let all the dirty laundry come to view. Logan was permitted to keep his showy sinecure as Chief Justice, with its tidy income, and he remained a member of Penn's council. More pertinent to present concerns, he was consulted as the Penns' chief adviser in Indian affairs. Although they no longer trusted him to act as their deputy, his intimate understanding of all the colony's business was still valuable.[13]

Shortly after Thomas Penn's arrival in Philadelphia, he and Logan met with Sassoonan, Pisquetomen, and other Tulpehocken Delawares to arrange compensation for their tribal lands. (Pisquetomen's name receded to fourth place among Indian signatures to the deed.) Payment was arranged in installments. Soon afterward, a formal delegation from the Six Nations appeared in Philadelphia to lay the groundwork for Logan's proposed new alliance, and the result was so satisfactory to him that he assumed a new manner toward the Delawares when they returned in 1733 to collect the last installment of their pay. As Logan reported to Penn, Sassoonan complained of inferior quality in the goods previously given. "He Sayes we have got all his Land, that it is good Land, and he ought to have good

12. P. Wallace, *Weiser*, pp. 46, 49.
13. Jennings, "Incident at Tulpehocken," pp. 353–54; power of attorney, May 8, 1732, mss., Pa. Patent Book A–6:170–72; Robert Charles's commission as secretary of the province: ibid., pp. 167–68; commission for John Georges as secretary of the Land Office: Pa. Commission Book A–1:1–2, mss.; replacement of Logan's henchman John Taylor by Benjamin Eastburn as Surveyor General, ibid., p. 4. Logan's close associate James Steel was recommissioned Receiver General, Dec. 16, 1732, which suggests that he had turned informer; he had earlier had differences with Logan: Pa. Patent Book, mss., A–6:166; Logan to J. Penn, Nov. 17, 1729, mss., Penn Mss., Off. Corr. 2:99, HSP. Above refs. in Dept. Internal Affairs, Harrisburg, except HSP as noted. See also J. Penn to Logan, Feb. 15, 1731, mss., Penn Letter Books 1:24; Logan to Proprietaries, April 17, 1731, mss., Logan Letter Books 3:336–40; J., T., and R. Penn to Logan, Aug. 23, 1731, mss., Penn Letter Books 1:34–37, 40; Logan to Thomas Penn, Oct. 9, 1731, mss., Logan Letter Books 3:345–46, all HSP.

Gods for it. [It is, in fact, still very good farm land.] He has no more to Sell, and when these Goods are gone . . . he shall have nothing. . . . They have no Interpreter but Pesqueetoman whom we too well know; yet he seems well enough inclined to interpret faithfully, the contrary of which is a very great crime with them."

Logan overbore them harshly. Sassoonan had expected "to receive in the whole £700. . . . I took the most proper means I could to give him a righter notion of the bargain." The magnanimous public Logan of 1728 was a different man from the private Logan of 1732. Sassoonan departed with the realization "that having parted with all his Land, and also with all the Pay for it, tho he holds the same rank with his people, he is slighted and disregarded when there is no further advantage to be made of him."[14] The description is Logan's; it cannot be said that his policies were the product of misunderstanding.

From then on, Sassoonan lived at Shamokin under the constant over-sight of Shikellamy, and thus of Logan. Every year or so he paid a cour-tesy call on Logan, received some handouts, and went back to Shamokin to live in increasing drunkennesss, the solace of which he purchased with the tribal wampum in his care. Pisquetomen resided at Shamokin too, but the younger man lived a more sober and active existence. The eastern Delawares stayed quiescent because the loss of their land made them increasingly dependent on the Six Nations whose guests they had become, and the new partnership of Pennsylvania and the Six Nations whittled away steadily at Delaware self-government.[15]

New proposals to the Iroquois

The Iroquois delegation to Philadelphia in 1732 consisted of chiefs from the Seneca, Cayuga, and Oneida nations, who had come, somewhat war-ily, to explore issues rather than commit to a formal alliance. One matter that gravely concerned the Pennsylvanians could not be treated with full candor by the Iroquois. They could not easily blurt out that Shawnee bands had fled west because of their own domineering blunder.[16] Logan's traders had pursued the Shawnees to the Ohio region and found that the refugees had "put up a french flag or Colours in their town, as if they

14. Logan to T. Penn, Aug. 16, 1733. Insignificantly discrepant versions are printed in *Pa. Archives*, 2d ser., 7:145 and *Manuscripts from Goodspeed's Catalogue 510*, p. 60. (My request to Goodspeed's to see the mss. was not answered.) Logan to T. Penn, July 7, 1734, *Pa. Archives*, 2d ser., 7:168–69. The goods promised Sassoonan are listed in Exhibit n, HSP transcripts, Bd. of Trade Papers, Proprieties, mss., 21–I, pp. 251–56.

15. See Francis Jennings, "The Delaware Interregnum," *Pa. Mag. of Hist. and Biog*, 89:2 (April, 1965), pp. 179–82; Weiser to Peters, July 20, 1747, *Pa. Arch.*, 1st ser., 7:145.

16. See ch. 15 above.

would say, they are in league with the french and all one as french men."[17]
By 1730 these distant Shawnees owed Logan's men the staggering amount
of £2,000, if the traders' accounts are to be believed.[18] There is no good
reason to put much faith in traders' unaudited accounts, but it seems likely
that some amount was due them. The skins that should have been used to
pay off this debt were, in effect, being hijacked by unlicensed johnny-
come-lately traders who could not be controlled at that distance. Nor could
the Shawnees, nor certainly the French. For both political and financial
reasons, Pennsylvanians wanted "their" Shawnees back in the colony.
Thomas Penn set aside a reservation specifically for them on the Susquehanna—a beneficence that might have kept them there if it had been offered
earlier. At the 1732 council he asked the Iroquois to go after the Shawnees
and "oblige them to return," for which service he would pay. The interested Iroquois asked whether the Pennsylvanians were willing to make
this a cooperative venture; they were told yes.[19]

The question and answer struck to the heart of all further negotiations.
Pennsylvania was now willing to step up relations with the Iroquois a
notch above simply recognizing Iroquois supremacy over the Shawnees.
Now the province would join in enforcing it. As Thomas Penn recapitu-
lated his offer, Pennsylvania would light a new fire for the Iroquois and
keep it burning at Philadelphia. For the record he proclaimed solidarity
with all the other English colonies, but he gave a subtle twist to the old
tie between the Six Nations and New York. He called it a league with the
king of England, demoting New York to the role of king's agent—a role
that Pennsylvania could play as well. He did not refer to his new arrangement as the Covenant Chain. Thomas Penn thus continued the process
of eroding Albany's controls that had been under way in Pennsylvania
since 1701.

17. Logan to Weiser, Dec. 15, 1731, in P. Wallace, *Weiser*, p. 47; abstracts of dispatches,
Oct. 1, 1728 and Oct. 25, 1729, *N.Y.Col.Docs.* 9:1013–14, 1016; Beauharnois to Maurepas,
Oct. 1, 1731, ibid., p. 1027; examination of Edmond Cartlidge, Dec. 7, 1731, *Pa. Archives*,
1st ser., 1:305.

18. Memorial of Cartlidge, Davenport, and Bailey, 1730, *Pa. Archives*, 1st ser., 1:261. See
William A. Hunter, "Traders on the Ohio, 1730," *Western Pennsylvania Historical Magazine*
35(1952), pp. 85–92.

19. Private conference minutes, Aug. 26, 1732, *Pa. Council Minutes* 3:442. Neither Mohawks
nor Onondagas were present. Several phrases in these minutes are worth noting. The Pennsylvanians remarked that the Shawnees had previously "joyned themselves to the Sasquehannah Indians who were dependent on the five Nations, they *thereby* fell also under their
Protection." [My emphasis.] Seneca Chief Tyoninhogarao remarked that the Iroquois had
"told Sassoonan, the old Chief of the Delaware Indians, that they must all come back from
the Ohio, for they should not Settle there." Both Shawnees and Delawares in the west
flouted the Iroquois authority so proclaimed. The conspiratorial nature of Logan's arrangements with the Iroquois is plain in Logan to Weiser, Dec. 15, 1731, mss., Logan Papers
2:14, HSP. Shawnee reservation deed, Oct. 5, 1732, mss., Penn Papers from Friends House,
London, HSP.

Bostonians had lit a new fire at Deerfield, Massachusetts, in 1723, but otherwise Albany had maintained a monopoly over official negotiations with the Iroquois. Boston had simply wanted to recruit warriors for its perpetual wars with French-allied Indians who were never going to become "props" of the Iroquois, no matter how bullied they were. This fact contrasted strongly with the availability of the broken tribes along the Susquehanna to reinforce Iroquois manpower and perhaps eventually be assimilated into the Iroquois League. Another contrast is also significant: the Boston connection was under the management of Mohawk Keepers of the Eastern Door, but the Mohawks were absent from treaties in Pennsylvania until the Seven Years War. It appears that their absence was due to exclusion by the other Iroquois nations. In 1732, the new arrangements proposed by Thomas Penn had the effect of a diplomatic revolution within the Iroquois League as well as between it and the English colonies.[20]

Four years elapsed before the Iroquois responded formally to his offer. I do not know what caused the delay. Perhaps a conservative reluctance to avoid Albany's displeasure played a part. Very likely the Mohawks continued their perpetual effort to keep Albany dominant and to control access to Albany. Perhaps there was some justified suspicion of Penn's and Logan's motives. Fairly likely, the impossibility of getting the Shawnees back to Pennsylvania was an embarrassment.[21] It was all very well for Pennsylvania to promise help, but French assistance to the resisting Shawnees was closer, stronger, and more deliverable. There was a further consideration: Iroquois interests in the region between Lake Erie and the Ohio River suggested the advisability of maintaining reasonable terms with the Shawnees, who were so strategically placed. Whatever the reason may have been, the Shawnees stayed put, and the Iroquois procrastinated with Pennsylvania.

The Penns' debts

Thomas and John Penn could not afford the luxury of delay. They were under a mountainous burden of debt. With their brother, Richard, they

---

20. *Pa. Council Minutes*, Aug. 31, 1732, 3:447–50; Boston Treaty, Aug.–Sept., 1723, mss., Thomas Gilcrease Institute of American History and Art, G329, Tulsa, Okla. Photocopy at Newberry Library.

21. Seneca Chief Hetaquantegechty admitted candidly that the Iroquois could not get the Shawnees back "unless we [Pennsylvanians] call our Traders from Thence, and hinder them from furnishing them with Goods and receiving their Peltry there. It will therefore be our own faults if they do not return." *Pa. Council Minutes*, Aug. 28, 1732, 3:443. When an Iroquois delegation did pursue the Shawnees, its speaker "pressed them so closely that they took a great Dislike to him," and they killed him. There is no record of retribution. *Pa. Council Minutes*, Sept. 10, 1735, 3:608.

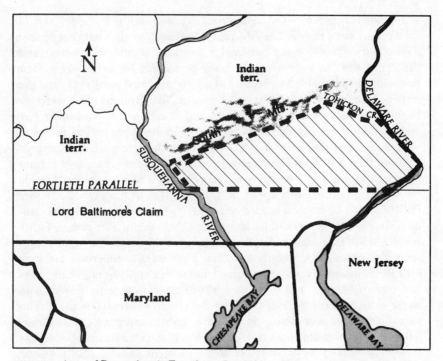

MAP 13. Area of Pennsylvania Free from Conflicting Claims, 1701–1732. The area shown within heavy black lines was the only territory at the unchallenged disposal of the Penn family.

owned by charter a feudal domain of imperial proportions, but the extent ceded by Indians—and therefore available to provide an income—consisted of only a tiny portion of the chartered whole. It was probably less than 5 percent. They had Indian quitclaims for no more than the southeast region between the Delaware and Susquehanna rivers, from the border with Maryland, north and northwest to the Blue Mountain, including Sassoonan's Tulpehocken. But this description overstates the facts. Maryland disputed the location of the boundary, and between the Schuylkill and Delaware rivers the land ceded by Indians ended abruptly at the Delaware River's tributary stream, Tohickon Creek, about twenty miles south of the first mountain range. The ceded land was good, but there was not enough of it for the Penns' financial needs. To visualize the situation, one may think of today's Easton, Bethlehem, Allentown, Harrisburg, and York as in Indian territory, de jure beyond the province. The valley in which Reading lies was acquired only after Sassoonan's deed of 1732.[22]

22. A draft or copy of Sassoonan's 1732 deed is in Logan Papers, mss., 11:21, HSP.

The Penns had received relatively only a handful of money out of their colony since their father's death, for the canny settlers held out against paying quitrent until every last legal technicality should be removed, and the Penns were in court over one issue or another for many years. The boundary dispute with Maryland was not to be settled until 1763, and the settlers in the wide strip disputed between Maryland and Pennsylvania happily refused quitrents on the plea that they did not know whom to pay and would not risk having to pay twice.[23] The Penns felt an inclination as well as an obligation to live in the fashion befitting eighteenth-century gentry, and they did. John Penn defended Thomas against charges of extravagance by saying that Thomas lived "in as frugall a Manner as was Possible for any Person that Must appear as the first Man in the Place he resides in."[24] It was a tolerable standard of austerity, but it did not help the family finances. The Penns had backbreaking debts inherited from their father besides what they accumulated on their own account. They were constantly embroiled in expensive lawsuits. They were a numerous clan with little or no income except what came from their Pennsylvania estate. Several were profligate, and those who leaned toward economy feared to go so far as to give the pack of creditors the scent of defenseless prey. The Penns were land poor, living on pretense, agility, and great expectations. Their only appreciable income from their colony came from the purchase money laid down for large tracts at the moment of sale. And the only open spaces large enough to accommodate such tracts were over the Indian line.

Penns sell Indian lands

They did not hesitate. When they could find buyers, they sold in Indian territory. This practice could be justified because William Penn had previously sold to speculators on the understanding that he would clear the Indian title "incumbrance" before colonial settlers should move in.[25] As early as 1729, the younger Penns sold 20,000 acres in Indian territory to

23. Logan to J. Penn, Nov. 25, 1727, mss., Logan Letter Books 4:150–64; Logan to J., T., and R. Penn, July 29, 1728, mss., ibid., p. 184, HSP.

24. J. Penn to T. Penn, Feb. 20, 1736 (O.S. 1735), mss., Penn Letter Books 1:143–44, HSP.

25. William Penn distinguished very carefully in his patents between lands that had been ceded by the Indians and those that had not. The telltale phrase is "free of incumbrance." When that is omitted from a patent, the meaning is that the land lies in unpurchased tribal territory. The opportunities thus presented to land speculators are discussed in Jennings, "Miquon's Passing," pp. 318–32. Logan differed from Penn in the matter of guaranteeing title on his personal sales. Knowing how much of those lands lay under Indian right, he gave "no covenants but against myself and those claiming under me." Logan to J. Steel, Sept. 22, 1736, mss., Logan Coll., HSP.

young William Allen who was studying law in London before returning
to become Pennsylvania's richest merchant.[26] In 1730 they sold 2,000 acres
more to Casper Wistar, an affluent German immigrant button maker.[27]
They knew what they were doing: they told Logan, "We see the Absolute
Necessity of Hastining the purchases with the Indians."[28] Before Thomas
Penn departed from England the brothers sold another 5,000 acres to William Allen's partner, Joseph Turner, besides making out survey warrants
totaling 25,000 acres for themselves as private persons, and a brother-in-
law.[29] Turner's purchase money probably paid the expenses of Thomas's
voyage.

On his arrival in Pennsylvania, Thomas tried to sell more land, but it
moved slowly, in all likelihood because prospective purchasers were only
too well acquainted with the problems of clear title. Persistent encroach-

26. Allen bought 10,000 Indian acres from the brothers Penn with title guaranteed against
"all Incumbrances whatsoever" in a sharp departure from William Penn's practice. Deed,
Aug. 29, 1728, mss., Pa. Patent Book F–5:92ff. Allen bought another 10,000 acres in a
complicated maneuver by which Springett Penn first made over title to Wm. Penn (grandson) for the nominal sum of £1.10. Deed, April 4, 1729, mss., Pa. Patent Book F–5:562.
Young William Penn then sold the land to Allen for £750. Deed, April 16, 1729, mss., Pa.
Patent Book F–6:1. Warrants were issued, March 5, 1729, to survey the parcels of the estate
on Saucon Creek, tributary to the Lehigh River and well inside Indian territory. Sale of the
parcels was dated Jan. 22, 1735. Northampton County Deed Book A–1:149–52, mss., Easton Court House, Pa.

27. The Penns sold to Wistar at about £7 sterling per hundred acres. Seven years later he
resold to one George Zewitz at about £53, Pa. currency, per hundred acres. After allowance
for the exchange rate, the profit is on the order of 500 percent. Wistar's patent, Jan. 30,
1732, dates survey warrants at April 23, 1730, and actual surveys at August and October
1730 and February 1731. Pa. Patent Book A–1:162, mss.; Zewitz's deed, May 24, 1737,
mss., Northampton Co. Deed Bk. B–1:177–78, Easton Court House.

Valuable indexed maps of land dealing in the area are given in A. D. Chidsey, Jr., *The
Penn Patents in the Forks of the Delaware*, Publications of the Northampton Co. Historical and
Genealogical Society 2 (Easton, 1937), pp. 67ff. See also David G. Williams, *The Lower
Jordan Valley Pennsylvania German Settlement*, Proceedings of the Lehigh County Historical Society
18 (Allentown, 1950). Both Chidsey and Williams are meticulous in detail.

28. J., T., and R. Penn to Logan [summer, 1730], mss., Penn Mss., Letters of the Penn
Family to James Logan 2:77, HSP.

29. On May 18, 1732, the brothers, acting as proprietaries, granted Thomas Penn (as a
private person) a tract of 5,000 acres. He sold it, the same day, to Wm. Allen's merchant
partner Joseph Turner for £350 sterling. Turner sold it to Allen, Sept. 10, 1735, for £500
Pa. currency. Allen sold it in parcels to the settlers of the "Irish settlement" that grew into
Allentown. *Minutes of Property*, Bk. K, July 24, 1739, *Pa. Archives*, 3d ser., 1:106–7; Warrants
and Surveys of the Province of Pa., 1682–1759, mss., 9 vols., 2:226–27; 7:96, 189; 8:90,
Archives Division, Philadelphia City Hall. Chidsey, *Penn Patents*, sheet no. 8; Pa. Patent
Books A–6:210; A–9:68ff; A–16:329ff. The follow-up documents show that Allen laid out
this tract in Indian territory.

Other grants: Penn Letter books, mss., 1:50–51, HSP. Of these grants, 10,000 acres for
brother-in-law Thomas Freame and 10,000 of the Penn acres were restricted to "Land purchased of the Indians and whereon no Persons are Seated." A grant to T. Penn for 5,000
acres omitted this restriction. When Freame had difficulty selling his acres, John Penn suggested that the "particular limitations" be removed. J. Penn to T. Penn, July 20, 1732, Penn
Letter Books 1:58, HSP.

ment from Maryland threatened the potential fortune locked up in the lands beyond the Susquehanna River, so Thomas moved to forestall the encroachers by issuing "a Sort of General Grant for people to Settle over the River" opposite Paxtang.[30] His more specific grants provided at first that patents would issue "as soon as the Indian claim shall be satisfied," but he omitted that qualification in July 1734 when he granted 3,000 acres at a distance of 80 miles beyond the Susquehanna.[31] A month later he sent a hundred pre-signed, printed blank warrants to his land agent to sell to "any Persons that have an Inclination to settle over Sasquehannah without regard to the distance Westward."[32] The scruples so honorably acknowledged at the beginning were soon sloughed off.

Thus we may trace to the Penns' desperation the origins of that colonizing surge, of which one branch would carry immigrants down the Shenandoah Valley to diversify Virginia's ethnicity. This was the region identified by Frederick Jackson Turner as the most expansive region of "The Old West"—a "kind of peninsula thrust down from Pennsylvania." What Turner failed to take into account was that all this land lay under unpurchased Iroquois claim. Penn relied on Iroquois willingness to go along for a price. Events justified his calculation, but the price was high and, as always, complicated. Intricate negotations would yet be required to open up this Old West that Turner thought so important for "the beginnings of much that is characteristic in Western society."[33] The settlers did not simply move in a "wave." They were able to travel without molestation because a new fire did get kindled at Philadelphia, and the Iroquois Covenant Chain arranged accommodation.

Nutimus resists

Thomas Penn acted with some caution until September 21, 1734, when brother John appeared unexpectedly from England, in fearful flight from possible imprisonment for debt. John stirred up a bustle. The brothers immediately invited the chiefs of the Delawares above Tohickon Creek to a meeting with Thomas at Durham, where, according to chief Nutimus, "He keep begging and plagueing us to Give him some Land and never

30. S. Blunston to T. Penn, Nov. 29, 1733, mss., Smith Mss. 1:37, Library Company of Philadelphia.

31. Permission for Benjamin Burgess to settle, Oct. 22, 1733, mss., Etting Collection, Gratz-Croghan Papers 1:2, HSP. *Minutes of Property* Bk. K, July 20, 1734, *Pa. Archives*, 3d ser., 1:38–39.

32. T. Penn to S. Blunston, Aug. 8, 1734, mss., Penn Mss., Thomas Penn, 1730–1766 (boxed), HSP.

33. F. J. Turner, "The Old West," in *The Frontier in American History* (New York: H. Holt and Co., 1920), p. 68.

gives us leave to treat upon any thing till he Wearies us Out of Our Lives."[34] Nutimus knew that his lands were worth more than the two pounds per thousand acres that James Logan suggested as a purchase price.[35] (Within the year the Penns were selling the same lands at 155 pounds per thousand acres.) Until the Penns would offer a more realistic price there could be no agreement for a cession. The Durham meeting was a flat failure.

In 1735, another meeting was held, this time at Pennsbury, the Penn family seat on the Delaware. Here the Penns laid a legalistic foundation for revised intentions toward Nutimus. Their new policy was to take his lands by main force without any compensation. (The device will be discussed in the next chapter.) The atmosphere at Pennsbury was understandably hostile. Logan threatened Nutimus that if the Indians resisted, "you'll make the big Trees and Logs, and great Rocks and Stones tumble down into our Road."[36] Nutimus remained stubborn nonetheless. It was wily old Logan who finally found the means to overpower him without resort to such overt violence as the Quakers of Pennsylvania would never have tolerated.

Once more the Iroquois descended to resolve the dilemma. They had finally made up their minds to light a new fire at Philadelphia, and in 1736 the alliance was formally solemnized. As Thomas Penn had expected, they were willing to cede the lower Susquehanna Valley on both sides of the river, and they thus legitimized his previously peddled grants.[37] The Iroquois disposed readily of Conestoga Indian claims to Susquehanna territory by asserting a right of conquest over the Conestogas.[38] (The "conquest" was fabricated insofar as past events were concerned, as was shown in part one above, but it cannot be denied that when Pennsylvania ganged up with the Six Nations, conquest became real, no matter how bloodless.)

The Delawares, however, still held different status. Even in the secret sessions of the 1736 treaty conference, the Iroquois refused to claim Delaware lands. Logan reported, secretly, "The utmost Extent of their Claims

34. Nutimus et al. to Jeremiah Langhorne, Nov. 21, 1740, mss., Penn Mss., Indian Affairs 4:30, HSP. See also analysis of Durham "minutes" in Appendix, "Documents of the Walking Purchase."

35. Logan to the Proprietaries, Oct. 8, 1734, *Pa. Archives*, 2d ser., 7:171–72.

36. *Johnson Papers* 3:767. Logan's remark was quoted by Delaware Chief Teedyuscung as he remembered it in 1762. See analysis of Pennsbury "minutes" in Appendix, "Documents of the Walking Purchase."

37. *Pa. Council Minutes*, Oct. 12, 1736, 4:87–88; Deed, Oct. 11, 1736, mss., Philadelphia Deed Book G–1:277ff., City Hall. Logan concocted a mini-epidemic of smallpox in order to delay the Iroquois at his house "in the country" for very private negotiations to offset the effects of increasing accord between the Conestogas and Maryland, which might have strengthened Maryland's claim to disputed Susquehanna lands. Logan instructed Weiser, Sept. 5, 1736, insisting that "great care is to be taken that this Letter be not seen." Cf. Logan Papers, mss., 10:60, HSP, with *Pa. Council Minutes*, Sept. 28, 1736, 4:81.

38. Weiser to Logan, Sept. 2, 1736, mss., Logan Papers 10:59, HSP.

. . . they Said were the   ids of the Branches or Waters running into
Sasquehannah."³⁹ Nutin   s right to Delaware Valley lands went unchallenged despite Logan's F   ; that the Iroquois should lay claim.

The Iroquois become police

I have said that the price paid by Pennsylvania for the Susquehanna
territory was complicated; in 1736 the complications came to light. The
Six Nations wanted more than material compensation for Susquehanna.
They claimed right to lands in Maryland and the Shenandoah Valley,
down into Virginia—the "peninsula" of the Old West—and they wanted
Pennsylvania's intercession with the other colonies for negotiation of the
cession of those very extensive claims. This demand embarrassed the
Pennsylvanians more than they could say—literally—because of the long
border dispute between Pennsylvania and Maryland.⁴⁰ No promises could
be given, and the departing Iroquois were forced to bide their time. They
were not satisfied.

Logan perceived this and tried a new gambit to compensate them. In
the finest Loganian mode, the new device would be at the Delawares'
expense instead of Pennsylvania's. Logan wrote to Conrad Weiser, who
had accompanied the Six Nations delegates to Shamokin, where they rested
before proceeding further. Logan's plan was to convert the Iroquois *refusal*
to claim Nutimus's lands into a *release* of claim, so worded as to imply that
the claim had once existed; and as he framed the papers, the conversion
worked wonders. "It was understood that they laid no manner of Claim
to the Lands on Delaware River or on the Waters running into," he wrote
Weiser. "However it may be proper for them, under their hands, to Declare
that they release to the Proprietors of Pennsylvania . . . all their Claim
and Pretensions whatsoever to all the Lands Between Delaware and Sasquehannah . . . as far Northward as to that Ridge or Chain of mountains
called the Endless . . . Hills [Blue Mountain]." Logan was always facile
with excuses and rationalizations. Ever so plausibly he explained that "They
do not grant us any Land on Delaware, therefore observe to them that
this is not at all intended by it, but they only release and quit all their
Claims there and as they make none it is in reality nothing and yet may
prevent disputes hereafter."⁴¹ Knowing that Nutimus planned to appeal
to the Six Nations as his "uncles" or protectors in the Covenant Chain for
defense against the Pennsylvanians, Logan offered to recognize an Iroquois right over Nutimus's lands, and by implication over other territories

39. Directions to Conrad Weiser, Oct., 1736, mss., Logan Papers 11:26, HSP.
40. *Pa. Council Minutes*, Oct. 14, 36, 4:93–94.
41. See n. 39.

higher on the Delaware. He twisted Nutimus's appeal for defense of Delaware territory into seeming to be an application for a "grant" of Iroquois territory.[42]

It was no problem at all for the Iroquois to release claims and pretensions they had never made, but Logan knew well that they would understand the implications of his finagling. He baited his hook with power. As he instructed Weiser, the reason to be given, "especially for their not making any Grant to the Indians further than to allow them to live on the Land [their own land] is this: that the five Nations are our Brethren—honest, wise, discreet, and understanding men—and we can treat with them with pleasure. But the others are weak and too often knavish (such as [Conestoga chief] Civility, Pesqueetomen, Nootamis, and the like), to whom, though we are always very kind and take great care of them as of ourselves—that they may in no point be abused—yet we are not willing to enter upon Treaties with them as with our Brethren of the five Nations for whom we keep our fire and therefore *would treat with them only in behalf of all or any of the others*."[43] This was the big bribe. At no time during the formal meeting in Philadelphia had the Iroquois requested or the Pennsylvanians offered exclusive recognition of the Six Nations as sole bargaining agent. The treaty had created an alliance; Logan now offered to use it for mutual conquest.

It must be said to the credit of the Iroquois that they temporarily resisted this large temptation. "It went very hart," wrote Weiser from Shamokin, "about syning over their right upon delaware because they Sayd they had nothing to doe there about the land. They war afaired they shoud doe any thing a mis to their cousins, the delawars." The kinship term should be noticed; neither in English nor Iroquois kinship systems are cousins in a state of subjection. But Weiser prevailed, and his methods are visible in his own report: "I must goe to Carry up some of their goods with about ten Horses. There is no help for it. They are disabled to Carry for sicknes and strong liquors sake. They Charges will be some what larger than you most Expect."[44] Nevertheless the bargain was struck, and as Paul A. W. Wallace has remarked, the Iroquois undertook to "police Pennsylvania's woods in return for Pennsylvania's recognition of their sole right to do so."[45]

42. Logan to Weiser, Oct. 18, 1736, mss., Logan Papers 10:64, HSP.
43. Loc. cit.
44. Weiser to Logan, Oct. 27, 1736, mss., Logan Papers 10:65, HSP.
45. P. Wallace, *Weiser*, p. 44.

The Six Nations' price

The Six Nations were not bought with only a drunken spree. They understood diplomacy as well as Logan, and they knew their services' worth. They raised his ante. Logan's transparent excuse for the secrecy of his proposal was that he had "forgotten" to mention it while the Indians were in Philadelphia. Now they, too, remembered a lapse. They dictated a petition by Weiser to "beseech our Brethren . . . to write in our behalf to Governor or Owner of the Land in Maryland and to the Governor of Virginia to let them both know that we expect some consideration for our Land now in their occupation"—an interesting reversal of the theory of English sovereignty. "We desire further of our Brethren Onas [Governor of Pennsylvania] and James Logan to use their utmost endeavour to sell the Goods cheaper to us or give more for our Skins." And then the *quid pro quo*. "We desire further of our Brethren Onas and James Logan never to buy any Land of our Cousins, the Delawares, and Others whom we treat as Cousins; they are people of no Virtue and . . . deal very often unjust with our Friends and Brethren the English. . . . They have no Land remaining to them, and if they offer to sell, they have no good design."[46]

The deal was made and the Penns were in luck. Virginians were tired and fearful of the incessant warfare in their back country between their Catawba and Cherokee allies and the Iroquois. Virginia's Governor Gooch wrote to Pennsylvania in December, less than two months after Weiser parted from the Iroquois at Shamokin, to propose peace negotiations. Gooch's letter arrived while Pennsylvania was between governors, and it happened that the current leading official was President of the Council James Logan. Logan promptly engaged Conrad Weiser to carry Virginia's overture directly to Onondaga (bypassing Albany) "and gave him proper Instructions to that End."[47] The Iroquois alliance was working out smoothly; Logan and the Penns turned their full attention to seizing Nutimus's lands, secure in the awareness that they had boxed him in.

The Indians, however, were not the only people to be managed. There were still some sensitive consciences to contend with in Pennsylvania, for which some legalistic legerdemain had to be contrived. Arrangements were made.

46. Indian Request . . . , Nov. 19, 1736, mss., Penn Mss., Indian Affairs 1:39, HSP.
47. *Pa. Council Minutes*, May 12, 1737, 4:203–4.

Chapter 17 ᴥ CHAIN into FETTERS

There never was any pretence of a Purchase made on thy father's account within thirty miles of the nearest of those Indian settlements.

James Logan to Honoured Friend [John Penn], December 6, 1727

Once the French reached Niagara Pennsylvania's geographical position offered her no security at all. Her true bulwark was her own Indians, the Delawares. When she lost their friendship she lay as exposed as any British colony in North America.

Joseph E. Johnson, "A Quaker Imperialist's View of the British Colonies in America: 1732"

John and Thomas Penn acquired possession of Nutimus's lands, and the adjoining lands of a number of other Delaware families as well, by a device known in the histories as the Indian Walk or Walking Purchase. It has served as the subject of great controversy for more than two centuries, but I think it is time to say that the Penns' apologists have lost their case. My reasons are given in the appendix "Documents of the Walking Purchase." Although annotating heavily in this and the preceding chapter, I have generally ignored the arguments of the Penns' advocates in order to write a straightforward readable account of the events. I have found the papers concocted by the Penns' lawyers to be as fraudulent as the Walk itself, and I see no reason to pussyfoot about it. Readers desiring a closer look at the evidence are referred to the appendix.

Delaware land tenure

A few words on Delaware customs concerning land ownership and William Penn's negotiations concerning land transactions will be helpful. Customs of land tenure differed from one Indian tribe to another. Among the Iroquois the tribe's territory was common land that could only be validly alienated by formal action of the tribal council. The Delawares recognized certain rights of private property in land, but their conception

325

of ownership must not be construed as exactly identical to modern European notions. Anthony F. C. Wallace remarks that

To the Delaware Indian, land was an element, a medium of existence, like the air and the sunlight and the rivers. To him, "ownership" of land meant, not exclusive personal title to the soil itself, but occupation of a certain position of responsibility in the social unit which exploited the soil. "Inheritance" of land was really the inheritance of this place in society. The "sale" of land (to use the white man's term) might, to the Delaware, be almost any mutually satisfactory change in the relationship of two groups of persons subsisting on the land. In the earliest sales, the Indians seem to have intended only to give the whites freedom to use the land in conjunction with the native population.[1]

This, by the way, was not so very different from conceptions of tenure in the Middle Ages as described by Sir Paul Vinogradoff; "that is of a holding conditioned by service and always combining the claims and interest of two persons in each unit of property."[2]

Under *aboriginal* Delaware custom, the "sale" of land conveyed only the rights of use for residence and subsistence as long as the parties lived and were satisfied with the terms of compensation. No sales were permanent. Even if all demands were met and the seller completely satisfied, he might show up a second time for further compensation and be entirely fair and honorable according to his standards. Apparently there were complications in these customs that were better understood by Englishmen at the time than by students nowadays. For example, though questions have been raised about the validity of some Delaware deeds, because various Indians seem to have sold the same tract of land several times over, William Penn, who had much reason to complain about double purchase, understood the reason for it. He wrote: "It hath been the Practice of America, as well as the Reason of the thing itself, even among Indians and Christians, to account not taking up, marking and (in some degree) planting a Reversion of Right; for the Indians do make People buy over again that land [which] the People have not seated in some years after purchase, *which is the Practice also of all those [colonial] Governments towards the People inhabiting under them.*"[3]

Penn knew law. The colonial governments did invalidate title to land

1. Anthony F. C. Wallace, "Woman, Land, and Society: Three Aspects of Aboriginal Delaware Life," *Pennsylvania Archaeologist* 17 (1947), p. 2.
2. Paul Vinogradoff, "Customary Law," in *The Legacy of the Middle Ages*, eds. C. G. Crump and E. F. Jacob, rev. ed. (Oxford: Clarendon Press, 1932), p. 300.
3. Instructions to Capt. Markham, ca. 1683, mss., Cadwalader Collection, HSP; printed in *Papers of Wm. Penn* 2:472–76.

grants that were not settled within specified periods.[4] The same general rule was instituted by the United States government under its Homestead Law grants of the nineteenth century, which lapsed and became void if their lands were not occupied and built upon.

Penn intended from the beginning to deal honorably with the Indians. He knew that their declining populations had made them willing to cede lands, and he paid fair prices. But it took him a little while to master the complexities of Delaware customs. After his first return to England, he received word from his surveyor general, in 1685, that Delaware Sachem Tamenend was creating disturbances and demanding more compensation for a particular conveyance. Penn's response was brisk and firm. "You must make them keep their word," he ordered. "If they see you use them severely when Rogueish and kindly when just, they will demean themselves accordingly." As for Tamenend's threats to set fire to English settlers' houses, Penn insisted that "Tamine . . . sould all, and If the Indians will not punish him, we will and must, for they must never see you afraid of executeing the Justice they ought to do."[5] But Penn must have come to see the point of Tamenend's objections; instead of punishing Tamenend, Penn's agents paid him again, in 1692, and still again in 1697.[6]

Delaware custom seems to have altered gradually to conform to enforced European expectations and demands, but Penn had to cope with the variety of rights involved in native tenure. (Modern "simple" ownership may be just as complicated. The sale of an office building may require a team of lawyers working all day to process the papers dealing with title, easements, mortgages, ground rent, etc.)

Delaware individuals and families owned and could dispose of certain rights to well-bounded hunting territories that might be either contiguous or in scattered tracts. Taken all together, these territories made up communally controlled areas. A head chief such as Tamenend, with many family connections and hereditary rights, might show up as owner of a hunting territory included within a tract being sold, and again as chief of a band ceding a larger area inclusive of his hunting territory. Even more bewildering to the uninitiated European was the Delaware technique of clarifying the disposition of land rights, conditioned as it was by the fact of illiteracy. Sales of Delaware land, whether individual or communal, were always witnessed by friends and neighbors who could then remem-

4. E.g., see Darrett B. Rutman, *Winthrop's Boston: A Portrait of a Puritan Town, 1630–1649,* published for the Institute of Early American History and Culture (Chapel Hill: University of North Carolina Press, 1965), pp. 83, 85.

5. William Penn to his son, Jan. 2, 1701, *Pa. Archives,* 2d ser., 7:11; Wm. Penn to T. Holme, Aug. 8, 1685, mss. photostat, Penn Papers in Boxes, HSP.

6. Deeds, June 15, 1692, July 5, 1697, *Pa. Archives,* 1st ser., 1:116–17, 124–25.

ber and testify to the transactions; and seemingly all these bystanders shared in the compensation.[7]

Cessions to Pennsylvania

To Europeans this opened a bleak prospect of endless outlay and uncertain possession. What the Delaware land tenure system amounted to was an assertion of inalienable sovereignty over the land; and, of course, alienation of the sovereignty was precisely the object of European purchase. Delaware expectation of perpetually renewed presents for use of the land might theoretically be supplemental to European expectations of perpetual income from quitrents, but the theory would have to be a different one from that of exclusive European sovereignty.[8] European pressure and power gradually forced the acceptance of European terms of purchase, but the transitional period is puzzling in retrospect. To contemporaries, as it seems to me, the issue was not an absolute failure of European and Indian to understand each other's ways. Although Penn was new to the customs of the Delawares, he employed old Swedish settlers who had been living intimately with the Indians for decades, and the Delawares had had half a century's experience with Dutchmen, Swedes, and Englishmen. The parties quickly learned what each wanted. The real issue between them was the unthinkability to the Europeans of sharing the rent. Not even William Penn could accept that sort of arrangement. He had promised English purchasers of Pennsylvania estates that he would eliminate completely the Indian "incumbrance" on their land titles. Delawares were quickly made to understand that, however complex their rights might be, when they sold, they "sould all."

A series of treaties between Delaware chiefs and Penn's commissioners, sometimes including William Penn himself, obtained Delaware quitclaims for territory on the Pennsylvania side of the Delaware River, extending westward to the headwaters of tributaries of the Susquehanna.[9] The language of the purchase deeds leaves much to be desired by a modern student; evidently the written words were supplemented by oral agreements

7. Wallace, "Woman, Land, and Society," pp. 2–6. See also Leon de Valinger, Jr., "Indian Land Sales in Delaware," with addendum by C. A. Weslager, "A Discussion of the Family Hunting Territory Question in Delaware," *Bulletin of the Archaeological Society of Delaware*, June 20, 1941.

8. For a statement of the European theory see the New York Council's opinion concerning . . . Indian purchases [1675], *N.Y.Col.Docs.* 13:486–87.

9. Mss. Indian deeds dated from 1682 to 1685 (RG–26) are in Safe D–7 of the Dept. of State, Harrisburg, Pa. These do not include the lost Brandywine or "Treaty Elm" deeds, both of which are known only by inference from other sources. All the surviving Indian deeds of cession to Pennsylvania were recorded in the minutes of the Supreme Executive Council, Jan. 3, 1783, and printed in *Pa. Council Minutes* 13:461–71.

and tacit understandings. When a deed specifies, for example, that the granted lands are to be measured by a two-day journey back into the woods, its reader must know that the journey could go no farther than the Indian grantor's property extended, and every grantor knew his bounds. So did his neighbors. As time went on, the precise extent of Penn's purchases became established well enough for demarcation on a modern map. For present purposes, we may note only that by 1718 the lands free of Indian encumbrance extended northward on the Delaware to its Tohickon Creek tributary, and that this boundary became the bone of contention in the Walking Purchase.

Most Indians retreated to the periphery of the territory ceded to Penn. Some remained within his territory on enclaves set aside, or re-deeded, for Indian occupancy. These were not reservations in the Massachusetts manner because their Indian occupants were neither governed nor missionized by Pennsylvanians. Maintaining native customs and institutions, Indians were free to come and go among Pennsylvanians at will, whether from reserved lands or from outside. No curfew tolled for the Indian visitor. No magistrate enslaved him. Even Logan observed certain limits of domination.

Covetous eyes soon fixed upon Indian lands, both in the enclaves and beyond the recognized bounds, and sinister hands seized tracts at an accelerating rate by means unknown to William Penn personally. Quakers were identifiably among the offenders. In Pennsylvania, however, the acquisition of Indian property and jurisdiction proceeded, for the most part, without intrusion upon the Indians' personal liberty. Although dispossession and eviction certainly occurred, they never entailed outright subjection. In view of ancient historical quarrels it may be emphasized that all of Pennsylvania's quitclaims from the Delaware Indians were transacted wholly without reference to the Iroquois until 1742, when the most-notorious of a series of eviction actions took place. In that year the Walking Purchase came to climax. We return now to the beginnings.

In 1735, John and Thomas Penn used an old piece of paper as their purported authority for seizing Indian lands on the Delaware River above Tohickon Creek. This scrap referred to an agreement, supposed to have been made during William Penn's lifetime, for the cession of lands beyond the then current boundary, the limits of his new purchase to be determined by a walk into Indian territory to be performed over a period of a day and a half. I have called it merely a piece of paper because it was not a deed, as the Penns insisted it was. But they used it as the basis for a conspiracy to defraud, which they worked out in elaborate detail. The conspiracy was a necessity imposed upon them by circumstance. To make an open seizure of recognized Indian territory would defeat its own purpose. The whole point of seizure would be to raise money by selling the lands, and no one would buy those lands if title continued to be clouded by Indian claims unextinguished by legal purchase.

The lands of Nutimus

The event to which the Penns' paper referred began in 1700, during their father's second visit to his colony estate. William Penn wrote then to James Logan that "an Indian township called Tohickon, rich land, and much cleared by the Indians," had not been surveyed. "It joins upon the back of my manor of Highlands. The Indians have been with me about it."[10] By Penn's reference to Highlands Manor, which had been surveyed and mapped, the area is identified precisely. It was north of a creek called Neshaminy, and Penn's letter settles the fact that he and the Indians were agreed in 1700 that this land had been sold. The question at issue was its extent to the northward. Where was the new boundary? The Indians claimed in 1700, as they steadfastly confirmed ever after, that the new line lay along Tohickon Creek, the next considerable stream above Neshaminy.[11]

Their version, which I accept as true, was recited by a Presbyterian Delaware convert named Moses Tatamy, a peaceful man who never took up arms against colonials even after they wantonly killed his son, and who achieved special status by paying the Penns in order to get their deed to the land he owned by native right. He is a credible informant.[12] Tatamy related as follows.

"[Chief] Mechkilikishi sold to Wm. Penn Lands along the Banks of the Delaware and the Tohiccon as far as a man could Travel in one day and a half *following the Course of the River;* there were to be two Whites and two Indians and a led Horse, and as they were to walk a common days Journey, they were to stop at Noon, unload their Horse, eat their dinner, after that smoak a pipe and after that was done load their Horse again and set forward and wherever they stop'd at the end of the Walk they were to draw a straight Line to where the Sun sets and that Line was to be the Boundary. Accordingly a Day was fixed and as soon as the Sun appeared

10. Penn to Logan, Sept. 6, 1700, mss., Logan Papers 1:15, HSP.
11. Land immediately above the Tohickon Creek line was granted to a German named John Streiper, whose heirs were unable to sell "for that not only the Indians lay a Claim to the Tract where now Scituated, but that the said John Strieper dying an alien they cannot Procure a good Title." Warrant to survey, May 15, 1727, mss., Streper Papers, p. 235, HSP; location of tract: Bucks County Papers, mss., 1:185, 289, HSP. See also William J. Buck, *History of the Indian Walk* (Philadelphia: E.S. Stuart, 1886), pp. 28–29.
12. William A. Hunter, "Moses (Tunda) Tatamy, Delaware Indian Diplomat," in *A Delaware Indian Symposium,* ed. Herbert C. Kraft, Anthropological Series 4 (Harrisburg: Pennsylvania Historical and Museum Commission, 1974), pp. 71–88.

they set out, James Yates was one of the white men. They travelled along the Banks and at noon rested according to Agreement. At length they arrived at Tohiccon. Here a dispute arose between the Proprietor and Nutimus. The Proprietor insisted they should cross the River, Neutimus insisted they had no right, for that Land on the other side was his, and Mechkilikishi had no right to sell it. The Bargain was they should travel up Tohiccon not cross it. The Dispute grew so high that the Travellers proceeded no farther. And it was agreed they should meet next year and adjust matters. In the meantime William Penn went to England and afterwards died, and also Mechkilikishi died."[13]

But neither James Logan nor Nutimus died. Logan quickly learned about the boundary when some Germans attempted to settle beyond Tohickon Creek. He wrote to Penn in 1702 that the Indians "Clamour [it] is not purchased."[14] Penn's significant reply was "to keep well with the Indians and suffer no hardships upon them from any of the Inhabitants." This is not the language of a man being cheated of his rights. Penn did issue a patent for trans-Tohickon lands in 1705 but omitted from it his usual guarantee of title against Indian claim—a certain acknowledgment of the existence of the claim.[15] It was the faulty title of this patent that Logan deviously bought in 1726, with open eyes, in order to start his ironworks at Durham. Never one to part with a penny unnecessarily, Logan nevertheless acknowledged the justice of the Indian claim by "satisfying" chief Nutimus with a payment of £60 for this small tract within Nutimus's territory. The payment insured Logan against trouble from the Indians, but it did not fully consummate his title even so, because the transaction had no standing in Pennsylvania law.[16] Indians did not bother themselves about such matters—their concern was simply to get compensation for their rights—but Logan had only a squatter's right under Pennsylvania law until he could have a formal survey recorded, and that could not be

13. Moses Tatamy's Account, mss., Etting Collection, Miscellaneous Mss. 1:94, HSP. In 1762, chief Teedyuscung said that old Indians had told him they had performed a trial walk before the 1686 sale to William Penn was agreed upon. By this tradition, the Indians' trial walk ended in a place called Cusho-hoppen, "which they knew to be no further than belong's to the Indians that made the Agreement." *Johnson Papers* 3:778–79.

14. Logan to Penn, Dec. 1, 1702, mss., Logan Letter Books 1:60–61; Penn to Commissioners, Jan. 10, 1703, mss., Gratz Collection, Papers of the Governors, Case 2, Box 33–a, both HSP. Penn mentioned in a hasty postscript, Jan. 22, 1703, that he had received Logan's letter, and he responded specifically to Logan's remark about resurveying lands. In a further postscript, dated Jan. 28, Penn made his comment about the Indians.

15. Patent copies in Bucks County Papers, mss., 1:187–89, HSP, and Pa. Patent Book A–3:334 ff., mss. As it was Penn's regular policy and practice to include a guarantee against Indian claims in all the lands he had purchased, the omission here is decisive evidence in itself.

16. *Statutes at Large of Pennsylvania, 1682–1809*, 17 vols. (Harrisburg: State Printer, 1896–1915), vol. 4, ch. 312, pp. 154–56; Logan to Honoured Friend [John Penn], Dec. 6, 1727, mss., Logan Papers, Correspondence of James Logan 1:89, HSP.

done until the Indian incumbrance was removed. Purchases of Indian land by individuals were forbidden. Though the Indians of the upper Delaware tolerated many squatters upon payment of compensation, they had grown canny enough to prevent surveys from being made until cession of the whole territory should be purchased by a Penn.

Logan knew that Tohickon Creek was the boundary between Pennsylvania and Indian territory. Besides the evidence of his payment to Nutimus, we have the repeated remarks of his letters to the Penns. Referring specifically to the upper Delawares, he wrote in 1727 that "There never was any pretence of a Purchase made on thy father's account within thirty miles of the nearest of those Indian Settlements."[17] Since Logan had been in Pennsylvania as Penn's personal secretary in 1700 when the presumed agreement was supposed to have been made, this statement in itself should be conclusive, but this was Logan writing in private, and he changed his tune later in public.

The "ancient deed"

In 1732, Thomas Penn brought with him to Philadelphia the piece of paper referring to the day-and-a-half walk of 1700. The central issue in all events to follow was the authenticity of this scrap. Was it an Indian deed, as the Penns insisted on calling it? If so, they had right on their side. It is instructive, therefore, that neither Logan nor the Penns regarded it as a deed and did not present it as such to the Indians in their first meeting with them about the trans-Tohickon lands. For good reason. No judge would have looked at this paper a second time. It lacked signatures and seals, and it had blank spaces in the all-important phrases specifying the direction of the bounding Walk. The Penns came to allege that this paper was a *copy* of a lost deed, but in a suit between Englishmen in an English court, such an argument would have been thrown out without fuss. The document itself has vanished like the supposed original into that limbo of important papers concerning Indian land transactions, but the Penns' own descriptions of it mark it on its face as a preliminary *draft* of a deed; and by Tatamy's unrefuted testimony we know that the deed had never been consummated because Nutimus raised objections in 1700 as he did again in the 1730s.[18] Penn's sons pretended that the supposed "lost" original

17. Ibid., Logan to W. Penn (grandson), Dec. 6, 1727, mss., Logan Parchment Letter Book, 1717–1731, p. 515; Logan to J., T., and R. Penn, July 29, 1728, mss., Logan Papers 10:45; same to same, Nov. 16, 1729, mss., Logan Letter Books 3:316; Logan to J. Penn, Nov. 17, 1729, mss., Penn Mss., Official Correspondence 2:99; James Logan to Honoured Friend [John Penn], Dec. 6, 1727, Logan Papers, Correspondence of James Logan, mss., 1:89, All HSP.

18. The 1686 draft is not in the state archives at Harrisburg nor among the Penn papers at HSP. A purported copy of this draft was submitted to Sir William Johnson at his hearing

had been consummated, knowing full well that this was false. In order to make a case in later years, they jumbled their supposed deed for a transaction in 1700 with a prior transaction in 1686 for which supporting documents existed. And they insisted that a new Walk should take place under their management when, in reality, a day's worth had been walked already, in 1700, to establish the Tohickon Creek boundary. If all this seems confusing, the reader understands the situation; the confusion was intentional. But Nutimus knew the boundaries of his own lands, knew that no one else had the right to sell his lands, and knew that he had not sold. *He* was not confused.

Rehearsal for a Walk

As shown in chapter 16, the Penns were desperate enough to ignore all niceties of morals and law, and to override all objections. When they decided in 1734, after their first conference with Nutimus's Indians at Durham, that they must have his lands by any means, they decided also to put forward their old paper to pretend legitimacy for their actions. They would organize a Walk in spite of Indian protests.[19] But first they organized a secret rehearsal to see how they could twist the paper's ambiguous phrases to best advantage. They gave charge of the rehearsal to their Receiver General, James Steel (an old henchman of James Logan), Bucks County Sheriff Timothy Smith, and surveyor John Chapman.[20] Two men were hired to do the actual walking: Joseph Doan, who became murderous and infamous in later years, offered himself willingly (in writing) to satisfy the Penns' desires for a price; and Solomon Jennings (very possibly one of my ancestors) was hired with the knowledge that he was a brawler regarded by James Steel as "a Person of ill fame."[21] Typically the Penns kept Sheriff Smith waiting for three years before paying him £16 out-of-pocket

in 1762 on the Walking Purchase case and forwarded by him to the crown. HSP mss. transcripts of Board of Trade Papers, Proprieties, 1697–1776, vol. 21–1, p. 189b.

19. James Steel to Barefoot Brunsdon, April 12, 1735, mss., James Steel's Letter Book, 1730–1741, p. 95, HSP. Brunsdon was to act as interpreter. He was brother-in-law to Thomas Lawrence, Mayor of Philadelphia and close associate of Logan and the Penns. Significantly, Brunsdon was an outsider who would not be near Philadelphia after the treaty to talk about it. He was Sheriff of Somerset County, N.J., and I have not found mention of his presence at any Pennsylvania Indian treaty after the meeting at Pennsbury. Inserted mss. note, Mary Morris Lawrence Collection, Correspondence, Thomas Lawrence Case, Barefoot Brunsdon folder, HSP.

20. Steel to John Chapman and Timothy Smith, April 29, 1735, mss., James Steel's Letter Books 2:96, HSP.

21. Joseph Doan to ———, May 29, 1735, photostat of mss., Indian Walk Mss., April 26, 1735–Sept. 19, 1737, Friends Historical Library, Swarthmore College; James Steel to Henry Van Wye, May 25, 1734, mss., James Steel's Letter Book, 1730–1741, p. 272.

expenses for all this.[22] The "first man" in the colony was never first in line to pay bills.

It is impossible to sniff an odor of sanctity in preparations such as these, but they were appropriate to their purpose. From the rehearsal walk the Penns discovered they could twist the language of their old paper to prescribe a gratifying boundary line. With due attention to topography and even more attention to semantics, the line could be made long enough to encompass not only the lands of troublesome old Nutimus but also the entire "Forks of Delaware" region of the Lehigh Valley, between the South and Blue mountains and a large area of the Minisink territory beyond the Blue. The cities of Easton, Bethlehem, and Allentown now occupy part of the area. Stimulated by this knowledge, the Penns met Nutimus in 1735 at Pennsbury and cried him down. What happened there was not negotiation in any proper sense of the word. It was bullying. The Penns had decided to make the Walk, regardless of Nutimus's objections.[23] It only remained to create the most favorable circumstances.

A real estate lottery

The Penns were not in a hurry—the Iroquois had not yet been recruited into the scheme—but they did want money fast, and they began to sell those lands that had not yet been acquired by even a pretense of legality. Within a month they had authorized surveys of a total of 13,000 acres,[24] and soon thereafter they set up a lottery of 100,000 acres more.[25] How-

22. T. Penn paid what he called "a handsome Gratuity" of £5 to each of the walkers, but Sheriff Smith had to wait three years for reimbursement of the party's expenses. T. Penn to J. Steel, reverse side of Doan to ——— (n. 21, above); T. Penn to J. Steel, July 23, 1735, mss., and "An Acct. of Charges accrued in walking the Day and ½ Journey," May 5, 1735, with receipt dated Feb. 13, 1738, Indian Walk Mss., Friends Historical Library, Swarthmore College.

23. See ch. 16, "A New Fire" and Appendix B, "Documents of the Walking Purchase."

24. Northampton County Papers, Bethlehem and Vicinity, 1741–1886, mss., pp. 19–20, HSP: Warrant issued Dec. 31, 1733, survey made May 20, 1735, mss., Warrants and Surveys of the Province of Pennsylvania, Philadelphia Archives, City Hall; Pa. Patent Books, mss., A–7:266 ff.; B. Eastburn's map of the upper part of Bucks County, 1737, mss., HSP call no. AM2349; tracts plotted on Eastburn's map of 1740, mss., HSP call no. OF,549*, 1740.

25. As this lottery has faded out of modern histories, I give full documentation. The scheme is written out, and managers named, in Pa. Patent Book A–7:224–26, July 12, 1735, with an addendum, Aug. 13, 1735, at pp. 239–40. Maps show the location of the affected tracts: an anonymous undated draft of "sundry Tracts" and B. Eastburn's draft of same areas, both in HSP maps, call no. OF,549*, 1740. Fifty-four thousand acres were surveyed: N. Scull's bill, Jan. 10, 1736, mss., Charles S. Ogden Papers, Series 4, Scrapbook 4, p. 30, Friends Historical Library, Swarthmore College. Several mss. drafts by N. Scull are in Cadwalader Collection, Copies of the Returns of Surveys, pp. 73, 74, HSP. Names of purchasers are listed in Penn-Physick Papers, mss. 8:39, HSP. The lottery was advertised in Andrew Bradford's *American Weekly Mercury*, nos. 814, 816, 817, 831, 833, 834. T. Penn

ever, the lottery failed to sell. Prominent Quakers opposed it as immoral. Their opposition might or might not have mattered much to land speculators, who have never been a notably moral lot; but in this instance the moral principle was backed up by law. The Penns had, oddly enough, overlooked a provincial statute against lotteries; it was rather awkward for them to guarantee good title to land acquired by illicit means, regardless of Indian claims.[26] Thomas Penn was not daunted. He organized a secret "little" lottery and sold a number of large tracts to an inner circle of confidants who were as little bothered as he by either morality or law. He authorized surveys, the records of which were kept in his secret files in the Land Office, and he withheld patents until after the Walk should be performed. When the patents were finally issued, the illegality of the transactions was cloaked behind the vague phrase, "by agreement some time since made."[27]

Surveyors' activities could be kept secret from Philadelphians, but not from Indian residents of the land being measured. Indian anger mounted and became audible. Logan recommended that some handouts be given to Sassoonan. Sassoonan claimed no right to land ownership in Nutimus's territory, but he was "considered and respected as the Chief of all our Delaware Indians."[28] Some presents were given with the hope of recruiting Sassoonan's influence to mollify Nutimus.[29] Whether Sassoonan cooperated went unrecorded but Nutimus did not become silent. In 1636, however, the Iroquois arrived to conclude their alliance, and thereafter the Penns felt confident enough to consummate their plans.[30]

More Shawnees flee, and the Mohawks grumble

Trouble threatened for a moment from an unexpected direction. A substantial Shawnee community of 130 warriors and their families living on the Susquehanna River's North Branch sent to Detroit for permission to remove thence, and the French offered not only a welcome but provisions for the march. The event disturbed the Mohawks, who had been the nearest of the Six Nations to those Shawnees. They complained of it to New

mentioned it in letters to Samuel Blunston, July 20, 1735 and Jan. 24, 1736 (1735 Old Style), Penn Mss., Thos. Penn, 1730–1766, boxed, HSP; Penn had survey warrants printed for purchasers, ibid.; J. Penn to T. Penn, March 18, 1736 (1735 Old Style), mss., Penn Letter Books 1:146.

26. *Statutes of Pa.* 4:141–47; Asa E. Martin, "Lotteries in Pennsylvania Prior to 1833," *Pa. Mag. of Hist. and Biog.* 47(1923), pp. 307–27, and 48 (1924), pp. 66–93, 159–80; Clement Plumsted to J. Penn, Sept. 10, 1736, mss., Penn Mss., Corr. of Penn Family 18:26, HSP.

27. Details in Appendix B, "Documents of the Walking Purchase."

28. Logan to Penns, June 25, 1735, *Pa. Archives*, 2d ser., 7:178.

29. *Pa. Council Minutes*, Aug. 20 and 21, 1736, 4:53–56.

30. See ch. 16.

York's Governor Clarke with the acid observation that the Shawnee flight was "Governor Pens own Fault." The Mohawks had not participated in Iroquois delegations to Philadelphia, and their comments to Governor Clarke were so much out of coordination with that delegation's secret agreements that we must presume the Mohawks were not let in on the secrets. "It is a Custome amongst the Christians," they said, "that when they buy Land of the Indians to take in more than is agreed for. And we believe Mr. Penn has Encroached on their [the Shawnees'] Lands and therefore they go for Protection to the French."[31] Clarke passed this on to Logan, who denounced it as "absolutely groundless and false." But the Mohawks kept somewhat aloof from Pennsylvania.[32]

A confidence game and the Walk

Logan's denunciation notwithstanding, the Penns' encroachments were real. By the time he wrote, they had bulldozed their plans for the Walking Purchase past Delaware resistance. John Penn adroitly flattered two of the chiefs present at the 1735 Pennsbury meeting by having their portraits painted. These two, Lappawinzo and Tishcohan, still look out sadly from the wall of the Historical Society of Pennsylvania.[33] Apparently Lappawinzo was highly susceptible to the Penns' attentions. He reappeared in Philadelphia on other business at the end of May 1737, and Thomas Penn seized the opportunity to caress him once more. Thomas took him off for dinner at the Proprietary table and loaded him with £20 worth of presents. Lappawinzo conceded Thomas's demand that the Walk be performed "to fix the bounds of the former purchase."[34]

There was pressure also from the (non-Mohawk) Iroquois.[35] Old Nutimus capitulated, and the Delawares gathered at Philadelphia in August 1737 to settle the procedure for the Walk. Thomas Penn carefully obtained another document from them—one with genuine original signatures that would be more presentable than the old paper he had been arguing from—

31. Conference minutes, June 25–30, 1737, N.Y.Col.Docs. 6:98–109 (esp. 99), 105–6.
32. Logan to Clarke, Aug. 4, 1737, mss., Logan Papers 10:58, HSP.
33. William J. Buck, "Lappawinzo and Tishcohan, Chiefs of the Lenni Lenape," Pa. Mag. of Hist. and Biog. 7 (1883), pp. 215–18.
34. A deposition of Edward Marshall, the man who completed the walk of the Walking Purchase, refers to Lappawinzo as "then the King or principal Chief of the Delaware Indians." The circumstances discount Marshall's value as a witness and his remark conflicts with Logan's assignment of paramount status to Sassoonan. Deposition, March 1, 1757, HSP mss. transcripts, Bd. of Trade Papers, Proprieties, 21–1, p. 230; Logan to Penns, June 25, 1735, Pa. Archives, 2d ser., 7:178; Minutes of Property, May 29, 1737, Pa. Archives, 3d ser., 1:86–87. For further discussion of Delaware leadership see Francis Jennings, "The Delaware Interregnum," Pa. Mag. of Hist. and Biog. 89 (1965), pp. 174–98.
35. Teedyuscung's statement, 1762, Johnson Papers 3:779.

and the new document was carefully preserved, though the old one disappeared. Thomas explained its quality in careful language that his brothers would understand. "I would not take their Conveyance as it would have lessened the Validity of the former deed, but only a Release of their Claim with an Acknowledgment of their Ancestors' before-mentioned sale."[36] Ever afterward the Penns relied on this document to authenticate their Walk.

Even to obtain this supposed confirmation of a supposed agreement, Thomas and his aides resorted to chicanery comparable to a carnival swindler's shell game. They presented a map to the Delawares, pretending that it portrayed the area to be walked. On this "draught," streams were drawn in a pattern that the Indians recognized as representing the lower end of Bucks County, but false labels were given to the streams, which extended the representation far beyond its picture. What the illiterate Indians saw as *Tohickon Creek* was labeled "West Branch River Delaware"—i.e., the Lehigh River. What the Indians therefore thought they were signing was an agreement to bound a tract of land that all agreed had been sold long ago. What they signed, in fact, was something else again as they soon found out. Only the colonial antagonists of the Penns would have been able to expose the misrepresentation, and they were never permitted to see it.[37]

With this trickery, Penn gained the signatures he needed to make a presentable case in court. All preparations were now complete. The walk's rehearsal had been performed. The Iroquois were lined up. The paperwork was done. The Walk was walked. We need not go into detail about it. The Walkers covered sixty-four miles in their day and a half of "walking"—clearly something more than a stroll—and the lines drawn from the finishing point with great punctilio were angled so as to include all of Nutimus's lands, all of the Lehigh Valley between the Lehigh and Delaware rivers (which Nutimus would have no right to sell even if he had wanted to), and a great tract beyond the Blue Mountain. Naturally enough, the Delawares cried fraud. This response had been anticipated and was disregarded.[38]

36. T. Penn to Brothers, Oct. 11, 1737, mss., Penn Mss., Off. Corr. 3:55, HSP.

37. The map trick is described in P. Wallace, *Weiser*, p. 98, and in A. Wallace, *Teedyuscung*, pp. 25–26. The source is Pa. Council Minutes, Aug. 24, 1737, mss., never printed, HSP mss. transcripts, Bd. of Trade Papers, Proprieties 21–1, indorsed x–12, pp. 195 ff. See Appendix B, herein.

38. An excellent pro-Delaware description is in A. Wallace, *Teedyuscung*, pp. 25–30. A pro-Penn version is in *Indian Treaties Printed by Benjamin Franklin, 1736–1762*, ed. Julian P. Boyd (Philadelphia: Historical Society of Pennsylvania, 1938).

A bibliographic note: Boyd's beautifully printed volume includes documents on which the Proprietary case was based. Boyd carefully noted, however, that he had not consulted the manuscript sources when writing his Introduction. Though the acknowledgment was commendable, the fact must be deplored because the Indians' case never got into printed sources.

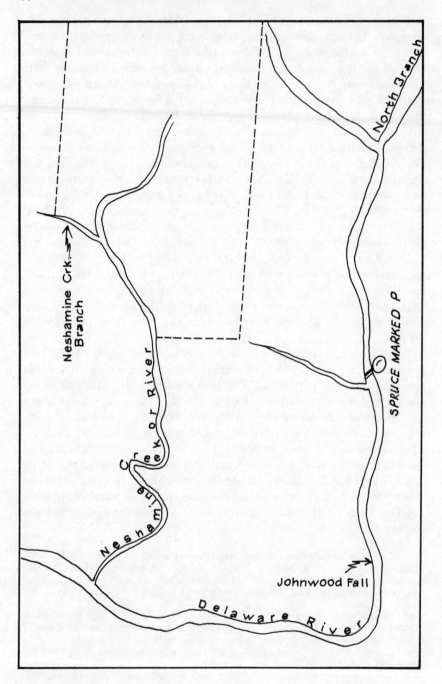

Thomas Penn contentedly informed his brothers that the Walk "at no very great Expence . . . takes in as Much Ground as any Person here ever expected." But his accompanying remark that all had been done by Indian consent and "to their satisfaction" is somewhat shaded by his afterthought that "The Minutes of the Treaty are not settled in so exact a Manner as I shal have them reduced to." We cannot doubt how Penn's reduction affected the minutes' reliability. Even so, they must still have been altogether too informative for later purposes; though Thomas promised to send a copy of them along with a copy of the quitclaim "confirmation," only the quitclaim survived among the Penn papers, and the minutes vanished from the province's official records.[39]

39. T. Penn to Brothers, Oct. 11, 1737, mss., Penn Mss., Off. Corr. 3:55; quitclaim: Penn Mss., Indian Affairs 1:41, HSP. A purported copy of the vanished minutes was dredged up from somewhere by the Proprietary lawyers to be submitted to Sir William Johnson's hearing in 1762. It was forwarded by Johnson to the Board of Trade and is the only available source. Considering how those lawyers fabricated and falsified other papers, it is anyone's guess what they did to their "copy" of Penn's "reduction" of the original. *Pa. Council Minutes*, Aug. 24, 1737, HSP mss. transcripts, Bd. of Trade Papers, Proprieties 21-1, ind. x-12, pp. 195 ff.

MAP 14. (facing page) In 1762 the Proprietary lawyers introduced this sketch as evidence in the hearing before Sir William Johnson. They stated that it had been shown to the Indians in 1737 as an explanation of where the Walking Purchase would extend, and that the Indians had then signed their confirmation deed of 1737, which was what the Penns relied on ever afterward for the validity of the Walk.

The lines on this chart do not correspond to the topography of the region. Neshaminy Creek, as labeled, does fall into the Delaware River above the big bend, but it does not extend above what in actuality would be Tohickon Creek because there is no considerable stream between Neshaminy and Tohickon. Here, however, this is labeled "Great Creek or Mackerickitton." In actuality, Neshaminy lies entirely below Tohickon, and considerably so. On this chart Neshaminy seems to extend nearly to what is labeled "West Branch River Delaware." It seems that what was labeled so was presented to the Indians as Tohickon Creek. As A.F.C. Wallace remarks, "The illiterate Indian owners of the lands north of Tohiccon Creek *saw* a map of the country south of Tohiccon; but the map's lettering *read* north of Tohiccon." [*King of the Delawares*, p. 25.]

Note that a hastily drawn line extends upward from the west branch of Neshaminy. This corresponds to the language of the "ancient deed," and was probably shown to the Indians as meeting Tohickon somewhere off the edge of the chart. Probably the other, more carefully drawn line—"The Supposed Day and a half's Journey back into ye Woods"—was drawn in afterwards, as indeed all the labeling may have been. TRANSCRIPTS OF BOARD OF TRADE PAPERS, PROPRIETIES, 21, PT. 1, P. 199, HSP. REPRODUCED BY COURTESY OF THE SOCIETY.

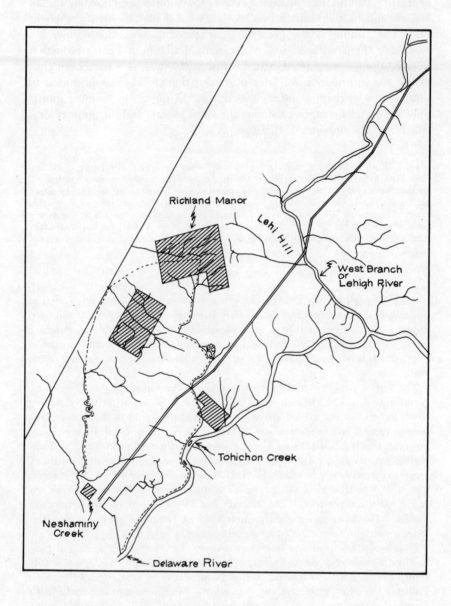

Anger, threats, and violence

Thomas Penn issued formal patents for the lands he had already sold and surveyed "by agreement some time since made." The speculators in his scheme resold to settlers at extortionate markups, and the settlers moved in. The desperate Delawares sent a letter to Bucks County Justice Jeremiah Langhorne (one of Logan's closest cronies), renewing their claims to ownership in a curious mixture of deference and bravado. They threatened to drive the intruders out.[40]

From the fragmentary record, it appears that Nutimus's protest aroused some of the colonial settlers to rage. It is not to be wondered at and need not necessarily be ascribed to deepseated malice. These were people who had paid high prices for deeds that now bore guarantees of good title, and they had no knowledge of the skullduggery that preceded the issuance of those deeds. They responded to Nutimus's threats with righteous menaces of their own. Nutimus dictated another letter complaining that "We dare not Speak for our Rights but there is an Uproar and [we are] in danger of being Cut to pieces." Still talking tough, he climaxed, "if this practice must hold why then we are no more Brothers and Friends but much more like Open Enemies."[41] No Delaware chief had ever before used language like that toward the Pennsylvania government.

Nutimus soon discovered how right he was. A settler, one Jacob Sebering, dared to speak up in behalf of the Indians. He was menaced in a "Great Uproar" of other settlers. In a manner that foreshadowed many

40. Delaware Indians to Jeremiah Langhorne, Smithfield, Nov. 21, 1740, mss., Penn Mss., Indian Affairs 4:30.
41. Loc. cit.

MAP 15. (facing page) THE INDIANS' UNDERSTANDING OF THE "ANCIENT DEED." This is a detail from a large map of the Walking Purchase now at the Historical Society of Pennsylvania. The original was made in 1873 by the Friendly Association and was owned by a Friend named George Scattergood in 1873.

Its accompanying text remarks: "The pricked Line from Delaware to Neshaminy, and up the west branch thereof was much further as makes a day and half walk according to the Indians intent and from thence to Tohickon and down the said Creek to the River Delaware to the Place, denotes the Tract of Land sold, as is alleged by the Indians; and all the Land belonging to the Indians, who contracted with Wm. Penn."

The long straight parallel lines show the course actually walked by the Proprietarys' agents.

Note: Stream identification does not appear on the chart. I have added it for clarity. The rectangular enclosures denote Proprietary manor lands. COPIES OF MAPS AND PAPERS RELATING TO THE "WALKING PURCHASE," 1737, MSS., SOCIETY MISCELLANEOUS COLLECTION, HSP. REPRODUCED BY COURTESY OF THE SOCIETY.

American tragedies to come, this believer in color-blind justice was doubly victimized, by the law as well as the mob. Instead of being offered protection, Sebering was taken into custody. The outraged Indians freed him, whereupon Governor Thomas, who had kept himself studiously ignorant of the proceedings till then, intervened to demand Sebering's delivery to the Sheriff of Bucks County.[42] I have not been able to find what happened to Sebering in the county's court records.[43] It is clear, however, that Nutimus was right in thinking, "We May not have an Honest Man to take Our part in any Just Cause but he must be killed or fly his Countrey."

Governor Thomas moved the machinery of official menace. "Consider well what you do," he wrote to Nutimus. "The English . . . are vastly superior in numbers and consequently would be soon able to overpower you." It was "not necessary" to discuss lands any further. Then he exploded Logan's carefully prepared mine: "your Uncles the Five Nations [whose] Assistance you expect to have, signed a release for those [lands] . . . and also in a Letter sent this Government [asked] that we would never treat with their Cousins the Delawares [about] Land." Nutimus replied that he would abide the outcome of a fair hearing by the Iroquois when next they should come to Philadelphia.[44]

Conquest of the eastern Delawares

In August 1741, pathetic old Sassoonan came to Philadelphia for a ceremonial farewell to Thomas Penn, who was about to return to England.

42. Nutimus to Langhorne, Jan. 3, 1741 (1740, Old Style), mss., Penn Mss., Indian Affairs 4:30; Gov. Thomas to the Delawares March 27, loc. cit. Thomas's reply is dated three months after Nutimus's letter. He was apparently intent on letting the belligerent locals dispose of Nutimus.

Thomas was completely the Penns' creature. He had solicited his post with a promise to give security "for the performance of whatever shall be demanded by you." He was hired for a minimum of four years on condition that he would obey all instructions and secretly rebate to the Penns half of his "Profitts" from the province. He could "dispose of no place, nor pass no Law" without Thomas Penn's approval. Thomas to J. Penn, London, Oct. 5, 1736, mss., Penn Mss., Off. Corr. 3:27; John to Thomas Penn, Feb. 17, 1737, mss., Penn Letter Books 1:182, HSP.

43. Sebering was of Dutch extraction, and the "uproar" against him apparently was made by Scotch-Irish settlers. Minor Swick, "The Sebring Family," Somerset County Historical Quarterly (N.J.), 3 (1914), pp. 118–24.

44. Governor Thomas to the Delawares, March 27, 1741 (1740 Old Style), and reply, mss., Penn Mss., Indian Affairs 4:30. These letters, now blotched and mutilated, formed Exhibit no. 14 of the defense prepared by Proprietary agents in 1758, but they were omitted from the papers submitted to Sir William Johnson in 1762. Their bad condition has made it necessary to guess the words in brackets, but the context is clear enough to make the sense fairly dependable. The Indians' reply has a tantalizing reference to a legal proceeding against Sebring on the 12th of some month in 1741 in a county the name of which is illegible. I have not found court records of Bucks Co., Pa., preceding 1742.

Once more, Sassoonan repeated the special status of the Delawares, remarking "That he lives in the middle between the Five Nations and his Brothers [of Pennsylvania]. He loves his Unckles and he loves his Brothers and desires to have the paths that lead to both places [clear] and open." His brothers promptly suppressed this too-revealing speech from the official records. (The manuscript is in a box full of miscellaneous scraps at the Historical Society of Pennsylvania.)[45]

Sassoonan's speech contained even more damaging material. He presented Pisquetomen "as the Person who is to have the chief command and to be the mouth of his people after [Sassoonan's] decease and desires his brethren would hearken and give credit to what he says." Logan's long intrigue against Pisquetomen had come apart. Powerless Sassoonan had been obsequious but not quite so stupid as he appeared; he simply bided his time. As for Pisquetomen, his disposition toward his "brethren" had not been improved by events since Logan first moved against him. He had witnessed Logan's cheating in the payment for Tulpehocken lands, and he had been present in Philadelphia at the final negotiations for the Walking Purchase.

Logan was alarmed by Pisquetomen's reemergence. When he received word of the long-awaited coming of the Six Nations in June 1742, he ordered Conrad Weiser to keep Sassoonan's people away. But a "further thought" struck Logan, and he rescinded the order in a postscript to the same letter. It might be "proper enough" for Sassoonan and some of his council to attend, "for probably we may have an important treaty."[46] Thus it came about that multilingual Pisquetomen acted as Nutimus's interpreter at that treaty.[47]

In the most intimate way possible, he experienced the bloodless conquest and humiliation of his people, and the transformation of the Covenant Chain. He saw Governor Thomas rise and address the Six Nations: "We now expect from You that you will cause these [Delaware] Indians

45. Sassoonan's speech, Aug. 7, 1741, mss., Records of the Provincial Council and Other Papers from the Numismatic and Antiquarian Society (boxed), fol. 1740–1749, HSP. This odd scrap is in the not-to-be-doubted scrawl of Secretary Richard Peters, which is easier to identify than to read. For the scattering of Pa.'s official records see Roland M. Bauman, "Samuel Hazard: Editor and Archivist for the Keystone State," *Pa Mag. of Hist. and Biog.* 107:2 (April 1983), pp. 195–215.

46. Logan to Weiser, June 10, 1742, mss., Peters Mss. 1:84, HSP.

47. *Pa. Council Minutes*, July 12, 1742, 4:578. Official treaty minutes are scattered through *Pa. Council Minutes* from July 2 to July 12, 1742, 4:559–86. A good short account is in Weslager, *Delaware Indians*, pp. 190–94. Unprecedented numbers of Indians attended this treaty. The very harsh winter of 1740–1741 had created conditions of actual deaths from famine. Richard Peters counted "upwards of 220 Indians" in town—i.e., in Philadelphia—"of one sort or another," though only 50 had been expected, and mentioned Weiser's opinion that they had come "for support." Governor Thomas maneuvered to put the expense of their entertainment on the assembly. *Pa. Council Minutes*, Oct. 14, 1741, 4:501; Peters to T. Penn, July 9, 1742, mss., Peters Letter Books, 1737–1750, Bk. 5, sheet 16.

to remove from the Lands in the fforks of the Delaware, and not give any further Disturbance to the Persons who are now in Possession." Upon which the Onondaga speaker Canasatego turned to the Delawares and blustered, "Cousins, Let this Belt of Wampum serve to Chastize you; You ought to be taken by the Hair of the Head and shaked severely till you recover your Senses and become Sober; you don't know what Ground you stand on, nor what you are doing." Canasatego did not really seize Nutimus by the hair as some writers have over-enthusiastically interpreted this passage. His message was grim enough without resort to acrobatics.[48]

He discovered suddenly that the land the Iroquois had refused to claim till 1736 because of acknowledged Delaware ownership had never belonged to the Delawares at all—and he fabricated an ancient conquest to justify the real one under way. "How came you to take upon you to sell Land at all? We conquered You, we made Women of you. You know you are Women, and can no more sell Land than Women.[49] Nor is it fit you should have the power of selling Lands since you would abuse it. This Land that you Claim is gone through your Guts. You have been furnished with Cloths and Meat and Drink by the Goods paid you for it, and now You want it again like Children as you are."

In one speech the Delawares descended from cousins to children. However, Canasatego was being carried away by his own rodomontade. The Iroquois did not later try to enforce the status of children. Rather they assumed the admonitory role of uncles and continued as before to address the Delawares as nephews, also as grandfathers! In this case there was no contradiction. Grandfathers deserved veneration and ceremonial deference but could not give orders. Nephews were obliged to give heed to their uncles' wishes. Both metaphorical roles could easily be assigned to the same persons. Indian metaphors have their own logic.

Even by Indian logic, however, Canasatego violated all the rules except the one about ends determining means. First he denied the Delawares' right to sell land; then he berated them for using the goods received from a sale fifty-five years earlier, in 1687; then, with the inconsistency possible to brute force, he bullied them for not sharing those goods with the Iroquois at that early date when (as he knew privately) the Iroquois had laid no claim to Delaware lands. "What makes you sell Land in the Dark? Did we ever receive any Part, even the Value of a Pipe Shank, from you for it?" Shikellamy and Saristaquo, the Oneida chiefs who had signed Logan's

48. *Pa. Council Minutes* 4:575–76; 578–80.
49. Cf. with the speech of Onondaga and Cayuga chiefs in 1684 when they specifically abjured claims on any land in Pennsylvania except the Susquehanna Valley. Treaty minutes, Aug. 2, 1684, *N.Y.Col.Docs.* 3:53.

"deed" in 1736, listened quietly as Canasatego thus converted black to white.

He was not yet finished. "We charge You to remove instantly. We don't give you the liberty to think about it. You are Women; take the Advice of a Wise Man and remove immediately. . . . We, therefore, Assign you two Places to go—either to Wyoming [on the Susquehanna North Branch] or Shamokin. You may go to either of these Places, and then we shall have you more under our Eye, and shall see how You Behave." Intoxicated with rhetoric as he was, Canasatego did not repeat the mistake that had been made with those distant Shawnees. The locations he assigned lay directly between Pennsylvania's settled territory and Iroquoia. These eastern Delawares, unlike those that had already migrated west, were not to be allowed to make contact with the French.

As the purpose of this book is primarily to follow Iroquois fortunes, we shall leave the Delawares here until another book may properly recite their revival. The Walking Purchase was their nadir, to be sure, but to regard it as *the* turning point in Pennsylvania's relations with the Delawares is "something of an exaggeration," as C. A. Weslager has remarked. Before Nutimus's eviction, chief Checochinican's Brandywines and chief Sassoonan's Tulpehockens had been deprived of their land by different sorts of power plays. One might reasonably place the turning point of Pennsylvania's Indian affairs at the moment of William Penn's second and final return to England in 1701. James Logan began to circumvent and alter Penn's Indian policies almost as soon as Penn took ship. But Weslager is right in a very real sense when he says that "the real turning point occurred when William Penn's humanitarian policy toward the Delawares gave way to Logan's new policy of strengthening their uncles, the Six Nations."[50] The fateful alliance between Pennsylvania and the Iroquois changed history on the large scale. When James Logan seduced the Iroquois into serving his purposes against their tributaries instead of protecting the tributaries against him, he opened the gate to colonial settlement beyond the Appalachians, insured that the French would respond in arms, and guaranteed the deaths of hundreds of Pennsylvania's back settlers at the hands of Delawares seeking righteous, though misdirected, vengeance.

Logan's masters, the Penns, fared better than the poor wretches of the frontiers. A single set of statistics shows how they achieved sudden real wealth by the adoption of their new Indian policies. Between 1701 and 1732 their total income from land sales was £12,610 / 3 / 6, Pennsylvania currency. In the like period of thirty years from 1732 to 1762, their land

---

50. Weslager, *Delaware Indians*, p. 193.

sales brought in (Pa.) £214,709 / 1 / 2¼. The Penns rose from the shabby gentility of perpetual debt to a status of substantial riches and power.[51]

As for the Iroquois, the triumphal speech of Canasatego seemed glorious. They appeared for the moment to have stopped the vise of competing empires from closing upon themselves. Not even their overmastering of the Shawnee bands in Pennsylvania had been so heady a victory as domination over the important and prestigious Delawares. But even as the Iroquois achieved their moment of triumph, the Shawnees were slipping through their fingers, and many of the Delawares also, to regain independence under new political identities in a new homeland in the west.

In the Ohio region there was a constant competition by French and English colonials, as well as the Six Nations, for the allegiance and support of the resident tribes; and the Indians of the region accepted no domination from any source, colonial or tribal. George Snyderman's judgment seems sound. The Six Nations' compliance in the Walking Purchase "unquestionably hastened the decay of the League, for its failure to protect the interests of the Nephews meant the eventual death of the family tree."[52]

51. An Account of the Grant of Pennsylvania made at the request of the Honorable John Penn, Jr., and John Penn, Sr., 1779, photostat of mss., Penn Papers from Friends' House in London, HSP.

52. George S. Snyderman, "The Manuscript Collections of the Philadelphia Yearly Meeting of Friends Pertaining to the American Indian," *Procs. of Amer. Phil. Soc.* 102 (1958), p. 616.

Chapter 18 ❧ SUMMIT and SLOPE

The intensity with which a sense of distinct identity was maintained by any given Indian group was quite unrelated to the extent to which its customs and beliefs had been replaced by those of the conquerors; the sense of identity was not at all proportional to the number of aboriginal traditions persisting. The processes of cultural assimilation were in fact distinct from the processes of group identification.

The factors affecting the Indian sense of identity were numerous and no one factor among those operating within the Indian societies can be said to be decisive in all instances. A major influence in all cases, however, was the conditions affecting the relationship of Indians to the land.

Edward H. Spicer, *Cycles of Conquest*

It might be very adviseable . . . that His Majesty would be pleased . . . to direct all the Governours on this continent to send for the Sachems and Heads of the Indians in their respective governments, and having renued the Covenant Chain with them, as they call it, to make a strict enquiry into all their complaints and gievances, both in respect of their lands and on other accounts; assuring them of redresse. . . .

Something of this sort my Lord would be very proper to have done; that we may if possible keep the Indians quiet and in temper, till we have our country better settled and secured and the French rooted out, and then we may expect to have the heathen on better terms, altho' justice ought forever to be don 'em.

Caleb Heathcote, Manor of Scarsdale, July 16, 1715

Settlers: Scotch-Irish and Moravian

Logan wrote contentedly to the Penns in England, "This has been, throughout, an excellent treaty."[1] Most of the Indians who lived in the Forks of Delaware region departed, as instructed. Some were to show up later on the Allegheny River. Others went with Nutimus to Nescopeck on the Susquehanna North Branch.[2] But a number remained stubbornly and evasively behind, in spite of all menaces and pressures. They had to contend with a new wave of colonial immigrants.

It is as true of Europeans as of Indians that they are not all alike. To homogenize them as "Whites" is to force history into the mold of racist ideology, no matter how good a writer's intentions may be. The new settlers moving into the Forks of Delaware differed from each other in ethnic origins, religions, and attitudes toward Indians. Most were either Scotch-

1. Logan to Proprietaries, July 12, 1742, mss., Peters Mss. 1:89, HSP.
2. A. F. C. Wallace, *Teedyuscung*, p. 63.

Irish Presbyterians or Central European "United Brethren" Moravians.

The Scotch-Irish began to arrive in Pennsylvania in 1718, and the earlier immigrants were located by James Logan along the province's southern strip in dispute with Lord Baltimore. In 1728, however, under the patronage of Logan's competitor William Allen, a new group of Scotch-Irish people founded Craig's Settlement on the Lehigh River. Later to become the city of Allentown, it was undeniably in unpurchased Indian territory, and the Delawares protested strongly. The Penns' Walking Purchase eventually provided a pretense of legality for the settlement but did not reduce the Indians' bitterness nor the settlers' reciprocal hostility.[3]

The Moravians began coming in 1741, after the consummation of the Walking Purchase, and they were shocked to hear from the Indians that the land they had bought was not so clear of encumbrance on their title as had been guaranteed. (They bought it from evangelist George Whitefield, who had earlier purchased it from William Allen.) But the Moravians reacted to the news with a degree of compassion. When informed that the local magistrate had received an order "for dispossessing the Indians, who have made themselves Masters of our purchased land in Nazareth . . . purchased and warranted to us by the Honourable Proprietor," they offered to let the Indian in residence remain as formally their tenant, free of rent, "because the said Place has been a Settlement of his Forefathers; and we will not drive any body from such a Right, was it only a simple Imagination." The government insisted on eviction, so the Moravians made a payment to the Indian they were replacing.[4]

The variant attitudes of the Scotch-Irish and Moravians may be seen in the light of their histories before coming to America. The Scotch-Irish, so-called, were descendants of Scots who had settled in the north of Ireland after it was devastated by Oliver Cromwell. Their people were accustomed to the invader's role and practices, and continue to the present day to be at bloody odds with the surrounding "mere" Irish. I speak of fact without attributing fault; but when English overlords racked their rents intolerably high, a tide of the Scotch-Irish flooded into Pennsylvania bringing along their hatred of both overlords and natives. They were not softened by their inherited Calvinist creed of exclusive election with its blessing on violent means by the elect to attain their predestined rewards.

The Moravians were a rather different lot. Their Protestantism dated

3. *Publications of the Northampton County* [Pa.] *Historical and Genealogical Society* 1 (Easton, 1926), pp. 6, 46, et passim; Logan to J. Penn, May 14, 1729, mss., Penn Mss., Off. Corr. 2:68; Logan to Penns, mss., Logan Ltr. Bks. 3:309–18; Logan to T. Penn, Dec. 18, 1730, mss., Penn Mss., Off. Corr. 2:145.

4. *The Bethlehem Diary*, trans. and ed. Kenneth G. Hamilton, 1:1742–1744 (Bethlehem, Pa.: Archives of the Moravian Church, 1971), pp. 31–32, 129; Joseph M. Levering, *A History of Bethlehem, Pennsylvania, 1741–1892* (Bethlehem, 1903), pp. 50–51, 154–55; A. F. C. Wallace, *Teedyuscung*, p. 38.

from John Wycliffe and John Hus, who had preached long before John Calvin was born. Instead of being descended from persons enjoying the fruits of conquest, the Moravians' ancestors had been persecuted unmercifully in their native land and finally hounded out of it. Those who came to Pennsylvania were themselves refugees from religious persecution. Though not absolute pacifists, they stressed doctrines of love and peace, and their missionary zeal was as fervent as that of the Jesuits. A painting by one of them still survives to show a radiant Christ in Heaven surrounded by adorers of every kind of human pigmentation and native costume, and ranked without discrimination.[5]

The Moravians had come as a body into Pennsylvania unaware that they were intruding into Indian territory. They bought from William Allen the land on which Bethlehem was to be built. Then came enlightenment through the protests of a Delaware named Captain John, whose home, cornfields, and peach orchard were on that land. The flustered Moravians paid again to Captain John. It was not a second payment to him for the same land, as is so often charged against Indians selling land; this was the first and only compensation he received. Thomas Penn, when he heard about it, was irritated, recognizing that this simple act of justice might expose the nature of his own transactions.[6]

Soon the Moravians organized missions to the neighboring Indians, providing refuge for them in the mission town of Gnadenhutten at the Lehigh Gap in the Blue Mountain range. The imperatives of faith appear here in processes similar to those of missions of other religions. The Moravians required Indians to adopt "civilized" dress and behavior. Unlike the Puritans, however, Moravian missionaries exerted no compulsion except banishment for misbehavior.[7] Indians were free to come and go. The Moravian missions were to become a major factor in the lives of Delaware Indians through the rest of their history.

5. The original painting is in the Archives of the Moravian Church, Bethlehem, Pa.

6. The Moravians bought two tracts—the sites of present-day Nazareth and Bethlehem. Apparently they purchased again to connect the two tracts, for Richard Peters suggested to Thomas Penn that the third tract should be conveyed in London, "because poor and best to be bought by those who have not seen it." Peters's second motive was to push the survey away from a tract of his own, which, presumably, was not so poor. R. Peters to T. Penn, July 9, 1742, mss., Peters Letter Books, 1737–1750, Bk. 5, sheet 16, HSP. Other lands: Northampton Co. Papers Bethlehem and Vicinity, 1741–1886, pp. 19–20. Nazareth tract can be traced in Pa. Patent Book, F–6; 120, and Northampton Co. Deed Book, C–1:156–64, Easton Court House. Joseph M. Levering, *A History of Bethlehem, Pennsylvania, 1741–1892* (Bethlehem, Pa.: Times Publishing Co., 1903), pp. 50–51, 154–55; A. Wallace, *Teedyuschung,* pp. 37–39.

7. Ibid., pp. 39–44, 47–50. Curiously, the issue of hair length was exactly opposed in Pennsylvania to what it had been in Massachusetts's 17th-century reservations. In Pennsylvania the "wild" Indians shaved their heads, and converts grew long hair. In Massachusetts the Puritans had required "civilized" converts to cut their hair short. "Civilization" has its ups and downs.

The Scotch-Irish intruded upon the Delawares more harshly. A single family of Scotch-Irish brothers—the Brainerds—preached Presbyterianism and apparently made some converts. (Moses Tatamy was one.)[8] But the Brainerds' example was not followed by others of their faith. Quite to the contrary, the Scotch-Irish colonials were intent on driving all Indians away, and they made no offer of compensation. Their major contribution to the Christian missions was a succession of attempts to massacre the converts. Theologically, they represented the Old Testament Yahweh in conflict with the New Testament Christ. It appears that all the missionaries made many converts because of Indian desires to acquire sanctuary from bellicose Scotch-Irish neighbors, and that the neighbors were intent on destroying the sanctuaries as well as their occupants.[9]

Yet the missions themselves, despite the good intentions behind them, were like missions everywhere in tearing apart the fabric of tribal society. Delawares who held fast to traditional religion and custom detested the converts. In the traditionalists' view the Christian Indians were renegades who had defected just when unity was most needed against a common enemy. Worse, the Moravian converts became absolute pacifists—more pacifist indeed than their teachers. To a society of warriors peace might be desirable, but pacifism was contemptible. The converts were caught between abuse by the Scotch-Irish on the one side and abuse by traditionalist Delawares on the other. They had no one to turn to for protection except their missionaries and the supporting Moravian community.[10] Notably the Moravian missions were outside the Covenant Chain, and the pacifist converts were of no use to the Iroquois. The missions became one of the funnels down which the strength of the Six Nations drained away.

The turbulent Ohio country

The biggest of those funnels, however, was the "Ohio country." This region was not identical with the State of Ohio as now bounded. To eighteenth-century Pennsylvanians the Ohio country began with the Allegheny tributary of the Ohio River (the tributary itself was often called the Ohio)

8. Weslager, *Delaware Indians*, pp. 192, 262–63, 271; W. A. Hunter, "Moses (Tunda) Tatamy," in *A. Delaware Indian Symposium*, p. 74.

9. A series of letters from James Logan comments on how his Scotch-Irish "countrymen" dealt harshly with the Indians. Examples: Logan to J. Penn, Aug. 13, 1729, mss., Penn Mss., Off. Corr. 2:83; Logan to T. Penn, mss., ibid., 2:145, HSP.

10. James Axtell has suggested provocatively how Indians "used" missions for their own reasons. "Some thoughts on the Ethnohistory of Missions," a paper read at Wilfred Laurier Conference Ethnohistory and Ethnology, Oct. 31, 1980, Waterloo, Ontario. Forthcoming in *Ethnohistory*. See also A. Wallace. *Teedyuscung*, p. 38.

and extended indefinitely westward to merge with an equally vague "Illinois country."[11] Delawares and Shawnees from the east settled new villages on the Allegheny and upper Ohio rivers, approaching a reverse migration of Wyandots and Twightwees from the west.[12] The Ohio country river valleys became a refuge, as the Susquehanna Valley formerly had been, and Pennsylvania's traders followed their old customers to the new habitations.[13] But there were no tight controls in the Ohio country such as Logan had exerted over Conestoga. At the Ohio, both the Indians and the traders were laws unto themselves.

At the end of the seventeenth century the Iroquois had been driven out of territory beyond Cleveland, Ohio, by combined action of the French and their Indian allies; they had striven ever afterward to achieve by diplomacy what they had lost in war. Their first major effort, and one they clung to for decades, was alliance with the Fox tribe, whose bands spread over a range from Green Bay, Wisconsin, to Detroit. The alliance was based primarily on mutual antagonism toward the French; it had problems from the beginning because the Foxes had few friends and many enemies among the surrounding tribes. In 1712 the Fox band at Detroit was destroyed by Indian enemies, with some French assistance. The French thereafter restored a degree of order in their alliance system, but the Foxes continued to break the peace, especially by raiding the Illinois confederacy. In 1729 the French mobilized their resources for an all-out war of extermination against the Foxes and succeeded to a degree that frightened their own allies. As a base for Iroquois influence in the west, the Foxes had liabilities.[14]

Other tribes were also willing to do business with the Five Nations, but not always on terms acceptable to the latter. The favorable prices of English goods were a perpetual attraction, especially during the period when a market glut brought on an embargo against shipment of furs to France. English colonials repeatedly advised the Iroquois to "open a path" for the western tribes to journey to English traders, and a number of instances show such tribes as the Ottawas treating warily with the Five Nations for

11. The two areas were distinguished as centers of activity. The French were paramount and omnipresent in the Illinois country. The Ohio country was taken over by Pennsylvania traders in the 1740s until the French evicted them forcibly.

12. Edmunds, *Potawatomis*, pp. 41–47. Note that Twightwee and Miami are English and French names, respectively, for the same people.

13. The fullest account is in Hanna, *Wilderness Trail*, vol. 2.

14. Edmunds, *Potawatomis*, ch. 2. Documentation of the Fox alliance is indirect and hazy. I suspect that the treaty minutes of July 5, 1710, refer to the Foxes in the phrase, "the farr Nations who are come into the Covenant Chain." *N.Y.Col.Mss.* 10:525. The ink was so faint that B. Fernow misread "farr" as "five" in compiling his calendar. *Calendar of Council minutes, 1668–1783*, comp. Berthold Fernow, *New York State Library Bulletin* 58 (Albany: University of the State of New York, 1902), p. 239.

this advantage.[15] Such liaisons were inherently unstable. They were constantly eroded by French pressures, and they were always subject to the effects of division among the Iroquois themselves. No such alliance could be equally beneficial to all the Iroquois nations, and all of the Five Nations were actutely aware that direct contact between the western nations and the English might easily eventuate in the elimination of the Iroquois middlemen.

By the 1720s the Iroquois began to speak confidently at treaty conferences about the way they had penetrated French defenses to extend their Covenant Chain to western tribes. We have seen how they "ordered" western allies to rise in insurrection against the French in 1726, but we have also seen that the command was disregarded.[16] In short, these alliances were made with independent Indian nations. The Covenant Chain in the west, such as it may have been, did not consist of tributaries in the ordinary subordinate sense of that English word.

The Six Nations and the French were equally disturbed by all this independence. Neither benefited by direct trade between the Ohio Indians and Pennsylvania traders. French concern heightened with the realization that British subjects were successfully penetrating the mountain barriers at last, to set up permanent trading posts in French-claimed territory. That the traders at such posts exerted political influence over the tribes, the French knew well; it was the principle underlying their whole system of territorial expansion. One British trader in particular, an Irishman named George Croghan, drove his pack horses all the way to Lake Erie, where, by 1744, he had built a store to trade with Senecas at Cuyahoga on the site of modern Cleveland, Ohio.[17] New France could not permit such competition. The French took measures to expel the intruders.

New France had the more reason for concern because its controls seemed to be coming apart farther west. A valiant French effort to extend the trade all the way to the upper Missouri Valley came to grief when militant Sioux bands assumed the obstructive role formerly played by the Fox tribe. The uneasy Huron-Wyandots moved upward along the Ohio to gain a measure of independence from France by proximity to British trad-

15. Norton, *Fur Trade*, pp. 20–21, 37–38, 159; treaty minutes, June 8, 1710, *Wraxall's Abridgment*, pp. 73–74. Norton errs, I think, in giving the Ottawas a path without interruption over a relatively long period of time. They alternated peace and war with the Iroquois.

16. See ch. 15.

17. Croghan has had two biographers whose works are complementary to a certain extent: Nicholas B. Wainwright, *George Croghan: Wilderness Diplomat*, published for the Institute of Early American History and Culture (Chapel Hill: University of North Carolina Press, 1959), and Albert T. Volwiler, *George Croghan and the Westward Movement, 1741–1782* (Cleveland: Arthur H. Clark Co., 1926).

ers.[18] The same reasoning made the French see clearly that a showdown with Britain was imminent. They strengthened their positions everywhere, including their Fort St. Frederic at Lake Champlain's southern end (Crown Point)—150 miles from Albany and less than half that distance from New England's settlements on the Connecticut River. No one could doubt its significance: this fort's function was not so much to control Indians as to threaten Englishmen.[19]

Mohawk travail

The Iroquois observed all and liked little. Their Pennsylvania alliance had secured one flank, but had not rescued them from the pressures squeezing so inexorably upon them. It had given no benefit at all to the Mohawks. As Pennsylvania's Governor James Hamilton explained (in 1754), the Mohawks had an agreement with the other Iroquois nations "that the Mohocks shall have nothing to do with the Lands in Pennsylvania, nor take any Part of the Presents received for them, because they have already had more than their Share for other Lands, and therefore the Mohocks never come here in Treaties for Land."[20]

The Mohawks' proximity to Albany, once an asset, had become a hazard. Albany was almost gone as a commercial partner. Its western trade had practically ceased to exist. Only the direct trade with Montreal remained; it was dominated by the Canadian Caughnawagas and passed under the guns of Fort St. Frederic. The western trade had moved to Oswego on the shore of Lake Ontario and to a new merchant named William Johnson, who set up shop west of Schenectady in the Mohawk Valley. For the Iroquois the changes meant a net loss. Though Johnson cultivated the Mohawks carefully, Oswego traders dealt directly with "far Indians" and coureurs de bois; there was no intermediary function for the Iroquois in their way of doing business. Despite Johnson's partnership, it was a time of travail especially for the Mohawks, who, of all the Iroquois nations, were closest to the growing settlements of New York colonials; for the Mohawks were losing land as well as trade. Though nothing so

18. Edmunds, *Potawatomis*, pp. 37–38, 41–43; S. Dale Standen, "Beauharnois de La Boische, Charles de, Marquis de Beauharnois," in *Dict. Can. Biog.* 3:43–46.

19. Lanctot, *History of Cannada* 3:35, 70; Guy Omeron Coolidge, *The French Occupation of the Champlain Valley from 1609 to 1759*, reprinted from *Proceedings of the Vermont Historical Society*, n.s., vol. 6, no. 3, Montpelier, 1938 (Harrison, N.Y.: Harbor Hill Books, 1979), chs. 11, 12.

20. James Hamilton to Roger Wolcott, March 4, 1754, in *The Pitkin Papers*, vol. 19 of *Collections of the Connecticut Historical Society* (Hartford, 1921), pp. 254–55. Hamilton's understanding may have been too simplistic to cover all the intricacies of Six Nations politics, but it must be taken into account.

elaborate as the Walking Purchase was concocted in New York, the lands seized by simpler, cruder frauds were just as extensive, and the Mohawks became just as bitter as the Delawares.[21]

Virginians attack an Iroquois party

Even the Pennsylvania alliance failed to fulfill its promise, for the Pennsylvanians had been unable, after all, to achieve a treaty with Virginia for the Iroquois. So the Six Nations–Catawba War ground on endlessly with its minor but constant bloodletting; and as the Shenandoah Valley filled up with immigrants from Europe the new settlers became more hostile to Six Nations warriors passing through to hit the Catawbas. Until one day, in the winter of 1742–43, a raiding party was attacked by Virginians so that the issue no longer could be blinked by responsible statesmen in either the colonies or the tribes. Conrad Weiser was hurried off to condole the Iroquois and to get the facts of the matter from Shikellamy at Shamokin. Weiser's report is worth quotation at length as a vivid example of how back-country incidents gathered momentum.

He wrote that one of the incident's Indian survivors "told Shikellimo, his Grandfather, that when they (twenty-two Onondagoe Indians and seven Oneidos) got over Potomack River, no body would give them a mouthful of Victuals.

They wanted to go to some Justice to have their [safe conduct] Pass renewed but could find none. They travelld along in great want of Victuals. There was no more Deer to be killed and they had been Starved to Death if they had not killed a Hog now and then. . . . Some while after they came to a big House, the Indians observed a great Number of People in the House. they were invited to come in. the main Body staid out some Distance from the House. some the oldest went in but more and more white People gathering the Indians without Door called to their ffriends to come away. The white People would not permit them to go but sent out a Captain with a Sword on his side to bring the others in which they refused. In the Meantime those that were in the House thought proper to show their Pass which they obtain'd in Pennsylvania. But the white Men told them they must not go any farther. Upon which the Indians went out of the House. the Man with the Sword endavourd to Stop them by force and drew his Sword. when the others saw the naked Sword they made a field Cry and took up their Arms in order to defend themselves but were Commanded by their Captain to be quiet till they were hurt and to Let the white People begin Violence. The Indians did not mind the Man with the naked Sword but went away . . . [three days later] a white Man came to their ffires and counted them all . . . The Indians hasted away and when they got

21. Norton, *Fur Trade*, pp. 172–73, 185–86; Nammack, *Fraud, Politics, and Dispossession*, ch. 4.

into the Road again two Boys that were in the Rear heard a Great Talk and Noise of Horses and looked about and saw a Great number of white Men on horseback and they called to the foremost that there was the white Men a coming, who order'd them to come up. then the Boys ran and the white Men fir'd at them but missed them. The Captain of the Indians seeing the Boys receav'd no hurt and a white Colour flying told the Indians to be quiet for that a white Colour was always a token of Peace with the white Men. Whilst the Indians were laying down their Bundles and their Captain talk'd to them not to fire till the white Men had hurt them the white Men alighted from their Horses just by and fired the second Time and Killed two upon the Spott, one of which was Shikellimo's Cousin. The Indians then made a field Cry and were commanded by their Captain to fight for Life who, after he had fired off his Gun, took to his Hatchett and exhorted the Stoutest to follow him and they ran in amongst the white People and did execution with their Hatchetts which put the white men to flight immediately. But the Captain would not suffer them to pursue them, Told them they did not come to fight white Men but the Cawtabaws."[22]

By this account the Indians lost three dead; a fourth was wounded so badly as probably to die; four more Indians were wounded less seriously. They counted eight dead Virginians. Weiser accepted the account as true, and so did Governor Thomas when he received the report. Thomas wrote to Virginia's Governor Gooch, "If the Inhabitants of the back Parts of Virginia have no more Truth and Honesty than some of ours, I should make no Scruple to prefer an Iroquois Testimony to theirs." Thomas may have been right, although his tone rings oddly coming from the man who had used the Walking Purchase to evict the Delawares. Lower-class back inhabitants were not the only colonials to lack Truth and Honesty. In this instance, however, Thomas's newly acquired faith in the honesty of Indians gave him the opportunity to suggest that the time had come for Virginia to negotiate the troublesome issue of Iroquois claims to the Shenandoah Valley.[23]

Gooch agreed. Instead of denouncing Iroquois perfidy, barbarism, and so on, in the familiar litany of justification, Gooch offered the aggrieved families of the slain warriors a wergeld payment of £100 sterling! He also retreated from his former rigid position that treaty making must be done at Williamsburg. Something new was cooking in Virginia. Middleman Weiser went ajourneying to Onondaga once more.[24]

22. Weiser's journal, in *Pa. Council Minutes*, April 5, 1743, 4:644–46.
23. Thomas to Gooch, April 25, 1743, in *Pa. Council Minutes*, June 6, 1743, 4:653–54.
24. Gooch to Thomas, May 7, 1743, in ibid. 4:654–55.

Treaty at Lancaster

The Iroquois solved the problem of face-saving. If Virginians would not insist on their going to Williamsburg, they would concede that the Virginians need not come to Albany. There is a hint of Weiser's influence in the Six Nations' suggestion that the parties could meet each other half way, on neutral ground, at Lancaster in Pennsylvania.[25] The arrangement suited Onondaga as much as Virginia because it excluded New York and the Mohawks from the proposed treaty and thus assured the Onondagans primacy among the Indian parties. Pennsylvania, obviously enough, was not unhappy about terms that made its new fire blaze as brightly as the old one at Albany.

So it came about that a great multiparty treaty took place at Lancaster in June 1744. Commissioners from Virginia and Maryland as well as the delegation from Pennsylvania made this the most important Iroquois treaty since the one held at Albany in 1722, and the change of locale was not the least noteworthy feature of the meeting. Pennsylvania's commissioners, especially Conrad Weiser, assumed significant leadership in Indian affairs for all the British colonies. The "Flaming fine Gentlemen" from Virginia wanted to run the conference their own way without Weiser, but the Pennsylvanians insisted—rightly it seems—that Weiser was indispensable.[26]

On the twenty-second of June the Iroquois entourage marched into town—deputies, wives, and children, followers, and attendants—252 strong. "A great concourse of people followed them," we are told by Maryland's Witham Marshe. "They marched in very good order, with Cannasateego, one of the Onondago chiefs, at their head; who, when he came near to the court-house wherein we were dining, sung, in the Indian language, a song, inviting us to a renewal of all treaties heretofore made, and that now to be made." The Indians pitched camp by making wigwams in "some vacant lots in the back part of the town." Then there was much conviviality, "a good quantity of punch, wine, and pipes and tobacco, were given to the sachems, and the Governor and all the commissioners drank to them, whom they pledged." After supper the next day, Saturday, thirty or forty of the younger Indians danced "one of their lighter war dances," hopping "round the ring after a frantic fashion, not unlike the priests of Bacchus in old times."[27] Marshe's ability to understand what he saw is rather doubtful. It does not seem likely that Indians would dance a war dance, even a "lighter" one, at a peace treaty. His authority on

25. Weiser's journal, in ibid., Aug. 13, 1743, 4:667.
26. P. Wallace, *Weiser*, p. 184.
27. Witham Marshe, "Journal of the Treaty . . . at Lancaster in Pennsylvania, June, 1744," *Collections of the Massachusetts Historical Society*, 1st ser., 7:178–81.

Bacchic revels is also a little dubious. But, his caustic manner notwithstanding, he gives us the best picture available of the socializing at Lancaster.

The more serious side is in the treaty minutes. Canasatego was in his element. When the governor of Maryland disputed the Iroquois land claims on grounds that Maryland had possessed the land more than a hundred years, Canasatego lectured on history. "What is One Hundred Years in Comparison of the Length of Time since our Claim began? since we came out of this Ground? For we must tell you, that long before One Hundred Years our Ancestors came out of this very Ground, and their Children have remained here ever since." This was rather all-inclusive geography, and is the only known occasion upon which the Iroquois claimed ancestors in Maryland, but Canasatego had not been strong on factuality or logic since his rhetorical heights in "womanizing" the Delawares two years earlier.

He continued his speech, however, in a noteworthy example of the Iroquois tradition of the Covenant Chain, mixed with a little propaganda.

Canasatego's traditionary history

"You came out of the Ground in a Country that lies beyond the Seas, there you may have a just Claim, but here you must allow us to be your elder Brethren, and the Lands to belong to us long before you knew any thing of them. It is true, that above One Hundred Years ago the Dutch came here in a Ship, and brought with them several Goods; such as Awls, Knives, Hatchets, Guns, and many other Particulars; which they gave us; and when they had taught us how to use their Things, and we saw what sort of People they were, we were so well pleased with them, that we tied their Ship to the Bushes on the Shore; and afterwards, liking them still better the longer they staid with us, and thinking the Bushes too slender, we removed the Rope, and tied it to the Trees; and as the Trees were liable to be blown down by high Winds, or to decay of themselves, we, from the Affection we bore them, again removed the Rope, and tied it to a strong and big Rock [*here the Interpreter said, They mean the Oneido Country*] and not content with this, for its further Security we removed the Rope to the big Mountain [*here the Interpreter says they mean the Onandago Country*] and there we tied it very fast, and rowll'd Wampum about it; and, to make it still more secure, we stood upon the Wampum, and sat down upon it, to defend it, and to prevent any Hurt coming to it, and did our best Endeavours that it might remain uninjured for ever. During all this Time the New-comers, the Dutch, acknowledged our Right to the Lands, and sollicited us, from Time to Time, to grant them Parts of our Country, and to enter into League and Covenant with us, and to become one People with us.

After this the English came into the Country, and, as we were told, became one People with the Dutch. About two Years after the Arrival of the English, an

English Governor came to Albany, and finding what great Friendship subsisted between us and the Dutch, he approved it mightily, and desired to make as strong a League, and to be upon as good Terms with us as the Dutch were, with whom he was united, and to become one People with us: And by his further Care in looking into what had passed between us, he found that the Rope which tied the Ship to the great Mountain was only fastened with Wampum, which was liable to break and rot, and to perish in a Course of Years; he therefore told us, he would give us a Silver Chain, which would be much stronger, and would last for ever. This we accepted, and fastened the Ship with it, and it has lasted ever since. Indeed we have had some small Differences with the English, and, during these Misunderstandings, some of their young Men would, by way of Reproach, be every now and then telling us, that we should have perished if they had not come into the Country and furnished us with Strowds and Hatchets, and Guns, and other Things necessary for the Support of Life; but we always gave them to understand that they were mistaken, that we lived before they came amongst us, and as well, or better, if we may believe what our Forefathers have told us. We had then Room enough, and Plenty of Deer, which was easily caught; and tho' we had not Knives, Hatchets, or Guns, such as we have now, yet we had Knives of Stone, and Hatchets of Stone, and Bows and Arrows, and those served our Uses as well then as the English ones do now. We are now straitened, and sometimes in want of Deer, and liable to many other Inconveniences since the English came among us, and particularly from that Pen-and-Ink Work that is going on at the Table [*pointing to the Secretary*] and we will give you an Instance of this. Our Brother Onas, a great while ago, came to Albany to buy the Sasquahannan Lands of us, but our Brother, the Governor of New-York [Thomas Dongan], who, as we suppose, had not a good Understanding with our Brother Onas, advised us not to sell him any Land, for he would make an ill Use of it; and, pretending to be our good Friend, he advised us, in order to prevent Onas's, or any other Person's imposing upon us, and that we might always have our Land when we should want it, to put it into his Hands; and told us, he would keep it for our Use, and never open his Hands, but keep them close shut, and not part with any of it, but at our Request. Accordingly we trusted him, and put our Land into his Hands, and charged him to keep it safe for our Use; but, some Time after, he went to England, and carried our Land with him, and there sold it to our Brother Onas for a large Sum of Money; and when, at the Instance of our Brother Onas, we were minded to sell him some Lands, he told us, we had sold the Sasquahannah Lands already to the Governor of New-York, and that he had bought them from him in England; tho', when he came to understand how the Governor of New-York had deceived us, he very generously paid us for our Lands over again.

Tho' we mention this Instance of an Imposition put upon us by the Governor of New-York, yet we must do the english the Justice to say, we have had their hearty Assistances in our Wars with the French, who were no sooner arrived amongst us than they began to render us uneasy, and to provoke us to War, and we have had several Wars with them; during all which we constantly received Assistance from the English, and, by their Means, we have always been able to keep up our Heads against their Attacks.

We now come nearer home. We have had your Deeds interpreted to us, and we

acknowledge them to be good and valid, and that the Conestogoe or Sasquahannah Indians had a Right to sell those Lands to you, for they were then theirs; but
since that Time we have conquered them, and their Country now belongs to us,
and the Lands we demanded Satisfaction for are no Part of the Lands comprized
in those Deeds; they are the Cohongorontas [i.e., Potomack] Lands; those, we are
sure, you have not possessed One Hundred Years, no, nor above Ten Years, and
we made our Demands so soon as we knew your People were settled in those
Parts. These have never been sold, but remain still to be disposed of; and we are
well pleased to hear you are provided with Goods, and do assure you of our Willingness to treat with you for those unpurchased Lands; in Confirmation whereof,
we present you with this Belt of Wampum.

Which was received with the usual Ceremonies.[28]

Not without some harsh words, an accommodation was reached. When
Virginia accused the Iroquois of violating their 1722 agreement to stay
outside Spotswood's Line, the Iroquois answered with another geography
lesson—a better one this time. That Line, they said, lay upon the mountains closest to Virginia's lowlands; nothing in the agreement had been
intended to keep them from traveling through the mountain valleys behind
the first ridge. Now they were willing to make a new agreement to remove
their Warriors' Path once more, this time "at the Foot of the Great Mountain," but no farther because of "those Parts of the Country being absolutely impassable by either Man or Beast." Virginians might have their
valleys in peace, but the Six Nations must be allowed a road.[29]

Rights of conquest, again

The Six Nations countercharged that colonials were trespassing on lands
the Iroquois had conquered from formerly resident tribes, and they wanted
satisfaction for their rights of conquest in both Maryland and Virginia.[30]
How many of those departed residents had, in fact, been conquered by
the Iroquois, I cannot say. The Piscatawa-Conoys went north to become
guests of the Iroquois after conflicts with Marylanders became no longer
tolerable. Perhaps the word translated as "conquest" meant something a

28. Treaty minutes, *Pa. Council Minutes*, June 26, 1744, 4:706–09. Bracketed comments in
italics are in the original.
29. The ambiguities in Spotswood's 1722 treaty at Albany now came out openly. At
Lancaster, the Iroquois accused Virginians of violating the treaty by crossing Spotswood's
line. The Virginians responded that "the White People, Your Brethren of Virginia, are in
no Article of that Treaty Prohibited to pass and Settle to the Westward of the Great Mountains. It is the Indians Tributary to Virginia that are restrained." This remark is interesting
in another connection as an early identification of "White" people; in 1722 they had been
"Christians." Treaty minutes, June 27 and 28, 1744, in *Pa. Council Minutes* 4:712–13, 717.
Cf. treaty minutes, Sept. 6 and 10, 1722, *N.Y.Col.Docs.* 5:670–73.
30. Treaty minutes, June 27, 1744, in *Pa. Council Minutes* 4:711–12.

bit different in the Iroquois languages. The assertion of conquest cannot logically be reconciled with Canasatego's bland declaration that the Iroquois had sprung out of that very ground. The contradiction points up how oral tradition must be used with as much care as written documents. There is nothing sacrosanct about either.

As for those supposedly conquered Conoys, we may note that some ignored both Pennsylvania and the Six Nations to join the Ohio Delawares, and still others, after their nation lost Maryland's recognition, remained in their homeland as "Wesorts," or "Brandywine People"—a hint that some of the Brandywine Delawares may have moved in with them. A group of these has reemerged in the twentieth century as the Piscataway Tribe.[31] What "conquest" means in such circumstances seems to depend a little on lack of challenge.

Among other considerations, "rights of conquest" last only as long as a conqueror can hang on to what he won with the sword, and the Iroquois, notably, were not taking over Virginia's real estate. Or Maryland's. At another time the fine, flaming southern gentlemen would probably have told the Six Nations what they could do with their conquest claims; but at Lancaster in 1744 the Virginians, especially, had objectives that required an uncharacteristically indulgent attitude and blandishing approach. After polite, preliminary haggling, they agreed to compensate the Iroquois. Maryland's price was £300 in Pennsylvania currency. Virginia lavishly laid out goods worth £200 in Pennsylvania currency, plus £200 in gold, and added another £100 in gold as a special present. Pennsylvania sweetened the pot with £300 more in currency. It added up to a tidy sum for an unenforceable claim.[32]

Iroquois cessions

The colonials were thinking of something more than Governor Thomas's admonition that "These Indians by their situation are a Frontier to some of [the English colonies]."[33] Though such wisdom provided an ample reason to refrain from hostilities with the Iroquois, nobody at Lancaster feared an Iroquois attack. The Virginians had a more positive goal in mind. Virginia's moving spirit in the Lancaster treaty was Colonel Thomas Lee, manager of the giant Fairfax estate. Lee had observed the migration of Germans to and through Pennsylvania and down the Shenandoah Valley. He knew well that great fortunes could be made by land speculators who

31. Christian F. Feest, "Nanticoke and Neighboring Tribes," in *Northeast*, pp. 240, 243, 245–47.
32. Treaty minutes, in *Pa. Council Minutes* 4:715–16, 726, 729.
33. *Pa. Council Minutes* 4:700.

successfully colonized their estates, and he knew that Virginia's charter gave the Old Dominion a claim on the Ohio country. Lee planned to extend Virginia's actual jurisdiction to correspond to its charter claims, and an Iroquois quitclaim would be a useful instrument in the process.[34]

The price paid by Virginia at Lancaster was a great bargain for what the Virginians obtained. The Six Nations chiefs thought they were ceding the Shenandoah Valley, but what they put their marks to said something grandiosely different. In their deed the Iroquois "renounce and disclaim not only all the right of the said six nations, but also recognize the right and title of our sovereign the King of Great Britain to all *the lands within the said colony [of Virginia] as it is now or hereafter may be peopled and bounded* by his said Majesty . . . his heirs and successors."[35] No one explained to the Iroquois that Virginia's charter limits had been expressed in terms of distance from "Cape or Point Comfort" two hundred miles to northward and two hundred miles to southward and from "*sea to sea, west and northwest.*" Had Virginia realized its full claims, all of midwestern United States, a substantial chunk of western Canada, and all of Alaska would now be part of Virginia, not to speak of the northern half of the United States to the Pacific coast.[36] Canasatego's joke about "that Pen and Ink work, that is going on at the Table" was funnier than he thought.[37]

Within three months after the Lancaster treaty, the Virginians began to capitalize on their Iroquois quitclaim; on April 26, 1745, the provincial government granted petitions for western lands totaling 300,000 acres.[38] Governor Gooch hesitated before taking the final step of sending settlers beyond the mountains, for "such Grants might possibly give some Umbrage to the French." Gooch thought that a fort would have to be built, "without which or some such work for their defence, it would be dangerous for them to venture out so far."[39] Events would prove him right

34. Alfred Procter James, *The Ohio Company: Its Inner History* (Pittsburgh: University of Pittsburgh Press, 1959), pp. 5, 9. Interestingly, the migration to Virginia seems to have started with some of the same Palatines who moved first from New York to Pennsylvania. They understood the Indian tenure issue well, and two of them planned with Pennsylvania's Ezekiel Harlan for large-scale migration of their countrymen. Klaus Wust, *The Virginia Germans* (Charlottesville: University Press of Virginia, 1969), pp. 29–31. Wust does not mention Indian treaties or the Covenant Chain, apparently not being as aware of such subjects as were the Germans in this book. Ezekiel Harlan was intimately involved in the land claims of the Brandywine Delawares. See Jennings, "Miquon's Passing," pp. 238–39, 247–49, 296, 301.

35. Deed, July 2, 1744. Original in Va. State Library, Richmond, Colonial Papers, Folder 41, Item 10. I have used the facsimile in the Newberry Library Iroquois archive.

36. P. Wallace, *Weiser*, p. 259; charter of 1609 in *The Genesis of the United States*, ed. Alexander Brown, 2 vols. (Boston: Houghton, Mifflin, and Co., 1890) 1:229.

37. *Pa. Council Minutes* 4:708.

38. James, *Ohio Company*, p. 8.

39. Berthold Fernow, *The Ohio Valley in Colonial Days* (Albany: Joel Munsell's Sons, 1890), pp. 243–44.

on both counts, and a third as well. When Virginia did begin to settle at the Ohio River, regardless of Iroquois deeds or Virginian pen-and-ink work, the resident Indians would be as unbrageous as the French.

Worm-eaten triumph

That must be matter for another book. To the Six Nations the Treaty of Lancaster seemed to be their moment of greatest triumph. Their preeminence over all the northern Indians was formally recognized by powerful colonial allies. Their land claims were recognized at least to the degree that they got compensation for colonial encroachments. Their oldest quarrel with an English colony was composed on what seemed to be highly satisfactory terms. They departed from Lancaster laden with goods, deference, gratification, and illusions.

The illusions lasted little longer than the goods. Lancaster opened a gate to the trans-Appalachian west for British colonization, and it guaranteed a violent French response. Lancaster demonstrated less the strength of the Iroquois than their dependence on English colonials, and it showed how a blowhard such as Canasatego could be manipulated by letting him posture to his heart's content so that he would forget to demand independent explication of the text he signed. Lancaster confirmed a division within the ranks of the Six Nations themselves, for the Mohawks again did not participate although issues of power were involved that went far beyond the cession of lands.[40] There is reason to believe that the other Iroquois had withheld information from the Mohawks about the whole sequence of agreements made in Pennsylvania that began in 1736.[41] In any case, the Mohawks dealt with New York's agents while the other Five Nations dealt with Pennsylvania, Maryland, and Virginia.

It is difficult to tell whether the damage done by this division outweighed certain advantages. As long as the Iroquois League could reconcile internal differences, it had a chance to gain strength from its own flexibility—facing alternately toward different colonies, just as it had survived earlier by dealing alternately with the French and the British.[42] The Mohawks were not merely absent from Lancaster; their chief, Hendrick,

40. Paul Wallace thought that "It was the Iroquois alliance, not the cession of Iroquois lands, that gave the Lancaster Treaty its importance." *Weiser*, pp. 185–86.

41. 41. I base this supposition on the ignorance displayed by the Mohawks at the 1758 grand treaty in Easton, which caused Conrad Weiser much uneasiness in the effort to avoid a candid response. This would not be the only instance of its kind: in 1745 the Mohawks and Tuscaroras complained that the Onondagas were conferring secretly with the governor of Canada and withholding information of what was transacted. Minutes of N. Y. Commissioners of Indian Affairs, Aug. 9, 1745, mss. copy in Peters Papers 2:41, HSP.

42. I owe this insight to Dr. Mary A. Druke.

seems to have been in Boston with a delegation purporting to speak for all the Six Nations.[43]

Speculation aside, the results of the treaties in Pennsylvania are clear in one respect. The policies enunciated by Canasatego were ultimately disastrous for the Iroquois. For thirty years previously, the League had followed the opposite policies of Decanisora, tediously and painstakingly building an Indian confederacy that protected Indian interests and faced the British colonials with united strength. The vast network of French-allied Indians then obliged the British to seek alternative commercial and military resources under Iroquois direction. But after the Iroquois about-face demonstrated in the treaties of 1736, 1742, and 1744, the Iroquois became heavily dependent on the English to enforce their short-term increase in power over the tributaries. Other chiefs besides Canasatego participated in the turn, but his was the bray that publicized it. No one can know what might have happened if the tradition of Decanisora had been preserved, but it could hardly have been worse.

So long as the Six Nations spoke in the Covenant Chain in behalf of the interests of all the Indians, the English authorities had no choice but to listen more or less respectfully. After the Six Nations faced the other way and spoke to the tributaries in the Chain in behalf of the English—more particularly, the Pennsylvanians—the willing allegiance of the tributaries soon became a sullen deference in form negated by independence in action as soon as the tributaries regrouped in the west.

Onondaga's about-face

There were repercussions within the Six Nations themselves. Canasatego died mysteriously a few days before Weiser and Daniel Claus were to treat with him in 1750. Many years later, Claus wrote that the death occurred "by Poison which was suspected to have been conveyed into his Victuals by some French emissaries that then resided at Onondaga Lake under the Disguise of Traders debauching the 6 Nations to the French Interest and inviting them to Swegatchy which settlement the Abbe Picquet was then forming after the peace of 1748."[44]

Conrad Weiser passed on a report current in Onondaga of Canasatego's being bribed by Moravians to sell land without approval by the Iroquois council. Weister discredited the report but thought it "perhaps occasioned his Canasategos Death."[45] To me this seems like someone's cover-up. It is

43. Treaty mss., July 1744, Massachusetts Archives 29:381–84. Incomplete and mutilated, it shows Massachusetts's effort once again, to recruit the Iroquois to fight the colony's Indian enemies. I have used the photocopy at the Newberry Library.
44. Colonel Daniel Claus, "Memoir of Descent," 1775?, mss., Public Archives of Canada M6 19 Fl, vol. 23, pt. 1. Again, thanks to Mary Druke.
45. P. Wallace, Weiser, p. 314.

much more likely that Weiser's hint that Canasatego's death had been "occasioned" referred to broader political developments. Claus thought of it as murder. Weiser suggests an execution.

Whatever the exact circumstances, there was no doubt about Ononda-ga's about-face in policy. During his journey, Weiser was told by old friends among the Mohawks "that the Onondagers, Cayugers, and Sene-cas were turned Frenchmen, and that some of the Oneiders inclined that way, and that they abused the Mohocks and used them ill for being true to the English." The French had erected a new fort "at a place called Swegatsy, not far from the Lake Frontinac, for the Indians," and "the French Priest at Swegatsy had made about a hundred Converts among the Onondagers, Men, Women, and Children that came to live at Swegatsy last Spring, and that the aforesaid French priest had cloathed them all in very fine Cloathes laced with Silver and gold and took them down, and presented them to the French Governor at Montreal, who had received them very kindly, and made them large Presents."[46]

"He that is on the head of affairs" at Onondaga now, reported Weiser to the Pennsylvania council, "is a professed Roman Catholick, and alto-gether devoted to the French."[47]

Weiser's journal contains an account of a significant symbolic event. "I was told by Tahashrouchioony the [new] Chief, that all the Belts of Wam-pum belonging to the Publick from the several English Governors that remained unanswered at the Death of Canassatego, and found in his Pos-session, were by his orders burned with him. This the said Chief said to make Canassatego a Thief after his Death; some imagine that his Widow and Family stole them."

This yarn is simply not credible. Much more likely, those belts were thrown contemptuously into Canasatego's grave, or simply destroyed, by his successor and possible executioners who were intent on putting an end to old ties with the English colonies. By destroying the belts, they ended the obligations implied by the belts without having to come back to the colonials in a hostile posture. A new start would have to be made.

Thus half of Canasatego's policy had been rejected—the half that com-mitted the Six Nations to do whatever dirty work among the Indians that was required by English colonials. But the Onondagas were reluctant to

---

46. Weiser's Journal, Oct. 10, 1750, mss., in Pa. Provincial Records, mss., vol. M, p. 87 Harrisburg. I have used the facsimile in the Newberry Library. The manuscript contains more than the printed journal, but the latter contains an interesting indication of the strength of Conndaga-Mohawk antagonism: Mohawks complained to Weiser "of the ill management of the English in Indian Affairs, and said that they were afraid to be cut off [i.e., destroyed] by foresaid Nations [Onondagas, Cayugas, and Senecas] because they charge them the Moh-ocks to be Slaves of the English; Several other Complaints they had but I could say nothing to them." Pa Council Minutes 5:470–80, quotation at p. 479.

47. Weiser to Peters, Sept. 30, 1750, in Pa. Council Minutes 5:467.

abandon the rest of Canasatego's policy—the part that involved Iroquois assertions of conquest and domination over the Delawares and Shawnees and the tribes of the Ohio country. But here they encountered a serious difficulty. They could browbeat the broken fragments of tribes still living along the branches of the Susquehanna and get away with it because they were stronger than those little villages. In the Ohio country, however, the authority of the Six Nations was more ceremonial than real. Only the backing of a colonial power could give them the power to enforce their "orders" in a land to which more of their own people had migrated than remained at home, not to speak of the great bulk of other populous tribes.

Privilege withdrawn

That difficulty came home to the Iroquois swiftly after Conrad Weiser reported how they had turned to the French. Pennsylvanians and Virginians realized that the Iroquois had become unreliable allies, and further that Iroquois power had become an empty shell where it was most needed: in the Ohio country. Wereupon the colonials abandoned their reliance on the Iroquois and opened direct negotations with the Ohio Indians, omitting Iroquois interposition. Conrad Weiser led the turnabout.[48]

There is no word more proper for these results than Iroquois defeat, however it may be interpreted. Many factors entered into it. Although the foregoing discussion has focused on relations between the Six Nations and their eastern tributaries, one must take into account the French expertise at manauever, the English intercolonial strife and clumsiness, and the probable drive for independence by the western Indians regardless of what happened back east. However these combined to create the fact of defeat, the fact is plain. "The Old Six Nations," wrote Richard Peters in 1749, "lose their Influence every day and grow contemptible."[49] True, the new defeat was neither as dramatic nor as immediately visible as deafeat by the French in the seventeenth century, so the Iroquois chiefs could maintain their illusions for a few years. To them it appeared that their grandeur in 1744 derived simply from the position they had won as sole recognized spokesmen for all the tribes. They had come to believe not only in their superior wisdom but in their own real supremacy. After a generation or two, they probably came to believe genuinely in the "conquests" of which they boasted. They thought they could control instead of merely leading their tributaries, and they continued their self-destructive course for a little while after the Treaty of Lancaster. But within a decade they learned

48. P. Wallace, *Weiser*, ch. 32.
49. Penn Mss., Off. Corr. 4:237–39, HSP.

that they would be sole spokesmen only so long as that role suited the convenience of the English colonies. Exclusive recognition could be, and was, withdrawn as easily as given. Such recognition had never even been considered by the French.

When imperial war renewed between France and Britain, Iroquois illusions shattered. Beginning in 1742, and resting to regroup their forces between 1749 and 1755, the empires once again clawed at each other in truly global conflict. During their long peace between 1713 and 1742, the Iroquois had had an opportunity to maneuver within a constantly contracting space. Now, however, a new era began, and all was again in turmoil.

Chapter 19 ❧ CONFLICT and ACCOMMODATION

Let Sepúlveda hear Trogus Pompey: "Nor could the Spaniards submit to the yoke of a conquered province until Caesar Augustus, after he had conquered the world, turned his victorious armies against them and organized that barbaric and wild people as a province, once he had led them by law to a more civilized way of life." Now see how he called the Spanish people barbaric and wild. I would like to hear Sepúlveda, in his cleverness, answer this question: Does he think that the war of the Romans against the Spanish was justified in order to free them from barbarism? And this question also: Did the Spanish wage an unjust war when they vigorously defended themselves against them?

Bartolomé de Las Casas, *In Defense of the Indians*, 1552.

Indian collaboration with Europeans

The typical picture of American Indians in our histories presents them as barriers to westward expansion of "civilization." This concept of civilization is so narrowly anglicized in ethnocentrism as to eliminate even the expansion of Spain and France. Certainly Spain drove northward from Florida and Mexico; and France moved both north and south along the Mississippi Valley. England and the United States had to conquer and purchase vast territories occupied and effectively controlled by Spanish and French nationals before "civilization"—read, Anglo-American political organizations—could go west. And when the time came to acquire Alaska, the Russians who had driven eastward into the continent from Asia had to be dealt with.

It must be emphasized that civilization was not an exclusive monopoly of the British empire and its colonies; and it follows that the westward march of civilization, as portrayed in our histories, is a fantasy. Not surprisingly, its corollary of the Indian or "savage" barrier is equally absurd when the hot air is blown away to permit a view of the fact supported by evidence. Indian *cooperation* was the prime requisite for European penetration and colonization of the North American continent. Despite the fascination of European observers and writers with the otherness of Indians, it was human similarity that created great institutions of commerce and

368 THE AMBIGUOUS IROQUOIS EMPIRE: PART THREE

politics through which Indians guided Europeans to the interior and collaborated in their exploitation of its vast resources.

One of those institutions was the Covenant Chain. It has been hiding
in thousands of source documents ever since the mythology of civilization-
savagery and the legal fiction of nation-state sovereignty were interposed
to block it out. We have seen a sampling of those documents. We know
the effectiveness of the Chain: it was the primary instrument for opening
the trans-Appalachian West to British colonization. But, if the Chain did
not conform to ordinary categories of historical analysis, just what was it?

A colleague and friend has expressed doubt that the Chain properly
constituted an institution. Was it, then, merely a catch-all rubric including miscellaneous happenings that had no integral relationship with each
other?

Apparently it was more than that. There was enough identifiable structure in the Chain to warrant being called a constitution—not in the American sense of one basic law, but rather as the British use that word to
embrace a whole body of traditions, customs, and practices basic to the
polity. The Chain's mutations need not put us off. We have no trouble
seeing an identity over centuries for the British Empire, despite all its
convulsions, because we recognize its durable core. So also, from beginning to end, the Iroquois were at the heart of the Covenant Chain.

The League and the Chain

But the Chain must not be confused with the Iroquois League nor with
that League plus its tributary system of alliances; the identifying quality
of the Chain was its combination of membership of both Indian and European polities. During its entire existence, the Chain was uniquely an institution created by contract for eliminating violence and reducing conflict
between Indians and Englishmen within specified and bounded territories
(often, however, by exporting violence beyond those bounds). That its
individual parties attempted also to turn the Chain to their special advantage is plain enough; but transient phenomena must not be confused with
basic functions, and there has never yet been a government anywhere
whose participants did not strive for special advantage.

Late in the nineteenth century, some Iroquois chiefs tried to reduce to
writing the political traditions of the old League. They produced several
different versions of the so-called Great Law of the League, none of which
mentions the Covenant Chain as such. The version of the Great Law most
current today gives rules for relations with "foreign [Indian] nations," for
their adoption into and expulsion from the League, and for the disposition
of "conquered nations"; but it does not mention an extended tributary

system. Neither does it speak specifically of relations with European polities, whether colonial or imperial. It is evident that the Covenant Chain was a novelty in Iroquois organization and thought, as strange to Iroquois customary law as to British statutory law. It was the creation of a historical moment. Though it endured for a century during which many parties were obliged to cope with its requirements, it did not bring about any fundamental alteration of either British or Iroquois legal structure. Long-established traditions resisted its novelties, and after the China's termination they resumed as though it had never been. One must infer what it was like from contemporary records that testify to the way it worked.

New York's dual center

The intricate relationships of the Chain became complex soon after its founding and varied confusingly as time went on. Its structure can be seen as an integrated group of sets. There was a set of English colonies effectively independent of each other but affiliated through their common crown. There was a parallel set of Indian tribes with the common characteristic of alliance to the Five Nations, although they had additional friendships and treaty arrangements within the general confederacy. Like a grid superposed upon these parallel sets of colonies and tribes were protectorates asserted by individual colonies over the tribes claimed to be within their several jurisdictions. And finally there was a special relationship between the Five Nations, at the head of their confederated allies, and the colony of New York, in what came to be a de facto, if not a de jure, leadership position amongst the English colonies in the field of Indian affairs. (New York's preeminence was to be challenged and to decline in the mid-eighteenth century.) Because of his special relationship with the Iroquois, New York's governor, who was a royal appointee, effectively served the crown in a dual capacity. From the city of New York he governed the colony, and from the town of Albany he intermittently imposed restrictions and controls on the frontiers from Virginia to Maine. One of the more hopeless gaffes of Frederick Jackson Turner was his proclamation that the 1754 Congress of Albany was the beginning of a new system of cooperation amongst the colonies in controlling the frontier.[1] It marked, in fact, the expiration of the old system in which the colonies had come to Albany from time to time to accommodate difficulties that had arisen in the Covenant Chain. As a result of the 1754 Congress's transparent failure to achieve anything positive, the crown took Indian affairs into its own

1. Frederick Jackson Turner, "The Significance of the Frontier in American History," in *The Frontier in American History* (New York: Henry Holt and Co., 1920), p. 15.

hands directly and appointed its own agent to superintend them—the famous Sir William Johnson.

For political as well as geographical reasons the province of New York was "esteemed as the centre of his Majesty's plantations on the continent," as the Board of Trade reported to the House of Commons in 1702. The Board recognized "the necessity of preserving the friendship of the Five Nations of Indians, which are a barrier between his Majesty's plantations and Canada, by treating them kindly, and shewing them a force constantly maintained in New-York, ready to protect them upon all occasions."[2] As we have seen, the Board's intentions to maintain that force were rarely fulfilled, but the partnership between Albany and the Mohawks was maintained by other means—not always welcomed by other tribes.

So much complexity obviously could not have been administered by a centralized bureaucracy even if the resources had been available for its maintenance. New York set up commissioners of Indian Affairs who worked out of Albany and kept records, but their method of operation conformed to Indian custom rather than the modes of European state hierarchies. Everything was done by council and agreement. At periodic intervals, formal treaty conferences convened to renew, revise, and enlarge the agreements formerly made, and in the intervals there were informal consultations to do subsidiary business.

Tribal insubordination

At first appearances, the tribes living outside New York's protection held an ambiguous position in the Chain. The governors of Connecticut, Massachusetts, Virginia, and Maryland claimed jurisdiction over all Indians, subject or free, within their respective territories as claimed by charter. In their own theory, the governors were deputies of the Crown that held sovereign jurisdiction, and that sovereignty was parcelled out to them for all inhabitants within their several colonies, Europeans and Indians alike. It made little difference in this respect whether an Indian tribe had ever acknowledged submission formally. On this assumption, such Indians were legally incompetent to treat with foreign powers or other colonies within the same empire, and their linkage to the Covenant Chain could only be through the intervening membership of the colonial government in charge. Thus Connecticut negotiated for the Mohegans, and Maryland negotiated

2. Reports to the House of Commons, March 22, 1700, and Feb. 5, 1702, in *Proceedings and Debates of the British Parliaments respecting North America, 1452–1754*, ed. Leo Francis Stock, 5 vols. (Washington, D.C.: 1924–1941) 2:368, 437.

in behalf of the Piscataways, after having gained New York's permission to treat with the Five Nations.[3]

Such situations have created great historical confusion because the governors' legal pretensions ran far beyond their capacity for enforcement. As a consequence, events sometimes deviated from the governors' theory to conform more closely to a counter theory held by the Iroquois. Regardless of English assumptions of sovereignty, the Iroquois negotiated directly with Canada at their pleasure and in spite of instructions to the contrary from governors of New York. Although the Iroquois treated respectfully and deferentially with the governors of other English colonies, what they did outside the treaty chamber shows that they did not accept the governors' assumption of full powers to treat in behalf of other tribes. The Iroquois required free tribes outside New York to negotiate directly and in person for themselves, regardless of vicarious stipulations made by governors. In their view, "People do not make peace until they see those who ask it."[4] Thus, although the Iroquois signed Maryland's treaty of peace for the Piscataways, the matter did not end there. The Iroquois went on to demand that the Piscataways confirm the peace by their own treaty action and to enter the Covenant Chain not merely as an adjunct of Maryland but also through direct alliance with the Five Nations. Piscataway resistance was worn down by incessant war until finally the tribe's chiefs showed up at Albany to speak for themselves according to demand. Similar pressures were exerted upon Indians in parts of lands that we call New England, Virginia, and New France, but which the Iroquois recognized as the territories of the free tribes in residence.[5]

The results of these pressures varied widely. Some tribes capitulated completely; others fought fiercely and remained independent to the end; some ducked skittishly in and out of the Chain. Iroquois success was conditioned by distance, circumstance, and the amount of colonial protection available to resisting tribes. At the far perimeters of Chain territories, Cherokees, Catawbas, Illinois, and Hurons were never forced into the Chain as tributaries (even though the Hurons took a terrible beating and

3. *Md. Archives* 5:243–46; 15:157; *Livingston Indian Records*, pp. 62, 153; *N.Y.Col.Docs.* 13:521–23.

4. Extract of the Conference between Lt. Gov. Clarke and the Five Nations, "towards the end of August 1740." *N.Y.Col.Docs.* 9:1062–63.

A bibliographic note: This is a French document, evidently drawn from a report made by French Mohawks attending the meeting. It contradicts New York's minutes of the same meeting. New York's account does not have the language quoted; instead it presents the Iroquois accepting Governor Clarke as peacemaking spokesman for other tribes, although the language attributed to the Five Nations is equivocal. Iroquois practice confirms the French document's version. New York: *N.Y.Col.Docs.* 6:172–79.

5. *N.Y.Col.Docs.* 13:519–29; 3:327; *Md.Archives* 15:282–84, 299–300, 358–59; 17:14; *Livingston Indian Records*, p. 83; *CSPA&WI, 1681–1685*, no. 184, p. 92; no. 185.

many became Seneca adoptees). The availability of French protection and aid enabled the Ottawas to affiliate and disaffiliate as they pleased. Shawnee bands accepted Chain membership along the Susquehanna and Delaware rivers, then moved westward to ally with the French and break away from the Chain. One rule prevailed despite Iroquois efforts to break it: tribes allied to New France never joined the Chain for any extended period of time. The French countered every Iroquois initiative with decisive action. The Chain remained limited within the effective jurisdictions of English colonies—and not even in all of those. The Carolinas stayed clear of the Chain. Iroquois inability to overcome the French barrier implied ultimate failure for Iroquois efforts to build what would today be called a "third force" between the European empires, and it made a mockery of claims to Iroquois empire. No matter how cleverly the Iroquois devised strategy and dedicated themselves to carrying it out, no matter how they maneuvered and twisted about, no matter how much they blustered and threatened, they were in the last analysis prisoners of systems of empire that were not of their own making. They could pursue their own interests as long as English colonial interests coincided. When they ventured out beyond English goals, as some of them often tried to do, they were soon beaten back.

Functions of Treaties

The means for reconciling interests and combining efforts was the treaty. This was all-purpose machinery. New York made treaties with the Iroquois and other Indians within its jurisdiction. The Iroquois made treaties with other colonies at Albany, with New York's consent and under New York's close supervision. In the eighteenth century, the Iroquois treated with other colonies, absent New York. The Iroquois made treaties with other tribes, wheresoever situated, whenever and wherever the tribal chiefs appointed. The tributary tribes treated with each other. The colonies also made tacit agreements with each other by means of the formal treaties they signed with the Iroquois.

When a treaty was confirmed it was enforced in the participants' several territories by their several customary or legal procedures. These bicultural sanctions remained as much alive after a treaty signing as a statute made by any legislature remains in force after the legislature's adjournment, but with a difference.[6] Whereas a legislative statute continues in force until repealed, the Iroquois required that all treaty agreements be regularly renewed. Specifications of obligation were thus altered from treaty to treaty

6. In the United States today, a treaty has the force of law, and it overrides conflicting statutory law.

although commitment to alliance continued. The Covenant Chain became something close to a condominium of multiple Indian tribes and English colonies.

Ambiguity of the Chain

A treaty is a contract, and it presumes parity of status and responsibility between the contracting parties. Subjects do not sign treaties with their rulers. As the Lords of Trade told commissioners from Massachusetts in 1677, "His Majesty did not think of treating with his own subjects as with foreigners."[7] But the Covenant Chain was legally ambiguous. Because of its bicultural membership it was dual in aspect and must be defined twice. From the Indian point of view, it was an organization of peers, unequal in real power, but equal in responsibility. The Iroquois saw the Chain as a fundamental institution of cooperation for apportioning tasks and rewards. Fully aware of disparities between colonial resources and their own, they could never forget their economic dependence on the intersocietal trade controlled by Europeans, but they conceived themselves as politically independent nations and demanded recognition as such in return for the services they could perform. In their view, instead of the Chain's being part of the British empire, the empire's colonies were part of the Chain. In the view of English statesmen, however, the Chain was an expedient to be maintained until the empire could muster enough local power to actualize the crown's pretensions to sovereignty. The English gave only de facto recognition to Indian nations. Never, at any time, did they relinquish their own crown's de jure pretensions to sovereignty.

Neither colonials nor Indians conceived the Chain as an altruistic organization. It is quite clear that the English regarded it as an instrument to serve their purposes and then to be "given law." From the Iroquois point of view the Chain was also a means of temporizing, of slowing down the inexorable advance of Europeans whose numbers increased swiftly while Indian populations declined. Within the limits of their real power—which limits were largely determined by what services they could perform for the English—the Iroquois manipulated Chain relationships to attain leadership among the allied tribes whom we call "tributaries." (I have strong doubts about the propriety of that semantic importation from European legal preconceptions.) As for the "tributaries," they wavered between perception of the Iroquois as intercessors between them and colonial power, and resentment of Iroquois pretensions; nor were they unaware of the

7. *CSPA&WI, 1677–1680*, p. 135. This is the voice of the emerging nation-state. Not long earlier, the crown's agents in Ireland had made treaties with lords who were claimed as subjects.

occasions when the Iroquois betrayed them. Yet the interests of all the parties coincided often enough, and mutual concessions were made frequently enough, to hold the rickety edifice more or less together for a century.

Although the Chain's members collaborated economically and militarily against French Canada, they wrestled constantly with each other for advantage: between tribe and colony, tribe and tribe, and colony and colony. Some of those contests have been mentioned in this book, but a chronological limit has precluded paying attention to the intensification of struggle within the Chain that occurred as the Seven Years War precipitated a showdown with France. This is a large subject, never heretofore examined with regard to the Chain's role. It will require at least one more book from this writer, who knows also of several being prepared by other scholars. Its time has come.

What can be said here is that efforts of Pennsylvania, Virginia, and Massachusetts to wrest control of the Chain away from New York, each for its own special advantage, produced chaos and weakness in the face of French advances. The alarmed crown thereupon acted to take the Chain directly under its own control by appointing the redoubtable Sir William Johnson as sole agent for dealing with the Iroquois, which meant, in effect, for royal management of the Covenant Chain. Johnson's claims to exclusive right were challenged by various colonial powers but upheld by others; consequently, still more complication entered into the Chain's affairs during this, its royal phase.

Johnson wrought well enough so that when the colony members of the Chain rebelled against their king, most of the Iroquois remained loyal. But some Iroquois and many tributaries joined the colonies, and the Chain broke apart, never to be reassembled. If an institution had descended from the Chain, one might regard it as formative, but after the cataclysm (for the Indians) of the American Revolution, the Chain became merely a vestigial form whose original function was quickly forgotten. Even the memory of the form soon faded.

Our side and their side

Considered in one way, the Covenant Chain was a by-product of the development of the modern nation-state in America. Because it was not integral to that political development it became invisible to scholars whose attention has been fixed narrowly on how present-day institutions of government came into being. Particular institutions aside, the Chain was integral to the growth and shaping of modern American society as a whole.

Considered in another aspect, the Chain was an example of accommodation and cooperation between peoples of different ethnicity, different cultures, and different social and political structures. The chronicler of accommodation has a great problem in trying to write fairly and objectively because of the categories that govern our thinking. At bottom is the assumption of sidedness: issues are seen at first glimpse as matters of Our Side and Their Side. (I live on the island of Martha's Vineyard, where this assumption is given delightfully clear expression. Happenings here are "on-island"; all the rest of the whole wide world is simply "off-island.") Primitive assumptions of sidedness develop into artificial, polarized categories of definition: savagery vs. civilization, heathen vs. Christian, subject vs. sovereign; upper class vs. lower class; Red (or Black) vs. White; and so on. Opposition and conflict inhere in the categories and in the attitudes so generated. In consequence, accommodation usually gets a bad press by being equated to capitulation or betrayal. Honor and glory are given to the heroes who stand staunch and fight hard for Our Side, whatever it happens to be. Compromisers become contemptible. Compare, for example, the epithet and invective so often heaped by historians upon Quakers in contrast to the gloriously militant Puritans.

With our eyes fixed upon conflict between two sides, and our sympathies fixed upon one of them, we glory in triumphs and fail to see the benefits to be derived from cooperation, or at least accommodation, between those sides. It seems to me that historical scholarship can be most useful in our day by finding ways to avoid political and social conflicts that all-too-predictably become disasters. This cannot be done by smudging the facts; conflicts of interests and ideas must be portrayed faithfully, or necessary adjustments cannot be made seasonably. But means and devices to avoid such conflicts, or to resolve them with minimum damage, must be given their due. The need is to reject the assumption of inevitability. That need has never been more pressing than in this era of nuclear armaments.

As an example of accommodation, the Covenant Chain had many obvious defects, and no attempt has been made herein to present it as an ideal model. It is nevertheless one kind of example. Perhaps comparative history will disclose more. Faced with creatures like amoebae and paramecia, the taxonomist tried at first to make them into animals, then realized that such organisms needed a protista category of their own. If historians compile enough examples of intercultural political accommodation, they may wish some day to devise a new category distinct from those of tribe and state and empire. For the present, seeing the Chain as it was is enough.

APPENDICES

APPENDIX A ❧

A Council at Onondaga, as reported by Conrad Weiser in 1743

Note: Weiser was sent by the government of Virginia to pacify the Six Nations after an incident in which Virginia backwoodsmen attacked an Iroquois party passing through. (See ch. 18.) His report of the treaty proceedings gives a rare, detailed picture of the ritual as it was conducted at Onondaga, away from European influence. As an adopted Mohawk, Weiser was one of the most sensitive of all European observers to Iroquois protocol, and his skill at adapting to it made him exceptionally successful in negotiations.

This journal is reprinted from *Pennsylvania Council Minutes* 4:660–69 primarily for its qualities of imagery and rhetoric; ethnographic analysis is not attempted. For that, see the essays in *The History and Culture of Iroquois Diplomacy*, edited by Francis Jennings, William N. Fenton, and Mary A. Druke (Syracuse, N.Y.: Syracuse University Press, forthcoming.)

August the 13th

Conrad Weiser's Report of his Journey to Onondago on the affairs of Virginia, in Obedience to the Orders of the Governor in Council, 13 June, 1743, delivered to the Governor the 1st September:

"On the 21st we arrived at Cachiadachse, the first Town of the Onondagoes. About noon I heard that the Messenger I had sent from Oswego had missed his Way and did not arrive there. I therefore immediately sent a Messenger from this place to the Chief Town about five miles off to acquaint the Chiefs of that Nation of my coming with a Message from Onas[1] on behalf of Assaryquoa.[2] They dispatched Messengers that Day to Summon the Council of the Six Nations. My Messenger came back & inform'd me that the House of Annwaraogon was appointed for our Lodging; we set out and arriv'd there at three o'Clock in the Afternoon. After we had eat some dry'd Eels boiled in Hominy, and some Matts had been spread for Us to lye upon, Canassatego & Caheshcarowanoto, of the Chiefs, with several more, came to see Us & receiv'd Us very kindly. They asked how their Brethren did in Philadelphia, and in particular the Governor, & whether Onas

1. The governor of Pennsylvania.
2. The governor of Virginia.

379

was arrived. I answer'd that their Brethren in Philadelphia were all well & in the same Disposition of Mind as they had left them in Last Year, and in particular the Governor their Brother was so, who according to the Trust reposed in him by Onas, when he left Philadelphia, was always engaged for the good of the Publick. We smoak'd a Pipe of Philadelphia Tobacco together, & had some further discourse on things of no Consequence. The 22d, early in the Morning, Tocanontie (otherwise call'd the black Prince of Onondago), came to see Us with Caxhayion and expressed their Satisfaction at my coming to Onondago, saying You never come without good News from our Brethren in Philadelphia. I smil'd & told him it was enough to kill a Man to come such a Long & bad Road over Hills, Rocks, Old Trees, and Rivers, and to fight through a Cloud of Vermine, and all kinds of Poisen'd Worms and creeping things, besides being Loaded with a disagreeable Message, upon which they laugh'd; and Tocanontie told me that he was extremely glad last Night to hear I was come to Onondago. Canassatego and Caheshcarowno, with several more, came to see Us again and spent the Day with us. We had for the Subject of our Conversation the Occurrences of our Journey and General News. The twenty-third it was good weather. I, with Shikellimo,[3] visited Canassatego, desired him to meet Us in the Bushes[4] to have a private Discourse, which he approved of. We met a little way distant from the Town; I brought with me my Instructions and the Wampums I had, and told him that as he was our Particular ffriend and well acquainted both with Indians & white People's Affairs & Customs, I would tell him all my Business, and beg his Advice how to speak to everything when the Council should be met. He assured me of his good will and Affection to the Governor of Pensilvania and all his People, and that he would do for me what lay in his power. I then explained my Instructions to him, and show'd him the Wampum. He told us that what he had heard of me was very good, he must first go and acquaint Caheshcarowano with it, and they would then both send for me and Shikellimo, and put us in the Way; we broke up imediately, and Canassatego went directly to Caheshcarowano and we to our Lodging. In the afternoon they sent for me and Shikellimo to the House of Caheshcarowano, and I was desired to bring my Instructions and my Wampums with me. I went along with the Messenger to the House of the said Chief, where I found, to my Surprize, all the Chiefs of Onondago met in Council. Tocanontie spoke to me after this Manner: 'Brother, the Chiefs of Onondago are all of one Body and Soul, and one Mind; therefore Canassatego and Caheshcarowano have acquainted us with the whole of what had passed betwixt You and Canassatego in the Bushes; you have done very well and prudent to inform the Onondagoes of your Message before the rest of the Counsellors meet, since it Concerns chiefly the Onondagoes, and it will altogether be left to Us by the Council of the United Nations to answer your Message; be, therefore, not surprised in seeing Us all Met in Council unexpectedly, and explain the Paper to Us you have from our Brother the Governor of Pennsylvania, which I did accordingly, and acquainted them with the whole Message; they seemed to be very well pleased, and promised they would put every-

3. The Six Nations resident agent at Shamokin, the village at the junction of the West and North branches of the Susquehanna River.

4. "In the bushes": a figure of speech meaning a private, informal meeting apart from formal councils.

thing in such Posture that when the Council of the United Nations arrive, I should have an Answer soon, and such an one as they did not doubt would be satisfactory to the Governor of Pennsylvania and Assaryquoa; that they had always so much regard for Onas & his People that they would do anything for them in their Power, and they looked upon the Person that kept House for Onas (meaning the Governor) as if Onas was there himself. I thanked them for their good will and Left them for this Time, knowing they had something to do amongst themselves; Tocanontie was Speaker. The 24th the Council of the Onandagoes sat again. Jonnhaty, the Captain of the Unhappy Company that had the skirmish last winter in Virginia, was sent for with two More of his Companions. He was desired to tell the story from the beginning how every thing happen'd, which he did; he seem'd to be a very thoughtful and honest Man, and took a deal of Time in telling the Story; after he had done, I told him I would write it down before I left Onondago, in his Presence, to which he agreed, and desired that some of the Chiefs might be present when he was to rehearse it again. In the Evening the Cajuga Deputies arrived. The 25th Visited Caheshcarowano this Morning, and Caxhayion in the afternoon. Jonnhaty gave a ffeast to which Assaryquoa whom I represented, and Onas whom Shikellimo represented, was invited with the Chiefs of the Town, about 18 in number; the ffeast consisted of a Cask of Rum, of about two gallons; several Songs were sung before the ffeast begun, in which they thanked Assaryquo for visiting them; they also thanked Onas (the Governor of Pennsilvania) for conducting Assaryquoa and Showing him the Way to Onondago; the Sun was praised for having given Light, and for dispelling the Clouds; then the Cask was open'd, & a Cup of about ¾ of a Gill was fill'd for Canassatego, who drank to the Health of Assaryquoa; next him drank Caheshcarowano to the Health of the Governor of Pennsilvania, and after this Manner we drank round; the next Time the first Cup was reached to me by Jonnhaty, who attended the ffeast, I wished long Life to the wise Counsellors of the united Nations, and drank my Cup, so did Shikellimo & the rest; after that the Kettle was handed round with a wooden Spoon in it; every one took so much as he pleased. Whilst we were drinking & smoking, news came that a Deputation of the Nanticoke Indians arrived at Cachiadachse from Maryland; the House of Canassatego was ordain'd for them, since the Town House was taken up by Onas & Assaryquoa;[5] after all the Rum was drunk, the usual thanks was given from every Nation or Deputy with the usual sound of Jo-haa, and we parted. The 26th. In the Morning I went to see the Nantikokes; there was six in Number, none could speak a word of the Language of the united Nations. I found there besides Canassetego, his Brother, Zila Woolien, and others; they desired me to stand Interpreter for the Nanticokes (they heard us talk English together), to which I consented; no Deputies were Yet arrived from any other Nation. I desired Canassatego to send again to have at least the Oneidos there, as they were concern'd in the Late Skirmish, which was done immediately. The 27th. No Business was done to-Day. The 28th. The Deputies from the Oneidos and Tuscaroros arriv'd. Aquoyiota, an old Acquaintance of mine, came with them; he is a Man of about 70 Years of age, a Native & Chief of the Oneidos. The 29th. The onondago's held another Private Council, and sent for me and Shikellimo; every thing was

5. I.e., Weiser and Shikellamy, the spokesmen for the governors.

discoursed over again, and we agreed that Canassatego should speak in behalf of the Government of Virginia; and the Wampums were divided into so many parts as there were Articles to be spoken of; and the Goods were to be divided between the family's in Mourning and the Publick Council of the united Nations. A Messenger was sent to hasten the Mohawks away from the Oneider Lake, where it was supposed they tarried; they arrived, five in Number. The 30th, About noon, the Council then met at our Lodging and declared themselves compleat, and a deal of Ceremonies Passed; [6] ffirst the Onondagoes rehearsed the beginning of the Union of the five Nations, Praised their Grandfathers' Wisdom in establishing the Union or Alliance, by which they became a formidable Body; that they (now living) were but ffools to their wise ffathers, Yet protected and accompanied by their ffathers' Spirit; and then the discourse was directed to the Deputies of the several Nations, and to the Messengers from Onas and Assaryquoa, then to the Nanticokes, to welcome them all to the Council ffire which was now kindled. A String of Wampum was given by Tocanontie, in behalf of the Onondagoes, to wipe off the Sweat from their (the Deputies & Messenger's) Bodies, and God, who had protected them all against the Evil Spirits in the Woods, who were always doing mischief to people travelling to Onondago, was praised. All this was done by way of a Song, the Speaker walking up & down in the House. After this the Deputies & Messengers held a Conference by themselves, and appointed Aquoyiota to return thanks for their kind reception, with another String of Wampum. Aquoyiota repeated all that was said in a Singing way, walking up and down in the House, added more in Praise of their wise ffathers and of the happy union, repeated all the Names of those Ancient Chiefs that establish'd it; they no Doubt, said he, are now God's and dwell in heaven; then Proclamation was made that the Council was now Opened, and Assaryquoa was to speak next morning in the same House, and due Attendance should be given. All those Indian Ceremonies took up that afternoon. Jo-haas [7] from every Nation was given. The 31st, about Ten of the Clock, the Council of the united Nations met, and Zila Woolien gave me Notice that they were now ready to hear Onas and Assaryquoa Speak. I called Canassatego and desired him to speak for me in Open Council, as I would tell him, Article by Article (according to what was first agreed upon), which he Proclaim'd to the Council, and they approv'd of it, because they knew it required some Ceremonies with which I was not acquainted. The Speaker then begun and made the following Narrative: "*Brethren the United Nations*, you Togarg Hogon our Brother, Nittaruntaquaa our Son, also Sonnawantowano and Tuscaroro, our Younger Sons, you, also, our absent Brother Ounghearrydawy dionen Horarrawe, Know Ye, that what was transacted last Winter at this ffire by Us and our Brother Onas, on behalf of our Brother the Governor of Virginia, known to Us by the Name of Assaryquoa, was all carefully put down in Writing and sent to Assaryquoa, our Brother, by our Brother Onas, upon the Receipt whereof our Brother Assaryquoa wrote again to our Brother Onas and thank'd him kindly for his Mediation in healing the Breach occasion'd by the Late unhappy Skirmish, and requested the Continuance of our Brother Onas' good Offices; and that the Interpreter might be sent to Sagog-

6. After all the informal preparations, the treaty ritual begins here.
7. Jo-haas: synchronized cries of assent, or applause.

saanagechtheyky with such Instructions as Onas our Brother (who knowing the Nature, Customs, and the very Heart of his Brethren) shall think fit. This is all what I have to say about what is past. Now you will hear our Brother Assaryquoa himself, who has been brought to our ffire by our Brother Onas. Then I took up a Belt of Wampum and told the Speaker, Canassatego, a few Words, and he proceeded and Spoke in behalf of the Governor of Virginia as follows:

"S.—Brethren, The United Nations now met in Council at Sagoghsaanagechtheyky; when I heard of the late unhappy Skirmish that happened in my Country between some of your Warriours and my People, I was Surprized. I could not account for it to my self why such a thing should happen between Brethren. This Belt of Wampum, therefore, I give to the ffamilys in Mourning amongst You my Brethren at Sagoghsaanagechchayky, to condole with them and moderate their Grief.' The Belt was given and the usual Sound of Approbation was returned by the whole House;—2. Then I handed another Belt to the Speaker and Spoke to him; he spoke much the same as before, and desired that Belt might be given to the ffamilys in Mourning at Niharuntaquoa, or the Oneidos, for the same Use. Thanks was given again by the whole Assembly with the usual Sound, then I handed a large Belt to the Speaker.—3. 'Brethren of the united Nations, the Sun kept back his beams from Us, and a dark Cloud overshadow'd us when the Late unhappy Skirmish happened between my People and Your Warriors. My People are charged with having begun Hostilities; I will not Dispute with you about it. It is most certain that an Evil Spirit which governs in Darkness has been the Promoter of it, for Brethren will never fall out without giving Ear to such Evil Spirits. I and the Old and wise People of my Country highly Disapproved the Action, I therefore came here to your fire to fetch home the Hatchet, from an Apprehension that it might have been unadvisedly made Use of my People, and I assure You, by this Belt of Wampum, that there shall be no more use made of it for the future, but it shall be buried. In Confirmation of what I say I give You this Belt of Wampum.' The solemn Cry, by way of thanksgiving & Joy, was repeated as many Times as there were Nations present. The Speaker then proceeded:—4. 'Brethren, the united Nations, this String of Wampum serves to bury all that unhappy accident under the Ground, and to Lay a heavy stone upon it to keep it under for Ever.' He laid down some Strings of Wampum. The usual Cry was given.—5. 'Brethren, the united Nations, these Strings of Wampum serve to dispell the Dark Cloud that overshadowed Us for some Time, that the Sun may shine again and we may be able to see one another with Pleasure.' He laid down some Strings of Wampum. The usual Cry, by way of Approbation and Thanks, was given. The Speaker proceeded:—6. 'Brethren, the united Nations, these Strings of Wampum serve to take away the Bitterness of your Spirit, and to purge You from the abundance and overflow of your Gall; all wise People judge it to be a dangerous Distemper; when Men have too much of that it gives an Open Door to evil Spirits to enter in, and I cannot help believing that my Brethren, the united Nations, are often sick of that Distemper.' He laid down four Rows of Wampum; the usual Cry was given by way of Approbation; the Speaker proceeded:—7. Brethren, the united Nations, this String of Wampum serves to mend the Chain of ffriendship again, which was lately hurt and was in danger of being broke. Let good understanding & true ffriendship be restor'd and subsist among us for Ever.'

Layd four Rows of Wampum, the usual Cry of approbation was given, and the Speaker proceeded:—8. 'Brethren, the United Nation, The old and wise People of my Country joined with me, and we Lodged a fine present in the hands of your Brother Onas for your Use, as a token of my own and my People's sincere Disposition to Preserve Peace and ffriendship with you. We will send Commissioners to you next Spring to treat with you about the Land now in Dispute and in the Possession of my People. Let the place and Time be appointed for certain, that we may not miss one another.' Layd some Strings of Wampum; The usual Cry, by every Nation in Particular, was given by way of thanksgiving & Joy; the Speaker Concluded & said, 'Brethren, I have no more to say at present, but only desire You to give me a Speedy Answer, I have been here many Days.'

"All the Wampum were hung over a Stick laid across the House about six ffoot from the Ground, several Kettles of Hominy, boil'd Indian Corn & Bread was brought in by the Women, the biggest of which was set before Assariquoa by the Divider; all dined together; there was about sixty People. After Dinner they walked out, every Nation's Deputies by themselves, and soon came in again and sat together for about two hours; then Zilla Woolie proclaimed that Assaryquoa was to have an Answer now imediately;[8] Upon which all the men in Town gather'd again, and the House was full, and many stood out of Door (so it was in the forenoon when the Message was delivered to them). Zilla Woolie desired Assaryquoa to give Ear, Tocanumtie being appointed for their Speaker, Spoke to the following Purpose: S—

" 'Brother Assaryquoa, the unhappy Skirmish which happen'd last Winter betwixt your People and some of our Warriors was not less surprizing to us than to You; we were very sorry to hear it; all amongst us were surprised; a Smoke arose from the bottomless Pitt, and a dark Cloud overshadow'd us; the Chain of ffriendship was indanger'd & disappeared, and all was in a Confusion. We, the Chiefs of the united Nations, took hold of the Chain with all our Strength, we were resolved not to let it slip before we received a deadly Blow. But to our great Satisfaction, in the Darkest Time, our Brother Onas enter'd our Door and Offer'd his Mediation. He judged very right to become Mediator betwixt us. We were drunk on both sides, and the overflow of our Galls and the Blood that was shed and corrupted our Hearts, both Your's and our's. You did very well to come to our fire and Comfort the Mourning ffamilies. We thank You; this Belt shall serve for the same Purpose to Comfort the ffamilyes in Mourning amongst You.' Laid a Belt of Wampum. After I thank'd them their Speaker proceeded:—2. 'Brother Assaryquoa, you have healed the Wounds of the Hearts of those ffamilys in Mourning both here & at Niharuntaquoa. We thank you kindly for your so doing. Let this Belt of Wampum have the same Effect upon your People, to heal the Wounds and Comfort them, as your's had upon our's.' Laid a Belt of Wampum, the usual thanks was given, & the Speaker proceeded:—3. 'Brother Assaryquoa, you judged very right in saying that an evil Spirit was the promoter of the late unhappy Skirmish. We do not doubt but you have by this Time full Satisfaction from your own People besides what You had from Us, that your People had begun

8. This was unusual. Customarily a day elapsed between the speaking of a proposition and the response to it.

Hostilities; but let have begun who will, we assure You it was the Spirit that dwells amongst the Catabaws, and by which they are ruled, that did it, for Brethren will never treat one another after this Manner without an Evil Spirit enters them. We agree with you and your Counsellors, the old and wise People of your Country, and disapprove the Action highly; we thank You Brother Assaryquoa for removing your Hatchet and for burying it under a heavy Stone. Let this Belt of Wampum serve to remove our Hatchet from You and not only bury it, but we will fling it into the Bottomless Pitt, into the Ocean, there shall be no more Use made of it. In Confirmation of what we say, we give You this Belt of Wampum.' After the usual Approbation was given, the Speaker proceeded:—4. 'Brother Assaryquoa, let this String of Wampum serve to heal the very mark of the Wounds, so that nothing may be seen of it after this Day, for it was done betwixt Brethren; let no more mention be made of it hereafter for ever, in Publick or Private.' Lay'd down four Strings of Wampum. The usual Cry by way of Approbation was given, and the Speaker proceeded:—5. 'Brother Assaryquoa, this String of Wampum serves to return you our Thanks for dispelling the dark Cloud that overshadow'd Us for some Time. Let the Sun shine again, let us look upon one another with Pleasure and Joy.' Lay'd some Strings of Wampum. The usual Approbation was given, and the Speaker proceeded:—b. 'Brother Assaryquoa, you have taken away the bitterness of our Spirit, and purged us from the abundance and overflow of our Gall. We judge with all the rest of the wise People, that when Men have too much of that it is like a dangerous Distemper; but it is not only your Brethren, the united Nations, that have too much Gall, but the Europeans labour likewise under that Distemper, in particular your back Inhabitants; you did very well in taking away the overflow of Gall. Let this String of Wampum serve to purge your People also from the overflow of their Gall, and to remove the bitterness of their Spirit; also, we own it to be very necessary on both sides. We thank You for the good advice.' Laid four Rows of Wampum. The usual approbation was given, and the Speaker proceeded:—'7. Brother Assaryquoa, this String of Wampum serves to thank you for mending the Chain of ffriendship which was lately hurt and in danger; we agree with you very readily. Let good understanding & true ffriendship be restored and subsist among us for Ever. Laid four Rows of Wampum. The usual approbation was given, and the Speaker proceeded:—8. 'Brother Assaryquoa, we thank you kindly for the present you and the Old and Wise of your Country lodged in the Hands of our Brother Onas, your good ffriend, as a token of your sincere Disposition to preserve Peace and ffriendship with Us. Let this String of Wampum serve to assure you of the like good Disposition towards you and your People, and as an assurance that we will come down within the Borders of Pennsylvania to a place called Canadagueany, next Spring, and we will be very glad of seeing your Commissioners there, we will treat them as becomes Brethren with good Chear and Pleasure. We will set out from our several Towns after eight Moons are past by, when the ninth just is to be seen, this present Moon, which is almost expired, not to be reckoned, Upon which you may Depend; in Confirmation whereof, we give you this String of Wampum.' The usual Approbation being given, the Speaker proceeded:—'Brother Assaryquoa, we have no more to say at present, but we will not permit you to Leave Us yet, but stay a Day or two longer with us. We have just now received Intelligence that the Jonontowas are on the

Road with some of the Cherikees' Deputies in order to strike a Peace with Us; They, the Cherikees, hindered the Jonontowas from coming sooner, and you will then hear the Particulars.' Then the Speaker directed his Discourse to the Deputies of the Nanticokes, who had been there all along present, and said: 'Brethren, the Nanticokes, We desire you will prepare for to-morrow and deliver your Message to us; and as you have neither the united Nations, their Tongue nor Ear, we have thought fit to hear you speak with our English Ear, and to speak to you with our English Tongue. There is the Man (pointing to me) who is the Guardian of all the Indians.' I was desired to acquaint the Nanticokes with it, which I did, and they were well pleased. They could talk some English, but not one word of the united Nation's Language. The 1st of August, the Nanticokes spoke, and had their Answer the same Day; the whole day was spent about it. The 2d, the Council of the united Nation met again, and Zillawoolie desired me to give my Attendance, and take Notice of what should be said to put it down in Writing immediately, and with Particular Care he spoke as follows: 'Brother Onas, Assaryquoa, and the Governor of Maryland: We are ingaged in a Warr with the Catabaws which will last to the End of the World, for they molest Us and speak Contemptuously of Us, which our Warriours will not bear, and they will soon go to War against them again; it will be in vain for Us to diswade them from it. We desire you, by this String of Wampum, to publish it amongst your back Inhabitants to be of good behaviour to our Warriors, and look upon them as their Brethren, that we may never have such a Dangerous Breach hereafter. We give you the strongest Assurance that we will use our best Endeavour to perswade and charge them to be of good Behaviour every where amongst our Brethren the English, with whom we are one body and Soul, one Heart and one Head, for what has happened is no more to be seen, and no token or mark remains thereof. Let the Spirit of the Catawba's be banished away from Us which will set Brethren to fall out; Let Treaties of ffriendship be observed, and believe no Lies. Our Brother Onas knows very well that some Years ago we made a new Road on the outside of your Inhabitants,[9] tho' they had seated themselves down upon the new Road and shut it up, and there is no more room for a new Road because of the Terrible Mountains full of Stones and no game there, so that the Road cannot be removed. To inforce this upon You, we give you this String of Wampum, which serves likewise for an Assurance that we will observe Treaties of ffriendship with You and believe no Lies, and will perswade our Warriors to behave well every where amongst your People our Brethren.' Laid a String of Wampum of three Rows—they desired that this might be sent to Maryland and Virginia immediately, from Philadelphia. 'Brother Onas, this String of Wampum serves to return you our Hearty thanks for your Kind Mediation. We thank our Brother Assaryquoa for the Kind visit. Let good ffriendship and Peace be amongst Us to the End of the World.' After all was over, according to the Ancient Custom of that ffire, a Song of ffriendship and Joy was sung by the Chiefs, after this the Council ffire on their side was put out. I with the same Ceremonee put out the ffire on behalf of Assaryquoa & Onas, and they departed. The 3d of August I put down, in the Morning, the Speech of the Nanticokes and visited Tocammtie, All the Chiefs of the Onondagoes came to see

9. The Warriers' Path negotiated at Albany in 1722. (See ch. 14).

Us—took my Leave of them—set out about nine and departed from Onondago. They desired to be remembered to their Brethren in Philadelphia, in Particular to the Governor and James Logan. The time that We staid on Onondagoe we were well entertain'd with Hominy, Venison, Dryed Eels, Squashes, and Indian Corn bread. They gave Us provision on the Road homeward, so much as we wanted. We passed Cajadachse—took my Leave thereof—Zillawoolie and I arrived that Day on the first Branch of Sasquehannah.

APPENDIX B 🎺

Documents of the Walking Purchase

The Walking Purchase has caused one of the oldest controversies in American historical literature. It began in 1756 when Delaware spokesman Teedyuscung accused Pennsylvania's Proprietaries of having defrauded the Delawares of their land. It was picked up by Benjamin Franklin and a Friendly Association for Regaining and Preserving Peace with the Indians by Pacific Measures; they demanded a royal commission of inquiry. The colony's Proprietary-appointed Council and Quaker-dominated Assembly took opposite sides. The crown's Superintendent of Indian Affairs for the Northern District, Sir William Johnson, settled the affair in negotiations with Teedyuscung but did so by paying him off in highly suspect arrangements. At the time and later, the dispute was contended with much rancor. Historians sometimes took sides according to whether they were pro- or anti-Proprietary, sometimes according to whether they sided with the Iroquois or the Delawares, sometimes according to their feelings about Quakers. Anthropologists came into the fray because of the Iroquois charge that the Delawares were "women" and therefore had no right to sell land; thus the issues of Indian cultural traits have merged with the issues of politics and religion in politics. Just to add an extra touch of spice, this may be the only case on record where the local Euramericans have steadfastly insisted that their ancestors swindled Indians despite all assurances from eminent national historians to the contrary: Bucks County Quakers have never wavered in their denunciation of the Walking Purchase. Even the son of one of the Walkers, who as a boy saw his mother murdered by vengeful Delawares, insisted in his old age that those Delawares had been defrauded.[1]

In such confusion, the source documents must be given more than ordi-

---

1. A typed copy of the account of Moses Marshall, son of the walker Edward Marshall, is in the third folder headed "Indian Walk of 1737" in the Bucks County Historical Society Library, Doylestown, Pa. The second folder has a photostat of a death notice of Moses, with an account of his telling of the Walk. The original was printed in *The Ariel* (July 12, 1828) 2:47.

nary attention, and comprehension requires analysis of the sources generated by events through 1762 when Johnson finally succeeded in silencing
Teedyuscung. I have discussed in the latter chapters of this book the events
up to 1742, and I will take up their documents below, along with the rest.
After 1742 the Pennsylvania-Iroquois partnership suppressed Delaware
resistance, but the defeat of General Edward Braddock at the Battle of the
Wilderness in 1755 reopened all wounds. Indians attacked Pennsylvania's
outpost settlements, and the Quakers were astounded to learn that Delawares led the attack. Leading Quakers became suspicious of their Proprietary's government and began an inquiry by the simple means of consulting
some nearby Indians.

What they found out was far from comforting, for nearly everyone
involved in the Walking Purchase had been a Friend. But Thomas Penn
had since left the Friends and was at loggerheads with his Quaker-dominated Assembly over a number of issues; and James Logan was dead. The
political Quakers seem to have set themselves two tasks: to restore friendship with the Indians, especially the Delawares; and to put the onus of
Indian alienation on Thomas Penn while diverting attention from Logan
and the other Friends who had connived with Penn. Unfortunately for
the new generation of Friends, the effort to preserve their fathers free of
blame created such difficulties that they laid themselves open to accusa-
tions of ruthless grasping after power—even to a charge that they offered
Indians arms to kill colonials so long as Quakers should be spared.[2] These
canards were quite false. The Friendly Association's minutes and its
members' private correspondence testify to their sincerity and integrity,
which would appear more plainly in the public record if they had not had
to twist about so much to protect their parents and in-laws.[3] *These* Friends
made enemies precisely because of their righteousness—and rightness.
When they realized that public officers were trying to suppress the evidence of fraud, they aggressively and extralegally intruded themselves as
private citizens into the negotiations of those corrupt public officers with
the Indians. They openly championed the rights of Indians at a time when
some Indians were scalping homesteaders. In hindsight their objectives
seem to be beyond criticism, always excepting the filiopietist variety, but
their discretion approached zero. Whether they or anyone else could have
done better in the circumstances, I shall not try to guess.

In alliance with Benjamin Franklin, whose opinion of Thomas Penn
made the Quakers seem like idolaters of the man, they forced a series of
treaties with the Delawares and Iroquois at Easton, from 1756 to 1758,
the minutes of which tell different stories according to which scribe took

2. A. F. C. Wallace, *Teedyuscung*, p. 140.
3. See Minutes of the Friendly Association, 1755–1757, mss., Indian Records Collection,
HSP. Call no. Am 525. Other Friendly Assn. papers are in Haverford College library.

them down.[4] The Assembly sent Franklin to London to demand a royal inquiry, which was duly ordered by the crown. It was placed in due form in the hands of Sir William Johnson, which worried Penn because Johnson had been writing condemnations of Pennsylvania's Indian policies.[5] But Johnson became jealous of his prerogatives when the Friends challenged his conduct of the inquiry and thrust themselves vigorously into his meetings with the Indians. Ever the pragmatist, Johnson outwitted the Friends by collaborating with Penn: Johnson got Penn a clean bill, and thereafter Penn served Johnson's interests at court.[6] For "a handsome present" at Penn's expense, Johnson prevailed on Teedyuscung in 1762 to withdraw the charges of fraud.[7] Teedyuscung was a bit of a pragmatist too. His objectives were simpler than the Quakers'. Meanwhile, *all* the issues were being fought out in Philadelphia between the Council and the Assembly. The Assembly had ceased to be Quaker-dominated when a number of Friends resigned in 1756; leadership passed then to Benjamin Franklin's Anglican supporters, who were much less compromising than the Quakers. When the Council worked up sets of documents exculpating Penn and sent them secretly to London,[8] the Assembly countered by seizing the secret records of the Proprietary's Land Office and having them transcribed as Warrants and Surveys of the Province of Pennsylvania. Penn managed to get the originals back through legal action,[9] but the transcripts evaded him and came ultimately to rest in two parts: one at the Interior Department of the Commonwealth at Harrisburg, the other in the archives at Philadelphia's City Hall. It was my good fortune to come upon the Philadelphia papers shortly after they were rescued from oblivion by a new archivist who had found them lying on the floor in City Hall's attic. He had them restored and indexed and I arrived by pure chance just as the index was being completed. It led me to key information about the Penns' sales of Indian lands prior to the Walk and to deeds scattered in county courthouses that enabled reconstruction of the pattern of the Penns' land transactions. Together with the private papers of Logan, the Penns and the Taylor family of surveyors, the land records made possible an analysis of the public documents upon which my description of the Walk's arrangements is based. I must stress that the careful work of

4. There are variant copies of the Easton treaties' minutes, in the American Philosophical Society, the Historical Society of Pennsylvania, and *New York Colonial Documents*.

5. See *Doc.Hist.N.Y.* 2:745–61; Johnson to T. Pownall, Sept. 8, 1757, *Johnson Papers* 2:737–38.

6. T. Penn to W. Johnson, Jan. 8, 1763, Penn Mss. (boxes), HSP.

7. Johnson's report to the Lords of Trade, Aug. 1, 1762, *Johnson Papers* 3:850.

8. *Pa. Council Minutes*, Jan. 20, 1759, 8:244–45.

9. Text of the laws: *The Charters and Acts of Assembly of the Province of Pennsylvania* (Philadelphia. Peter Miller and Co , 1762), 2;119–13. Repeal noted: 2:164. Controversy: *Votes and Proceedings of the House of Representatives of the Province of Pennsylvania, 1682–1776*, ser. 0 of *Pa. Archives* 5:50–52; *Pa. Council Minutes* 8:337–76. See esp. p. 348.

foregoing scholars, especially Paul A. W. and Anthony F. C. Wallace, was indispensable.

Here are the public documents, in chronological order.

1. *"The ancient deed."* So far as is known, the original has disappeared. By "the original," I mean the paper shown to Nutimus. A purported copy of this was included as document (b) in the papers delivered to Sir William Johnson in 1762, which he forwarded to the Board of Trade. There was a very close connection between the Proprietary lawyers' allegations about this paper and the so-called minutes of the meeting at Durham. Penn's lawyers told Johnson, "The Truth is there was no Vestage of the said Deed until Thomas Penn Esquire, one of the present Proprietaries, came from England in the year 1732 and happened to bring with him among his Father's Papers the said ancient Copy of this Deed."[10] The point is that Thomas knew about the old paper when he and John Penn went to Durham but did not produce it then. He understood, and Logan had stressed, the paper's invalidity.[11] In 1762 the Penns' lawyers saw this weakness and concocted the Durham "minutes" to enable them to argue that the old paper had been "the Occasion of *the several* Meetings with the Chiefs who claimed the Lands now in Dispute at *Durham*, Pennsbury and at last at Philadelphia."[12] Their argument was refuted by Teedyuscung, who had been present at both Durham and Pennsbury, and on this point Sir William Johnson tacitly accepted Teedyuscung's word. In Johnson's final report to the Board of Trade, he wrote in such a way as not overtly to contradict the lawyers in so many words, but he omitted mention of the old paper *at Durham*, and his report introduced it for the first time (without saying as much) *at Pennsbury*.[13]

In their argument to Sir William Johnson in 1762, Thomas Penn's lawyers insisted that the "ancient deed" was proved valid by various old documents contemporary with it. One of these was an old letter mentioning goods paid to the Indians on April 21, 1688. From this the lawyers inferred "it was the Residue of the Goods paid for the purchase of these [Walking Purchase] Lands."[14]

Thomas Penn's papers, preserved by Secretary Richard Peters, refute this argument by specific reference to the Bucks County lands in question. They were not in the Forks of Delaware nor anywhere near. Surveyor General Thomas Holme wrote, on November 12, 1685, that "betwixt

10. Proprietary Commissioners' answer to the Assembly's Commissioners, June 24, 1762, mss., Board of Trade Papers, Proprieties, 1697–1776, XXI–1 (Indorsed x. 20), p. 332, HSP.

11. J. T., and R. Penn to Logan [summer, 1730], Penn Mss., Letters of the Penn Family to James Logan 2:77.

12. See n. 10.

13. *Johnson Papers* 2:767, 841.

14. Ibid., 3:840.

Neshamineh [Creek] and Delaware [River], backward of the Purchase made per Colonel Markham, is not done, some of the chief Kings refuseth to sell, so that lyes not done." As all of Neshaminy Creek lies south of Tohickon Creek, which in turn lies about twenty miles south of the Forks of Delaware, "between" Neshaminy and Delaware could not possibly have meant the lands embraced in the Walking Purchase. [Peters Papers, mss., 5:8 HSP.]

On August 28, 1686, some Delaware "kings" did cede land, as attested by a document in the Penns' possession, reading as follows: "1686 Aug 28 Copy of an Indian Purchase of Lands near Delaware." This is followed by "1692 June 15: Indian Conveyance of all the Land between Neshamineh and Poquessing [creeks]" and the further entry "1697 July 5: Taminy and his Brother and Son grant their Lands between Pemmapecka and Neshamineh [creeks]." All of these creeks are south of Tohickon, and it is clear from the series, as well as other records, that William Penn's agents were clearing *lower* Bucks County of Indian claims. No mention is made in any document to Tohickon Creek or the Forks of Delaware which were then in Indian territory or *upper* Bucks County depending on one's point of view. ["List of Grants, Deeds, Papers etc. left in the Proprietors Closet in his House at Philadelphia examined by R. Peters and Lyndford Lardner, 20th October 1741," Penn Collection, Tempsford Hall Papers, mss., Box 1, Folder 20.]

When these arrangements are understood, the goods paid to the Indians in 1688 become payment for lands south of Tohickon. Indeed, all land transactions with the Indians in the seventeenth century were south of Tohickon. The Indians themselves insisted, without exception, that William Penn, rather than any of his agents, had treated for the Walking Purchase. He could not possibly have done so until his second stay in Pennsylvania, in 1699–1701.

It is plain from the above that the documents purported to confirm the "ancient deed" of 1686 do no such thing. This piece of paper, which vanished so conveniently immediately after it was no longer of use, was no deed at all. Most likely it was an unconsummated draft of a negotiation that never produced agreement.

2. *"The Proprietaries Journey to Durham."* This document was produced for the first time by the lawyers in 1762. Secretary Richard Peters identified it under oath in highly equivocal language, which may easily be read as an effort to make an untrue impression without literally lying. He swore, on June 12, 1762, that he "did some time ago (but the particular Time he cannot now set forth) find deposited among others in his care the hereunto annexed ancient Paper purporting to be Minutes of the Transactions in a Journey of the said Proprietaries to Durham in the year 1734 and of a Conference then held between them and certain Indians therein men-

tioned." Peters carefully avoided any commitment to the validity of the document or the means by which it got into the papers in his care, and he did not plead lack of memory about when he found it; he swore only that he could not "set forth" the time.[15] Why he could not must be guessed. Such fine distinctions were undoubtedly very important to Peter, who was simultaneously an ordained Anglican minister and an absolute dependent of Thomas Penn.

Another of Penn's officials identified the handwriting of the Durham document and its endorsement as that of two men deceased.[16] This official was Lynford Lardner, who was Receiver General in the Penns' Land Office—a private agency that they kept inaccessible to public scrutiny. Lardner made an affidavit that the purported minutes of the Durham conference were in the handwriting of one James Steele, the Younger, who had served in the Receiver General's office as an assistant in 1740 and 1741. [Bd. of Trade Transcripts, Proprieties, vol. 21, pt. 1 (1761 and 1762), x.10.e., HSP.] But the Durham affair had taken place in 1734, and Lardner did not think it needful to explain why Steele might have been there. Even more suspect is the nonappearance of these "minutes" until 1762, although the Walking Purchase had been in dispute since 1757 and the same Lynford Lardner had signed a report exculpating the Penns on January 6, 1758. [Pa. Council Minutes, Jan. 20, 1759, 8:246–61, a signature at p. 259.]

It is possible that James Steel the Younger may have written the purported Durham minutes long after the event—someone had to write them—but the relevant question is whether he took those minutes in the first place, and the answer is that he did not. His father, James Steel the Elder, took them. For this we have the word of Thomas Penn in a private letter to Richard Peters. [Dec. 10, 1757, mss., Peter Papers 5:6, HSP.] Penn noted also that the elder Steel had taken the minutes of the subsequent meeting at Pennsbury in 1735, for which a deposition of William Allen was substituted in the papers submitted to Sir William Johnson. See below. Johnson accepted all the concocted papers at face value; he forwarded the Durham document to the Board of Trade as "minutes."[17]

The contents of the document do not stand up well under analysis. The usual Indian treaty format was that of a dialogue with occasional editorial comment; this paper is written as a narrative, and all discourse is remotely indirect. It violates the practice standard in Pennsylvania of listing by name all the Indians present—a practice that the same interpreter had

15. Bd. of Trade Papers, Proprieties, 1697–1776, mss., XXI–1, pp. 177–78. HSP.
16. Loc. cit.

17. *Johnson Papers* 3:841. Johnson's report is printed without the enclosed papers. For those one must go to the HSP transcripts (as cited in note 10, above) or the originals in the Public Record Office, Kew, England.

followed in 1733 in Philadelphia.[18] The omission was important to the placemen's efforts in later years to belittle Teedyuscung by implying that he was unimportant and uninformed. The document's omission of his name among those present at Durham reflected adversely on his testimony to Johnson that he had been at Durham and could bear witness as to what happened there. The "Journey" document is controverted both by Nutimus's and Teedyuscung's word and by the letter of Governor George Thomas, cited at p. 342 above, which obviously was written before the placemen concerted their strategy.

There is further reason to believe that someone took original minutes and converted them to this useful paper. The "Journey" has John and Thomas Penn arrive at Durham on October 8, 1734. Nutimus comes on "the 10th at Night and on the 11th Tishecunk [Tishecomen] came." They spent a social evening. "The next day," which would be the 12th, was spent in dispute. The Proprietaries left on the following day, the 13th, but the chronicler called it the 12th and, with a circumstantiality missing from the rest of the document, conveyed the Proprietaries home, one day offbeat all the way.

3. *The "Minutes" of the Pennsbury Treaty in 1735.* Here again, the original had disappeared by the time of Sir William Johnson's inquiry. In its place Johnson accepted an affidavit from William Allen, the great land speculator who had become Chief Justice of Pennsylvania (by the Penns' appointment). Johnson mentioned the office of Chief Justice as good reason for accepting Allen's word.[19] He failed to mention that Allen had bought many thousands of acres in the Walking Purchase region before the Walk was walked. Allen had substantial reasons for wanting to prove the validity of the Walk. He swore that the "ancient deed" had been proved at Pennsbury by a man who had been a witness to it and had subscribed his name as such. This man was dead by the time of Johnson's inquiry, and, as we have seen, the original "ancient deed" had been replaced by a substitute. We have only Allen's word as underpinning, and it was the word of a man almost as deeply implicated in the Walk as were the Penns. The written statement by the so-called witness was not produced for Johnson and cannot be found now. From another source, we know that Delaware Chief Lappawinzo made a speech at Pennsbury on May 9, 1735, that does not appear in William Allen's "Minutes." Lappawinzo's speech is noted on an inventory of papers once included in the Proprietary records; but the paper itself was not produced for Johnson and has since disappeared from the Land Office archives in Harrisburg, where the rest of the inventoried papers are housed.[20]

18 Penn Mss., Indian Affairs, 1:37, HSP.

19. *Johnson Papers* 3:840.

20. Exhibit G., Bd. of Trade Papers, Proprieties, XXI–1, indorsed x–12, HSP. "Lappawinsa's speech to the Proprietors at Pennsbury, 9th May 1735," *Pa. Archives*, ser. 3, 3:222.

4. *The lottery lands deeds.* Sale of the lottery tracts violated Pennsylvania law as well as Indian rights. After the advertised lottery failed, Thomas Penn conducted a secret "little" lottery. Surveyor General Benjamin Eastburn prepared a map of these tracts with a number on each as the only identifying data.[21] A Bucks County deed provides the clue to identification. In 1736, James Bingham bought and surveyed four five-hundred-acre tracts that were patented to him as of June 22, 1737. The patent is silent about the lottery; Bingham, however, died soon afterward, and his sons sold the tracts. To make title secure, they inserted mention in their deeds of sale of "the four five hundred Acre Lotts laid out to the Testator in the Fork of Delaware in Right of the Lottery Tickets he purchased from the Proprietary." Secrecy was maintained both by certifying the deed before Justice William Allen and by not recording it until 1748.[22] Starting from this clue and Eastburn's map, we find that cross references to locations and dates establish the lottery purchasers as follows:[23]

William Allen, Lots No. 7, 13, 17, 20, 21, 24. (3,000 acres)
James Bingham, Lots No. 10, 15, 16, 19. (2,000 acres)
Thomas Clark, Lot No. 3 (500 acres)
John Georges Lots No. 1, 2 (1,000 acres)
Patrick Graeme, Lots No. 4, 11, 22, 23 (2,000 acres)
Jeremiah Langhorne, Lot No. 14 (500 acres)
Casper Wister, Lots No. 5, 8, 18 (1,500 acres)
Total: 10,500 acres.

In addition, Thomas Penn, acting through a front, had tracts surveyed to himself as a private person.

5. *Logan's quitclaim from the Iroquois.* Logan's deal with the Senecas, Cayugas, Onondagas, and Oneidas in 1736 was kept secret. Paul A. W. Wallace unearthed it from Logan's and Conrad Weiser's private papers. I have given it a somewhat different interpretation from Wallace's.[24] I do not think that the Mohawks were informed of the transaction. Secrecy was necessary because nothing that had happened in the formal treaty in Philadelphia warranted Logan's trick. At no time in Philadelphia had the Iroquois requested or the Pennsylvanians offered to treat exclusively with the Iroquois at the expense of other tribes, nor had the Iroquois either claimed to have conquered the Delawares or impugned the Delawares'

21. Cf. an anonymous, undated draft of "sundry Tracts" with Eastburn's draft of the same areas, dated 1740. Both in HSP maps, call no. OF 549*, 1740.

22. Deed, James Bingham's sons to John Benezet, June 1, 1741, Bucks County Deed Books 7:408, Doylestown courthouse.

23. Cross references between the deed cited in n. 22 and the following sources establish the purchasers. Pa. Patent Books A–8: 218, 220, 222, 231, 234, 245; A–10:405. Northampton County Deed Books A–1:346–47; B–1:352–53; D–23:335–39, Easton courthouse. All mss.

24. Cf. ch. 16, above, with P. A. W. Wallace, *Weiser*, chs. 6, 9.

right to dispose of tribal lands as they pleased.

6. *The Walk rehearsal.* Another secret. Paul Wallace unearthed and reported it, and Quaker historian Frederick Tolles generously took the initiative to show me the manuscript evidence under his care at Friends Historical Library, Swarthmore College. It has been discussed in chapter 17.

To sum up, *all* the important contemporary documents of the Walking Purchase were fabricated, altered, or hidden. It is small wonder that historians have been confused by them; the wells of research were poisoned. Offsetting this handicap, however, a modern historian has certain advantages. The private correspondence of the Walk's principal conspirators has been preserved in family papers and is no longer secret. The land records have become public, and the clues to understanding their often cryptic language are at hand—thanks to the rebellious Assembly that seized and transcribed the Penns' Warrants and Surveys. Oral traditions of the Indians and the local colonials of the Walk region were written down within a generation from the event, and they confirm each other as they refute the official records. For this boon and the mass of documents compiled by Sir William Johnson's inquiry, we owe gratitude to the strenuous efforts of the Friendly Association's members, who, however mixed their motives, fought the Penns' singleminded effort to deceive. (Thanks go also to the Friends' ubiquitous ally in this struggle, Benjamin Franklin.) Nor should we forget that those Quakers put their money where their mouths were. Contrary to the libels heaped upon them, they contributed and spent what were then very large sums to compensate the Indians for injustice and thus to restore conditions prerequisite to peace.

Yet *these* Quakers of the 1750s have been harshly condemned in many histories while the Quakers who schemed and executed the Walk have been defended. And the oral traditions indispensable to reconstruct the Walk's actual events have been sneered off the pages of some of our most famous historians. The element of racial and religious biases in all this can be neither ignored nor condoned. Something more than drinking at poisoned wells was involved; some writers have delighted in renewing the poison with their own evil brews.[25] I shall generalize no further here because there have also been serious and conscientious researchers who were genuinely taken in by the elaborate falsifications of the walk.

As remarked earlier, ethnological issues have contributed also to the confusion about the Walk: in particular, questions concerning the status

25. For example, Daniel Boorstin, *The Americans: The Colonial Experience* (New York: Random House, 1958), chs. 0, 9, which manages to attack Quakers and Indians alike without bothering to mention the Walking Purchase or any other Indian affairs in Pennsylvania except war. Ignorant and malicious, this is not history.

of the Delawares in relation to the Iroquois. Did the Delawares have land titles recognized by Indian custom? Had they been conquered by the Iroquois and thus made "women"? What did the status of a woman mean to the Iroquois and Delawares? What significance is to be read into the kinship terms used by the Indians to express their own understanding of their intertribal relationships? Because anthropologists typically have accepted historical sources uncritically (when they bothered with them at all), the falsified sources of the Walk long provided the assumptions for ethnological interpretation of Iroquois and Delaware cultures. But the information collected by anthropologists through their own methods provided data at variance with the historical sources; the contradictions created puzzles that, by the mid-twentieth century when Frank Speck and Anthony Wallace challenged old assumptions, compelled historians to reexamine the evidence.[26]

26. In this appendix, I have tried to be conclusive without becoming tedious. Reference to still more evidence will be found in Jennings, "Scandalous Indian Policy of William Penn's Sons," and "Miquon's Passing," passim; see index.

APPENDIX C 🙒

On the undoing of history

    *In the traditions of Anglo-American historiography normal eth-*nocentrism has been complicated and strengthened by myths of statecraft, religion, and race. These were muddled yet more by source writers who justified invasion, domination, and worse practices by adjusting the sources to conform to their ostensible moral and legal codes. They, too, practiced creativity in transmitting information to subsequent generations. Adjustment was accomplished by half-truths, suppression of some evidence, fabrication of other, and substitution of "good" reasons for the real ones. An example is analyzed in Appendix B, on the documents of the Walking Purchase.

    As the bulk of this book has been devoted to analyses of the texts written by preservers and makers of Anglo-American traditions, it would be redundant to examine them again. Instead, I shall discuss more ancient assumptions held by the source writers—those that motivated them to produce the materials of the traditions. By way of introduction, let me note that Europeans were as diverse as tribesmen. William Penn was as Protestant an Englishman as Captain John Smith or Governor John Winthrop, but his policies were rather different from theirs. Yet he and they shared many cultural assumptions that can be seen with hindsight to have been unwarranted. Penn believed in fair treatment for "the poor Indians," but he also believed in their inferiority, and there is revelation in his ownership of black slaves.

    The source writers often acted in the complacent belief that their practices were sanctioned by one or another of the general myths of their culture. They rationalized that they had various "rights" to act as they did. *Right* was one of the most equivocal words in the English language, and still is. It wobbles back and forth between a privilege recognized and enforced by legal process, on the one side, and, on the other, a privilege that a person believes he *ought* to have because of some sort of status, conduct, or assumed virtue. English colonials believed that they had a duty, and a right derived from the duty, to acquire mastery over the natives of America, and that the duty and the right justified the means used.

The duty was to their god and king. Englishmen generally (after we allow for Quaker minority difference) were required by their god to spread his worship and suppress other religions. Similarly, their king required them to expand his state and suppress competitors. For sanction of the rights derived from these duties, Englishmen appealed to "natural law," the "law of nations," and a conception of state sovereignty based on the divine right of Christian kings, especially that recognized and spoken for by the Church of England headed by the king. In the case of Puritan reformers, divinity shifted slightly to endow the Puritan magistrates instead of the king, but effects were identical: God was English. All of these sanctions required considerable amounts of purposefully directed imagination. However, seventeenth-century Englishmen believed in them without strain. When belief began to waver among later generations, the sanction of racial superiority was developed to fill the place of what was no longer credible, and nineteenth-century science labored mightily to play the role of seventeenth-century theology.[1] Imagination continued active in the new forms as in the old.

Perhaps there are persons who doubt that all the listed sanctions were mythical. Let us attend to them, one by one. "Natural Law" was neither natural nor law. It was a theological doctrine developed by Saint Thomas Aquinas from Greek and Roman Stoic philosophy. In a capsule *The New Columbia Encyclopedia* remarks, "Natural law is opposed to positive law, which is man-made, conditioned by history, and subject to continuous change."[2] In Christian doctrine—Catholic and Protestant alike—Natural Law became what the church fathers said it was, and some of them derived from it a "natural"—i.e., divine—right to do whatever they desired most fervently. The Puritans of New England relied upon it to validate their seizure of Indian lands.[3]

Natural Law also spawned the Law of Nations. This generally accepted information is noted in encyclopedias without comment as to the implication of this sort of law. It should really be called the assumptions of the nation-state. Its theological origins are hidden nowadays because many nation-states have agreed to make a legal fiction out of it and use it as a means of mediating disputes in a World Court at the Hague. This so-called law is neither enacted nor enforced by any government; its procedures are an expedient for nations to accommodate disputes short of war—if they wish. In the seventeenth century, the Law of Nations was understood very clearly to endow Christian kings with the sovereign right to

1. See Berkhofer, *White Man's Burden*, part 2.
2. P.1896.
3. John Winthrop, Sr., "General considerations for the plantation in New England, with an answer to several objections," in *Winthrop Papers*, ed. Allyn Bailey Forbes, 5 vols. (Boston: Massachusetts Historical Society, 1929–1947) 2:120.

rule heathen peoples. The semantic possibilities of these "laws" show instantly in the Reverend Samuel Purchas's rationalization for seizure of Virginia Indians' land.

"The Barbarians . . . *having not the Law* were a Law to themselves, practically acknowledging this Law of Nature . . . from which if they since have declined, they have lost their owne Naturall, and given us another Nationall right; their transgression of the Law of Nature, which tieth Men to Men in the rights of *Natures commons* [i.e., the Indians' lands] exposing them (as a forfeited bond) to the chastisement of that common Law of mankind; and also on our parts to the severitie of the Law of Nations, which tyeth Nation to Nation. And *if they bee not worthy of the name of a Nation, being wilde and Savage:* yet as Slaves, bordering rebells, excommunicates and out-lawes *are lyable to the punishments of Law, and not to the priviledges. . . .* That natural right of cohabitation and commerce we had with others, this of just invasion and conquest, and many others praevious to this, we have above others; so that England may both by Law of Nature and Nations challenge Virginia for her owne peculiar propriety, and that by all right and rites usuall amongst men."[4]

Law of Nations gave Protestants a means of appealing to Rights of Conquest. Since such rights depended upon a determination whether a war had been "just," and the ultimate authority over such moral questions in Christendom had been the Pope, Protestants needed a way of rationalizing their conquests that would avoid the certainty of Papal hostility, and they fervently invoked Biblical authority for Rights of Conquest in wars against each other as well as everyone else.

I assume that Divine Right of Kings needs no discussion in the United States of America. Natural Law, Law of Nations, and / or Rights of Conquest bolstered the Divine Right of Kings to Sovereignty. Here is another legal fiction, still much cherished, and it is especially relevant to this discussion because it drew a curtain that has prevented recognition of the Covenant Chain for what it was. Sovereignty doctrine dictates that there can be no *imperium in imperio*—no fully autonomous government within the territories of the sovereign. Under such doctrine a national ruler "gives law" to his subjects—he does not negotiate agreements with them—so the facts of the Covenant Chain were simply ignored in favor of the rationales of creeping conquest.[5] The same mythical rationales have contributed heavily to a more general rejection and distortion of American Indian cultures.

4. Samuel Purchas, *Hakluytus Posthumus or Purchas His Pilgrimes*, 4 vols. (London, 1625), vol. 4, Bk. 9, ch. 20, p. 1811. And see the comment on Law of Nations in D. V. Jones, *License for Empire*, pp. 5–7.
5. See Sir William Johnson's candid remarks in a private letter to New York's Attorney General John Tabor Kempe, Oct. 7, 1765, *Johnson Papers* 11:925.

Almost as much history has been tortured by lawyers as by theologians, and when the two professions combined to support the emerging nation-state, they dictated the language of politics. Modern historical semantics owes too much to the vocabulary developed as a weapon in the long war of kings against their own peoples. To the Anglo-Saxon tribes of post-Roman England the word *law* identified the folk custom. In complex cases, inquiry discovered the law; no man made it. As the kings gradually acquired resources to form bureaucratic state structures, their legal retainers worked out mystical and fictional rationalizations for destroying the ancient folk customs and for imposing the commands of the kings' "civil" law. Thus the "rule of law" was transformed from the rule of custom over kings to the rule of kings against custom. Self-governing communities that relied for sanction upon the obligations of kinship ties were denounced as "uncivil," and the king's power was turned against them in the name of his "sovereignty" and "state." The king's bishops gave God the credit for inventing sovereignty and cursed its resisters as enemies of true religion.[6]

It was natural for the king's servants venturing to America to cram the facts of new-found societies into the categories of pre-existing legal thought, for their missions involved the reduction of native American communities to the king's jurisdiction, which they phrased as "reducing the savages to civility."[7] Kings disagreed with each other over which of them should seize which lands, but they agreed upon the Law of Nations that refused recognition of sovereignty to governments lacking the form of a state and the sanctification of one of the cults of Christianity. The kin-ordered governments of Indians were therefore "uncivil" in the vocabulary of their conquerors—soon to become "uncivilized"—and since they were stateless they lacked sovereignty. In the new semantics there could be no law without a sovereign to decree it, so the Indian tribes had no law. Lacking sovereignty, law, and state, they had no government "worthy the name." Europeans competed strenuously to fill that void. The kings hurled their sovereignty across the seas at every turf their servants trod upon or looked at.

As an abstraction, sovereignty flew lightly from one shore to the other. In practice, however, it had to be confined within the limits of the kings' effective, deliverable power, which were real and strong. European power was sea-borne and coast-bound. It faced the power of native Indian polities, which was generated both from the size of their communities—far

6. S. B. Chrimes, *English Constitutional Ideas in the Fifteenth Century* (Cambridge: Cambridge University Press, 1936), pp. 192–94; Fritz Kern, *Kingship and Law in the Middle Ages*, trans. S. B. Chrimes (Oxford: Basil Blackwell, 1939), pp. 70–75.

7. Discussed in Sheehan, *Savagism and Civility*, introduction and ch. 5. James Axtell has written directly on the point in "The Invasion Within: The Contest of Cultures in Colonial North America," in *The European and the Indian: Essays in the Ethnohistory of Colonial North America* (New York: Oxford University Press, 1981) pp. 45–46.

greater in the early days than the few boatloads of European colonists—and from the Indians' resourcefulness.[8] In these circumstances, it was impossible for a king's deputy to "give law"—i.e., the king's law—to the tribes. The two kinds of power could not co-exist without adapting to each other through processes of negotiation between their bearers, and so they did. (I am speaking here of North America beyond the Spanish empire.) Though distant kings never forgot for a minute their claims to sovereignty, colonists on the spot filed such claims away for use at appropriate times and places. Meanwhile the colonists made treaties with Indian tribes in the same manner that their kings treated with each other.

A system in which persons and territories are ordered by agreement between practically functioning governments is a system of governance regardless of the imperatives of ideology. If the crown's lawyers did not recognize divided sovereignty, the crown's agents in America acted on the assumption that the power to rule was in fact divided. In New France this recognition led to the adoption of the medieval conquest strategy of placing forts (castles) strategically among the populations claimed as royal subjects while the customary day-to-day government of each tribe continued unchanged except where missionaries had become strong. In New England and Virginia, the colonists quickly became strong enough to conquer and dictate terms to local tribes. In the middle colonies the Covenant Chain became the major instrument for getting English policy executed by Indian agency.

But the Iroquois never recognized British sovereignty over their tribes, and some still do not recognize the sovereignty of either the United States or Canada. Along with many other Indians of the present day, they proclaim themselves sovereign nations. The assertion is neither absurd nor insignificant, but it is ironic. When British colonials had to bide their time, they recognized Iroquois independence *de facto* by bowing to the necessity for negotiation while preserving *de jure* claims to sovereignty. (Much as English monarchs styled themselves kings of France during centuries when they could not step foot on French soil without permission.) Now the shoe is on the other foot. The necessitous Iroquois deal *de facto* with United States officials while preserving, as loudly and clearly as ever, their *de jure* claim to sovereignty. The forms have changed, but negotiation still continues.

The American and French revolutions ended the myth of kingship's divinity, and the nineteenth century became an era of secularization. What happened to ideas was described in a book title as the warfare of science with theology, and a climactic battle that seems to be reviving was fought over the books and theories of Charles Darwin.[9] But the nineteenth cen-

8. See Jennings, *Invasion*, ch. 2.

9. Andrew Dickson White, *A History of the Warfare of Science with Theology in Christendom* (New York: D. Appleton and Co., 1896).

tury did not end mythology. Like the process described as the survival of the pagan gods, old myths transmuted into new forms. The theologians' Natural Law became the scientists' Laws of Nature. God's Chosen People, endowed by grace, became nature's White people, endowed by race.[10] Race conferred the same duties and rights formerly given by religion. From palm to pine the European White man kept his Christian burden.

Racial conceptions permeated all fields of thought, including anthropology and history. Morgan and Parkman saw eye to eye on White supremacy, though Morgan attributed it to cultural evolution while Parkman preached survival of the fittest. Their difference of formulation, however, held significance, for the notion of cultural evolution permits any people to lift itself to higher levels, but the survival of the fittest dooms all but one.[11] That difference became the fork in the road where anthropology and history diverged at the century's end.

Historians became enamored of Frederick Jackson Turner's races locked in eternal combat—with White civilization pitted against Red savagery. Anthropologists were startled, and then persuaded, by Franz Boas's denunciations of race, Social Darwinism, and cultural evolution. (Boas was not a man to do things half way.)

Enough has been written elsewhere about these subjects. The absurdities and contradictions of race have been demonstrated forcefully in hundreds, perhaps thousands, of books; and its proponents have never even succeeded in defining it except in terms of the quantum fallacy embodied, for example, in (1) the Nazi Nuremberg Laws—one Jewish great grandparent makes the great grandchild a Jew whether he knows it or not; (2) the former miscegenation laws of Louisiana and South Carolina—*any* identifiable Black ancestor, no matter how remote, made the descendant Black. As I write this, the newspapers report that a court challenge is being mounted to a Louisiana law enacted in 1970, and still in effect, that any person is defined as Black if he has at least one–thirty-second part of "Negro blood"; i.e., one Black great, great, great grandparent. It seems that the Louisiana legislature thought that Nazi mathematics were deficient.

Fallacy aside, what can be said validly about race is that it has been conceived as an absolute given to individuals by heredity and thus unchangeable by human agency. Racists adopt the assumption of animal breeders; to wit, that if races mix the offspring are but degenerate mongrel descendants of pure-blooded parents. This is purely a European and

10. Two books are especially helpful: George W. Stocking, Jr., *Race, Culture, and Evolution;* and William Ragan Stanton, *The Leopard's Spots.*

11. Spicer, *Cycles of Conquest,* p. 582. See Francis Jennings, "A Growing Partnership: Historians and Anthropologists in the Writing of American Indian History," *The History Teacher* 12 (Nov., 1980), pp. 87–104.

Euramerican conception. Though Indians have learned how to call themselves "full-bloods," "half-bloods," and "quarter-bloods" in the English language, they use tribal names in their own tongues, and no Indian language has a word equivalent to "half-breed."[12] They simply hyphenate Mohawk-Delaware as one might hyphenate German-American. A child of Mohawk and Euramerican parents is either Mohawk or American, depending on which culture he adopts. Indians adopted the "paleface" terminology rather late. The Algonquians of the East Coast called the first European colonizers *Swannakens*, a word that carried the meaning of salty-bitter.[13] Indians were certainly ethnocentric but not civilized enough to be racists then. It must be ruefully confessed that they have learned racism in the interest of their own defense.

World War II and the glaring absurdities of "honorary Aryans," as well as the horrors of the "final solution," taught reasonable historians the implications of race. Once more, a number of us have turned to anthropology for ordering conceptions, but it is a new, revised anthropology. From the old notion of cultural evolution, twentieth-century anthropologists have extracted culture and dropped the evolutionary mechanism.

This basic culture concept has been developed into a chest full of very useful analytical tools, such as acculturation, diffusion, syncretism, accommodation, innovation, and so on. The mere recital of these words exhibits the glaring contrast between culture and race. Culture is the product of human intelligence and activity, changing within individual lifetimes and from generation to generation. Any person's race is an unchangeable given; his culture must be learned and taught. Culture not only can, but must, be transmitted or diffused by means other than genetic reproduction.

There is another highly significant contrast: namely, that theories of race were and are based on deductive logic.[14] Race theories could be maintained only in defiance of the evidence. It is almost a definition of mythology. Culture, on the other hand, has been founded from its inception in inductive logic applied to observed and compared phenomena whose substance can be verified by independent investigators. The shift of anthropology from race to culture was like the shift from astrology to astronomy, or from alchemy to chemistry. Though some data may be salvaged from the pseudo-science, the change requires a total reorganization of assumptions, definitions, and interpretations. For historians who think in terms of culture, the contact between two societies with different cultures becomes something different from a war for survival of the fittest. Conflict

12. Not a linguist, I base this statement on the gracious response to my direct question by Dr. Ives Goddard, of the Smithsonian Institution.
13. Weslager, *Delaware Indians*, p. 106 and n. 10, p. 112.
14. My thanks to Henry F. Dobyns for this perception.

often does occur, but so do varieties of cooperation and accommodation, all willed by human agents. Such accommodation need not always be offered in good will. It may often—perhaps most often—be dictated by the harsh realization of its being the lesser of evils. Nevertheless it is qualitatively different from incessant conflict, as is well understood by people making the choice; that difference must be given its due.

The discovery of intercultural activity makes possible the recognition of the Covenant Chain among other things. More broadly, it opens up a new vista on American history as a whole.[15] Through the culture concept an ethnohistorian may replace the homogenized rigid absolutes of "Indian-White Relations"—which is a barely camouflaged racial formulation of Red-White relations—with a fluid mixture of peoples and cultures interacting variously with each other to create something new. However unconsciously made, the pluralistic American society and culture of modern times are the historical product of all the society's constituent persons and their ancestors in this land. Since 1492 Indian history cannot truthfully be extricated from *American* history, nor vice versa.

Perhaps an objection will be made that this concept is but the twentieth-century ethnohistorian's myth, similar in function to the racial myths of nineteenth-century historians. Only posterity will be able to have a full perspective on such a supposition, but several valid comments can be made now. The first two have already been mentioned: the concept of culture correlates better than that of race to recorded data, and it serves as a more flexible analytical tool. This book, like its predecessor volume, is offered in evidence of these claims. But, supposing no difference in such matters, and supposing culture to be only a myth equal in quality to race, I would argue that it is a preferable myth on grounds of social morality. Culture presupposes that all men *are* created equal, and women too, *in moral worth*, and that this kind of equality overrides differences of physique, ability, sex, and social status. There are differences in cultures, to be sure. They function in different ways and they are unequally attractive, but the honest scholar must study alien types with the same respect for accuracy that he gives to his own, as the honest judge must not discriminate his rulings because of class or race. (He passes judgment after he has studied the evidence fairly.)

Such assumptions, attitudes, and behavior would make impossible the erection of an autocratic empire on the basis of assumed superiority of one genetic stock. They imply the real democracy that Frederick Jackson

15. "Today it is increasingly being realized that many activities of Euroamerican settlers cannot be understood adequately without a sound understanding of native history." Bruce G. Trigger, "Ethnohistory: Problems and Prospects," a paper read at the Laurier Conference on Ethnohistory and Ethnology, Oct. 30, 1980, Waterloo, Canada. Forthcoming in *Ethnohistory*.

Turner rejected in favor of a racist myth; i.e., the *Herrenvolk* democracy of egalitarian Whites forming a caste above all others.[16]

Yet I do not think that democracy requires homogenization. Beguiling as is the old Mohawk ideal of one people in one land (translated into terms of a Euramerican melting pot in modern times), total assimilation is neither possible nor desirable. Cultural identities are stubborn things, no matter how much their details change. However indefinable, "Indianness" lives still, after three centuries of pressures for its eradication. And there is obvious value in variety, which we recognize among individual persons. The moral ideal that rejects imperial domination has a feasible and desirable alternative in democratic cultural pluralism.[17] Most of the Iroquois have learned that lesson the hard way. How long must the rest of us wait?

16. See Christopher Saunders, "Political Processes in the Southern African Frontier Zones," in *The Frontier in History: North America and Southern Africa Compared*, eds. Howard Lamar and Leonard Thompson (New Haven: Yale University Press, 1981), p. 169; and George M. Frederickson, *White Supremacy: A Comparative Study in American and South African History* (New York: Oxford University Press, 1981), pp. xi–xii.

17. See Hazel Whitman Hertzberg's thoughtful study, "Nationality, Anthropology and Pan-Indianism in the Life of Arthur C. Parker (Seneca)," *Proceedings of the American Philosophical Society* 123:1 (Feb., 1979), pp. 47–71.

BIBLIOGRAPHY 🦢

Materials cited in the notes

Because of the wide range of sources and disciplines represented in the bibliography, detailed analysis in the list would be unwieldy. It is divided into the following sections: (1) manuscript materials (classified by locations); (2) printed source materials originating before 1800—official records are classified by place and all others are in alphabetical order; and (3) printed materials originating after 1800 (in alphabetical order).

In a few instances further analysis and commentary pertaining to a particular citation can be found in the text notes. Such cross-referencing is indicated in the citation as, Bib. note: ch. , n. . Data on governors are from David P. Henige, *Colonial Governors from the Fifteenth Century to the Present* (Madison: University of Wisconsin Press, 1970.)

I. Manuscript Materials

Canada
Public Archives of Canada, Ottawa: Daniel Claus, "Memoir of Descent" (1775?).

England
Longleat House, Wilts.: Coventry Papers, vol. 67. Public Record Office, Kew: Colonial Office Records, Classes 1 and 5. Has printed calendars.

Illinois
The Newberry Library, Chicago: Documentary History of the Iroquois Archive.

Maryland
Enoch Pratt Free Library, Baltimore: Young Collection, Document 7.

Massachusetts
Massachusetts Archives, Boston: Treaty mss., July 1744.

New York
New York State Archives, Albany: (1) New Netherland Council Minutes: typescript translated from Dutch by A. J. F. van Laer. (2) New York Colonial Manuscripts, 1638–1800; 103 vols. greatly damaged by fire; 52 vols. in fair to good

condition; has printed calendar. (3) New York Council Minutes, 1668–1783; 28 vols. with damage by fire; has printed calendar.

Oklahoma
Thomas Gilcrease Institute of American History and Art, Tulsa.: Minutes of treaty at Boston, Aug.-Sept., 1723.

Pennsylvania
Doylestown
Bucks County Court House: (1) Deed Books; (2) Court Records.
Bucks County Historical Society Library: Indian Walk of 1737.

Easton
Northampton County Court House: Deed Books.

Harrisburg
Department of Internal Affairs: (1) Patent Books; (2) Commission Books.
Department of State: Indian cession deeds, 1682–1685. (Class RG-26)
Historical and Museum Commission Library: Provincial Record (Minutes of the Provincial Council, March 10, 1683, to Dec. 9, 1775).

Philadelphia
American Philosophical Society Library: (1) Miscellaneous Manuscripts Collection; (2) Penn Letters and Ancient Documents.
City Hall (1) Archives Division: Warrants and Surveys of the Province of Pennsylvania, 1682–1759. 9 vols. with card index. Set is incomplete—supplemental set is in Dept. of Internal Affairs, Harrisburg, not indexed. (2) Records Department: Deed Books.
Historical Society of Pennsylvania Library: (1) Anonymous draft of "Sundry Tracts" of Forks of Delaware region, and Benjamin Eastburn's draft of same region. Call no. OF, 549*, 1740; (2) Bucks County Papers; (3) Cadwalader Collection, Thomas Cadwalader; (4) Dreer Collection; (5) Etting Collection, Miscellaneous Manuscripts; (6) Gratz Collection, Governors of Pennsylvania; (7) Indian Records Collection, Minutes of the Friendly Association, 1755–1757; (8) James Logan's Account Book, 1712–1719; (9) James Logan's Ledger, 1720–1727; (10) James Steel's Letter Books; (11) Logan Letter Books; (12) Logan Papers; (13) Logan Papers, Correspondence of James Logan; (14) Logan Papers, Records of the Court at Upland; (15) Logan Parchment Letter Book, 1712–1715; (16) Mary Morris Lawrence Collection, Correspondence, Thomas Lawrence Case, Barefoot Brunsdon folder; (17) Nead Papers; (18) Northampton County Papers, Bethlehem and Vicinity, 1741–1886; (19) Penn Letter Books; (20) Penn Manuscripts, Additional Miscellaneous Letters; (21) Penn Manuscripts (boxes); (22) Penn Manuscripts, Large Folio; (23) Penn Manuscripts, Letters of the Penn Family to James Logan; (24) Penn Papers from Friends House, London; (25) Penn Papers, Indian Affairs; (26) Penn Papers, Official Correspondence; (27) Penn-Forbes Collection; (28) Penn-Physick Manuscripts; (29) Peters Letter Books, 1737–1750; (30) Records of the Court at New Castle, 1676–1681; (31) Records of the Provincial Council and Other Papers from the Numismatic and Anti-

quarian Society (boxed); (32) Society Collection; (33) Streper Papers; (34) Taylor Papers; (35) Thomas Holme's 1687 Map of Pennsylvania; (36) Transcripts of Board of Trade Papers, Proprietaries, 1697–1776; (37) Wayne Manuscripts, Indian Treaties, 1778–1795, B.

Library Company of Philadelphia: Smith Manuscripts.

Swarthmore

Friends Historical Library, Swarthmore College: (1) Charles S. Ogden Papers, Series 4, Scrapbook 4; (2) Indian Walk Manuscripts, Apr. 26, 1735, to Sept. 19, 1737.

West Chester

Chester County Court House: Quarter Sessions Docket, 1714–1723.

Virginia

Virginia State Library, Richmond: Colonial Papers.

II. Printed source materials originating before 1800

OFFICIAL RECORDS

Canada

Canada: Indian Treaties and Surrenders from 1680 to 1890. 2 vols. Ottawa: Queen's Printer, 1891. Reprinted facsimile with vol. 3 (to 1902). Toronto: Coles Publishing Co., 1971.

The Correspondence of Lieut. Governor John Graves Simcoe, with Allied Documents Relating to His Administration of the Government of Upper Canada. Comp. and ed. E. A. Cruikshank. 5 vols. Toronto: Ontario Historical Society, 1923–1931.

Connecticut

The Public Records of the Colony of Connecticut. Ed. J. Hammond Trumbull. 15 vols. Hartford, 1850–1890.

England

Acts of the Privy Council of England, Colonial Series, 1613–1783. Eds. W. L. Grant and James Munro. 6 vols. London, 1908–1912.

Calendar of State Papers, Colonial Series, America and West Indies, Preserved in the Public Record Office. Eds. W. Noel Sainsbury, et al. London: Her Majesty's Stationery Office, 1896–.

Proceedings and Debates of the British Parliaments respecting North America, 1452–1727. Ed. Leo Francis Stock. 5 vols. Washington, D.C., 1924–1941+.

Royal Instructions to British Colonial Governors, 1670–1776. Ed. Leonard Woods Labaree. 2 vols, 1935. Reprint. New York: Octagon Books, 1965.

Maryland

Archives of Maryland. Eds. William Hand Browne, et al. Published by authority under the direction of the Maryland Historical Society. 72 vols. to date. Baltimore, 1883–.

Calvert Papers, Number One. Fund Publication No. 28. Baltimore: Maryland Historical Society, 1889.

New Netherland
Minutes of the Court of Albany, Rensselaerswyck and Schenectady, 1668–1673. Trans. and ed. A. J. F. van Laer. 3 vols. Albany: University of the State of New York, 1926–1932.
Minutes of the Court of Fort Orange and Beverwyck (1652–1660). Trans. and ed. A. J. F. van Laer. 2 vols. Albany: University of the State of New York, 1922–1923.
Minutes of the Court of Rensselaerswyck, 1648–1652. Trans. and ed. A. J. F. van Laer. Albany: University of the State of New York, 1922.

New Plymouth
Acts of the Commissioners of the United Colonies of New England. Ed. David Pulsifer: vols. 9 and 10 of *Records of the Colony of New Plymouth in New England*. Eds. Nathaniel B. Shurtleff and David Pulsifer. Boston, 1859.
William Bradford. *Of Plymouth Plantation*. Ed. Samuel Eliot Morison. New York: Alfred A. Knopf, 1966.

New Sweden
The Instruction for Johan Printz, Governor of New Sweden. Trans. Amandus Johnson. Philadelphia: The Swedish Colonial Society, 1930.

New York
Documents Relative to the Colonial History of the State of New York. Eds. E. B. O'Callaghan and Berthold Fernow. 15 vols. Albany: Weed, Parsons and Co., 1856–1887. Vols. 1–2 are Dutch records. Vols. 3–8 and 12–14 are English records. Vols. 9–10 are French records. Vol. 11 is Index to 1–10. Vol. 15 pertains to American Revolution.
The Livingston Indian Records, 1666–1723. Ed. Lawrence H. Leder. Gettysburg, Pa.: Pennsylvania Historical Association, 1956. Reprinted from entire issue of *Pennsylvania History* 23:1 (Jan. 1956).
Minutes of the Executive Council of the Province of New York: Administration of Francis Lovelace, 1668–1673. With 98 "Collateral and Illustrative Documents." Ed. Victor Hugo Paltsits. 2 vols. Albany: State of New York, 1910.
New York Colonial Manuscripts, vols. 23 and 24. In *Third Annual Report of the State Historian of the State of New York, 1897*. Ed. Hugh Hastings. New York: Wynkoop Hallenbeck Crawford Co., 1898. Appendix L. Pp. 159–435.
Wraxall, Peter. *An Abridgment of the Indian Affairs Contained in Four Folio Volumes, Transacted in the Colony of New York, from the Year 1678 to the Year 1751*. Ed. with Introduction (pp. ix–cxviii) by Charles Howard McIlwain (1915). Reprinted facsimile, New York: Benjamin Blom, 1968.

Pennsylvania
The Charters and Acts of Assembly of the Province of Pennsylvania. 2 vols. Philadelphia: Peter Miller and Co., 1762.
Indian Treaties Printed by Benjamin Franklin, 1736–1762. Ed. Julian P. Boyd. Philadelphia: Historical Society of Pennsylvania, 1938. Bib. note: ch. 17, n. 38.

Minutes of the Commissioners of Property. In *Pennsylvania Archives,* q.v. 2d ser., vol. 19, and 3d ser., vol. 1.

Minutes of the Provincial Council of Pennsylvania. (Spine title *Colonial Records.*) Ed. Samuel Hazard. 16 vols. Harrisburg and Philadelphia, 1838–1853. Note: vols. 1–3 were printed in two editions with different pagination. Bib. note: ch. 14, n. 9; ch. 17, n. 45.

Pennsylvania Archives. 9 series, 138 vols. Philadelphia and Harrisburg, 1852–1949.

Statutes at Large of Pennsylvania, 1682–1809. 17 vols. Harrisburg: State Printer, 1896–1915.

Votes and Proceedings of the House of Representatives of the Province of Pennsylvania, 1682–1776 (1752–1776). 8 vols., 8th ser., *Pennsylvania Archives,* q.v., Harrisburg, 1931–1935.

United States

Anthony Wayne, A Name in Arms: Soldier, Diplomat, Defender of Expansion Westward of a Nation; The Wayne-Knox-Pickering-McHenry Correspondence (1960). Transcribed and ed. by Richard C. Knopf. Reprint. Westport, Conn.: Greenwood Press, 1975.

The New American State Papers: Indian Affairs. Ed. Thomas C. Cochran. 13 vols. Wilmington, Del.: Scholarly Resources, 1972.

UNOFFICIAL SOURCE MATERIALS ORIGINATING BEFORE 1800

American Weekly Mercury. Philadelphia. Nos. 814, 816, 817, 831, 833, 834.

Bartram, John. *Observations on the Inhabitants, Climate, Soil, Rivers, Productions, Animals, and other matters worthy of Notice . . . in his Travels from Pensilvania to Onondago, Oswego and the Lake Ontario, In Canada* (1715). Reprinted facsimile as *Travels in Pensilvania and Canada.* Readex, 1966.

The Bethlehem Diary. Trans. and ed. Kenneth G. Hamilton, 1:1742–44. Bethlehem, Pa.: Archives of the Moravian Church, 1971.

Champlain, Samuel de. *The Works of Samuel de Champlain.* Gen. ed. H. P. Biggar. 6 vols. Publications of the Champlain Society, Extra Series (1922–1936). Reprinted facsimile, Toronto: University of Toronto Press, 1971.

[Claypoole, James.] *James Claypoole's Letter Book: London and Philadelphia, 1681–1684.* Ed. Marion Balderston. San Marino, Calif.: The Huntington Library, 1967.

Colden, Cadwallader. *The History of the Five Indian Nations Depending on the Province of New-York in America* (1727–1747). Reprint. Ithaca, N.Y.: Great Seal Books, 1958. Bib. notes ch. 2, n. 8; ch. 8, n. 68; ch. 9, n. 33.

Collections of the State Historical Society of Wisconsin. Vol. 16. Ed. Reuben Gold Thwaites. Madison, 1902.

Collections of the New-York Historical Society. 2d ser., 2. New York, 1849.

Correspondence Between William Penn and James Logan, and Others, 1700–1750. From the Original Letters in Possession of the Logan Family. Ed. Edward Armstrong. Notes by Mrs. Deborah Logan. 2 vols. Memoirs of the Historical Society of Pennsylvania 9–10. Philadelphia: J. B. Lippincott and Co., 1870–1872. Bib. note: ch. 12, n. 37; ch. 13, n. 14.

Correspondence of Jeremias van Rensselaer, 1651–1674. Trans. and ed. A. J. F. van Laer. Albany: University of the State of New York, 1932.

[Coxe, Daniel.] "Dr. Daniel Coxe his Account of New Jersey." *Pennsylvania Magazine of History and Biography* 7 (1883), pp. 327–35.

The Documentary History of the State of New-York. Comp and ed. E. B. O'Callaghan. 4 vols. Albany: Weed, Parsons, and Co., 1849–1851. Note: the Quarto edition published in 1851, by Charles van Benthuysen, is paged differently, though in the same order.

Documents Relating to New Netherland, 1624–1626, in the Henry E. Huntington Library. Trans. and ed. A. J. F. van Laer. San Marino, Calif., 1924.

The Genesis of the United States. Ed. Alexander Brown. 2 vols. Boston: Houghton, Mifflin, and Co., 1890.

George Mercer Papers Relating to the Ohio Company of Virginia. Comp. and ed. Lois Mulkearn. Pittsburgh: University of Pittsburgh Press, 1954.

Gipson, Lawrence Henry. *Lewis Evans: To Which is Added Evans' A Brief Account of Pennsylvania . . . Also Facsimiles of Evans' Maps.* Philadelphia: Historical Society of Pennsylvania, 1939.

"A Glimpse of Iroquois Culture History through the Eyes of Joseph Brant and John Norton." Ed. Douglas W. Boyce. *Proceedings of the American Philosophical Society* 117 (Aug. 1973), pp. 286–94.

Hamilton, Andrew. "Narrative of Sir, W. Keith's coming to the Govt. of Pennsylvania." Ed. Joshua Francis Fisher. In *Memoirs of the Historical Society of Pennsylvania* 2: pt. 2. Philadelphia: Lea and Carey, 1827.

The Indian Tribes of the Upper Mississippi Valley and Region of the Great Lakes, as described by Nicholas Perrot, French commandant in the Northwest; Bacqueville de la Potherie, French royal commissioner to Canada; Morrel Marston, American army officer; and Thomas Forsyth, United States agent at Fort Armstrong. Ed. Emma Helen Blair. 2 vols. Cleveland, O.: Arthur H. Clark Co., 1911–1912.

"Inventory of Martin Chartier's Estate." *Publications of the Lancaster County* (Pa.) *Historical Society* 29 (1925), pp. 130–33.

The Jesuit Relations and Allied Documents: Travels and Explorations of the Jesuit Missionaries in New France, 1601–1791 (1896–1901). Ed. Reuben Gold Thwaites. 73 vols. Reprinted facsimile in 36 vols. New York: Pageant Book Co., 1959. Bib. note: ch 6, n. 2.

Johnson, Joseph E. "A Quaker Imperialist's View of the British Colonies in America: 1732." *Pennsylvania Magazine of History and Biography* 60 (1936), pp. 97–112.

Keith, William. *A Just and Plain Vindication of Sir William Keith, Bart., Late Governour of Pennsilvania.* Philadelphia: Samuel Keimer, 1726.

———— *A Letter from Sir. Wm. Keith . . . to Mr. James Logan* (Dec. 13, 1725). Philadelphia: Andrew Bradford, 1725.

Lahontan, [Louis-Armand de Lom d'Arce], Baron de. *New Voyages to North-America* (1703). Ed. Reuben Gold Thwaites. 2 vols. Chicago: A. C. McClurg and co., 1905.

Las Casas, Bartolomé de. *In Defense of the Indians.* Trans. and ed. Stafford Poole. DeKalb: Northern Illinois University Press, 1974.

The Letters and Papers of Cadwallader Colden. Collections of the New-York Historical Society 50–51, 67 68 (1918–1937). Reprint. New York: AMS Press, 1937.

Lindestrom, Peter. *Geographia Americae with an Account of the Delaware Indians, Based on Surveys and Notes Made in 1654–1656.* Trans. and ed. Amandus Johnson. Philadelphia: Swedish Colonial Society, 1925.

Logan, James. *Remarks on Sir William Keith's Vindication*. Philadelphia, 1726.

Marshe, Witham. "Journal of the Treaty . . . at Lancaster in Pennsylvania, June, 1744." In *Collections of the Massachusetts Historical Society*. 1st ser., 7:171–201. Reprinted as *Lancaster in 1744*. Ed. William H. Egle. Lancaster, Pa.: New Era Steam Book and Job Print, 1884.

"Narrative of Bacon's Rebellion." *Virginia Magazine of History and Biography* 4 (1896), pp. 117–54.

Narratives of Early Pennsylvania, West New Jersey, and Delaware, 1630–1710. Ed. Albert Cook Myers. Original Narratives of Early American History series. New York: Charles Scribner's Sons, 1912.

The Papers of Sir William Johnson. Eds. James Sullivan, et al. 14 vols. Albany: University of the State of New-York, 1921–1965.

The Pitkin Papers. Vol. 19 of *Collections of the Connecticut Historical Society*. Hartford, 1921.

Plantagenet, Beauchamp [Edmund Plowden]. *A description of the Province of New Albion* (1648). Separately paged in *Tracts and Other Papers*. Comp. Peter Force, q.v., vol. 2.

Pownall, Thomas. *A Topographical Description . . . of the Middle British Colonies, &c., in North America* (1776). Reprinted as *A Topographical Description of the Dominions of the United States of America*, Ed. Lois Mulkearn. Pittsburgh: University of Pittsburgh Press, 1949.

Propositions made by the Five Nations of Indians . . . in Albany, the 20th of July, Anno Dom. 1698. New York: William Bradford.

Proud, Robert. *The History of Pennsylvania* (1797–1798). 2 vols. Reprinted facsimile. Pennsylvania Heritage Series 2–3. Spartanburg, S. C. : The Reprint Co., 1967.

Purchas, Samuel. *Hakluytus Posthumus or Purchas His Pilgrimes*. 4 vols. London, 1625.

Sagard, Gabriel. *The Long Journey into the Country of the Hurons* (1632). Trans. H. H. Langton. Ed. George M. Wrong. Publications of the Champlain Society 25. Toronto, 1939.

Smith, John. *A Map of Virginia* (1612). In *The Jamestown Voyages Under the First Charter, 1606–1609*. Ed. Philip L. Barbour. 2 vols. Works issued by the Hakluyt Society. 2d ser., 136–37. Cambridge: Cambridge University Press, 1969, 2:327–464.

Talbot, George. "Report of a conference between Coll. Talbot and William Penn" (1684). *Maryland Historical Magazine* 3 (1908), pp. 21–32.

Thornton, John. "First Map of Pennsylvania Under William Penn, 1681." Ed. Albert Cook Myers. Philadelphia, 1923. (Copy in HSP.)

Tracts and Other Papers Relating Principally to the Origin, Settlement, and Progress of the Colonies in North America. Comp. Peter Force. 4 vols. (1836). Reprinted facsimile, Gloucester, Mass.: Peter Smith, 1963.

Treaty with the Five Nations at Conestoga, 5 July 1721. Philadelphia: Andrew Bradford, 1721.

Van der Donck, Adriaen. *A Description of the New Netherlands* (1653). Trans. Jeremiah Johnson. Ed. Thomas F. O'Donnell. Reprinted. Syracuse, N.Y.: Syracuse University Press, 1968.

Van Rensselaer Bowier Manuscripts. Trans and ed. A. J. F. van Laer. New York

State Library 90th Annual Report. Vol. 2. Supplement 7. Albany: University of the State of New York, 1908.

Virginia and Maryland, or, The Lord Baltamore's printed Case, Uncased and answered. In *Tracts and Other Papers*, ed. Peter Force, q.v., vol. 2, separately paged.

The Voyages of Jacques Cartier. Trans. and ed. H. P. Biggar. Publications of the Public Archives of Canada 11. Ottawa: F. A. Acland, 1924.

Weiser, Conrad. "An Account of . . . the Six Nations." *The American Magazine.* Boston, 1744.

Wilderness Chronicles of Northwestern Pennsylvania. Eds. Sylvester K. Stevens and Donald H. Kent. Harrisburg: Pennsylvania Historical Commission, 1941.

The Winthrop Papers. Ed. Allyn B. Forbes. 5 vols. Boston: Massachusetts Historical Society, 1929–1947.

III. Printed materials originating after 1800

Alvord, Clarence W., and Lee Bidgood. *The First Exploration of the Trans-Allegheny Region by the Virginians, 1560–1674.* Cleveland, O.: Arthur H. Clark Co., 1912. Bib. note: ch. 12, n. 20.

The American Heritage Book of Indians. Ed. Alvin M. Josephy, Jr. New York: American Heritage Publishing Co., 1961.

Andrews, Charles M. *The Colonial Period of American History* (1934–1938). 4 vols. Reprint. New Haven: Yale University Press, 1964.

Andrews, Matthew Page. *Tercentenary History of Maryland.* 4 vols. Chicago: S. J. Clarke Publishing Co., 1925.

Axtell, James. *The European and the Indian: Essays in the Ethnohistory of Colonial North America.* New York: Oxford University Press, 1981.

———. "Some Thoughts on the Ethnohistory of Missions." A paper read at the Wilfred Laurier Conference on Ethnohistory and Ethnology, Oct. 31, 1980, Waterloo, Ontario. Forthcoming in *Ethnohistory*.

Bachman, Van Cleaf. *Peltries or Plantations: The Economic Policies of the Dutch West India Company in New Netherland, 1623–1639.* Johns Hopkins University Studies in Historical and Political Science. 87th ser. Baltimore, Md.: Johns Hopkins Press, 1969.

Bailyn, Bernard. *The New England Merchants in the Seventeenth Century.* Cambridge, Mass.: Harvard University Press, 1955.

Benson, Evelyn A. "The Huguenot Le Torts: First Christian Family on the Conestoga." *Journal of the Lancaster County* (Pa.) *Historical Society* 65:2 (spring 1961), pp. 92–103.

Berkhofer, Robert F., Jr. *The White Man's Indian: Images of the American Indian from Columbus to the Present.* New York: Alfred A. Knopf, 1978. Bib. note: ch. 1, n.7.

Bieder, Robert E. "Anthropology and History of the American Indian." *American Quarterly* 33:3 (1981), pp. 309–26.

Biggar, H. P. *The Early Trading Companies of New France: A Contribution to the History of Commerce and Discovery in North America.* University of Toronto Studies in History. Toronto, 1901.

Billington, Ray Allen. *Land of Savagery, Land of Promise: The European Image of the*

American Frontier in the Nineteenth Century. New York: W. W. Norton and Co., 1981.

Boorstin, Daniel. *The Americans: The Colonial Experience.* New York: Random House, 1958. Bib. note: Appendix B, n. 25.

Bozman, John Leeds. *The History of Maryland, from Its First Settlement, in 1633, to the Restoration in 1660.* 2 vols. Baltimore, Md.: James Lucas and E. K. Deaver, 1837.

Braithwaite, William C. *The Second Period of Quakerism.* 2d ed. Ed. Henry J. Cadbury. Cambridge: Cambridge University Press, 1961.

Brasser, T. J. "Mahican." In *Northeast,* q.v., pp. 198–212.

Brodhead, John Romeyn. *History of the State of New York.* 2 vols. New York: Harper and Brothers, 1853–1871.

Brown, Jennifer S. H. *Strangers in Blood: Fur Trade Families in Indian Country.* Vancouver: University of British Columbia Press, 1980. Bib. note: ch. 5, n. 12.

Browne, Bennett Bernard. "Historical and Genealogical Notes." *William and Mary Quarterly.* 1st ser. 3:3 (Jan. 1895), pp. 206–7.

Buck, William J. *History of Montgomery County within the Schuylkill Valley.* Norristown, Pa.: E. L. Acker, 1859.

———. *History of the Indian Walk.* Philadelphia: E. S. Stuart, 1886.

———. "Lappawinzo and Tishcohan, Chiefs of the Lenni Lenape." *Pennsylvania Magazine of History and Biography* 7 (1883), pp. 215–18.

Calendar of Council Minutes, 1668–1783. [Comp. Berthold Fernow]. New York State Library Bulletin 58. Albany: University of the State of New York, 1902.

Calendar of Historical Manuscripts in the Office of the Secretary of State, Albany, N.Y. Ed. E. B. O'Callaghan. 2 vols.: vol. 1: Dutch Mss.; vol. 2: English Mss. Albany: Weed, Parsons, and Co., 1865–1866.

Calendar of New York Colonial Manuscripts Indorsed Land Papers in the Office of the Secretary of State of New York: 1643–1803. Albany: Weed, Parsons, and Co., 1864.

Calendar of State Papers, Colonial Series, America and West Indies . . . Preserved in Her Majesty's Public Record Office. Eds. W. Noel Sainsbury, et al. London, 1860.

Callender, Charles. "Shawnee." In *Northeast,* q.v., pp. 622–35.

Canny, Nicholas. "The Permissive frontier: The problem of social control in English settlements in Ireland and Virginia, 1550–1650." In *The Westward Enterprise: English Activities in Ireland, the Atlantic, and America, 1480–1650.* Eds. K. R. Andrews, N. P. Canny, and P. E. H. Hair. Detroit: Wayne State University Press, 1979. Pp. 17–44.

Chidsey, A. D., Jr. *The Penn Patents in the Forks of the Delaware.* Publications of the Northampton County Historical and Genealogical Society 2. Easton, Pa., 1937.

Chrimes, S. B. *English Constitutional Ideas in the Fifteenth Century.* Cambridge: Cambridge University Press, 1936.

Clifton, James A. "Potawatomi." In *Northeast,* q.v., pp. 725–42.

Cochran, Thomas C. "The History of a Business Society." *Journal of American History* 54 (1967).

Condon, Thomas J. *New York Beginnings: The Commercial Origins of New Netherland.* New York: New York University Press, 1968.

Coolidge, Guy Omeron. *The French Occupation of the Champlain Valley from 1609 to*

1759. In Proceedings of the Vermont Historical Society. N.s., vol. 6, no. 3. Montpelier, 1938. Reprint. Harrison, N.Y.: Harbor Hill Books, 1979.

Copway, George [Kah-ge-ga-gah-bowh]. *The Traditional History and Characteristic Sketches of the Ojibway Nation*. London: C. Gilpin, 1850. Reprint. Boston: Benjamin B. Mussey and Co., 1851.

Crane, Verner W. *The Southern Frontier, 1670–1732*. Ann Arbor: University of Michigan Press, 1929.

Cutcliffe, Stephen H. "Colonial Indian Policy as a Measure of Rising Imperialism: New York and Pennsylvania, 1700–1755." *Western Pennsylvania Historical Magazine* 64:3 (July 1981), pp. 237–68.

Dangerfield, George. *Chancellor Robert R. Livingston of New York, 1746–1813*. New York: Harcourt, Brace, and Co., 1960.

Day, Gordon M. "The Identity of the Sokokis." *Ethnohistory* 12:3 (summer 1965), pp. 237–49.

———. "Iroquois: An Etymology." *Ethnohistory* 15:4 (fall 1968), pp. 389–402.

———. *The Mots Loups of Father Mathevet*. Publications in Ethnology 8. Ottawa: National Museum of Man, 1975.

A Delaware Indian Symposium. Ed. Herbert C. Kraft. Anthropological Series 4. Harrisburg: Pennsylvania Historical and Museum Commission, 1974.

De Valinger, Leon, Jr. "The Burning of the Whorekill, 1673." *Pennsylvania Magazine of History and Biography* 74 (1950), pp. 473–87.

———. "Indian Land Sales in Delaware." With addendum by C. A. Weslager. "A Discussion of the Family Hunting Territory Question in Delaware." *Bulletin of the Archaeological Society of Delaware*. June 20, 1941.

Dictionary of Canadian Biography. Eds. George W. Brown et al. Toronto : University of Toronto Press, 1966–.

Drinnon, Richard. "Ravished Land." *The Indian Historian* (fall 1976), pp. 24–26.

Du Creux, François. *The History of Canada or New France* (1664). Trans. and intro. by Percy J. Robinson. Ed. J. B. Conacher. 2 vols. Publications of the Champlain Society 30–31. Toronto, 1951–1952.

Dunn, Mary Maples. *William Penn: Politics and Conscience*. Princeton: Princeton University Press, 1967.

DuPonceau, Peter S., and J. Francis Fisher. "A Memoir . . ." In *Memoirs of the Historical Society of Pennsylvania* 3. Philadelphia, 1836. Pp. 141–203.

Eccles, W. J. "A Belated Review of Harold Adams Innis, *The Fur Trade in Canada*." *Canadian Historical Review* 60:4 (1979), pp. 425–30. Bib. note: ch. 5, n. 55.

———. *Canada under Louis XIV, 1663–1701*. Canadian Centenary Series. Toronto: McClelland and Stewart, 1964.

———. *The Canadian Frontier, 1534–1760*. Histories of the American Frontier series. Ed. Ray Allen Billington. New York: Holt, Rinehart and Winston, 1969. Bib. note: ch. 5, n. 28.

———. *France in America*. New American Nation Series. New York: Harper and Row, 1972.

———. *Frontenac, the Courtier Governor*. Toronto: McClelland and Stewart, 1959.

Edmunds, R. David. *The Potawatomis: Keepers of the Fire*. Norman: University of Oklahoma Press, 1978.

Eid, Leroy V. "The Ojibwa-Iroquois War: The War the Five Nations Did Not Win." *Ethnohistory* 26:4 (fall 1979), pp. 297–324.

Ellis, George E. "The Red Indian of North America in Contact with the French and English." In *Narrative and Critical History of America*. Ed. Justin Winsor. 8 vols. Boston: Houghton, Mifflin and Co., 1889. 1:283–328. Bib. note: ch. 2, n. 3.

Engels, Frederick. *The Origin of the Family, Private Property, and the State* (1884). Trans. Ernest Untermann. Chicago: Charles H. Kerr and Co., 1902.

Eshleman, H. Frank, A. K. Hostetter, and Charles Steigerwalt. "Report on the True Character, Time and Place of the First Regular Settlement in Lancaster County." *Publications of the Lancaster County* (Pa.) *Historical Society* 14 (1910), pp. 21–71.

Essays on the Problem of Tribe: Proceedings of the 1967 Annual Meeting of the American Ethnological Society. Ed. June Helm. Seattle: University of Washington Press, 1968.

Extending the Rafters: Interdisciplinary Approaches to Iroquoian Studies. Eds. Jack Campisi, Michael K. Foster, and Marianne Mithun. Albany: State University of New York Press. Forthcoming.

Feest, Christian F. "Nanticoke and Neighboring Tribes." In *Northeast*, q.v., pp. 240–52.

Fenton, William N. "Locality as a Basic Factor in the Development of Iroquois Social Structure." In *Symposium on Local Diversity in Iroquois Culture*. Ed. W. N. Fenton. Bureau of American Ethnology Bulletin 149. Washington, D.C.: Smithsonian Institution, 1951. Pp. 35–54.

———. "The Lore of the Longhouse; Myth, Ritual, and Red Power." *Anthropological Quarterly* 48:3 (July 1975), pp. 131–47.

———. "Northern Iroquoian Culture Patterns." In *Northeast*, q.v., pp. 296–321.

Fernow, Berthold. *The Ohio Valley in Colonial Days*. Albany: Joel Munsell's Sons, 1890.

Fiske, John. "Francis Parkman." *The Atlantic Monthly* 73 (1894), pp. 666–74.

Fredrickson, George M. *White Supremacy: A Comparative Study in American and South African History*. New York: Oxford University Press, 1981.

The Frontier in History: North America and Southern Africa Compared. Eds. Howard Lamar and Leonard Thompson. New Haven: Yale University Press, 1981.

Garcia-Mason, Velma. "Acoma Pueblo." In *Southwest*, q.v., pp. 450–66.

Garrad, Charles, and Conrad E. Heidenreich. "Khionontateronon (Petun)." In *Northeast*, q.v. Pp. 394–97.

Giraud, Marcel. *A History of French Louisiana*. Vol. 1: *The Reign of Louis XIV, 1698–1715* (1953). Trans. Joseph C. Lambert. Baton Rouge: Louisiana University Press, 1974.

———. *Le Métis Canadien: Son Role dans L'Histoire des Provinces de L'Ouest*. Paris: Institute d'Ethnologie, 1945.

Goddard, Ives. "Delaware." In *Northeast*, q.v., pp. 213–39.

Gottman, Jean. *Megalopolis: The Urbanized Northeastern Seaboard of the United States*. New York: Twentieth Century Fund, 1961.

Gould, Stephen Jay. *The Mismeasure of Man*. New York: W. W. Norton and Co., 1981.

The Great Law of Peace of the Longhouse People. Mohawk Nation at Akwesasne: White Roots of Peace, 1971. Bib. note: ch. 6, n. 26.

Grumet, Robert Steven. " 'We Are Not So Great Fools'; Changes in Upper Delawaran Socio-Political Life, 1630–1758." Ph.D. diss. Rutgers, The State University of New Jersey, 1979.

Haan, Richard L. "The Problem of Iroquois Neutrality: Suggestions for Revision." *Ethnohistory* 27:4 (fall 1980), pp. 317–30.

Hale, Horatio. *The Iroquois Book of Rites* (1883). Reprinted with introduction by W. N. Fenton. Toronto: University of Toronto Press, 1963.

Hamilton, Milton W. *Sir William Johnson: Colonial American, 1715–1763*. Port Washington, N.Y.: Kennikat Press, 1976.

Hamilton, Raphael N., S. J. *Marquette's Explorations: The Narratives Reexamined.* Madison: University of Wisconsin Press, 1970.

Handbook of American Indians North of Mexico. Ed. Frederick Webb Hodge. 2 vols. Washington, D.C.: Government Printing Office, 1907.

Handbook of North American Indians. Gen. ed. William C. Sturtevant. 20 vols. planned. Washington, D.C.: Smithsonian Institution, 1978–.

Hanke, Lewis. *All Mankind is One: A Study of the Disputation Between Bartolomé de Las Casas and Juan Ginés de Sepúlveda in 1550 on the Intellectual and Religious Capacity of the American Indians.* DeKalb: Northern Illinois University Press, 1974.

———. "Indians and Spaniards in the New World: A Personal View." In *Attitudes of Colonial Powers toward the American Indian.* Eds. Howard Peckham and Charles Gibson. Salt Lake City: University of Utah Press, 1969. Pp. 1–18.

Hanna, Charles A. *The Wilderness Trail, or The Ventures and Adventures of the Pennsylvania Traders on the Allegheny Path.* 2 vols. New York: G. P. Putnam's Sons, 1911. Bib. note: ch. 7, n. 12.

Harris, Richard Colebrook. *The Seigneurial System in Early Canada: A Geographical Study.* Madison: University of Wisconsin Press, 1968.

Hart, Simon. *The Prehistory of the New Netherland Company: Amsterdam. Notarial Records of the First Dutch Voyages to the Hudson.* Amsterdam: City of Amsterdam Press, 1959.

Hazard, Samuel. *Annals of Pennsylvania from the Discovery of the Delaware, 1609–1682.* Philadelphia: Hazard and Mitchell, 1850.

Heckewelder, John. *An Account of the History, Manners, and Customs of the Indian Nations Who once Inhabited Pennsylvania and the Neighbouring States* (1819). Rev. ed. edited by William C. Reichel. Memoirs of the Historical Society of Pennsylvania 12. Philadelphia, 1876.

Heidenreich, Conrad. *Huronia: A History and Geography of the Huron Indians, 1600–1650.* Toronto: McClelland and Stewart, 1971. Bib. note: ch. 6, n. 9.

———. "Huronia." In *Northeast*, q.v., pp. 368–88.

Heisey, Henry W., and J. Paul Witmer. "The Shenk's Ferry People." In *Foundations of Pennsylvania Prehistory.* Eds. Barry C. Kent, et al. Anthropological Series 1. Harrisburg: Pennsylvania Historical and Museum Commission, 1971. Pp. 477–507.

Hertzberg, Hazel Whitman. "Nationality, Anthropology and Pan-Indianism in the Life of Arthur C. Parker (Seneca)." *Proceedings of the American Philosophical Society* 123:1 (Feb. 1979), pp. 47–71.

Hewitt, J. N. B. "Tuscarora." In *Handbook of American Indians North of Mexico*, q.v. 2:842–53.

Hinsley, Curtis M., Jr. *Savages and Scientists: The Smithsonian Institution and the*

Development of American Anthropology, 1846–1910. Washington, D.C.: Smithsonian Institution Press, 1981.

A Historical Atlas of Canada. Ed. D. G. G. Kerr. 2d ed. Don Mills, Ont.: Thomas Nelson and Sons Ltd., 1966.

Historical Statistics of the United States: Colonial Times to 1970. Ed. William Lerner. 2 vols. Washington, D.C.: Bureau of the Census, 1975.

The History and Culture of Iroquois Diplomacy: An Interdisciplinary Guide to the Treaties of the Six Nations and Their League. (Eds. Francis Jennings, William N. Fenton, and Mary A. Druke. Published for the Newberry Library Center for the History of the American Indian. Syracuse University Press, forthcoming.

Hofstadter, Richard. *Social Darwinism in American Thought.* Rev. ed. Boston: Beacon Press, 1955.

Honour, Hugh. *The New Golden Land: European Images of America from the Discoveries to the Present Time.* New York: Pantheon Books, 1975.

Horsman, Reginald. *Race and Manifest Destiny: The Origins of American Anglo-Saxonism.* Cambridge, Mass.: Harvard University Press, 1981.

————. "Scientific Racism and the American Indian in the Mid-Nineteenth Century." *American Quarterly* 27:2 (May 1975), pp. 152–68.

Hudson, Charles. *The Southeastern Indians.* Knoxville: University of Tennessee Press, 1976.

Hunt, George T. *The Wars of the Iroquois: A Study in Intertribal Trade Relations.* Madison: University of Wisconsin Press, 1940. Bib. notes: ch. 3, n. 38; ch. 6, n. 43.

Hunter, William A. "Documented Subdivisions of the Delaware Indians." *Bulletin of the Archaeological Society of New Jersey* 20 (1978), pp. 20–40.

————. "Traders on the Ohio, 1730." *Western Pennsylvania Historical Magazine* 35 (1952), pp. 85–92.

Illick, Joseph E. *William Penn the Politician: His Relations with the English Government.* Ithaca, N.Y.: Cornell University Press, 1965.

Indians, Animals and the Fur Trade: A Critique of Keepers of the Game. Ed. Shepard Krech III. Athens: University of Georgia Press, 1981.

Innis, Harold A. *The Fur Trade in Canada: An Introduction to Canadian Economic History* (1930). Rev. ed. prepared by S. D. Clark and W. T. Easterbrook. Toronto: University of Toronto Press, 1956. Bib. note: ch. 5, n. 32.

International Encyclopedia of the Social Sciences. Ed. David L. Sills. 17 vols. New York: Macmillan Co. and Free Press, 1968.

Jackson, Donald. *Thomas Jefferson and the Stony Mountains; Exploring the West from Monticello.* Urbana: University of Illinois Press, 1981.

Jaenen, Cornelius J. *Friend and Foe: Aspects of French-Amerindian Cultural Contact in the Sixteenth and Seventeenth Centuries.* New York: Columbia University Press, 1976. Bib. note: ch. 5, n. 12.

James, Alfred Procter. *The Ohio Company: Its Inner History.* Pittsburgh: University of Pittsburgh Press, 1959.

Jenkins, Howard M. "The Family of William Penn." *Pennsylvania Magazine of History and Biography* 21 (1897), pp. 1–19, 137–60, 324–46, 421–44; 22 (1898), pp 71–97, 171–95, 326–49.

Jennings, Francis. "The Constitutional Evolution of the Covenant Chain." *Pro-*

ceedings of the American Philosophical Society 115:2 (April 1971), pp. 88–96.

———. "The Delaware Interregnum." *Pennsylvania Magazine of History and Biography* 89:2 (April 1965), pp. 174–98.

———. "Glory, Death, and Transfiguration: The Susquehannock Indians in the Seventeenth Century." *Proceedings of the American Philosophical Society* 112:1 (Jan. 1968), pp. 15–53.

———. "A Growing Partnership: Historians and Anthropologists in the Writing of American Indian History." *The History Teacher* 12 (Nov. 1980), pp. 87–104.

———. "Incident at Tulpehocken." *Pennsylvania History* 35:4 (Oct. 1968), pp. 335–55.

———. "Indians and Frontiers in Seventeenth Century Maryland." In *Early Maryland and the World Beyond.* Ed. David B. Quinn. Detroit: Wayne State University Press, 1982. Pp. 216–41.

———. "The Indian Trade of the Susquehanna Valley." *Proceedings of the American Philosophical Society* 110:6 (Dec. 1966), pp. 406–24.

———. *The Invasion of America: Indians, Colonialism, and the Cant of Conquest.* Published for the Institute of Early American History and Culture. Chapel Hill: University of North Carolina Press, 1975; rpt., New York: W. W. Norton, 1976.

———. "Jacob Young: Indian Trader and Interpreter." In *Struggle and Survival in Colonial America.* Eds. David G. Sweet and Gary B. Nash. Berkeley: University of California Press, 1981.

———. "Miquon's Passing: Indian-European Relations in Colonial Pennsylvania, 1674 to 1755." Ph.D. diss. University of Pennsylvania, 1965.

———. "National Policies: Sweden and Netherlands." In *History of Indian-White Relations.* Ed. Wilcomb E. Washburn. Forthcoming as vol. 4 of *Handbook of North American Indians,* q.v.

———. "The Scandalous Indian Policy of William Penn's Sons: Deeds and Documents of the Walking Purchase." *Pennsylvania History* 37 (1970), pp. 19–39.

———. "Sovereignty in Anglo-American History." In *Indian Sovereignty: Proceedings of the Second Annual Conference on Problems and Issues Concerning American Indians Today.* Ed. William R. Swagerty. Newberry Library Center for the History of the American Indian Occasional Papers 2. Chicago, 1979.

———. "Susquehannock." In *Northeast,* q.v., pp. 362–67.

———. "A Vanishing Indian: Francis Parkman Versus His Sources." *Pennsylvania Magazine of History and Biography* 87:3 (July 1963), pp. 306–23.

———. "Virgin Land and Savage People." *American Quarterly* 23:4 (1971), pp. 519–41.

Johnson, Amandus. *The Swedish Settlements on the Delaware. Their History and Relation to the Indians, Dutch and English, 1638–1664.* 2 vols. Philadelphia: University of Pennsylvania Press, 1911.

Jones, Dorothy V. *License for Empire: Colonialism by Treaty in Early America.* Chicago: University of Chicago Press, 1982.

Jordan, Winthrop D. *White Over Black: American Attitudes Toward the Negro, 1550–1812.* Published for the Institute of Early American History and Culture. Chapel Hill: University of North Carolina Press, 1968.

Katz, Stanley Nider. *Newcastle's New York: Anglo-American Politics, 1732–1753.* Cambridge, Mass.: Harvard University Press, 1968.

Kennedy, J. H. *Jesuit and Savage in New France*. New Haven: Yale University Press, 1950.

Kenney, Alice P. *The Gansevoorts of Albany: Dutch Patricians in the Upper Hudson Valley*. Syracuse, N.Y.: Syracuse University Press, 1969.

————. *Stubborn for Liberty: The Dutch in New York*. Syracuse, N.Y.: Syracuse University Press, 1975.

Kent, Donald H. "Historical Report on the Niagara River and the Niagara River Strip to 1759." *American Indian Ethnohistory: North Central and Northeastern Indians*. Ed. David Agree Horr. In *Iroquois Indians* II. New York: Garland Publishing Inc., 1974.

Kern, Fritz. *Kingship and Law in the Middle Ages*. Trans. S. B. Chrimes. Oxford: Basil Blackwell, 1939.

Klein, Philip S. and Ari Hoogenboom. *A History of Pennsylvania*. New York: McGraw-Hill Book Co., 1973.

Konrad, Viktor. "An Iroquois frontier: The north shore of Lake Ontario during the late seventeenth century." *Journal of Historical Geography* 7:2 (London 1981), pp. 129–44.

Kupperman, Karen Ordahl. *Settling with the Indians: The Meeting of English and Indian Cultures in America, 1580–1640*. Totowa, N.J.: Rowman and Littlefield, 1980. Bib. note: ch. 1, n. 8.

Lanctot, Gustave. *A History of Canada*. Trans. Josephine Hambleton and Margaret M. Cameron. 3 vols. Cambridge, Mass.: Harvard University Press, 1963–1965. Bib. note: ch. 6, n. 23.

Landis, Charles I. "Postlethwaite's and our First Courts." *Publications of the Lancaster County* (Pa.) *Historical Society* 19 (1915).

Lange, Charles H. "Relations of the Southwest with the Plains and Great Basin." In *Southwest*, q.v., pp. 201–5.

Leder, Lawrence H. *Robert Livingston, 1654–1728, and the Politics of Colonial New York*. Published for the Institute of Early American History and Culture. Chapel Hill: University of North Carolina Press, 1961.

Lescarbot, Marc. *The History of New France* (1609). Trans. W. L. Grant. 3 vols. Publications of the Champlain Society 1, 7, 11. Toronto: 1907–1914.

Levering, Joseph M. *A History of Bethlehem, Pennsylvania, 1741–1892*. Bethlehem: Bethlehem Times Publishing Co., 1903.

McGrath, Patrick. "Bristol and America, 1480–1631." In *The Westward Enterprise: English Activities in Ireland, the Atlantic, and America, 1480–1650*. Eds. K. R. Andrews, N. P. Canny, and P. E. H. Hair. Detroit: Wayne State University Press, 1979. Pp. 81–102.

McNeill, William H. "Make Mine Myth." *New York Times*. Dec. 28, 1981, Op-ed. p. A19.

Martin, Asa E. "Lotteries in Pennsylvania Prior to 1833." *Pennsylvania Magazine of History and Biography* 47 (1923), pp. 307–27. 48 (1924), pp. 66–93, 159–80.

Martin, Calvin. *Keepers of the Game: Indian-Animal Relationships and the Fur Trade*. Berkeley: University of California Press, 1978. Bib. note: ch. 5, n. 62.

Marye, William B. "Warriors' Paths." *Pennsylvania Archaeologist* 13:1 (1943), pp. 4–26; 14:1 (1944), pp. 4–22.

Merrell, James H. "Cultural Continuity among the Piscataway Indians of Colonial Maryland." *William and Mary Quarterly*. 3d ser., 36 (Oct. 1979), pp. 548–70.

Michelson, Gunther. "Iroquois Population Statistics." *Man in the Northeast* 14 (fall 1977), pp. 3–17.

Mooney, James. "The Aboriginal Population of America North of Mexico." In *Smithsonian Miscellaneous Collections* 80:7 (1928), pp. 1–40. Bib. note: ch. 7, n. 13.

Morgan, Edmund S. *American Slavery, American Freedom: The Ordeal of Colonial Virginia*. New York: W. W. Norton and Co., 1975.

Morgan, Lewis Henry. *Ancient Society; or Researches in the Lines of Human Progress from Savagery through Barbarism to Civilization* (1877). Reprint. Ed. Eleanor Burke Leacock. Cleveland, O.: World Publishing Co., 1963.

———. *League of the Ho-dé-no-sau-nee, Iroquois* (1851). Reprinted facsimile, with introduction by W. N. Fenton. New York: Corinth Books, 1962. Bib. note: ch. 2, notes 20, 23.

Morison. Samuel Eliot. *Samuel de Champlain: Father of New France*. Boston: Little, Brown, and Co., 1972.

Nammack, Georgiana C. *Fraud, Politics, and the Dispossession of the Indians: The Iroquois Land Frontier in the Colonial Period*. Norman: University of Oklahoma Press, 1969.

Narrative and Critical History of America, ed. Justin Winsor. 8 vols. Boston: Houghton, Mifflin and Co., 1889. Bib. note: ch. 3, n. 11.

Nash, Gary B. "The Free Society of Traders and the Early Politics of Pennsylvania." *Pennsylvania Magazine of History and Biography* 89:2 (April 1965), pp. 147–73.

———. *Quakers and Politics: Pennsylvania, 1681–1726*. Princeton: Princeton University Press, 1968.

———. "The Quest for the Susquehanna Valley: New York, Pennsylvania, and the Seventeenth-Century Fur Trade." *New York History* 48 (1967), pp. 3–27.

Newcomb, William W., Jr. *The Culture and Acculturation of the Delaware Indians*. Anthropological Paper 10 of the Museum of Anthropology. Ann Arbor: University of Michigan, 1956.

Northeast. Ed. Bruce G. Trigger. Vol. 15 (1978) of *Handbook of North American Indians*. Gen ed. William C. Sturtevant. 20 vols. Washington, D.C.: Smithsonian Institution, 1978–. Bib. note: ch. 3, n. 3.

Norton, John. *The Journal of Major John Norton, 1816*. Eds. Carl F. Klinck and James J. Talman. Toronto: Publications of the Champlain Society 46, 1970.

Norton, Thomas Elliott. *The Fur Trade in Colonial New York, 1686–1776*. Madison: University of Wisconsin Press, 1974.

Old Trails and New Directions: Papers of the Third North American Fur Trade Conference. Eds. Carol M. Judd and Arthur J. Ray. Toronto: University of Toronto Press, 1980.

O'Neill, Charles Edwards. *Church and State in French Colonial Louisiana: Policy and Politics to 1732*. New Haven: Yale University Press, 1966.

Parker, Arthur C. *The Constitution of the Five Nations, or the Iroquois Book of the Great Law* (1916). Reprinted facsimile (separately paged). In *Parker on the Iroquois*. Ed. W. N. Fenton. Syracuse, N.Y.: Syracuse University Press, 1968.

Parkman, Francis. *The Conspiracy of Pontiac and the Indian War after the Conquest of Canada* (1851). Rev. New Library ed. 2 vols. Boston: Little, Brown, and Co., 1909. Bibliographical note: ch. 5, n. 21.

————. *Count Frontenac and New France under Louis XIV* (1877). New Library ed. Boston: Little, Brown, and Co., 1909.

————. *The Jesuits in North America in the Seventeenth Century* (1867). New Library ed. Boston: Little, Brown, and Co., 1909.

————. *Letters of Francis Parkman*. Ed. Wilbur R. Jacobs. 2 vols. Published in cooperation with the Massachusetts Historical Society. Norman: University of Oklahoma Press, 1960.

————. *Montcalm and Wolfe* (1884). 2 vols. New Library ed. Boston: Little, Brown, and Co., 1909. Bibliographical note: ch. 5, n. 22.

Pennybacker, Samuel Whitaker. "Bebber's Township and the Dutch Patroons of Pennsylvania." *Pennsylvania Magazine of History and Biography* 31 (1907). Pp. 1–18.

Peterson, Jacqueline Louise. "The People in Between: Indian-White Marriage and the Genesis of a Métis Society and Culture in the Great Lakes Region, 1680–1830." Ph.D. diss. University of Illinois at Chicago Circle, 1981.

————. " 'Wild' Chicago: The Formation and Destruction of a Multiracial Community on the Midwestern Frontier, 1816–1837." In *The Ethnic Frontier: Essays in the History of Group Survival* in Chicago and the Midwest. Eds. Melvin G. Holli and Peter d'A. Jones. Grand Rapids, Mich.: William B. Eerdmans Publishing Co., 1977. Pp. 25–71.

Pollock, Frederick. *An Introduction to the History of the Science of Politics* (1890). Rev. ed. reprinted. Boston: Beacon Press, 1960.

Porter, H. C. *The Inconstant Savage: England and the North American Indian, 1500–1660*. London: Duckworth, 1979.

Publications of the Northampton County [Pa.] Historical and Genealogical Society 1. Easton, 1926.

Quimby, George Irving. *Indian Culture and European Trade Goods*. Madison: University of Wisconsin Press, 1966.

Quinn, David B. "James I and the Beginnings of Empire in America." *Journal of Imperial and Commonwealth History* 2:2 (London, 1974). Pp. 135–52.

————. *North America from Earliest Discovery to First Settlements: The Norse Voyages to 1612*. New York: Harper and Row, 1977.

Ray Arthur J. *Indians in the Fur Trade: Their role as trappers, hunters, and middlemen in the lands southwest of Hudson Bay, 1660–1870*. Toronto: University of Toronto Press, 1974.

Rich, E. E. *The History of the Hudson's Bay Company, 1670–1870*. 2 vols. Hudson's Bay Record Society Publications 21, 22. London, 1958–1959.

Richter, Daniel K. "Rediscovered Links in the Covenant Chain: Previously Unpublished Transcripts of New York Indian Treaty Minutes, 1677–1691." *Proceedings of the American Antiquarian Society* 92:pt. 1 (1982), pp. 45–85.

Ritzenthaler, Robert E. "Southwestern Chppewa." In *Northeast*, q.v. Pp. 743–59.

Rogers, E. S "Southeastern Ojibwa." In *Northeast*, q.v. Pp. 760–71.

Rogin, Michael Paul. *Fathers and Children: Andrew Jackson and the Subjugation of the American Indian*. New York: Alfred A. Knopf, 1975.

Russ, William A., Jr. *How Pennsylvania Acquired Its Present Boundaries*. University Park, Pa.: Pennsylvania Historical Association, 1966.

Rutman, Darrett B. *Winthrop's Boston: A Portrait of a Puritan Town, 1630–1649*.

Published for the Institute of Early American History and Culture. Chapel Hill: University of North Carolina Press, 1965.

Ruttenber, E. M. *History of the Tribes of Hudson's River; Their origin, Manners and Customs; Tribal and Sub-Tribal Organizations; Wars, Treaties, etc., etc.* (1872). Reprinted facsimile, Port Washington, N.Y.: Kennikat Press, 1971.

Sauer, Carl Ortwin. *Sixteenth Century North America: The Land and the People as Seen by the Europeans.* Berkeley: University of California Press, 1971.

Scharf, J. Thomas, and Thompson Westcott. *History of Philadelphia, 1609–1884.* 3 vols. L. H. Everts and Co., 1884.

Sheehan, Bernard W. *Savages and Civility: Indians and Englishmen in Colonial Virginia.* Cambridge: Cambridge University Press, 1980.

Shepherd, William R. *History of Proprietary Government in Pennsylvania.* Ph.D. diss. Columbia University, 1896.

Smith, Donald B. "Who Are the Mississauga?" *Ontario History* 17:4 (Dec 1975). Pp. 211–22.

Smith, Joseph Henry. *Appeals to the Privy Council from the American Plantations* (1950). Reprinted. New York: Octagon Books, 1965.

Snyderman, George S. "The Manuscript Collections of the Philadelphia Yearly Meeting of Friends Pertaining to the American Indian." *Proceedings of the American Philosophical Society* 102 (1958). Pp. 613–20.

———. "An Ethnological Discussion of Allegany Seneca Wampum Folklore." *Proceedings of the American Philosophical Society* 126:4 (1982), pp. 316–26.

Southeastern Indians Since the Removal Era. Ed. Walter L. Williams. Athens: University of Georgia Press, 1979.

Southwest. Ed. Alfonso Ortiz. Vol. 9 (1979) of *Handbook of North American Indians.* Gen. ed. William C. Sturtevant. 20 vols. Washington, D.C.: Smithsonian Institution, 1978–.

Spicer, Edward H. *Cycles of Conquest; The Impact of Spain, Mexico, and the United States on the Indians of the Southwest, 1533–1960.* Tucson: University of Arizona Press, 1962.

Stanton, William. *The Leopard's Spots: Scientific Attitudes Toward Race in America, 1815–1859.* Chicago: University of Chicago Press, 1960.

Starna, William A. "Mohawk Iroquois Populations: A Revision." *Ethnohistory* 27:4 (fall 1980), pp. 371–82.

Stenton, Doris. *English Justice between the Norman Conquest and the Great Charter, 1066–1215.* Jayne Lectures for 1963. Philadelphia: American Philosophical Society, 1964.

Stocking, George W., Jr. *Race, Culture, and Evolution: Essays in the History of Anthropology.* New York: Free Press, 1968.

Sutton, Imre. *Indian Land Tenure: Bibliographical Essays and a Guide to the Literature.* New York: Clearwater Publishing Co., 1975.

Swagerty, William R. "Marriage and Settlement Patterns of Rocky Mountain Trappers and Traders." *Western Historical Quarterly* 11:2 (April 1980), pp. 159–80.

Swick, Minor. "The Sebring Family." *Somerset County* (N.J.) *Historical Quarterly* 3 (1914), pp. 118–24.

Thompson, Benjamin F. *The History of Long Island*. rev. 2d ed. 2 vols. New York: Gould, Banks and Co., 1843.

Tolles, Frederick B. *Quakers and the Atlantic Culture*. New York: The Macmillan Co., 1960.

Tooker, Elisabeth. "The League of the Iroquois: Its History, Politics, and Ritual." In *Northeast*, q.v., pp. 418–41.

——. "Wyandot." In *Northeast*, q.v., pp. 398–406.

Trelease, Allen W. *Indian Affairs in Colonial New York: The Seventeenth Century*. Ithaca, N.Y.: Cornell University Press, 1960.

——. "The Iroquois and the Western Fur Trade; A Problem in Interpretation." *Mississippi Valley Historical Review* 49 (1962), pp. 32–51.

Trigger, Bruce G. "Champlain Judged by His Indian Policy: A Different View of Early Canadian History." *Anthropologica*. N.s., 13:1 (1971), pp. 85–114.

——. *The Children of Aataentsic: A History of the Huron People to 1660*. 2 vols. Montreal: McGill-Queen's University Press, 1976. Bib. notes: ch. 6, n. 9, 23.

——. "The Destruction of Huronia: A Study in Economic and Cultural Change, 1609–1650." *Transactions of the Royal Canadian Institute* 33 (1960), pp. 14–45.

——. "Early Iroquoian Contacts with Europeans." In *Northeast*, q.v., pp. 344–56.

——. "Ethnohistory: Problems and Prospects." A paper read at the Wilfred Laurier Conference on Ethnohistory and Ethnology, Oct. 30, 1980, Waterloo, Canada. Forthcoming in *Ethnohistory*.

——. "Hochelaga: History and Ethnohistory." In *Cartier's Hochelaga and the Dawson Site*. Eds. James F. Pendergast and Bruce G. Trigger. Montreal: McGill-Queen's University Press, 1972. Pp. 1–93.

——. *The Huron: Farmers of the North*. New York: Holt, Rinehart and Winston, 1969.

——. "The Mohawk-Mahican War (1624–1628): The Establishment of a Pattern." *Canadian Historical Review* 52:3 (Sept. 1971), pp. 276–81.

Trudel, Marcel. *The Beginnings of New France, 1524–1663*. Canadian Centenary Series. Toronto: McClelland and Stewart, 1973.

Tuck, James A. "Northern Iroquois Prehistory." In *Northeast*, q.v., pp. 322–33.

Turner, Frederick Jackson. *The Character and Influence of the Indian Trade in Wisconsin: A Study of the Trading Post as an Institution* (1891). Reprint. Eds. David Harry Miller and William W. Savage, Jr. Norman: University of Oklahoma Press, 1977.

——. *The Frontier in American History*. New York: H. Holt and Co., 1920.

Ubelaker, Douglas H. "The Sources and Methodology for Mooney's Estimates of North American Populations." In *The Native Population of the Americas in 1492*. Ed. William M. Denevan. Madison: University of Wisconsin Press, 1976. Pp. 243–92.

Usner, Daniel, Jr. "Frontier Exchange in the Lower Mississippi Valley: Race Relations and Economic Life in Colonial Louisiana, 1699–1783." Ph. D. diss. Duke University, 1981.

Van Loon, L. G. "Tawagonshi, Beginning of the Treaty Era." *Indian Historian* 1:3 (1968), pp. 23–26.

Vinogradoff, Paul. "Customary Law." In *The Legacy of the Middle Ages*. Eds. C. G. Crump and E. F. Jacob. Rev. ed. Oxford: Clarendon Press, 1932.

Volwiler, Albert T. *George Croghan and the Westward Movement, 1741–1782*. Cleveland, O.: Arthur H. Clark Co., 1926.

Wainwright, Nicholas B. *George Croghan: Wilderness Diplomat*. Published for the Institute of Early American History and Culture. Chapel Hill: University of North Carolina Press, 1959.

Wallace, Anthony F. C. *King of the Delawares: Teedyuscung, 1700–1763*. Philadelphia: University of Pennsylvania Press, 1949.

———. "Origins of Iroquois Neutrality: The Grand Settlement of 1701." *Pennsylvania History* 24 (1957), pp. 223–35.

———. "Origins of the Longhouse Religion." In *Northeast*, q.v., pp. 442–48.

———. "Woman, Land, and Society: Three Aspects of Aboriginal Delaware Life." *Pennsylvania Archaeologist* 17:1–4 (1947). Entire issue.

Wallace, Paul A. W. *Conrad Weiser, 1696–1760, Friend of Colonist and Mohawk*. Philadelphia: University of Pennsylvania Press, 1945.

———. *Indian Paths of Pennsylvania*. Harrisburg: Pennsylvania Historical and Museum Commission, 1965.

———. *Indians in Pennsylvania*. Harrisburg: Pennsylvania Historical and Museum Commission, 1961.

Waller, G. M. *Samuel Vetch: Colonial Enterpriser*. Published for the Institute of Early American History and Culture. Chapel Hill: University of North Carolina Press, 1960.

Washburn, Wilcomb E. *The Governor and the Rebel: A History of Bacon's Rebellion in Virginia*. Published for the Institute of Early American History and Culture. Chapel Hill: University of North Carolina Press, 1957. Bib. note: ch. 8, n. 1.

———. *Red Man's Land / White Man's Law: A Study of the Past and Present Status of the American Indian*. New York: Charles Scribner's Sons, 1971.

Webb, Stephen Saunders. *The Governors-General: The English Army and the Definition of the Empire*. Published for the Institute of Early American History and Culture. Chapel Hill: University of North Carolina Press, 1979.

Weeden, William B. *Indian Money as a Factor in New England Civilization*. Johns Hopkins University Studies in Historical and Political Science. 2d ser. 9–10. Baltimore, 1884.

Weslager, C. A. *The Delaware Indians: A History*. New Brunswick, N.J.: Rutgers University Press, 1972.

———. *The Delawares: A Critical Bibliography*. Published for the Newberry Library. Bloomington: Indiana University Press, 1978.

———. *The English on the Delaware, 1610–1682*. New Brunswick, N.J.: Rutgers University Press, 1967.

———. *Red Men on the Brandywine* (1953). Reprinted facsimile, Wilmington, Del.. Delmar News Agency, 1976.

———, in collaboration with A. R. Dunlap. *Dutch Explorers, Traders and Settlers in the Delaware Valley, 1609–1664*. Philadelphia: University of Pennsylvania Press, 1961.

White, Andrew Dickson. *A History of the Warfare of Science with Theology in Christendom*. New York: D. Appleton and Co., 1896.

Williams, David G. *The Lower Jordan Valley Pennsylvania German Settlement. Proceedings of the Lehigh County Historical Society* 18. Allentown, Pa., 1950.

Wolf, Edwin, 2nd. *The Library of James Logan of Philadelphia, 1674–1751.* Philadelphia: Library Company of Philadelphia, 1974.

Wright, J. Leitch, Jr. *The Only Land They Knew: The Tragic Story of the American Indians in the Old South.* New York: The Free Press, 1981.

Wust, Klaus. *The Virginia Germans.* Charlottesville: University Press of Virginia, 1969.

Zeisberger, David. *History of the Northern American Indians.* Trans. Nathaniel Schwarze. Ed. Archer Butler Hulbert. *Ohio Archaeological and Historical Quarterly* 19:1–2 (Jan. and April 1910), pp. 1–189.

Zimmerman, Albright G. "Daniel Coxe and the New Mediterranean Sea Company." *Pennsylvania Magazine of History and Biography* 76 (1952), pp. 86–96.

———. "The Indian Trade of Colonial Pennsylvania." Ph.D. diss. University of Delaware, 1966.

———. "New Approaches to the Indian History of Early America." *Hayes Historical Journal* 3:3 (spring 1981), pp. 49–61.

Zoltvany, Yves. "New France and the West, 1701–1713." *Canadian Historical Review* 46:4 (Dec. 1965), pp. 301–22.

———. *Philippe de Rigaud de Vaudreuil, Governor of New France, 1703–1725.* Carleton Library 80. Toronto: McClelland and Stewart, 1974.

INDEX

Accommodation: between colony and tribe, 6, 9, 72; violence of, 81–83; between Pa. and Iroquois, 249; requisite for European penetration, 367; its desirability, 374–75. *See also* Covenant Chain; Trade

Adoption: systematic Iroquois practice, 95; issue at Shackamaxon, 154–56

Ahookasoongh, Onondaga chief, 237, 239, 304

Albany: magistrates pressure Mahicans, 135; rejects Maryland's demands, 169; merchants stay in place, 177; trade with Montreal, 178–79; lures Canadian Indians, 188; traders waylaid by Denonville, 190; welcomes Shawnees, 201–2; population loss, 206*n*53, 218; Indian shelters deteriorate, 240; intercepts Pa. presents, 263; short of goods, 281; deed to Mohawk Flats, 308; bypassed by Logan and Weiser, 324; useless to Mohawks, 353; 1754 Congress, 369–70. *See also* Smuggling; Trade

Alexander, James, 287

Algonquian linguistic stock, 28

Algonquins, 129–30

Allen, William: buys and sells unceded land, 318–19 & *n*26, 348–49. *See also* Appendix B

Allentown, Pa., 348

American Philosophical Society, 22

Andastes (Susquehannocks), 27

Andros, Edmund (gov. of N.Y., 1674–77, 1678–81, 1688): distrusts Canadian refugees, 64; pacifies Indians, 141; offers refuge to tribes, 148–50; ltr. to Notley, 152–53; orders Susquehannock relocation, 155; hazes Coursey, 157–59; and Covenant Chain, 165-67, 177; calls Iroquois "children"; 193; arrested in Mass., 194

Anne, queen of England: dies, 283

Aquinas, St. Thomas, 3

Atkinson, Stephen, 269–70

Atrakwaeronon Indians, 27, 121

Bacon, Nathaniel, 147

Baltimore, Lord, 165, 225

Barentsen, Peter, 50

Bartram, John, 13 & *n*9

Beauharnois, Charles de la Boische, Marquis de (gov. of New France, 1726–1747): welcomes Shawnees, 307

Bellomont, Richard Coote, Earl of (gov. of N.Y., 1698–1701), 209–10, 216

Berkeley, William (gov. of Va., 1642–52, 1660–77), 147

Berkhofer, Robert F., Jr.: on Indian diversity, 5*n*7

Bethlehem, Pa., 349

Bisaillon, Michel: trader in Illinois country, 234; Logan's informant, 287

Bisaillon, Pierre, 64; joins Le Tort, 232; connections, 234–35; reports Onondaga intentions, 239; denounced by W. Penn, 255; needs protection, 257; brings brother Michel to Logan, 287

Bisaillon, Richard, 234

Black Minquas, 27

Bozman, John Leeds: on Maryland-Susquehannock war, 119–20

Brainerd, David and John: missionaries, 350

Brandon, William: on Iroquois conquests, 20

Brethren: significance of term, 193

Burlington, N.J., 234

Burnet, William (lt. gov. of N.Y., 1720–28): suppresses smuggling, 287; deposes Decanisora, 288; supervises 1722 treaty, 292; struggle with smugglers, 298–99; fort strategy, 299–300

Cadillac, Lamothe- (Antoine Laumet): instigates attacks on Senecas, 207; and smuggling, 283

Calvert, Cecilius (2d Lord Baltimore): demands New Amstel's surrender, 126; orders hostilities against Dutch, 128

Calvert, Charles (gov. of Md., 1661–76, 1681–84): "invites" Susquehannocks into Maryland, 139–40

Calvert, Leonard (gov. of Md., 1634–47): seizes Claiborne's posts, 116

Calvinism, 348

Canasatego, Onondaga chief: Easton speech, 21, 22–23; Lancaster speech, 23; his chain of silver, 167; makes "women" of Delawares, 344–45; at Lancaster, 356–61; death, 363–64

Canondondawe, Mohawk chief, 229

Cantwell, Capt. Edmund: brings Susquehannocks to Andros, 149; brings them to Maryland, 151

Capital accumulation: alien to Indian culture, 69

Carantouanais Indians, 27

Carolinas: accused of enslaving Tuscarora children, 279

Carondawana, Oneida chief: becomes "king" of Shawnees, 265

Cartier, Jacques: visits Hochelaga, 4; Stadaconas obstruct him, 85

De Vitoria, Francisco, 4
Decanisora (Teganissorens), Onondaga chief:
meets with Frontenac, 203–4; his diplomacy,
251; at 1710 treaty in Pa., 259–60; double dealing between Vetch and Vaudreuil, 258, 261;
deposed, 288; on need for neutrality, 288
Deeds: Iroquois, 1701, 12–13 & n7; 14, 54, 212;
Iroquois, 1726, 14; Susquehanna Valley, 228–
29 & n12, 235 & n35, 303, 358; Susquehannock, 1701, 236; Mohawk Flats, 308; Iroquois,
1736, 321–24; Delaware, 328–29; Penns' "ancient deed", 329, 332–33, 336–37. and Appendix B; Virginia, 1744, 361
Delaware (Three Lower Counties): bought by
W. Penn, 225
Delaware Bay: Maryland's designs on, 128;
Whorekill raids, 136–37; Maryland's war aim,
139, 153
Delaware Indians (Lenni Lenape): and Susquehannocks, 116–128, 134; population, 118 &
n13; kill Marylanders, 128; and Maryland, 139;
"Masquas", 153; want adoptees, 154; party to
1677 treaty, 159–62, 164; "Mattawass", 160; as
tributaries, 160–62; reject Iroquois demands,
204–5; a powerful tribe, 215; territorial tenure
right, 225n6, 325–28; postpone tribute to Iroquois, 239; Penn's great treaty, 245–49; bring
presents to Iroquois, 263; discontent in 1720,
273; reject war, 301; "women," 301–2; dispersed westward, 302; evict Shawnee "guests",
303, land cessions to W. Penn, 328–29. See also
regional groups; Sassoonan; Nutimus
Delaware tradition: 21, 40
Delawares, Brandywine: at 1710 treaty in Pa.,
259; distinct from Tulpehockens and Jerseys,
263; dispossession, 271. See also Delaware Indians
Delawares, Jersey: distinct from Brandywines
and Tulpehockens, 263–64. See Delawares,
"Tohickon"
Delawares, "Tohickon", 311: land sold by Iroquois, 321–24; evicted, 344–45. See also Delawares; Nutimus; Walking Purchase
Delawares, Tulpehocken: distinct from Brandywines and Jerseys, 263; compete with Iroquois,
264; land seized by Palatines, 293–94; 1728
treaty, 305–6; compensation for land, 311,
313–14. See also Delawares; Sassoonan
Denonville, Jacques-René de Brisay, Marquis
(gov. of New France, 1685–89): his instructions, 186–87; contemptuous of Dongan, 188;
attacks Senecas, 190–91
Dependence: effect of trade, 61; Dutch and Mohawks, 71; effect on intertribal war, 134; substance distinguished from form, 290; demonstrated at Lancaster and after, 362–65
Des Groseilleurs, Médard Chouart, 64
Detroit: smuggling at, 283. See also Cadillac; Fox
Indians; Deeds, 1701
Disease, epidemic, 1630–40: 88–89; 1663: 129;
1717: 268–69
Doan, Joseph, 333
Dongan, Thomas (lt. gov. of N.Y., 1683–88), 64;
taunts Iroquois, 111; succeeds Andros, 178;
abets smuggling, 179; expands trade, 187–89;

asks Denonville for money, 188; aids and lectures Iroquois, 191–92; on Iroquois cession,
194; his deed for Susquehanna Valley, 228–29
& n12, 235, 358; secret war on Penn, 232–33
Dowaganhaes. See Ottawa Indians
Drake, Samuel G., 18
Drinnon, Richard: on myths, 24
Duffels, 51
Durham: Logan's purchase, 309, 331; conference
with Nutimus, 320–21
Dutch West India Company, 48; policies, 71,
124; guns for Mohawks, 98-99 & n43; faulty
charter, 117. See also New Netherland

Eelkens, Jacob, 51, 54
Eid, Leroy V.: on Iroquois defeats, 207 & n58
Ellis, George E.: on Indian tenure rights, 11n3
Engels, Friedrich: debt to L. H. Morgan, 19
Erie Indians: Location, 29; conquered, 104–5
Esopus Indians, 57: war against Dutch, 109–11;
chided by Susquehannocks, 123
European: as category, 5
Evans, John (lt. gov. of Pa., 1704–1709), 256
Evans, Lewis: his General Map and Analysis, 14;
reprinted, 1776, 16

Farmer, Edward, 255
Fenton, William N.: "kinship state" concept, 37
Firearms, 80–81
Five Nations. See Iroquois Indians; League of the
houdénosaunee
Fletcher, Benjamin (lt. gov. of N.Y. and Pa.,
1692–98): and Shawnees, 201, 206; meets with
Minisinks, 202–3; friction with Iroquois, 203–5
Forks of Delaware, 334; false "draught", 337–38.
See also Walking Purchase, Nutimus
Fort Casimir. See New Castle
Fort Frontenac, 174
Fort Nassau, 47–48 & n1
Fort Niagara: built by La Salle, 174; rebuilt, 299
Fort Orange: founded, 48–49; immunity from
Indian attack, 50; probable treaty ca. 1630, 53;
supports Mohawks, 104–5
Fort Oswego: strategic value, 300; trade with
western tribes, 353
Fort Richelieu, 56, 92
Fort St. Frederic: location, 307–8; menaces
English, 353
Fort St. Louis: attacked by Iroquois, 180; Shaw-
nees at, 197
Fort Stanwix: treaty, 1784, 16–17
Forts: for control of trade, 286–88, 299–300; dif-
ferent kinds, 299
Fox Indians: ally to Iroquois, 261, 351; wars, 283,
307
Franciscan missions, 73
Freame Thomas, 319n29
French, Colonel John: at 1710 treaty in Pa., 259;
refrains from Vetch's campaign, 260–61; com-
missioned against Md., 269; forbids torture,
279
French Indian policy: as seen by Eccles, 20n29;
opposition to Iroquois, 42; instigation of western Indians, 209; influence of traders, 352
French Mohawks. See Caughnawaga Mohawks

New England: incites Indians against Dutch, 126; insists on treaty, 1677, 148
New France: population, 1650, 85; trade with Hurons, 86–87; population, 1642, 91; war against Iroquois, 195–210; treaty, 1701, 210–12. *See also* French Indian Policy; Missions; Trade; names of governors and missionaries
New Haven, 126
New Jersey, 258
New Netherland, 9; preparations and purpose, 50–51; treaty with Mohawks, 1643, 53; conquers New Sweden, 108, 122; controls tribes, 123; contradictions in, 124–25; population, 125*n*37; House of Hope, 126; conquered, 130; reinstated, 137; final end, 140. *See also* Dutch West India Company; Trade; Stuyvesant, Peter; Chains of Alliance
New Sweden: conquered by Dutch, 108, 122; founded, 117; site at Christina Creek, 118; trade with Susquehannocks, 119; population, 119; aids Susquehannocks against Md., 120; trade with Delawares, 121
New York: established, 130; conquered by Dutch, 137; re-established, 140; expansionism, 187–89; peace mission, 1698, 208–9; gains by Iroquois neutrality, 211; jealous of Pa., 239–40; special imperial position, 369–70. *See also* Covenant Chain; Trade; Smuggling; Treaties; names of governors
Newcheconner, Shawnee chief: discloses Iroquois war proposals, 301–3
Nichols, Richard (lt. gov. of N.Y., 1664–68), 133
Norton, John, 207*n*58
Notley, Thomas (deputy gov. of Md., 1676–81): plans to invade Delaware Bay, 153
Nutimus, Delaware chief: will cede only to a Penn, 309; resists Walking Purchase, 331–35; consents to Walk, 336; threatens enmity, 339–41; wants Iroquois hearing, 342; dispossessed by Pa. and Iroquois, 343–45; removes to Nescopeck, 349. *See also* Walking Purchase: Delawares, "Tohickon"

O'Bail, Seneca capt. *See* Cornplanter
Ochtaghquanawicroone Indians, 297
Ohio country, 350–51; Shawnees sent to, 302; Indian migrations to, 351
Ohongeoguena Indians, 27
Ojibwa nations, 111
Ojibwa tradition, 21; on defeats of Iroquois, 207, 209
Old West, the, 320
Olumapies: ceremonial name for Sassoonan, q.v.
Onas ("feather"): Iroquois name for W. Penn, 23*n*19
Oneida Indians: location, 29; southern orientation, 35; adoptees, 95; raid Chesapeake Bay, 130; peace with Frontenac, 203; thank Va., 229. See also Iroquois Indians, League of the Houdénosaunee; Iroquois Indians, Western
Oneniuteronnon. See Seneca Indians
Onondaga Indians: location, 29; Iroquois "capital", 35, 105; adoptees among, 95; negotiate with Hurons, 97; friction with Mohawks, 104–9, 159, 181, 356, 362 & *n*41, 364*n*46; on inde-

pendence, 183; on Covenant Chain, 185; refuse to plunder English traders, 189; demand help from Delawares, 204–5; lay claim to Susquehanna Valley, 230; negotiate with Pa., 1704, 239; double dealing with Vetch and Vaudreuil, 258; turn toward French, 364. *See also* Iroquois Indians; League of the Houdénosaunee; Iroquois Indians, Western; Decanisora; Canasatego; Covenant Chain
Onontio (gov. of Canada), 96
Opessa, Shawnee chief, 265
Oreouache (Ourehaoare), Cayuga chief, 228
Ostanghae Indians, 297
Ottawa Indians, 111; impressed by English prices, 189; tradition of Iroquois defeats, 207; hound Iroquois, 209; treat with Iroquois, 351–52

Palatine Germans: settle at Tulpehocken, 293–94, 305; settle Shenandoah Valley, 361*n*34
Parker, Arthur C.: on Iroquois conquests, 18
Parker, Ely S.: and Iroquois tradition, 17–18
Parkman, Francis: on Iroquois conquests, 18, 162; a racist, 19; on Copway, 22 & *n*37; on Indian tradition, 22*n*39; on coureurs de bois, 64*n*21; on Huron defeat, 100
Patron-client relationship, 7
Peach War, 108
Peachoquelloman, 302; abandoned, 306
Penn, John (Proprietary of Pa.): treats with Nutimus, 320–21, 334; cozens Lappawinzo and Tishcohan, 336. *See also* Penns; Walking Purchase; Appendix B
Penn, Thomas (Proprietary of Pa.): reorganizes Pa. govt., 313; allies to Iroquois, 315–16, 321–24; extravagance, 318; sells unceded lands, 318–20; treats with Nutimus, 320–21; brings "ancient deed", 332–33; at Pennsbury conference, 334; cozens Lappawinzo, 336; gets Delaware release, 337; alters map and minutes, 337–39; issues patents, 339. *See also* Penns; Walking Purchase; Appendix B
Penn, William (Proprietary and gov. of Pa., 1681–1718): charges Md. betrayal of Susquehannocks, 140; loses govt., 201; a great lord, 217; competes with N.Y., 218; govt. restored, 219; and Indian trade, 223–25, 254–55; buys Indian quitclaims, 225 & *n*4; 326–29; buys Dongan's deed, 235; treats with Susquehannocks, 235–37; praise from Indians, 238; character and powers, 240–41; Indian policies, 242–48; letter to the Indians, 242–43; bankruptcy and death, 265; his will, 276; and Indian "incumbrance", 318*n*25, 328; omits guarantee from trans-Tohickon sales, 331; final return to England, 345
Penn, William, Jr.: contests father's will, 276–77
Penns (John, Thomas, and Richard): debt, 316–18; wealth, 345–46
Pennsbury: conference with Nutimus, 321, 334
Pennsylvania: asylum for Indians, 215; immigration into, 218; boundaries, 225–26; council protects Shawnees, 239; tacit accommodation with Iroquois, 249; attracts western Iroquois, 251; commissioners of property, 257; assembly stalls